READING "REMBRANDT"

Reading "Rembrandt": Beyond the Word–Image Opposition explores the potential for interdisciplinary methodology between literature and visual art. In a series of close analyses of works by "Rembrandt," and of texts related to those works, Mieke Bal questions the traditional boundaries between literary and visual analysis, and examines "Rembrandt"'s complex handling of gender and the representation of women in "Rembrandt"'s painting.

Although *Reading "Rembrandt"*'s methods originate outside the history of art, this book demonstrates the author's sensitivity to the visual aspects of "Rembrandt"'s work. Through the analyses, the works by "Rembrandt" gain in depth and interest, and an original perspective on the role of visuality in our culture emerges, which ultimately has consequences for our views of gender, the artist, and the act of reading.

CAMBRIDGE NEW ART HISTORY AND CRITICISM

General Editor:
Norman Bryson, *University of Rochester*

Advisory Board:
Stephen Bann, *University of Kent*
Joseph Rykwert, *Cambridge University*
Henri Zerner, *Harvard University*

Also in the series:

Stephen Bann, *The True Vine*
Michael Camille, *The Gothic Image*
Mark A. Cheetham, *The Rhetoric of Purity*
Whitney Davis, *The Canonical Tradition in Egyptian Art*

Reading "Rembrandt"

Beyond the Word–Image Opposition

The Northrop Frye Lectures in Literary Theory

MIEKE BAL

Professor of Theory of Literature,
University of Amsterdam, and
Adjunct Visiting Professor of Comparative Arts,
University of Rochester

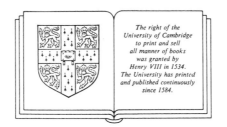

The right of the
University of Cambridge
to print and sell
all manner of books
was granted by
Henry VIII in 1534.
The University has printed
and published continuously
since 1584.

CAMBRIDGE UNIVERSITY PRESS

Cambridge

New York   Port Chester   Melbourne   Sydney

Published by the Press Syndicate of the University of Cambridge
The Pitt Building, Trumpington Street, Cambridge CB2 1RP
40 West 20th Street, New York, NY 10011, USA
10 Stamford Road, Oakleigh, Melbourne 3166, Australia

© Cambridge University Press 1991

First published 1991

Printed in the United States of America

Library of Congress Cataloging-in-Publication Data
Bal, Mieke. 1946–
Reading "Rembrandt" : beyond the word–image opposition : the
Northrop Frye lectures in literary theory / Mieke Bal.
p.   cm. – (Cambridge new art history and criticism)
Includes bibliographical references and index.
ISBN 0-521-39154-7
1. Rembrandt Harmenszoon van Rijn, 1606–1669 – Criticism and
interpretation.   2. Women in art.   3. Ut pictura poesis (Aesthetics)
4. Art and literature.   I. Title.   II. Title: Northrop Frye
lectures in literary theory.   III. Series.
ND653.R4B18   1991
759.9492 – dc20   91-24210
                                                            CIP

A catalog record for this book is available from the British Library.

ISBN-0-521-39154-7 hardback

Page 495 constitutes a continuation of the copyright page.

For Ernst

CONTENTS

LIST OF
ILLUSTRATIONS

PREFACE

We can never understand a picture unless we grasp
the ways in which it shows what cannot be seen.
(W. J. T. Mitchell, *Iconology*, 1985:39)

The world is all-seeing, but it is not exhibitionistic,
it does not provoke our gaze. When it begins to
provoke it, the feeling of strangeness begins too.
(Jacques Lacan, *The Four Fundamental Concepts*,
1979:75)

As a result both of their oppression, their specular-
ization and their forced confrontation with their own
lack, Fassbinder's male characters acquire the capacity
to become something other than what the male subject has classically been – to slip out from under the
phallic sign, away from the paternal function. (Kaja
Silverman, "Fassbinder and Lacan," 1989:80)

I began by dropping the picture theory of language
and ended by adopting the language theory of pictures. (Nelson Goodman, "The Way the World Is,"
in *Problems and Projects*, 1972:31–2)

THIS study is the result of an adventure across borders. Coming from the field of literary studies, I began to work on
visual art in relation to literature, because I felt increasingly
dissatisfied with the generalizing assumptions about literature on
which this field operates, which often struck me as not specific at
all to the object of inquiry. However, locked up within the academic
field of "literary studies," I did not find it easy to gain the necessary
perspective on assumptions so widely shared by students in that
field. Studying images has made me aware of how strongly privileging the word impedes insight into the enormous influence of
visual images on thought, imagination, and social interaction in
our culture. Even art historians in their writing, I was surprised to
notice, in certain ways and often unawares, privilege the verbal.
At the same time, having sensitized myself to visual elements in
literature and literary criticism, I could not remain blind to the fact
that the overt emphasis on the word hardly conceals an overwhelmingly visual dimension in our culture, including both literature and the study of it. This prompted me to study systematically
the interplay of visual and verbal elements.

Several lectures given to audiences in literature and art history
have provided me with the serious feedback needed to develop my
ideas and to interact with scholars of other fields, primarily art
history, but also film studies. This generous and open-minded response in art historical and literary gatherings has convinced me
that a fruitful dialogue between the two disciplines is possible and
welcome, and that common concerns can be addressed in an increasingly common language. Unfortunately, I cannot begin to
enumerate all the people who have been important to this study.

This book originated from what was in many ways the most
pleasurable teaching experience of my career: the twelve lectures I
was invited to give as Northrop Frye professor at the University
of Toronto. When invited to hold that chair in theory of literature
for 1987, I asked if I could do it on "Rembrandt." The unqualifiedly
positive answer was evidence of the interest, in literary studies, in
things visual. Among the group of faithful interlocutors, graduate
students and faculty, I owe special gratitude to Milena Doleželova
Veringerova, Linda Hutcheon, and Peter Nesselroth. But the development of those lectures into a book could not have been accomplished without my colleagues and students at the University
of Rochester. In addition to the people in the Comparative Literature Program, I wish to mention especially those who participated
in the creation of the Program in Comparative Arts: Norman Bryson, Michael Holly, the late Craig Owens, Constance Penley, Grace
Seiberling, Kaja Silverman, and Sharon Willis. The creation of that
program ran parallel to the writing of this book. It retarded my
progress on the book when the inevitable bureaucratic procedures
claimed priority, but it also provided major inspiration by fostering
the intellectual environment I shared with these colleagues: one that
was stimulating, challenging, demanding, and friendly. Major inspiration came especially from Kaja Silverman from both her work
and her conversation. It is impossible to acknowledge her influence
fully; pursuing the same goal, she had often thought through problems with which I had only intuitively grappled. Her friendship
and intellectual generosity have been crucial to me.

I don't know how to thank two people who have been particularly important, maybe without knowing just how important.
The first is Michael Holly. Should I thank her as chair of the Art
History Department who gave me a second home department, or
as the person who was most deeply involved in the creation of the
Program in Comparative Arts from its inception, or as the friend
who supported me at bad moments, or as the scholar who kept
asking me the questions that I kept trying to evade? The second is
Norman Bryson. Should I thank him as a colleague, or as editor
of the series "Cambridge New Art History and Criticism"; as a
friend, a continuous interlocutor, a source of inspiration from beginning to end; or as a person who managed to keep all these
functions neatly separated?

On several occasions, I have profited from the generous advice of Svetlana Alpers, Evelyn Fox-Keller, Ria Lemaire, Jan van Lux-emburg, Henk van Os, Simon Schama, and many others. Very special help at just the right moment came from Elisabeth Bronfen. Thanks to her painstaking efforts to make sense of unreadable drafts and the inspiring interaction with her, this book has been finished much earlier than it would have been otherwise. In the final stage, the discussions in the Summer Institute "Theory and Interpretation in the Visual Arts," sponsored by the National Endowment for the Humanities and organized by Michael Holly and Keith Moxey, have been crucial to the formulation of important issues underlying this book. The continuous challenge from the participants, and in particular from coorganizer Keith Moxey, was just what I needed. I dare not hope that my view of social context will satisfy Keith now, but it was articulated in dialogue with his.

Claudia Swann gave the final version a critical eye from the perspective of the technicalities of art history. Needless to say, I am solely responsible for the end result. Jane Carter deserves very special thanks. She was the very best editor I have ever had the pleasure to work with, did several rounds of style editing of the entire book that were incredibly precise, strong, and creative. I won't confess to what small disasters her work has been subjected, only that she put up with them cheerfully. Without her invaluable help, the text would not have reached the degree of readability it presently enjoys.

The University of Rochester allowed me to take more leaves of absence than my colleagues and students would have liked; I am grateful to all those concerned, for their tolerance. The J. Paul Getty Foundation awarded me a senior research grant to complete the manuscript in its final stage, and to prepare a revised version in Dutch.

Very special and continuous help and encouragement came from Ernst van Alphen, without whom I never would have persevered. His lessons in looking were as valuable as his relentless criticism and his never failing support. Since he is also my most eager and sharp reader, I cannot but dedicate this book to him.

INTRODUCTION

This is the dream's navel, the spot where it reaches
down into the unknown. (Sigmund Freud, *The Interpretation of Dreams*, 1905:525)

BALANCING VISION AND NARRATIVE

Vermeer's *Woman Holding a Balance*, housed in the National Gallery in Washington, represents a woman in a
blue dress, holding a balance above a table; on the wall,
in the background, is a painting of the *Last Judgment*. Light streams
in from a stained-glass window at the upper left. It is a strikingly
still painting. It avoids narrative – both the anecdotal and the dynamic. Instead it presents an image in terms of visual rhythm,
equilibrium, balanced contrasts, and subtle lighting (Figure 0.1).
As Arthur Wheelock, Jr. (1981:106–7) remarks, the painting stands
in marked contrast to other works on related themes. In those other
works the woman tends to look greedily at the precious objects on
the table, whereas here she is self-absorbed. In those others the pans
of the balance, here empty, tend to be heaped with gold or pearls
so that action is implied. In this work the parallel between the *Last
Judgment*, hung on the wall behind her, and the woman's act of
weighing/judging is elaborated on the basis of similarity, not of
narrativized contrast.

Svetlana Alpers, I assume from her *Art of Describing* (1985), would
call this a descriptive painting. It is a painting that appeals to visuality if ever there was one, a case for Alpers's opposition to Italian
infatuation with narrativity. Any attempt to read the painting as a
narrative can only misread it. It is a surface carefully balanced for
visual experience, where the appeal to visuality is worked out in
the tiniest details. On the upper left part of the painting, in the
white wall near the represented *Last Judgment*, is a nail, and near
that nail, a hole in the wall. The minutely detailed work of painting
is so highly emphasized in these tiny details that both inside the
hole and next to the nail we can see a shadow. The soft, warm
light streaming in from the window on the upper left touches these
two irregularities in the wall, as if to demonstrate that realistic
description of the world seen knows no limits.

This light also generates other details in the overall darkness of the painting. The woman's dress underneath the mantle is fore-grounded by it; between the two fur rims a slice of orange tissue protrudes, showing the dress's color that is in shadow. The dress may be in keeping with the fashion of the times, but for some viewers, questions may keep nagging: Why this soft light, why this striking color and shape, why does it fall *here*? These questions may lead one to interpret this detail: Since the part of the dress that is illuminated is the one that covers her womb, it may, through metonymy, come to represent the slit that opens the womb – her navel. And if we focus particularly on this element, we may come to associate the woman in this painting with the pregnant madonna as represented in the Italian Renaissance.[1] The woman's hairdress and the blue color of her mantle then may be taken to underscore the visual similarity in the distribution of surface space between her and God in the represented *Last Judgment*. An ordinary Dutch woman for some, an allegorical figure representing *Vanitas* for others, she may become Mary for those who pursue the interpretive game further. To some viewers who notice this detail, such an association will appeal; to others it won't. The point is not to

0.1 Vermeer, *Woman Holding a Balance* ca. 1662–4 (Washington, D.C., National Gallery of Art)

2

convince readers of its appropriateness, or its truth, but to offer the speculative possibility.

For me it was the nail and the hole that the light made visible, produced; that instigated a burst of speculative fertility. When I saw this nail, the hole, and the shadows, I was fascinated: I could not keep my eyes off them. Why are they there? I asked myself, Are these merely meaningless details that Roland Barthes would chalk up to an "effect of the real"? Are these the signs that make a connotation of realism shift to the place of denotation because there is no denotative meaning available? Or do they point to a change in the significance of the *Last Judgment*? Do they suggest that the represented painting which, according to Wheelock, is there to balance the work, to foreground the similarity, the rhyme, between God and this woman, has been displaced from an earlier, "original" position to a better, visually more convincing balance, leaving only the telltale trace of a nail hole? As it is, the woman stands right below God, a position that emphasizes the similarity between judging and weighing. Also, the separation between the blessed and the doomed is obliterated by her position, suggesting, perhaps, that the line between good and evil is a fine one. But in the midst of this speculative flourish, I am caught up short by the remembrance that we are looking at a painting of this balance, not at a real room. The painter surely did not need to *paint* the nail and the hole, even if, in setting up his studio, he actually may have displaced the *Last Judgment*.

If the room were a real room, the hole and the nail would evince traces of the effort to hang the painting in the right place. As such, they demonstrate the materiality of the difficulty and delicacy of balancing. Hanging a painting in exactly the right place is a delicate business, and the result is of the utmost visual importance. For the representation of this statement on visual balance, the nail alone would not do the trick; the failure of the first attempt to balance the represented painting correctly must be shown through an attempt still prior to it. The hole is the record of this prior attempt. The suggestion that the *Last Judgment* was initially unbalanced, with balancing as its very subject matter, threatens to unbalance the painting as a whole. While the metaphoric connection between the idea of judgment and this woman's activity is tightened by the final result, the difficulty of balancing and of judging is thus foregrounded.

In the painting, narrativity so blatantly absent on first – and even second – glance is found to have been inserted by means of a sign that makes a statement on visuality. The visual experience that encodes the iconic association between woman and God is not displaced but, on the contrary, underscored by this narrative aspect. We imagine someone trying to hang the painting in exactly the right place. We are suddenly aware of the woman's artificial pose: Instead of changing the painting's position, the artist arranging his studio could simply have changed the woman's place, or his own angle of vision. All of a sudden something is happening, the still scene begins to move, and the spell of stillness is broken.

The nail and the hole, both visual elements to which no iconographic meaning is attached, unsettle the poetic description and the passively admiring gaze that it triggered, and dynamize the activity of the viewer. Whereas before the discovery of these details the viewer could gaze at the work in wonder, now he or she is aware of his or her imaginative addition in the very act of looking. The work no longer stands alone; now the viewer must acknowledge that he or she makes it work, and that the surface is no longer still but tells the story of its making. That is what narrativity does to a work of art, be it visual or literary. Attracting attention to the work of representation as well as to the work of reading or viewing, the nail and the hole are traces of the *work* of art, in all senses of that expression and in all its specificity.

This, then, raises questions about the place of narrative in visual art. Narrativity is generally considered an aspect of verbal art, which can be mobilized in visual art under great representational pressure only. Something comparable is alleged for visual imagery, which literature strives for but can never completely realize. I propose to shift the terms of these questions and reconsider the typically medium-bound terms of interpretive scholarship – like spectatorship, storytelling, rhetoric, reading, discursivity, and visuality – as aspects rather than essences, and each art's specific strategies to deal with these aspects, as modes rather than systems.

This study, then, is concerned with theoretical and interpretive problems pertaining to relations between verbal and visual art. Shifting attention from the study of the medium-bound, allegedly intrinsic properties of each domain to the question of reception, allows a systematic scrutiny of the ways in which the arts function in a culture where the public is constantly surrounded by images, yet trained to privilege words over images. Dehierarchizing the arts, and dispossessing a mythified author of a work given over to public use, this study is situated within the rapidly growing field of critical studies of culture. My goal is to contribute to cultural theory, to a different understanding of the powerful effects of certain works of art, and to the teachability of the arts across departments.

THE SUBJECT OF THIS STUDY

This study centers upon Rembrandt. Each chapter confronts one or more of his works with texts related to them in various ways: as "source" or pre-text, as response, as thematic companion or counterpart, as theoretical subtext, surrounding context, or as critical rewriting. As for the verbal works selected, the choice is purposefully eclectic, not only to balance the concentration on visual images all by one artist but also because the arguments I am developing are theoretical rather than corpus-bound. I wanted to confront the visual works with a variety of verbal works, from different genres and contexts, and with different types of relations to the visual works. It is those relations, rather than the particular texts and works, that I wish to discuss. I take Rembrandt to stand for an exemplary painter in "high culture" and not as a particularly discursive or narrative artist. This art lends itself, therefore, to the kind of questions I wish to ask, without "begging" them.

The juxtaposition, in an interpretive venture, of verbal and visual "texts" has among many other advantages that of making the student of visual art and literature aware, not so much of those aspects of the works that inhere in the medium but more importantly of those that do not. This kind of interpretive juxtaposition can generate insight into the strategies of representation and of interpretation, as distinct from medium-bound devices, and can help generate a broader perspective on other cultural issues. This book is designed to explore some of the possibilities of this field of study.

The primary assumption underlying the book is that the culture in which works of art and literature emerge and function does not impose a strict distinction between the verbal and the visual domain. In cultural life, the two domains are constantly intertwined. In order to assess what a work means for the culture in which it circulates, we therefore need to overcome the artificial boundaries that form the basis of academic disciplines.

A second assumption underlying this work is that art is both entirely artificial – that is, not "natural" – and entirely real – that is, not separated from the ideological constructions that determine the social decisions made by people every day. Hence, nothing about art is innocent: It is neither inevitable, nor without consequences. In order to drive this point home, for example, Chapter 2, entitled "Visual Rhetoric," discusses the issues of rhetoric and rape in the Western representational regime, the one through the other.

Two other, intertwined assumptions need some comment. The one holds that any analysis and interpretation of visual or verbal works of art, even historical interpretations, are necessarily and by virtue of the semiotic status of art informed by the views, standards, ideologies, and background – in other words, by the subjectivity – of the person doing the analysis. Not that attempts to recover the past are futile; rather they tend to displace the issue of the epistemological status of the knowledge they produce and thus undermine the status of their own results. Most historical interpretation aims at restoring the author's intentions. But by obliterating and repressing the subjectivity of the analyst, the author's alleged intentions are burdened with, and sometimes buried under, projections by the former passed off as intentions of the latter. Thus intention and meaning, and work and analyst, are conflated.[2]

The question is not just whether "pure" historical knowledge is possible – and the answer has to be negative, even to historians less skeptical than Hayden White.[3] We must also ask what is to be gained

by making explicit what happens when one tries. This study attempts to explore some aspects of that question by focusing here
and there on the gestures of critical readers, foregrounding this
difficulty, by endorsing a radically reception-oriented approach.

One can argue that the historical endeavor is not exhausted by
the surprisingly tenacious search for intentions. But today a more
sophisticated historical inquiry into the work and workings of a
body of visual material would define the underlying historical question in a more social sense, as a search for the social situation and
context out of which the work emerged. This inquiry includes
economical and political factors and their influence on the structure
of public life as analyzed, for example, by T. J. Clark; as well as
what Martin Jay would call the "scopic regime," or Svetlana Alpers
the visual culture of the time.[4] All these elements together constitute
the answer to the question "What made this possible?"[5] This question situates the work in a social situation rather than in an individual
genius. I acknowledge the value of such inquiry, which, indeed, I
find indispensable.

Yet social history does not escape the problem of the presence
of the critic as inseparable from historical knowledge. In addition,
the very concept of context is as problematic as that of text. Jonathan
Culler formulates the problem acutely when he writes:

> But the notion of context frequently oversimplifies rather than enriches
> discussion, since the opposition between an act and its context seems to
> presume that the context is given and determines the meaning of the act.
> We know, of course, that things are not so simple: context is not funda-
> mentally different from what it contextualizes; context is not given but
> produced; what belongs to a context is determined by interpretive strat-
> egies; contexts are just as much in need of elucidation as events; and the
> meaning of a context is determined by events. Yet when we use the term
> *context* we slip back into the simple model it proposes. (Culler, 1988:xiv)

Context, in other words, is a text and thus presents the same
difficulty of interpretation as any other text. The context cannot
define the work's meaning because context itself defies unambiguous interpretation as much as the work. Culler goes on to argue
that an alternative to the notion of context is that of framing:

> Since the phenomena criticism deals with are signs, forms with socially-
> constituted meanings, one might try to think not of context but of the
> framing of signs: how are signs constituted (framed) by various discursive
> practices, institutional arrangements, systems of value, semiotic mecha-
> nisms? (Culler, 1988:xiv)

This is, de facto, what Pollock (1988) as well as Alpers, Clark, and
many others are doing, at least on the sender's side. But this still
does not solve the question of meaning.

I would like to explore what the question "What *made* this possible?" fails to address by changing it into "What *makes* this possible?" – referring not to the work as a given but to its existence
as both affect and effect. The meaning of the work is now situated

as an effect of meaning. This effect is complicated by the social construction of visuality, the modalities of looking that we are trained to adopt, and the variability of identifications.[6]

Another, related assumption that underlies this study concerns the status of the artist as genius and of art as "high art." The choice of works by Rembrandt as the central body of visual art for this study may seem provocative. But although his authorship is currently under pressure, the status of his art goes unquestioned. True, some Rembrandt critics (the members of the Rembrandt Research Project are among them; see Bruyn et al., 1982), voluntarily question the quality of some of the works, and even take pride in their demythologizing attitude. Yet the very fact that these aesthetic criticisms lead to rejection of the authenticity of the works as "Rembrandts" provides evidence of the basically unchallenged status of both author as genius and of aesthetic quality as determinable. Hence these acts of judgment rest on the possibility to delimit "high art" from other art. An ever "higher," purer Rembrandt is thus safeguarded.

In the wake of a growing awareness of the mechanisms of exclusion inherent in both these notions of authorship and of aesthetic quality, a number of attitudes have come to prevail instead. One very powerful attitude has been to reject the preoccupation with the works of geniuses altogether, turning toward the products of popular culture, formerly denigrated as "low art" and today valued as more representative evidence of the cultural life of the people. Examples among many are Keith Moxey's (1989) study of popular early German woodcuts and Nathalie Kampen's (1981) study of sculpture in the Roman provinces, and, in an altogether different domain, the current revaluation of the nineteenth-century "sentimental novel," on which more appears in Chapter 5. The successful work in film studies, a field that deservedly has a leading position in cultural studies, ignores the boundaries between artistic and popular film and analyzes both indiscriminately.[7] Another approach is to criticize "high art" as ideologically flawed, examining racism, sexism, classism in canonical works, and, subsidiarily, in art history and literary criticism (e.g., Said, 1978; Gates, 1985; Trinh, 1989).

In spite of the obvious importance of those endeavors, there seems to be room for a third attitude, which I can formulate most briefly as a paradox: "High art" is part of popular culture. In other words, I am interested in why a culture, largely but not exclusively colonized by the cultural leaders who have the power to impose their taste and stakes, continues to respond to a set body of works of art; I am also interested in what kind of response that body of works elicits. These works may be part of the elitist culture, but the responses they elicit are not. Issues like the relationship between storytelling and voyeurism; the thematic centrality of the nude as an object of vision, as well as a source of blindness, of the impotence to see; transparent representation and its limits – all are pervasively present in contemporary Western culture. It is my claim that the

7

works traditionally attributed to Rembrandt elicit a response to, and reflection on, issues like these.

The opposition high–low is intrinsic not to the object under scrutiny but to the assumptions we bring to these (or any) works. Thus bringing the concerns of popular culture to bear on works of "high" culture debunks the latter and undermines the opposition between them. A similar dichotomy exists in feminist criticism: Is it necessary to expend ever more attention on the works of the male canon instead of looking at works by women? There, too, I would argue that both endeavors need to be pursued in tandem.[8]

To a certain extent, a culture makes its art and its artists. It is to be expected, then, that the art also makes the culture, by initiating or addressing issues that pertain to the culture at large. Thus I will argue, in Chapter 4, that the relationship between looking and power, which pervades this culture where positions in visual art are quite strongly gendered, is both exemplified and addressed by the works attributed to Rembrandt. The sections "Viewer," "Voyeurism," and "Focalizer" address current theories of the gaze, of spectatorship, and confront these with literary theories of point of view and focalization. The story of Susanna and the Elders, which thematizes looking, makes a good case.

That many of these works are now in the process of being disavowed as part of the Rembrandt corpus does not bother me; it rather supports my argument that "Rembrandt" is a cultural text, rather than a historical reality. "Rembrandt" constitutes these works *and* the response to them, responses that range from their mistaken (?) attribution to attempts to challenge their authenticity on the basis of a holistic and elitist concept of authorship. In this study, the name of an author is meant as a shorthand for this complex of readings of certain works *as* works by a particular artist. In order to keep in mind this definition of the author, I shall put the name "Rembrandt" in quotation marks, as the title of a text, whenever I am using the name in my own argument. I shall avoid using quotation marks when I render the views of others, lest using them would distort these views.[9]

This book represents an attempt to reflect systematically on these and a number of other related issues, which today receive ever wider attention, yet have not been pulled together. I hope to knit these strands together into a reception-oriented perspective of cultural critique. This book is based, not on a denial of difference between verbal and visual art, but on a provisional bracketing of the question as to what that difference might possibly be. Shifting attention from the question of intrinsic properties to that of response, the focus will be on the interaction between the visual and verbal "behavior" of those who deal with, process, or consume the works of art. The book is reading-oriented; the transfer of approaches traditionally limited to analyzing works of visual or of verbal art to the other is primarily to enrich the methods of analysis and interpretation currently in use, as well as to promote the reader's self-awareness as a critic. Each chapter focuses on a theoretical problem. For example: What can we do with rhetoric for the interpretation of visual images? How can images narrate? What are the status and the effect of a represented viewer in visual and literary art? These will be discussed as an issue of cultural criticism.

In order to be teachable, the approach needs to be elaborated through detailed analyses of works of art whose artistic status in the culture in which they function is undeniable. Therefore, the book will also contain a number of interpretations as well as discussions of extant interpretations of works of art. In these interpretive analyses, the relationship between (i.e., the approaches to) verbal and visual arts, and between the work and the world, will be explored with the help of specific examples. No claim to exhaustiveness is intended, nor are my interpretations meant to suggest that alternative or conflicting interpretations are invalid. On the contrary, conflicting meanings are, in my view, what art is about.

The book is designed to pursue a number of intertwined goals. First, I shall practice "reading" – that is, describing and interpreting images and stories both verbal and visual. At the same time, I shall reflect on what "reading" means. I shall reflect on the relationship between literature and the visual arts, a relationship between different, but not opposed, ways of producing signs and meaning. Thus I shall pursue insight into the rhetorical and pictorial devices used in the two arts. At the same time, I shall explore the different ways in which works by "Rembrandt" and certain verbal texts are or can be related. These reflections will point toward unexpected but crucial relationships between technical and ideological issues. Although each of the chapters of this book deals with a particular theoretical point, three issues derived from the above assumptions recur and intersect with the main points to constitute a subtext, uniting the various reflections. These three issues are the choice of "Rembrandt" in an anti-individualist study; the status of interpretation in a reception-oriented study; and the choice of certain terms of analysis, some of which have been compromised by their use in misogynist analyses, in a feminist study. I shall begin by discussing the first two of these issues, and, after presenting the various chapters in light of these, conclude with a brief discussion of the third.

WHY "REMBRANDT"?

In our culture, painting is art *par excellence*, and in a capitalist society, that excellence is taken quite literally, not only in the form of prices reached at auction, but also in the central position painting retains institutionally and ideologically within Western culture. There is nothing in the literary institution, for example, that really compares with the *museum*.[10]

Within the institution of art "Rembrandt" is a most representative figure, fetching among the highest prices ever paid per canvas, with the authenticity of the works – their autographic reliability – fully determining their worth. "Rembrandt" scholarship has become a paradoxical power; without being invested with power itself, it makes or breaks fortunes. If only for these reasons, "Rembrandt" presents a challenge to the analyst. Forgetting "Rembrandt" in order to pay more attention to popular works would leave these institutional aspects unchallenged.

A second answer to the question Why "Rembrandt"? can be found in his period. This artist belongs to an era still innocent of Freudianism – an innocence that makes his work a proper object for a psychoanalytic criticism that wishes to avoid circularity. There may not be in "Rembrandt" 's painting such wonderful coincidence of discourse as was the case with Freud and Sophocles.[11] But equally prestigious, and in many ways equally tragic, complex, and riddled with riddles, "Rembrandt" 's visual art, nevertheless, constitutes a suitable challenge to psychoanalysis.

A third answer to Why "Rembrandt"? rests in the *kind* of art his corpus contains. "Rembrandt" 's art being figurative, it presents us with both a problem and an opportunity. Representational art is "about" something and thus is open to reductionism. The reductionism that threatens the analysis of art is threefold: the reductionism of geneticism, as in intentionalist art history and classical psychoanalysis; the reductionism of interpretation, as in the unificatory tendencies of positivistic analysis; the reductionism of logocentrism, of "reading" the image only for its (monolithic) meaning. On the other hand, these tendencies can and should be challenged in their turn, and thus we come to our opportunity. By retaining the kind of openness and vulnerability described above, we can escape reductionism and engage a liberating analysis. "Rembrandt" is appropriate for exploring the ways in which interdisciplinary analysis can counter the tendency to reductionism.

A fourth answer to our question can be elicited by remembering that "Rembrandt" belongs to a tradition that considers skill the primary asset for a painter, an asset far more crucial than the "touch of craziness" that classical psychoanalytic criticism, as heir to the Romantic tradition, so often presupposes. With so little known about his life, and with that "knowledge" so riddled with romantic presuppositions that wild speculations about his neuroses can only be ridiculous, we are left only with what remains on the canvas and what can be inferred from the texts that frame the canvases. This state of affairs protects the enterprise of criticism against another well-known trap, what we might call the pseudobiographical fallacy. On the other hand, at least Rembrandt scholarship has been enlivened by Schwartz's "nasty" account of Rembrandt's person (Schwartz, 1985) and more profoundly by Alpers's (1988) book. Therefore, this kind of scholarship at the very least escapes the problem lying in wait for the many respectful but not sufficiently distanced studies that get bogged down by the laudatory discourse of connoisseurship. The "Rembrandt" corpus is worth some kind of attention in which respect is not an issue, and in which, ultimately, craziness, incoherence, and contradiction are possibilities, if only because the critic and viewer are never exempted.

Finally, the number of works in which blindness is thematized makes "Rembrandt" doubly appropriate for a study like this one. First, there is the question of the insistent presence of a theme that postmodernism relates to self-reflexivity, feminism to voyeurism, and psychoanalysis to castration. Second, there is the metaquestion of the critical blindness brought forth by sheer thematic psychoanalysis which obscures the work of representation. Both these questions deserve exploration.

"Rembrandt," then, is here treated as a cultural text that transgresses the imaginary boundaries between "high" and popular culture, a boundary I locate between the work as thing and its reception as event. It is the center of a body of reflection on art, visuality, and discourse. "Rembrandt" inserted itself into the cultural discourses and visual practices in the seventeenth century in Holland, and has been in constant movement and transformation since. Whenever historical "facts" – speculations about the biography of the painter named Rembrandt – partake of the event of reception, these facts and speculations themselves become part of the text. Conceiving the historical dimension of analysis in this way, I do not ignore it, but I do keep in mind that no historical position is innocent of the contemporary perspective of the subject doing the historiography. In fact, it is that historical position in which I am primarily interested.

In his famous attack on the concept and authority of the author, Foucault (1979) banishes four different concepts of authorship. Not only does he dispose of the psychological idea of the author, of the authorial intention, and of the historical author as origin of the work, he also jettisons the last stronghold of the concept of the author – the author function as the centering of meaning – by demonstrating it to be a projection of a reader who needs semantic centrality to deal with the work. Foucault's alternative is a radical proliferation of meaning, where the author/work becomes a fluctuating function, always interacting with other functions in the larger discursive field.

So far so good; but is there a limit to these fluctuations? Or are we constrained by an anything-goes attitude that makes any future shift in power relations within the culture invisible from now on? My position here is that there *are* limits, but not limits that can be authenticated by appeal to the author, even when interpreting "author" in the widest sense of the historical context. Instead, those limits are strategic, but fundamental. They are fundamental, for any position that does not assess the political basis of the status quo cannot challenge the established cultural powers, because, simply, these powers were established on political grounds. But once shifting, strategic limits are accepted as replacement for both "natural" limits and Foucault's "antilimits," then these new bounds offer a starting point from which to develop a politics of reading that draws its legitimacy from political positions, not from any fictitious "real" knowledge. And once we acknowledge both the necessity and the strategic nature of limits to interpretation, we move from the question of the author back to the question of interpretation.

WHY INTERPRETATION?

The need for interpretation requires some additional comments at this point as well. A study that focuses on reading cannot but question the location of meaning and the related concern regarding the subject of interpretation. Such a task inevitably leads to the further question: Why bother to interpret if interpretation is subjective anyway?[12]

Here, again, strategy prevails. Whenever a literary scholar, moved by the commendable intention of putting an end to the current proliferation of interpretation, stands up to claim that some details in realistic texts have no narrative function, that they merely serve to produce an "effect of the real" (Barthes, 1968) or an effect of verisimilitude (*vraisemblance*; Genette, 1969b), someone else responds that the examples given do have a narrative function after all, if only one looks hard enough. There seems to be a resistance to meaninglessness that invariably looks convincing. As a consequence, we continue to assume that everything in a work of art contributes to, and modifies, the meaning of the work.

But if everything in a work of art participates equally in the production of meaning, then how do we know what texts and images are "about" and why? In other words, which signs convey, or trigger, which meanings? One answer is that there is no answer because texts and images do nothing; the interpreter invents the meaning. Putting the question differently, we may ask, On what basis do we process verbal and visual signs? The debate is particularly troublesome in literary theory because the question interferes with the apparent obviousness of the answer. We assume we know what signs are and which signs we process because we know what a letter, a word, and a sentence are, and we assume that words are the units we call signs in verbal works.

Here, visual poetics reminds us of this assumption's untenability, by forcing us to ask what the visual counterpart of a word is: Is it an image, as the phrase "word and image" too easily suggests? Mulling over this difficult equation, we become less sure that words are, in fact, the "stuff" of verbal signification.

The problem of delimiting signs and delineating interpretation – of distinguishing interpretation from description – is related. Since readers and viewers bring to the texts and images their own cultural and personal baggage, there can be no such thing as a fixed, predetermined meaning, and the very attempt to summarize meanings, as we do in encyclopedias and textbooks, is by definition reductive. Yet as soon as we are forced to draw from these views the inevitable conclusion that "anything goes" and that interpretation is a futile scholarly activity since it all depends on the individual interpreter, we draw back. We then turn around, trying to locate, in the text or image, not a meaning, but the "occasion" of meaning, the thing that triggers meaning; not fixity, but a justification for our flexibility.

As Jonathan Culler has argued, when confronting the dilemma of interpretation we face two mutually exclusive positions which nevertheless are complementary, continuous – that is, mutually inclusive.[13] Ernst van Alphen has argued convincingly in response to Culler that the dilemma can be resolved only by our letting go of a unified concept of meaning and being ready to distinguish at least two different "moments of meaning production" occurring at the two loci of the debate, text and reader. Van Alphen's solution is not a harmonizing of the conflict demonstrated by Culler; it is not a dialectic resolution but rather a radicalization of the poles of the opposition. Moreover, van Alphen leaves room for more than two kinds of meaning, and stimulates thinking about other possibilities.[14]

As I hope to show in the third chapter of this study, I subscribe to the general skepticism concerning the possibility of circumscribing meaning, but as my second chapter will demonstrate, I do not find interpretation futile. On the contrary, the continuity and interdependence between producing and processing works of art makes interpretation as important, as valuable, as writing and painting. But my continued adherence to interpretation is more polemical than that. While I find much that is intellectually attractive in the currently widespread resistance to interpretation presented in response to the recognition of the free play of signs and meanings, I also see in it a renewed threat to the freedom of cultural participation, a new form of censorship.

Censorship of art, be it overtly political or subliminally social, is confirmed, strengthened, and perpetuated by censoring forms of interpretation. In a world where access to writing and painting is made difficult – by the institutional censors of art – for all individuals deviating from a self-asserting mainstream, making interpretation a privileged form of art processing subjugates it to the same mechanisms of exclusion.

But there is more to it. True, the academic practice of interpretation, linked with journalism and other more popular forms of interpretation through a common ideology and often even through shared personnel, can be a form of censorship in itself. Even where the margins built within art and the reigning concepts of beauty leave some space for the production of works that cannot be exhausted by mainstream response, the exclusions operating within the very activity of interpretation as a practice taught and learned can easily take care of all interpretations that might enhance the unsettling aspects of these not-so-mainstream works; of interpretations that make the works threatening. This is precisely the mo-

tivation for the resistance coming from progressive scholars. But
for the same reason, censorship *of* interpretation can be used to
conceal the censorship *by* interpretation. And that is why the resistance to interpretation can receive such wide acclaim, from progressive as well as from conservative ideologues.

A more open academic and educational policy can make room
to include the views of those who respond to art from a less predominant social position. Such a broadening is an indispensable
next step toward a better, more diverse and complex, understanding
of culture. In spite of its challenging and persuasive logic, we must
place the resistance to interpretation within this dynamic. I am afraid
that it cannot be an accident that the increasing participation of
women and minorities in the academy coincides with a growing
resistance to the very practices from which they had formerly been
excluded. To put it overly simply, as soon as women began to
speak, the subject of speech was no longer relevant; as soon as
women began to interpret, there was no more need for interpretation. In other words, the same threat is acutely present as the one
that the "death of the author" poses: As women gained access to
signs, the sign was put to death.[15] This demonstrates precisely how
the problematic of interpretation and the challenge to the sign are
related.

In the following chapters, I shall not make a regressive claim for
the reinstatement of the Saussurian sign with its system-ontological
status and its safely sutured signified. My endeavor will be much
more down to earth; I shall explore modes and possibilities, analyzing what does or can happen in the encounter between text and
reader – an encounter that is never a true encounter and that always
leaves rests, gaps, and "meaninglessness" anyway. I shall try to
show that the determination of signs and the attribution of meaning
to signs – acknowledged as readerly activities – follow various paths
whose diversification is precisely the point. We do many different
things under the unifying heading of interpretation that we call the
response to signs. This is how the problem of interpretation joins
the problem of the sign.[16]

The view of signs to which I shall adhere in this study posits the
basic density of both verbal and visual texts. I use the term "density"
in Goodman's (1976) sense: as conveying the fundamental inseparability of individual signs, as the opposite of discreteness. This view
eliminates at least one difference between discourse and image.
Resisting the early Wittgenstein's anguish about, and sympathizing
with his later happy endorsement of, the cloudiness of language, I
shall contend that the same density that characterizes visual texts
obstructs the propositional clarity of verbal texts.[17] Thus, separate
words cannot be taken to rule interpretation, and the ideal of "pure"
propositional content longed for in the *Tractatus* is untenable: The
elements of a proposition cannot have independent meaning. This

recognition means that the difference between verbal and visual texts is no longer one of the status and delimitation of the signs that constitute them. And the visual model, apparently predominant, overwhelms the concrete particularity of the signifier, giving rise to "cloudiness" in each medium. Hence, the Wittgenstein of the *Tractatus* mourns the fact that there is no nondense language, whereas later, in the *Investigations*, Wittgenstein denounces the positivistic illusion that makes visuality the basis of interpretation, sacrificing both the signifier and the activity of semiosis. In this later work he endorses the view he earlier regretted, that language is as dense as pictures. This may not make language visual, but it does displace the difference between the two media.

Yet the density of both visual and linguistic signs is not really the issue. Rather, it is the dynamism of signs that the recognition of their density makes possible that is at issue. The perception of signs as static can be traced to the atomistic view of verbal signs, itself a relic of early structuralism which, in its turn, had inherited it from more explicitly positivistic schools of cultural scholarship.[18] The problem and source of this atomistic view are the semiotic positivism that claims ontological status for the sign. If the sign is a "real thing," then signs must be numerable, hence discrete and intrinsically static. A radically dynamic view, however, would conceive the sign not as a thing but as an event, the issue being not to delimit and isolate the one sign from other signs, but to trace the possible emergence of the sign in a concrete situation of work–reader interaction. Wittgenstein's concept of language games posits a dynamic view of the sign, which makes signs as *active*, and requires them to be both deployed *according to rules* and *public*. *A sign, then, is not a thing but an event.* Hence the meaning of a sign is neither preestablished and fixed, nor purely subjective and idiosyncratic.

Although this view seems to open the discussion to a paralyzing infinitude of phenomena, this apparent problem disappears as soon as we acknowledge that sign events occur in specific circumstances and according to a finite number of culturally valid, conventional, yet not unalterable rules, which semioticians call "codes." The selection of those rules and their combination leads to specific interpretive behavior.

THE CONTENT OF THIS STUDY

In light of the preceding considerations, this book progresses from more general to more specific explorations of problems pertaining to the interpretation of verbal and visual art. The opening chapter, "Beyond the Word–Image Opposition," provides an overview of issues included in the general theme of the book, and relates these issues to some major works of art analysis that are currently influential in both art history and literary studies.

Chapter 2 begins to explore the hermeneutic exchange between

gender that are readable in ''Rembrandt'''s works, through the
challenge posed by death.

THE TERMS OF ANALYSIS

The status of my own interpretations is strongly bound up with
the terms I use to elaborate them. Most of the terms of analysis
used here are necessarily derived from theories pertaining to a single
discipline; the disciplines from which these terms are derived include feminist theory, rhetoric, narratology, and psychoanalysis. I
shall discuss their relevance and the conditions for bringing them
to the other disciplines in due course. Neither restrictive discipli-
narity nor free eclectic borrowing will be taken for granted, and I
shall try to justify explicitly any modifications of concepts. Although most concepts are derived from visual analysis and literary
theory, the use of psychoanalytic and feminist concepts is so current
in contemporary critical cultural studies that it seems that they need
not be problematic. Yet I find that the self-evidence of those concepts sometimes precludes their efficacy, as imprecise, casual use
alternates with precise, technical deployment.

I shall try to argue deliberately for my uses and possibly misuses
of theoretical terms, but the general question of the relation between
visual response and psychoanalysis must be mentioned right away.
As I have argued before, the object of a reader-oriented analysis of
art is *our relation to the image*. The ''our'' in this statement needs
further analysis. Although this phrase is meant to suggest how
deeply entrenched we are in any act of interpretation of images
stemming from other times and places, ''we'' is emphatically not
a monolithic subject. Within a psychoanalytic framework, this collective subject can be further differentiated. By ''us'' I mean a subject
traversed and fraught by the unconscious, including the superego
and its social implications: narcissism and its defensiveness against
affect, desire, and the fantasy character of response. The way we
perceive and interpret images is based on fantasy, and fantasy is
socially based. Thus there is dissymmetry between men and women
before male and female figures. But this dissymmetry is also unstable, varying according to which aspects of the unconscious are
more or less strongly implicated in the act of looking. As I will
argue, the response to the *Danae* is more likely to differ according
to gender, whereas the response of women and men to *The Blinding
of Samson* might differ less strongly, because this painting appeals
to a pre-Oedipal fantasy. The differentiation, here, occurs not so
much directly according to gender lines but primarily according to
other divisions, like narcissistic fulfillment and the relative solidity
of the ego.

Thinking about the uneasy fit between psychoanalysis – a basically verbal discourse – and visual art, and the equally uneasy fit
between psychoanalysis – an overwhelmingly masculine discourse
– and feminism, the strategies and concepts of deconstruction have

often been quite helpful. The continual suspicion of binary oppositions, which informs this study as a whole, is, of course, a major tenet of deconstructive criticism. And for a study that puts interpretation in the center and questions the status of meaning, no concept seems more attractive than that of dissemination.[19] For dissemination also takes place in the space between verbal and visual reading, and calls into question the tenability of those categories through an alternative concept of textuality.

Earlier in this Introduction I discussed Vermeer's *Woman Holding a Balance*, a painting that might be considered the "purest" of images. As we have seen, it was textualized by the workings of narrativity, imported into the work by an act of reading. That discussion exemplifies the way in which I shall generally handle standard concepts; such a method is called for by this book's interdisciplinary status, but it accommodates neither purism nor eclecticism without problems. For, in an important sense, an image is not a text; but while irreducibly different, the visual and the verbal domains interpenetrate, influence, and inform each other. Why, then, speak about "reading" images as "texts"? Without trying to assimilate images to verbal texts, I want to make a case for an idea of visual textuality without that visual text losing its visual specificity.

Later on in this study, I shall more fully interpret "Rembrandt"'s *Danae*, but here I would like briefly to analyze that work as a text, offering this analysis as a model in miniature of just how this method will let visual texts be read without sacrificing their visuality. First, I shall present the *Danae* in the more traditional sense: as a narrative. But this concept of textuality will prove to be slightly problematic. If the concept of text illuminates the painting, so the painting shows the defects of the concept of text, with its fixed relation between sign and meaning, its hierarchical structure, its suppression of details, of the marginal, of the "noise." It is to such an oppressive notion of text that Derrida opposed the concept of dissemination, which enhances the slippery, destabilizing mobility of signs in interaction with sign users: here, viewers. Derrida replaces the metaphor of the phallus as the ultimate meaning with that of the hymen as the sheet – or canvas – on which meaning circulates without fixity.

The *Danae* (Figure 0.2) is more than a narrative in the traditional sense of a re-production, an illustration of a preexisting, narrative text. Let me briefly compare the verbal and the visual approach. The pre-text has it that this woman, forever barred from love by her frightened father, is, at the very moment the picture presents, visited by Zeus who managed, thanks to his disguise as a shower of gold, to break the taboo the woman's father had imposed on his daughter. In this pre-text's context, Zeus, the ever-loving master-god, is also the first Oedipus slaying his jealous father. But this is a verbal story, and we want to pursue a *visual* text.

Looking at the picture, we see a female body, nude, displayed

for the lust of the viewer who is allowed to peep into the intimacy
of the doubly closed bedroom. But this is a visual story, the story
of vision in Western culture. It is the story of the male voyeur and
the female object, of the eroticization of vision; it is the story of
the central syntagm – subject–function–object – in which the positions are fixed along gender lines – through which, indeed, gender
itself is constructed. It is the scheme that is invariably nearly dominating, nearly exclusive, but never absolutely so, because the dynamic of narrative precludes its foreclosure. If only in order to
break the monopoly of this visual construction of gender, undermining this verbal/visual opposition is worthwhile.

Between the text (the story of the welcomed arrival of Zeus) and
the image (the exhibition of a female body for voyeuristic con-
sumption), the painting produces its own narrative, reducible to
neither–the work's visual/narrative textuality. The pre-text is literally a pretext: Its anteriority allows the painting's appeal to the
general understanding of the story as a frame for its reversal. The
story's centrality, as the theme of the work, allows everything
decentered to slip in; it allows, that is, for the dissemination of
meaning.

There is another way to phrase this. The work's genesis in a
preexistent narrative helps to sever the tie between the two and to
produce another narrative, irreducibly alien to it, void of the deceptive meaning the pre-text brought along. With its genesis, the
severing of the tie, a central void, and the dissemination of what

0.2 *Danae* 1636, Bredius 474,
canvas, 185 × 203 cm
(Leningrad, Hermitage)

20

matters, an alternative to the hymen as the central bodily metaphor is creeping in here – and that alternative is the navel.

Starting from the pre-text, the divine lover who is supposedly welcome is visible only as a sheen. But the sheen, the border of light, so crucially "Rembrandtish," dissolves into futility. For in spite of deceptive appearances, Zeus's gold does not illuminate the woman. Rather, the sheen delimits the space in which the woman is enclosed; it demarcates her private space, emphasizing the form of the opening in which the woman's feet disappear – her opening. The sheen emphasizes the opening, but it does not produce it; so in this way the sheen does not *count*, and the pre-textual story is undermined.

Looking at the image from a different angle, we must take our own position into account. The viewer is *also* supposed to come in and be welcomed – as voyeur, allowed to see the female body on display. But, at the same time, this viewer is deprived of his iden-tity, as his eyes come in contact with his mirror image in the two represented onlookers. These two, the putto and the servant, form, according to a formal analysis, an insistent triangle with the female body as its base, paralleling and reversing the triangle of the exit-curtain. The putto refers iconographically to the pre-text, his tied hands a "symbol" of forbidden sexuality. While also offering a way of viewing the woman, it is an immature, childish way. For though he wrings his hands in despair, he is not looking at the woman's body. Perhaps he despairs over this lack, a lack imposed by the bonds on his hands, which, in fact, prohibit both touching *and* looking. Exasperated by the interdiction, the putto is visually self-enclosed. The servant, of whom more needs to be said later on, does not look at the woman at all.

These two stories – the purely textual, verbal pre-text and the story of the purely visual present – collude and collide in the work's textuality. They are in tension, but not in contradiction. They produce a new story, the text of the *Danae* as an interaction between the canvas and the viewer who processes it. In this text, Zeus, invisible as he/it is, thus becomes the pre-text the woman uses to get rid of the indiscreet viewer. The woman who at first sight seemed to be on display – as spectacle, in a static, visual reading – takes over and dominates both viewer and lover. Her genitals, prefigured by the slippers and magnified by the opening of the curtain at the other end of the sight line, are central in the framed text. They are turned toward the viewer, but they can be seen by neither viewer nor lover, because the viewer is sent away while the lover comes to her from the other side/sight. In this way her sex-uality, in spite of its centrality, is a trace of the pre-text, for the conflicting lines of sight cut it off; it is also the locus of the metaphor that kept creeping into the vocabulary of my analysis: It is the navel of the text. But between sex and navel lies a difference – the dif-ference between voyeurism and its deconstruction.

The metaphor of the navel is more satisfying than that of the

hymen for the deconstructed image; diluted into a multiple textuality, it is a false center attracting attention to its void of semes
– to its dis-semination. The metaphor of the navel pushes Derrida's
dissemination to its limits, and beyond. Although he undermined
the phallic view of the sign and of meaning inscribed in Saussure's
semiotics, Derrida still could not quite let go: For his dissemination,
meant to dissolve the penetrating power of the dualistic sign, comes
dangerously close to an overwhelming dispersion of semen; coming
all over the text, it spreads out so pervasively, so Biblically, that
it becomes like the stars in heaven or the sand at the seashore: a
promise to fatherhood. Derrida clings to the concept of the hymen,
the veil that protects from penetration as an alternative for the
phallic privileging of the invisible signified; but by invoking Hymen, he also embraces the moment when the virgin bride is torn
open and pervaded by semen. Invoking Hymen invokes marriage.
And marriage imperialistically prevails, threatening to become the
metaphor for semiosis.

Deconstructing this metaphor with the help of visual images read
as texts, I propose to replace it with the navel – both a trace of the
mother, and the token of autonomy of the subject, male and female
alike; a center without meaning, it is yet a meaningful pointer that
allows plurality and mobility, that allows the viewer to propose
new readings to meet his or her needs, but without letting those
readings fall into the arbitrariness that leads to isolation.

This concept of textuality leaves room for the specificity of the
visual; indeed, it builds the reading it suggests upon the image's
visuality. Yet it enhances the irreducible textuality – its play between story and static image, its visual mobility, and the indispensable collaboration between the work and its socially and
historically positioned viewers. The navel, then, is a metaphor for
an element, often a tiny detail, that hits the viewer, is processed
by her or him, and textualizes the image on its own terms. In the
Danae, it is not the woman's "real" navel but her genital area (Figure
0.3); in *The Toilet of Bathshebah*, another nude with an ostentatiously
represented navel, the navel of the text is the left-hand corner of
the letter the naked woman is holding (Figure 0.4); in the Vermeer,
it is the nail-and-hole (Figure 0.5). Later on, I shall argue that the
navel of the Berlin *Susanna* is the fist of one of the Elders (Figure
0.6). In many works that I shall analyze in this study, the textual-

0.3–0.6 (*left to right*)   *Danae*,
detail; *The Toilet of Bathshebah*,
detail; Vermeer, *Woman Holding a
Balance*, detail; *Susanna Surprised
by the Elders*, detail.

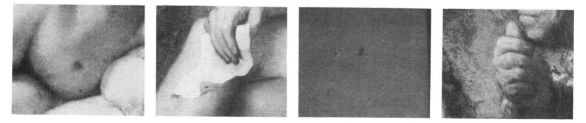

izing navel is an emptiness, a little surface which the work leaves unfilled.

This play with metaphors should not be taken for a meaningless linguistic game. By chosing a bodily metaphor, I also wish to demonstrate both my allegiance and my polemic opposition to much of psychoanalytic theory. Here the navel is the symbolization of a body part, just as the phallus is, and it too is loaded with the connotations of gender. Yet these are radically different in status. The phallus refers to gender in terms of haves and have-nots, or "to have it" versus "to be it." The navel, in contrast, is fundamentally gender specific – the navel is the scar of dependence on the mother – but it is also democratic in that both men and women have it. And unlike the phallus and its iconic representations disseminated throughout post-Freudian culture, the navel is starkly indexical.

Thus, the metaphor of the navel, as the detail that triggers textual diffusion, variation, and mobility of reading, is therefore a tribute not only to an antiphallic semiotic but also to an antiphallic genderedness that does not assign to women a second-rate position. My position toward gender, then, is comparable to my attitude toward "high art." In both cases, the hierarchy is not denied, which it cannot be because it is a cultural reality, but it is shifted and thereby undermined.

In her seminal article on Freud's *Beyond the Pleasure Principle* (1922), Elisabeth Bronfen (1989) suggests that we focus on the navel as an image of primary castration. In support of that suggestion, she argues for the psychoanalytic importance of the experience of primary narcissism. She makes her case through a close analysis of Freud's repression, in that essay, of the place of the woman – his daughter and the mother of the child out of whose game the theory emerges. Freud's identification with the child as between father and son is based on the conflation of mother and daughter, and demonstrates the genderedness of the very formation of this theory and, by analogy, of theory in general. But when Freud, the day after the death of his favorite daughter, shifts attention from her death to his woundedness, calling her death an incurable assault on his narcissism, another identification – that between father and daughter/mother – is at stake. When the father/son is wounded, only then are gender boundaries crossed.

What emerges from this study, finally, is a "Rembrandt" full of ambivalence. Both highly disturbing and highly gratifying, this body of work gains in depth by readings in the mode of the navel; the readings in each chapter acknowledge visuality and do not shy away from discursive elements; they recognize where cultural commonplaces are mobilized, yet leave room for the marginal other; they endorse the "density" of visual signs and let that density spill over into literature, while not fearing to point out specific, discrete signs in visual works and the loci of density in literature. Each chapter pursues simultaneously a theoretical question, the interpretation of at least one "Rembrandt" work and at least one verbal text with which the visual work entertains a relation. Together these chapters offer an overview of issues and concepts relevant for the study of the interaction between image and discourse.

The interpretations set forth in this study are not meant to be full, comprehensive descriptions of what we see in the paintings; nor are they narratives reconstructing the pre-texts that give the works meaning. Instead, my interpretations start at the navel, the little detail that doesn't fit the "official" interpretation: the view of the work put forward by the terms of agreement among readers before me. For invariably those official readings leave a rest, a lack. They have one thing that isn't there and should be, or that is there but shouldn't, and thus trigger the alternative reading. What the classical narrative readings cannot unproblematically accommodate sets in motion another narrative, via the suspenseful encounter between the narrative and the visual. In this way, the concept of the "navel of the text" is programmatic: It proclaims an interaction, not an opposition, between discourse and image.

CHAPTER 1

BEYOND THE WORD–
IMAGE OPPOSITION

[T]his beat has the power to decompose and dissolve
the very coherence of form on which visuality may
be thought to depend. (Rosalind Krauss, "The Im/
pulse to See," 1988:51)

INTRODUCTION

I T is fashionable today to speak of art history as a discipline in
crisis. At first sight, the symptoms of such a crisis are overwhelming. Books with titles like *The End of the History of Art?*
(Belting, 1987), *Rethinking Art History* (Preziozi, 1989), or *The New
Art History* (Rees and Borzello, 1986) find eager publishers and
buyers; scholars from adjacent fields enter the field of art history
to propose alternatives to current approaches they consider dead
ends (e.g., Bryson, 1981, 1983, 1984) or to deconstruct the art
historical enterprise itself (e.g., Melville, 1990); some of the most
interesting art historians disclaim their allegiance to the discipline
(e.g., Fried 1987:10); and, most significantly, alternative fields
emerge out of ongoing but hitherto rather marginal preoccupations,
under various headings, which propose the study of art in relation
to other disciplines. Programs in cultural studies, visual poetics,
word and image studies, and comparative arts are testimony to
attempts to revitalize art history by expansion into another field.
Without such an emergency measure the field is in danger of being
rigidified, impoverished, dying.

But these supposed symptoms are deceptive; when examined
more closely, they indicate something quite different from a crisis:
an astonishing vitality, perhaps the all but overwhelming predominance of art history within the humanities today; indeed, they
perhaps indicate a shift from linguistics in the 1960s and early 1970s,
via anthropology in the 1980s, to art history in the 1990s as the
central discipline on which other fields draw heavily for their *own*
revitalization. One can argue that the willingness of art historians
to challenge their discipline provides evidence of the discipline's
strength; it can afford the risk.[1] If scholars from other fields are
attracted to the study of art, something more attractive must be
going on there than in their home fields.[2] And if strong art historians
take some distance from what they consider less interesting or

tenable in their home field, they are by the same token themselves contributing the new perspective that was lacking. For in spite of their disclaimer, they, too, are art historians, and unless they wish to give away the field to those whose practice they don't like, their own practice must remain art history. Art history is expanding its boundaries with the creation of new fields, not giving up the ghost. Art history itself is not in crisis; it is challenging, addressing, and overcoming the threat of its own foreclosure. The works of Svetlana Alpers, T. J. Clark, Michael Fried, Linda Nochlin, Griselda Pollock, and Leo Steinberg, to name just a few contemporary historians of older art, attest to art history as a lively, exciting discipline.

This is not to say that all is fine in art history, and that those who think the discipline is in crisis are out of their minds. Those who claim that art history cannot survive the challenge of feminism, for example, may have a point. Of course, to the question whether art history is sick or in the pink, the answer will have to be neither, or both. I am situating my own enterprise within the cracks produced by these opposing views. I am speaking, that is, as one of those "aliens," who come to visual art from a literary background, with what some may want to call the arrogance of ignorance, and others a fresh, or at least different, perspective. I am speaking as one who enthusiastically participates in establishing an integrative discipline where the study of words and images is no longer separate.

Scholars from various disciplines have been able to enter the adjacent field thanks to semiotics, a multidisciplinary methodology, which is in no way the property of literary studies.[3] The usefulness of semiotics as a method, a paradigm, a perspective, or just an eye-opener, for art history in its current exciting crisis, is worth assessing.

In *Tradition and Desire* (1984), Norman Bryson takes up the issues raised by Harold Bloom in *The Anxiety of Influence* (1973) to show how the dialectical relationship between the wish to follow and the desire to outdo great models establishes the unique interaction between sameness and difference that characterizes each work of art. These interactions can properly be called a dialogue, in the Bakhtinian sense of the many-voicedness of any work, but including the tensions that Bakhtin's slightly embellishing concept tends to obscure.[4] The tensions between tradition and desire, as Bryson phrases it, generate *new* work, renewal of work, and reworking of newness, with the very newness being relativized in the very process of analysis.[5]

Of course, there is a context for the dialogue between the desire to follow and to outdo glorious predecessors that I wish to actualize here. First, it is well known that scholars, just like everybody else, need to establish their own difference from others by lumping together all the work they wish their own to differ from. Thus they practice what Hayden White (1978) calls "ostentatious self-definition by negation." Labeling their own work as "new," their predecessors' "old," if not "ancient," they try to separate and valorize their own work at the expense of their models. But difference between "old" and "new" is never unproblematic. With *les anciens et les modernes* in seventeenth-century France, for example, *les modernes* found it less easy to define their newness than the oldness of *les anciens*. Today the New Historicism in literary studies is, from the perspective of nonhistorians, just a little too close to the old historicism to gain a distinct profile. And in certain quarters the New Art History is too busy disqualifying its great predecessors to emerge itself as detached from them.

Don't misunderstand me here. I find this tension largely productive, as it motivates the "new" people to radicalize their positions, while it challenges *les anciens* to renewal as well. But in the case of art history it is partly responsible for the defensive conservatism of large contingents of art historians who rightly refuse to recognize their work in the caricatures set up by *les modernes*.

A second context for the tension between tradition and desire is the dialogue between word and image. Mirroring the preceding struggle, word-and-image works tend to suggest that "straight" art historians neglect the verbal aspects of visual art. But this can hardly be the case in a field whose strongest tradition is today icono*graphic*, the method that consists of *reading* images as what, visually, they are *not*, and which has, moreover, always been strongly anchored in verbal sources. Traditional, iconographic art history may suffer from underestimating the readerly quality of its own work. But, at the same time, overemphasis on the novelty of word-and-image studies encourages the repression of the verbal aspects of traditional art history, hence making difficult the insertion of traditional work within the new paradigm. And word-and-image studies may undermine their own project in the way they accuse their predecessors of failing: The very phrase "word and image" suggests that two different, perhaps incompatible things are to be shackled together; the phrase emphasizes the difference, not the common aspects of the two. This dichotomistic fallacy continues to weaken the renewal word-and-image studies promise.

Having learned so much from art history, I am now caught in the very tension Bryson demonstrated in *Tradition and Desire* (1984), both in relation to the works I shall discuss here and in relation to the discussion itself. I wish to make my endeavor clear from the outset: This is not a work of art history, "new" or not, although it is deeply indebted to some outstanding work in art history. Therefore, I shall begin with a brief presentation of work by three authors: Svetlana Alpers, an art historian; Michael Fried, who is trained as an art historian and a literary critic; and Norman Bryson, who came to art history as a literary scholar.[6] I also want to acknowledge that disciplinary input is indispensable if one is to avoid importing old problems into new attempts. And an increase in such acceptance might make it easier for me to show to both outsiders and insiders of art history that *verbality* or "wordness" is indispensable in visual art, just as *visuality* or "imageness" is intrinsic to verbal art.[7] As I shall use the terms, verbality (or "wordness") refers to a kind of discursivity that is not logocentric, visuality (or "imageness") that is not imagocentric; neither is tied to a particular medium.

Following my discussion of the works of Alpers, Fried, and Bryson, I shall replace that awkward conjunction "and" with some more specific links. As Shoshana Felman (1977) has demonstrated for the equally unsatisfying phrase "literature and psychoanalysis" (of which more in Chapter 8), such an apparently neutral conjunction or linking word often hides an unwarranted hierarchy that undermines the connection's enriching potential. I shall therefore propose different possibilities to rebaptize, hence to reorient, the enterprise. For my goal is not to claim more "newness" than is there, but to systematize currents, or even perhaps undercurrents – "tropisms" in Nathalie Sarraute's (1957) sense – in extant work, and thus contribute to the acknowledgment and further development of more thorough and explicit relations between fields, and more self-confidence for each, which is a precondition of acceptance of otherness.

STATE OF THE ART

In 1985, Svetlana Alpers published *The Art of Describing: Dutch Art in the Seventeenth Century*, a book that received much attention both inside and outside art history. In this book she undertook to revise the concepts with which we approach the art of the past. She argued against the art historical bias that privileged narrative art in the Italian mode, thus obliterating the specificity of Dutch art. Earlier she had demonstrated the heuristic productivity of this hypothesis as a reading strategy in a piece on Velázquez's *Las Meninas*, where she had shown that the sense of paradox this painting seems to produce (e.g., Foucault, 1973; Searle, 1980; Snyder and Cohen, 1980) stems from an integration of narrative and description.[8]

In *The Art of Describing*, Alpers draws upon contemporary documents, both verbal and visual, concerning the "visual culture" in the Netherlands: ideas about vision, about scientific reliability, about the invention and the impulse to invent instruments for the perfection of vision, about the impulse to document structures visually as in maps. On the basis of this reading of the visual culture of the time, she analyzes a large number of works of art of various genres in order to demonstrate the descriptive impulse in that art.[9] What is at stake in *Describing*, in my interpretation of Alpers's thesis, then, is the influence of a verbal context, a diffuse cultural text about vision, on the visual art of the time. This visual culture is an *episteme* à la Foucault, which pervaded the culture as a doxa[10] à la Barthes. It is this aspect of Alpers's study – with its roots in widely circulating discourses of the time, in diffuse rather than pointed sources – that makes a good case for art history's inherent "word-and-image-ness."[11]

The book concludes with two case studies, of Vermeer and of Rembrandt, where the former is shown to be descriptive to the point of representing its extreme while the latter escapes it, or takes it to its limits.[12] Alpers's later book, *Rembrandt's Enterprise* (1988), begins by challenging this conclusion. Here, the author takes Rembrandt not to have been an exception to his time, but to have been both its product and an instrument of change. It is a creative response to the current debate on (dis)attribution, authenticity, and the sense of loss entailed by the nonautographic status of many of Rembrandt's masterpieces. And it is an excellent piece of evidence that the discipline is well able to take care of its own problems and dead ends.

Rather than deploring the loss of great "Rembrandts" or settling for the resolution of the authenticity question, Alpers proposes an explanation for why the misattributed paintings have fooled us for so long.[13] This study is "materialist," in an unorthodox sense of that word, in that it analyzes both the materiality of painting and the economic activities of the artist; the economic organization of the art business and Rembrandt's eccentric and, at the same time, founding place in it.[14] The book's four chapters each deal with a different aspect of Rembrandt's active intervention in the status of art: his relation to the materiality of paint, his use of theatricality, the direction of his studio, and his way of creating value on the market. As interesting as all four issues are, I shall return only to the first two, and shall discuss them only insofar as they touch upon the relation between discourse and image.

Michael Fried's book, *Absorption and Theatricality: Painting and Beholder in the Age of Diderot* (1980), declares its object to be painting plus commentary. In this book Diderot's writing on painting in the *Salons* is not taken as a secondary metatext, but as an inherent part of the art production of the time; the interaction between critic and artist is dialectic rather than hierarchical. As Fried's title indicates, the central theme of the study is the relation between painting and beholder which, in the period Fried discusses, becomes more and more problematic and paradoxical. Fried begins at the moment in French art when interest focused on characters so absorbed in their own mental occupations that the visual representation of their states of mind was the ultimate challenge painters had to face. The twenty or so years of production he studies show a shift away from this challenge to one seemingly opposed, but in fact a response to it: the representation of dramatic movement. Fried shows that this preference for the theatrical is the diegetic[15] consequence of a representational preoccupation with unity. This concern for unity can be seen as a response to the absorption tradition, where unity remained thematic (i.e., all figures were absorbed) but could not be diegetic (i.e., figures did not interact). Fried argues, however, that the concern for unity is in turn grounded in a specific view of the painting's relationship to the beholder, which is paradoxical from the start and, as we will see, bound to disrupt the unity itself.

Theatricality addresses a beholder willing to identify with positions offered, and most of these paintings include a figure representing that identification diegetically. Yet the theatrical mode also implies an awareness and acceptance of, even a demand for, the viewer's absence from the scene of (the) painting.

In his book *Realism, Writing, Disfiguration* (1987), Fried focuses only indirectly on these issues, his main theme being a kind of deconstructionist self-representational quality in a major painting by Thomas Eakins, *The Gross Clinic* (Figure 1.1), and in the writings of Stephen Crane. The self-representations in both cases are paradoxically intertwined; simplifying Fried's complex thesis, one could say that Eakins's preoccupation is with writing, Crane's with drawing. A similar "word-and-image-ness" is at stake in my remarks

1.1 Thomas Eakins, *The Gross Clinic* 1875, canvas 96 × 78½ in. [243.8 × 199.4 cm] (Jefferson Medical College, Thomas Jefferson University, Philadelphia)

30

on the Tobias drawings in Chapter 8. Yet the analysis of Eakins's work, which is the part of the book I shall limit myself to here, works its way to that thesis through an analysis of the relationship to the beholder as suggested by two major figures in the painting, the master surgeon Gross and a seemingly secondary figure, who, according to Fried and his predecessors, is the patient's mother.[16] The paradox of theatricality in Eakins's painting takes on a twentieth-century affective quality that is related to familial roles and becomes the acute dilemma of both intense seeing and intense not-looking. I shall revert to this affective aspect in the concluding chapter of this study, where I shall take mis-seeing, unseeing, and not-looking as the founding themes of visual representation. Although in this book Fried presents himself thematically as a word-and-image scholar since he focuses on the representation of writing in painting and on visual representation in writing, it is within the former that I wish to take up his work.

Norman Bryson has published three books within a few years' time: *Word and Image* (1981), *Vision and Painting* (1983), and *Tradition and Desire* (1984), already mentioned.[17] The first and third books deal with a historical body of painting, from Lebrun to Delacroix. The second is a shorter essay, largely a polemic against the resemblance theory of representation predominant in art history, of which Gombrich's schemata are taken to be the last remnant. In the first of this series of books, Bryson addresses word-and-image issues in more than one way. These discussions are representative of the various steps which will be outlined in this chapter and will be indicated with the somewhat provisional catch phrases "word and image," "visual poetics," and "comparative arts." In this book the author analyzes both paintings and texts; two chapters are on Diderot. Thus the book belongs to "straight" word-and-image approaches. He confronts texts with their pre-textual background (Lebrun) or with their posttextual responses (Watteau), and shows the interaction between them.

To the extent that he is able to demonstrate how the texts interfere both with the painting and with its perception by the viewers, and how textuality determines the rhetorical effect of paintings, Bryson comes close to what I shall call "visual poetics." Most characteristically, throughout the book he works with a distinction within the paintings between two modes of representation, both visual and both present in each of the works discussed: "discursivity" and "figurality." The distinction between the two draws upon French semiotics and is related, not always in entirely clear ways, to pairs like paradigm and syntagm, denotation and connotation, signified and signifier, realism and narrativity.

It might be worthwhile to compare Bryson's distinction between discursivity and figurativity to Peirce's symbolicity and iconicity, to which his formulations sometimes come close. But such a conflation would be misleading. Iconicity – in the vulgar sense of pictorial resemblance – is precisely what all the books discussed here are determined to challenge. In the specifically Peircean sense, iconicity represents a subset only of figurality. Iconicity is a ground of meaning production, a code, if you like, that establishes a relation between sign and meaning on the basis of analogy – of a common property. Thus, a map is iconic, not because it resembles the land, but because it shares with it a particular property: the shape of its boundary. Symbolicity is also a code, but one that establishes a relation between sign and meaning on the basis of conventional agreement. A good example is perspective, long considered the device of realism par excellence. It may be iconic in the specific sense, but it is more significantly symbolic.[18] We accept perspective as "natural," as realistic, because we are accustomed to it, even though we know that there are many art forms, within and outside our own culture, that are not perspectival.

Peircean iconicity is emphatically not the same thing as visuality. It is worthwhile to straighten out this possible misunderstanding from the start, because I shall use Peirce's vocabulary incidentally. Here is an example of an iconic meaning production that is not visual, yet that has repercussions for art historical writing. Jonathan Culler (1988:100) demonstrates that Bachelard's philosophical discourse is iconically contaminated by the earlier philosophers he writes on. The text's style is in some specific ways analogous to the style of its object. Although the relationship between sign – Bachelard's text – and meaning – the discourse he is commenting on – is iconic, there is nothing specifically visual about this production of (additional) meaning. In the following example, the visuality is there, but not in the iconic relation itself. In the wake of Hayden White's emphasis on the rhetoric of history, Michael Holly (1988, 1989) shows how the great early cultural historians such as Burckhardt and Adams are iconically prefigured by the paintings and stained windows they respectively discuss. They write their historical accounts in a style whose poetics is iconically referring to, if not shaped by, the works of art they set out to describe. Here the sign is discursive, the meaning is visual, and the iconic relation is shaped by the visual object. A symmetrical counterpart of this iconicity is implied in Michael Baxandall's *Giotto and the Orators* (1971), according to which the paintings are shaped in the form of the Latin sentences written by contemporary humanists. Here the sign, an aspect – composition – of the paintings, is visual whereas the meaning is not. Again, the relationship between sign and meaning is iconic, because analogous. Figurality, in Bryson's visual sense, then, must by all means be kept distinct from iconicity.

Bryson uses "figurality" in the etymological sense of formness, materiality, defining discursivity as propositional content. The most extreme figurality is what Bryson calls the painterly trace, the "deixis" of a work of art. The trace is the clearest example of another Peircean type of ground of meaning production – indexicality. The index is the sign that signifies on the basis of an existential relationship of contiguity with its meaning. Alpers's claim about the continuity between the visual culture in the Netherlands and the paintings produced in it is based on indexicality as a code. And Bryson's deictic painterly trace is closer to indexicality than to iconicity.[19]

In his second book, a theoretical and polemical treatise, Bryson uses the linguistic concept of deixis to depart from realism. In that work the idea of deixis leads to a plea for a kind of materialism[20] that would foreground the trace of the work of painting over the transparency of realism. The latter appeals to the ahistorical, disembodied gaze; the former to the more engaged, bodily glance. This pair is quite helpful to a discussion of feminism's hot issue – voyeurism – although it requires some further clarification. For whether Bryson is speaking of the interaction between painter and beholder or of the diegetic representation of that relation in the work is not always clear. But the integration of the linguistic concept of deixis with the two modes of viewing is a good example of comparative arts as a discipline. By stretching Bryson's theory a bit, we can even make the opposition, established by Benveniste (1970), between *discours* and *histoire*, or first–second person and third person modes of language use, relevant for visual art.[21]

As already indicated, Bryson's third book, *Tradition and Desire* (1984), was inspired by Harold Bloom's *Anxiety of Influence* (1973), and analyzes, through often fascinating discussions of major works, the tension between various trends in art in the early nineteenth century in France and, in particular, between specific painters (see his Chapter 4: "Ingress in the atelier of David") or painters and their context (see his Chapter 6: "Desire in the Bourbon Library"). Methodologically, Bryson slightly changes his approach by drawing more upon psychoanalysis than in his earlier books.

The three authors are presented here in order of increasing allegiance to literary studies, as well as in order of increasing commitment to an analysis of visual art. Bryson's own development shows this same progression: From a heavy input from literary studics and a distinct focus on verbal texts, his work moves via a discussion of art (only) criticism through a body of critical texts, to a work of art history *pur sang*, albeit with a difference, which is the methodological background imported from (psychoanalytic) literary studies.

WORDS IN IMAGES:
BEYOND ILLUSTRATION

One of the obvious approaches to word-and-image studies that has yielded sometimes fascinating results is the study of texts and their illustrations, preferably done by the same artist or, reversedly, images and the captions that "illustrate" them. Blake is a favorite author/artist studied by means of the first approach (Guest and Barrell, 1988); seventeenth-century emblems are a favorite genre apt for the second (Gelderblom, 1988). The question of what can be rendered in which medium is central for these approaches (e.g., Kibédi Varga, 1988). But the most obvious conclusion drawn over and over again is the inexhaustibility of the one medium in terms of the other. Poems will never be fully illustrated, nor can the plates ever fully be understood with reference to the poem. Image and caption hardly match, not only in terms of exhaustibility of meaning, but also in terms of coherence of message. Yet reading the image without the words can lead to hilariously erroneous interpretations, and vice versa. Text and image, even when presented as a whole, do not match, do not overlap; they can neither do with nor do without each other.

The study of images supposedly meant to illustrate well-known stories (e.g., Biblical episodes) shows the same obvious fact. Although those images, especially when painted on walls or windows of churches, did function as a replacement for texts in partly illiterate societies (Miles, 1985), they did so on the basis, not of total redundancy, but, on the contrary, of overwriting the previous text. Images are readings, and the rewritings they give rise to, through their ideological choices, function in the same way as sermons: They are not a retelling of the text but a use of it; not an illustration

1.2 *Joseph Accused by Potiphar's Wife* 1655, Bredius 523, canvas, 106 × 98 cm (Washington, D.C., National Gallery of Art)

but, ultimately, a new text. Stained windows may be "the poor man's Bible," but they are so in the Catholic sense: They must be mediated by the priest, not read directly by the poor man. So the image does not replace a text; it *is* one. Working through the visual, iconographic, and literary traditions that produced it, these images propose for the viewer's consideration a propositional content, an argument, an idea, inscribed in line and color, by means of representation. They function by means, also, of an appeal to the already established knowledge that enables recognition of the scene depicted. And paradoxically, this recognition of what is already known is an indispensable step in the communication of a new, alternative propositional content that is not yet known.

One example among many is "Rembrandt"'s Biblical history paintings.[22] Take the two paintings of Joseph accused by Potiphar's wife (Figures 1.2 and 1.3), two clearly narrative paintings on whose narrativity I shall dwell at greater length in Chapter 3. The story told in Genesis 39, in turn a rewriting of an ancient mythical tale,

1.3 *Joseph Accused by Potiphar's Wife* 1655, Bredius 524, canvas, 110 × 87 cm (Berlin-Dahlem, Gemäldegalerie)

35

runs more or less as follows.[23] Joseph, a slave in Egypt, escapes a seduction by the wife of his owner. He refuses to comply, alleging Potiphar's total trust in him as his excuse. Having entered the house as a nobody, his master has given him everything; to return favor with deceit by having sex with his master's wife would betray his gratitude. The woman grabs his coat, which she later uses as evidence that Joseph tried to rape her. The story belongs to a world-wide tradition commonly referred to as "lustful stepmother seducing innocent young son" (Yohannan, 1982). And it offers both a story about gender relations and a case for Freudian analysis.

If words and images could be separated, it should be possible to read the two paintings without reference to this tradition, as would be done by people unfamiliar with the literary tradition. It is hard to predict what kind of response such ignorance would produce, and to what extent it would still partake of the obvious Oedipal flavor with which it is represented in the Joseph tradition. This would be a thoroughly ahistorical reading, since no seventeenth-century Dutch, nor any contemporary person raised in cultural connection with any of the major monotheistic religions would possess this happy ignorance. For whoever has the slightest, probably doxic, inkling of the story, the paintings are recognizable as *Joseph*s, both globally, in character cast, and in detail, through iconographically readable signs. At this point a distinction must be made, however, between an attempt to read these works historically and the attempt I am pursuing, to account for our contemporary dealings with these works. Whereas knowledge of the story in seventeenth-century Holland was much more textually based, as it was embedded in the struggles of the aftermath of the Reformation, today the story is recounted, but in a much less textual manner. Thus the relation between the image and its pre-text, the primary characteristic of history painting, is unstable over time.

Reading the three characters and their postures on the global level, it is clear that the woman's action of pointing is easily decoded as accusatory, and the age difference between the two men and the intermediate age of the woman complete the sexual plot. For those who have gone through a substantial visual acculturation, a first viewing of these works cannot but include response to iconographic detail. For example, the key hanging at Joseph's waist in the first work represents the notion that Potiphar has trusted Joseph with his entire house.[24] As such it might be considered a "translation" into a visual idiom of an important element of the text, even though the text does not mention a key. But one must know both text and painterly tradition to make this connection.

Bryson relates this kind of iconographic reading to recognition. As it happens, the issue of recognition is one of the thorny problems of semiotics. Semioticians ask whether it is recognizing the *code* that enables us to relate signs with meanings in a rule-governed fashion; this is the thesis of linguistic competence. Or do we recognize the code because we know the "language" of visual representation in the Western tradition? Do we recognize the signs and their meanings, because we know the vocabulary of visual language? Do we decode the painting, recoding it in verbal language that intertextually refers to a story we know? These questions will be dealt with in Chapter 5. What matters at this point is that this "immediate" reading, based on recognition of the subject matter, finds only partial support in the verbal story.

Bryson uses the concept of recognition to distinguish denotative signs from connotative ones. Denotation is for him iconographic, and in semiotic terms that identification makes sense. Implicitly, he opts for the vocabulary thesis, making a case for the inherently readerly quality of visual semiosis. Under this reading, the key Joseph holds in the painting is not a key but a token of trust. But it is the Brysonian reading of the key as denotative (as opposed to connotative), turning it into a seemingly irrelevant (in realistic terms) painterly detail, that seems more problematic to me. True, the difference between recognition and decoding, or rather, between direct recognition of the image as standing for something else (i.e., the vocabulary thesis) and indirect recognition of the code (i.e., the linguistic competence thesis) has some differentiating value. But it encourages falling back into a naive notion of visual iconicity that is both unwarranted and misleading. The denotation–connotation pair does not solve the problem raised by the question, Why is it that viewers recognize the works as *Joseph*s even though they differ from and in some sense contradict the Biblical story?[25]

The Biblical story, however, differs considerably from these two pictorial versions. In fact, it never presents the three characters at the same time, nor is there any mention of keys. There, three confrontations follow one another: first, Joseph versus the woman; second, the woman versus her husband; and third, the husband versus Joseph. Especially in light of the obvious psychoanalytic aspects of this story, the direct confrontation between the three characters, due as it may be to the needs of visual simultaneity, brings about a major change in the reading of the story.[26] Briefly and provisionally summarized, the change is as follows: The three-fold confrontation increases the anxiety and enhances the position of the woman who, in the Genesis story, is merely a pre-text[27] for the main confrontation; she is the scapegoat whose rejection strengthens the intergenerational bond between the men. Rather than one of two single-episode oppositions, her position becomes central both structurally – as the apex of a triangle – and sequentially – as the three episodes are conflated into one. Hence, the knowledge of the verbal story partakes of the reading of the painting, but in doing so brings about a radical change in its meaning.

So, clearly the paintings respond to the story, but they do not copy, illustrate, or visualize it as it is presented in the Bible. Rather, they propose a counterreading, a displacement of interests, a shift in emphasis and affect.[28] In fact, the paintings suggest the position that feminist literary theory has termed "resistant reading" (Fet-

37

terley, 1978).[29] Although the paintings are, on an obvious level, totally visual, they also function in a combination of modes that includes various levels of verbality. One such level is that of the pre-text: Genesis 39, globally known. Another one is that of the new structure, offered by the works' propositional content. Then there is psychoanalysis, a theory and practice verbal par excellence. And finally, there is the new meaning – the increased and shifted affect mediated through verbal conventions of emotional expression.

The iconographic detail of the keys (Figure 1.4), on the other hand, represents in itself a different level of verbality. It requires reading *strictu sensu* to relate the keys to the Biblical expression "He gave everything into my hand," to which this visual sign has no *visual* connection. A key is not everything; nor is the figure holding it in his hand. But reading is a semiotic activity broader than literate reading, yet narrower than interpretation in general. Therefore, two interpretations interact here. On the visual level a painted key refers to a "real" key, by a combination of iconicity, indexicality, and symbolicity, the first and the third modes of signification dominating, the second indispensable nevertheless. On the verbal level, a represented key "stands for" trust, in a precise, because material, interpretation of both sign and interpretant,[30] by a combination in which the indexical is predominant. It is only by virtue of conventions of reading that this mode of reading is literary rather than merely verbal; some would say metaphorical or symbolic, rather than literal.[31]

This shows us something not only about the "pure" visuality of visual art, but also about the difficulty of speaking about paintings in terms of word and image. There are neither pure words – no verbal caption is visible – nor pure images, if by that we understand images readable without referential recourse to words. Yet materially as well as according to cliché norms of word-and-image distinctions, the works are entirely visual.[32] An interpretation of the

1.4 *Joseph Accused by Potiphar's Wife*, detail

works cannot confine itself within a traditional art-historical perspective, as the imput of verbality would remain unnoticed.[33] On
the other hand, a problematic of word and image would tend to
assess the relationship between the Biblical text and the paintings
in terms of the priority of the one and the derivative nature of the
other. The dichotomy inherent in such an endeavor would preclude
the *visibility* of the interaction of more than two modes operating
simultaneously.

Norman Bryson means something in this spirit, it seems to me,
when, in his first book on painting (Bryson, 1981), he tries to assess
the relative degrees of discursivity in French painting of the *Ancien
Régime*. The programmatic title of this book is thoroughly problematic. His analyses are mostly rich, dense, subtle, original; and
truly art historical. Showing the rich possibilities of art history, the
book is extremely valuable, evidence of the discipline's healthy
state.[34] But to the extent that it is a work on word and image, it
is confusing. Falling here and there into the trap of binarism, Bryson's account of discursivity, while subtle and pluralistic, suffers.

Bryson does, however, exploit the word–image dichotomy fully.
He does not stop at analyzing Diderot's prose on painting in visual
terms and in its relation to the paintings reviewed;[35] nor does he
flinch at the visual implications of the double meaning of history
as both event and representation. Of the many facets of discursivity,
the interpretation of visual representations of propositions commonly known through verbal accounts – for example, the notion
of *gloire* known through Corneille – is convincingly exploited and
related to a theatrical mode of spectator address (Bryson, 1981:38).[36]
Yet Bryson's work suffers slightly from the lack of structure that
results from binary overstructuring: Since the various facts are subsumed under one heading, such as "Discursivity," grasping the
argument otherwise than simplistically remains difficult. For example, in his theoretical introduction I miss a specification of the
different modes of discursivity as outlined for "Rembrandt"'s *Joseph*s, such as the distinction between pre-textual and intratextual
discursivity: between the image as response to a text and the image
as a text. Not that Bryson neglects this specificity; he only fails to
name them. Discursivity is now equal to semiosis and opposed to
realism (Bryson, 1981:10), then equal to verbality and opposed to
visuality (passim), sometimes equal to syntax and opposed to
paradigm (10), equal to relevance and opposed to realistic persuasiveness (10–11). All these meanings make much sense. I only
wish to suggest that Bryson is doing much more, rather than less,
than his title promises. The point of my problem is that the very
name – or phrase, for that matter – word and image does not help
clarify, and puts subtlety and complexity at risk of getting lost
between confusion and simplicity. It is the very book that carries
this problematic title, which shows convincingly that we have to
move beyond the terms of a word-and-image enterprise.

WORDS ON IMAGES: FROM ART
CRITICISM TO EPISTEME

When Fried (1980) set out to study the changing relationship between painting and beholder in the age of Diderot – in the age of
the invention of art criticism, that is – he also promised to study
the paintings as paintings plus commentaries: to study words *on*
images. For the connection between art and commentary is, he
demonstrated, not simply the hierarchical one we have been accustomed to through methodological positivism and its rigorous
distinction between object and metalanguage. Fried's argument
about the relationship is more subtle than that: He shows that it is
one of interaction, rather than of hierarchy. The art critic is, first,
a beholder. So painters who listen to their critics will learn about
the other side of the relationship between painting and beholding.
Diderot's thematization of beholdership supposedly furthers the
painters' thinking about, and acting upon, this crucial position.

For Fried, then, the beholder's position, here, his own position,
is the key. And clearly the concept of the beholder is central to art
analysis, but still it is no less problematic. On one level, the position
is, as Fried and others convincingly show (see, e.g., Alpers, 1988),
basically historical, and any serious art historical study must account
for historical beholdership, both actual and constructed by the period's *episteme*. This is what Fried does: He tries to reconstruct the
position of the beholder in a specific historical period (roughly,
from 1755 to 1781) through an analysis of word–image interaction.

But Fried's intellectual focus resembles somewhat that of recent
reader-response theory in literary criticism; it shifted from text to
reader but, in its attempt to reconstruct contemporary readership,
remained caught in the dialectic of historicism. This is a legitimate
focus but not one that can account for the writing critic's own
position.[37] Nevertheless, in Fried's study, the appeal to contemporary criticism provides a convincing reconstruction of the beholder's historical position in the age of the author of both the
Salons and of *Le paradoxe sur le comédien*, described as the uneasiness
between absorption and theatricality. I shall return to these terms
in the next section; here, it seems useful to recognize that Fried
bases his reconstruction of the beholder on the words of the critic
and on the images of the painters, which serve as support and
substantiation more than as a source for the words.[38] Ultimately,
then, Fried implicitly argues for a double predominance of words
over images: the words of the critic who encourages the painter to
follow his lead, and those in which the beholder emerges as the
relevant position in the construction of images. But this also implies, through a deconstruction of the conventional dogma of communication in literary theory since Jakobson, that the reception of
art precedes, generates, and confines its production.

Similar implicit positions regarding the status of the beholder
and the relationship between painting and beholder can be read in

the other works under discussion here. But I sense that these historical claims might be slightly defensive, forwarded to obliterate
the claim that the beholder's discursive activity formulates, and
thus prefigures, the art. Although this claim for the prefiguring
power of the beholder remains implicit, it is for me the more
interesting one, even if it may be a position unacceptable for art
historians. Such a claim relates nicely to Bryson's contention of a
connection between the political events around, and the critical
events in, the *Académie* in regard to the production of art. And in
fact, the psychoanalytic framework of the thesis in his third book
is, of course, verbal in precisely the same implicit, yet pervasive
sense, a sense that is inevitable in the discussion of the visual in a
thoroughly verbal culture. This issue becomes even more challenging when we think of Holly's symmetrical claim regarding the
prefiguring of the poetics of the great nineteenth-century cultural
historians by their visual objects of inquiry.[39]

What I mean by this perhaps unconscious level of word-and-
image interaction can best be demonstrated by examining the difference between Svetlana Alpers's two recent books. In *The Art of
Describing* (1985), Alpers leans heavily on written sources of a philosophical and epistemological tradition to substantiate her claim
that Dutch art in the seventeenth century is descriptive rather than
narrative. Although the more diffuse relationship between these
sources and the works of art is less direct, the argument is not
fundamentally different from Fried's in *Absorption* (1980): Here, too,
contemporary writing provides evidence of the (verbal) construction of the horizon of expectation against which the art of the time
sets itself off, and without which, the explicit claim runs, it cannot
be understood. Although Alpers's sources cannot be dubbed words
on images in the same way as art criticism can, they certainly fit
the idea of metalanguage, hence, of language on visual ("language"
of) images.

For art historians, and perhaps for Western culture as a whole,
the relationship between words and images is problematic, and this
leads sometimes to repression of the inevitable verbal side of the
argument. The repressed verbality of Alpers's (1985) argument is
visible in the absence of definitions of, and even of explicit reflection
on, the very concepts of description and narration on which her
work is grounded. This is not surprising; seemingly obvious, these
notions suffer from a conspicuous lack of convincing definition
within their "home" field of literary theory, as well.[40] This, in turn,
is not surprising either; it is much easier to presume a "natural"
meaning for these terms than to deconstruct this dichotomy.[41] Reversing the hierarchy between narrative and descriptive art, as Alpers does in this book by showing the value of descriptive art,[42] is
a first, powerful, but insufficient, step. Its insufficiency shows in
the solution she offers to the dilemma of the misfit, the "exception."
As she herself states in her later book, to categorize Rembrandt as
culturally exceptional – as a more narrative artist than the rest of

41

the Dutch – undermines the reversal. For classifying one of the greatest artists of the time outside the emancipated class comes close to reinstating the dominance to be undermined, while the potentially subversive power of exceptionality remains unexploited as long as the dichotomy stands, reversed or not.[43] Any serious attempt to define the terms of such a suspect pair should lead to a questioning, not of the order of the hierarchy, but of the very opposition underlying it.

In *Rembrandt's Enterprise* (1988), Alpers takes issue with her previous position regarding this artist. Within her continuous struggle to define the difference of images in a predominantly verbal culture, she need not also take issue, as from my perspective I must, with the (verbal) dichotomy that led to his exceptional position in the first place. Nevertheless, the relationship she posits between paintings and historical context, and between words and images, becomes more diverse, and for me more interesting, in this study. Although demonstrating the precedence of words is more problematic, as Alpers rightly states, in the preclassical age where artists did not follow a body of theoretical writing, she manages to show a more complex relationship between painting and writing in which now the paintings generate the texts, and then the texts generate the paintings. For a typical tradition-and-desire artist like Rembrandt, full of ambivalence toward predecessors, this relationship becomes even more complex.

Inevitably, the modern critic partakes of the problems produced by that complexity, and the subsequent need for simplification in the service of clarity. It thus becomes tempting to discuss "Rembrandt"'s works in terms of that other deceptive distinction, between "fine" and "rough" (*fyn* and *grof*), but taking that distinction a step further into semiotics. The terms would then indicate not just manners of painting but meaningful signs. Paint handling would become a statement, and the propositional content of that statement would move from self-reference to affective attitudes. Alpers does this, semiotizing Rembrandt's manner of painting by emphasizing the materiality of paint and its relation to sculpture, to touching as a specific way of seeing, and to a problematization of representation; in short, Rembrandt's manner of painting becomes a sign of self-reflection. Alpers argues that the pure materiality of the work of paint, what Bryson calls the "painterly trace," produces a sort of self-implosion that counters the overt representational dimension of the work. Her general point is well taken. Defending "rough" painting or the famous late-Rembrandtish impasto, with the emphatic substantiality of its paint, by making it so much more interesting and meaningful in the semiotic sense, the critic carefully avoids binary valuation.

But in the (verbal) interpretation of the (visual) particularities of the works, the repressed hierarchy resurfaces. The focus on material seeing – touching – gets rephrased in the idealizing terms of love, understanding, human relation (e.g., 23, 29). However, this seems a problematic stance to take in regard to an artist with a clear predilection for subjects wherein the contiguity between seeing and touching is thematized in terms of power and sexuality – as in Bathsheba, Susanna, and Lucretia. Alpers's viewing here seems to be informed by a certain humanistic discourse.

What does this problem have to do with word and image, and specifically with the subject of the present section, words *on* images? I would contend that the unawareness of the input of verbality in this interpretation, which presents itself as based on visual observations, obscures the extent to which words take precedence over, even produce, the construction of the image. Of course, the words taking precedence here are obscured by those of the more explicitly alleged contemporary texts. But the words constructing the (Alpers's) images here are those of the doxa of our culture: the diffuse presence of stories as arguments. As I shall argue in Chapter 2, that doxa, among other things, condones rape with reference to the implicitly alleged "natural" continuity between seeing and touching, which in turn allows the members of that culture to construct touching as concern and affection, rather than as power and possession.[44] With this in mind, then, a second, unintended meaning can be read in Alpers's chapter title, "The Master's Touch."

I would like to revert to the relation between these two issues, the more technical one of Rembrandt's impasto and its relation to self-reflection through emphasis on the tactile, on the one hand, and the ideological representation of sexual power, on the other. I shall do so with a particularly troubling painting, the Berlin *Susanna*, where the subject is, on one level, the abuse of power through the extension of seeing to touching (Figure 1.5).

The subject of this painting is related to the verbal pre-text in a manner similar to that of the two *Josephs* discussed earlier. Both the Joseph and the Susanna subjects enjoy a particular popularity; they are attractive to painters and viewers because they thematize vision: power and the abuse of power as it is related to seeing. For Joseph, this issue is raised by the physical presence of the coat as material though deceptive evidence. The story of Susanna focuses on the arousal, by seeing, of the lust to touch, and the power to touch is warranted by social power. Here, visuality and also its epistemological potency, visibility, are the decisive factors generating the narrative. The fact that the one Elder, in the Susanna, touches his victim is less important than the specific part of her he touches: her clothes; thus by undressing her he makes her vulnerability *visible*; he exposes her "touchiness," so to speak.

According to Alpers's argument, the man's hand is thematically related to the painter's touch as well as to the diegetic hold on the woman, but the isotopy of touching is clearly related to a theme more negative than love. Of course, as her interpretation of *The Goldsmith* suggests, Alpers would agree with this. But then we may wonder how the hand can be related to image making, and what the ideological implications of that relation might be. The critical dimension of reading the painting which this question raises cannot be ignored.

But the case becomes slightly more interesting as soon as we notice, thanks to Alpers's semiotization of it, the handling of paint in this work. It is not the impasto, the thickness of the paint, that is meaningful here, but the contrast between "rough" and "fine" paint handling itself. Large parts of the *Susanna* are painted in the manner Alpers is analyzing: They are painted a bit "roughly" or, as I would call it in Alpers's line, touchily. (Bryson would call it deictic, rather than "fine" or diegetic, transparent.) But amazingly, and undermining the dichotomy, not all of it is "rough." There is one detail painted more in the "fine" manner: Susanna's hair. The transparency of realism is here doubled by and commented upon by the deictic indexicality of the painterly manner. From a semiotic perspective, that is, taking these striking details as signs, one is led to ask, What do they mean?[45]

As we are speaking of a painting, and a painting on vision at

1.5 *Susanna Surprised by the Elders* 1645, Bredius 367, canvas, 102 × 84 cm (Berlin-Dahlem, Gemäldegalerie)

that, the answer to this question must be anchored in the visual image presented. The position of Susanna's hair within the structure of the image is crucial: It is the object of the Elder's gaze; Bryson's critique of the gaze is quite effective here. Surprisingly, the Elder is not looking at the body he is busy unveiling. But, looking above it, he is doubly overlooking it: He is staring at the one location in the work where "fine" takes precedence over "rough" (Figure 1.6). This is an unsettling confirmation of Alpers's claim that the handling of paint works as a sign of self-reflection and self-representation in the work of painting.

From the relation between painter, paint, and painting, the discussion shifts toward Fried, toward the relationship between painting and beholder, but with a difference. The subject – that is, the "ideostory"[46] – is verbal by virtue of its medium (the text) or of its structure (narrative), but it is neither an incidental choice, exclusively motivated by commission or market, as Schwartz would argue, nor an underscoring of the artist's personal obsessions, as one might misconstrue my present argument as claiming. Rather, it is evidence of the inseparability of images and words, and of the impact of words on images. I shall argue in Chapter 4 that the detail in the *Susanna* can be read as a reference to a verbal – philosophical as well as practical, ideological, and political – discussion going on in the society that generated the work: the token of an *episteme*.

WORDS AS IMAGES:
THEATRICALITY AND VISUAL POETICS

Fried's earlier book *Absorption and Theatricality* (1980) establishes a tension between two modes of the painting–beholder relationship: absorption, where the figures are ostentatiously engaged in an inward activity (seeing as one of the possibilities), and theatricality, where they are acting out their relationship to one another, and thus drawing the viewer in. Fried then studies this tension as it is manifested in the late eighteenth century. Fried remains carefully historical, yet his text opens up the possibility of using what I see as his systematic semiotic for works from other periods.[47] But given his historical precision, this cannot be done unproblematically. He exemplifies this himself in his more recent book, *Realism, Writing, Disfiguration* (1987).

1.6 *Susanna Surprised by the Elders*, detail

Nevertheless, I would like to demonstrate the validity and relevance of the distinction between absorption and theatricality as a device for systematic analysis by briefly returning to the two Joseph paintings (Figures 1.7 and 1.8).

The Berlin canvas uses a typically theatrical device, a favorite of "Rembrandt's," the "speaking hands." In fact, the woman's hand speaks so directly, is so clearly indexical in its pointing to Joseph, that its effect does not go beyond explicit signaling, functioning as an arrow on a traffic sign does. With her left hand, she seems to protect her breast from attack. As a "speaking hand," that gesture tells, in a theatrical manner, that Joseph tried to violate her.

The Washington painting is different. There the narrativization of the scene is much more ambivalent. The hand with which the woman supposedly accuses Joseph does point, but not directly at him. It points perhaps toward the red garment, the token of Joseph's misbehavior, but even that direction of her gesture is not unambiguous. Instead of gesticulating in despair, Joseph stands still; he does not participate in the scene. This painting is so much more enigmatic that it is worth trying a different approach, not from Joseph's side but from the other side of the bed, and not from Genesis but from the image itself. Potiphar's hand is not, here, behind the woman but slightly in front of her, as if on its way toward grasping her. The woman protects her breast again, but in combination with the lesser distance between her and Potiphar, his grappling hand, and his determined face, it seems as if *he* were the one approaching her sexually against her will.

The work of light is also much more subtle here than in the other *Joseph*. The light falls on the bed and on the woman in both, but here, Joseph also is very subtly illuminated. The light, thus, produces a pattern in which the woman and the young man are illuminated to the exclusion of the older man. Here Joseph's face has an intense, but unclear expression: Is it desirous, anxious, admiring? The curtain, much more clearly indicated in the Berlin painting as

1.7 (*left*) *Joseph Accused by Potiphar's Wife* 1655, Bredius 523, canvas, 106 × 98 cm (Washington, D.C., National Gallery of Art)

1.8 (*right*) *Joseph Accused by Potiphar's Wife* 1655, Bredius 524, canvas, 110 × 87 cm (Berlin-Dahlem, Gemäldegalerie)

46

the (realist) representation of a bed curtain, is here so vaguely indicated that its only function seems to be to set off Joseph as standing in a space, lighter and further away, *at the other side*. In Chapter 3, I shall bring this separation into a psychoanalytic perspective. Here, it is striking that the lower seam of his garment forms a figural line: His body seems to end there.

The eyes of each protagonist thematize a specific concept of visuality. Each figure looks intense, but inwardly. No one looks clearly at an object. The woman does not look at her husband; rather, she seems to stare at an inner vision, at the vision of her desire. The older man does not look at the woman either; he, too, seems to concentrate on his desire. And Joseph's look, not specifically directed anywhere either, is even more inward than that of the two others; at the same time, however, his eyes seem to stray toward the viewer (Figure 1.9). The separation between Joseph on the one hand, and the couple on the other, is radical; when viewed from the other side of the bed, his image is almost detached; like a portrait on the wall, he takes on a different ontological status than the other characters depicted. His image, itself, gives the inner view, the preoccupation of the two others. When viewed in isolation, Joseph seems full of feelings, yet not involved in any event.

Considering these paintings in terms of absorption and theatricality, they seem to fit almost too perfectly. The Berlin painting is highly theatrical, with the interaction between the figures grounded in the liveliness of their movements – the speaking hands – and in the unity of the scene. No special relation to the beholder seems to be thematized, however. The Washington painting is entirely absorptive, and as a consequence, there is no unity based on the interaction between the figures. Ontologically, Joseph does not

1.9 *Joseph Accused by Potiphar's Wife*, detail

47

belong to this fantasy as a diegetic figure, but rather functions as an embedded image. But in order to see the paintings in this way, we must remove ourselves from Genesis – from word and image, that is – and be ready to reverse the traditional perspective and reconsider Genesis on the basis of the paintings. In the story, there is no moment where all three characters are present, and the Berlin painting therefore presents itself as a theatrical condensation of different scenes. The Washington painting, apparently more removed from the Bible, shows an interesting though repressed aspect of the story in which the woman's lust gets full attention: The story thus has become her fantasy.

In *Realism, Writing, Disfiguration* (1987), Fried characterizes Eakins's *Gross Clinic* as a painting that is difficult to look at, yet impossible to look away from (Figure 1.10). The thematics of surgical violence and the representational practice of making key details invisible, together appeal to the viewer's ambivalence, which Fried relates to the psychoanalytic framework of father–son relations in Eakins's life. This shift to a more personal problematic does not, however, do away with the complex of absorption and/versus theatricality. The so-called woman/mother figure, with her strange gesture of refusing to look, yet expressing horror at what she is seeing, is a powerful representation of precisely the kind of theatricality discussed in Fried's earlier work (Figure 1.11).

But before considering this figure in terms of the word–image problematic outlined above, let us first consider the figure itself; let us make this figure strange. For it is incomprehensible to me that critics take this figure to be a woman, the patient's mother, or even a human figure at all. It has no face, and its skull is covered by a leatherlike substance. To the right of the head there is a strange flap that reminds me of a devilish ear rather than anything human. And its hands are clawing. The figure is out of proportion with the other human figures: There is not enough distance between this figure and the doctor to account for the emphatic difference in size. True, the collar suggests that the figure is not one of the doctors or students, and that collar could be taken to signal femininity. But this is a meager foundation on which to assign gender, especially in light of the characteristics that deny this creature plausible humanity.

Yet this figure is unanimously gendered feminine by the critics. We can give the critics the benefit of the doubt and decide to go along with the gender, but that is about all that can be done to make the figure reassuringly "normal," but I do so "under erasure." If a mother she/it is, then the mother in *Psycho* is a more suitable figure to keep in mind than that pitying, concerned mother we would all like to have, and we would therefore like this figure to represent.

Regardless of what character we assign to the enigmatic figure, in *The Gross Clinic* it functions, literally, as the image of a concept. The concept it represents, makes present, is a specific relation be-

tween painting and beholder, which Fried proposes we call "theatricality": engagement in action played out with the other figures.
Theatricality refers to a mode of looking, a mode of composition,
and a mode of representation. It shows that it is no longer possible
to base a discussion on the distinction between words and images,
nor to return to an illusory "pure visuality." Although the theater
uses words (a script) and images (e.g., backdrop, costume, staging),
the theatrical collapses words and images through the three modes
of looking, composition, and representation.

Theatricality as a mode of looking is based on identification: The
viewer wants to see what the other figures are engaged in seeing
so intensely: here, the violent and healing operation on the sick
body. But the viewer cannot quite see it, the inability being both
visual and psychological. The intricate connection between the visual and the psychological colors the concept of theatricality with
a historically specific nuance. It takes the early twentieth century
to produce such a connection, exemplified by, but not exclusive
to, the work of Freud.

Of all the figures represented, that of the so-called mother mediates between the play and the spectator.[48] Spectator herself, the
figure is also an actor. She is an embedded, diegetic spectator symmetrical to Brecht's staged narrators.[49] Fried is careful to spell out
the different beholder positions to be distinguished in this painting,
in order to avoid what I would call the diegetic fallacy, the collapse
of represented, proposed, and actual looking.[50] So, on the basis of
Fried's suggestions, I would provisionally systematize these
distinctions.

The various positions offered by the painting can be differentiated

1.11   *The Gross Clinic*, detail

in the following way: First, we have the *addressed* viewer, the equivalent of the *narratee* in narrative (Prince, 1982). This position is defined, in the *Susanna*, by the female figure's appeal to the viewer as represented by her eyes and lips, expressing vulnerability and need (Garrard, 1982). This position, then, demands sympathy. The woman (?) figure in Eakins's painting addresses this viewer by her gesture of hiding her face as well as blocking her sight. Here, the position demands identification with the mode of (non)vision. The *implied* viewer would be slightly different; it would be the kind of viewer the painting as a whole seems to call for. In the *Susanna* the implied viewer would be the voyeur who is attracted by her exposure, but, as I shall argue, meets obstacles in his way. The mother, as well as the hidden and exposed body of the sexually ambiguous patient, in the *Gross Clinic* implies a viewer both fascinated and repulsed.[51] The *represented* viewer is diegetic; it partakes of the represented scene. In the *Gross Clinic*, various viewers are represented: the four visible doctors, watching their object unambivalently;[52] the woman who displays the impossibility of looking; and Gross, reassuringly mediating for the benefit of the external viewers.

The mother (?), then, stands for theatricality, but since Fried claims that theatricality necessarily implies unity, she cannot represent it by herself. She is the sign of problematic vision that the one Elder in the Susanna painting also is, but the mode of the problematic has shifted since Rembrandt's time and place, through Diderot's, to Eakins's. The mode of looking at stake here is gender specific, as was the case in Rembrandt's *Susanna*, but the way in which it is gender specific is radically different. And this difference is what makes it possible for the figure to be gendered female, even to be seen as a mother figure.

The mother figure (?) here is not gendered female iconically, but because she indexically refers to a mode of looking that stands outside the male world represented. Eakins's painting stages an exclusively male world, where tensions at work between masters and students – fathers and sons – are played out in terms of (medical) technology and of life giving (healing). More strongly than Fried, I would suggest that these roles are themselves problematic. This becomes obvious when we realize that the father figure par excellence, the master surgeon, is not doing anything. Although displaying the bloody knife he has, by implication, been wielding – and Fried's discussion of the motif of castration is highly plausible here – he is at this very moment just looking, possibly at the theatrical figure, possibly at the audience she stands for; he is turning away from the acting sons toward the diegetically excluded woman and the equally excluded audience. Being, himself, unable to look, he takes the unexpected side of the viewers, both diegetical and external, whose power of judgment is, in fact, paternal.

The exclusion of the mother from the medical scene is thus undermined by her identification with the master surgeon-painter.

The figure whom we can now give the *meaning*, not the shape, of a mother also signifies the unifying mode of composition. On the basis of what precedes, I must use this idea of unity as a means to relativize it. The paradoxical position of the woman who, standing for theatricality, would be excluded from the unity theatricality implies, is broken by Dr. Gross's pose. This pose is symmetrical to hers. While she makes a clawing gesture, he quietly displays the bloody knife. And while she violently refuses to see the thing the seeing of which constitutes her horror, he quietly looks at her horror, but away from its object. The complex interaction between these two figures almost absorbs the scene's theatricality. The operation, the audience in the background, the writers, seem an embedded painting, an alternative object of vision for the two parental figures whose sole interaction constitutes both the unity of the theatrical scene, and its breaking up of the unity of the work as a whole.

Just how strongly this break in the unity of the composition directs the viewer can be glimpsed when one compares this painting to the other one of Eakins's clinics: *The Agnew Clinic* (Figure 1.12). In this later work, the patient is unambiguously female, and the onlooking woman is neatly and clearly a nurse. Not that this painting has no problem of represented looking. For again the surgeon's

1.12 Thomas Eakins, *The Agnew Clinic* 1889, canvas 84⅜ × 118⅛ in. [214.3 × 300 cm] (University of Pennsylvania, Philadelphia)

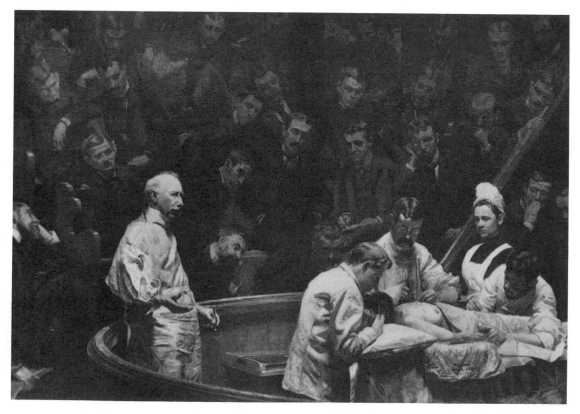

look seems irrelevant, and the students invariably seem asleep. Perhaps they betoken in this way the difficulty of looking. In contrast, the nurse's quiet but concentrated look at the face of the patient warrants the latter's protection in this male world. Solely the nurse makes certain that the patient is not alone. Yet this painting has lost the enigma, the horror, and the productive incoherence of the earlier work.

The break in the compositional unity of the *Gross* implies a statement about theatricality as a mode of representation. For paradoxically, the basic break is that which links painting and beholder, drawing the latter within the former, and thus challenging the autonomy of the work. The theater itself is the nonautonomous, multidisciplinary art par excellence. For most of us, a performance without an audience is more obviously unthinkable than is a text without readers, or a painting without a beholder; yet the case of performance makes the case for the other two. Theatrical painting draws attention to the theater's extreme position and, by implication, claims the same status for painting. Thus, it is not a coincidence that the theater is also the art in which word and image can neither be sundered nor ignored. What is at stake in Fried's concept of theatricality is an analysis of painting in terms of a *poetics* of painting: of a conception of visual representation as working toward an ever-changing problematization of the relations between the work as sign and the painting's working as pragmatic event; of a rhetoric of visual art. In other words, Fried's concept of theatricality begins to articulate a visual poetics, a poetics that gets beyond the word–image opposition. In this context, Bryson's interpretation of *gloire* as necessarily ostentatious, as void without spectatorship (see his *Word and Image*, 1981:37–8) also becomes relevant as a plea for just this kind of visual poetics.

Alpers's (1988) book also devotes attention to the theatrical model. Rigorously historical without following older, rather superficial historical views in which theatricality was merely associated with gestures, light, and dress (Alpers, 1988:35), the author shows convincingly how Rembrandt drew upon the popularity of the theater of his time, upon the discussions about acting, and upon what Diderot would later call the "paradox of the actor" – the fundamental unnaturalness of acting as imitation of nature. Yet, Alpers argues, he also managed to confine his practice of painting to the domain where he alone reigned: the studio. Here, he had models act out scenes to be painted. Thus discussions about the theater focused, precisely, on the relationship between word and gesture – hence, image – and between oral and visual presence (Alpers, 1988:48).

Discussing the represented viewer, so frequently present in Rembrandt's works, Alpers proposes that we see this idiosyncratic feature as *spectatorial*, rather than *voyeuristic*, and this remark joins Bryson's (1981:37) criticism of the use of the term "voyeurism" for cases where the privacy characteristic of voyeurstic looking is not only absent but by definition excluded because spectatorship is part of the meaning of the display. Rembrandt's preference for scenes involving spectatorship indeed points in this direction.

Beyond this thematic argument, Alpers interprets other aspects of Rembrandt's work as theatrical as well, such as the unconventional movement of his figures, which have no sources in the pictorial tradition and which bear comparison with Delacroix as Bryson discusses him. The movement of Rembrandt's figures, in turn, works beyond their own mobility. In a detailed discussion of one of the rare written phrases in which Rembrandt expressed his views on art, Alpers (1988:49–51) shows that the artist linked the movement of his figures to another kind of movement, to a triple sense of the word "moving"; For Rembrandt, then, the idea of movement included mobility of figure, gesturality, and affect, making movement a part of the rhetorical model of visual poetics of which theatricality is the central mode.[53]

FROM VISUAL POETICS TO COMPARATIVE ARTS

As in the case of Alpers's discussion of "The Master's Touch," I have no problems with the overall argument Alpers makes about Rembrandt's theatricality. But, while most of her discussions of actual works are illuminating, I do have a problem with one of her interpretations. Indeed, I might be blamed for nit-picking my example, and I am aware of the injustice I am doing Alpers by foregrounding a case that is secondary for her. But, as it happens, the case has an interesting bearing on the problematic of this introductory chapter – that is, the attempt to overcome the word–image dichotomy – while the work in question is the subject of a more extensive analysis in Chapter 5. In this section, and with the help of this example, I shall try to rehearse and wind up this chapter's discussion by advocating the study of comparative arts as a fruitful academic venture, not instead of but in addition to, or rather, as integrated within, art history and the study of literature.

Among the first examples Alpers discusses is an early work, *Judas Returning the Pieces of Silver* of 1629, in which the theatrical gestures of the figure emphasize the untrustworthiness of his intentions. "Once a traitor, always a traitor" is what the painting's excessive theatrical movement seems to say. By the same token it addresses the paradox of acting and, we might say, opposes words (of repentance) to images (of hypocrisy). The link between representational and moral opposition suggested by this example is, of course, not inherent to Alpers's concept of theatricality. Yet it presents, I fear, a rhetorical trap nevertheless. The second example is a work of a decade or so later, *Samson Posing the Riddle to the Wedding Guests* of 1638 (Figure 1.13). Alpers gives a visual description of the work, immediately followed by an account of its verbal background:

To the one side we see Samson posing his riddle to the Philistines, while just off center, behind the festive board, is the self-conscious, stiffly posed figure of his new wife, identified in the Bible only as the woman from Timnah. It is she who will betray Samson to her people after tricking him to tell her the answer to his riddle. Posed in the posture of a bride... she is a woman who will contradict her appearance as a newly wedded wife by doing her husband in. Once again, at the center of his picture, Rembrandt has focused on a betrayer – on one whose appearance or actions must be understood as being a performance. And this fact is underlined here by the compositional echo of Leonardo's *Last Supper*, in which Rembrandt placed Samson's wife, his betrayer, in the place of Christ. (Alpers, 1988:37)

I quoted this passage at length because of the interaction of word and image it displays and because this interaction entails a view of the painting in which the visual is overruled by the verbal. The first sentence describes the painting ("we see"), while the final clause of that sentence introduces the verbal source. The conflation of the two is marked by the words describing the bride, in which a narrative shifter bases the evaluation of the figure on the verbal account. The words "self-conscious, stiffly posed" are quite concretely shifters: self-consciousness and stiffness are each semantically double

BEYOND THE WORD—
IMAGE OPPOSITION

1.13 *Samson Posing the Riddle to the Wedding Guests (Samson's Wedding)* 1638, canvas, 126 × 175 cm (Dresden, Gemäldegalerie)

(although they are so in different ways). The self-consciousness is strongly related to the figure's relationship to the addressed viewer: The woman literally addresses the viewer. Hence, the bride's "self" calls for identification between figure and viewer through the implied viewer that is called forth by the very contrast between the woman and the other figures. The stiffness of the woman's pose, in contrast, inserts the figure into the mode of theatricality which it alone challenges. The figure is isolated from the other actors, who all interact ostentatiously with one another and exclude the viewer who can enter the scene by identification alone.

The problem can be summarized as follows: Why is the "stiffly posed" bride chosen to represent theatricality, while the other figures, engaged in busy action with one another, seem to qualify for the part much better?[54] If it is the connection with Judas that motivates this focus, the verbal – the notion that both characters are traitors – has overruled the visual. This is why I suggested above that the Judas example turned out to be a rhetorical trap.

But where does this damning verbal input come from? It does not come directly from the text of Judges 14. For Judges 14 mentions neither tricks nor betrayal; only blackmail, only life-threatening intimidation of the woman by her kinsmen. Hence, it is not that text that is brought in here, but a more diffuse and by no means universal doxa, a cultural commonplace which has it that this bride is a prelude to Delila.[55] One might support a claim that Rembrandt has represented this particular doxa with contemporary views on the story, but that would miss my point. Rather, what I am contending is that Alpers's interpretation of this work is based on neither the visual evidence of the painting, nor on the verbality imported to supplement vision, drawn from the specific and prestigious religious document, and that her own allusion points this out.

As I shall argue in Chapter 5, the visual allusion to Christ that Alpers posits and takes as evidence that a (theatrical) betrayer is intended, seems to me to undermine her case. The woman is compositionally taking the place of Christ. If she were to be a traitor, then this position in the painting would have to be ironic. But for me such an ironic reversal of values as implied in Alpers's interpretation is unwarranted.[56] Rather, the woman is depicted in this honorable position because she is about to be sacrificed, just like Christ at the Last Supper. The wedding feast is, so to speak, *her* last supper. And that is much more likely even in Alpers's intentionalist historical terms, in a seventeenth century fond of so-called typological interpretation, where characters of the Old Testament are taken to prefigure Christ. What makes the case special, and shows "Rembrandt" 's ambivalent relationship to women in an interesting light, is that it is not Samson but the woman, the woman who is – we must not forget – his victim, that is here presented typologically.

In terms of theatricality using the criteria of Alpers (movement and performance) as well as Fried (interaction, unity, and the relation to the beholder), I would suggest that the painting does appeal to a notion of theatricality, but only through a questioning of that status. The figures busily performing in the mode of genre painting, all engaged in role playing, contrast with the one figure who is *not* acting, and who is, ostentatiously, excluded from the scene. Alpers senses this exclusion when she places her "behind the festive board." In strictly visual terms this placement is not entirely convincing, but it nevertheless rings true. Fried's criterion of unity is, then, not belied but "explicitly" foregrounded by its denial. The relation to the beholder is, indeed, comparable to that in *The Gross Clinic*. Although the issues connected with the beholder are different here, owing to differences in historical context, the figure who, like a Brechtian narrator, steps out of the play does so in order to address the viewer and ask for help, or, at least, for an opinion.[57]

I am not presenting this dissident view as a simple difference of interpretation, nor do I wish to quibble with an otherwise fine study. Instead, I want to argue that the concept of theatricality, presented in the previous section as an exemplary meeting place for verbality and visuality, as the token of visual poetics, has hit its limits before we know it, and that this entails yet another turn in my case for an approach beyond the word–image opposition. The limits of visual poetics are bound up with its implicit relation to word and image, its historical exclusivity, and its methodological isolation. The exploration of these limits will help bring the present argument to a provisional close and prepare the ground for the chapters that follow.

The concept of theatricality is fit for a visual poetics precisely because it unites word and image into one, composite sign. A theatrical unit, be it diction, gesture, or movement, can only artificially be confined to either verbality or visuality. So students of the theater accept this unity implicitly and, thus, find the very word–image opposition meaningless. To some extent this implicit unity allows the colonization of the image by the word to pass unnoticed. Alpers's description of the *Samson* betrayed this domination of the visual image by the diffuse discursivity that informed her interpretation. The colonization of the image by the word turns the image into a myth, into the locus where illusory stability of meaning can anchor itself.

The specific form this verbality took in the case just discussed was double. On the one hand, it was the doxa surrounding the Biblical story; on the other, the preestablished status of betrayal as the syntagm of role playing. The concept of theatricality came in only after these two verbal pre-texts had been given relevance. And this turned out to be too late: It was unable to correct the verbal dominance and to assert its own specificity. In contrast, Bryson's distinction between discursivity and figurality held the advantage of its explicitness. Thus it worked heuristically – the analyst knew what to look for – and it kept the analyses accountable for noting what interpretation each of the terms yielded.

In general, the historical approach is considered to be in conflict with a systematic approach; but this dichotomy – together with those between theory and practice, literal and figurative, form and content, text and context – is in my mind among the most powerful and paralyzing ideologies in the humanities today. Of course, studying a historical object in context is necessary, and I find the research underlying Alpers's study, as well as the other studies discussed, both solid and relevant. But the lack of a systematic concept of theatricality made for a line of argument that led, in spite of the author's overt disavowal of the dichotomy truth–falsehood, to a syntagm in which role playing was connected with the stiff pose, rather than with the movement of the other figures; that the opposition between "appearance" and "reality" was embraced. If, as the author claims, "taking the part of another . . . is the measure of success" (Alpers, 1988:37), then such a method requires a unification of historical and systematic perspectives if we are to answer the question, Whose part is this woman playing – that of Christ, compositionally present through the prestigious predecessor and historically present through contemporary exegesis, or that of Judas, discursively present through the modern doxa? In other words, what address is proposed to the viewer by the woman's stiff pose and anxious eyes? Working the systematic perspective proposed by Fried (unity and engagement of the beholder) into the historical one (Alpers's point about performance in the studio *and* that of contemporary theology and exegetic tradition) would have led to a different, and in my view more challenging, interpretation. This is exactly what Bryson does in his two historical books, with the result showing the importance of such an integration. And Bryson, even less than Alpers or Fried, is *not* opting for systematic against historical work.

Methodological isolation, finally, is the result of opting for either a systematic or a historical approach. By remaining within the art historical paradigm, although exploiting it optimally, Alpers cannot add to the concept of theatricality the verbal and the visual perspectives in such a way as to exploit fully their respective potential and overcome their respective limits. Semiotics could have helped by making recognizable which phenomena were taken as signs and given meaning. It would have been helpful to know the sign status of the stiff pose and how it overlaps with or deviates from the compositional sign that is Christ's place. But it takes more than just a semiotic toolbox to go beyond the word–image dichotomy.

The contribution of indexicality (which points out the metonymical relation of the *Wedding* to the earlier painting and its synecdochical relation to the doxa) to the overruling of iconicity (which would identify the woman with Christ (com)positionally) raises the question of relative power of sign systems and codes. Is it because index overrules icon or because words overrule images that the concept of the theatrical did not push the interpretation beyond the implicit domination of verbality? Precisely because semiotics offers only a general theory of signs, it cannot answer this question.

The semiotic perspective, then, raises questions that can be answered more specifically only within an interdisciplinary framework, a framework in which semiotics would serve by letting the traditions and methods of the various disciplines be consciously confronted with one another. Although the three scholars whose works were discussed here are aware of disciplinary differences and of the importance of a balanced integration, Bryson goes farthest in taking this necessity to heart. His work shows that visual poetics can be placed within such a framework, and within it, theatricality can still be a privileged term. But in order for this to happen more generally, the various disciplines must learn to take themselves and one another equally seriously.[58] Declaring one's own or the interlocutor's discipline in crisis may be more helpful than unwarranted self-congratulation or overadmiration of the other, but it is less helpful than a recognition of limits that have yet to be overcome.

It is against this background that I would like the following chapters to be positioned. After having outlined, in this introductory chapter, the general project of studying images and texts in interaction with each other, and with each other's modes of reading, I shall now elaborate a visual rhetoric that will be a first step toward a systematic exploration of the potential of this program.

CHAPTER 2

VISUAL RHETORIC: THE SEMIOTICS OF RAPE

If the object becomes allegorical under the gaze of melancholy, if melancholy causes life to flow out of it and it remains dead, but eternally secure, then it is exposed to the allegorist, it is unconditionally in his power. That is to say it is now quite incapable of emanating any meaning or significance of its own; such significance as it has, it acquires from the allegorist. He places it within it, and stands behind it; not in a psychological but in an ontological sense. (Walter Benjamin, *Origin of German Drama*, 1977: 183–4)

The very notion of a "rhetoric of violence" . . . presupposes that some order of language, some kind of discursive representation is at work not only in the concept "violence" but in the social practices of violence as well. (Teresa De Lauretis, *Technologies of Gender*, 1987:32)

INTRODUCTION

ALLEGORY is a historical attitude; yet allegory can never replace the "literally" real.[1] Rather, allegory is an extended metaphor; it is a reading based on the continuous *similarity* or *contiguity* between its vehicle – say, here, the myth of Lucretia – and its tenor – political tyranny.

The subject of the chaste Roman Lucretia who stabbed herself in the presence of her husband and father after she had been raped by her husband's fellow-soldier was familiar in Rembrandt's time; it was, so to speak, part of the culture,[2] receiving, of course, political and religious allegorical interpretations. But such cultural currency is never sufficient to explain an oeuvre's interest when the subject both offers a persistently powerful image, a cultural emblem, even a cliché, and addresses a real and serious problem such as rape.

In keeping with the assumptions set out in the introduction, I propose to examine here, not a particular work of art, but a "case." That case will expose a cultural problem related to the representation of a topic that is at once popular in the culture, difficult to represent yet often represented, and real. My analysis will aim at understanding the margins of that case, the seams where art is attached to reality: I shall foreground the artificiality of the artistic utterance as well as its anchorage in, and effect upon, the real. For this first exploration, the case is rape; the subject, the myth of Lucretia; the tool, rhetoric.

Lucretia is a good subject to begin our discussion with, first, because it is a story, a verbally propagated theme; second, because it has been and still is, popular; third, because it was often painted, represented visually. In fact, even in the corpus of "Rembrandt" paintings, Lucretia figures twice. Hence, this subject invites key questions: What are the relations among cultural fascination, verbal representation, and visual representation? And how does rhetoric, a mode of analysis traditionally applied to verbal art, serve to connect these?

In order to avoid special pleading and hence the construction of a social relevance for humanistic analysis on a circular argument, neither literary theory nor "Rembrandt" will be privileged a priori in this chapter. Both will be brought to bear on the real-life issue: The case of rape will be rigorously foregrounded and seen as a semiotic event.[3] The semiotic aspects of rape will be considered on two levels. One level is the semiotic behavior surrounding rape, such as the difficulty survivors have recounting the experience, the refusal of others to listen to survivors, and the semiotic use of the rape for other purposes. Another level is the semiotics of rape itself, its status as, among other things, body language, as a speech act of aggression, as an attempt at destroying the victim's subjectivity, which equates rape with murder. I shall examine the difficulties of getting access to the semiotic of rape on both levels, because of the nature of the act, as well as the cultural attitude toward the act, through a detailed analysis of the two "Rembrandt" paintings of the suicide of Lucretia and through a comparison of these works with both the textual pre-texts in Livy and Ovid and with another Renaissance representation in Shakespeare's *Rape of Lucrece*. Thus a manner of reading will develop that is particularly suited to grasping the artificial construction of rape, as well as to recovering the unspeakable aspects of the experience of rape.

Since the case of rape is doubtlessly the one that touches reality most closely, I shall make separating art from reality even more difficult by choosing rhetoric as my major tool of analysis. Rhetoric has traditionally been divided untenably between argumentation and decoration.[4] My claim in this chapter will be based on the intricate connection between "beautiful" – that is, decorative – speech and real persuasion. Therefore, I shall try to show the limits to, if not the lack of, any distinction between modes of expression and rhetorical effect.[5]

A rhetorical perspective on a classical "rapish" situation on the one hand, and brief remarks on textual versions of the same story along with another ancient rape tale on the other, will help generate a view of rape that will then, even more briefly, be confronted by a few women's rape stories. But since the share of a visual rhetoric in the reading of rape will prove indispensable, the analysis of the "Rembrandt" *Lucretia*s will show the point of visual poetics as cultural critique.

THE WANDERING WOMB

Before beginning an analysis of the two *Lucretia*s, however, I would like first to take a brief detour into Jeffrey Masson's collage of Freud's letters to Fliess.[6] Those letters reveal among other things the following scene, which is *not* literally a rape scene. Emma Eckstein, whose nose was operated on for pains in her abdomen deemed hysterical, began to feel extremely unwell and suddenly started to have life-threatening nosebleeds. Freud called upon a competent specialist to examine the patient. This specialist suddenly pulled out of Emma's nose a piece of half-rotten gauze, two feet long.

In this episode Freud, contrary to expectation, did *not* find support for his real-trauma theory of hysteria. On the contrary, in his written reports to Fliess he gradually turned the nosebleeds, consequences of the misplaced operation and mistreatment of the patient, into symptoms of the hysteria the operation was supposed to cure.

Two aspects of this event will detain us here. First, the displacement: The operation on the nose for stomach pains is strongly reminiscent of ancient theories of hysteria, of the wandering uterus that had to be domesticated, as recalled by Charles Bernheimer in his introduction to *In Dora's Case* (1985). The displacement, in its etymological sense of spatial dislocation, as well as in its psychoanalytical sense of distortion and, through distortion, of censorship, of hiding the uncomfortable truth, seems a key figure in both the story of the operation and the scene of the two men observing the suffering and almost destroyed woman.[7] Displacement seems a key figure for understanding the signs in the Emma Eckstein scene as well; that scene has the blood, the woman's powerless position insofar as she is confined to her bed, the separation between the two men together on the one hand and the woman alone on the other, and so forth.

The second aspect of the Emma Eckstein scene on which I would like to dwell is that of language. Emma does not speak to us. She does not tell her story, her experience, her feelings. We observe the scene only through Freud's language. And his story is distorted: His interest turns out to be displaced, systematically, from Emma to Fliess, from *her* suffering to *his* apology. The intriguing question is, How can we know about Emma's situation? On what basis can we infer her experience from the account exclusively given by the "other"? The answer to this question is crucial for the endeavor of this book. We can *see* it, visually, on the basis of Freud's verbal account.

But what kind of semiotic must we need apply in order to read the unsaid, to recover the repressed, and to interpret the distorting signs of that unspeakable experience? We need to account for the obliqueness of representations whose rhetoric aims at erasing the woman's experiences, yet which cannot entirely repress those experiences. The *visuality* of the Emma story allows us to gain access to her experience despite Freud's censorship. For although entirely verbal, Freud's account promotes a visual imagination that lets us identify with the victim. Hence, three aspects of this mode of reading or poetics that would allow us to read from the victim's perspective would have to intertwine: visuality, imagination, and identification.[8] Such a poetics would cut across the traditional word–image opposition in order to fill in images where words predominate, and words where images repress language.

So far as the location of signs is concerned, this poetics would also be dynamic: It would be based on shifting and displacing back. It would be a *rhetorical* reading of the visual. In honor of the wandering womb of ancient hysteria, let us name this poetics *hysterics*.[9] Such a "hysterical" poetics is semiotic in that it utilizes signs – nonverbal signs as much as verbal ones – so that if Emma does not speak, her silence would be sign number one. The visual image of the scene shows the two standing men, collaborating and observing, versus the observed woman alone, too sick to participate, utterly powerless and on her way to total destruction. The piece of gauze is an alien body, introduced by violence and destroying the subject from within. The refusal or incapacity or unwillingness to focus attention on the victim, along with the determination to displace that attention to the perpetrator whose reputation is at stake, becomes itself a sign of the powerful displacement that a hysterical reading aims to counter. That would be sign number two. For what Freud's very attempts to apologize for Fliess reveal is, not only the particular distribution of interests, but also the lack of logic of his endeavor. What this lack of logic demonstrates is the very displacement Freud's efforts are trying to conceal. But what Freud cannot unwrite is the revelatory "detail," the evidence, the piece of gauze.

Rather than "reading for the plot" (Brooks, 1984), a "hysterical" semiotic reads for the image; rather than reading for the main line or the proposition, it reads for the detail; and rather than reading for the hero or main character, it reads for the victim. Rather than reading for logic, linearity, and literality, it displaces these, replacing them with a scene-oriented simultaneity in which the categories of literal and figural change places. Thus our "hysterical" semiotic counters, reverses, and thereby denounces and undermines the violence of rhetoric that obliterates the rhetoric of violence.[10] Rather than placing the event in the historical past, this kind of reading places it in the "hysterical" present of identification, which receives its figuration from the spatial. Read "hysterically," the scene of Emma's nosebleed becomes a *figuration* of a rape scene.[11]

THE RAPE OF LUCRETIA

The "heroine of rape" celebrated throughout Western culture is Lucretia. She killed herself, calling for revenge, because she was raped; her death initiated the revolution that led to the Roman Republic. As a mythical story, we may assume that the Lucretia legend speaks to the culture that brought it forth, as well as to the cultures that maintain and repeatedly reproduce it. Its popularity is demonstrated in the Renaissance and in Northern Renaissance painting in particular, and this popularity in fact continues. In order to arrive at a satisfactory explanation, let us first try out what a "hysterical" poetics can do to reconstruct Lucretia's experience in the representations of a story that deploys all its strategies to ignore and erase that experience; I shall discuss two visual representations of it. For now, I shall use the two "Rembrandt" *Lucretias* to develop an understanding of the continuing mythic significance of rape.

"Rembrandt" 's two *Lucretias* are both late works dating from 1664 (Washington; Figure 2.1) and 1666 (Minneapolis; Figure 2.2).[12] It is striking that these paintings are late works. For although "Rembrandt" painted scenes that in English are referred to as rapes more than twenty years earlier (the *Rape of Proserpine* and the *Rape of Europa*, both probably painted in 1632), the differences between these works and the *Lucretias* in both style and content are enormous. Thus it is significant that in *Proserpine* and *Europa* "Rembrandt" depicts the events that *precede* any actual, sexual rape (which neither the stories nor the paintings represent), whereas in the *Lucretias* he depicts what *follows*. And ultimately, the latter works thematize the effect of rape whereas the former works do not. If, as I shall argue, the *Lucretias* can be seen as metaphoric/metonymic representations of real rape, the abduction scenes do not necessarily lead to an insight into rape.[13]

These visual images of Lucretia lend themselves to the kind of "hysterical" reading that Emma's sickbed suggests. For just as the sick Emma was confronted by two healthy men, Lucretia, too, faces more than one man in three respects. First, according to the myth, Lucretia killed herself in the presence of her father, her husband, and the latter's friend. Second, just as Freud wrote his story of Emma so much for Fliess that we can almost say that they collaborated on it, so Rembrandt, a man, and probably his students, also men, represented Lucretia cooperatively.[14] Third, just as the spectators at Emma's bed are outsiders, so too are the men who observe Lucretia's suicide: Ignoring her experience, they go forward to take revenge against the tyrant of Rome, the father of Lucretia's rapist. The spectators outside the painting are also comparable to the readers of Freud's letters, for they can choose to read "hysterically."[15] And it is only such a "hysterical" reading that reveals the extent to which rape and murder are semiotically related.[16]

My very first impressions of the 1664 painting (Figure 2.1) were Lucretia's movement away from my voyeuristic gaze and the deadly color of her face. But despite her deadly pallor, as the curator of the department in Washington rightly remarked, the cleaning had actually brought her back to life. Her hands had come forward, emphasizing the force and the surprise of her act of suicide – literally, self-killing. Immediately I was struck by two tiny details. First, the earring on Lucretia's left ear does not hang straight. This suggests movement of her head, in addition to her hands. Second, the point of the dagger seemed doubled, thus suggesting a shadow which, in turn, suggests strong emphasis on frontal lighting.[17]

Like the first Lucretia, the later one (Figure 2.2) also represents the suicide rather than the rape. In this work the frontal presentation is even stronger, the white undergown larger. The necklace, which in the Washington piece enhances the frontal pose by its symmetry, is here replaced by a diagonal sash. Lucretia's face is turned in the other direction here, to her left instead of to her right. And the movement, notable in the earlier picture, is replaced in the later one with a frozen pose. The left hand, open in the Washington *Lucretia* as if to persuade or implore, now holds a cord – a curtain or bell cord? The red gown, which hangs down normally in the Washington painting, here bulges, thus suggesting either Lucretia's sitting posture or, more likely, the beginning of her collapse, her body beginning to sink into a red mass. Her tears are gone, her earring hangs straight, her dagger points in a different direction, and there is blood on her undergown.

Reading the earlier painting "for the plot," we would interpret Lucretia's movement as a consequence of the presence of the men. Father and husband are trying to comfort her when suddenly she kills herself. For she has to act swiftly before they can restrain her. Such a reading is realistic in its argument. It is an explanation of the detail in terms of the "real" story,[18] taking the motivations from the story, rather than from the scene as it is depicted. It is also verbal in the traditional sense, since it superimposes on the painting an "underlying" verbal story which the painting is then supposed to "illustrate." The appeal to such a realistic reading demonstrates how much even traditional art interpretation owes to the relations between visual and verbal texts, without, however, examining its own foundations.

But I shall argue that the discursivity of the painting is much more intricately connected with its visuality. In other words, I shall try, in reading the *Lucretia*s, to make a case for a concept of "visual verbality" in which rhetoric, a representational strategy traditionally associated with verbal communication, is analyzed in visual terms. As a consequence, the relationship between the paintings and the verbal sources must be conceived of in a radically different

2.1 *Lucretia* 1664, Bredius 484,
canvas 120 × 101 cm
(Washington, D.C., National
Gallery of Art)

66

manner, not as offering two layers of meaning, but as providing an intricate interaction.

What would the meaning of the signs of speed be in such a framework? Starting with the details of the 1664 *Lucretia* – the earring and the doubling of the dagger's point – the emphasis on the act itself becomes the primary sign. This emphasis recapitulates an aspect of the ideology of rape, in which the victim is conceived of as having committed the crime against herself. This is a crucial displacement, betraying its own project of censorship: Thus, rape is identified with suicide, not with murder as it should be. I contend that Lucretia has become the heroine of rape, not only because she is posited as a model of chastity, but even more so because of this identification between rape and suicide. This identification, made most explicit in Livy's story, the oldest source (Foster, 1959), is also represented in the "Rembrandt" *Lucretias*, where suicide is the outcome of a rape story; thus these "Rembrandts" partake of the ideology that makes the social disease of rape so hard to cure. In a few moments I shall go on to argue that the painting does, however, not merely do that.

What, then, are the semiotics of rape that we can infer from this displaced and misplaced, yet inevitable, suicide? *Suicide* – or, translated into its Anglo-Saxon synonym, "self-killing" (or, as the Dutch and German have it, "self-murder") – replaces the rape in this and other representations because rape itself cannot be visualized. It cannot be visualized, not because a "decent" culture would not tolerate such representations of the act, but because rape makes the victim invisible.[19] It does that both literally – first the perpetrator covers her – and figuratively – then the rape destroys her self-image, her subjectivity, which is temporarily narcotized, definitively changed, and often destroyed. Finally, rape cannot be visualized because the experience is, physically as well as psychologically, *inner*. Rape takes place inside. In this sense, rape is by definition imagined; it can exist only as experience and as memory, as *image* translated into signs, never adequately objectifiable. As a consequence, the signs are all we have, and we had better take that "hysterically" too. We must turn the "logical" consequence – if rape is an imaginary crime, it must therefore be dismissed before the bar – upside down and take rape as an inherently semiotic case that derives its strength from that status. The need to listen to survivors, then, becomes doubly urgent, as the only way to reach a solution to the juridical dilemma rape represents.[20]

Because of this difficulty in representing rape, its depiction is often displaced; it is then depicted as self-murder, as in Lucretia's case where self-murder stands for rape, the suicide becoming its metaphor.[21] But replacing the experience, the metaphor displaces the rape itself. Thus its very occurrence conveys the idea that the victim is responsible for her own destruction. As far as the subject of action is concerned, the act of killing herself shifts attention from the rapist to the victim.[22] But as a consequence of the nonrepresentability of rape, spectators/readers reinterpret the self-murder rhetorically as metaphor. This consequence, then, shows that the notion of rhetoric can be extended, as was the notion of semiotic, to signify the real.[23] By this I do not mean that rhetoric is exactly identical with "literal" language, but that rhetoric is important because of the very difficulty it presents in deciding which reading is literal and which is figural. But before such an extension of rhetorical concepts can be useful in analyzing the "Rembrandt" *Lucretia*s, we must consider whether we can really use rhetorical concepts for the analysis of visual works.

Using rhetoric for the analysis of visual works assumes two things, first, that figures of style or, rather, figurations of meaning, are used not only in language but in other media as well. That is to say, concepts from one field, literature, are not merely being metaphorically transposed to the other, visual arts; rather, both already use the same devices to shape meaning. Hasenmueller, for one, would contend that we already use the same devices to shape meaning in both fields. In discussing Van Eyck's *Rolin Madonna* (1980), she shows how choosing to activate either metaphor or metonymy modifies the way we see the painting[24]:

In that *visual* sense, the relationship to the successive spaces is metonymic: if we specify the context of visual experience of the picture from a given point, then the spaces in the picture and that between us and the picture are part of a single whole or view.

If we step outside the fragile set of circumstances that support our suspension of ordinary perception in order to appreciate van Eyck's illusion, the continuity dissolves. Nature and illusion are different orders. They are parallel to each other, but different in kind and never precisely congruent. Their relationship is metaphoric. . . . (Hasenmueller, 1980:80)

In the following pages, I shall try to substantiate the claim that rhetoric is as visual as it is verbal, and that the two can be separated only on the basis of an artificial a priori distinction.

The second claim, equally basic to this study, is that rhetoric, by shaping meaning, constructs reality through the construction of the meanings it offers reality to work with. That is to say, the rhetorical analysis does not stand in opposition to the real issue of rape. Rather, it partakes of it, the rhetorical figurations helping to construct the views of rape dominant in the culture in which the rhetorical discourse or image functions, and to condition the responses to real rape (Estrich, 1987). Like the first claim, the second posits the inextricable intertwining of verbal and visual representation. Real rape is already, according to this claim, a representational act. If the first claim is one of method, the second is both concerned with method, based on semiotic principles as it is, and directly related to the concern of feminist scholars about their work's ability to contribute to changing reality.

The importance of seriously attending to rhetoric becomes obvious as soon as we look again at the metaphor of suicide in the

"Rembrandt." The use of metaphor raises the question of motivation: Why compare this tenor – the content of the metaphor – with this vehicle – the metaphoric image? This motivation is more often than not metonymical: A sign represents the rape not by similitude but by temporal contiguity, just as a consequence can represent its cause, or a later event its predecessor (Genette, 1972). Read metonymically, then, we would interpret the scene depicted in the *Lucretia* paintings as follows: Rape *is like* self-murder (metaphor) because rape *leads to* self-murder (metonymy). In other words, the choice of a rhetorical term is itself already an ideological decision. By limiting ourselves to metaphor, we displace responsibility onto the victim – emphasizing "self" rather than "murder." In contrast, if we use metonymy as well, responsibility is returned to where it belongs: to the rapist and the rape as destruction – to murder, rather than "self."

But if rhetorical terms are so important, then we need not stop at a metonymic reading. Synecdoche – that is, taking the detail to stand for the whole, *pars pro toto* – can become another important tool in reading the painting. By using that rhetorical strategy, self-murder becomes the "detail" representing the entire process. Lucretia's raped body part comes to stand for her whole person, just as her suicide, *her* act that stands for herself, comes to stand for the entire story, the rape and its consequence. Not only is the rape itself thus brought back into sight, but the rape also recovers its place as the act that brings about the *murder* of the *self.*

Reading synecdochically, then, emphasizes the fact that rape *has* consequences, that it alters the victim definitively. In this sense, Lucretia's suicide does not suggest her own culpability, but emphasizes instead her position as victim, and the perpetrator's responsibility for both the rape and Lucretia's death – for the rape *as* her death. Reading synecdochically includes the rapist in the representation. He becomes again a part of the represented whole, despite the fact that – or even because – he is invisible in the painting. And as he is synecdochically reinstated in the scene, his vacant place needs to be filled. The urge to fill that place involves the viewer.

In order to avoid the social clichés associated with rape, we must complicate our rhetoric even further. We can do so by returning briefly to the details of the earring and the dagger in the 1664 *Lucretia* to see how another trope is also at work here. The movement of the earring and the doubling of the dagger's point, which produce a tension between the static composition and the dynamic effect, might allow us to ask to what extent Lucretia is subject of the act, object of the representation.

The frontal light becomes significant in answering this question by helping to produce the tension between these two contradictory positions. If we can see the figure of Lucretia as a body on display, other details become meaningful. The woman – the subject, or rather, object of the representation – stands right in the middle of the canvas, her body turned directly toward the spectators. So does her upper gown which, closed beneath the bosom, has an opened "lock." This opened closure refers rhetorically to the violent opening of Lucretia, to her rape and to her display at the same time, with the latter coming to stand for the former as we have seen. The chaste Lucretia, thus, has become public property by her rape; she has been opened to the public. The visual representation of the woman at the moment of her self-killing partakes of this "publication." Lucretia is put on display for the eyes of the indiscreet onlooker.

Once we are reading in this mode, there is little to stop us. In the face of this display, Lucretia has her arms spread as one crucified. Within the Christian culture in which this painting of a secular subject functions, the connection with Christ's martyrdom can readily be established, initiating another metaphor, one that operates to pernicious ideological effect. For in the crucifixion the victim is doubly complicitous: He accepts his own death, and as a human being he is complicitous in the human sinfulness that supposedly makes his death deserved. Hence, for those viewers who establish this metaphorical connection, there is yet another reason to concentrate guilt on the victim. The crucifixion seems a valorization of the same process of displacement of guilt, of accepting guilt as necessarily redounding upon the victim of violence. In this process the acceptance of guilt is a means of asserting identity between victim and assailant.

But again, using metaphor by itself obscures another set of meanings that using the other rhetorical concepts brings about. Although the pose is in iconographic concordance with Christ, Lucretia turns her face away with just a little more insistence – as the earring's movement shows. Read "hysterically," this movement appeals to the spectator, makes present the painting's external spectator through a direct address, as an *apostrophe* (Culler, 1981; Johnson, 1987). This device, so common in lyric poetry, makes the semiosis personal and makes the reader/spectator aware of her or his own position. The movement is the equivalent of a powerful speech act. This speech act establishes a continuity between the subject of address and the addressee. Thus Lucretia's pose can be activated as a metonymy that writes the spectator into the painting.

But if Lucretia's turning away is a sign of such an apostrophe, who is being addressed? Within the story and within this scene, the father and husband are present, hence addressable. But the part-of-the-whole reading of synecdoche which would conflate the gesture as an appeal to father and husband – legal owners – with repulsion of the rapist – illegal appropriator – would make those two an inappropriate choice. Outside of the story the spectators become potential addressees. But as they are metaphorically identified with the witnesses inside, because they, too, are witnesses, looking at somebody who does not want to be looked at, the

spectators become "hysterically" contaminated by the similarity between their position and that of father and husband, and through the positions of husband and father, that of the rapist.

But the addressee of apostrophe, traditionally out of reach, might merely signify the speaker's isolation and emphasize the rhetorical status of her hopeless address. Lucretia turns her head away in order to break contact with the spectators, preferring isolation to remaining an object of their voyeuristic gaze.[25] Her upraised left hand, then, comes to signify resistance to that gaze, a request to the viewer to turn away. Denying contact with others in this final moment of death by her own hand, she seems to say that she alone can perform it. Even the pitying, sympathizing onlookers are, at this moment, indiscreet and superfluous.

The duplication of the dagger's point is the second detail which, read "hysterically," becomes a major sign. It points to the rape victim, who is so much destroyed as a subject that her personality disappears behind that of the rapist. The rapist dictates her self-image to her. *His* murder of her subjectivity becomes *her* self-murder. This is often expressed in the self-blame rape victims express: "I must have deserved it." The idea that the rape was a punishment stems from the feeling of worthlessness, of being nothing, which in turn comes from the experience of having been taken possession of. Only by *becoming* the rapist is the woman able to perform an act which, however negative and destructive it may be, is the only illusion of self-determination she has left.

The replication of the one – the rapist – by the the other – the woman – is signified in the duplicated shadow of the dagger. Dagger and penis, the weapon of the victim and the weapon of the rapist, become each other's metaphor. The violent penetration of the alien and hard, destructive object into her body occurs *twice*. The dagger thus represents the feeling of guilt, which seems to be part of the experience of rape and which rests on a causal reversal: the thought of being nothing and *therefore* of having deserved, caused, the rape. This reversal is an ultimately desperate means of fighting the destructiveness of rape at least partially, for one who is guilty must exist. This reversal of cause and effect, a reversed metonymy, continues to be a cultural commonplace. The person who has been raped cannot live any longer, and she is the first to agree; she has to be raped again, by the dagger, by the public conception of rape, by others – police, court officials, the rapist's lawyer – and by herself.

The direction of the dagger in the 1664 *Lucretia* emphasizes this point even more. Lucretia directs it to the bottom of her bosom, to its vertical middle and the composition's center. This composition makes us aware of the display of Lucretia's body. Just as the rapist's penis was directed toward her vagina – that part of her body which, in the eyes of the rapist, defines her synecdochically as a woman and makes her "rapable" – just so the dagger aims at this figuration of it, this part so similarly shaped but decently displaced to higher regions, representable and visual: her bosom. The bosom, close to her heart, is thus metonymically related to the heart, an organ which, according to the commonplace, is the site of or metaphor for feeling, for self-experience.[26] There, at the heart of the body, of Lucretia's selfhood, the dagger will perform its destructive penetration. This figure, the displacement of the "literal" wound to the metaphorical one, reminds us again of the wandering womb, emblem of Freudian displacement and of this reading which attempts to recover what has been repressed.

One more detail, in all its ambiguity, can make us aware of the extent to which a reading such as this one can help us use this point to illuminate the experience of rape. Earlier I raised the problem of realistic reading by addressing, and dismissing, an alleged reason for the choice of the weapon. By now, however, it should be clear that this was a complete rejection, not of realism, but only of a defensive realism that too readily dismisses challenging interpretations that belie "common sense." In order to make my attitude toward realism clear, I shall for a moment read realistically, and see what happens. Realistically speaking, then, it is possible to wonder at some of the painting's less than likely details, details that initiate what Genette (1969b) would call the tension between verisimilitude and motivation. Let us take a second look at the hand holding the dagger.

One could argue that the "normal" way to hold a dagger in order to kill oneself would be to position the hand at a right angle to the body, with the fingers and thumb up, so as to have more force.[27] As it is, the hand is parallel with the body, palm in; so the placement of the hand also signifies the opposite intent. Had the dagger been positioned at the other side of the hand, the hand would be ready to kill the aggressor. Although the painting does not explicitly propose this second possibility, the ambiguity of meaning is possible. Thus, the reader who pauses over the awkwardness with which Lucretia wields her weapon can stretch the visual language to its limits without overstepping the intersubjective communicability of that language. A historical reading would force the reader to inquire into the Renaissance codification of gesture, following which that reader might conclude that this gesture has no further relevance. But the modern reader, who is more interested in the work's semantic and pragmatic potential than in its intentional meaning, can choose to ignore these limitations. As is demonstrated by the very fact that some viewer came up with this detail, one does with an image what one can when one is looking at it.

Finally, then, the status of this ambiguity can be assessed as follows. What the modern reader can do is make the most of the work's lack of realism; what she or he cannot do is pretend that the victim is de facto going to kill the rapist. The dagger, after all, *is* pointed toward the person holding it. So readers are constrained by the implicit contract that this image offers: Its facture suggests that the work recognizably represents an act of suicide.

But beyond that skeleton of meaning, the reader will fill in what she or he wills.

A second way to deal with the hand holding the dagger is to read it with intertextual reference to the Venus tradition. Garrard (1982) proposed to read Gentileschi's *Susanna* through such an iconographic reference. And Lucretia is, after all, also one of the women of antiquity famous for her beauty. As the beautiful woman Lucretia is supposed to be, she should be looking into a mirror. The allusion, then, emphasizes the contrast between happy and fatal beauty. In contrast, she turns her head away to look not at the part of her body she means to strike, but at the shining dagger, that substitutes here for Venus's mirror. So the direction of her look can be taken to allude to the Venus, but, misused by the rapist, Lucretia is cut off from her self-image. She sees only the dagger; the lethal weapon replaces her self.

These two examples offer different interpretations of the same detail that for some viewers may not be significant enough to warrant any attention. But their insignificance to some is not important here. For they show, not what the painting means, but what members of the consuming culture can do with it. For a culture that is struggling with acute problems such as frequent rape, such an *approach* is significant, even if the details used are not. Processing art, not objectifying it as untouchable icon; framing art, not idealizing art as "above" politics, is what this study is about. The analysis of these two details does not proffer a unified image of the painting. The first proposes the image of a woman about to act, although in two different directions, with each possible act metaphorically evoking the other; the other proposes her as a static image, an icon of traditional beauty, perversely subverted in its own denial. The second is easier to integrate, say, with the idea of crucifixion than with the act of self-killing. The woman on the cross, the Venus looking into the mirror to see nothing but death: two still images that, superimposed one upon the other, prevent us from limiting the reading to some allegorical explaining away. And it is from those two images, as background, that Lucretia's act comes forward, only to shock us more deeply.

LUCRETIA'S LAST MOMENT

The second *Lucretia* is not only a later product; it also represents a later phase in the story. Lucretia has already struck; she is bleeding. She still clutches the dagger she has already removed from the wound, an act that is done by Brutus, one of the onlookers, in Livy's story. In that tale Brutus uses the bloody dagger as a sign to instigate the revolution that will end the tyranny of the kings and inaugurate the Republic. But by removing it herself, Lucretia robs Brutus of this opportunity to use her drama semiotically for political purposes.

By keeping the dagger in her own hand, it not only serves to remind the viewer, then, of the rapist's weapon; it also draws a parallel between rape and this use made of it to further political ends. We might even suggest that in a sense Lucretia is also using the bloody dagger semiotically for political purposes; but Lucretia's politics holds that the political is personal, whereas Brutus makes this personal experience highly political.

In the image of her hand holding the bloody dagger, we can clearly see the two levels of meaning that run through the painting. On the one hand, Lucretia can be thought of as wielding the dagge against herself in her guise as a substitute for the rapist; in this reading she continues to conform to the image of the rape victim who exists only as the mirror of her assailant. On the other hand, in a "hysterical" reading she can be read as wielding it for herself, as one excluded from the rather limited democracy about to be initiated.

The dagger in the second *Lucretia*, pointed toward her vagina, emphasizes the idea that the victim compulsorily repeats her rape. The oblong wound denoted by the bloodstain on the white gown, becomes now a more iconic representation of the wounded vagina[28]; displaced upward, and to the left of her body (to the right for the viewer), it is nevertheless metaphorically identifiable by its shape, color, and location, as an analogue of the *locus* of Lucretia's destruction.[29]

The gown, by virtue of the more emphatic exploitation of the three-quarter format, seems magnified, compared to the one in the Washington painting, where it was only a small part of her clothing. Thus it suggests an indiscreet display of the belly and represents much more explicitly that the woman's body has been raped: wounded, destroyed, and made public.

Bell cord and curtain cord join in the double sense of the dramatic which is at stake in the case of rape. The cord Lucretia holds has been interpreted in various ways. Held (1969:54) interprets it as belonging to a stage where it would control the curtain. Alpers (1988:146), within her discussion of the studio, sees it rather as a model's sling, a studio device. I do not find this either/or argument useful; rather, the collusion – or maybe even collision – of the two meanings is what interests me, as both together would enhance the work's complexity in challenging ways. To be sure, Lucretia does seem to be holding the cord as if for support. Within the present perspective, the cord thus becomes a metonymical representation of the two central events in the aftermath of the rape. As a bell cord, it can indicate an appeal to the men – father and husband – called upon to avenge her. As a curtain cord, it can indicate the opening of the curtain of the stage, Lucretia's "publication," her display. Lucretia has become drama, both inside and outside the story. That the model's sling, which the cord doubtlessly also is, would be used in this manner may be typical of Rembrandt the studio master, as Alpers would suggest; it is also typical of the viewer's interpretive impulse that we let it have these meanings. Inside, the drama already performed by the rapist unfolds itself

75

again for the men whose property she is. Outside, the dramatic relation between the painting and the public, the spectators to whose gaze she is subjected, is manifest.[30]

In Livy's story Lucretia kills herself for two reasons: She fears for her reputation, and she wants to set an example for other women. In Livy's text, the rape equals the destruction, not because it denies the woman's subjectivity, but because it is an assault on her chastity, her exclusive possession by some other man. Livy makes her say that her suicide must prove her innocence. A culture that makes women believe they have either caused or imagined their rapes pushes victims toward self-destruction; and that *self*-destruction, which completes the destruction initiated by the rapist, is supposed to show their victimization.

If we read in complicity with the Livy story, then, the red stain on the white gown, the sign of the suicide that proves her chastity, can be seen as an allusion to a very old tradition of visual positivism: the widespread practice of showing the bloodstained sheets after the wedding night as evidence of the bride's virginity. The large stain on Lucretia's body "proves," by a metonymical allusion to that tradition, that Lucretia's chastity has been violated, even if "technically" she is not a virgin. Again, then, we see a duplication, not of the weapon but of the raped organ.

This duplication helps us see the representation as a story, but not exactly the traditional one told since from Livy. Recognizing the 1666 *Lucretia* as another story changes the relationship between Livy's text and the "Rembrandt." No longer are the two texts related hierarchically, with Livy's as "primary" and "Rembrandt"'s "secondary," or with Livy's as story and "Rembrandt"'s as illustration. Rather, the painting re-presents the culturally available story, the doxa, and proposes its own story as a response to it. This response partially reaffirms, partially denies, or revises the tradition; counters it polemically and undermines it. To the extent that no re-production of a story can completely duplicate its "sources," the cultural life of the legend is always active, always transforming the cultural view of the fictitious "source" to which each work contributes.

Thus a painting can contribute to the transformation of a view held by the culture in which it functions; this painting does so by representing its own interpretation of rape. By conveying a suggestion of a succession of two moments, the moment before the rape and the moment after, the 1666 *Lucretia* emphasizes rape's deadliness. Read "hysterically," the slit in the top of the gown depicts the intact nightgown–hymen of the innocently sleeping Lucretia, and the lower, bloody slit depicts her wound, her femininity chaste before and violated after the rape. The two moments are related to each other in several ways, which form the links constituting the structure of visual narrative.[31] From a narrative perspective they succeed each other. Metonymically they are causally related, and metaphorically they represent each other. Together all three of these relationships figure the displacement of hysterics. The diagonal cord or chain relates these two moments of innocence and safety to wounding and mortal terror by leading our gaze from the first moment to the second. By thus making us aware of the movement of our gaze, the cord has a critical potential: By following it with our eyes, we can break the painting's stillness and the abstraction of our own gaze.[32] As a result, we become participants in Lucretia's story, but the role we are to occupy remains a disturbing question.

CONTAGIOUS LOGORRHEA

In this attempt to map out relevant aspects of the semiotics of rape, we have seen how the "Rembrandt" *Lucretia*s illuminate some aspects of the tradition verbally perpetuated by Livy's and Ovid's versions of this tale, while leaving other aspects of the story in the dark. On the other hand, we have seen that the "Rembrandt" works also propose different meanings for specific elements of the Lucretia story. These paintings reactualize the issue of rape which, although a permanent feature of the story, has been unequally emphasized, or even hidden under layers of displacements and allegorization. So perhaps by discussing these texts briefly, we can begin to assess the ideological positions taken by each storyteller.[33]

Taking the classical texts – or even Shakespeare's, for that matter – as "Rembrandt"'s *sources* is highly problematic. Of course, it is through Livy and Ovid that the story has survived, but we have no evidence that the painter "Rembrandt," or indeed any painter, actually studied texts before setting out to depict a story. Looking upon the text and image as participating, to a certain extent, in a common "textual community" (Stock, 1983) is more plausible. Oral transmission is an important part of the "life" of stories in a community. Therefore, positing the unverifiable use of a particular source is not helpful. Rather, we should merely assume that the artist knew such a source existed. Some might feel that even this entails going too far out on a limb. However, I would counter that the authority of a text or set of texts was well established in the time of the paintings' production, as it is today. And even if few people actually read them, "Rembrandt"'s textual community would have assumed the existence and relevance of those classical texts.[34] In this study, Rembrandt's personal literary experience in the strict sense of reading does not really matter, for I am seeking to place these works in a community and speculate about the continuity between that community and ours, in order to grasp how visual and verbal art function both in the past and in contemporary society, with the primary emphasis on the latter. So knowing that "Rembrandt"'s contemporaries would have recognized the relevance of the classical texts to the *Lucretia*s is enough to begin to see a closer scrutiny of Livy and Ovid as relevant, as long as we see ourselves in (partial) continuity with that culture.

Livy's *Annales* are mythical historiography, an endeavor directly brought forth by the need to justify the Roman Republic. In doing so, providing the status quo – the Republic – with an origin, hence, a cause for its existence, was urgent. Lucretia's rape became the cause that satisfied the need for origin, this need becoming, in turn, the cause of the rape. In this process the temporal sequence of the story – its beginning and ending – becomes conflated with the logical order – cause and effect – and the logical order becomes inextricably bound up with the mythical explanation of origins.

In the same way, guilt, a moral interpretation of causality, leads logically to punishment here, as cause leads necessarily to effect. Since Lucretia as victim identifies with her assailant, as I argued earlier, she must accept punishment for the crime committed by the man whose surrogate she has become. So when her father and husband try to comfort her, she says: "Though I acquit myself of the sin, I do not absolve myself from punishment" (Foster, 1959:203).

Obviously, the true "logic" of guilt and punishment does not hold here; her identification with her assailant, Tarquin, has perverted it. So now she who had been made victim takes the other's guilt upon herself and thus metes out and *causes* her own punishment. But although the logic here is twisted, it still makes a kind of sense. Lucretia can remain sinless while still culpable, for she had already divided herself in two. She says: "My body alone has been violated; my spirit is guiltless" (Foster, 1959:203; translation adapted). This separation of body and mind is, however, impossible, as the impossibility of separating guilt and punishment shows: If her mind is guiltless, punishment is impossible. For violence directed against the body alone, which cannot instigate but merely respond to command, is like rape: sheer violence, torture, but no punishment (Scarry, 1985). Hence, the two statements quoted above, uttered in rapid succession to the same addressees, are violently contradictory. They are contradictory, however, only until we recognize these statements as indicative of Lucretia's identification with the rapist and with this guilt.

The paradox that this is the only way in which the victim can retain a minimum of subjective power is strongly at work in Livy's text and can be seen in many details of the fragment. One example among many is the wordplay "Sextus Tarquinius is he who last night returned hostility for hospitality" (*hostis pro hospite*) (Foster, 1959:202–3). The two words "hostility" and "hospitality" are derived from the same root but express opposed attitudes toward strangers, toward the *other*. The strong similitude between the words emphasizes the gap between the two related concepts, where hostility (*hostis*) wounds the sacred value of hospitality. But it also emphasizes the unexpected identity that the root betrays: Though usage has obscured it, hospitality has become a metaphor for hostility. This similitude in turn suggests a causal, metonymical relation: Hospitality, in this case, instead of conjuring hostility, causes it. And that possibility, even if occurring only in a flash, brings us back to well-known territory: Lucretia has provoked her own rape.

Perhaps the most disturbing aspect of Livy's version of the Lucretia tradition is the particular management of the *voice*, of the subject of semiosis. I started with a silenced woman, Emma, who was made audible, by means of a "hysterical," visual reading, through a male voice. Although by definition voiceless because exclusively visual, the "Rembrandt" Lucretia can be "heard" even more clearly than Emma. Her representations in the 1664 and 1666 works are particularly evocative because so many aspects of her situation are manifested there.[35] Livy's Lucretia, in constrast, is a woman who speaks, but from a male perspective, through the mediation of a man, and nowhere is this clearer than when she represents and justifies male fear and hostility. Her experience of the rape is thus again silenced. The scene is narrated as follows by Livy:

With this terror his lust gained the victory, victorious [*victrix*] as if by violence over her obstinate chastity, and [when] Tarquinius [had] left after the conquest of the woman's honor . . . (Foster, 1959: 200; my translation)

Two aspects of the quotation above interest me here. First, the rape itself, both as an act and as an experience, is glossed over. And second, the vocabulary is military. The latter aspect will be exploited to the point of parody in Shakespeare's version, as Catherine Stimpson (1980), Nancy Vickers (1986), and others have shown. Although this military rhetoric is commonplace, however, it is still significant, for it shows that rape is a fight, a war between the sexes to which the man comes fully armed. The drawn sword with which Tarquin approaches the defenseless, sleeping Lucretia is not only a metaphor for his real weapon. As metonymy, it foreshadows the suicide and shows that *his* sword causes it. But also, it expresses his own insecurity, by suggesting that the victim is dangerous.

Livy's rhetoric itself serves ideological purposes here. Violence is represented as a comparison: "victorious as if by violence." The rhetorical comparison, the "as if" structure, is used as an ideological code (van Alphen, 1987). In the common notion of "literal" and "figurative" language, violence would be only a figure of speech here, superfluous and ornamental. Ovid exploits this possible interpretation by representing his Tarquin as a passionate lover. The military language, however, deconstructs this hierarchy between "literal" and "figurative" language by showing what is primary and what secondary. In loyalty to our commitment to concreteness, we shall take seriously the "color" or "shade" of the language, and this commitment to taking the language seriously will prove a vital strategy of the "hysterical" semiotic. Rather than seeing in Livy's sentence the suggestion that Lucretia's resistance called forth Tarquin's violence, thus making the scene military, it seems clear to me that his violence needs the rhetorical device – the "as if" – as an apology.

The comparison "as if by violence" must then be read literally in its figurality. It thus becomes a "hysterical" direction for reading this passage, a comment on the relation between "literal" and "figurative," between "reality" and the "decoration" of reality. The comparison proves that rhetoric surpasses reality, in that the rhetorical phrase says more, rather than less, about it. But if rhetoric can surpass reality, then our hysterical rhetoric may also override the "real" rhetoric of Livy's language. Then the interpretation, "It is no real violence; it only seems as if it were real violence," would be superseded by a second, hysterical interpretation: "The rhetoric, the language is more important than the reality" which, once appropriated, comes to mean, "The important thing [about rape] is not the 'objective' fact but the language used [by the victim] to express her experience." This reversal in turn allows us to activate the other meaning of the ambiguous Latin word for violence, which also means "force," "strength." Read "hysterically," the phrase "victorious as if by violence" then also means: "My strength is just a manner of speaking." The insecurity about his own strength that made Tarquin draw his superfluous weapon thus turns the rape into a test of power, a test of the rapist's insecure masculinity. That insecurity is the violent enemy faced by the woman experiencing rape.

The alienating use of the victim's voice for the verbalization of a male view can thus be countered by the operation of the reversals and displacements of "hysterics." The two kinds of reversing figurative and literal – decorative and "essential," and verbal and visual – are crucial for this endeavor. The important point to make is that these two operations of reversal go together and reinforce each other.

In Freud's verbal account the visual image of the scene helped reconstruct Emma's experience; in "Rembrandt"'s visual representations we have seen how his paintings allow for a reading based upon rhetoric – almost a verbal reading. The rivalry between the verbal and the visual domain is by no means coincidental to the sex war of rape. It is no accident that the rape of Lucretia is represented as caused by a visual image – the sight of her beauty and chastity, of her exclusive possession by one man, that is – an image evoked, first, verbally, by the competing husband-owner. This husband, Collatine, boasts in beautiful rhetorical language that words are superfluous and sight is crucial: "Let every man regard as the surest test what meets his eyes when the woman's husband enters unexpected" (Foster, 1959:199).

But the beauty of the image does not work without the other element of attraction, the woman's chastity. The voyeurism that leads to Lucretia's rape is not simply the gaze directed at the (arousing) sight of female beauty, but the sight of her as a possession of another man. The emphasis on the visual hardly conceals the crucial discursive factor, as the attraction of the woman hardly conceals the real target – the other man (Sedgwick, 1985). This becomes clearer in Ovid's fragment of the story, where Collatine's statement in Livy's version has been replaced by an equally ambiguous one: "non opus esse verbis, credite rebus," translated by Frazer (1931) as "[N]o words are needed; trust deeds." This translation (which contains a possible but not a necessary choice among the possible meanings of the noun "res") shifts from sight – trust things – to action. This translator's choice is relevant. The advice to trust deeds is eagerly adopted by Tarquin, thus showing that seeing and acting are tantamount to the same thing. This identification will be developed further in Chapter 4.

Shakespeare resolves the paradox in his own way. For him the words alone produce the visual image, and the rape is planned *before* the rival has so much as seen the woman. He "sees" her through her husband's verbal description, and it is through his words that he sees her, even when he "really" sees her:

> Therefore that praise which Collatine doth owe
> Enchanted Tarquin answers with surmise
> In silent wonder of *still-gazing eyes*. (lines 82–4)

In the face of Collatine's logorrhea,[36] Tarquin is dumbfounded. His eyes stare at the image produced by Collatine's words, but the rhetoric, entirely military, produces a (visual) image of war – a war, in turn, represented through sexual imagery of the queens for whom the knights fight. This mixture of sexual and military imagery is cemented by an additional isotopy: that of color, of painting. Here is a passage in which these three semantic fields are equally represented[37]:

> This heraldry in Lucrece's face was seen,
> Argu'd by beauty's red and virtue's white;
> Of either colour was the other queen,
> Providing the world's minority their right.
> Yet their ambition makes them still to fight;
> The sov'reignty of either being so great,
> That oft they interchange each other's seat. (lines 65–71)

Does the dumbfounded Tarquin, with the still gazing eyes, see an attractive woman or a medusa?[38] Is he overcome by desire or by fear? In any case, he is contaminated by the logorrhea that makes him sick – dangerously and deathly sick – although the danger and the death are displaced onto the object of the discourse: Lucretia.

After the rape, the despair of Shakespeare's Lucretia is in the first place caused by her frustration about her inability to represent her experience. In contrast with the verbally evoked visuality that condemned her to her victimization, she feels sharply the inadequacy of her mastery over the language that the men have mastered so well, and as an alternative she seeks comfort in a visual image. It is a painting of the Trojan War – a painting full of eyes. The following fragment from the lengthy description of the painting displays the insistent inscription of the visual:

And from the towers of Troy there would appear
The very *eyes* of men through loop-holes thrust
Gazing upon the Greeks with little lust:
Such sweet *observance* in this work was had
That one might *see* those far-off *eyes look* sad. (lines 1382–6; my emphasis)

Through the visual image, Lucretia identifies with old Hecuba's sorrow, and the motivation for that identification is obvious: "Of what she was no *semblance* did remain." She identifies with the destroyed subject whose destruction she *sees* negatively, by not seeing a "semblance" of her former self. The image has lost its stability; the subject's self has been irretrievably destroyed by the narrative of violence – and by the violence of narrative. The *change* of the *image* is the "telling" element that enables the identification of the young woman with the old.

But the visual cannot replace language, for which Lucretia blames the artist: "to give her so much grief and not a *tongue*." The painted Hecuba is like the sick Emma in Freud's letters, deprived of speech, reduced to spectacle. But this spectacle is also productive; it allows Lucretia to express her inexpressible experience. "Semblance," the key notion of rhetoric, thus bridges the gap between self and other, making expression possible.

SEMIOTIC APPROPRIATION

The tension between language and image is nowhere played out more impressively than in the episodes *following* Lucretia's rape and suicide. In the Roman legend, her rape and murder are appropriated for a male cause by the semiotic use of her blood. Thus, her rape and death become so fully incorporated into the public domain that they are seen as acts violating her husband's property. Here lies the importance of the "Rembrandt" that makes Lucretia draw the dagger out of the deadly wound herself. Again, whether the historical painter Rembrandt consciously and polemically deviated from the "source" or merely represented his memory of the doxic legend is ultimately irrelevant from my perspective. In both cases, we are dealing with a work that, unlike the verbal texts, does not let Brutus appropriate the rape for his political purpose.

What does it mean, for our reading of the work, that it is precisely in this detail that "Rembrandt"'s story "deviates" from the others, or rather, replaces those other stories with its own? It means that between story and story a battle takes place over meaning, not over facts. And in the "Rembrandt" paintings the meaning of Brutus's intervention, not merely the gesture itself, is overruled. By using the rape for political purposes Brutus became *Lucretia*'s allegorist. Was he the first? Nothing, of course, is more tricky than assigning origin, but it is Tarquin who allegorized Lucretia before Brutus. He disembodied her, turning her into an emblem of male possession, an appropriable object of male rivalry and battle. But then, would it not have been Collatine who allegorized her first, by making her into a story about who had the most desirable and secure possession? With each new gesture of allegorization, Lucretia was robbed more and more of her self, and of her story, until, in infinite regression, the search for origin that brought forth this text itself allegorized the allegory.

As we saw in the beginning of this chapter, allegory is a mode of reading that takes the represented event out of its own history to put it into a different one. Dehistoricizing Lucretia's experience, an allegorical reading appropriates it, gives it a new history, divorces it from the experiencing subject. As Craig Owens puts it in his defense of allegory:

[T]hroughout its history it has functioned in the gap between a present and a past which, without allegorical reinterpretation, might have remained foreclosed. (Owens, 1984:203)

Seen in this light, allegorical interpretation is an indispensable gesture of appropriation. If the allegorical impulse functions positively, it allows the work to situate itself in relation to it: Thus a particular work can encourage a reader to, or discourage a reader from, that gesture. But the decision remains with the reader. An allegory (or, as I would specify, an "allegorogene" detail of a work) that functions negatively, however, has a metatextual function that, according to Northrop Frye (1957), prescribes the direction of its own commentary. If the representation of Brutus's appropriation constitutes the Latin story's allegorical direction, then the painting's denial of that gesture is an equally metatextual denial of allegorical appropriation. At Lucretia's own handling of the dagger, the allegorist should be pulled up short.

In the still older story of the rejection, torture, gang rape, murder, and dismemberment of a young woman in the Biblical story of Judges 19, we see an even more disturbing instance of this allegorical appropriation, this semiotic misuse. The story begins with a young woman leaving her husband to rejoin her father. The husband then goes after her to bring her back to his home. The father tries to detain the couple, but has to give up after several days. And on their way to the husband's dwelling, the couple has to spend the night in a dangerous environment, as guests of an old man. Men from the city threaten to rape the husband. In order to save himself, he later throws his wife out as a sop to the men, who begin a nightlong torture scene. The next morning the husband takes (the body of?) his wife home and cuts her/it into pieces. Then the fragments of the body itself are used in a manner not unlike the way Lucretia's bloody dagger is used. They are sent to the twelve tribes of Israel as a call to war, a war that, after more murder and rape, will lead to the establishment of the kingdom.[39] The symmetry with the Lucretia tradition is striking: In Rome, the tyranny of the kings had to be replaced by the Republic, whereas in Israel, internal chaos had to be resolved by instituting monarchy. In both cases, rape, considered a crime of property, represents the disorder. And that social disorder must be eradicated by the introduction of a new political structure.

As in the case of Lucretia, some claim that this public, political use of the raped woman is merely evidence of the story's allegorical genre. But this interpretation, however plausible, hardly explains anything. It does not, for example, explain the choice of vehicle for tenor. Nor does it explain the insufficiency which allegory itself betrays. This deficiency becomes obvious to the reader who is both trained to allegorize and equally willing to reflect on the allegorial impulse. For a semiotic analysis of the relations between the episodes shows that it is precisely because allegory – metaphor – alone is not satisfying, that the next episode – the semiotic use of the raped body – is needed. As before, we can see that we need to open up rhetoric to more than metaphor.

Both in the Lucretia traditions and in Judges, the public arrogation of the woman's body is a "natural" next phase in an act of public appropriation which the rape itself constitutes. The bloody knife and the pieces of flesh are used because metonymy and synecdoche are stronger – more "penetrating" – signs than mere metaphor. As you will recall, allegory and metaphor operate through similarity; metonymy and synecdoche through contiguity. By connecting this with Peircean semiotics, we can see that the deficient modes of reading, the modes based on similarity, are predicated upon iconicity, whereas the modes based on contiguity are based upon indexicality. The index is the sign of the touch. When the fight over signs has to be, somehow, a *real* fight with *real* issues, the male rivals literally need to *touch* the woman's body – to partake in its rape. In this instance we see how indexicality is implicated in interpretation. The touch here has become a blow.

I connect the idea of the "touch" that draws blood with the question of "Rembrandt"'s impasto as interpreted by Alpers. In the second *Lucretia*, the thick paint of the bloodstain not only represents the real, dried-up blood in a disturbingly "lifelike" fashion. It also looks like real, applied paint. And while that gestalt shifts, the touch of the maker is represented as strongly as is the touch of the rapist. In one sense, then, Rembrandt as Alpers (1988:14–33) sees him, Rembrandt the *sculpteur manqué*, the toucher, also makes a political use of Lucretia's rape. He uses her death to attract attention to his skill, the craft which he is at this very moment promoting into an art. This very act, on the other hand, also draws attention to Lucretia's status as representation, hence to the representational aspects of rape itself. The blood–paint, then, serves a dual critical function. In contrast, the verbal texts, which narrate the semiotic use of the body without problematizing it *as use*, mobilize narrativity to mystify rape.

"Men rape what other men possess," wrote Catherine Stimpson (1980:58); "false desire" is Shakespeare's qualification, offered as early as the second verse of his *Lucrece*. "Aimer selon l'autre," is René Girard's (1961) phrase; *Between Men* is the title of Eve Sedgwick's (1985) book. All these expressions suggest *why* men rape; they also imply *what* rape is: a public, semiotic act. In addition to being physical violence and psychological murder, rape is also an act of body language spoken to other men through, and *in*, a woman's body.

In *Death and Dissymmetry* (1988c), I developed the argument that the specific act of rape as a semiotic message conveyed from one man to another is related to the insecurity, the arbitrariness, of male possession as denoted in fatherhood. The father's possession of the woman purported to be bearing *his* child is insecure indeed. And such tenuous possession can be extrapolated to apply to all relationships in which a man claims to possess a woman. The act of rape, within such a doxa, is the violent appropriation of a body that belongs to another man – father or husband – by bodily contiguity.

The anthropological background of Judges 19 makes it a particularly convincing example of this. The men in the city where the couple spends the night, belonging to the culture of the woman's father, participate in what is called nomadic marriage, but which I prefer to call *patrilocal* marriage: a form of marriage whereby the daughter remains in the house of her father while the husband visits her incidentally. The attempt of the husband to take the daughter out of the father's house violates a basic tenet of patrilocal culture: the contiguity of fatherhood. To these members of a patrilocal culture, any sexual relation outside of the fatherhouse is perceived as arbitrary, reflecting the arbitrariness of the semiotic relation between sign and meaning. The daughter taken out of the house belongs, not simply to another man, but to any man, hence to every man. This idea of public property as the only alternative to contiguity, to the woman as private property, is precisely the foundation of rape. The act, then, ironically presents an iconic image of both possibilities. It presents rape as an arbitrary appropriation, the theft of a man's property, by means of contiguity (squatter's rights, if you like); and it presents rape as indicating the arbitrariness of the relation between sign and meaning, for what does the woman have to do with the rivalry between the men? This arbitrariness is signified by means of metonymy.

This semiotic aspect of rape resolves the paradox of the competition between words and images, between rhetoric and "real facts" which Livy, Ovid, Shakespeare, and, in his own way and medium, "Rembrandt," brought to the fore. The meaning of the speech act of rape is hatred of the male competitor, of the woman who may not be possessible; it is a hatred spoken through metonymy. The hatred comes from fear and is acted out – spoken – through the actual body of the object of fear. Rape is a speech act that reduces its sign to silence. Reducing her to sign status through dismemberment, as the husband in Judges does when he sends the raped woman's body out as a message, is only an extreme variant of the common cultural attitude toward rape. As the "speaking" of rape is exclusively done by men, consisting, as it does, of reducing the victim to silence, speaking *about* rape is also generally a male privilege. The women have become spectacles, images. But when we take these images of them as *raped* as primary, as literal, and as real, we can give them back their voices.[40]

One way to do this is to attend to the representations of rape proposed by women; another is to attend to the "deviant" detail of works predominantly representing the male perspective. The importance of those details in the "Rembrandt" paintings, which seem either harmlessly insignificant (e.g., the doubling of the dagger) or due to the assumed limitations of the visual medium (e.g., the omission of Brutus's appropriation, considered visually unrepresentable because occurring in the next moment), can be emphasized by a reading that reappropriates what was appropriated.

Thus the refusal to let Brutus take the dagger can be read as a doubly metatextual commentary. Brutus's gesture was itself seen as a direction for allegorical appropriation, metatextual and thus drawing attention away from the "real" event. *Not* allowing this gesture even to be implied is quite different from submitting the work to the "limitations" of the medium; it is exploiting the medium's conventions in order to provide a commentary on the predecessor's commentary. Denying allegory is itself allegorical, but such a reversal still changes the meaning. Self-reflexively drawing attention to the work *as* work, to the representation's representational quality, Lucretia's hold of her own dagger, her own death, is what brings her, her experience, and what the reader must realize about it, back to life.

REAL RAPE: THE IMPORTANCE OF TELLING STORIES

In order to contribute to this returning of voices, I have also examined a few rape stories written by women in present-day culture. The two most striking differences are worth mentioning. It is not so much, or not only, the fact that the women's experience is done more justice in these stories. More subtly, the relationship between the rapes and political violence is shown to be much more intricate than our classical texts would suggest. First, in the women's stories that I have read, the rape does not *lead to* revolution; it *is* one. Second, the woman's perspective does not obliterate the male one. The men, the rapists, are attended to with surprising detail. But this becomes less surprising when we realize that for women, attending to the *why* of rape is the only way to overcome the feeling of personal destruction without having to identify with the rapist. And they deal with the question why in semiotic terms. It is failing to understand the signs, rather than the rhetorical rivalry between words and image, that causes rape in these women's texts. Although it is again the *sight* of the women, their images, that entice the rapists, the texts represent not the silenced image of voiceless women but active women whose activity is denied meaning. The most impressive example of this view of rape as the denial of subjectivity in terms of the denial of meaning is the representation in Buchi Emecheta's *The Rape of Shavi* (1985) of the future rape victim, the prospective queen of Shavi, sweeping the entrance of the rapist's cabin as a *sign* of respect. This sign is, of course, mistaken for a sign of humble status, and, taking the girl for a maid, the man feels free to rape her, showing how inextricably intertwined are racism, classism, and sexism.

Let me wind up this discussion, then, with a few of these stories, in order to demonstrate how visuality and discursivity need to be considered together, how images sometimes determine what happens, and how recounting these images makes the change in that inexorable train of events. My stories range from real reportage to fiction, and I have chosen for these concluding remarks two texts from each pole: a real rape story and a fairytale. The real story was written five years after the double rape of a young woman – I call her Leta – during a vacation in the south of Spain. The fairytale is in the Grimm collection (1974). The comparison helps us see the urgency of "hysterics" as a strategy, as well as its heuristic value for visual poetics.

The story of Leta, extremely soberly written in three pages, has the following description, an *image* if ever there was one:

While the first was fucking me, I saw el gordo [the older, fat man she has named "the belly"] walking rounds around the car [in which she was raped] waiting for his turn. (Leta; text in Bal, 1988a)

This image represents the victim's experience; read hysterically, it does so in three ways. In the first place, the image is what she sees while being raped. It is precisely this moment that is repressed in the Lucretia texts. Second, her fear of the second rapist forces Leta to "rape herself" (as she wrote in the previous sentences) by trying to talk the first rapist into some sort of solidarity so that the second man would be excluded. The first man seems to comply, but is of course only deceiving his victim.[41] The sight of the fat man walking around the car foreshadows the next rape by conveying the feeling of alienation, for, third, "el gordo" is represented as a guard who keeps her locked up. The collaboration between men turns the rape from an incident, almost an accident, into a relational structure in which Leta is imprisoned. These three aspects together represent her perspective of repetition without hope for liberation. This visual image was, Leta wrote, the most frightening moment of the experience.

Written down by men in the nineteenth century, but doubtlessly an earlier, oral tale used by older women to warn young girls,

Grimm's fictional rape story can serve as an allegory – why not use this ploy in my turn? – for the importance of hysterics. The tale "The Robber Bridegroom" ("Der Räuberbräutigam"; Grimm, 1974) is about a miller's daughter who is "promised" by her father to a frightening man. The repulsion the girl feels tells her that the man is bad ("so oft sie ihn ansah oder an ihn dachte fühlte sie *ein grauen in ihrem Herzen*"; "her heart contracted with horror every time she looked at him or thought of him").[42] Taking seriously the warning of her own eyes and heart, she takes measures to protect herself when she has to go to the man's house for a visit. And after witnessing the rape and dismemberment of another girl, she manages to escape with help from a bird – a voice – and an old woman. Once back home, she tells her story in the presence of her father, brothers, and murderer-fiancé. She is listened to. Thanks to her story and the men's attention, the criminal is caught, and justice is done.

Three aspects of the tale distinguish it from the male texts discussed so far, aspects that I take to be characteristic of the underlying female voice. The first is the presence of the helping mother-figure. An old woman who lives in the robber's house helps the girl and is helped by her. Interestingly, the absence of a mother in both the Lucretia tradition and the Judges story contrasts with her presence in rape stories written by women, as, for example, in Isabel Allende's *The House of the Spirits* (1985). Readers should also note the importance of the mother in Marilyn French's *The Women's Room* (1977) and the function of the mother of the rape victim in Buchi Emecheta's *The Rape of Shavi* (1985). There, the mother explicitly excludes the men, concealing her daughter's rape from them, while telling the daughter's prospective mother-in-law. She motivates this concealment by telling her daughter that the men would only make things worse.

The second element that distinguishes the tale from the male texts previously discussed is the solidarity among women, a solidarity we also noted in Emecheta's story. In "The Robber Bridegroom," that solidarity is between the betrothed girl and the girl whose dismemberment she witnesses and whose finger she takes home as evidence.

While the girl in the Grimms' grim tale watches sexual violence committed against the other girl, a severed finger falls into her lap. This moment of extreme danger is also a moment of metonymical, synecdochical, as well as metaphorical, identification with her fellow victim: She is contaminated by the other's blood. A similar idea is visualized in Frida Kahlo's painting *A Few Little Nips* (reproduced in Herrera, 1983), in which a naked woman, entirely covered by cuts, is lying on a bed, the killer standing behind her. Blood is everywhere, all over the body, all over the floor, and even all over the picture's frame, thus signifying not only the illusoriness of framing as a limit of relevance, but also signifying the viewer's contamination.[43] The thick impasto of the bloodstain in the second "Rembrandt" *Lucretia* receives yet another meaning in this context: the painter who, as emphatic readers we can imagine, has stained his finger with her blood and cannot but take Lucretia's side. Similarly, the miller's daughter is not simply metaphorically related to the other girl as a possible victim like her; she is also metonymically, causally related to her, fully identified with her: She is bloodstained *because* the other is murdered. By appropriating this finger and using it semiotically in the name of the murdered woman, this girl points to the need for metonymic identification among women, with all those who are "rapable." This semiotic use of the finger replaces the political use of the bloody dagger in the Lucretia stories.

The third and final trait that characterizes "The Robber Bridegroom" as a text reflecting a woman's perspective is the fact that the girl gets to tell her own story. The girl in "The Robber Bridegroom" replaces Brutus as the teller of the tale, just as the finger has replaced the dagger. She tells it in the mode of fiction, so that it will be listened to. Narrating her story as if it were a dream, she repeatedly utters the refrain: "Mein Schatz, das träumte mir nur" ("My dear, it was only a dream"). She repeats this phrase so often that its overt purpose of framing the story by reassuring fictionality is reversed. By presenting the "real" story in this fictional mode, she is able to force the murderer to listen to her and to betray himself to her father and brothers, as Shakespeare's Claudius betrays himself to Hamlet.

This fictionalization is also Emecheta's strategy in her "fable" about the rape of a young black woman in the innocent, virginal African community of Shavi, by an "albino" who has failed to understand the culture. If the Grimms' tale ends happily, it is because the girl's story is well understood. If Emecheta's fable ends unhappily, it is because misunderstanding – that of the man toward the woman and that of the albino toward the black culture – is the basis of behavior:

Ronje fell on her and, in less then ten minutes, took from the future queen of Shavi what the whole of Shavi stood for. To him, the Shavians were savages and Ayoko was just a serving girl. Though she fought, cried and begged, her pleading was jibberish to him, her resistance enhanced the vengeance he was taking on Shona. (Emecheta, 1983/1985:94)

Shona is his ex-wife who had run off with a black man. Again, rape is related to the possession of women.

Rather than considering fiction as innocent, like the robber in the tale who got caught because of his "willing suspension of disbelief," we readers can use rape stories in fictional texts and images as sources that allow us to interpret, to understand the real but inexpressible experience of rape; we can use those texts, those images, to replace rivalry and repression of experience with the primacy and understanding its signs require.

CONCLUSION

As pointed out by Winifred Woodhull in the collection *Feminism and Foucault* (1988), the problem of how to view rape and how to act upon that view is far from being solved. The 1970s gave rise to a lively debate in France which centered around Foucault's proposal to separate rape and sexuality, and instead to treat rape as an ordinary civil offense. This view was based on Foucault's relational concept of power, that would "shift the emphasis from power's repressive function . . . to its productive function."[44] Woodhull goes on to argue that

Instead of sidestepping the problem of sex's relation to power by divorcing one from the other in our minds, we need to analyze the social mechanisms, *including language and conceptual structures*, that bind the two together in our culture. (Woodhull, 1988:171; my emphasis)

One can see how the foregoing analyses fit into this program.

The conclusions that can be drawn from these analyses are three-fold; they relate to the domain of the social, to the domain of the semiotic in general, and to the specific relations between the verbal and the visual. Rape, as I have tried to argue, is encouraged by cultural attitudes that are hostile not to the phenomenon of rape but to its victims. These attitudes can remain in force because of the frequently held misconceptions about meaning that allow the rapist's usurpation of the authority over meaning to pass unnoticed. The radical separation of seeing and speaking, not only in academic disciplines but also in gender relations, fosters these misconceptions.[45] Reversing these cultural attitudes is crucial.

The semiotics of rape, available through a "hysterical" reading, can help us to redefine rape in a way that will change cultural attitudes toward it and allow those changes to be translated into measures – juridical, medical, therapeutic – that will make rape not only intolerable but untolerated. To that end, it is crucial that we recognize that besides being violent and aggressive, rape also has the following characteristics: First, rape is a language, a body language. It speaks hatred caused by fear and rivalry. As a speech act, it is the "publication," the public appropriation, of a subject. It turns the victim into a sign, intersubjectively available. The speech act of rape signifies the arbitrary relationship of sign to meaning, of men to offspring through the indispensable mediation of the woman whose children his children really are. Therefore, the primary meaning of rape for the perpetrator is revenge, a crime of property; the victim becomes anybody's property because she is no longer one man's. Second, it is important to remember that the goal of rape is the destruction of the victim's subjectivity, a destruction necessitated by the problematic self-image of the rapist. This destruction is accomplished by the alienation from self that ensues as a result of the experience of hatred being spoken in one's body by means of another's, by forced contiguity. As a consequence of the semiotic nature of rape, the victim, a member of the semiotic community in which the rape takes place, understands and internalizes the message of annihilation absolutely. She is destroyed, hence unable to participate in semiosis anymore. Just as her body has been appropriated, so, too, her semiotic competence has been usurped and her semiosis becomes the other's. As a consequence, the most characteristic result of rape is the victim's agreement with the rapist's hatred of her. The victim is not only blamed by others, she also blames herself, because she is not addressed, not spoken to, but *spoken*.

Any change in the culture that aims at putting an end to the proliferation of rape should start at this last point and help survivors undo their assimilation to the rapist by emphatically refusing their guilt. The cleaning of the Washington Lucretia shows us how this transition can take place, for it brought the dying woman back to life by granting to the movement of her arms the attention it called for. But rather than turning violently against herself, as Lucretia did, the raped woman should be helped to listen to the other story of her own movement. As the emblematic cultural story of rape, Lucretia's case must be replaced by the story of Ayoko in Emecheta's novel, because it is both allegorical and real; and because it describes both the woman's experience and its meaning for the culture as a whole in which that experience takes place. It is here that semiotic analysis, as an interdisciplinary endeavor that suspends the specifics of different media, becomes relevant. Through semiotic analysis it becomes possible to understand a social phenomenon like rape in terms of representation, which is an important dimension of the problem of rape that has remained otherwise unexplored.

But what is the point of discussing rape through paintings and novels? For one thing it is important, because these works are public, intersubjectively available for scrutiny; but is it really possible to move back and forth between the real issue of real rape and the representations of fictional rapes in "high" art? The crux of this problem is the relationship between meaning and experience. Analyzing such a relationship might shed light on my ongoing appeal to empathy with the victim of rape. Therefore, I would like to return briefly to an issue raised earlier, that of the location, the status, and the nature of meaning.

Teresa De Lauretis is one of the few semioticians willing to explore the tenability of the apparent watershed between a materialist-historical semiotics such as that developed by Umberto Eco (1976), which locates meaning rigorously in the social domain, and a subject-oriented semiotics such as that developed by (Lacanian) psychoanalysis. In her centrally important paper "Semiotics and Experience" (1983), De Lauretis rereads Peirce's famous definition of the sign:

A sign, or representamen, is something which stands to somebody for something in some respect or capacity. It addresses somebody, that is, it creates in the mind of that person an equivalent sign, or perhaps a more developed sign [the interpretant]. (Peirce, 1931–58, 2:228)

In spite of the problems of mentalism in some of Peirce's formulations, this widely endorsed definition stages the interaction between the social and the subjective. De Lauretis rightly argues that this definition provides ample support for the notion, quite insistently argued away by Eco (1976), that meaning is produced by the users of signs, not solely by the sender:

[T]he interpreter, the "user" of the sign(s), is also the producer of the meaning (interpretant) because that interpreter is the place in which, the body in whom, the significant effect of the sign takes hold. That is the subject in and for whom semiosis takes effect. (De Lauretis, 1983:179)

De Lauretis makes the decisive move to theorize the concept of experience in these Peircean terms by placing experience within the realm of Peirce's enigmatic concept of the habit. This concept is Peirce's bridge between the individual and the social. De Lauretis (1983:179) writes: "The individual's habit as a semiotic production is both the result and the condition of the social production of meaning." The habit is shaped by experience. Experience, then, is not predicated upon some innate femininity that qualifies everything that subsequently occurs for the female subject, but is a product and producer of meanings in which the subject is implicated and through which the subject is produced and reconfirmed as gendered.

Within such a view of experience as the producer and product of meaning, it is not only possible, but necessary, that we posit experience as centrally operating in interpretation. Rape, a cultural phenomenon that partakes of the production of meaning, is then inextricably intertwined with the representations circulating about it. For rape itself is immersed in meanings, again, not transhistorical or universal; it is immersed in meanings through fluctuations of its embeddedness in doxic representations and interpretations of those doxic representations that condone rape because it duplicates the enforcement of the violent, alien meaning inside a body; it duplicates the dislodging of the subject that occurs in myriad forms in the process of acculturation.

The place of visuality in the semiotics of rape has turned out to be crucial. But this dimension became apparent only once I had integrated rhetoric with vision. As long as we keep respecting the arbitrary and mystifying dichotomy between "literal" and "figural," the positivistic ideal of objectivity will always be a hindrance, rather than a help, to understanding experience. We have seen that a visual reading with the help of rhetorical concepts can mediate between what the culture, in the name of the rapists, tries to suggest and what the experience really is. The counteraction I propose is radically readerly: Works of art that offer public texts for reading propose images whose ambiguity allows for this resistance.

But this visual rhetoric has a second effect, equally crucial. The movement of Lucretia's earring, the movement typically denied to painting by the cliché views on the sister arts, introduces the idea of a narrative that ends in Lucretia's death. Like that narrative, rape is not a single event; instead, with a cause and a consequence that narrative shares, rape is the cause of the end of a story. That is why it equals murder: It leads to the ideal end – to death. The realization of this murderous quality of rape is the first step toward an adequate treatment of it in our culture, a treatment that looks into the space between verbal and visual expression.

This is why I chose to open this book on "Rembrandt" with the case of rape. The problem of rape is too urgent to be dismissed as irrelevant. Art forms repeatedly choose it as their privileged theme; rape must be taken as emblematic for our culture. Too pregnant with relevant and problematic meanings for all members of our culture to be dismissed merely as "high" culture, as elitist, these representations of rape are central in any definition of culture one can come up with. Fully realistic yet fully rhetorical, utterly readable yet totally ambiguous, the works discussed here can bring us closer to the experience of an art that is not only part of social life, but constitutive of it. As I hope to have shown, arbitrary or ideological delimitations of the domains of the visual and the verbal can only serve to obscure the urgency with which these works confront us. In a certain manner, just as the sick Emma can be taken to stand for a raped woman, so can a raped woman stand for every interpreter who can opt to identify with her. For in a sickly acute and definitive way, every interpreter is what the rape victim is: to repeat De Lauretis's phrase, "the body in whom and for whom semiosis takes effect."

CHAPTER 3

VISUAL STORYTELLING: FATHERS AND SONS AND THE PROBLEM OF MYTH

The fantasy . . . is there in front of me, in the mode of *Vor-stellung*: I (re)present it to myself. Better still, I (re)present myself through some "other," some identificatory figure who enjoys in my place. But the point from which I can contemplate the scene – the fantasy's "umbilical cord," we might say, through which it is linked with what is invisible for the subject – is not offstage. I am *in* the fantasy, there where I am the other "before" seeing him, there where I am the mimetic model even "before" he arises in front of me, there where I am acting out before any distancing, any drawing back: a nonspecular identification (blind mimesis) in which consists (if he/it consists) the entire "subject" of the fantasy. (Mikkel Borch-Jacobsen, *The Freudian Subject*, 1988:44–5)

INTRODUCTION

THE preceding chapter focused on the margins of the story represented in history paintings – the work of the relationship between painter/writer and viewer/reader, the rhetoric that differentiates each "version" of a story from all others. Thus, the "Rembrandt" *Lucretia*s, although invariably interpreted as renderings of the "same" classical myth, addressed the issue of rape and its destructiveness much more sympathetically than did the classical texts, by inserting and foregrounding the focalization of the woman.

In this chapter, I shall explore further the question of cultural images between the visual and the verbal by pursuing one particular line of the preceding inquiry: the idea of using preexisting stories on which the genre of history painting is based. In this genre the painter represents (an episode of) a story, such as that of Lucretia, a story that, known from mostly venerable sources, is assumed to be fixed, almost objectified. I shall begin exploring this issue by questioning the idea of the "core" of a subject, of an eternal, universal story that can be "rendered" over and over again. And since no story is supposedly more universal than the mythical ones transmitted to us from antiquity, myths seem a good place to begin examining storytelling itself. We shall see that what we assumed, in the previous chapter, to be the invariable "hard core" of the story will lose its stability here. Instead, storytelling will be considered as an inevitably hallucinatory act, producing a work that is always new, different, but never autonomous, regardless of whether it is verbal or visual.[1]

But this analysis of storytelling cannot occur without paying attention to theoretical considerations. Thus I shall analyze, intertwined with images, a variety of verbal texts – pre-texts and re-writings, both theoretical and artistic. I shall confront the various works without assuming a hierarchical relation between them, neither of chronology nor of medium-bound superiority. Nor will I confront these works without recognizing the theoretician's, the artist's, and my own projections.

Again, I shall engage the theoretical problem – visual storytelling – through the analysis of a case, in turn made concrete by focusing on an often represented subject. Keeping to extremes in my choice of social problems, the case this time will not be the innocent victim whose innocence is somehow challenged over and over again, but the idea of the guilty, wicked woman, whose guilt is never questioned, but should be. The prototype is the stepmother who seduces her innocent stepson: Phaedra, or, in the monotheistic traditions, Potiphar's wife:

The universal story of the Chaste Youth and the Lustful Stepmother is best known to Western readers in the Biblical account of Joseph's temptation by the wife of Potiphar and in the Greek myth (later embodied in drama) about Hippolytus and Phaedra.

Thus begins an article on Thomas Mann's version of this "universal story" (Yohannan, 1982). Although Yohannan is well aware of the difference between the innumerable versions and traditions, as his earlier (1968) book shows, he shows no sign of awareness of his own projections in the very enterprise of his paper. Myth in literature has generally been discussed in terms of the "universal," the eternal, the true, the similar, the imitative. By beginning his paper with that very word, Yohannan inserts himself into the discourse that he might also have endeavored to critique. What does it mean for a culture to assume that stories are always available – permanent essences – ready to be taken up again and again? Some of the works "Rembrandt" did on, or rather with, this theme, I shall place in the center of a much larger patchwork of verbal and visual texts in order to find an answer to this question.

THE PROBLEM OF MYTH

Taking the universality of the story for granted, Yohannan detaches
Mann's text, written at the time of the rise of Nazism, from its
discursive contingency. Symptomatic of this move is the very word
story in Yohannan's title: "Hebraism and Hellenism in Thomas
Mann's Story of Joseph and Potiphar's Wife." Mann never wrote
such a story in his *Joseph and His Brothers* (1948), though perhaps
he commented on one. What he actually wrote was a voluminous
novel of over 1,200 pages in which he dealt with what he described
as "only an episode, if an important one, in the life of Jacob's son"
(Mann, 1948:87). In other words: what is a story for Yohannan is
an episode for Mann. The difference is crucial and affects the status
of storytelling and of history painting, as we shall see.[2]

In the Foreword to the novel, Mann (1948:xi) states:

> *Joseph in Egypt* seems to me unquestionably the artistic zenith of the work,
> if only on account of the humane vindication that I had undertaken in it,
> the humanization of the figure of Potiphar's wife, the mournful story of
> her passionate love of the Canaanite major-domo and her *pro forma*
> husband.

Mann is claiming here that this ideological stance has contributed
to *Joseph in Egypt*'s artistic accomplishment. Although I am reluctant to endorse such a conflation of aesthetics and ethics, the case
of Mann's novel and his claim regarding it are worth examining.
As we have seen, "Rembrandt" worked with the idea of Joseph
and Potiphar's wife as well. And in these works, too, we can read
reflection on the ideological position regarding the triangular relationship, a position that makes the "story" irreducible to any
stable myth. The very difference between the three works of "Rembrandt" I shall discuss here – two paintings and an etching – shows
that there is no way to consider them as similar in content, as
representing the "same story."

In Mann's statement, the use of the term "story" needs comment.
As opposed to Yohannan, Mann is not referring to some stable,
universal content that can become discursively and rhetorically different while remaining identical with itself. He is referring specifically to his own account, which he describes with the telling
adjective "mournful" and in which he includes the basically absent
character of Potiphar himself. By writing about him, Mann includes
Potiphar's presence in the story, signifying his absence differently
in the adjective *pro forma*. As a husband, Potiphar is only a signifier,
an empty form, and it is the absence of the signified that triggers
the story and makes it "mournful."

Yohannan takes for granted the innocence of the youth as Mann
does not. Hence, it is clearly his – Yohannan's – projection. The
same holds for the lustfulness of the female character. Calling her
a stepmother, Yohannan willfully deviates from the very case he

is interested in, for there is no stepmother involved with Joseph. This sort of projection seems to be inherent in myth criticism (Kirk, 1972; Vickery, 1966). Barthes said long ago that "the very end of myth is to immobilize the world" (Barthes, 1972:155), and, according to Rahv, the same holds for myth criticism (Rahv, 1953:109–18). The interest in myth is, according to Rahv, a persistence of romanticism and conservatism occasioned by the fear of history and freedom, of change, of choice, and he concludes: "The craze for myth is the fear of history" (Rahv, 1953:114). Calling myth "universal" obviously would affect the status of myth as discourse, privileging it as essential to all human experience, thus discouraging criticism that questions, while encouraging criticism that assumes this alleged universality.

"Rembrandt," like Mann, also represents the absent character of Potiphar, but his representation poses a temporal problem. In the two paintings the solution adopted is simple: The "Rembrandt" works displace the scene of passion denied to the next episode, and represent the "denunciation" rather than the "seduction," recalling a similar displacement in the *Lucretia*s. But in the little etching on which I shall focus primarily, the solution to the problem of including the absent husband is more striking. Potiphar is not included literally, which thus would entail the displacement of the earlier scene to the next sequence; instead, he is included symbolically. This difference between the paintings on the one hand and the etching on the other might be related to the differences inherent in the media: Etchings are less openly displayed; their small size makes them more likely to be viewed by individuals, almost as secretive as the scene itself.

The interest in visual representations of stories could be related to the fear that informs myth criticism, too. For painting is also assumed to immobilize the story, *including* those aspects that need most urgently to be confined, while confining experiences to the framework of allegorical unification.[3] Thus the fixed scene of a painting reflects the ambivalent attitude toward time inherent in most representations of myth, as well as myth criticism; all this comes to the fore in the appeal to longevity as part of the definition of myth apparent in the notion of universality. Myth critics assume that myths have been so long-lived that time becomes irrelevant. Representing myths visually helps reinforce this notion: The idea of the extreme length and thus irrelevance of time is strengthened, while the idea of time within the story is removed or at least confined in a spatial frame. Or, so it seems.

Although psychocritics have perhaps taken too readily for granted that their approach signals the overcoming of formalist-structuralist narratology,[4] they have made a convincing case for an approach that accounts for narrative as dynamic, and this approach seems to be the appropriate framework in which the concept of myth can be renewed. Renewed it should be, by taking the concept *and* its object *à la lettre*, as discourse and as symptom.

MYTH AND TRANSFERENCE

The idea of myth in myth-critical discourse has the attraction of truth. Susanne Langer, in a statement that is common in myth criticism, put it in a characteristic way: "Myths are not bound to any particular words, nor even to language, but may be told or painted, acted or danced, *without suffering degradation or distortion*" (Langer, 1953:160; my emphasis). This statement suggests that the relations between discourse and image are quite simple: The media are just signifiers, unimportant in the face of the stable meaning. The overall negativity of this statement that describes myth by what it is not obliterates the difference between the first and the second part of the sentence. Whereas we can agree on the first part, which detaches myths (and stories, for that matter) from a definite signifying system, the second part has to be rejected since it implies a positive meaning or signified, which can suffer damage but can also remain undamaged. What Rahv (1953:114) described as the fear of history is in Langer's statement quite close to the fear of the signifier. Indeed, historicity and discursivity are part of the same problem.

But the fear of the signifier hides in its turn another fear. The shifting signifier, inaccessible and versatile, is as frightening as the presence of the signifying subject of/in the myth. If the meaning of a myth is unstable, it is because of this very split between the subject who tells the story about itself and the subject it tells about. This fear of the split signifier is acted out, as we shall see, by the Joseph figure in the etching. The attraction of myth is that its universalism conceals this split by using eternity, objectivity, and universality to help the subject obliterate the time and space in which the subject itself is constructed; the universalism of myth allows the subject to obliterate its contingent nature by obliterating itself. The idea of myth allows this illusion to be entertained and also the need for it to be repressed.

If Langer's belief that changing signifying systems does not "distort" myths is to have credence, it is only because there is nothing to be distorted. Instead of a positive, reified mythic content I propose the emptiness of myth. Thus conceived, myth cannot be defined but as an empty screen, a structure that appeals to the individual subject because of its pseudostability, a stability that helps overcome the feeling of contingency. And the screen can be seen as an empty canvas or etching plate, as well as a finished work which the reader or viewer approaches as if it were empty – ready to be filled.

In her contribution to an issue of *Poetics: Psychopoetics* Jane Gallop (1984) insists on the difference between the spirit and the letter, as between the (American) Humanities and the (French) Letters; as between *man* and *other* as the possible content of psychoanalysis; as, we could now add, between myth as pseudo-transhistorical content and myth as discourse. A concept of myth according to the "Humanities" is to be replaced by a concept of myth according to the "Letters."[5]

Transference is the key word here. Interpretation is always an exercise of power; transference is the structuration of the authority relation; to analyze transference is to unmask that structure, to interrupt its efficient operation (Gallop, 1984:305–6). Analyzing the relation of transference displaces temporarily the position of the patient from the text onto the critic/reader, and interpretation becomes, then, self-criticism.[6] For the text does not take the place of the analyst. Instead the text occupies, at times, the place of the empty screen. At other times, it occupies the other position with which the first is constantly in dialectic exchange: that of the transferring, projecting patient. Since texts are by necessity responses to other texts, they cannot but share with the critic/reader/viewer the same relation of transference from which the viewer/reader/critic cannot separate him-/herself.

On the one hand, myth is a subcategory of art; on the other, it is a more general form of it.[7] The difference between myth and literary text or artistic image, like that between primal and other fantasies, is to be situated on the level of the transferring subject and its relation to the myth – to the empty screen. The *illusion* of the stable signified allows the user of a myth to project more freely onto the screen. But what s/he takes to be a signified, actually functions as a signifier: a material support borrowed from language – a *letter*. It has no meaning, but it supports meaning, providing the subject's projection with a means of getting rid of its subjectivity and thereby granting subjective projections universal status. The hypothesis of transference, and the nonmastery it implies, frees the theoretical texts from the constraints its status places upon them. If anything, they become, through that analysis, more lively, literary, narrative; and, acutely relevant in the framework of this chapter, more *telling*.

In the following pages, I shall analyze the discourse *on* myth and the discourse *of* myth as if they were the same discourse; I shall expose my reactions to various discursive units, each with a different relation to myth: The scholarly discourse of psychoanalysis on myth; Freud's own mythical discourse; Thomas Mann's novel, with explicit myth-critical intentions, in interaction with a discourse that Mann and many others have responded to, Genesis 39; and I shall offer, interwoven with these texts, an analysis of the three "Rembrandt" works presumably based on Genesis 39.[8] In order to counter the fear of the signifier, I shall give narrative a central place in these analyses. But while the "Rembrandts" can be read in a strongly narrative mode, I shall also go on to show that Mann's narrative operates through visuality at its most crucial moments. Through these analyses I shall dialectically elaborate my point, which is that such a dynamic, and also a more visual and literary, comment can provide a better explication of the mythical process than the current approaches can ever do.

"REMBRANDT"'S MYTH: NARRATIVE DEVICES

Whereas Mann's polemical attitude toward the traditions where he found his mythical screen can be followed through his own statements, we have no such evidence for "Rembrandt." On the contrary, we must assume that the painter had no conscious wish to deviate significantly from the myth at his disposal. So, although "Rembrandt"'s choice of topics is sometimes significant, we have no reason to challenge his faith in Holy Writ.[9] It is the more striking, then, that his representations of Joseph's encounter with Potiphar's wife are no more re-presentations of a previously set story than Mann's novel is.

A central signifying practice in these works is narrative – the representation of events in temporal sequence. Representing narrative time sequences in visual art is subject to a number of conventional devices that compensate for the difficulty of unfolding time into space. Whereas Langer declared such devices irrelevant, I see them as primary signifiers, as the very stuff of the work as text. The difficulty of narrating visually is at its most acute when speech is to be represented imagistically.[10]

Rembrandt's sketch of a beheading (Figure 3.1) shows how three phases of a process are made to represent the continuum of the event. There are of course more devices at work in this sketch that contribute to the sequential effect, devices that reduce the three-dimensional space to a two-dimensional surface: The two phases during which the victim is still standing and, hence, the image vertically structured, are each construed at one side of the surface, emphasizing the horizontal space. The third phase, the moment after the act, is drawn more in the foreground, to represent a time frame distinct from, and following, the two earlier ones. This se-

3.1 *Beheading* ca. 1640, Benesch 479, drawing, 153 × 225 mm (London, British Museum)

quentiality is then also emphasized by the bolder lines in this third image.

These simple devices allow less obvious interventions to pass unnoticed. One tends to assume, for example, that the three sub-sketches are part of one sketch, that the three events are phases of the same event, because the primary device, the division into three phases, obliterates other aspects, such as the change in the killer's face. Although the primary device pushes us to assume that the figures in each of the three images represent the same characters, the sympathetic man at the left of the first section bears no resemblance whatsoever to the frightened soldier with helmet at the left of the second. The face of the man at the right does seem to denote the same person in the two upper images, but his expression has changed so radically, from concern to cruelty and from a sense of powerlessness to a strong commitment to his task, that the very notion of identity becomes dubious. In order to fill in this gap[11] we can fantasize about what may have happened between the two: Perhaps a conversation took place during which the executioner has become angry with the victim he first pitied?

We can deal with this gap only if we let ourselves project a concern of our own onto the incomplete image. In other words, the difference between the first and the second image creates a screen for our transference. And what we transfer is then the baggage that we bring to the final image, the one that is both pushed onto a smaller and lower part of the surface, yet enhanced by bolder lines; in this section the beheaded man is represented as both a peacefully sleeping body and a portrait of a beautiful face we really see for the first time only here. The bolder lines give the head a statuary quality, like a tombstone, and thus challenge the process of narrative with an insistent stability. The head, clearly severed from the body, becomes here a "letter," a sign of "death." Thus the moment of the figure's death occurs only with this recognition. By the same token, the head renarrativizes the very representation whose narrativity it had first put under pressure by its suggestion of death, of stasis. As a result, the narrative built up by means of the first convention of representing events sequentially becomes problematic with the second of these interventions, which undermines that illusion of temporal sequence. Thus, we could say that "Rembrandt" obeys the simple rules of conventional drawing in order to transgress other conventions more freely.

For example, in keeping with reading conventions, looking, in the West, tends to proceed from left to right, with the emphasis slightly off the center to the right. This convention is overruled by the sequentiality of this narrative sequence. Although the left–right convention is in itself related to reading, hence, to discursive attitudes, the overturning of this convention by sequential reading is also related to discursivity, to narrative. This sketch, then, demonstrates a competition between two discourse-bound conventions and visual modes of meaning production.

A less conspicuous occurrence of this device can be seen in the shadow of Lucretia's dagger in the Washington painting. We have seen that the light, there, is frontal. The shadow, therefore, is understandable only as an indication of movement. The movement is rendered, as in comic strips, by tiny lines or a blot representing a shadow, brought forth by the speed of the movement. The oblique earring belongs to the same category of device.

Although extremely common in modern culture, this sequential device is not enough of an alternative for the history painter. A much more common device, which can be used only on the basis of assumed knowledge of the story the work is supposed to represent, is the concentration of the entire story or episode in one single, scenically representable event, the so-called pregnant moment. In "Rembrandt" this device is used in reference to the story of Jacob's encountering and wrestling with the messenger of the Lord at the river Jabok on his way to meet his brother Esau, whom he had wronged so deviously years earlier (Figure 3.2). The painting represents the fight between the man and the angel.

3.2 *Jacob Wrestling with the Angel*
ca. 1659, Bredius 528, canvas,
137 × 116 cm (Berlin-Dahlem,
Gemäldegalerie)

The iconography is convincing enough. The wings are conventional symbols for angels, even if no mention of wings is made in this or any "angel" story in the Hebrew Bible.[12] The story mentions a distortion of Jacob's hip, as evidence of the divine provenance of his antagonist. The knee and the hand on the figure's hip immediately convey this symbol. The man does not look the angel straight in the face; this also conforms to the story. The viewer who sees the painting, it is then assumed, will fill in the entire story and remember the sequence well enough to assess the meaning of this particular element of it. So far, the myth provides the motivation for the viewer's particularization.

Again, the obedience to conventions gives the artist the freedom, then, to place his accents and to "distort" the story at will, as it gives the viewer the freedom to handle these "distortions" in her or his own way. Because we know the story, we do not challenge the representation as a "version" of it.

This concentration of multiple events into a single scene is, however, a highly problematic device. Had we not known the story, what would we have made of this image? Let me try out some of my own reactions. As in the *Moses* of the same year, the dramatic tension of the image is in the body of the Biblical figure. The actions of both Jacob and Moses are ambiguous: Is Moses about to smite the tables of the law, or is he quietly holding them up, the tension in his body expressing the mere fatigue of his patient gesture? Is Jacob wrestling with or embracing the angel? In addition, the figures facing the viewer in these two works look intensely but do not make any eye contact with the viewer. Another oddity is that both paintings, by the contrast between activity and introspection, seem emphatically unviolent.

The face of the angel in the *Jacob* is tender, maybe feminine, but in any case not emphatically gendered, and is inclined toward Jacob's face. In itself, this conforms with a common seventeenth-century image of angels as sexually ambivalent creatures,[13] but such a commonplace is never obviously meaningless in any particular work. Here the eyes of the bearded man, himself clearly gendered, seem directed toward the breast of a feminine or ambiguous figure. Thus the entangling gesture suggests an embrace more than a fight; lovemaking rather than wrestling. In such a context, the gender of the angel may become relevant. The work uses the story precisely as we cannot help using stories: as a relatively empty screen. And the Biblical story comes to participate in that exchange of transference: The ambiguous gender of the figure backfires in a story where there is no unambiguous mention of the angel's maleness. If the angel is female, then the scene pulls in one direction; if male, then it pulls in another. Thus, the viewer will gender or degender this figure according to her or his own desire.

At any rate, the encounter, which was already a bit mysterious in the Biblical story, loses the aggression that at first sight we might have read into it.

The point of the encounter in the text is the application of a *mark*.
Jacob is marked, according to the exegetical tradition, by both the
promise of divine election and the criticism of Jacob's previous
misbehavior toward his relatives. The mark is the distortion of
Jacob's hip – a visible, visual, and permanent token of narrative
events that were precisely based on invisibility: If we are members
of the textual community in which this work functions, we remember that Jacob deceived his father Isaac into disinheriting his
brother Esau, by taking advantage of his father's blindness. The
moral ambivalence of the character is, thus, represented in the painting by a sexual ambivalence, and the reference to Isaac's blindness
in a previous episode has marked Jacob as well. His strangely low-
ered eyes focus on nothing in particular; they look toward an empty
spot rather than toward a specific bodily aspect of the angel. They
focus on paint, on an empty surface of paint.

This empty surface, then, is the navel of this text, the place of
the strange mis-fit that allows entrance into the other story. Hence,
the meaning of the distortion brought about by the angel *in* the
story becomes the key to the distortion of the painting *of* the story.
An unexpected iconicity emerges. Paradoxically, story and painting, once brought together as text and metatext, match better than
they could have without the "distortion."

In spite of the inherent difficulty of representing speech in painting, history painting represents scenes characterized by speech. The
third common device for achieving narrative is the use of iconographic symbols of narrative events, to which I shall return in
Chapter 5. In "Rembrandt" the hands of figures often function as
iconographic symbols conveying the idea that those figures are
speaking. In most of several drawings of Joseph explaining dreams
to his fellow prisoners, the youth stands in front of the two dream-
ers, the baker and the wine server, one of whom is condemned in
his dream while the other's dream announces his liberation (Figure
3.3).

3.3 *Joseph Expounding upon the
Prisoners' Dream* ca. 1632–3,
Benesch 80, drawing, 174 × 206
(Chicago, The Art Institute of
Chicago)

The viewer recognizes in the gesture of Joseph's hands the sign of oratorical speech. Hence, we have no doubt that the drawing does indeed represent the Biblical story of Genesis 40. The detail of the hands is, as it were, "translated" into "speech." Yet, again, recognition may blur the sight of the nonrecognizable, iconographically unmapped signs. For one thing, the hands not only express the movement that makes them suitable for representing speech; they also point in different directions. One hand points upward, the other downward. These directions in turn have a standard meaning and conventionally symbolize good and bad – in this case, good and bad news. If that meaning is activated, then Joseph's standing position also denotes his superior power over the two older men. If we expand the story to include its outcome – Joseph's rise to power – there is no reason not to see in Joseph's hands a gesture of command as well.

Taken together, these possible interpretations of the hands of the standing figure demonstrate the superiority, in semiotic capacity, of this one visual detail over the many verses of the Biblical story. In other words, the visual medium is not a confining limitation to the representation of narrative. On the contrary, it seems that this "Rembrandt" could use the one device – iconographic symbolism – to combine, beyond the recognizable meaning of the detail, other concerns, of which the predictions of the power of the youth is the most "telling."

Returning to the two paintings of the denunciation of Joseph to Potiphar we might return, also, to the comic strip device we saw at work in "Rembrandt"'s three-part sketch of the beheading. If we take the two paintings, both currently dated 1655, as a sequence, we could see the painting from Washington (Figure 3.4) as a first phase, the accusation itself, and the one from Berlin (Figure 3.5) as the next phase, Joseph's protestations, in the same way that the two Lucretia paintings represented two successive phases of her story. In the case of two different paintings, this does not say much about visual storytelling as such, however.

3.4 (*left*) *Joseph Accused by Potiphar's Wife* 1655, Bredius 523, canvas, 106 × 98 cm (Washington, D.C., National Gallery of Art)

3.5 (*right*) *Joseph Accused by Potiphar's Wife* 1655, Bredius 524, canvas, 110 × 87 cm (Berlin-Dahlem, Gemäldegalerie)

The second and third devices, concentration (or the "pregnant moment"), and speaking hands, are more to the point. In both paintings, several sequential events from the story are concentrated into one scene. According to Genesis 39, Potiphar is told about Joseph's seduction attempt long after the event and in Joseph's absence. Thus Joseph's presence in the painting suggests the combination of the earlier seduction attempt with the later accusation. His position – toward the back (on the far side of the painting), at the far side of the bed – might represent not only his subdued position but also the temporal anteriority of his presence.[14] Seen in this way, the comic-strip device of sequentiality has indeed been used within this painting.

At the same time, the expression of desperate protestation in his face in the Berlin painting also suggests that the later moment, *after* the accusation, is being depicted concurrently with the seduction. The three phases – the seduction, the accusation, and the confrontation between Joseph and Potiphar – are thus represented in two images, both doubled. Joseph, at one side of the bed, represents the earlier and first and the third incidents; Potiphar, clearly listening to his wife, represents the second incident but is drawn, by Joseph's second function, into the third moment as well. Thus, time is represented in space, but again, more effectively, more temporally, than the Biblical story had done. This narrativization of the scene is not at all based on the story; there, Joseph and Potiphar do not meet together with the woman. In this case, visual representation is capable of bringing together narrative elements that the verbal text had to present successively, and the image is thereby powerfully narrativized; what the text had to separate, the painting can integrate: two men, and a woman.

In the painting from Berlin, the third device, the representation of speech through gesturing hands, is also employed. The woman points to Joseph so clearly that its effect does not go beyond explicit signaling. With her left hand, the woman seems to protect her breast from the attack of the violator. But within the context of the speech representation, that gesture is part of her monologue: She is telling that Joseph tried to violate her, and she is telling it in a lively, theatrical manner. Potiphar's right hand is resting on the chair, slightly behind the woman, thus creating a sense of intimacy between the two which excludes the accused. By its systematic use of conventional narrative devices, the painting is as adequate as a narrative as it is uninteresting as a *painted* mythical text, as an empty screen. It leaves little for the viewer to act upon.

The Washington painting is different. The same devices are employed: sequentiality, narrative condensation, and "speaking hands." But narrativization there is much more ambivalent, and, as in the drawings, many more functions are accorded to the devices and to the other details. For example, the hand with which the woman supposedly accuses Joseph, does point, but not at him. It points perhaps to the red garment, the token of Joseph's misbehavior, but even that direction is not unambiguous. And instead of gesticulating in despair here, Joseph is standing still; he does not participate in the speech acts. And his left hand, which is just a little bit above his arm, suggests that he was about to say something, but he has hesitated.

This painting is so much more enigmatic than the Berlin work that it is worthwhile approaching not from Joseph's side but from the other side of the bed, and reading it not in terms of the Genesis story but on its own terms. Potiphar's right hand is not, as it was in the Berlin image, behind the woman, but slightly in front of her, as if on its way to grabbing her. The woman protects her breast again, but, in combination with the lesser distance between her and Potiphar, his grappling hand, and his determined face, it seems as if – again, when we ignore the Biblical story – he was approaching her sexually against her will. Joseph, who is just standing there, is then indicated, not as the accused, but as the more desirable, more handsome, younger love object. However fanciful this interpretation may seem, there are several details that make it possible.

One of those details is the work of the light, which is much more subtle here than in the Berlin picture. The light falls on the bed and on the woman in both, but in the Washington picture, Joseph is also, very subtly, illuminated, whereas Potiphar, in contrast, becomes almost ghostly. The light produces a pattern in which the woman and the young man are illuminated to the exclusion of the older man. As a ghostly figure, he comes to evoke the dead father of *Totem and Taboo*, to be discussed shortly, who threatens both son and woman. Joseph's face has an intense, yet unclear expression. It is hard to tell whether he is anxious, desirous, or admiring. This intense obscurity points to dreaming, to fantasy. Moreover, just like Jacob's angel, Joseph here seems sexually ambiguous; his gender wavers. The curtain, much more clearly indicated in the Berlin canvas as a (realistic) representation of a bed curtain, is here so vaguely indicated that its only function seems to be to set off Joseph as standing in a space, lighter and farther away, *at the other side.*

The most intriguing detail are the eyes of each protagonist. Each figure looks intensely, but inwardly. No figure looks at a clearly definable object. The woman does not look at her husband; rather, she seems to stare at an inner vision – the vision of her desire. The older man does not look at the woman; he, too, may be concentrating on his desire or, from another perspective, he may be looking at nothing; he may already be dead. Joseph's look, not directed anywhere either, is even more inward than those of the two others, while also *almost* directed toward the viewer.

The difference in Joseph's look reinforces the radical separation between Joseph on the one hand and the couple on the other. When viewed from the other side of the bed, his image is almost detached, as if it were a portrait on the wall. Visuality is in this way pluralized by the different modes of looking, and the three figures do not have the same visual status. The figure of Joseph is itself the inner view, the object of preoccupation of the two others. When viewed in isolation, Joseph seems full of feelings, yet not involved in any event.

Between these three still and intense-looking figures there is an object that attracts attention, if not from the figures, at least from the viewer. That is the red garment, lying over the bedpost, standing, therefore, as an erect object between the woman and the youth. The color of the garment reminds one of the blood that, as we shall see, testifies in Mann's novel to the desire of all the women. Should the garment testify here, by the color it shares with blood, as the event the woman is supposed to evoke as having really happened? Or does it represent her desire, her hallucination, that it happened?

All these details point in the direction of fantasy. But they have led us far from Genesis, unless we reprocess Genesis on the basis of the painting, which we may well wish to do. These details differentiate this painting more radically from the Berlin painting than from, say, Mann's novel with which it shares the hallucinatory quality the other painting lacks. As I suggested in Chapter 1, in the terms of Michael Fried's study on painting and beholder in the age of Diderot (1980), the Washington painting is an extreme case of absorption, whereas the Berlin work is much more theatrical.[15] The absorptive quality of the Washington work enables us to rework the Genesis story through the detour of Mann's episode, where the fantasy character of the woman's account is as impressively signified as it is – paradoxically – staged.

It is no coincidence that the inquiry into the signifiers operating in the "Rembrandt" *Joseph*s leads us to fantasy, not to myth. As it happens, psychoanalytic discourse itself follows this same detour. The following analysis of a sample of that discourse will demonstrate that it cannot be otherwise, for by a strange case of discursive iconicity, the slipperiness of myth denounces the fantasy character of the idea of myth itself.

MYTH AND PSYCHOANALYTIC DISCOURSE

"Myth" is a concept of psychoanalysis, but it is not a psychoanalytic term. Although the word occurs frequently in psychoanalytic publications, it is never, so far as I know, explicitly defined for its own sake. There is no entry on myth in the paradigmatic sample of psychoanalytic discourse, Laplanche and Pontalis's *The Language of Psychoanalysis* (1973). Nevertheless, the features it has, when the word is used self-evidently, relate it axiomatically to a concept like fantasy. With the latter, it shares connotations of subjectivity, that is, of untruth and personal input, projection, identification, and the like. At the same time, it also has relations, via its universal character, with the more specific concept of primal fantasy with which it then shares connotations of original truth, phylogenesis, trans-historicity, and the collective unconscious.

The Freudian concepts of fantasy and primal fantasy as defined in Laplanche and Pontalis's dictionary have, however, perhaps less in common than in contrast. Perhaps, then, it is in the space left by the tension between these two basic psychoanalytic concepts that the status of the concept of myth as written and unwritten, signified but not defined, can be situated. Between writing and discourse, implicit concepts have no *letter*; they have no such "essentially localized structure of the signifier," as Lacan defines the letter in his major essay on the letter, which he advises us to take *à la lettre* (Lacan, 1966:259). The concept of *myth*, indeed, has no such letter, in that it has no place in Laplanche and Pontalis's alphabetically ordered series of letters, of concepts arranged by letter. On the other hand, it does have letters in the sense of "material supports which the concrete discourse borrows from language" (Lacan, 1966:254), since its signifiers of sorts haunt the analytic text. This conspicuous discursive *lack* in a dictionary, a text devoted to the all-importance of the definition as the beginning of discourse on the concept, is symptomatic: The very concept the use of which is based on the assumption of universality has no such beginning in the scholarly text. This double absence, then, becomes the *letter* of the concept, its material support by antithesis, its primal signifier. We don't need to take this signifier as referring *only* to its place in the field of the concept that has no origin. For it does point, at the same time, to an absence, not of origin but of articulation; hence it is dissolved in related concepts that adopt it.[16] In order to articulate it, then, we must give it a beginning, borrowed from the language of these related concepts.

The following definitions constitute the first piece of verbal discourse to be analyzed:

1. *Phantasy*: "Imaginary *scene* in which the subject is a *protagonist*, representing the fulfillment of a wish (in the last analysis, an unconscious wish) in a manner that is *distorted* to a greater or lesser extent by defensive processes" (Laplanche and Pontalis, 1973:314; my emphasis).
2. *Primal phantasy*: "*Typical* phantasy *structures* (intrauterine existence, primal scene, castration, seduction) which psychoanalysis *reveals* to be *responsible* for the *organisation* of *phantasy life*, *regardless* of the *personal* experience of different subjects; according to Freud, the *universality* of these phantasies is *explained* by the *fact* that they constitute a phylogenetically transmitted *inheritance*" (Laplanche and Pontalis, 1973:331; my emphasis).

The two concepts should stand in a relation of specification, hence of implication; logically, the definition of the first, more general term, "fantasy" ought to hold for the second, which is one of its specifications. Surprisingly, the two definitions are different and to some extent mutually exclusive, as we shall see below.

The definition of fantasy contains the narratological notions of scene, protagonist, and subject. The two latter terms refer to the split, typical of any autobiographical discourse, between the subject *of* and *in* the fantasy. Note that the distortion, syntactically, refers to the *manner* of representation, not to the wish or its fulfillment. In other words, the agent of distortion is the focalizer, not the protagonist. It is the subject of the *image*, the subject of *vision*, who is held responsible for it. Fantasy shares the eccentric split between subject and protagonist with both language and representation. It is particularly acute in so-called first-person narrative, but equally, via the concept of projection and that of fantasy itself, in all narrative. Narrative is even the exemplary type of discourse where *différence* is generally thematized – a feature that allows conceptual reversals like Brooks's (1984:37) junction of "the narrative of desire" and "the desire of narrative." The double teleology implied in the phrase "representing the fulfillment of a wish" enhances the new-narratological flavor of the definition: Both representation and wish coincide in a satisfactory ending.

The term "scène" implies both a plot and its staging, its *mise en scène*. It also begins to introduce visuality. "Imaginary" and "distorted" enhance the fictional status of the scene, which makes it still more narrative, in the sense that in English, narrative and fiction are synonyms (Rimmon-Kenan, 1983). Reading this definition, we can hardly wonder that the most celebrated myths in Western culture have come to us through the stage. That they have been reconfirmed so often in painting only underscores this alliance between myth and the visual.

The definition of "primal fantasy" is quite different in tone from that of "fantasy." Its beginning is much more static and metalinguistic, and it comes to us as more "scholarly" in wording. If fantasy is a scene, primal fantasy is its structure; if fantasy is literary or otherwise "artistic" discourse, primal fantasy is critical discourse. More importantly, the subject, enhanced in the first definition, is disposed of in the second. The primal fantasy is described in a positivistic discourse that is characterized by the attempt to do away with subjectivity at the cost of personification: Primal fantasy is "responsible" for something that happens to the life of the subject, but "regardless" of the latter's experience. In terms of the first definition, we could venture that the definition of primal fantasy, here, reveals an attempt to get rid of the double subject. This riddance is accomplished through elimination of the focalizer who, as the subject of experience, would be capable of bridging the gap between the subject of the unconscious discourse – the scene – and the protagonist. The universality implied in this separation of fantasy from subject, of scene from representation – including distortion – is not argued for, nor even stated, but simply *explained*. Its existence, its truth, is taken for granted by the assertion that it is in need of explanation – which indeed it is, but on a different, more conceptual level. This definition, then, shares the feature of presumed universality with all definitions of myth.

Narrativity comes into focus only at the end of the definition, only when the explanation of the existence of the primal fantasy is given. Hence, narrativity receives an altogether different place here than it had in the definition of fantasy. The phrase "phylogenetically transmitted inheritance" introduces a plot, a dynamic element, and two fallacies. The first is the fallacy of the "third-person narrative," or "objectivity." This mode implies the very attempt to get rid of the split between subject and protagonist by eliminating the former, and thus forcing a break with the latter. The protagonist becomes the "third person," radically inaccessible.

The word "fact" symptomatizes this *objective fallacy*, a fallacy with implied attitudes close to the positivism, objectivism, and mythical thinking displayed in myth criticism itself. The colonizing and hierarchizing effects of this fallacy are well known, especially in a psychoanalytic context.[17] The second is the *narrative fallacy*, which consists of replacing explanation with story. These two fallacies are needed in order to fit the second definition within the first, but they are not consistent as a set. If fantasy is a *distorted manner of representing a wish fulfilment*, each embedded verb implying an agent/subject, how can one of its subtypes be "inherited"? The answer provided by the two fallacies is that it can be inherited only on the level of representation, *in casu*, through the idea of primal fantasy itself. That is why narrativity, in the second definition, was assimilated on a metanarrative level.

We now come to grasp why "myth" needs no definition – indeed, cannot afford definition. It is because "myth" is the paradox itself in which the Freudian argument is caught: The argument tries to explain *structures* by *stories*, or, to use Thomas Pavel's terms, to replace *articulation* with *origin* and the inherent subjectivity with the pseudo-objectivity of the "scientific myth" of phylogenetic explanation/beginning. We shall soon see how strongly the story by which Freud accomplishes this very narrative explanation of human phylogenesis displays the marks of this background ("scientific myth"). The replacement of (logical) articulation by (nonfalsifiable) assumptions of origin is an attempt to impose, on notions that are alien to it, a family structure: Ideas, fantasies, get a father and become *sons*.

The conflict between universalism and historicity is thus *staged* in this "explanation": The utmost universality *is* in this view equal to the utmost historicality, via the assumption that the further removed from the present, the older, the truer the story is and the more general its range of application. Within this line of thought, origin counters – replaces – articulation. This is exactly how mythical thinking functions. The basic message of myths from this perspective is as follows: What *I* think (fantasies, wishfully distorted) *is* the truth *because* it has always been so. The authority of time becomes a historical projection of the unwillingness to assume the historicality of the *I*'s wishes. Every accent placed, in a representation of a myth, on its historical contingency and its subjective discourse undermines this authority.

FREUD'S STORY OF THE SONS

Read the evocation of the primitive horde and the murder of the father in Freud's *Totem and Taboo* (1914a). (To give the reader a taste of the discourse, two passages from this text are appended to this chapter.) There is no more revealing myth, no better case of a primal fantasy and of an autobiographical narrative thereof. Hence, there is no more convincing case of the site of the concept of myth in the space between definitions of fantasy and primal fantasy of Laplanche and Pontalis's dictionary.

On the one hand, the myth is veiled by scientific discourse. The subject of the fantasy is hidden behind predecessors, the anthropologists who had come up earlier with the idea of a primitive patriarchal horde. But, on the other hand, this disclaimer of subjectivity is countered by the claim to originality Freud makes when he corrects and extends the views of his authorities, thus assuming subjectivity.

The conflict is *mise en abyme* in the opening sentence of the personal version which is at the same time the outcome, catastrophe, and *end* of the whole myth.[18] Freud intervenes with his magical explanation only at the end, when the authority of the predecessor must be replaced by his own. Significantly, the sentence that reveals the origin and truth of the whole of civilization is surprisingly short. The sentence runs: "One day the expelled brothers joined forces, slew and ate the father, and thus put an end to the father horde" (Freud, 1914a:183). The passage ends with a footnote, enigmatically referring to another authority – Atkinson – whose account of the *same act* is quoted. The difference between Freud's and Atkinson's account is of a narrative-temporal order: Whereas Atkinson represents the attack as a durative act ("combined attacks, renewed again and again"), Freud's contribution to the discussion amounts to the turning of this durative act into a *singular event*. No wonder he uses the fairytale convention of "one day," while, at the same time, trying to avoid the "erroneous impression which this exposition may call forth by taking into consideration the concluding sentence of the subsequent chapter," as the text of the footnote has it.

There is, again, ambiguity in the use of spiritual paternity. Meant to be the most universal story, it is, in fact, the most personal one Freud has ever "revealed." Freud claims *and* disclaims for this story, his most fanciful, most creative fantasy, the authority of storytellers like Darwin and Frazer. His use of sources completes the picture. The discourses of Darwin and Frazer, and of Atkinson for that matter, are all contaminated (as they are quoted by Freud) by their object of study and by the confusion of historical and analogical reasoning. The discursive devices Freud uses in this passage – and in the book as a whole – are borrowed not only from the convention of the fairytale, but also from that of the eighteenth-century novel, where the device of claiming reliable sources has come to signify fictionality.

Indeed, the chapter opens with a sentence that stages the focalizer whose position Freud wants his readers to share:

Let *us* now *envisage* the *scene* of such a totem meal and *let us embellish* it further with a few probable features which could not be adequately considered before. (Freud, 1914a:181; my emphasis; for the sequel to this sentence, see Appendix 1a, this chapter)

The sentence displays discursive features that embed the definition of the primal fantasy into that of fantasy in general. The first-person plural subject ("us") shifts onto the first definition, discussed above, the universality of the second, a move that reconciles it with the first definition's basic subjectivity. Invited to partake in the feast, we become protagonists in the scene *and* focalizers capable of embellishing it according to our personal needs, and hence capable of introducing "distortions" in the manner of representation. In short, we take the place of Freud, Mann, or "Rembrandt" – the last, most specifically: It is by the appeal to visuality that Freud makes his case. However, it is not of the "Rembrandt" *Joseph* that this appeal makes us protagonists, but of his *Samson's Wedding Feast* evoked in Chapter 1 (Figure 1.13). The bride, in this painting, invites us, even urges us, to join the meal and thus break her fatal isolation.

Freud's discourse of this founding myth of the origin of all the myths he is interested in (the myth explaining, by storytelling, his key myth of Oedipus) becomes the paradigmatic case of mythical discourse, where fantasy and primal fantasy come together in a pseudohistorical escape from history. Utterly mythical and utterly personal, Freud's father-murder scene, visual and still as he made it, becomes the token of the conflation of myth and fantasy, the myth of myth: *myth en abyme.*[19]

MANN'S MYTH VERSUS MAN'S MYTH

The relation (or the distinction or lack of distinction) between *myth* and *myth criticism* can be clarified by an examination of the case of Thomas Mann. Mann's explicit claim that he has attempted to humanize Potiphar's wife in his novel, amounts to a disclaimer. His polemic against the tradition that condemns the woman in the story of Genesis 39 and, through the typically mythical universalistic twist, women in general, is also a reaction against the function of transference implied in the myth. As Mann complained, the Biblical meager "what" was lacking the "how" and the "why"; life's circumstantiality was missing (Yohannan, 1982:431). But this complaint would seem ill-grounded if we took the Biblical account at its letter.

The ratio of "circumstantiality" to the "factual" *event* is as unequal in Genesis as in Mann's novel. The chapter in Genesis is characterized in the first place by the number of circumstantial clauses that literally circumscribe the event, which is, after a long preparation, presented in a few simple sentences. The dialectic between the singular and the durative that we have seen at work in Freud's mythical text is overwhelmed, enclosed, by the predominance of speech events. The latter are not durative but repetitive: Narratologically, they are repetitive because they are narrated several times; stylistically, they are repetitive in that the declarative verb is repeated in each case, a feature typical of Biblical Hebrew but nevertheless functional here for a more specific effect as well.

Speech acts are central in both the Biblical and the novelistic texts. As I have argued before, they can be considered the exasperating feature of texts that challenge works of visual art. By representing speech, painting and literature change places in regard to the common assumption that painting works with icons and literature with symbols. Although time is involved in the sequentiality of verbal art, the iconic representation of sequential events in the sequential signs of language is itself subject to convention-bound "distortion." And in the representation of speech, in quoted, or direct discourse, the conventionality of that iconicity is at its most pronounced. Representing speech in words would, then, be a case of iconicity, whereas representing speech visually by using necessarily conventional devices – for example, speaking hands – would suggest symbolicity.

If Mann is responding to the missing circumstantiality in the Genesis text, then, it is not for any reason inherent in the medium or genre itself. Could it be, therefore, because of a specific aspect of "life," the one he explicitly claims to be interested in – the woman's subjectivity, that is? Indeed, juxtaposing her to the men, to Joseph and to her *pro forma* husband, Mann transfers a preoccupation of his own onto the screen provided by the Biblical story. From the very beginning of this exceedingly long novel, Joseph is represented as a sexually ambivalent character. The first scene represents him daydreaming at night, fantasizing in the moonlight:

a youth famed for his charm and charming especially by right from his mother, who has been sweet and lovely like the moon when it is full and like Ishtar's star when it swims mildly in the clear sky. (Mann, 1948:4)

We don't need to guess whether the sometimes even more explicit femininity of Joseph is Mann's response to the phrase "and he was beautiful of appearance and well-favored of face" (Genesis 39: 6). Mann extensively discusses his view that the relation between beauty and femininity is a subjective association confirmed by intersubjective agreement:

Joseph, moreover, as *he knew himself*, and as *everybody told him*, was both
beautiful and well-favored – a condition which *certainly* embraces a con-
sciousness of femininity. (Mann, 1948:48; my emphases)

This chiastic expression of the association's subjective roots seems
to emphasize a consciousness of the "distortion," of the transference
of Mann's own preoccupations onto the screen provided by the
bare Biblical sentence.[20] The episode with Potiphar's wife is, as
Mann claims, an integral part of Joseph's life, and therefore there
is no limit to the projection of features of the ambiguous youth
whose status as "the true son of Jacob" is defined by his very
ambiguity, by being an exceedingly attractive man confronting
desire in and *as* the other.[21]

Wherever Mann polemically or otherwise *discusses* the mythical
traditions – the Greek, the Arabic, as well as the Hebrew texts that
represent the screen for him – he is not *transferring* onto it, but
deconstructing the transferences of others. There is no point, then,
in taking the entire episode, as it is represented in the novel, as
another myth. Much of it amounts to myth criticism, although it
is much less disposed to accept traditional interpretations than most
scholarly myth-criticism tends to be.

Thus, Mann represents an excessively narcissistic Joseph, guilty
of *hubris*, too confident of his capacity to defend his somewhat
unmotivated chastity. The strangest feature of this character seems
to me to be the fact that he loses his charm as soon as he becomes
socially accomplished. Once viceroy of Egypt, he becomes fat,
physically middle-aged, pleased with himself, sure of his power.
Something must have gone wrong. Of the old Joseph "no semblance did remain": The stability of the subject is under threat; and
Mann shows that he cannot escape the mythical dynamics he tries
to undo by replacing them with his own conscious preoccupations.

Indeed, Joseph has lost his ambiguity and the double attraction
it warranted on the way to social success. He has in fact lost himself;
there is hardly any continuity between the ambiguous youth and
the accomplished man. His narrative position has completely
changed and has been severely reduced to that of an ordinary character, with no traces of the position of central knot in the network
of subject positions he held earlier. When he was still this narrative
center, not only all women desired him, but all men as well, including the "jealous creator and lord, insistent upon sole possession" to whom Joseph's chastity was dedicated and due. What made
the young Joseph so very special was his status as the "true son"
who was identified with his mother and hence the unique love
object of his father who projected onto him his love for the deceased
favorite wife. The competition between father and mother, male
and female lovers who struggle for the possession of his beauty, is
won by the father, or rather, is given up to the fatherly position.
Joseph's story ends when he loses his sonship. He stops being loved
by the father when he becomes a father himself.

Arguing against the universalistic fallacy of myth criticism that leads to hatred of women in love, Mann makes his Joseph represent an attempt at a different kind of universality: that which arises when the limits between subjects are suspended. The general recognition of his lovability calls into question the limits between the self and others. Being man and woman, loved by men and women, he becomes himself the screen onto which the other characters project their most problematic feelings. Joseph then represents the mythical transference of which Mann's novel is an example, a polemic against other views of myth; Joseph himself becomes a metatextual comment on storytelling.[22]

The most characteristic scene in this respect is one that I see as a general defloration scene (Mann, 1948:802–3; see Appendix 2 to this chapter) that takes place before the famous bed scene.[23] This scene exemplifies the conjunction of artistry and ideological subtlety on which Mann prided himself in his Foreword; it is precisely where words are important and generate the story that Mann's verbal work receives its artistic and ideological power *from the use of visuality*. In this talkative text, the character of the woman cannot speak. Mut-em-enet is pressed by her women friends to tell them why she is so unhappy and sick. Unable to answer this request verbally, she stages a scene, a scene that can be *seen*, can signify visually where words fail. Apparently, in some cases visuality can tell a tale more effectively than words. Whereas speech was signified by hands in "Rembrandt," it is silenced and replaced by them in this novel.

Mut gives a party. At dessert, oranges and very sharp little knives to peel them are distributed. And when the ladies are busy peeling their oranges, Osarsiph/Joseph comes in to serve wine. Sheer fright at the *sight* of such beauty makes all the women cut their fingers, some of them to the bone. "My loves, what ever has happened to you all? What are you doing? Your blood is flowing" is the reaction of the plotting, lovesick virgin. Her intentionally insincere exclamation receives sincerity from the contiguous comment in which the speaker fails to distinguish between himself and this woman. For the narrator continues: "It was a fearful sight" (Mann, 1948:803). Mut-em-enet planned this event explicitly to make herself understood, because she wanted her friends to understand, to experience her love at the very same moment they knew it. For the difference between knowing and experiencing is, precisely, identification through affect, confusion of subjects, the passage from subjectivity to intersubjectivity, to meaning. They all had to *feel* her love, so that it became theirs. Thus the split created by discourse is cured by sight. There is no longer a narrative, a "third person," an object of gossip radically isolated. Visuality succeeds where words fail. But it succeeds, not because of iconicity, but because of indexicality.

This strategy fits well with Mann's attempt to humanize the woman by generalizing not her crime but her feelings, by transgressing the denial of female subjectivity. But at the same time, discursive signifiers produce emotional overtones that symptomatize a less explicit truth. Mut expresses her surprise at what *happens*: Their blood is flowing. And the narrator partakes of the event's effect: It was a fearful sight. The moon–nun not only desires the sexual initiation whose denial symptomatizes the denial of her subjectivity; she also fears it. Identification with the feminine man made the perspective less frightening, but Joseph's refusal was a refusal of identification. The general defloration he is innocently guilty of is another way of going through the frightful event. Mut's fright is, within this story, genuinely cathartic.[24]

This scene is, on another level, also a rehearsal for the accusation of Joseph to Potiphar which the two "Rembrandt" paintings represent. If we read the Washington *Joseph* (Figure 3.4) through this scene, the fantasy quality of the Joseph figure in the painting receives a stronger function. Like the painting, the scene has the same aspects of intersubjectivity, of lack of limits between subjects, which is so central throughout the novel. The defloration scene enhances and explains the accusation scene.

This aspect of the novel is not at all related to the Genesis story of which it is supposed to be a "version." There is hardly a "universal story" to refer this scene to; yet it is perhaps the most central and the most poignant scene of the book. Whereas Genesis derives its meaning from the very absence of female subjectivity – the woman acts, but does not *focalize* – the scene in Mann's novel stages a dramatic generalization of the woman's ambivalent fears. Although he is not explicitly polemic here, I would suggest that this comment on the Hebrew myth of the Jew in a foreign country, confronted by a foreigner in love with him, could arise only from a response to the historical moment. While Nazism, with its neurotic ideology of maleness, was beginning to make the limits between groups of subjects so absolute as to become those between life and death, the ambivalence, both sexual and ethnic, of the encounter between two ambivalent subjects became an acutely necessary alternative, an opportunity to dramatize the intensity of emotional community.

In Mann's story, the woman obviously has a different function from the one she has in Genesis, where she is merely a motivator of something else. Emphasizing the position of the woman and the identity of the woman's position with Joseph's, Mann's text calls into question the very distinction between the sexes. Mann's myth is not the myth of the young man. He uses the story of the son in order to tell the story of the daughter, while making subjective identity futile. Thus he introduces as his major theme an aspect totally absent from the Biblical story.

If we may play on the etymological meaning of "version" as turning, I would like to see Mann's novel as a turning away from Genesis, as an antiversion. The Biblical text (see Appendix 4a and b) is structured around three notions: talk, possession, and the house. The first one is worked out by Mann, the second is not at all central in the novel, and the third is relevant only as a setting, the dramatic function of the house in Genesis being taken over by that of sight in Mann. The repetition, in the Genesis story, of the filling of Joseph's hand with all it can possibly contain is a business of men. Joseph's reluctance to transgress is, therefore, an acceptance of the fathers above him. In Mann's novel the father-God does claim Joseph's sexual abstinence, but for a more indirect reason involving sexual jealousy and his opposition toward Joseph's narcissistic lack of realism.

The *house* of Genesis is the site of power *and* of bondage, with Joseph going back and forth between inside and outside. In Genesis the house is the mediating signifier between the two relationships Joseph is involved in. From his deliverance from the mother's womb, rehearsed three times over,[25] to his ascension to worldly power and possessions, the transition is signified, by condensation, in this recurring word. But just as it is not *his* house, what happens is not *his* doing; the words that narrate it over and over again are not his words. The function of the house as the frame to be transgressed, as the ambivalent structure of safety versus danger, of freedom versus confinement, has the potential for visual representation which we shall find also in the "Rembrandt" works. There, the house, including its unstable boundaries, is superseded by its narrative equivalent, the bedroom, and also by the representational equivalent, the frame. The whole structure, which the repetition of the word "house" in Genesis generates, is not used in Mann's novel. Quite to the contrary, Mann's Joseph needs no house and talks enough, too much even. Early on he once decides not to talk, but to act negatively instead. When on his way to Egypt, he has an opportunity to send a message to his father. He prefers not to. So sure of his power, he acts arrogantly. Displaying *hubris*, he prematurely breaks with his father, with his son-position, only to become a son again. Having been thrown back by his brothers into the pit, the emergence from which into slavery represents a renewed birth, he thus voluntarily assumes the position of the newly born once more, the fatherless in search of parents. But he does so under the assumption that he needs no father, that he is ready to become one himself.

An analysis of speech acts and other acts in both Mann's and the Biblical stories shows how deeply the two accounts differ. Mann's decision to attack, to diverge from what he takes to be his model, shows the function of the mythical screen: Mann *acts upon it* and cannot help acting beyond his intentions.

REMBRANDT'S MEN: JUMPING TO CONCLUSIONS

In this section I shall try to do what is strictly impossible: I shall propose a reading of the etching that both analyzes and demonstrates mythical projection. But this reading is not, any more than the other readings in this book, meant to propose *the* meaning of the work. Even more emphatically than the others, it is a sample of the phenomenon that this chapter is about.

The etching *Joseph and Potiphar's Wife* (Figure 3.6) is not always included among "Rembrandt"'s Biblical works but is treated, rather, as a nude (White, 1969) or as an eroticum (Ostermann, n.d.). However, this ambiguity in the reception of this little etching (it is reproduced larger than full scale) gives no information about the artist's position toward it, and that is so much the better for our discussion. I ventured earlier to propose that a myth is a screen for transference. In spite of our good luck with the case of Mann, we must, then, accept that in general there is no way to distinguish what the artist has transferred onto the screen – provided, say, by the Biblical story – from what the semiotician, desperately trying to argue against the stability of myth, has transferred. Similarly, it is hard to distinguish the work of "Rembrandt," in the preceding interpretation of the paintings, from my own, or the latter from the responses of my readers. But fortunately, transference is a dy-

3.6 *Joseph and Potiphar's Wife* 1634, etching (Haarlem, Teylers Museum)

namic relation, and it is that dynamic chain I want to point out now.

The first difference between the etching and the paintings is, of course, the relation between medium and subject. The paintings, by definition public, represent the later event, the accusation; whereas the etching, by definition more private, smaller, and more suitable to be tucked away, represents the earlier, more overtly sexual scene. This distribution is not irrelevant for the interpretation of the three works together and makes a further case for an interpretation in which repressed desire has a place. But if we want to get a more precise idea of the transference, we must start by positing what can be considered the screen of the etching.

One aspect of the screen is, then, the topic – for us, the title of the etching – and what we know of the stories and traditions this title evokes; the other, the composition of the image in its barest form.[26] Three aspects of the image struck me immediately: the body, the composition of the image on the surface, and the represented position of the spectator. The body of the woman is twisted: The upper part is turned toward Joseph, the lower part is turned away from him toward the lower part of the picture. The composition offers different lines – both vertical and diagonal. The erect line that begins at the bottom right is dominant as a line. The top left vertical is very slight, while the curved lines are still less striking.

So far, all I know is that apparently the subject "Rembrandt" has projected upon the more or less empty myth of Joseph and Potiphar's wife these things: a twisted body, a play of lines. That my readers are likely to see these things with me might seem like evidence that the artist really did this. But even that is not obvious; the twisted body, for example, might be a vestige of artistic clumsiness, a Monday-morning's work. Together, we readers who see the lines and find the body strange shall continue reading (into) the image, and see what happens. According to the conventions of academic interpretation, I shall pause to give arguments for my reading, to point out features in the image that support it, but that process is merely me, hopefully with the readers' consent, projecting onto the work's empty screen that in the process gets filled in.

Like most images, certain elements suggest how one can do that filling in. The picture proposes spectator positions, "lines of sight," that can be read into the image. As I wrote in Chapter 1, such a

3.7 *Joseph and Potiphar's Wife*, detail

line of sight does not in any way guarantee that the actual viewer looks that way, but only that aspects of the image – for example, light – *represent* an act of viewing. (In terms of reader response theory, this line of sight would be a represented reader, not an intended reader.) According to this line of sight, the external view – say, ours – is directed from the outside into the image, starting at a specific point. If we take light as such a guideline, the play of dark and light directs this view from the bottom right to the middle, then to the top left. Reaching the thematic center of the etching, Joseph's head, it reaches the internal, diegetic spectator-position: Joseph's eyes.

Here a first clash between "common sense" – the fear of the signifier – and the persistence of taking the image at its word occurs. Joseph's eyes, when taken as central and therefore examined more closely, are ambiguous. At first sight he simply looks away from the scene, looks toward the door toward which he seems to be heading (White, 1969). But the black blot in the corner of his eye doesn't quite match that impression (Figure 3.7). It is possible to say – or imagine or project – that his eyes look back, although it is unclear in which direction they are turned exactly. Do they look back at the body of the woman or at the vertical object where the external spectator position has entered the image? The ambiguity of the eyes can then become a strong shifter. Thanks to them, the initial viewer position and Joseph's eyes meet again (Figure 3.8).

Starting from the spectator position suggested by the line of sight, I decide to follow these directions, and enter the image from the bottom right-hand corner, which emphasizes the diagonal line; hence, the woman appears to turn away from me, so I see her sexual parts first, her protruding belly second. I follow this line as far as Joseph's face and look back with him – as I assume he is doing, because I had been struck by the misplaced blot in the corner of his eye.[27] Identifying with a text-internal character by looking

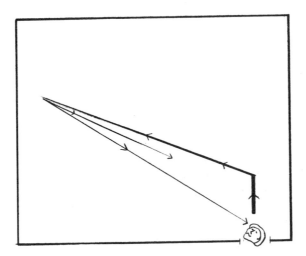

3.8 Structure drawing by Danielle Keunen

with him, I am suggesting, in terms of narrative theory, that there is an embedding into the outside focalization of an internal focalizer.[28]

From a different perspective, then, I see the woman's fat, protruding belly, a feature I had already seen, but that I now see differently; this time I see it with Joseph from the inside. Meanwhile I also see the vertical part of the bedpost which is where my eyes rested when I first began to peep in. Hitting my own spectator position and arriving thus at the beginning, I cannot but go back again to my point of entry and get involved in a movement back and forth that makes me aware of the doubleness of my view. I cannot help alternating between the external position and the internal one, between identifying with the outside onlooker and with Joseph, but I can never become absorbed by both positions at the same time. Since this experience of looking is ambiguous as logically described, ambiguity becomes the leading principle in my reading of the etching.[29]

But the ambiguity of the two focalizer positions should be analyzed more closely. It is different from the famous rabbit-or-duck gestalt shift in that the principle of embedding is at work here. Thus the ambiguity of the etching comes closer to that of the drawing "What's on a Man's Mind," in which Freud's face is represented as embedding a woman's body. Since the dual nature of the ambiguity in the latter case suggests a hierarchy, the difference between the external focalizer and the internal one must be accounted for. One difference is in who sees whom. As in the *Lucretia*s and in the *Jacob* and the *Moses*, there is no direct eye contact between Joseph and the spectator. In other words, we cannot meet Joseph's eyes directly. We see his eyes; he does not see ours. So in these works the external focalizer is absent from the image. She or he is potentially a *voyeur*.

The external focalizer's role as voyeur is reinforced if the viewer endorsing that position enters the image from the bottom right-hand corner as I did when following the directions of the line of sight. If one enters the image that way, at the bottom of the vertical object, then identifying the represented spectator position with that object becomes easy, because the vertical object's contiguity with the outside – its ending at the very edge of the image – makes it a suitable candidate for the function of *mediator*, as an element in the image that mediates among the viewer, the work, and an outside frame of reference. Its strong vertical presence, as opposed to the weak lines of the other vertical object – the door at the other side – suggests the psychoanalytic frame of reference: I can hardly avoid associating that strong, vertical object with a phallus. More specifically, it comes to symbolize both the outsider position and the scepter, the scepter signifying both power in general and the power inherent to the position of the voyeur in particular. Voyeurism as analyzed by contemporary feminism is characterized by noncommunication; the position is attractive because of its safety: It is looking without being looked at. The object represents the outside viewer *in absentia*. And that position is gender specific: The *voyeur* becomes a man who looks right into the woman's genitals. I may actually be a woman, I may actually be a feminist, but at this moment, to use De Lauretis's terms as presented at the end of Chapter 2, the interpretants I make are shaped also by a male habit.

Becoming aware of the masculinity of the external spectator's position might also make one aware of a significant absence in the etching. Indeed, there is a conspicuous absence in the etching that the two paintings lack; it is an absence signified, made present, stated by the etching's title/subject: It is Potiphar. Once I evoke Potiphar by recognizing his absence, the outside focalizer becomes a *motivator* as well: The *pro forma* husband, absent for the attempted seduction, must return – at least within the minds of the characters – for the second part of the event, the denunciation, to occur.[30]

Joseph's ambiguous eyes can also gain meaning from the mediating phallic object. Joseph reacts to the woman with attraction and repulsion, *and* he reacts to the object – the father, the fatherly position, the outside position.[31] The fatherly position is the position of legal rights, of "having done it." The father sets the rules, possesses the woman, excludes the son from sex with her. And it is the position that belongs to a different *time frame*, to the elder generation of which the son is not a member. Joseph is confronted by the witness of the scene, a witness that is the internalized law which forbids him to do what he seems to be doing: looking at, seeing the naked body of the father's wife. This, then, is the meaning of the line of sight, of the representation of viewing that I have tried to describe.

In this context we can again assess the difference between the two paintings. Whereas the Berlin painting represents the explicit confrontation that, in the Genesis text, never took place, the Washington painting, by the internalized looks of the figures whose gazes do not meet one another, comes much closer to what this intimate little etching is most suited to suggest: the internalization of guilt.[32] Joseph's fear of Potiphar, which makes him shy away, is again a fear of the signifier, in this case the exemplary signifier or the symbolic phallus. The story represented here is an internal one, a story of conflicting feelings, not a drama so overt that only the Biblical background can save it from melodrama.

Joseph is looking where he should not be looking, but perhaps he is doing even more. For in this framework, we cannot simply attribute to the figure's hands the symbolic meaning of speech. For his whole body – his hands, his eyes, his head, and his feet – are equally ambiguous. The head is turned away, already reaching toward the door of escape, but the eyes turn back, looking at the woman *and* at the father. We can see that, in combination with the ambiguity of the focalization and other signs of ambiguity, his hands might be grabbing for the body as well as thrusting it away.

The reader who is not convinced of the latter conjecture is invited to follow, with a pencil, the line of what might be the fold of Joseph's garment which the woman holds. This *is* a rabbit-or-duck case. Technically, the woman's hand does hold a fold of Joseph's garment. But given the firmness of the grip and the looseness of garments, should there not be, then, small folds right under her hand? The absence of these folds, although not at all conspicuous, does allow the rabbit to become a duck; without those folds the object the hand holds must be hard, no less hard than the bedpost. We now recall the garment – red, stiff, erect – in the Washington painting. And again, we may wonder at what Joseph is vaguely staring. On the level of the explicit reference in Genesis the woman in the etching is already grasping the garment by which she will betray Joseph. But if we contemplate in isolation the etching, with the detail that its medium allowed for, we might see the boy as still being tempted, as fantasizing an event that is ambiguous in its turn: The passive object of sex, he could both enjoy it and be innocent.

The ambiguity of Joseph's feet frames that of the fold within a "story of the son." One foot turns away from the scene, the other points toward it. But what exactly does that foot point to? It points to the bottom of the vertical object, in other words, to the aspect of the phallic object that brings together the inside and the outside, voyeurism and legitimacy. At this point, I am going to seem to jump to conclusions. However, another inconspicuous, but telling, visual feature provokes this interpretation. Physically speaking, Joseph's weight rests on the wrong leg. If he wants to move away toward the door, his weight should rest on his other leg, since then the woman who holds his garment would pull him back. The foot closest to the door should *not* be carrying the weight of his reluctant body.[33] But he cannot flee in that direction, for the door is closed. Thus the only escape for "Rembrandt"'s Joseph is at the other side of the bed. Joseph's attitude is that of an athlete ready to jump. The character is preparing to jump from the son position to the father position.

3.9 and 3.10   Structure drawings by Danielle Keunen

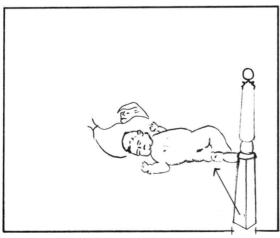
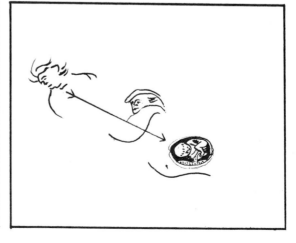

In order to clarify this and make up for my own leap, let me go back to the ambiguity of the image as a whole, which started at the dual focalization. One does not need to follow my jumping hypothesis in order to see the other representations of ambivalence. Identifying with the fatherly position, the spectator is committed to seeing what the peeping father / woman-owner sees. The structure of embedding receives its relevance here. *Within* this view, we look with Joseph and notice with fright that the latter *seems* to shrink back from the transgression, but in fact *is* attracted by the perspective. Identifying with the son, the father sees the *other side* of the fold in the garment. Paradoxically, the father's fright can be understood *and* experienced only when the outsider enters the image and identifies, through the father, with Joseph. In a different medium, and for a different effect, this "Rembrandt" is using the same device as Mann's text in the scene with the little knives. There, too, an identification was proposed by the work by means of a representation of the focalizer position. In that case, we saw that Mut could convey her pain only by making her cohorts experience it vicariously. What is the transference in the etching after? What problem is it that the character-focalizer can bear only when it is shared with others?

The father looks at the sexual parts of the body; the boy sees only the belly. That belly is fat, ostensively so, and Rembrandt's contemporaries criticized him for this kind of "ugliness."[34] Depending on the status of the focalizer who watches and interprets it, the protruding belly may associate the woman with pregnancy (Figure 3.9); or the hairless vagina, the short, fat thighs and the position of the left leg may connote a baby (Figure 3.10).

The meaning of these two different, even contradictory, interpretations of the same body depends on, and makes sense only in terms of, the focalizers. The young boy sees a mother: a woman of the elder generation who, as a primary love object, attracts him but who, as belonging to the father, is inaccessible to him. He rejects, if ambiguously, the prospect of being undressed by this naked woman, for that would be both a regression and a transgression. The father, in his direct focalization, sees a baby girl, a female of the younger generation. In his view, she belongs to Joseph's category: In his frightened fantasy she cannot but be attracted by the handsome youth. The father's anxious jealousy and the son's fear of initiation are represented by the ambiguous structure of focalization of the strangely twisted body that blocks both men's sight.

What about the leap, then – that most narrative of events and most visually represented? Jumping and skipping are variations on a theme. Going back and forth between the two starting points of the readings of the image, the spectator, just like the two focalizers, has been skipping, jumping over, the embedded body of the woman. At the woman's bedside, the two focalizers are dealing only with each other. The father is afraid of competition with the son, a competition that is expressed in the view of the woman as a child, a member of the younger generation, the other side. The son is afraid of the father's interdiction against competing with him to gain access to his domain, but he is equally afraid of both winning and losing that competition. Between him and the fatherly position there is the body of the woman: an obstacle spatially, an opportunity for initiation temporally.

As we can see from this discussion, to say that visual art uses space simplistically to symbolize time would be naive. It is not only through collapsing multiple events into a single scene or by representing a sequence of events on a single surface that visual art uses space to convey an idea of temporality. As we can see in the etching, the initiation – a temporal moment – is best represented spatially, as an obstacle. It is through the blockage of *sight* represented by the woman's strangely twisted body that we come to realize how serious this blockage is for a youth who cannot help being confronted by a jealous father. The text of the image represents metatextually the impact of both sight and sightlessness, just as the metatextual notion of distortion could be represented only analogically in *Jacob Wrestling with the Angel*. The woman, then, is a *monster*, just like the "mother" in the *Gross Clinic* discussed in Chapter 1, and for similar reasons. There, the "mother" figure was less than human, here she/it is both overrated as a mother-to-be and underrated as a baby; in both cases, projected motherhood leads to monstrosity. What Joseph as an image-internal, hence limited, focalizer cannot know is that once on the other side, the right side of the image or the right side *tout court*, Joseph will have to assume, with the fatherly position, the ambiguous backward-looking glance at the competing son. And his assumption of that position begins the whole story again.

Of the two focalizer positions, the embedding one with which the external spectator entered the image is decisive, and the embedding of focalization is the most narrative of the visual devices for storytelling employed in this little work. In spite of the competing vertical "fold" – still hidden in ambiguity – it is the object at the bottom right that clearly has won the competition between the two vertical objects. Doubly opposed to the door at the upper left, it is, if we may say so, discursively stronger. The door is closed, whereas the scepter is already *in* the woman's space, which is delimited by the curtain, and *outside* that space, at the exit it disposes of and guards. The door is not a viable exit. There is no represented spectator-position at the top-left outside: There is no way to turn back, for time moves on and sons become fathers.

CONCLUSION

Again I have three points to make, one on the social issue of representations of women, one on semiotic theory, and one on the respective status of verbal versus visual art. Parallel to the conclusions of the previous chapter on the nature of rape in relation to

language, we are left here with an insight into the nature of misogyny in relation to language, through the mechanisms of cultural
repetition. Blaming the woman for a structure of power that is
played out between older and younger men is possible only if we
ignore what the discursive devices of storytelling "add to" the
"story itself." On the basis of the analyses presented in this chapter,
we can no longer put the problem that way, for that story is virtually
nonexistent, and the telling of it is all there is to it. The telling, in
turn, is different each time, so that the meaning is unfixed, the
view of women various. And the importance of the telling reassigns
responsibility, taking it from the teller, who disposes of the means
to propose his or her own view, and assigning it to the viewer,
reader, or listener, who takes over by processing the works. In this
light, *myth* becomes a pre-text and a pretext – that is, in both senses
of the word.

This view also has implications for semiotic theory. If, for simplicity's sake, we assume that both Mann and "Rembrandt" use
the Biblical story of Genesis 39 as their common screen, it is obvious
that they share aspects with the source myth, but nothing, or hardly
anything, with each other. They do, however, both leave out several striking aspects of the Genesis story, which is in its turn doubtlessly very different from its own screen. And they both focus on
aspects *not* present in Genesis. Finally, both Mann's and "Rembrandt'"s works share an awkward relationship to the discourse of
psychoanalysis. While Mann shares with Laplanche and Pontalis's
definitions a challenge of the distinction between the subjective and
the intersubjective, his defloration scene stages that challenge "hor-
izontally," in a scenic articulation, whereas Laplanche and Pontalis
try to obliterate the distinction by means of a "vertical" perspective
of origin. And although Freud's myth of the primal horde is not
specifically related to the story of Joseph and Potiphar's wife, it
does depict the struggle between positivism and fantasy, a struggle
closely connected to the problems of the relations between father
and son. For, as we have seen, Freud's text shares with the "Rembrandt" etching a duality in representing the competition between
fathers and sons in the story and in the discourse that represents it.

My point is not that each occurrence of a mythical signifier is different, for that is commonplace. Instead, it is that the relation between a mythical unit and its so-called versions is not simply a
relation of interpretation but a relation of transference. The myth is
not a sign that can be interpreted adequately or inadequately, but a
sign that is, like the analyst in transference, mistaken for another.
Such a relation is mutual, dynamic, historically specific, and discursive. Consequently, a mythical unit is not a discrete unit of meaning,
but a signifying structure. And it is a structure by virtue of its appearing to be a unit of meaning. We are used to referring to myths in
terms of what we take to be a summary of their content and what we
can easily displace from one text onto another, as in the titles of history paintings. But it is the action imposed on the myth – as well as

on the painting – that *is* the myth. The summary of the myth, then, becomes an empty signifier that triggers other signifiers, bringing the mythical discourse into being. Consequently, the third point I wish to make is that neither the verbal nor the visual arts are privileged as the most suitable medium for storytelling. Not only do they each dispose of specific, complementary devices, but also in both cases the telling itself is discursive and visual.

In Peircean terms, we can say that an indexical relation between the screen and the myth is obscured by the *illusion* of an iconic relation. On the basis of this illusion of iconicity, the producer of the new myth works with the assumption that she or he can establish an indexical relation of another kind, as Mann tries to do in his polemic response. Myth criticism and psychoanalytic criticism both try to obscure that indexical relation under cover of the universalistic fallacy. And if you, reader, think that in my discussion of the etching I have not been able to avoid projecting onto it my own subjective preoccupations, entailed at once by my experiences of the jealous father-owner and of being skipped over, and of my feminist position, you get exactly my point. But given the state of criticism of mythical texts and its blindness to these positions, a case can be made for the relevance of these particular projections as more critical than traditional criticism, as capable of producing a differentiation otherwise obscured; a case for letting these projections counter the obviousness of the already known.

APPENDIX ONE

From *Totem and Taboo* by Sigmund Freud (trans. A. A. Brill, M.D., New York, Vintage Books, 1946).

(A)

Let us now envisage the scene of such a totem meal and let us embellish it further with a few probable features which could not be adequately considered before. Thus we have the clan, which on a solemn occasion kills its totem in a cruel manner and eats it raw, blood, flesh and bones. At the same time the members of the clan disguised in imitation of the totem, mimic it in sound and movement as if they wanted to emphasize their common identity. There is also the conscious realization that an action is being carried out which is forbidden to each individual and which can only be justified through the participation of all, so that no one is allowed to exclude himself from the killing and the feast. After the act is accomplished the murdered animal is bewailed and lamented. The death lamentation is compulsive, being enforced by the fear of a threatening retribution, and its main purpose is, as Robertson Smith remarks on an analogous occasion, to exculpate oneself from responsibility for the slaying.

But after this mourning there follows loud festival gaiety accompanied by the unchaining of every impulse and the permission of every gratification. Here we find an easy insight into the nature of the *holiday*. (p. 181)

(B)

By basing our argument upon the celebration of the totem we are in a position to give an answer: 'One day[77] the expelled brothers joined forces, slew and ate the father, and thus put an end to the father horde. Together they dared and accomplished what would have remained impossible for them singly. Perhaps some advance in culture, like the use of a new weapon, had given them the feeling of superiority. Of course these cannibalistic savages ate their victim. This violent primal father had surely been the envied and feared model for each of the brothers. Now they accomplished their identification with him by devouring him and each acquired a part of his strength. The totem feast, which is perhaps mankind's first celebration, would be the repetition and commemoration of this

77. The reader will avoid the erroneous impression which this exposition may call forth by taking into consideration the concluding sentence of the subsequent chapter.

memorable, criminal act with which so many things began, social organization, moral restrictions and religion.'[78] (p. 183)

78. The seemingly monstrous assumption that the tyrannical father was overcome and slain by a combination of the expelled sons has also been accepted by Atkinson as a direct result of the conditions of the Darwinian primal horde. 'A youthful band of brothers living together in forced celibacy, or at most in polyandrous relation with some single female captive. A horde as yet weak in their impubescence they are, but they would, when strength was gained with time, inevitably wrench by combined attacks, renewed again and again, both wife and life from the paternal tyrant' (*Primal Law*, pp. 220–1). Atkinson, who spent his life in New Caledonia and had unusual opportunities to study the natives, also refers to the fact that the conditions of the primal horde which Darwin assumes can easily be observed among herds of wild cattle and horses and regularly lead to the killing of the father animal. He then assumes further that a disintegration of the horde took place after the removal of the father through embittered fighting among the victorious sons, which thus precluded the origin of a new organization of society; 'An ever recurring violent succession to the solitary paternal tyrant by sons, whose parricidal hands were so soon again clenched in fratricidal strife' (p. 228). Atkinson, who did not have the suggestions of psychoanalysis at his command and did not know the studies of Robertson Smith, finds a less violent transition from the primal horde to the next social stage in which many men live together in peaceful accord. He attributes it to maternal love that at first only the youngest sons and later others too remain in the horde, who in return for this toleration acknowledge the sexual prerogative of the father by the restraint which they practise towards the mother and towards their sisters.

So much for the very remarkable theory of Atkinson, its essential correspondence with the theory here expounded, and its point of departure which makes it necessary to relinquish so much else.

I must ascribe the indefiniteness, the disregard of time interval, and the crowding of the material in the above exposition to a restraint which the nature of the subject demands. It would be just as meaningless to strive for exactness in this material as it would be unfair to demand certainty here.

APPENDIX TWO

From *Joseph and his Brothers* by Thomas Mann (trans. H. T. Lowe-Porter, Harmondsworth, Penguin, 1984 [1943])

Again Mut-em-enet had beckoned, and he who now appeared on the scene was the cup-bearer, the pourer of the wine – it was Joseph. Yes, the lovesick woman had commanded him to this service, requesting, as his mistress, that he should himself serve the wine

of Cyprus to her guests. She did not tell him of her other preparations, he did not know for what purpose of edification he was
being used. It pained her, as we know, to deceive him and deliberately make such misuse of his appearance. But her heart was set
on enlightening her friends and laying bare her feelings. So she said
to him – just after he had once more, with all possible forbearance,
refused to lie with her:

'Will you then, Osarsiph, at least do me a favour, and pour out
the famous Alashian wine at my ladies' party day after tomorrow?
In token of its excelling goodness, also in token that you love me
a little, and lastly to show that I am after all somebody in this house,
since he at its head serves me and my guests?'

'By all means, my mistress,' he had answered. 'That will I gladly
do, and with the greatest pleasure, if it be one to you. For I am
with body and soul at your command in every respect save that I
sin with you.'

So, then, Rachel's son, the young steward of Petepre, appeared
suddenly among the ladies as they sat peeling in the court; in a fine
white festal garment, with a coloured Mycenæan jug in his hands.
He bowed, and began to move about, filling the cups. But all the
ladies, those who had chanced to see him before as well as those
who did not know him, forgot at the sight not only what they
were doing but themselves as well, being lost in gazing at the cup-
bearer. Then those wicked little knives accomplished their purpose
and the ladies, all and sundry, cut their fingers frightfully – without
even being aware at the time, for a cut from such an exceedingly
sharp blade is hardly perceptible, certainly not in the distracted state
of mind in which Eni's friends then were.

This oft-described scene has by some been thought to be apocryphal, and not belonging to the story as it happened. But they are
wrong; for it is the truth, and all the probabilities speak for it. We
must remember, on the one hand, that this was the most beautiful
youth of his time and sphere; on the other, that those were the
sharpest little knives the world had ever seen – and we shall understand that the thing could not happen otherwise – I mean with
less shedding of blood than as it actually did. Eni's dreamlike certainty of the event and its course was entirely justified. She sat there
with her suffering air, her brooding, sinister, masklike face and
sinuous mouth, and looked at the mischief she had worked; the
blood-bath, which at first no one saw but herself, for all the ladies
were gaping in self-forgotten ardour after the youth as he slowly
disappeared toward the pillared hall, where, Mut knew, the scene
would repeat itself. Only when the beloved form had disappeared
did she inquire of the ensuing stillness, in a voice of malicious
concern:

'My loves, what ever has happened to you all? What are you
doing? Your blood is flowing!'

It was a fearful sight. With some the nimble knife had gone an
inch deep in the flesh and the blood did not ooze, it spouted. The

little hands, the golden apples, were drenched with the red liquid, it dyed the fresh whiteness of the linen garments and snaked through into the women's laps, making pools which dripped down on the floor and their little feet. What an outcry, what wails, what shrieking arose when Mut's hypocritical concern made them aware what had happened! Some of them could not bear the sight of blood, especially their own; they threatened to faint and had to be restored with oil of wormwood and other pungent little phials brought by the bustling maids. All the needful things were done; the neat little maids dashed about with cloths and basins, vinegar, lint and linen bandages, until the party looked more like a hospital ward than anything else, in the pillared hall as well, whither Mut-em-enet went for a moment to assure herself that blood was flowing there too. Renenutet, the wife of the overseer of bulls, was among the more seriously wounded; they had to quench the flow of blood by putting a tourniquet on the wrists to shut off the circulation from the slowly paling and yellowing little hand. Likewise Nes-ba-met, Beknechons's deep-voiced consort, had done herself considerable damage. They had to take off her outer garment, and she was tended and reassured by two of the girted maids, one black and one white, while she raved and raged in a loud voice at everybody indiscriminately.

'Dearest Head Mother and all of you my dear friends,' said the hypocrite Mut, when order had somewhat been restored, 'how could it happen that here in my house you have done this to yourselves, and this red episode has marred my party? To your hostess it is almost intolerable that it had to be in my house that it happened – how is such a thing possible? One person, or even two, might cut their fingers while peeling an orange – but all of you at once, and some of you to the bone! Such a thing has never happened before in the world, and will probably be unique in the social life of the two lands – at least, let us hope so! But comfort me, my sweethearts, and tell me how ever it could happen!' (pp. 802–3)

APPENDIX THREE

Quran SXii.23–35

> 23. But she in whose house
>   He was, sought to seduce him
>   From his (true) self: she fastened
>   The doors, and said:
>   "Now come, thou (dear one)!"
>   He said: "God forbid!
>   Truly (thy husband) is
>   My lord! he made
>   My sojourn agreeable!
>   Truly to no good
>   Come those who do wrong!"

24. And (with passion) did she
    Desire him, and he would
    Have desired her, but that
    He saw the evidence
    Of his Lord: thus
    (Did We order) that We
    Might turn away from him
    (All) evil and shameful deeds:
    For he was one of Our servants,
    Sincere and purified.

25. So they both raced each other
    To the door, and she
    Tore his shirt from the back:
    They both found her lord
    Near the door. She said:
    "What is the (fitting) punishment
    For one who formed
    An evil design against
    Thy wife, but prison
    Or a grievous chastisement?"

26. He said: "It was she
    That sought to seduce me –
    From my (true) self." And one
    Of her household saw (this)
    And bore witness, (thus): –
    "If it be that his shirt
    Is rent from the front, then
    Is her tale true,
    And he is a liar!

27. "But if it be that his shirt
    Is torn from the back,
    Then is she the liar,
    And he is telling the truth!"

28. So when he saw his shirt, –
    That it was torn at the back, –
    (Her husband) said: "Behold!
    It is a snare of you women!
    Truly, mighty is your snare!

29. "O Joseph, pass this over!
    (O wife), ask forgiveness
    For thy sin, for truly
    Thou hast been at fault!"

SECTION 4.

30. Ladies said in the City:
    "The wife of the (great) 'Azīz
    Is seeking to seduce her slave
    From his (true) self:

133

Truly hath he inspired her
With violent love: we see
She is evidently going astray."

31. When she heard
Of their malicious talk,
She sent for them
And prepared a banquet
For them: she gave
Each of them a knife:
And she said (to Joseph),
"Come out before them."
When they saw him,
Thy did extol him,
And (in their amazement)
Cut their hands: they said,
"God preserve us! no mortal
Is this! This is none other
Than a noble angel!"

32. She said: "There before you
Is the man about whom
Ye did blame me!
I did seek to seduce him from
His (true) self but he did
Firmly save himself guiltless! . . .
And now, if he doth not
My bidding, he shall certainly
Be cast into prison,
And (what is more)
Be of the company of the vilest!"

33. He said: "O my Lord!
The prison is more
To my liking than that
To which they invite me:
Unless Thou turn away
Their snare from me,
I should (in my youthful folly)
Feel inclined towards them
And join the ranks of the ignorant."

34. So his Lord hearkened to him
(In his prayer), and turned
Away from him their snare:
Verily He heareth and knoweth
(All things).

35. Then it occurred to the men,
After they had seen the Signs,
(That it was best)
To imprison him
For a time.

Genesis 39: working translation (a)

1. And Joseph was brought down to Egypt and bought him Potiphar, a eunuch of Pharaoh, a leader of the guard, a man of
   Egypt, from the hand of the Ishmaelites who had brought him
   from there.
2. And it came to pass [that] Jahweh [was] with Joseph and it
   came to pass [that he was] a man [whom god] made successful
   and it came to pass [that he was] in the house of his master the
   Egyptian.
3. And saw his master that Jahweh [was] with him and all that
   he was doing Jahweh made successful in his hand.
4. And Joseph found grace in his eyes and he served him and he
   made him supervisor over his house and all that [was] onto
   him he gave in his hand.
5. And it came to pass from the time [that] he had made him
   supervisor over his house and over all that [was] onto him and
   blessed Jahweh the house of the Egyptian for the sake of Joseph
   and it came to pass that the blessing of Jahweh [was] upon all
   that [was] onto him in the house and in the field.
6. And he left all that [was] onto him in the hand of Joseph and
   not knew he with him anything except the bread that he was
   eating and it came to pass that Joseph [was] beautiful of appearance and beautiful of face.
7. And it came to pass after these things and lifted up the woman
   of his master her eyes upon Joseph and she said, lie with me.
8. And he refused himself and said to the woman of his master:
   behold, my master knows not with me what [is] in the house
   and all that [is] onto him he gave into my hand.
9. No one [is] greater in this house than me and not kept he back
   from me anything except you because you [are] his woman
   and how shall I do this great wickedness and sin against God?
10. And it came to pass when she spoke to Joseph day by day and
    not he heard to her to lie by her [or] to be with her.
11. And it came to pass on such a day and he went to the house
    to do his work and no man of the men of the house [was] there
    in the house.
12. And she caught him by his garment in saying lie with me and
    he left his garment in her hand and he fled and went outside.
13. And it came to pass when she saw that he had left his garment
    in her hand and had fled outside.
14. And she called unto the men of her house and said to them
    saying: see, he made come to us a Hebrew man to laugh at us,
    he has come to me to lie with me and I called in a loud voice.
15. And it came to pass when he heard that/because I lifted my

voice and called and he left his garment with me and he fled
and went outside.

16. And she laid his garment by her until came his lord in his
house.

17. And she spoke to him according to these words saying: he
came to me the Hebrew servant which you made come to us
to laugh at me.

18. And it came to pass that I lifted my voice and I called and he
left his garment by me and he fled outside.

19. And it came to pass when his master heard the words of his
woman which she spoke unto him saying: according to his
words did unto me your servant and his nose burnt/his anger
rose.

20. And Joseph's master took him and gave him in the closed
house, a place where the bound ones of the king were bound
and he was there in the closed house.

21. And it came to pass [that] Jahweh [was] with Joseph and extended to him favour/solidarity and he gave him mercy in the
eyes of the leader of the closed-house.

22. And the leader of the closed-house gave in the hand of Joseph
all the bound ones who [were] in the closed house and all that
they were doing there he was the doer.

23. And not the leader of the closed-house was seeing all that [was]
in his hand because Joseph [was] with him and what *he* did
Jahweh made successful.

Genesis 39: King James translation (b)

And Joseph was brought down to Egypt; and Pŏt-ĭ-phär, an officer
of Pharaoh, captain of the guard, an Egyptian, bought him of the
hands of the Ĭsh-mêe-lites, which had brought him down thither.

2. And the LORD was with Joseph, and he was a prosperous man;
and he was in the house of his master the Egyptian.

3. And his master saw that the LORD *was* with him, and that the
LORD made all that he did to prosper in his hand.

4. And Joseph found grace in his sight, and he served him: and
he made him overseer over his house, and all *that* he had he
put into his hand.

5. And it came to pass from the time *that* he had made him overseer
in his house, and over all that he had, that the LORD blessed
the Egyptian's house for Joseph's sake; and the blessing of the
LORD was upon all that he had in the house, and in the field.

6. And he left all that he had in Joseph's hand; and he knew not
ought he had, save the bread which he did eat. And Joseph
was *a* goodly *person*, and well favoured.

7. And it came to pass after these things, that his master's wife cast her eyes upon Joseph; and she said, Lie with me.

8. But he refused, and said unto his master's wife, Behold, my master wotteth not what *is* with me in the house, and he hath committed all that he hath to my hand;

9. *There is* none greater in this house than I; neither hath he kept back any thing from me but thee, because thou *art* his wife: how then can I do this great wickedness, and sin against God?

10. And it came to pass, as she spake to Joseph day by day, that he hearkened not unto her, to lie by her, *or* to be with her.

11. And it came to pass about this time, that *Joseph* went into the house to do his business; and *there was* none of the men of the house there within.

12. And she caught him by his garment, saying, Lie with me: and he left his garment in her hand, and fled, and got him out.

13. And it came to pass, when she saw that he had left his garment in her hand, and was fled forth,

14. That she called unto the men of her house, and spake unto them, saying, See, he hath brought in an Hebrew unto us to mock us; he came in unto me to lie with me, and I cried with a loud voice:

15. And it came to pass, when he heard that I lifted up my voice and cried, that he left his garment with me, and fled, and got him out.

16. And she laid up his garment by her, until his lord came home.

17. And she spake unto him according to these words, saying, The Hebrew servant, which thou hast brought unto us, came in unto me to mock me:

18. And it came to pass, as I lifted up my voice and cried, that he left his garment with me, and fled out.

19. And it came to pass, when his master heard the words of his wife, which she spake unto him, saying, After this manner did thy servant to me; that his wrath was kindled.

20. And Joseph's master took him, and put him into the prison, a place where the king's prisoners *were* bound: and he was there in the prison.

21. But the LORD was with Joseph, and shewed him mercy, and gave him favour in the sight of the keeper of the prison.

22. And the keeper of the prison committed to Joseph's hand all the prisoners that *were* in the prison; and whatsoever they did there, he was the doer *of it*.

23. The keeper of the prison looked not to any thing *that was* under his hand; because the LORD was with him, and *that* which he did, the LORD made *it* to prosper.

CHAPTER 4

BETWEEN FOCALIZATION AND VOYEURISM: THE REPRESENTATION OF VISION

INTRODUCTION

Iɴ her essay "Artemesia and Susanna" (1982), a classic of feminist art history, Mary D. Garrard makes a case for the attribution of the Gentileschi painting *Susanna and the Elders* to Artemesia Gentileschi, not to her father and teacher Orazio. In doing so, she addresses the question of attribution, which seems to be one of the key problems of art history as a discipline.[1] Garrard (1982:120) begins by showing that the painting had been attributed earlier to Artemesia, mainly on the basis of biographical data.[2] The confirmation of the work's date and signature shows that it must be the earliest preserved of Artemesia's paintings, a work she did at the age of seventeen.

Yet dissident views are still heard: Although the new data make it impossible to attribute the work wholly to the father, some still contend that the stylistic influence of the teacher was so pervasive that this work differs from the father's, as Garrard writes, only in degree (Moir, 1967:100). However, taking art history to task for this fallacious argument here is irrelevant, for in order to examine what is really at stake in this case we must question, not this particular instance, but the research paradigm in general. Since attribution is taken to have an unchallenged relevance within this tradition, any effort to examine the ongoing attempts to deprive the Italian artist of her own works can only call into question the very issue of attribution.

Garrard cunningly manages to ask the questions her discipline requires, while at the same time turning those questions against themselves. She addresses the attribution problem, but while not seeming to challenge the question, she still comes up with a different kind of answer. What is new in Garrard's article, what makes it possible for her to answer the question differently, is not the attention to attribution itself, but her attention to what she calls "the treatment of the theme." Although the painting can be placed among a group of works of the circles to which Artemesia belonged, there is a striking difference, which Garrard (1982:148) describes thus:

[T]he position of the arms has been decisively changed, and her image accordingly revised, from that of a sexually available and responsive female to an emotionally distressed young woman, whose vulnerability is emphasized in the awkward twisting of her body.

Just as Garrard uses questions of attribution in order to undermine that approach, Frima Fox Hofrichter uses another entrenched tool of art history, iconographic analysis, to substantiate her claim, with a similarly subversive effect. In the article immediately following Garrard's in the volume *Feminism and Art History* (1982), Hofrichter challenges, not the attribution of Judith Leyster's *Proposition*, but its place within the genre to which it belongs. Hofrichter makes plausible that Leyster modified the genre and set the tone for a radical reversal of its moral message. Again, a traditional methodology, iconography, is used to argue for Leyster's novelty, not for her traditional use of symbolism.

These articles convincingly demonstrate that feminist art history can make a genuine and important contribution to the discussion of art history's own topics: iconography, attribution, genre development. At the same time, however, they also contribute, though more implicitly, important theoretical insights into the relationship between gender and representation. In both articles, the question of authorship metamorphoses into that of the genderedness of the image. The fact that the painters were women is a logical extension of the interpretation of the painting, rather than the other way around. Garrard brings in biographical detail, but only at the end of her argument, supplying further evidence for a claim that was already fully argued for on the basis of the image itself.

One might wonder whether art history can meet the challenge these works of feminist criticism present. But for the present study, it is more important to notice the way Garrard and Hofrichter change the question of actual authorship into that of the genderedness of the image; that change is largely related to the issue of looking. In both cases, the relation between represented men and women on the one hand, and the position of the viewer on the other, becomes the key to the particular gender quality of the works. And as I hope to have demonstrated in the previous chapters, the viewer is no more genderless than the figures.

In both works, it is the direction of the eyes of the figures in relation to their bodies that offers the most significant support for the argument. For example, the Leyster painting represents the propositioning man as looking intently at the woman, while she, equally intently, avoids looking at him. In the other pieces in this genre in its pre-Leysterian form, Hofrichter tells us, the woman returns the man's look. Similarly, in Gentileschi's *Susanna* the figure turns her eyes away from her assailants, unlike most Susannas in this very rich tradition, who all respond to the men's gaze in one way or another. Looking and being looked at – this theme, self-reflexive as it is in visual art, is so central to the representational practice of Western culture that it deserves some special attention, for it might be the theme that undermines the standard art-historical questions more radically than these two cases have shown thus far.

The entire visual tradition of the Susanna story rests on the kind of mythical work discussed in the preceding chapter: The Biblical story becomes a pre-text, and a pretext, for its radical reversal;[3] the exemplum of chastity becomes the occasion for the celebration of sexual opportunity; and, of course, the justification of rape is not far away. The use of voyeurism in the Susanna tradition to transform the rape of a woman (as in the *Lucretias*) into seduction by a woman (as in the *Josephs*) makes that tradition an appropriate third topic for the discussion of representation and gender that I have presented in these first chapters.

The Susanna tradition is characterized by the representation, as well as the use, of voyeurism. As Garrard (1982:150) argues, the inclusion in a visual representation of this story of the two lecherous old men makes the distortion of resistance into opportunity "both iconographically justified and pornographically effective." In this tradition the innocent and chaste Susanna is generally shown, first, as an attractive sex object and, second, as a daughter of Eve either struggling against her own impulses to sin, or overtly acquiescing to the "temptation."[4] Insofar as any resistance or anguish is represented at all, it is generally conventional and used only to enhance the excitement of the two men standing in for the viewer. In such cases we need to consider whether the representation of voyeurism itself encourages voyeurism, whether such a representation is indeed pornographic.[5] And we must consider such a relationship seriously since, as we saw earlier, voyeurism and actual rape may be closely related. In fact, it is to the experience of rape that Garrard attributes Gentileschi's choice and treatment of subject in the Susanna painting.[6]

Garrard acknowledges that occasionally Susanna has been depicted sympathetically in the long and generally male tradition; in those cases some attention has been paid to her vulnerability. She notes Rembrandt's *Susanna and the Elders* of 1647 (Berlin) as the most positive example, although she also points out iconographic details that evoke erotic associations, such as the reference in Susanna's pose to the Venus Pudica tradition. In this chapter I would like to consider whether the two "Rembrandt" paintings of Susanna stand firmly in the male tradition or whether they are, rather, closer to Gentileschi's work.[7] For example, Artemesia Gentileschi's Susanna refuses visual intercourse not only with the two elders, but with the viewer as well. Both of the "Rembrandt" Susannas also turn away from the assailants. But in both paintings she turns toward the viewer. Does this mean that "Rembrandt" is aligned more closely with the masculine tradition than with Gentileschi?

To determine this we must consider the relationship between Susanna's engagement of the viewer's vision and the ease with which
the viewer can adopt a voyeuristic stance. At this point, the distinction that Bryson (1983) makes between the gaze and the glance
and that Silverman makes between the gaze and the look (in her
[1989] revision of Lacan) will be useful.

And since it is a verbal text after all that stands at the beginning
of this long tradition of representing Susanna's plight, we may well
wonder what made this text so attractive for an elaboration of an
ideology of vision in the first place. If we are to bring the verbal
and the visual together, we must consider the relationship between
the position of the focalizer in verbal narrative and the viewer in
the visual. And by taking viewing in both verbal and visual narrative as our semiotic activity, we return again to a consideration
of voyeurism.

To begin, let us consider the visual representation of the nude
female body, a representation perhaps too easily relegated to the
pornographic because of an assumption of its availability to the
voyeuristic gaze. To this end I shall propose a visual reading of
the Biblical Susanna story and a narrative reading of the paintings.

VOYEURISM, THE GLANCE, AND THE GAZE

Since "Rembrandt" 's realism clashed with the art world's standards
of beauty, his nudes, with their stretch marks and imprints of
garters, have provoked many comments from "Rembrandt" 's time
to our own. One reaction has been to criticize this "realism," as
the following passage from a contemporary, the poet Pels, clearly
shows:

> When he a naked woman, as it sometimes happened,
> Would paint, chose no Greek Venus as a model,
> But sooner a washerwoman, or a peat-treader from a barn,
> Calling his error imitation of Nature,
> Everything else invention. Sagging breasts,
> Wrenched hands, even the pinch of the sausages [the mark of the
> pinches]
> Of the stays of the stomach, or the garter on the leg ... (quoted by
> Alpers, 1988)

On the other hand, what some find offensive, other celebrate.[8] The
most relevant comments for this chapter are those that betray a
deep ambivalence. Here is Kenneth Clark's appraisal of the *Danae*:

The closest Rembrandt came to a statement of his ideal was the *Danae* in
the Hermitage, where he certainly wished to make the figure as beautiful
as he could. But his love of truth got the better of him. She is sensuous
and desirable, but beautiful is not the word that comes to one's mind.
(Clark, 1980:23)[9]

In these two reactions we see the typical conflation of representation and object that comes with the eroticization of viewing. If
matching the body constructed for the mind's eye inspires lust, the
painting is praised; if that body does not, the painting or drawing
is criticized. In both of these reactions the work of representation
itself is ignored, so that the work of art disappears behind the object
represented. This attitude reflects the notion that what is seen is
the "real" thing; if that thing is a woman, one conventionally responsible for inspiring desire through her beauty, then the work
of art is judged on how successful that end is achieved. Pels's poem
is explicit: As an ardent classicist, he finds that reality is ugly, and
"excessive" realism produces ugly art.[10] The work is elided, and
thus seeing and perception are radically separated in this approach
to art.

In Bryson's terms these kinds of reactions verbalize the gaze, the
look that ahistoricizes and disembodies itself and objectifies, takes
hold of, the contemplated object.[11] Distinct from the gaze, the
glance is the involved look where the viewer, aware of and bodily
participating in the process of looking, interacts with the painting
and does not need, therefore, to deny the work of representation,
including its most material aspects like brush-, pen-, or pencilwork.
The awareness of one's own engagement in the act of looking entails
the awareness that what one sees is a representation, not an objective
reality, not the "real thing."

In Bryson's own work, it is not always clear whether he locates
the motivation for these two modes of looking in the work or in
the act of viewing. Discussing Chinese and Japanese calligraphy,
he seems to place it in the work, where traces of the work of
representation, the brushstrokes, refer to the work indexically (Bryson, 1983:89–95); but elsewhere (e.g., in his discussion of the *An-
nunciation* of the Master of the Barberini Panels; Bryson, 1983:101–
3) the mode of looking taken up does not seem to be motivated
by the work of art.[12]

I would like to appropriate this helpful distinction, understanding
the gaze and the glance as viewing attitudes or modes proposed,
encouraged, but not enforced, by the work. The gaze is, then, an
attitude that conflates model and figure, an attitude that is encouraged by "transparent" realism effacing the traces of the labor of
representation; whereas the glance is the mode that emphasizes the
viewer's own position *as* viewer, encouraged by the traces of the
work of representation which propose, for reflection, that the representation is focalized in specific ways. These two modes of looking are not mutually exclusive; they can be taken up alternately
before the same work and even combined within the same looking-
event; yet the choice is not entirely arbitrary: The work's structure
suggests either the one mode or the other.

If we want to avoid fallacious, self-fulfilling, repetitive confla-
tions of representation and actual viewing, we need to consider

carefully how particular works of art can encourage one viewing posture or another. I suggest that the actual viewer is addressed by positions offered for identification. The viewer, then, accepts or refuses that position, depending on its attractiveness. According to the present state of reader-response theory, it seems plausible to me to suppose that, although no simple one-to-one relationship between represented and actual viewing position can be assumed, a representation of viewing does affect actual viewing.[13]

How much actual viewing will be affected depends on the degree of congruence between the representation of viewing and the Lacanian gaze. According to Silverman's illuminating exegesis and revision of Lacan's impenetrable text, the gaze is the internalized social construction of vision, what others call visuality (Foster, 1988). This construction is "looking back" at the viewer in every act of looking. It is part of the experience that shapes the interpretants the viewer will contrive.

The gaze, a social construct, can hardly be unified and stable, so within the regime of the gaze there is room for a look that is not an appropriation. While a hostile, appropriating gaze is more tenacious than one could hope for, Silverman also discusses a look of desire that is communicative and not "rapish," and to which women, too, have access. But one can also imagine a look of aggression, a look that excludes: a look that looks the looked-at subject out of existence, or out of the social group doing the looking. We shall soon see an example of such a look.[14]

Bryson's gaze is a subset of Lacan's/Silverman's look, an act of looking of the colonialist variety that the social gaze so often encourages. In the following analyses, I shall use the terms "gaze" and "glance" in Bryson's sense, bearing in mind that they are predicated upon varieties of the Lacanian look within the gaze, a social construct currently dominated by a masculine, colonizing perspective. Bryson's gaze cannot be conflated with Lacan's gaze. For one does not escape so easily the Lacanian gaze. The glance is an incidental *act of looking*, performed on the mode of, say, the communicative variety of looking (looking as desire but not appropriation) within the Lacanian gaze as differentiated by Silverman.

As soon as we address "Rembrandt"'s nudes from the position of the glance, we cannot ignore how the many drawings and sketches of the so-called "ugly" female body relate to the representation of looking itself. Indeed, the sense of ugliness may be generated not so much by an excessive or aggressive realism as Pels sarcastically suggested, but, on the contrary, as by an emphatic reference to representation. Let us consider this possibility by comparing three drawings of female nudes; all three are "ugly" – that is, not idealized, not Venuslike – but, as we shall see, not necessarily more "real." I shall end that discussion with a fourth sketch, different from the others, which will mediate between those random sketches and the *Susanna* paintings. In this comparison I shall not

assume the reality of the object represented (the conflation de-
nounced above), but neither shall I totally discard a relationship to
the object as woman (an aestheticization that fails to account for
the relationship between representation and actual social behavior).

The following four sketches, at first sight quite similar, turn out
to be dramatically different in the modes of address they suggest.
Figure 4.1 represents a paradoxical exposure of a body as not exposed for looking. This drawing would most certainly be classified
as one of the "ugly" nudes. What is "ugly" about the represented
body is, however, not the body itself but its pose (or is it its
attitude?). There is nothing in the body itself that I would point to
as specifically "ugly." But the whole body expresses unwillingness
to be seen, unavailability for eroticism, lack of exhibitionist efforts.
But since it is represented for us to see, what exactly are we supposed to see? What is being represented?

I would contend that the work of representation makes precisely
this unavailability for seeing itself visible. The effort is toward
lowering the shoulders, letting the belly protrude; the proximity
of breasts to belly underscores the fact that the former are not
ornamental, but part of the mass of flesh that this body in intimate
relaxation chooses to be. Pels would call these breasts "sagging,"
for example, but they are just being allowed to hang. The sketchy
background is no more than what it is: background, a surface that
screens off the space of the woman. It signals the intimacy of her
position and represents the screen which should also shut her off
at the other side, the viewer's side. The curtain on the left should
fall and let the woman be alone.

If we consider the traces of this representational effort as constituting the work, then we have a drawing that, as far as it is
constructed as meaningful, is totally indexical. But the traces of
representational effort are not the pen- or brushwork as much as a
collusion between that work and the work of representation it is
doing. In other words, the drawing does not represent by means
of brushwork; instead, the brushwork *is* the representation of unwillingness to be seen. Between the drawing subject – say, "Rembrandt" – and the subject of the drawing – the woman – there is
collusion, conflation, coincidence. The traces signify that collusion
itself.

Within the resulting representation there are also signs of reluctance. Turning the head away, for example, is a conventional sign
of the reluctance to be seen – a Peircean symbol. Paradoxically
again, the woman in this drawing turns her head away, *toward* the
viewer. The symbol is undermined by the index. But the index is
undermined in its turn, for the figure turns toward the viewer only
to lower her eyes. Thus the refusal to look back is thematized by
this conspicuous gesture precisely because it is deconventionalized.

Everything in this drawing discourages erotic response. This is
not to say that an erotic response is impossible. It certainly is possible, but on different terms: on the terms of the glance, not of the

Facing page, from left to right:
4.1   *Female Nude Seated* ca. 1654–
6, Benesch 1122, drawing, 211 ×
177 mm (Chicago, The Art
Institute of Chicago)
4.2   *Female Nude Seated* ca. 1660–
1, Benesch 1142, drawing, 290 ×
175 mm (Amsterdam,
Rijksprentenkabinet)
4.3   *Female Nude Seated* ca. 1630–
1, Benesch 21 (*Diana at the Bath*),
drawing, 181 × 164 mm
(London, British Museum)
4.4   *Woman Standing Up
(Susanna?)* no date, Benesch 590,
drawing, 203 × 164 mm (Berlin,
Kupferstichkabinett)

gaze. One can respond erotically to this representation in different, contrasting ways; one can respond through the awareness of the viewer's own intrusion, an awareness that forces the viewer to come to terms with the unwillingness of the figure to be watched and, by *working through* it, thus to overcome one's position as voyeur;[15] or one can enjoy the woman's exposure despite her reluctance, in a slightly sadistic mode of looking.

In the next drawing (Figure 4.2), at first apparently similar to Figure 4.1, the representation of this reluctance is dramatically different. Again, the female figure is not exposed for viewing. The position of her legs, for example, is not only not at all gracious, but is doubly uninviting: It closes off what the peeper would want to see, and the legs are engaged in a self-contained movement that signifies their unavailability.[16] She is engaged in herself, and her body expresses relaxation and indifference to its visual effect. Again, the effort of the work is toward emphasizing this unavailability, as, for example, the strong line from the left hand to the foot suggests. The head is turned away again, but this time not in the direction of the viewer but away from him/her.

Unlike the passive, interiorized look of the preceding drawing, however, this figure does actively look – but not at the viewer. Ignoring the viewer, she is busy looking at herself. The left edge of the figure narrativizes the drawing and brings the female figure to life. If the preceding figure was represented in its utter narrative passivity, this one is represented as active. Instead of the refusal of the first figure we have the ostensive indifference of the second.

This difference between the two figures also alters the position of the viewer. The absence of any indication of an intention to expose the body, the absence of any exhibitionism, does not preclude voyeurism as strongly as does the refusal to exhibit the body of the other sketch. Nor does this lack of exhibitionism encourage it. Rather, the indifference confronts the viewer with his/her own choice: to watch or not to watch; to watch the indifference or to watch the body; to watch the work or to watch the object. This indifference constitutes in itself a resistance to voyeurism. It makes the work of drawing impenetrable; it complicates transparency. The very fact that the choice between glance and gaze is emphatically proposed to the viewer is in itself an obstacle to the smooth, self-effacing gaze. This is the paradox of self-reflexive art.

With the third of this series (Figure 4.3), we come closer to traditional nudes. The woman, rising from her seat, holding a veil that does not veil her body, and looking toward the viewer as if surprised by the latter's intrusion, is the rhetorical signifier of erotic provocation. The figure establishes a continuity between herself and the viewer. The drawing's narrativity, the figure's pretense of movement, is consequently weak, compared to that in the previous figure (4.2). The woman in Figure 4.3 looks outside the image, betraying no signs of distress or anguish, and the token act of taking up a cloth for covering her body is the pretext for the arm to be stretched out, for the breast to be shown, and for the shoulder to be raised.

Although the body is neither more nor less "ugly" than the two others, the relationship between it and the viewer is now completely different. Stretch marks; a weak, protruding belly; and a thigh marked by a garter now removed are equally represented. But this body is not warding off the possible visual-erotic initiative of "whom it may concern." There is no resistance to the gaze. In other words, as I suggested earlier, "ugliness" is a property, not of the body represented, but of the viewing attitude the representation of that body promotes. What is evaluated as "ugliness," then, is in fact an appeal to the glance; "beauty," an appeal to the gaze.[17]

Even here, we cannot claim that the work stands fully within the eroticizing tradition of the *Susanna*s which Garrard discussed. Traces of the work of representation remain, which disturb the perfect objectification of transparent realism welcomed by the gaze. Here, for example, the lines of armpit, breast, and thigh can be taken to deny what the attitude and look suggest and emphasize the representation itself. The strange lines on the upper left thigh belong to the cloth; yet they also seem to suggest disturbance in their position as guardians of the body's entrance. And although the figure looks in the direction of the viewer, her eyes are just not clear enough to be caught. Thus two modes of realism are in competition here: the one promoting transparency and the other promoting awareness of the representational effort. Pels and Clark are wrong, then, in suggesting that these women *were* somehow "ugly"; rather, it was the trace of the labor of the representing subject which bothered them. And the opposition between truth and beauty in the passages quoted above can thus be read as expressions of the discomfort experienced when, as a consequence, the glance is hard to escape.[18]

These works are sketches, and are thus even less for public viewing than are etchings. Because they are sometimes preparations or exercises for paintings or independent exercises, they bear a close relation to the artist-and-his-work – to "Rembrandt" – as we know him/it. In a sense, they are his *work*, and they can therefore never entirely fall into the realm of the gaze.[19] Studying them, here, before studying the paintings, is a way to retrace the steps of the work of representation and to remain in continuity with the representing subject as we construct it. It is, so to speak, a way to keep in touch.

But before turning to the text and the paintings of Susanna with these drawings in mind, let us take a brief look at another drawing; Figure 4.4 is considered a preparatory drawing for "Rembrandt"'s early *Susanna*.

This drawing (Figure 4.4) does not belong to the "ugly" nudes. The body is far removed from the mature and rather fleshy bodies of the three other drawings; it is hardly a nude at all. This drawing shows the effort of representing the moment of getting up from a seat. This effort is notable in the tension in the figure's back. The

artist has succeeded in the quasi-magical trick of representing movement in a medium reputed for stillness, thus challenging the common opposition between visual and verbal art.

The same craft shows in the head of the figure. The head is not turned toward the viewer; it is caught in the very moment of turning. Again the work of drawing goes into representing this cross between a situation and an event, as the different lines around and on the neck show. In comparing this head to that in Figure 4.3, the difference is striking. A significant difference can be noted also in the eyes. In Figure 4.3, the figure's eyes are not looking directly at the viewer but resting more vaguely somewhere between fictional onlooker and outside spectator; the sharp eyes in this drawing address the viewer directly and instantaneously. These two pairs of eyes stand in opposition to each other as representations of the gaze and the glance.

This is a first important point in relation to the question of the eroticization of Susanna's body in the paintings. The eyes, in this drawing, are apostrophic, active, and positioned in time. They protect the body against the eyes of the viewer who, after being thus addressed, can only raise his hat and walk by, blushing. The viewer of Figure 4.3 can take her or his time and look on as long as it pleases him. This does not mean that the actual viewing time for the two drawings is different; on the contrary, Figure 4.4 is much more confusing and will therefore require more viewing time. But the viewing, however long it takes, is positioned on a time scale. Viewers who watch Figure 4.4 for ten minutes will realize all those minutes that they are being indiscreet. Even the briefest look at Figure 4.3, in contrast, will take the stature of a gaze: Outside of time, undisturbed, the viewer can take in, usurp – Bryson would say, *prendre sous garde* – the represented body. Even if the actual viewing time is shorter, the viewing of the image before the mind's eye is longer. The viewer takes it with him as a fixed icon. The gaze is thus the visual equivalent of myth. It is a reading attitude that fixes the object and builds on the illusion that the object exists outside of time, space, and the viewer's body.

Looking, then, is an act that affects the looker more than the subject being looked at. Although verbal texts obviously accomplish this effect by different means, these means are, in the Susanna story, equally strongly bound up with visuality.

"A CLUSTER OF SIGNS FOR HIS NEIGHBOUR'S FALSE SUPPOSITIONS"

Assessing the function and nature of looking in the Biblical Susanna story involves a reversal of priorities. Such an assessment requires that we bring into consideration aspects that are mostly omitted in both verbal and visual interpretations of the text and that we ignore other, perhaps more conspicuous aspects. By concentrating on the visuality of the story, we shall see that in spite of the edifying Biblical context, the story is perhaps more pornographic than Garrard assumes.[20] And Susanna's chastity, although clearly a conspicuous theme, is crossed, if not overwhelmed, by another theme that we remember from the "Rembrandt" etching of Joseph and Potiphar's wife.

Like all Biblical stories, this one has theological, moral, and juridical themes that we must mostly leave aside. The text is a second- or first-century addition to the Book of Daniel called "Daniel and Susanna," and this alliance is more than mere coincidence: Daniel is not only a prophet, hence a spokesman of wisdom, but also a *young* man. It is young Daniel, the future prophet, who saves Susanna from the death penalty to which the vengeful Elders had condemned her.

The relation between the Elders' behavior and their position of power is crucial. They were elected judges and often held court in the beautiful garden adjoining the house of Joakim, Susanna's husband, because Joakim was a most respected citizen and his house and garden were spacious and pleasant. So not only had they easy access to the place of their crime and to the object of their lustful eyes, they also had a priori the power to acquit themselves of the crime. Their case was made beforehand, so to speak. Finally and, I think, most importantly, the two Elders were together.

The text introduces the tension in visual terms:

When the people went away at noon, Susanna used to go and walk in her husband's garden. Every day the two elders *saw* her entering the garden and taking her walk, and they were obsessed with lust for her. ("Daniel and Susanna," verse 8)[21]

Typically, the combination of iterative situation-description, and new information makes it unclear how, in the view represented in the text, the lust of the Elders began. But the sequence of the two sentences suggests a causal connection and suggests that it was *because* Susanna exposed herself unknowingly that they became inflamed.[22] So far, the act of viewing has not done any harm outside of the men themselves. The two men have not confessed to each other

what pangs they suffered, because they were ashamed to confess that they wanted to seduce her. Day after day they watched eagerly to see her. (11–12)

Viewing is, here, explicitly opposed to "seduction" (read: rape). This is indeed a common view even today: The causal connection between seeing and acting is violently denied in the debate on pornography. What is at stake here is, of course, a complex kind of causality. It is not the case that every act of viewing a desirable object, even if purely on the mode of appropriation, leads to taking possession of that or an equivalent object, or else all consumers of

149

pornography would be rapists or johns. Yet the lack of simple causality does not mean that there is none at all. There is a direct relationship among viewing, desiring, and the impulse to fulfill the desire. The difference is that not every consumer of pornography who subsequently has a rapish desire will actually try to fulfill that desire. Most subjects make concessions; however, some – too many – do not.

In his chapter on "The Sexual Aberrations" (in *Three Essays*; first German edition: 1905), Freud lists voyeurism with the perversions. He distinguishes "normal" from "pathological" voyeurism on the basis of the ultimate fulfillment of the desire.[23] If voyeurism does *not* function as a preliminary sexual aim, the subject is ill. In other words, lustful looking only is pathological, whereas looking as preparation for intercourse is normal. Of course, Freud means to distinguish between anonymous voyeurism and – possibly bilateral – looking as foreplay. He does not mean that voyeurs can save their mental health by raping the object of their looking. But by ignoring the cases where voyeuristic looking does lead to rape, the distinction he draws can easily be misunderstood. To avoid this kind of mis-understanding let us draw a fourfold distinction between engaged looking and voyeurism, and between voyeurs who, once a rapish desire has been aroused, channel their desires into harmless means of satisfaction, and those who do not. Now that we recognize such a distinction, we must next examine the factors that differentiate these two latter categories.

If the power to act upon the desire is one of those factors, then the Susanna story can help us understand the interaction among viewing, lust, and rape. For one thing, the relationship between looking and touching is, according to Freud, an inherent one. Look-ing is for him a derivative of touching, and, therefore, looking is able to arouse desire by contiguity. Rhetorically speaking, then, looking is a metonymic substitute for touching. But we have al-ready seen how easily the two elements of a rhetorical figure can be reversed. So let us reverse this relation and see touching as an inherent second phase of looking, while the desire aroused by look-ing is generated by the prospect of touching. Hence, a temporal perspective has to be reckoned with, and narrative can help us see how.

All the time the men were lusting after Susanna, but not yet acting, they were "hidden and spying." Their position is emblem-atic of the consumer of pornography and, by extention, of all view-ers of visual images.[24] The position of the outsider who can look in without being seen himself, turns looking into spying. The po-sition has the comfort of invulnerability. But at the same time, because of the symmetry between voyeurism and exhibitionism which Freud has pointed out, it also has the guilt that comes with this lack of commitment, this lack of self-exposure.

The pleasure of invulnerability is either caused by or causes guilt; either one hides because one feels guilt, or hiding makes one guilty.

Guilt can be avoided only if one manages to receive community support for the hiding, that is, unless it is culturally acceptable to "hide and spy." But this puts the hider into a paradoxical position, for why should he hide if the community accepts the hiding? The voyeur must hide because the community colludes in the peeping only indirectly or, rather, metaphorically, and the metaphorical relation is always unstable.

The community stands by the Elders. The men's power is based on the assumption that they are honorable, decent Elders. The agreement between them concerns the fact that they are not. But the one – the support inherent in their high social position – is continuous with the other – their *agreement* to attack Susanna. Their togetherness is what makes it at all possible for them to envisage the attack.

In the Susanna story, this pattern is followed with precision. The viewing arouses desire, and although the desire does not immediately lead to action, nevertheless action – touching – will follow inevitably, evoked as it is by metonymy. That action does not immediately follow viewing is related to the Elders' solitude, moral solitude: The two Elders are solitary, but not physically; obviously, they are together, but they are morally separate because they are ashamed of their feelings, and in their shame they do not dare confess their lust to each other. So the two men refrain from acting; they remain alone in their lust.

This situation changes when they discover each other's secret:

One day they said: 'Let us go home; it is time for lunch'. So they went off in different directions, but soon retraced their steps and found themselves face to face. When they questioned one another, each confessed his passion. Then they agreed on a time when they might find her alone. (14)[25]

The men have the power to carry out their desires because of their high position; but the power they each have over life and death as judges is not enough to prompt them to act separately on their lust; they need to act in concert, for the moral support they get from each other is the fictional representation of cultural support. But this also makes their power fragile; it breaks down as soon as each is alone. Later it is taken away from them completely when cunning young Daniel isolates them from each other.

Symmetrically opposed to their combined power is the powerlessness of their victim in her isolation. As soon as the woman has sent her servants away, the men "who had hidden and were spying on her" run toward her and attack her. Alone, she has neither rescuer nor witness; together, their power is absolute. The word they use to confront her with their power is "look."

As in the Lucretia story, the men threaten to ruin Susanna's reputation for chastity, hence the honor of her husband. Lucretia's rapist threatened to denounce her with a slave, the utmost shame, and the victim yielded for the good of her husband's reputation.

The logic cost her her life, however. In Susanna's case, significantly, the threat is:

> If you refuse, we shall give evidence against you that there was a *young man* with you and that was why you sent your maids away. (21; my emphasis)

What is the difference between a slave (of unspecified age) and a young man? Compared to the assailants, both are equally inferior in social status. The difference is not so much between the slave and the young man, but in the direction of the shame. The slave affected the victim's status; he signified her fictitious lust as so forceful that it brought her low. Similarly, the young man is brought in, on the level of the story's logic, as the most convincing evidence against Susanna's unassailable reputation. But on another level, a more relevant level in relation to voyeurism, importing a young man into the story affects the status of the elders, the rivals of the fictive youth, more than the youth affects Susanna's. The end of the story will make this fiction about the young man literally come true – but what we can by now mean by "literally" remains to be seen.

Why can Susanna stand firm where Lucretia yielded? She can afford to because the men themselves introduce what is at stake, thus allowing her the logic of escape. The unconscious and implicit argument of the Elders would run as follows: First, Susanna is the more desirable as she is chaste (see Lucretia). Second, she is desirable, therefore she must be accessible; she must have a desire. Third, she can hardly desire us, unattractive old men. Hence, fourth, she must desire a young man, so much more attractive than us. Finally, then, we can take her, because she is accessible. The split between desire and action is now overcome by the acknowledgment of their own lack. Nevertheless, the lack remains.

If the men are themselves setting up a dichotomy between old and young men, there is more to it than the youth's attractiveness for the woman. Susanna can now afford to say "no," because saying "yes" would challenge the men to perform as if they were young men. The suggestion here is that voyeurism may be related to real or feared impotence, and one reason why not all porno viewers set out to rape may also be that there is a relatively high rate of impotence or the fear thereof in that category. This impotence is not, however, a given, disconnected from the act of viewing. As feminist film theorists have argued, viewing women asymmetrically is itself so loaded with guilt and fear that it alone entails castration anxiety.[26]

EXHIBITING DESIRE

With this possible line, the story acquires a mood as close to fantasy as the Washington *Joseph* painting did. The young man represents for the Elders the other side of voyeurism: the danger and attraction of exhibitionism. The story offers a verbal equivalent of Fried's category of "absorption" which further complicates the question of voyeurism. Even if the Elders are quoted here as speaking aloud, the visual charge of the words they speak is entirely inner. And although the representational work is not foregrounded in the same way as in the drawing we just saw, what is foregrounded is the problematic of looking. If this reading needs more textual support, this is provided by the men themselves in the scene of the trial, when they establish an interesting connection between viewing and potency. This textual support, however, must be retrieved by a specifically absorptive-visual mode of reading their account:

Then a young man who had been in *hiding*, came and lay down with her. We were in a corner of the garden and when we *saw* this wickedness we ran up to them. Though we *saw* them in the *act*, we could not hold the man; *he was too strong for us*, and he *opened the door* and *forced* his way out. We *seized* the woman . . . (38–40; my emphasis of significant words)

This passage can be read as an account of what happened *to the old men*, if only we juxtapose the words, according to coloration, as if they were blots of paint. They describe the young man first in terms that identify him with themselves: Hiding and running up to her, opening the door, forcing, and seizing her is what they did; lying down with her is what they wanted and what they *saw*, hallucinating the fulfillment of their desire. The key phrase is "we saw them in the act." Seeing is hardly the pretended innocent witnessing in this context. They saw her while they were hiding, and, as viewers of pornography, desired/fantasized the act. They hallucinated the act, performed by procuration in their stead, by someone young, *stronger than them*.

The hallucination, in fact, comes true. "A devout young man named Daniel" will be seen to act and overwhelm the Elders. He does so by separating them, by bringing them back into their initial position. This is precisely how he formulates his scheme, apparently knowing where their power comes from: "Separate these two men and keep them at a distance from each other, and I will examine them" (51).

Daniel, in the name of justice, truth, and objectivity, protests the innocence of the young man when he says: "I will not have this woman's blood on my head" (46), an expression that, in the context of the fantasized rivalry over the woman's possession, can also carry ambiguity. How can he be so sure of what happened, if he is not the fictive youth, and the Elders are not identifying with him in a fantasy? By separating the old men, he undoes the crime of the Elders, restoring Susanna's chastity, her veil, in the public eye, by traveling the same path backwards, until, as a good analyst, he shows them that they have not really *seen* what they saw, that they had been hallucinating instead. Separating them from each other, he confronts them with the unbridgeable gap between the young man they created and themselves, now without power as without potency. In their hallucinated fantasy, they created Daniel. Now they are forced to deal with the consequences. Without their lie, Daniel, the young man, would not exist as a character, nor would he become the hero he is now, thanks to the Elders' evocation. On the level of the story's logic, it is their lie that necessitates Daniel's intervention.

This reading is not a narrative reading in the traditional sense, nor is it, of course, a historical reading. Semiotically speaking, its plausibility is strong, however, because it is a *doubly visual* reading. In the first place, bracketing the chronology of the story, this reading works by skimming over the elements of the text, as a viewer of a painting skims over the surface, not the sequence, in order to compose the work in his or her mind. In the second place, it works on the assumption that the men are hallucinating, as continuous with their voyeurism, the fulfillment of their desire. Hallucination is a peculiar way of seeing: Countering the positivistic assumption that seeing is based on the objective reality of the object, hallucination proposes seeing what is not present in reality. Hallucination is a visual experience that is also a lie.[27] It is seeing what is not there – seeing nobody – while, as a visual act, it produces the body to be seen. The articulation of the lie in visuality repeats the pornographic experience of voyeurism.

Initially, these two ways of reading visually appear completely different: The first one affects the actual work of the reader of the text; the second one introduces an isotopy, the psychoanalytic view of voyeurism, *into* the reading. But the two are related by the narrative strategy through which the second is represented. In narratological terms, we can say that these strategies combine to represent voyeurism through focalization.

I introduced focalization in earlier work to replace the cumbersome and ambiguous term "point of view." Focalization is the relation between the elements of the fabula presented in the story, and the perspective from which they are presented. The overall focalizer whose view is directly rendered by the narrative voice is distanced from the elders, as is obvious in evaluative passages which begin as early as the introduction of the two men. For example, when the narrator says, "She was closely veiled, but *those scoundrels* ordered her to be unveiled so that they may feast their eyes on her beauty" (32), a passage immediately followed by and contrasted with "Her family and all who saw her were in tears" (33), there can be no doubt that the overall focalizer stands on the side of the righteous and invites us to identify with that perspective of decency.

But at certain points the focalization of this verbal story works to combine the view of the overall subject of the text with the view of the Elders. Depending on the episode, the structure of focalization is now separated from, now coincides with, the voyeurism of the Elders. For example, the evaluative words "those scoundrels" leave no room for moral ambiguity. Only when focalization is embedded, and the elders are assigned the power to present their own focalization, does focalization come to provoke the specific reading attitude of male voyeurism. Yet the embedded clause "so that they may feast their eyes on her beauty" insinuates the focalization of the Elders into the framing "righteous" perspective. Although the unveiling is condemned, the visual feast is promised by the same token. Perniciously, the moral dimension of the tale absorbs the pornographic one and provides the innocent reader with an excuse to anticipate the pleasure *sanctioned*, rather than countered by the moral indignation.

The passage of the hallucinated wish fulfillment is a rather long one in which the Elders narrate their "version" of the story. This embedding structure leaves open the question to what extent the story as a whole works pornographically, a question to which no simple answer can be given. For as I have argued earlier, the interaction between text and reader, not the text alone, determines the effect of a cultural object. So all we can point out is how the text proposes a structure open to pornographic processing.

Mary Garrard wrote about the irony that Susanna, the model of chastity, has become, in painting, the occasion for a celebration of sexual opportunity. Garrard rightly emphasizes the differences between story and paintings, and since she is solely interested in the paintings, her judgment in that area may be helpful. But if we examine the story in as detailed a manner as Garrard examines Artemesia's painting, we must come to a different conclusion. Although the Biblical story relies, in moral terms, on the Biblical context in which morality and theology always frame the stories, however disturbing they may otherwise be,[28] I contend that the Susanna story holds the germs of the pornographic flavor that later became its sole motivation in the painterly tradition. In the hallucinatory quality of the Elders' account lies the implicitly pornographic aspect of the Biblical story. Ironically, this argument initially seems to undermine that set forth in the preceding chapter, where I contend that works of art could be processed by radically separating them from their pre-texts. For painters are readers, too; and since reading is both utterly subjective and utterly social, readers are bound to encourage one another to respond to works of art in a certain way: This is the shaping of the Peircean "habit," the experience that informs interpretants according to De Lauretis.

A clear relationship can be seen in the pornographic obsession with viewing a naked woman, an obsession shared by the story on the one hand and the painterly tradition on the other. And since the Biblical account was both visually based and visually readable, yet verbally produced, we cannot assume that pornography is solely a matter for the visual media. But neither are pornography and visuality unrelated. Their relationship lies in the mode, rather than in the medium, of visuality, however.[29] The possibility of verbal pornography (based, as pornography is, on the thrill of voyeurism, of detached viewing) is evidence for the visuality of the verbal as much as for the imaginative nature of seeing.

''THEY WERE HIDDEN AND SPYING''

The situation with the *Susanna*s is similar to that of the *Lucretia*s. The chronology of the making of "Rembrandt"'s two works coincides with the chronology in the represented stories. And as we have seen for the *Lucretia*s and shall see for the *Susanna*s, there are crucial similarities, as well as crucial differences, between the two works devoted to the same topic. Both characters, moreover, engage the works' lines of sight in complex ways. So again, I shall discuss the two paintings in relation to each other, indeed, consider them in continuity with the ongoing work of the particular storyteller, "Rembrandt," not so much because they are works by the same "hand" but because they are by the same, although unstable, ideological subject.

Both *Susanna* paintings (Figures 4.5 and 4.6) represent a young, vulnerable woman who looks toward the viewer as if seeking help. And neither female figure shares the voluptuous and assertive traits of the traditional Susanna bodies. And both have more or less the same pose; the Berlin *Susanna*, although slightly younger looking and more elegant than the Mauritshuis version, is at first sight closer to the Medici Venus Pudica. This pose is, according to Garrard, a remainder of the tradition of eroticization of Susanna's body for the lust of the viewer.

The similarity of the works again suggests that we read them according to the comic-strip device discussed earlier: The early Susanna is still sitting on the bench, just beginning to stand up, whereas the later one is already stepping into the water. Among the slight differences in the represented body that this chronology entails are the position of the left leg and arm. The left arm is closer to the body, and the left leg closer to the ground, in the early work than in the later one.

The major, conspicuous difference between the two works is the position of the Elders. In the earlier work, the men are almost invisible. They seem integrated into the bushes. In fact, only one man is visible, on the outer right side, and this figure is assumed to be a later addition. If we take the work as it is now, we must read the work as if at most one peeper were actually represented. In the later painting, the men are as clearly represented as the woman; one Elder is watching at some distance, the other is already touching Susanna. The face of the more distant elder is sharply illuminated, for there is a gradual shading of the light from background to foreground. Although the tension in the early work is related to the hidden presence of the Elders, it is their absence from the scene, of which Susanna is the center, which makes the earlier work so different from the later.

4.5 *Susanna at the Bath* ca. 1634, Bredius 505, panel, 47.2 × 38.6 cm (The Hague, Mauritshuis)

4.6 *Susanna Surprised by the Elders* 1645, Bredius 367, canvas 102 × 84 cm (Berlin-Dahlem, Gemäldegalerie)

The positions of the voyeur, viewer, and focalizer – to be distinguished but also related – on the one hand, and the problem of the erotic status of the female body on the other are thus the two most striking aspects of these two works taken as a set (Figure 4.7). As a first step toward understanding these two works, let us assess the position of the viewer in representations of the story of Susanna and the Elders.

THE FOCALIZER: THE FIGURATION OF THE VIEWER

The position of the viewer endorsing visuality as a mode of reading can shift back and forth and in variable degrees from narrative focalizer to erotic voyeur. In this section, we shall try to see how these two interact. But in order to avoid terminological confusion, methodological eclecticism, and ideological miasm, it is imperative that we first assess the *visual* status of the narrative focalizer, just as we had to assess the concepts of rhetoric and storytelling.

The concept of *focalization* here refers to both *narrative* as a genre and *discourse* as a semiotic system.[30] In fact, it relates those two aspects – the narrative represented and its representation – by acting as the steering perspective of the events (or fabula) that is verbalized in the text by the narrator or voice. Although its basis in the notion of perspective *seems* to simplify its transposition to the realm of the visual, such a transposition is not unproblematic.

In order to make the concept operational for visual art, we must be aware of the following:

1. In narrative discourse, focalization is the direct *content* of the linguistic signifiers. In visual art, it would then be the direct

4.7 *Susanna Surprised by the Elders*, detail

content of visual signifiers like lines, dots, light and dark, and composition. In both cases, focalization *is already an interpretation*, a subjectivized content. What we see is before our mind's eye; it has already been interpreted.

2. In narrative there is an external focalizer distinguished in function, not identity, from the narrator. This external focalizer can embed an internal, diegetic narrator.[31] For the analysis of narrative, this relation of embedding is crucial. In visual art, the same distinction between external and internal focalizer holds, but this distinction is not always easy to point out. For example, in the Joseph etching, the external focalizer, with whose view the spectator is asked to identify but from which the spectator's view remains distinct, *embeds* the internal Joseph-focalizer. As the internal focalizer, the focalization of Joseph is entirely contingent upon the fantasy of this external focalizer, which I have identified with Potiphar. We have seen the same structure of focalization in the Biblical Susanna, where young Daniel is produced by the focalization of the Elders.

3. In narrative, the fabula or diegesis is *mediated*, or even produced, by the focalizers. Similarly, use of the concept in analyzing visual art implies that the *event* represented has the status of the focalized object produced by focalizers. In the case of a diegetic focalizer, the "reality" status of the different objects represented is variable and contingent upon their relation to the focalizer. In the two Joseph paintings, we analyzed, for example, how Joseph as a character had a different status in each: He was "really" present, theatrical, and perhaps even melodramatic in the Berlin painting; he was fantasized by the internal focalizers, Potiphar and his wife, in the other. The status of the figure in the second case was thus suspended, leaving room for different interpretations.

4. Thus, the same object or event can be differently interpreted according to different focalizers. The way in which these different interpretations are suggested to the reader is medium-bound, but the principle of meaning production is the same for verbal and visual art. In *Madame Bovary*, the heroine's eyes are variably dark, black, blue, and gray, according to the internal focalizer with whom we watch her. The words conveying these incompatible descriptions do not themselves betray the difference between them. Flaubert could simply have been careless. But in order to make sense of the work as it is, only the hypothesis of different focalizers, substantiable in a textual analysis, can account for these differences. Similarly, we saw how in the Joseph etching, one object, the woman's body, was represented in two different, incompatible ways, according to the two different focalizers, one of whom was internal (Joseph) and one hinging between internal (Potiphar) and external. Again, the lines composing the body did not themselves betray the difficulty – the body could have been simply "ugly" or poorly etched

– but the hypothesis of two different focalizers showed the rabbit-or-duck problem underlying this mistake or "ugliness."

5. In narrative discourse, the identification of the external focalizer
   with an internal one can produce a discursive conflation called
   "free indirect discourse."[32] The identification between the external focalizer in visual images with an internal focalizer represented in the image can similarly give rise to such a conflation,
   which would then strengthen the appeal to identification. But
   nevertheless, the conflation is still on the level of the representational work itself, the "text."

The dynamics of focalization is at work in every visual work that
contains traces of the representational work, as seen and interpreted
by the viewer, since it is precisely in those traces that the work
becomes narrativized. In principle, all works contain such traces,
but some display these more openly than others. To begin with an
apparent counterexample: In the drawing *Judith Beheading Holophernes* (Figure 4.8), the internal focalizer is represented as failing
the act. The soldiers who are supposed to spy on Judith look in
the other direction. What is represented emphatically here is the
refusal of the onlooker – the guards – to *see* the threat to Holophernes. This could be a case of the look that excludes, mentioned
earlier. It is certainly not by chance that the drawing's theme is
exactly the opposite of that of the *Susanna*s. Here, the rapish aggression comes from a woman, and the viewer is *not* invited to share
it.[33] In contrast, the viewer is asked, or offered the suggestion, to
look away. In other words, the onlooker in both cases is addressed

4.8 *Judith Beheading Holophernes*
ca. 1652, Benesch 897, drawing,
182 × 150 cm (Napoli, Meso di
Capodimonte)

as sharing the male interest: The emotion suggested is fright, in the *Judith*; pleasure, in the *Susanna*s.

Of the three "ugly" nudes I have analyzed above, the first one, Figure 4.1, is not narrative on the level of the fabula; no narrative action seems to be implied. Yet the strong resistance to the viewer and the emphasis on the representation of that resistance narrativize the drawing: The position of the external focalizer, with which the viewer can easily identify, is implicated in the representation of what becomes an active resistance to exposure. In the second drawing, Figure 4.2, narrativization takes place on all three levels of narrative discourse: On the level of the "text," narrativization is located in the emphatic representation of the "activity of indifference"; on the level of the focalization, it takes place in the implications of both access to viewing and self-reflection on viewing; and on the level of the fabula, it takes place in the figure's internal focalization, directed "elsewhere," refusing to meet the external focalizer's eye. In the third drawing, Figure 4.3, the easy, yet not entirely convincing, encounter between external and internal focalizer left nothing to focalize; the only action is erased by the "event" of that encounter. The traces of the "text" are partly erased for the benefit of the external focalizer, and as a result, the event is not diegetic.

In Figure 4.4, in contrast, the same action – rising – leads to an event of internal focalization so strong that it undermines the external focalization. In stories this occurs when the focalization of a character produces so strong an illusion that the external focalizer seems absent, although this is technically impossible. James's *What Maisie Knew* is the classic example, a favorite of literary theorists. These brief accounts illustrate how narrativization can either support or counter voyeurism, in interaction with a viewer who is or is not sensitive to the dynamics of narrativization. The attention drawn to the representation itself by the dynamic effect of narrativization precludes the smooth realism the voyeur demands. In different terms, these remarks can also suggest that in variable degrees the glance, as a mode of viewing proposed by these works, can undercut the gaze.[34]

SUSANNA AND THE VIEWER

It seems obvious that the story of Susanna, in whatever "version," thematizes the position of the viewer. But as we saw in Chapter 3, there can be no fixed "story of Susanna," repeated and reworked; there can only be a "pre-text Susanna" used in each work for its own effect. These "versions" may either facilitate and reconfirm or problematize the position of the viewer. The first facilitates voyeurism, the second works against it, and, of course, many works oscillate between the two options, as do many viewers.

In a sense, the story of Susanna is *about* illegitimate viewing, and as such, it raises the question whether viewing is by definition an illegitimate activity. The history of Western culture suggests that attitudes toward vision vary and range from condemnation to idealization. The attitudes are deeply ambivalent from early Judaism on (Meltzer, 1987) and the inheritance of this ambivalence is still to be felt, even in contemporary philosophy (Jay, 1988). Therefore, are focalizer positions semiotic devices to trick us into an indiscreet activity that in "real life" we would avoid or feel guilty for not avoiding?

These attitudes are related to the preference for the female body as the object of looking, and the cultural commonplace that looking is an integral part of male sexuality. Is the female body so often the object of this indiscreet looking, not because it is what "we" want most to look at, but because it is simply the most convincing case for the illegitimacy of looking in general? John Berger's (1980) study of representations of animals suggests as much.

With these questions in mind, let us consider two drawings un-ambiguously similar to the Berlin *Susanna*, but in which we may note some areas where they resemble Gentileschi's painting more closely than "Rembrandt"'s own finished version (Figures 4.9 and 4.10). Since the Elders are explicitly represented in these drawings, as they are in the Berlin painting, the status of these internal fo-calizers is important. In contrast with the Berlin painting (Figure 4.6), the three figures in the drawings – the two Elders and Susanna – are contiguous. This contiguity makes us strongly aware of the immediate bodily threat to the woman, a threat Gentileschi's paint-ing also makes us feel. In both drawings, the hands of the men are significant, but they do not convey the same meaning in each case.

In Figure 4.9 both men are concentrating on Susanna, to whom they seem to speak with their hands. The raised finger of the man who actually touches her is ambiguous. Read in terms of Genti-leschi's painting, it indicates whispering: the indictment of the guilty secret and the threat to the woman's reputation. Read in terms of a more general cultural role of elderly men, in this case more specifically justified by the men's status as judges, it is the raised finger of the teacher, of the law, of the Father who designs, circumscribes, and imposes Susanna's status as a woman (i.e., her sexuality) upon her. We see something similar in what is perhaps the most repulsive representation of the Fall in Genesis 3, in "Rem-brandt"'s etching of what a mythical reading would see as Adam's seduction by Eve (Figure 4.11). We see the representation of the seduction of Eve by Adam, and Adam's hands are the instrument of this reversal. One hand, with the lifted finger, expresses the moral message of interdiction, and Adam stands for the knower "of good and evil," for the judge. The other hand, however, grabs for the apple/body, just as the Elder in the drawing of Figure 4.9 grabs for Susanna. In retrospect, that is, *after* seeing the grabbing hand, the lifted finger becomes the token of hypocrisy – indeed, the symbol of the erect penis that contradicts the moral warning; it becomes a smaller version of the bedpost in the etching of *Joseph and Potiphar's Wife*.[35]

The Susanna drawing of Figure 4.9 also resembles Gentileschi's painting in that Susanna does not look at the viewer, but looks half back, in fright, at her assailants. She uses both her hands to cover her nakedness, thus leaving little room for the unreflective voy-euristic gaze. The emptiness of the background can be related to what Garrard sees as the emphasis on material discomfort in Gen-tileschi's stone bench. And the close proximity of the two men leave Susanna no room for escape; nor is space left between them and the water.

In Figure 4.10 the Elders are equally continuous with each other and with Susanna. And again, they use their hands to speak. The man on the right seems to be engaged in convincing Susanna; the other one points at the absent public to which they threaten to denounce her. The erect finger is here replaced with a horizontal

4.9   *Susanna and the Elders* ca.
1647, Benesch 592, drawing, 198
× 188 mm (Amsterdam,
Rijksprentenkabinet)

4.10   *Susanna at the Bath, and the
Two Elders* 1637–8, Benesch 159,
drawing, 149 × 177 mm (Berlin,
Kupferstichkabinett)

finger; the reference to the higher Law, replaced by one to the concrete law to which, as judges, they have privileged access. The metaphorical status of the sign is replaced with a metonymic one, and the symbolic expression is replaced with a narrative reference to the future.

Susanna's body is shown in both drawings, and in both the representation itself is problematized; how are these two facts related? In Figure 4.9, the body is hidden by Susanna's hands and by its oblique position. In Figure 4.10, it is represented frontally, and one breast is visible. The covering of only one breast seems a conventional device often used in order both to show and to hide the body, to satisfy the demands of both voyeurism and morality. The drawing can, indeed, be taken to refer to that tradition. Yet the insistent proximity of the two men, who have already overwhelmed Susanna, provides a narrative motivation for her incapacity to be effective in her shame, thus redeeming what might come close to encouraging the voyeurstic impulse. This is further confirmed by the representation of her legs. Although shown frontally, there is no visual access to her genitals. It is not even quite clear that she is naked; the drawn lines in this area can be read either as legs or as cloth. If they represent legs, then the position of the legs is comparable to that in Figure 4.2, where visual access to the woman's genitals is explicitly denied. The close, bodily imposition

4.11   *Adam and Eve* 1638, etching (Haarlem, Teylers Museum)

of the two men is a more direct effect of the frontal pose. The pose emphasizes the discomfort of the woman who is imprisoned between the men and the water. This imprisonment is even more strongly suggested here than in the other Susanna drawing, precisely because of the frontal pose. If the woman in the other Susanna drawing has still almost half the space of the drawing's surface to flee to, the woman in Figure 4.10 can only come closer to the external viewer. This shift from the internal voyeurs to the external ones is hardly an improvement of her situation.

In the Berlin *Susanna* (Figure 4.6), the position of the Elders is split up into the two aspects of the complex of voyeurism: looking and touching according to Freud's theory.[36] The Elder on the right side of the painting is not only looking on; the man is recumbent in the seat of justice. The seriousness of the look on his face, which in terms of the Biblical story could represent his serious position, can as well be taken to be the representation, in the visual narrative, of the strength of the desire aroused by looking. The hands, in fact, are both interesting in this respect. The left hand is holding a stick, the staff that symbolizes power as conventionally as the phallus represents power through male sexuality. His right hand holds on to his seat, perhaps suggesting how little is holding him back from acting, while emphasizing the power this seat conveys to him.

If we follow the eyes of this internal focalizer, however, we notice that he is not just watching Susanna; he is also watching his colleague (Figure 4.12). The line of sight, which establishes the structure of internal focalization, moves from his eyes to the other man, from the latter's eyes to Susanna, from her eyes to the external viewer. This line of sight is connected to the distribution of light. The brightness of the looking Elder's face makes it plausible to begin reading this visual narrative with him. Reading brightness as relevant is part of the cultural construction of "Rembrandt": The distribution of light is one of our cultural assumptions about this art. Thus, we are offered this Elder as a possibility for identification, but this identification is not imposed.

4.12 *Susanna Surprised by the Elders*, detail

166

Just as in the Joseph etching, the primary position offered to the viewer is that of the elderly man in power. But unlike that etching, we have no continuous movement from internal to external focalizer. This virtual circle is broken by Susanna's direct address to the external viewer. I contend that it is to the extent that she participates in the structure of looking and connects the internal focalization to the outside, that the painting cannot be dismissed as a pornographic work.

This difference is related to the narrativization of viewing which attracts attention to itself. Once we become conscious of the narrativity of viewing, immediate access to the signifieds is blocked in favor of the opaqueness of the signs, and we, in turn, grant a greater importance to the ambivalent signs in the details. Susanna's left hand, rightly interpreted by Garrard as an iconographic – we may also call it an intertextual – allusion to the Venus tradition, hence, to eroticism, raises the question of the function of intertextual allusion. I suggest that her hand does not merely allude to that tradition. It *also* wards off that same eroticism by its defensive attempt to push aside the threat that comes from behind. By the slight shift the gesture comes to life: It is narrativized, and loses the fixity of its meaning as pure iconographic allusion.

Similarly, the second Elder's gesture of undressing Susanna, if viewed in isolation, could work for voyeurism. Semantically, it represents what the voyeur, enticed by the visual experience, would like to do: take the next step, from looking to touching. Yet, syntactically, in combination with Susanna's appeal to the viewer to turn his eyes away if the undressing eventually occurs, it can simultaneously be taken to criticize the gesture: It says, the body may be naked in a moment, but please don't look. The vulnerability of this young, helpless female figure is certainly a possible occasion for voyeurism in its sadistic variant. But this *ideologeme* is counterbalanced by the opposite ideologeme, the strongly active look.[37] Compared to the look of the woman in the most voyeuristic of the four drawings, Figure 4.3, we can see the difference clearly. The woman in this picture, although not as strongly addressing the glance as the woman in the fourth of these drawings, Figure 4.4, is most surely much more actively involved with the external viewer than is the acquiescent woman of Figure 4.3.

The narrative structure of focalization has a syntactic function; it binds the otherwise loose elements together. The meaning of the structure of focalization as such is not fixed, and it depends on the viewer to assign it meaning. I would suggest, however, that the viewing position is not quite left open once we combine it with some other elements suggesting a critical attitude, and thus supporting the antivoyeuristic interpretation. These elements include the ridiculous overdressing of the men, with their pompous mantles and hats, the staff and seat for the one, the chain referring to his honorable function for the other. These elements hamper the viewer's gaze in that they activate the narrative of abuse of power with which most viewers will not automatically wish to identify. The position the viewer is invited to share, that of the Elder at the right of the painting, is thereby just too uncomfortable to allow the viewer to take up his objectifying, abstract, and delectating gaze very easily.

This brings us to the other *Susanna*, the earlier one, where the voyeuristic gaze is almost imperceptible. But in order to assess the difference between the two *Susanna*s, a brief comparison between two other paintings may be illuminating. In *The Toilet of Bathshebah*, in the Metropolitan Museum of Art in New York, we see a naked woman, according to the Biblical story of II Samuel 11, being prepared for royal rape (Figure 4.13). The *story*, which will be extensively discussed in Chapter 6, includes a scene of voyeurism: King David, standing idly on the roof of his palace, sees the naked Bathshebah taking a bath, and his lust is kindled. Although the rooftop can be seen in the background of the painting, the voyeur himself is not visible. The nakedness of the woman, emphasized by her passivity, is the real subject matter of this painting. The two women who help her prepare her toilet only enhance the importance of her display: She is being made ready to be a perfect object, first of the gaze, then of the rape for which the gaze is a preparation or at least a substitute. Her hand on her breast does not seem to have meaning other than to attract attention to her nakedness itself. This woman also looks at the viewer, but this look is not related to any internal focalizer position. Hence, it works for voyeurism and is as acquiescent as the look of the woman in Figure 4.3. The invitation to the gaze is close to being conflated with the invitation to rape, for which the pre-textual David took his visual

4.13   *The Toilet of Bathshebah*
1643, Bredius 513, pancl, 57.2 ×
76.2 cm (New York,
Metropolitan Museum of Art)

168

experience. The *Lucretia* works have amply demonstrated the inherent relation between a certain kind of visuality – the appropriating gaze – and rape.

In contrast, the naked woman in the *Danae*, in the Hermitage in Leningrad, looks away from the viewer (Figure 4.14). According to Schama's well-documented study of 1985, this painting has suffered as much as the sketches from the charge of "ugliness," although it is hard, today, to imagine why. Even Kenneth Clark's somewhat ambivalent appraisal, quoted earlier, does not counter the sense of attraction the painting seems to convey.[38]

As for the inscription of (anti)voyeurism, not only does the figure look away from the viewer, but more importantly, as I have suggested in the Introduction, the figure's look is embedded in a structure of focalization that undermines the possibility of voyeurism generated by the display of her body. In fact, the painting thematizes and problematizes voyeurism; it does not cater to it. The woman is represented as naked in her most private space, on her bed. But her nakedness does not make her into a passive object for visual appropriation. Where Bathshebah was represented in her emphatic passivity, this woman derives power from her body, by the very fact that it is almost exposed offensively. Her beauty, desired by both the pre-textual desiring Zeus and the viewer, is not an object for possession taking. She emphatically disposes of it herself.

As I mentioned before, the hand she raises directs us. In combination with the look of the servant (an internal focalizer) behind the curtain, the hand dismisses the gaze. The implied onlooker is forced to follow the narrative structure of focalization and look with the servant, with the woman, somewhere else. Had the internal focalizer not been represented, then the gesture would have been deprived of its narrative status and become empty, a pretext for a better look at her body. The powerful arm, which makes us aware of this woman's self-disposal, certainly does not preclude the viewing of her body, but it does enforce awareness of that act of viewing, and that awareness shifts the viewing posture from the gaze to the glance.

Compared to this contrast, the earlier *Susanna* (Figure 4.15) lacks precisely those features that implicate the viewer and encourage awareness of the latter's own position. We must begin by acknowledging that this work is more directly connected to the voyeuristic Susanna tradition as documented by Garrard. If the preceding re-

4.14 *Danae*, detail

marks are correct, then the fact that the men are supposed to be hidden in the bushes modifies the ideological positions suggested by the painting, thus inviting the viewer to engage in the easy and safe position of the gaze. And Garrard's iconographic interpretation of the bushes themselves as lustful foliage, reminding viewers of the garden of earthly delight, supports this view. Additional aspects that contribute even more to this effect are the draperies, so luxurious that they evoke a bed rather than an outdoor stone bench; the conventional naked foot, which traditionally represents the act of undressing, hence, availability; and the ample space left between Susanna and the water, which suggests the possibility of escape. Not much is left of the sense of immediate danger, of strong appeal for help, or the ridiculing of the Elders.

Yet, even here, a global judgment precludes insight into the subtleties of visual narrative, for other aspects counter this voyeuristic setup. In terms of iconographic traditions, the pose of Susanna is less strictly tied to the Medici Venus, and thus there is a less direct evocation of a traditionally erotic meaning. Susanna's pose is in general less elegant than in the later picture, her gestures are more strongly defensive, and her face is equally turned to the external viewer.

But Susanna's look is not connected to any narrative structure of internal focalization. It is this denarrativized look directed toward the external viewer that, to my mind, makes for the more erotic, voyeuristic sense the work as a whole suggests. Compared to the later work, there is not, here, a structure of looking wherein Susanna has a place on the same footing as the men, and even has the last word. The position of the hidden voyeurs is completely severed from that of the woman. As a consequence, we have two separate and only superficially related narratives.

The one is the narrative of male voyeurism. We are invited to share the position of the internal focalizer hidden in the bushes; just like we viewers in the gallery, this voyeur is out of reach, unseen by Susanna. She does not participate in this narrative other than as a passive and unaware object of the gaze. It is because Susanna does not see the voyeur that her look, directed at the external viewer, is not related to that primary, internal focalizer. Her look initiates the second narrative: It is the story of an exposed woman who,

4.15 *Susanna at the Bath*, detail

although trying to hide her nakedness, looks back. In the later painting, her mouth was slightly opened, as if she were about to speak or scream for help. But in this earlier painting, her mouth is closed. One can argue about the meaning of the eyes, and some viewers will find them more connotative of vulnerability than will others. But neither her mouth nor her look explicitly seems to call for help, support, or protection.

In narrative terms, the painting has now lost its unity. Although this heterogeneity can itself function as a self-reflexive sign, drawing attention to the representation itself and thus discouraging identification with the voyeur position, for me it does not function in this way, because the lack of unity is itself hidden in the marginalization of narrativity. For me, this figure resembles the woman in Figure 4.3 more closely than it does the woman in Figure 4.4. The eyes are less intense, more conventional. In spite of its pictorial qualities, in terms of its narrative subtleties and the ideological consequences they may entail, this picture does not come up to the standards of either Gentileschi's or the later "Rembrandt" *Susanna*. The question that remains is, then, whether there is a relationship between narrative and ideological *finesse*.

THROUGH THE LOOKING GLASS

Ultimately, the sense in which focalization as a narrative position and voyeurism as an erotic one join forces is related to the status of visual technique itself. The distinction between gaze and glance is also related to the technical issue of visual representation: It is certainly not coincidental that the perfection of voyeurism was offered in the twentieth century through the technical perfection of the cinema. It is this question of representation that is raised by the later, Berlin *Susanna* (Figure 4.16). Two details remain to be considered, and it is those details that undermine the unity of the image as a traditional seduction scene, and insert an alternative reading: the navel of the text. First, the gaze of the Elder closest to Susanna undermines the assumed line of sight, to the point of undermining the subject as a whole. If we look at his look, we cannot fail to notice that this man is not looking at the body he is about to unveil at all. Instead, he is examining Susanna's hair. Second, unlike the drawing in Figure 4.9, where the Elder who

4.16 *Susanna and the Elders*, detail

171

touched Susanna lifted his finger of the law, the Elder who touches and undresses Susanna in the Berlin picture uses his hand not to point but to hold. He clenches his right fist around something; yet there is nothing visible in that hand. This leaves an empty space as a powerful visual zero-sign (*zero priem*; Lotman, 1980), encouraging the viewer to imagine the fictitious object he may hold. And this is precisely what can set the critical machine in motion.

I propose that we see these two details in relation one to the other and that we consider them as central to understanding the painting, as they are literally central. The intense look of the man's eyes goes through the object his fist is (ostensively *not*) holding. Hence, the object is related to looking, and specifically, looking at Susanna's hair. What can this hair suggest that makes it worth this enigmatically displaced looking? As I suggested in Chapter 1, compared to the Lastman *Susanna*, which hangs next to this work in the gallery in Berlin and which is assumed to be its iconographic model, the hair in the "Rembrandt" is triply elaborated.

Lastman's Susanna has loose hair, which might suggest that she is quite loose herself. The "Rembrandt" Susanna has her hair elaborately dressed; it has a scarf plaited through it and it is adorned with pearls. This attention paid to her hair does more than deny the possible suggestion of sexual looseness proposed by the Lastman.[39] It is also iconic for the elaboration of the painted surface. The surface to which the Elder's look is so intensely drawn is different from that of the rest of the painting: It is more delicately painted, more fully elaborated, "fine" rather than "rough."

Rembrandt's rough impasto is rightly famous, and Alpers (1988) has underscored its importance. What its emphatic use suggests is that we not take it for granted. For Alpers, the impasto is self-reflexive, drawing attention to the paint *as* paint. I would suggest that this meaning is emphasized in some cases by the represented look, which, diverted from the diegetic event it was supposed to be focalizing, focuses precisely on a fragment of painted surface, a fragment in which hardly anything figural is to be seen. Jacob's eyes, in *Jacob Wrestling with the Angel*, if not blind, are looking at a fragment of the painted surface where nothing much is visible but the rough impasto that other parts of the painting lack. The distortion of the character's hip (which, I suggested earlier, represented by the "distortion" of the story, is made erotic rather than aggressive) is thus reinforced by this "distortion" of the look, directed away from the diegetic antagonist toward an apparently irrelevant but in fact central detail: paint.

In the *Susanna*, the Elder looks at finely elaborated paint, deceptively realistic, yet emphatically *worked*. When seen through a magnifying glass, the shining pearls are merely blots of paint, but to the naked eye they are reflections of the desired woman's beauty. Related to the object of this special looking, the object the man is holding, then, can be imagined as a magnifying glass. Not that I want to suggest, of course, that the historical Rembrandt had that in mind; but within the culture in which these works serve now, such an instrument of vision is, so to speak, never far away. One may think of the magnifying glass that "fine" painters use when elaborating details, and that lovers of art use when, in the intimacy of the private sphere, they look at drawings and etchings: All of that can be evoked by this empty sign. And as if to emphasize this self-reflexive critique, the Elder's gaze barely hits the upper line of Susanna's hair, otherwise focusing on the empty surface above it.

A magnifying glass is one of those technical instruments for looking, considered an important advance of scientific knowledge in the visual domain. The technology of vision was in development in the seventeenth century. It was an object of discussion as well as a direction of cultural thinking (Alpers, 1985): It was an *episteme* in Foucault's sense. Visual technique was, then, a kind of visual "text" in the textual community. And as Schama (1987) has demonstrated, Dutch seventeenth-century culture, no less than contemporary culture, was preoccupied with the advantages and dangers of its own progress.

In this painting, the technique the sign evokes, whether through the idea of finesse and connoisseurship or by means of my fictitious magnifying glass, is misused to look at what should be left alone. In its reference to science, the sign reminds us of the metaphors of nature as the female body, analyzed by Evelyn Fox Keller in her seminal *Reflections on Gender and Science* (1985). Not only does voyeurism misuse the female body; science also does, and we only need to read Freud, among many other scientist authors closely, to see how strongly.

This critique concerning misuse of visuality by displacement was made possible in the Berlin painting by the magnifying glass, evoked despite its absence. Instead of using the eye and its extension to improve visual culture, its misuse through looking elsewhere produces unwarranted and harmful power. It modifies the status of the hidden voyeurs of the earlier painting into that of "scientific," technical observers. Establishing a connection between voyeurism and positivistic belief in observation, the empty fist of the Elder thus refers to the position of voyeurism, a position now contiguous with that of the scientific observer.

Excessive scientific interest, which is misused for appropriation, is strongly gendered. Commentaries on the famous Dürer woodcut of the draughtsman practicing perspective, a work cited in so many books on visual art (Figure 4.17), inevitably focus on perspective; most of them miss the genderedness of the image and the distribution of tasks represented.[40] Not only is the scholarly looking draughtsman safely hidden behind the grid that he uses as a technical ploy; he also sits upright, while the female model reclines, exposing her rhetorically covered genitals to him. Most strikingly, the second tool the man uses is an upright stand, supposedly helping him to measure distances but whose phallic status is hard to overlook. This phallic object stands between him and her and supports the prisonlike aspect of the grid. This is, indeed, the *law* of perspective. It turns the female body into a figure. This extreme fetishization of figuration is the perversion of a technical mastery that denies the female body in the very act of appropriating it.

But while the empty fist of the Elder makes us conscious of the link between the voyeur's position and positivistic belief in observation, the absent magnifying glass also becomes a looking glass, a device for self-reflection not only for the work itself, but, in keeping with my conception of the interaction between work and viewer, for the act of viewing. Disturbing the conventional ease with which Western culture uses women's bodies for erotic looking, with or without subsequent touching, the empty fist connotes the emptiness of such pleasure and announces the powerlessness it entails.

That powerlessness cannot be taken lightly, especially not if we read the figure of this Elder through Dürer's *Melencholia*, a figure with which he has both his pose and his sad expression in common (Figure 4.18).[41] Melancholia is a widely popular allegoric figure in the late sixteenth and early seventeenth centuries, and it has been argued to be a pre-text for Rembrandt's early self-portraits.[42] For a contemporary reader informed by Freud's interpretation of melancholia as a state of paralysis caused by failed mourning, the reference to Dürer cannot but evoke the relationship of the Elders to fictitious young Daniel – that is, to their own impotence to act, "Bad looking" is bad, then, because it is bad, not only for the victim in danger of rape, but also for the subject of looking. The reason is that looking is not a simple, positivistic subject–object relation: What is bad for the object is also bad for the subject because it is bad for the relationship between them.

The fictitious magnifying glass shows that *looking through* (a grid or magnifying glass) is a way of ignoring, hence denying, the other as subject. Dematerializing the female body, this "looking" attitude falls back into the mythifying gaze that takes all bodies as versions of the same, masculine or man-possessed essence. This "looking

4.17   Albrecht Dürer,
Draughtsman Drawing a Recumbent Woman 1525, woodcut, 7.5 × 21.5 cm (Berlin, Kupferstichkabinett)

through'' is thus presented as a *per-version*, literally a turning away from the body in the very act of penetrating it. The appropriation thus becomes an act of dispossession.

The possible allusion to melancholia hints at the absence, in the painting, of the redeemer Daniel, who saved Susanna through divine inspiration by striking the Elders with psychic paralysis. The position this figure takes in the story seems vacant in the painting, and for intertextual readers it asks to be filled. Where can "Daniel" be, if there is no divine inspiration but only an image and its viewers? The looking glass, suggesting *self-reflexion* to the Elder and distance from him to the viewer, is doubled, on the side of the viewer, by a *self-reflection* addressed to him or her only. Susanna's foot is reflected in the water, and that reflection is visible for the viewer, not for the Elders.[43] In the post-Freudian era, a foot set off from the rest of the body cannot but evoke fetishism. In this respect, this reflected foot reflects the strand of hair the Elder is looking at: Both are detached, and therefore, meaningless body parts; both belong to Susanna and not to the person watching them, taking visual possession of them. The reflection of the detached body-part signifies "fiction," "inaccessibility," "otherness," and precludes our appropriation of the body by synecdochic extension – fetishism – proposing instead that we reflect on what it is we are doing when looking at a female body, ready to touch it.

In the story, the position of Daniel was a horizontal one: He stood for righteousness, justified by divine command. It was also

4.18 Albrecht Dürer, *Melencholia I* 1514, engraving, 23.9 × 16.8 cm (Berlin, Kupferstichkabinett)

175

a polemically verbal one, for Daniel's participation in the viewing of Susanna was interrupted by the divine voice. In the painting, the position of Daniel has become a horizontal one, not justifiable any longer by transcendental righteousness, but an index of the negotiable position between the woman and the viewer. It is also a verbal one, another place where words come to interact with vision. But instead of the divine logos, the slippery language of criticism is available for that negotiation.[44] The language of criticism is, then, a double displacement of Daniel's position. From transcendental righteousness that needs no further justification, the position has shifted to a problematic but active, indexical position to which each viewer relates in her or his own way. And offering a possibility to oppose "good seeing" to "bad seeing," the critic displaces Daniel from his self-evident position within the male competition between him and the elders in the name of his god, to a much more risky position, but one that does not exclude the woman. "Daniel," now, has shifted gender, and gender has become unfixed in the move. The look Susanna addresses to the viewer, and the foot she offers for self-reflection, engage a complicated interaction between the different positions involved in gendered visuality.

If initially, upon considering this work, we might have aligned our viewing position with that of the Elder at the right side of the work, we now realize that that position is contaminated by an ideology of the gaze.

CHAPTER 5

RECOGNITION: READING ICONS, SEEING STORIES

INTRODUCTION

Iᴺ his thought-provoking book, *Vision and Painting: The Logic of the Gaze* (1983), Norman Bryson challenges the present state of art history as a discipline, with a long attack on what he calls perceptualism and its inheritance; Bryson's attack includes Gombrich's seemingly pathbreaking work that is, in Bryson's account, only a perpetuation of the same perceptualism.[1] For all his critique of traditional art history, however, Bryson explicitly leaves room for one of the strongest dogmas of traditional art history in the twentieth century: Panofskian iconography.[2] Put simply, an iconographic approach proposes that we *read* art, make sense out of what the image is *not* rather than *viewing* it. Reading iconographically is interpreting visual representation by placing its elements in a tradition that gives them a meaning other than their "immediate" visual appearance suggests. A vase of flowers is not merely a vase of flowers; the little insects on the flowers, not merely insects. Instead, they become signs. Those insects, for example, are the minuscule but undeniable symptoms of decay. As such they are indices, metonymies; and as metonymies they become the master trope that takes over the entire image. By virtue of the convention through which we allow such colonizing of the image, the motivated signs become symbols. Instead of "seeing" the motivated sign, we "read" the conventional sign "automatically." Thus the little insects turn the image into a *vanitas*, a reminder of the temporality of earthly goods. *Vanitas* is the theme, the meaning, and the little insects are the signs that allow that meaning to appear; they are the details (Schor, 1987) that take over, the readable signifier, the *letter*. Reading in this mode Vermeer's *Woman Holding a Balance*, in the National Gallery in Washington, does not merely "mean" a woman weighing her pearls, nor does it mean that we should identify God with women as judges of the world of men. It means, again, *vanitas*, and the signs that tell iconographic readers so are the contrasting elements: the mundane activity of counting her wealth juxtaposed against the allegorical painting of the Last Judgment, hanging on the wall of the represented space.

The interesting point of iconographic reading, though, is not so much the theme that the signs point up, but the signifying force that emanates from those tiny details. Those tiny details can gain their signifying force, however, only when the viewer reads them "correctly," and doing so requires several first steps. First, the viewer must resist the tendency to process the details sheerly as "effects of the real," as mere details to fill in the surface of a usual work, for such emptiness in visual works is intolerable. The viewer must not assume that the details are mere symptoms of realist representation designed to make viewers forget the work of representation itself. The little insects and the fading edges of flower petals can be explained away only too easily as the realistic details an iconographic reading would have us deny. Second, the viewer must know the conventional idiom of visual representation, must be "literate" enough in visual traditions to recognize the signs as part of a culture in which this act of viewing is taking place. And third, the viewer must be "well read" enough to recognize the "ideologeme" (Jameson, 1981), the Renaissance dogma of *vanitas* or *memento mori* or, in the case of a narrative, the story and its other details, so that the sign can evoke the doxic text as a whole.

This part standing for the whole, or the synecdochical relationship built into iconographic interpretation, is one of the ways in which the problematic of interpretation and that of the sign are conflated. The very fact that the sign can impart to the viewer an interpretation of the work as a whole through reference to another, textual work as a whole, makes this mode of reading basically a discursive one. But iconography is also discursive in a more fundamental sense, a sense not contingent upon the (to some extent, accidentally) verbal pre-text. Iconographic reading is itself a discursive mode of reading because it subordinates the visually represented element to something else, thus privileging the symbol at the expense of the icon, while displacing the indexicality that allowed this semiosis in the first place. Iconography means, literally, writing by means of images. It is this challenge to the unwarranted assumption that visual art is iconic and verbal art symbolic that turns the iconographic mode of reading into a powerful critical tool, a tool that can be used to undermine the opposition between word and image.

In this chapter, I shall discuss iconography as a useful yet limited code, a code which like all others can be used to ward off threatening interpretations, to fit the works into a reassuring tradition, but which can also be taken beyond its most obvious use to yield a powerful critical reading. Iconography is both a vulnerable and a productive central dogma in art history as a traditional discipline. It is in the name of iconography that some art historians cut off the dialogue with literary scholars who "invade" or, as I prefer to say, "visit" the field; yet iconography itself contains and generates verbality in the very core of art history which xenophobic scholars feel most constrained to defend against it.[3]

The most obvious place where iconography stands in continuity with discursivity is where the details signify not a doxic concept but a doxic story. In those works the narrative which the detail inserts into the reading of the image imports a textual story, like "Susanna," "Joseph," or "Lucretia." And the narrativity imported is not necessarily visual either, but can remain predominantly textual. However, the narrative imported does not preclude other readings; visual storytelling and the reading thereof are able to produce competing narratives that stand in tension with the doxic story. I shall argue for that tension – for its existence and for its productivity. I shall argue that both the iconographic and the visual-narrative modes of reading need to be acknowledged, exploited, and maintained concurrently. But, rather than advocating a dialectic solution, I shall argue for maintaining the tension, a tension that is unresolvable, dynamic, that makes possible a reading attitude wherein recognition is the primary, but never a stable nor reliable, tool.

THE TELLTALE DOG, OR ONE WOMAN TOO MANY

In a verbal text, the mention of a dog accompanying a character setting out on a journey will at first be processed merely as "the little detail that rings true." Thus the dog mentioned in the Book of Tobit, accompanying Tobias and his guardian Raphael on their journey, is read mostly as a realistic detail. Only if the story were to assign a narrative function to the dog later on would it be perceived as a functional agent and its earlier mention read as proleptic; in the Book of Tobit this does not happen.

The story is a complex and convoluted, relatively late and un-canonized Biblical narrative. The Book of Tobit presents the story of a righteous man, his wife Anna, and his son Tobias. One day when he is taking a nap in the courtyard, a swallow deposits a veil on Tobit's eyes, and he is blinded. Tobit loses his wealth and becomes poor, remaining god-fearing and good. He sends his only son Tobias to collect a debt in the land of a far-away relative. The concerned parents provide the boy with a guide, not knowing that the guide is the angel Raphael incognito. *In the meantime* Tobias's cousin Sarah, the daughter of the distant relative, has been married seven times, but to no avail: Her husbands die during the wedding night. The girl is desperate and wishes to die. Her mother comforts her. On the way, Tobias catches an enormous fish, and he is frightened. Raphael helps him with the catch and tells him to keep the liver for later use. When they arrive at the relative's house, Tobias wishes to marry his cousin. He uses the fish's liver to burn away the evil spirit, and he does not die. After collecting the debt, Tobias returns home, triumphant. Still under the instructions of Raphael, Tobias then removes the veil from his father's eyes. Of this story, many episodes have become favorite subjects for painting: the old man sleeping in the courtyard, the catch of the fish, the departure of the evil spirit, the "operation" on Tobit's eyes, and the various goodbye scenes.

So the little dog, in the book of Tobit, is merely a detail. In the tradition of interpretation of visual representations of Biblical stories, however, a little dog in some corner of the work is not accepted as merely "meaning" a dog, nor does it merely produce an effect of the real; it might also have a more specific meaning: For example, it might be read as a "device to foreshorten the space" as in copies of Leonardo's *Last Supper* (see Steinberg's formalist reading, "Leonardo," 1974:395), or, as in Figure 5.1, it might make the viewer process the work as an "episode from the story of Tobias." The former reading is based on an indexical signification of a pictorial element; the latter, on an indexical identification between image and pre-text. In both cases the interpretation of the dog establishes a continuity with the tradition in which, by some historical accident, a little dog tends to be represented as a sign for this particular verbal background. The sign is an index, and the rhetoric at work in this decoding is both synecdochical and metonymical. Just like the insects in flower petals, the dog places the work within a tradition as a whole (synecdoche), which in its turn operates by contiguity or "influence" (metonymy).[4] These would both be typical cases of iconographic readings.

Bryson proposes to accommodate iconography within his approach by revitalizing the obsolete distinction between denotation and connotation, which is so uneasy for verbal art.[5] His argument

5.1 *The Farewell of Tobias* (*Raguel Welcomes Tobias*) ca. 1651, Benesch 871, drawings, 192 × 271 mm (Amsterdam, Rijksprentenkabinet)

runs as follows: Iconographical elements operate through *recogni-tion*; that is, we do not so much see a dog as *know* that a dog means /Tobias/, just as we know that the word "table" means /table/. We do not doubt this interpretation, anymore than we doubt our in-terpreting a word in our own language; we learn to take both those conventional references as primary, self-evident, and absolute in-formation – as denotative.[6] This absolute quality of denotation is historically variable, as we learn to recognize in relation to what Bryson calls the "social formation," but at any given moment in time, recognition is in itself absolute, nevertheless. In Bryson's work, the signifying relationship between these signs and their meaning also tends to be textual or verbal, as opposed to visual. Thus, by recognizing the story through the little dog, we decode the sign as a synecdoche for the story as a whole. This is what makes the iconographic detail so fundamentally verbal: Not only does it import into the image an entire story with all its verbal elements, but it also operates through the discursive rhetorical strat-egies of meaning production to do so. In addition, this operation is antivisual: The image that we *see* is subordinated to the meanings we *know*.

At the other end of iconographic reading, Bryson sees conno-tation as what is, informationally, excessive. He uses the rather infelicitous term "semantic neutrality" (Bryson, 1983:62) to refer to all the elements that, after the subject has been determined on the basis of iconographical denotation, further fill in the image so that it becomes full text. These connotative elements are *nonexplicit* and *polysemic* (Bryson, 1983:71).

Although I have some problems with the dichotomy thus estab-lished, or rather, maintained, its didactic value as a demonstration of the readerliness of iconography is immediately obvious when we try to explain, for example, why a drawing represents an episode from the story of Tobias (Figure 5.1). We recognize the dog as related to traveling, and on the basis of yet another cultural com-monplace we recognize the farewell scene. The best known farewell scene in the story of Tobias comes to mind first: Let us assume that the drawing represents the moment that Tobias leaves his parents to visit his distant relative whose daughter he is eventually to marry. We see the older man embrace the youth. Among the many possible, culturally available farewell scenes, this one is re-lated "self-evidently" to the apocryphal Biblical story because of the little dog, which, although hardly visible between the father-and-son and the man at the left, takes up the only empty space between the five standing figures. The little dog is a sufficient indication for the "well-read" viewer to recognize this particular scene.

The other elements then fall easily into place, and the verbal story colonizes the image. The little dog helps us make sense of the specific figures included in the representation. The man standing at the left *must be* the angel Raphael who will accompany the young man on his quest for adulthood and will secure his safe return. He lacks the wings angels tend to have in the Christian tradition, but this does not bother the iconographic reader; it is consistent with the story wherein Tobias is explicitly said not to know that the fellow is an angel. The old woman on the right must be Anna, Tobias's mother, for her old age is mentioned several times in the story. That this act of reading is not inevitable, that it is not inscribed in the drawing but imported by the viewer, appears when we try to apply other possible readings, both from the book of Tobit and from other Biblical or non-Biblical books. Yet the certainty with which scholars assert their readings of the drawing, even if they differ widely in their precise location of the scene within the story, seems to confirm the idea that there is an *illusion of denotation* at work.[7]

Through the reassuring certainty the little dog brings to the viewer's identification of the scene, other possibly problematic elements in the work are taken care of. Once we recognize the image as the first farewell scene of the story, we are not in the least troubled by the woman-in-excess in this drawing, the veiled second woman who has no place in this episode of the story. The certainty provided by the iconographic detail allows us either to ignore her because she is not relevant or to process her in terms of the story.

There are several possibilities of interpreting the woman-in-excess here, too. One could ignore the woman or her strangeness, her excessiveness, which would confirm Lacan's notion of woman as excess, as outside the exchange of images. Or one could readily incorporate her by changing the reading through ignoring other details such as her veil, as Benesch does in his entry in the catalog. But this would merely confirm this Lacanian view in another way. Avoiding these two repressions, we can process the woman in at least two different ways. The more general interpretation is to see her as a servant. This fits the story as well as it fits the "effect of the real" hypothesis; and, thus, it provides a hinge between narrative and realist readings. It exploits the space produced by iconographic recognition of the story while exceeding iconographic reading itself, since no servant is mentioned in the story.

But we can also interpret the woman by employing a different, more directly narrative mode of reading; we can see in this figure a proleptic allusion to the woman-in-excess whose acquisition will be the outcome of the journey just beginning. She then becomes the demon-possessed Sarah, who, once domesticated by the safely initiated Tobias, will be brought by him to his parents' home. Such a reading of the second woman, although operating on nonexplicitness and polysemy (she does not require interpretation, and if she does she can be both a servant and Sarah), is no less based on recognition of the theme. It is equally verbal and, for those who adopt either reading, equally likely.

But is this reading of the woman, initiated by the little dog, another case of iconographic-denotative processing as well? The verbal pre-text, a remarkably complex narrative, seems to mention the dog merely as an index of the effect of the real: "The boy and the angel left the house together, and the dog came out with him and accompanied them" (6:1). Hence, the dog could be represented merely to help us recognize the text; neither artist nor reader needs to *read* the story; it is enough to have it as part of one's doxic knowledge. Decoding it in relation to the farewell is already a more specific demonstration of being "well-read."

But knowing the text doxically would mean knowing it only for what it narrates, the fabula; knowing it as verbal text would mean also knowing it structurally. The story makes explicit mention of the simultaneity of the two lines of the story. The first is Tobit's blindness and his subsequent prayer to God for deliverance; the second is Sarah's demonic lethality (which had already killed seven prospective husbands) and her prayer for deliverance after considering suicide. Hence, the symmetry between Tobias's departure as a consequence of his father's blindness and his arrival at his cousin's as a consequence of her lethality is significant. If Tobias's voyage is an initiation, his successful battle against the evil spirit and the subsequent marriage are its outcome.

Here is the description of the moment immediately preceding the departure scene which our reading projects as represented in the drawing: "At the moment when Tobit went back from the courtyard into his house, Sarah daughter of Raguel came down from the attic" (3:17). This simultaneity of the actions of both protagonists, which were temporarily separated from the daily environment, lends to both their experiences a flavor of initiation as defined in anthropological theory.[8] Given the seriousness of the problems they both have to deal with – the father's blindness and the woman's lethality (both of which shall be related to sexual impotence) – the emphatic simultaneity might concern a *rite of passage*, displaced from Tobias, the subject of initiation, onto his father and his future bride. Not only does the text develop these two lines, it explicitly ties them together in a very specific and emphatic simultaneity.

This narration of concurrence is the symmetrical counterpart of the comic-strip device of sequential narrative art; whereas visual narrative needs specific devices to represent episodes that succeed one another temporally, verbal narrative needs specific devices to represent simultaneously occurring events causally. Both are quite effective as long as the reader/viewer is capable of integrating visual and verbal modes of reading. And for the reader who is capable of such an integration, the narratological structure of the verbal story is thus integrated into the visual work.

The simultaneity in the narrative is enhanced in the drawing; at least, if we take the veiled woman as referring to Sarah. There are good reasons for this accentuation: As I noted above, Tobias, through his initiation, is going to cure both his father's blindness and Sarah's lethal quality. This link suggests that the two are related.

And indeed they are, quite strongly. Blindness traditionally (and in "Rembrandt" specifically) is related to castration, and this particular blindness is described in the text as a *veil* covering Tobit's eyes. The word "veil," strongly evoking the hymen that Tobias will successfully pierce, establishes a *verbal* connection between Tobit's and Sarah's problem. This connection is then *verbally* read and *visually* represented in those Tobias works where the young man uses a pointed instrument to *pierce* the blind eyes of his father, which he does after successfully piercing the woman's veil. The woman-in-excess, in the drawing, is holding the veil that covers her mouth with her left hand. Is she holding it up, or is she about to remove it? In the one case, one could venture, she insists that it be Tobias who removes it; in the other, she signifies the anticipation of the removal for which Tobias's travel is the preparation. Again, then, a narrative device is used, and a verbal mode of reading is at work.

This verbal simultaneity would allow us to consider the interpretation of the overcomplete woman as an iconographically denotative sign; however, the pictorial iconographic tradition does not systematically include Sarah in the farewell scene. Thus we may have to distinguish between various kinds or degrees of iconographic denotation. Although the signs of the dog and the woman are visual in both, in the first case the reference is needed to help the reader recognize the preceding visual tradition, which in turn refers to the verbal text; in the second case the recognition is directly related to the text and works with the text's verbal devices. We must then reserve the term "denotation" in Bryson's revised sense or, as I would prefer, the term "iconographical sign" for the sign that travels the visual–verbal route. The sign based upon the solely verbal reference then falls under the more encompassing concept of intertextuality and exemplifies the subcategory of pre-textual thematic reference.[9]

Semiotically, both the dichotomy between denotation and connotation, and the standard procedure of iconographic interpretation as such are insufficient. The reference to the story produced on the basis of the little dog does not determine the subject of the story by itself; nor does it do so immediately. We need more information, and we may need that other information first to determine the subject (even if we cannot know in any concrete sense what exactly the reader of the drawing does and in which order).[10] The Popperian procedure of conjecture and refutation seems a more likely account of the reading process than the Saussurian determining of the signified /Tobias/ as inhering unproblematically in the signifier "little dog," and this is one of the problems that exemplifies the undeniably Saussurian implications of Bryson's terminology and its dualistic flavor. The dog becomes relevant at the moment of "refutation" rather than at the moment of "conjecture"; the dog provides the supporting and decisive evidence rather than the primary sign. Nor is it, after all, a sufficient indication of the subject.

Its merit, however, can hardly be overrated: The dog hints at the woman *and* her proleptic meaning, her visual strangeness and excessiveness, which can then be acknowledged and emphasized, as well as meaningfully integrated.

HAGAR'S HARROW

The vocabulary of iconographic reading cannot, however, be fixed.[11] The following drawing, for example, is also a farewell scene, but not a Tobias (Figure 5.2). In composition it is quite similar to the Tobias drawing we just discussed. It also has a little dog, even a much more explicit one in terms of visual representation; yet the dog does not lead us to recognize a Tobias scene. Figure 5.2 depicts the expulsion of Hagar and Ishmael, and more than anything else the difference between the tender embrace of the father in the Tobias drawing and the patriarchal gestures of power in this one sharply distinguishes the sense of hopeful suspense in the former drawing from the despair in the latter. Reading the dog as decisive for the theme might make us forget that the difference between the two works is related primarily to the status of the sons: the only son, the hope of his parents, versus the superfluous, dispossessed son, whose mother is by definition rejectable.[12]

In a different sense, the woman in this second farewell scene is also in excess: Hagar was a handmaid of Sarah, Abraham's wife. When Sarah did not conceive, she asked Abraham to father a child with Hagar, so that Sarah would own the child. When much later Sarah conceived herself and bore Isaac, she did not want Hagar's son to share Isaac's inheritance, and she asked Abraham to dismiss

5.2 *Hagar's Dismissal* ca. 1652–3, Benesch 916, drawing, 172 × 224 mm (Amsterdam, Rijksprentenkabinet)

Hagar. The moment that is often visually represented is the one in which Abraham grants Sarah's wish.

Clearly the meaning of the little dog cannot be fixed. In the Tobias drawing, the dog was an unambiguous sign: a sign for the recognition of a particular cultural unit, which, unstable as it is, can be recognized.[13] In this Hagar drawing, the dog does not work in the same way. We do not need to read it as a sign in order to recognize the theme, but we may still recognize it and process it as a sign. In such a case the little dog might refer us to the Tobias tradition, extending the meaning of the dog to farewell scenes in general. Thus, from a specific narrative synecdoche, it would become a common noun in the vocabulary of departure. With this extension into generality, the dog's meaning becomes diluted and its operation less important, less narrative, and less informative; yet it is still iconographic. But we may also read the dog in the Hagar drawing as falling within Bryson's category of connotation, as the excess, the superfluous that works to provide the arbitrary denotation with the status of truth, the visual effect of the real. As Bryson formulates it:

[T]he "effect of the real" consists in a specialised relationship between denotation and connotation, where *connotation so confirms and substantiates denotation that the latter appears to rise to the level of truth.* (Bryson, 1983:62; emphasis in text)

In other words, the little dog is either a relatively autonomous sign, meaning /farewell scene/ or it is a connotative element that, in concert with other elements – like the house, the path descending

5.3   *Hagar's Dismissal* (London, British Museum)

186

into the space of traveling outside the frame, the staff carried by the boy, and the bag carried by the woman in the Hagar drawing – signifies situation, setting, and reality.

This drawing, too, can be recognized by "reading for the theme," but not through the little dog. One of the signs that lets us do so is the hunting equipment carried by the boy, which the iconographic tradition assigns to Hagar's son Ishmael. Although Panofsky's account of iconography does not assume a one-to-one correspondence between visual and verbal material, there often is a textual detail that becomes much more significant in the visual tradition. Thus the boy's hunting equipment seems so decisive because Genesis 21:21 has it that "he became an archer."[4] On that basis we can process the drawing in Figure 5.3 as representing Hagar's expulsion.

In that work we also recognize Abraham's ambivalence through his "speaking hands," blessing Ishmael with his right hand and admonishing Hagar with the other, resembling Adam in the etching discussed in the previous chapter (Figure 4.11) and the Elder with the raised finger in Figure 4.9. The combination of the three figures in the drawing and their gestures is enough to make viewers conjecture, and the quiver enough to confirm after trying to refute.

When "reading for the theme," this drawing is amply redundant; the quiver is enough to recognize Hagar's departure even in the next drawing (Figure 5.4), although Abraham, Sara, the house, and the road are not represented. We must recognize Hagar here because we have seen her so often in company of the quiver bearer. But this sort of iconographic reading does not, or should not, operate alone, for over*reading* leads to *under*reading. Exclusive attention to, or privileged interpretation of, these iconographic signs diverts attention from other signs that may be less recognizable but perhaps more important to a significant interpretation of the drawings. What do we make, for example, of Hagar's gesture of despair, contrasting with Abraham's patriarchal gestures in Figures 5.2 and 5.3, and complemented by Ishmael's surprised and sympathetic look in Figure 5.4? Her gesture is a sign, for it suggests meaning; it elicits recognition, for on the basis of our knowledge of the story we know how bleak Hagar's situation is. Yet it is not as "denotative" as the quiver; we can ignore it, while we cannot ignore the latter and still recognize the story.

The quiver in Figure 5.4 has the same status as the dog in Figure 5.1, whereas the dog in Figure 5.2 is polysemic. But the dog in this drawing is not polysemic in the same way as the veiled woman in Figure 5.1, whom we could also place as a kind of verbally based iconographic, pre-textual sign and whose status hovered between that of servant (an effect of the real, that is) and that of bride. The dog is here rather a generic marker of the type scene, which we may want to call a cotextual sign.[5] In both cases, that of the little dog in the first of the Hagar drawings and the veiled woman in the Tobias drawing, a strict distinction between iconographic and redundant, or, if you like, between denotative and connotative readings, encourages us to oversimplify and, hence, to obscure the different sign events in favor of the recognition of theme, type scene, dogma, or specific narrative content. This limitation and the blinding effect can occur if iconographic reading is privileged exclusively.

Iconography is, of course, not as simplistic a procedure as my example suggests. One complicating factor is the fact that iconography does not distinguish between (abstract and static) themes and the narratives from which these themes are often derived. The synecdochical principle makes any element of a story an iconographic sign for recognition, and, as we have seen, even the most unimportant element will do. Once the story is recognized, nothing prevents the reader from using the story in all its complexity to process other elements of the visual work. If understood as a reader's response, recognition can be helpful, not blinding but eye-opening, a means to enhance awareness of the cultural process every act of reading or viewing is involved in. Recognition can also trigger a critical response that would not be possible without iconographical support. In the following section I shall demonstrate this.

5.4 *Hagar and Ishmael* ca. 1649–50, Benesch 648, drawing, 140 × 96 mm (London, British Museum)

188

THE CONTINUING STORY:
HAGAR TODAY

Before presenting my argument for iconography-in-tension, I want to draw attention to the critical possibilities of iconographical reading. I shall use a verbal example – albeit visual in many aspects – in order to demonstrate that iconography does not apply exclusively to the interpretation of visual art. The figure of Hagar with its long tradition of representing the oppressed, the slave, the woman-in-excess is so much part of our cultural vocabulary that it makes a good case for the importance of iconography in cultural analysis in general. The figure also makes a good case for the critical connections between art and social reality. Hagar's expulsion is acutely present in the social novel *Uncle Tom's Cabin*, and reemerges in the 1980s in Alice Walker's polemical rewriting of this popular novel in her equally popular *The Color Purple* (1982). That novel was, in turn, visualized by Steven Spielberg's very popular film of 1986. Both Hagar and the works' popularity are relevant for my argument.

The contribution of iconography to cultural analysis lies in the way it helps us answer the question, Why did I, and many critics, consider Steven Spielberg's film *The Color Purple* an ideological and artistic failure, in spite of its obvious attractions to a large audience? I contend that this was so because the movie failed to represent the iconographic basis of the combative ideological position that Walker's novel proposed. Ignoring iconography, it ignored the novel's embeddedness in, and response to, a cultural tradition. A brief discussion of this case will allow us, therefore, to see how iconographic reading can be exploited to enhance a critical ideological position, rather than fostering the conformism that it is so often alleged to imply.

A work of art entertains at least three systematic relationships: one with the cotext or the literary and artistic environment, one with the historical context that frames it, and one with the preceding artistic tradition, the pre-text.[16] *The Color Purple* as a novel, as a response to social and literary issues, and as an ideological work, plays out these relationships in many ways. On the one hand, the novel revitalizes elements of African-American religious traditions; on the other hand, it responds explicitly to *Uncle Tom's Cabin*. I shall limit my remarks here to the latter elements, but it should be borne in mind that the former are constantly in interaction with the latter.[17]

Stowe's novel is alleged to have contributed to the abolition of slavery; hence, by referring to it, Walker provides her novel with a similar, yet modified goal: to contribute to the abolition of the oppression of black women. In both cases, a work of fiction responds to a social problem. And in this respect, *Tom* is among *Color*'s pre-texts.

This relationship, in turn, should show us that *Tom* needs to be replaced within a context out of which its very popularity has lifted it in later times: the context of slave literature. A few years before *Tom*, Frederick Douglass (1845/1982) published his autobiography – a nonfictional report on slavery; like *Tom*, it was also written for propaganda purposes. Douglass's text may well be the most widely read of slave narratives, although it is only one among many of the genre, which together form one cotext for *Tom*. Douglass's work is in many ways dramatically different from Stowe's, not only ideologically and historically. The one wrote from and about his own tragedy whereas the other, although writing for the sake of the slaves, could not but be confined in her own, privileged class.[18] But the slave narratives are, precisely for that reason, the cotext in which *Tom* appeared: As indexically related to the context of real slavery, they produced the sense of the real, the historical background of which the novel gave a fictional account which they, in turn, authenticated.

The intimate connections with this cotext are easily forgotten. Yet, they imply more than a relationship between facts of slavery and *Tom*. These connections also include the contemporary doxic views of the relationship between literature and social reality in general as expressed in the text's reception. And those views are not very far removed from today's views of the same relationship. Here is a contemporary response to Douglass's work:

The *picture* that it presents of slavery is too horrible to look upon, and yet it is but a faint *picture* of what to millions is a vivid *life*. It is evidently drawn with a *nice eye*, and the *coloring* is *chaste* and *subdued* rather than extravagant or overwrought. *Thrilling* as it is and full of the most *burning eloquence*, it is yet simple and unimpassioned. . . . There are passages in it which would *brighten* the reputation of any living author – while the book as a whole, judged as a mere work of art, would widen the fame of Bunyan or Defoe.[19] (my emphases)

This passage could be published today about a successful feminist novel, for example. The passage is laudatory, and the praise is based on two dichotomies: That between life and art is explicit, whereas that between verbal and visual expression is implicit and related to the first. "Picture," "colored," "nice eye," "brighten" are opposed to both "life" and "eloquence." In addition, the language is strongly sexual, gendered female: The words "chaste" and "subdued" redeem the dangers of "thrilling" and "burning." All this is visible only if we read visually in the same way as with the Susanna text, taking the colors and shades of language as an alternative propositional content.

According to this critic, the author's restrained tone, the "unimpassioned" discourse, is what rescues the work from its "burning eloquence" and the "thrilling" character. If fiction versus reality was the issue, than this opposition between unimpassioned discourse and burning eloquence would by implication seem to praise the nonfictional features of the book.[20] This is where the implicit preference for visuality comes in: It enters through the fear of expressivity, which is, more importantly, a fear of the signifier that Langer was shown to have in Chapter 3.

The first sentence uses the word "picture" twice, even in two opposed senses: as a fictional representation ("too horrible to look upon") versus a real, or realist, document ("but a faint picture . . . of life"). The latter is used in the sense of a real picture of "real life," and as such the book fails; its failure is fortunate, the critic argues, because, *therefore*, it is a better novel, a better work of art. Why is this so?

The expression "nice eye" shows what the literary criterion is: It is visual taste, or artistic arrangement of reality into something pleasant to see; it is tasteful coloring. The eye is the mediator between the horrible reality and the convincing fictional representation that makes the best case – for reality. The double sense of "eye" – the sense of visual perception and interpretation, and, by metaphoric transposition, the sense of taste – makes us aware of the relationship among realism, the social relevance of fictional representation, and visuality. Having "a nice eye" – the token of connoisseurship as of adequate perception – makes a good writer, in the nineteenth-century tradition, a tradition that is still with us. This connection between visuality and taste, hence, literary effectiveness, is as much an element of the cotext as the characteristics of early humanist thought and discourse were to painting in the age of Giotto (Baxandall, 1971).

But this artistic standard is only one side of that tradition, the other side being the generic background of the text. Indeed, the relationship between a work and contemporary reality (say, its context), and the relationship between a work and its predecessors (its pre-text) are the two most often alleged standards for the evaluation of art. Although Harriet Beecher Stowe was less lucky in her critics than was Douglass, the response to both works, and to their contemporary posttexts, have not changed. An analysis of the references to both diffuse, cotextual types and to generic conventions soon makes clear why. Here is a passage from the Introduction to the Harper Classics edition of *Tom* of 1965, written by Jeremy Larner:

Among moralistic fiction, *Uncle Tom's Cabin* is unique in its general compassion and lack of personal hatred. In this sense, it's a woman's novel. As an intelligent woman, Mrs. Stowe occupies a position marginal to the world of politics and vested interests; and she refuses to acknowledge that this world has the face-value importance that men so matter-of-factly attach to it. . . . Whatever weakness a given man may show, Mrs. Stowe, like other good women, *understands*. . . . The woman's touch shows up also in the feminine style of melodrama in *Uncle Tom's Cabin*. The book is long on love, death, and religious conversion; short on action, physical conflict, and feats of heroism . . . the novel's two purest heroes, Uncle Tom and

Little Eva, achieve their greatest glory in eager acceptance of death. (emphasis in text)

I quote this passage at length because it helps us distinguish between various sources of recognition, which a careful "iconographic" interpretor needs to disentangle if she or he is to help criticize the working of the doxa. Therefore, this case bears on the case of "Rembrandt," as we shall soon see. The postulated relationships between the novel and the reality the passage evokes are complex, and run from the book – via the author, her gender, and her personality as a stereotyped woman – back to the novel as belonging to a feminine genre. The position of the novel's author is defined as marginal, her personality as compassionate, and her style as melodramatic; needless to say, the three are related. The latter characterization implies a literary value judgment. Regardless of the fact that the characterization of the novel on which this judgment is based is incorrect,[21] the themes of death, love, and religion are seen as typically feminine, those of action, fighting, and heroism as masculine. Recognition is at work here, but not iconographic, nor even pre-textual recognition. Larner bases his judgments on the recognition of a doxa, a set of more diffuse, cotemporal, and vaguely contextual stereotypes that circumscribe for him the genres, styles, and modes of gendered works. It is here that a self-conscious iconographic reading can make a difference: We can oppose the doxa by "looking" – reading, that is, against the safety of stereotyped images that do not even need to be present in the text so long as they are present in the culture.

When Larner blames the author for leaving important events rather vague – like the relationship between the proud Cassy and her cruel master Legree which "had to wait for William Faulkner to be brought to light" (xii) – or for elaborating them in a stereotypical manner – like the relationship between George and Eliza – we begin to see how the contextual stereotyping precludes iconographic – that is, cotextual and pre-textual – recognition of elements. Reading with the clichés of the doxa precludes acknowledging the difference the work makes, precludes acknowledging the different "version" of the "same" old story which, I argued in Chapter 3, is an altogether different work. Thus, we arrive at a point where the recognition of preceding models to which a work alludes can help neutralize ideological misjudgments, and where iconography, by virtue of its traditionalism, becomes the tool that undermines the doxic tradition.

In the first place, the sentimental novel is less a feminine genre than a widely popular genre in nineteenth-century literature, except that when men wrote it, we called it realism. The description of Tom's cabin, at the opening of Chapter IV, applies better to Balzac's famous opening of *Le père Goriot* or to certain passages from Dickens, than it matches a vague sense of femininity. But in the second place, the romantic ending of reunited families – in fact, the symmetrical counterpart of the visual farewell scene – although indeed conventional in the nineteenth-century social novel, cannot be detached from a literary tradition either: Such an ending is typical of comedy. Contextual judgment must yield to co- and pre-textual recognition. Certain cotexts – the comedies of Shakespeare, Molière, and Corneille, for example – bind *Tom* together with themselves into a genre, as distinct from tragedy, even if, sometimes, there is not much else "comic" in the modern sense. And the nineteenth-century novel's inscription within this comic tradition endorses a literary allegiance that Larner ignores. When Stowe gave a tragedy about slaves a double ending – Tom's tragic death and the happy reunion of George and Eliza's family – she provided an ending suitable to the two genres, integrated into what *thereby* becomes the "sentimental novel" of the nineteenth century.[22]

Stowe actually connects the contemporary "sentimental novel" to Shakespeare and the Renaissance tradition, when, in Chapter XLII, two women, Cassy and Emmeline, frighten the wicked slaveholder Legree with spooky effects, brought about with white sheets. The narrator comments that the people were frightened because they did not remember that Shakespeare also did this in his comedies; because they lacked the necessary iconographic vocabulary and reading skill, they missed the allusion to comedies with complicated plots, models for the George–Eliza fabula, models for the white-sheet effect, and thereby were vulnerable to the illusion. The two women save their lives by means of literary iconography.[23]

This concrete reference to a particular sign – the white sheets – as a polysemous sign for the bad conscience that makes it effective, for the white skin that makes Legree himself spooky, for death and deception, for the masking of the refugees, refers to the generic pre-text and leaves little doubt about the literary traditions the novel is working on. Thus that play within a story is not without its own social meaning: In this reading, the novel, refusing the limitations of one genre, also refuses the paralyzing effect of pure oppression and victimization by depicting a possible happy end in juxtaposition to the tragic one.[24] The figure of "Hagar," the oppressed figure who will not be victimized, is central within this strategy.

THE RETURN OF HAGAR

The pre-text that is ubiquitous in *Tom* is, of course, Biblical, and here we find Hagar again. We have no quiver by which to recognize her this time, but we do have the starkly visual narrative of a mother on her flight to rescue her son. The story of Hagar is even explicitly mentioned. It is mentioned, however, with the opposite, negative morality: "But you know how the angel commanded Hagar to return to her mistress, and submit herself under her hand" (112).

This reference appropriately reminds us that the Hagar story has two sides to it, and has in effect been used to opposite purposes.

This reminder, in turn, makes the Hagar story a suitable signifier of the double standard to which the appeal to religious authority lends itself, and the double bind it entails for many.

The icon of Eliza crossing the river is thus more than an iconographic reference to Hagar; it critiques the use of Biblical reference itself. We do not need the elaborate allusions to the river Jordan to realize that the image of Eliza crossing the river is a compound sign, a condensation of the Hagar story as that of the flight of mother and child, and that of crossing the river to the Promised Land. Eliza–Hagar thus appropriates and improves the position of the mighty male leader Moses who was *not* to cross the river.

The condensation of Biblical images is ironically put into the hands of the comical secondary figure Sam. Indeed, in his account, Eliza's crossing of the river is related to the Exodus, Ohio to the Promised Land, and Eliza's miraculously successful escape over the ice to Elijah's chariots of fire. In other words, the eclectic scriptural references, presented with humor and readable as a parody of the misuse of scriptural reference in the proslavery preachings and the hypocritical self-justifications of the slaveholders, are diffuse and invoke the Bible, both Old and New Testaments, as one pre-textual potpourri of visual images.

This kind of seemingly holistic iconography is not to be confused with the conflation of sign and text, however. For it serves a more specific purpose here. It does not connect everything Biblical to everything *Tom* is concerned with; instead, it addresses just this important but specialized point of the novel. It can do this because, ultimately, the iconographic detail is specific. Hagar, de facto, *was* a slave, just like Eliza; her child was expelled and in danger of dying as Eliza's was in danger of leading a life "worse than death," if he were to survive at all. The similarity of the sign status of the flights is made apparent quite effectively *through* pre-textuality, which works upon recognition. The flight through the desert stood for danger, as does the flight over its equally sinister counterpart, the unreliable ice. Within the Christian typological reading of the Bible, which is the religious context of this novel, Hagar's flight offers an alternative to, and is redeemed by, Christ's death, as here Tom's acceptance of death stands in contrast with Eliza's flight. Hagar and Ishmael will make it safely through their plight, which gives the episode a predictive function as a *mise en abyme*. It announces that Eliza and Harrie will make it, too.

Finally, the Biblical pre-text offers the possibility of critically reviewing the relationship between Christianity and the problem of slavery. In other words, pre-textual recognition allows, even encourages, differentiation. The pre-text can be used, and then recognized by readers, as the negative counterpart of the work rather than the model. Tom's status as a second Christ then becomes not merely a "feminine" and sentimental effect.[25] Self-sacrifice for the deliverance of humanity from guilt is no longer the privilege of a unique yet white Christ figure. Typological reading, which began as a strongly imperialistic appropriation of the Hebraic tradition, is turned against itself: As Christianity appropriates all Biblical heroes for its own sake, Stowe appropriates Christ for the sake of American slaves, and, in so doing, she places her novel within a long tradition which she also subverts.

The critique of religious hypocrisy, a major theme both in *Tom* and in Douglass's autobiography, is placed within a context in which allusions to Biblical themes – Genesis, Exodus, Passion – can counter the hypocritical exegeses of the preachers. But they do more: When accumulated, they turn the novel into a socially relevant and critical rewriting of the Bible – that is, a book which makes the case for the importance of books for people's lives, hence of the social relevance of *Tom* as a novel. In this way *Tom*, in spite of its blatant racism typical of its time, offers a powerful critique of social positions that reaches far beyond the religiosity of the "sentimental" novel and provides an argument in favor of renaming the genre as "social." We shall see below how the "Rembrandt" image can be read through Stowe's novel in terms of this strategy.

The Color Purple refers directly to this tradition of self-assertive literature, to *Tom* and the tradition of slave narratives, which *Tom* overshadows but also keeps in contiguity with contemporary work. For example, when *Color* addresses the problem of education it evokes both slave narratives and *Tom*:

'Why can't Tashi come to school?' she asked me. When I told her the Olinka don't believe in educating girls she said, quick as a flash, 'They're like white people at home who don't want colored people to learn.' (Walker, 1982:162)

The theme of learning is represented in *Tom* as in slave narratives; it is acutely discussed by Douglass, and the very existence of the slave narrative as the exemplary genre of persuasive texts confirms the function of writing and reading for emancipation.

But while *Color* refers directly to *Tom* and indirectly to slave narratives, it does not merely "repeat"; it puts *Tom*'s religiosity in its place by juxtaposing it to elements of black religious culture. And insofar as the characters in *Color* repeat the characters of *Tom*, they are critically feminist rewritings of them. Celie is a female Tom ("I ain't never struck a living thing," 43). Her attempt to spare her little sister Nettie from rape by their father by offering herself to him is her version of Tom's Christlike self-sacrifice. Nettie is the female George who lifts herself up from humiliation, and like him she travels to Africa. The almost lifelong separation between Celie and Nettie and that between Celie and her children repeat the plot of George and Eliza, her mother and sister, reunited as in the comedy-based romance. And Celie's husband has much of Legree, Tom's cruel master, including the flicker of hope for conversion toward the end. Sophia with her strength and sense of humor as weapon incarnates Cassy, the proud slave who manages to save herself with Tom's help.

The allusions to *Tom* and to all it stood for are more subtle and complex than just the cast of characters indicates. The language, events, and conversations all respond to the choices made by Stowe and show the limits of Stowe's choices and more radical possibilities. The novel is much more tradition-based, and *thereby* more effective, than appears at first sight. It is effective because it balances and intertwines critically the cotext of modern popular culture, the context of the double oppression of black women, and the pre-text of the particularly effective "sentimental" social novel. Thus it appropriates a genre that in its turn had used its own cotext (slave narratives and contemporary taste), its own context (slavery, religious hypocrisy), and its own pre-text (the Bible).

I began this discussion with a statement on Spielberg's failure and the need to explain that failure. We can now see that Spielberg's movie is missing context, cotext, and pre-text. Because of this lack, as a visual representation of Walker's novel it is arguably both racist and sexist, as the representation of the character of Sophia alone demonstrates. The film makes use of those generic conventions of the social novel that relate the genre to sentimentality. Thus the movie visualizes "sentimentality" in bright colors, counterlight, a soft focus, a picturesque setting. Those characteristics of the social novel that Walker uses polemically to represent critically the relationship between sexism and slavery are stripped of their critical content, are merely repeated, endorsed without any subtlety, sense of humor, or critical perspective; most importantly, they are repeated without iconographic resonance from the other texts.

Some readers might wish to argue that the visual medium of film, and the popular character of Spielberg's movie, made it impossible to work in Walker's critical iconography. I don't believe that this is true, for visuality is as strongly embedded in cultural traditions as discursivity is, but even if this were the case, such obliteration comes with a pricetag: Ignoring what made the novel critical makes the movie uncritical. The sentimental genre stripped of its critical iconography is fundamentally different from the sentimental genre *with* it. It now comes to support negative ideological positions. Two examples will illustrate how Walker's attempt to connect racism and sexism are turned, in the movie's visualization, into the very racism and sexism her novel critiqued through discursivity.

If taken as a twentieth-century documentary view, Walker's representation of Africa is to a certain extent naive; what made it effective was not its realistic adequacy but its relationship with the combative pre-text. Stripped of this relationship, it is open to imperialist appropriation: With Spielberg, Africa comes to stand under an enormous orange sun; thus visually represented, it is insistently unreal. The Bible, the slave narratives, and the critical response to contemporary taste which replaced realism in Walker's novel disappear from sight. We are left with kitsch, which, under Spielberg's direction, easily picks up a connotation of black folklore as seen through white prejudice.

The representation of black sexism *without* reference to slavery allows the distancing that results in the eagerly adopted view that blacks are more sexist than whites, hence, that "we" are not implicated. The father–daughter rape which informed the novel from the start is hardly present in the movie, and neither is the alternative the novel proposed: the erotic friendship between Celie and Sug, the wife and the mistress. That these themes have been sacrificed in order to reach a larger audience may be justifiable. But these gender relations form the background for other elements that become overemphasized in the movie. Thus the figure of Sophia, who recalls the insubordinate Cassie, Tom's more combative *alter ego*, has changed dramatically from the novel to the movie. Without the intertextual relationship to *Tom* on the one hand, and the contemporary context of the questioning of gender relations on the other, Sophia's insubordination is an easy target for cheap and sexist comic effects. Spielberg introduces her as a gigantic woman, an overwhelming mother-figure who is dragging her husband-to-be along like a child through the fields, when the latter is supposed to introduce his fiancée to his father. The scene is filmed from above and accelerated for comical effect. Thereby allusion to Charlie Chaplin and silent comedy film supersedes the allusion to Cassie and thereby to *Tom* as a whole. Ultimately, the movie changes the aspect of comedy as a liberating alternative to tragedy, as it was in *Tom*, into a comic effect at the expense of the figure Sophia and what she stands for. Spielberg's Sophia is irretrievably ridiculous from the start, and so are, then, her insubordination, her husband, and her revolt. Visual effect is used to neutralize the critical potential of the novel.

The effect of the ridiculous which Walker so carefully avoided has free play in Spielberg's movie because the iconographic tradition has been made invisible; the basis for recognition of the images has been changed dramatically. It is important to realize how much of this ideological transformation is connected to the problematic of discourse and image. We cannot dispose of this case with contempt for popular culture, which is the obvious context of this movie, for both *Tom* and *Color* belong to the same domain. Spielberg is therefore not simply a bad reader, nor is the point, here, to denounce him as an ideologically "bad guy" who makes "politically incorrect" movies. The issue is both more specific and more general.

More generally, the case makes us aware of three aspects of the making of art. The first is the *active* work with "sources" involved in *any* making of a work of art, whether the pre-texts are verbal (the Bible, *Tom*) or visual (Chaplin and the silent comedy), whether the tradition is romantic film-making, or, as we shall see in the next section, that of da Vinci's *Last Supper* for "Rembrandt." The second aspect concerns the different rhetorics involved in this active work with sources, of which the figuration of characters who "stand for" ideas or values within the interplay of generic conventions has been my example.

And the third aspect is the interaction among verbal and visual pre-texts, rhetorics, and devices. The basis for a visual work responding to *Color* from the same critical perspective that informed the novel would have to *recognize* the ways in which Walker had responded to the literary past. Such a recognition could then have led to a search for visual alternatives. In other words, it is not by putting some *Tom* into the movie that Spielberg could have improved its ideological stances. What could have helped are allusions to a specifically visual tradition of critique.

The importance of being able to *read* in order to be able to propose *images* that in turn must be read – this is what iconography helps us realize. In a certain way, Spielberg's failure to read can be compared to Alpers's failure to read in her response to the woman in *Samson's Wedding*. Both responses to the works – Alpers's to the "Rembrandt" painting and Spielberg's to Walker novel – fall short because they ignore the embeddedness of the works within a longer tradition, because they assume that works can be read in isolation. The impossibility, in principle, of doing so makes both Alpers and Spielberg feed into their own texts nonreflective input from other texts: the doxa concerning the woman from Timnah, the doxa concerning "strong women," Africa, comedy. With the disappearance of Hagar, not only literature but also criticism has disappeared.

COMPOSITIONAL ICONOGRAPHY

In *Tom* and in *Color*, the adoption of a pre-text as a whole was signified through specific signs: events, characters, language use, metaphors. The three collaborating texts – Bible, social novel, feminist novel – are different in genre, composition, and ideology, and in many other respects, but they converge in rhetoric: All three are, explicitly and eagerly, texts with a message. The complex way in which the Bible is brought in, together with the strong ideological position of this particular pre-text, makes Stowe's and Walker's texts strong critically, each in its own way. This is emphatically not just because the pre-text is the Bible, but also because of the intricacy of the iconographic production of meaning.

One form of complex iconographic reading is the recognition of the composition of another work. The compositional mode of reading is at stake when the composition as a whole, rather than one of its particular details, is the sign on whose basis our recognition works. This is not to say that this mode of reading falls back into the conflation of text and sign mentioned in the Introduction. If the composition as a whole can be taken as a sign, it is precisely to the extent that it is the skeleton, not the entire text, that triggers the recognition-based interpretation.

Compositional signs are the closest one can get to syntactical signs: signs that establish connections among parts of a composition. Compositional signs are more holistic, whereas syntactical signs can consist of just one line of a composition.[26]

Compositional iconographic signs are, I contend, likely to lead to strongly critical interpretations. Consider the following case, also Biblically based. In 1635, "Rembrandt" drew a copy after (a copy after) Leonardo da Vinci's *Last Supper* (compare Figures 5.5 and 5.6). The copy looks like a simple sketch, most likely to help the copyist memorize the work and reflect on the possibilities its composition offered.[27] Among its distinguishing details, there is a little dog again, added not initially in the "Rembrandt" but in the older copy, which is therefore taken to be the model used for the "Rembrandt."[28]

I am not convinced that Steinberg's casual suggestion that foreground figures like the dog serve to modify the sense of space is an exhaustive reading of the dog. The dog can also be read in a pre-textual relation to Christ's words in Matthew 7:6: "Do not give that which is holy unto the dogs." This injunction draws attention to a confusion of moods, a mixture of holiness and everyday vulgarity. Responding to this mood-crossing in the Gospel, the addition of the dog, eating leftovers, can also be taken to refer to genre painting and the vulgarity and intimacy it allows to be signified; thus the dog might mainly indicate the possibility of diverting the composition from high history painting to low genre painting. In Peircean terms the dog would still be an index, but of a different kind: From an image-internal index (a pointer to the feet) and from a metacompositional index (Steinberg's explanation), the dog would become an intergeneric index. For now, I take the dog to be the index of the idea of using a dog as a genre shifter (never mind the unanswerable question whether this idea already occurred to Birago or not), and the sketch's adoption of it, the (in)reading of that idea.

What the sketch has in common with the composition of da Vinci's fresco is in the first place the isolation of the Christ figure, surrounded by the disciples who are ostensibly busy doing other things. In this respect, the "Rembrandt" sketch is closer to the fresco than to the Birago copy through which presumably "Rembrandt" read it. The static character of Christ is opposed to the down-to-earth commerce of the others. If the disciples on the left can be interpreted as listening and responding to the master with the exception of the figure next to Christ, those at the far right are definitely not attending to him. They are arguing among themselves, maybe plotting, maybe responding in their own way; Christ, in contrast, is not engaged with any of them. Christ is thus suspended from the narrative of talk, of worldly futility. He is absorbed, like the Washington Joseph (Figure 3.4). He is also em-

phatically alone. His hands, from a narrative standpoint, are engaged in the gestures of teaching; but his absorption undermines the teaching. It separates him from the others (who are not clearly listening anyway), as does the halo around his head.[29]

If his separateness calls attention to his difference, as his halo does, then the careful reader might note that behind Christ's head is another head (Figure 5.7). Since this is merely a sketch, nothing would be easier than to ignore it. For example, it can be easily dispensed with as an earlier but rejected attempt at drawing Christ's head. The pointed finger of the bald man next to Jesus *can* be directed toward Jesus or toward one of the figures on the other side, and the strangely unreal second head does not *need* to be a woman's head, although it alone has long, curly hair. Moreover, that second head can be taken as a proleptic allusion to Judas, who will later come up to kiss Jesus, thus identifying himself as the traitor. So one would think we need not worry about this second head, although the depiction of this Judas as a woman is remarkable; if we forget about this second head, the pointed finger of the bald man then merely signifies that the latter acknowledged the traitor.

Still we have learned that women-in-excess are quite "Rembrandtesque": They are readable, never mind how enigmatic they may otherwise be. In this case in particular, the woman-in-excess evokes memories. For a reader who knows what happened in "Rembrandt" with the Susanna story, the head of a woman syntactically related to an old man with a lifted finger sets the stage for a situation where a woman is almost, but not quite, victimized by men in power. The woman who technically should not be there is an *excurse*, leading the viewer outside of the story, into the space where the absorptive Christ figure has also gone. The sketch tells us no more; it just suggests the sheer possibility of an "elsewhere."

Three years later, however, this elsewhere is followed up. The composition of the Leonardo returns in a painting with a completely different subject: the painting of the episode of Samson's wedding in which Samson proposed the riddle to the wedding guests (Judges 14:12–20) now in Dresden (Figure 5.8), and of which I have already said a few things in Chapter 1. Since the subject is so different from

5.7 *Last Supper, After Leonardo da Vinci*, detail

Facing page, top and bottom:

5.5 *Last Supper, After Leonardo da Vinci* ca. 1635, Benesch 443, drawing, 365 × 475 mm (New York, Metropolitan Museum of Art, Robert Lehman Collection)

5.6 Leonardo da Vinci, *The Last Supper* 1497, mural painting, 460 × 880 cm (Milano, Convent of Santa Maria della Grazie; refectory)

the sketch, it is not sufficient to use the iconographic mode of reading to identify the subject matter itself. Yet, in spite of the tradition of wedding painting, it is compelling to relate the *Samson* to the Leonardo rather than to works, say, like Brueghel's *Peasants' Wedding* (ca. 1560), which is closer in subject but different in composition.[30] This is an important difference between compositional and figural iconography: We cannot use the iconographic mode of reading to identify theme, but we can use it to identify a very relevant meaning, to make the two subjects speak to each other, and to see how the "Rembrandt" painting appropriates the pretexts – both the Leonardo and the Gospel – for its own ends. But doing this requires a semiotic attitude that abhors meaninglessness. Not all viewers will share this attitude, but those who do cannot leave the similarity of composition to accident.

We need not make a detailed analysis to see the enigmatic female head behind Christ reappear here as a full-fledged woman. Nor need this gender-crossing surprise us; more remarkable cases will be discussed later on. The figure of Christ especially lends itself to gender ambiguities, as Stowe's social novel demonstrates, among many other examples. Tom's sacrificial death resembles that of little Eva, who thereby joins the typological category. In the Judges story the bride is a more ambivalent figure, who ends up betraying her husband, but she is forced to do so. And she pays a stiff penalty for her enforced betrayal.

The story is less widely known than the episode with Delilah, so I shall briefly recall it here: Samson wishes to marry a Philistine woman. On his way to the wedding, he tears a lion open with his bare hands, and a few days later he makes a detour to look at the cadaver. In its belly a beehive had been established, and Samson

5.8 *Samson Posing the Riddle to the Wedding Guests* (*Samson's Wedding*) 1638, canvas, 126 × 175 cm (Dresden, Gemäldegalerie)

202

eats the honey out of the corpse, thus transgressing his Nazarite vows. At the wedding feast Samson proposes a riddle to the guests, who are the bride's kinsmen. The riddle is unanswerable without foreknowledge of the episode with the lion and the honey, which is known to Samson alone. The guests then threaten the bride with death if she does not come up with the answer. She has no choice but to use Samson's infatuation to extort the answer from him, and betray it to her kinsmen. In rage, Samson returns to his parents, leaving the marriage unconsummated.

The painting represents Samson's proposal of the riddle. Crushed between her kinsmen who threaten her and her groom who denies her the secret that must save her life, the bride has no way out. In the afterlife of the story, she is either ignored or receives as much blame as Delilah, for like the latter she betrays the hero. Just like Jesus, however, she will be killed in the aftermath of the event here depicted and which she did not in the least initiate. Little attention has been paid to the fact that she has been killed by the intertwined operation of two speech acts: the riddle whose outcome is possessed by Samson, and the threat emanating from her kinsmen. She has no prospect other than sacrificial death,[31] announced and brought about by the men's speech. It is relevant to notice the fundamentally verbal nature of an event that constitutes the challenge to visual representation.

If the bride's status as sacrificial victim makes the honorable position of Christ in the composition a suitable place for her, this compositional sign brings about an astonishingly sympathetic reading of the Judges story that few critics have endeavored to propose. The use of the composition emphasizes this sympathy in more than just this placement (Figure 5.9). The woman is as isolated as Christ. She is not, as he was, engaged in a stillness outside of time and of the world, for she is not the son of God. But she, too, is lonely and about to die. Christ's inward gaze was directed to no one in particular; the bride's gaze is also directed outside of the story that the others are busy acting out; but whereas Christ's gaze is inward, the bride's is outward, toward the viewer. Thus she steps out of a diegetic situation that is as frightening and as threatening as Susanna's situation when she is trapped by the Elders.

5.9 *Last Supper, After Leonardo da Vinci*, detail; *Samson's Wedding*, detail

203

Many less conspicuous details also contribute to the specific interpretation *The Last Supper* brings to the *Samson* via the sketch (Figure 5.9), details that become iconographic in the more figural sense, along the lines of the little dog in the drawing of Tobias. The woman's head in the *Samson* is adorned with the curls of the head behind Christ in the drawing, as if the woman, still hidden there, has stepped foreward to tell her story of sacrificial death. Of course, no halo surrounds her head, but the figure in the background tapistry is just a little bit lighter around her head than elsewhere; and looking back, we notice that the window in the fresco had already been replaced with a baldachin, which enabled the introduction of the tapestry. Furthermore, the woman is wearing a crown, which is a worldly variation on the theme of the halo.

In the fresco as well as in the sketch, the gesture made by Christ's hands is striking; it seems to clear the space for the figure's difference from the other figures. The bride's hands are differently placed, but no less significant. They represent her isolation as contained in her own body. Resting under her breast, they point to the locus of the woman's function as bride: the provider of offspring.[32] The plate before her, conspicuously empty in the drawing, is adorned with a wild, snake-surrounded erect object, which is likely to indicate a pagan practice but at the same time is hardly irrelevant in this context as a phallic object.

According to the Gospels, Jesus was betrayed by a kiss, a gesture that is visually perceptible and easy to depict, and may be proleptically signified by the double head. Instead, this woman is betrayed by language. Significantly, the sketch is not without "speaking hands." In the painting, Samson's riddle is represented by his gesture, counting the stakes – thirty sets of garments – on his fingers. What about the other speech act, the threat? It is obviously not because the threat intervenes later in the story that it is not as explicitly signified as the riddle itself; we have seen that visual art has its own means of conveying proleptic signs. The threat, in fact, *is* represented – through "speaking hands." But these hands can be "heard" only if we step into the language of compositional iconography and intergeneric indexing.

At the left side of the painting, the scene is very much like the numerous lecherous scenes of genre painting. Most of the women present comply with the men's advances. But not the woman next to the bride: She is shying away from the man who, while imposing himself on her, is also pointing at what is going on at the other side. In the sketch, the figure next to Christ looks quite feminine. She also bends her head, responding to a man pointing at the scene at the other side. Here, the relation has changed, and the man is speaking with his hand to the woman who is holding her hand under her breast just like the bride. We can now see how the little dog in the sketch is used. I have suggested that the dog is a quick note taken in order to keep an idea current, the idea being the

204

transition between the high and low genres whose possibility produced the *Samson* painting. Whether or not Rembrandt the artist
took the dog from his model is irrelevant; for those of us who
know the subsequent work, the allusion to genre painting is a
meaningful "direction for use." Genre then becomes a crucial cotext
for this work.

This reading works with the combined devices for storytelling
discussed in Chapter 3. The reference to the Biblical pre-text's
combination of the two verbal acts that kill this woman works
together with the sequentiality – the comic-strip device – which
represents the bride *twice*: once as being threatened by the man next
to her, and once as the already condemned sacrificial victim. The
first instance of the bride is fully diegetic; the woman is engaged
in the event set up by the men. In the second, she has pulled herself
out of it, like Jesus, and appeals to the viewer, if not for help, at
least for understanding.

In what ways are we using an iconographic mode of reading in
these examples, and what are the signs which this mode of reading
helps us to process? First of all, the iconographic reference to the
Last Supper works globally; it brings in a frame of reference in
relation to which the work is read. Without the assumption of the
compositional sign, including its suggestion of sacrificial meaning,
its similarity in composition to the sketch, hence to da Vinci, the
representation of the scene would make much less sense. Why
would the bride be so royally adorned, so separated from the rest
of the figures, and so focused on the viewer, if not to signify the
similarity between her fate and Christ's? Without the generic sign,
the reference to the lecherous scene, the wickedness and the sexual
nature of the plotting going on around her seem less than relevant.

Unlike the Hagar references in *Tom* and *Color* which propose
ironic reversals of the religious morality of the day to drive their
points home, the references in *Samson's Wedding* (of which more
will be said in Chapter 10) may be ironic, but in a different way.[33]
The irony here is one of shifting, of displacement, of turning the
highest subject into a low one – the genre scene. But the displacement does not affect the woman at the center. She remains separated
from the promiscuous scene, isolated in this way just as she is
diegetically and pictorially isolated. In addition, there is no confusion, no extension of the reference to "the Biblical" in general.
The sign is compositional, but no less precise and delimited. In
Tom, and by extension in *Color*, a mixture of elements from the
pre-text were worked together, not at places in the novel, for a
specific purpose that had its bearing upon the work as a whole.
Indexicality worked mainly on the basis of synecdoche. In *Samson's
Wedding*, a specific moment of the one pre-text – of the Leonardo
and, through it, of the Gospel – is seen to be used to compose the
framework of the painting in which the other pre-text – the Judges
episode – is then made to fit. The cotext, the contemporary habit

of typological interpretation, is used in a way that makes a highly sympathetic representation plausible. Each case is complex and effective, but not exactly similar in semiotic strategy.

Iconography thus conceived does, indeed, read the image as something it is not. But by the same token, such a reading demonstrates that bypassing these allusions would be not reading at all: not seeing the woman's isolation. Attempts to see "only what is there" are irresistibly unifying. But they also violate the image by ignoring the extent to which the woman is framed within a different space than the other figures. Such attempts, therefore, can only fit the woman in with the rest of the scene, appropriating her to advance the negative readings of Judges that are current today, and thus, again reading the image as what it is not. If there is something wrong with iconography as a predominant practice, it is the dogmatic notion that reference to models replaces reading of the image; instead, reference to models should inform the reading. Instead of meanings, reference provides a "language" through which the reader is enabled to "speak" – to recognize and then to endorse actively. Of course, there are other modes of reading, and reading with alternative modes may lead to collision with recognition. But I would contend that the tension produced by reading in different modes is positive. In order to make that point, I shall now turn to one other such mode.

RECOGNITION AND NARRATIVE: SIGNS FOR THE STORY

In spite of the possibilities of using iconographic reading to enrich our interaction with the image and its pre-texts, this mode of reading does not overlap, and can even clash with, other modes. Signs

5.10 *Jesus Washing Peter's Feet* ca. 1653, Benesch 931, drawing, 156 × 222 mm (Amsterdam, Rijksprentenkabinet)

206

like the Hagar image, the little dog, and the quiver, and the composition of the *Last Supper*, do not tell the story; they refer to a story. This difference is crucial and demonstrates the risks of loss inherent in a mode of reading that focuses exclusively on this type of sign. These signs do not participate in a narrative syntagm constituting the skeleton of the fabula, nor do they direct the viewer, offering a specific manner of focalization. Neither do they participate in the telling itself, visualizing the narrator's voice, as did, for example, the painting of Jacob's wrestling with the angel by its double use of distortion. As I suggested earlier, iconography proposes that we read the image as what it is not; it is only logical, then, that it will prompt us as well to read narrative works as what they are not; that such a mode of reading will prompt us to recognize the "underlying" story, rather than the new, visual story we might read otherwise. Of course, I am not proposing that we ignore the evoked story in favor of some "fresh" or "direct" visual narrative. Rather, I would like to make a case for a double, differential reading, which juxtaposes the evoked against the narrated story, in order to let them interact and to let the tensions between the stories produce new meanings.

Iconographic reading tends to obliterate the other story because stories are sometimes so generally known that readers/viewers have difficulty realizing to what extent the visual work responding to the story signifies its own story. Compare the following two drawings, for example (Figures 5.10 and 5.11). They are immediately recognizable as "Jesus Washing Peter's Feet" and "One of the Magi Adoring the Infant Jesus," respectively. There are signs that make us recognize the stories, signs that work like the iconographic-

5.11 *One of the Magi Adoring the Infant Jesus* ca. 1635, Benesch 115, drawing, 178 × 160 mm (Amsterdam, Rijksprentenkabinet)

207

denotative signs discussed earlier. For example, in the first work, Jesus' long hair and beard, iconographic details in the convention of representing Jesus, "automatically" turn a number of men surrounding the event into the apostles.

So far, recognition only evokes the general setting: a Jesus story. The bowl and the feet as well as Jesus' action, however, are not only fixed elements that we process on the basis of previous viewings of representations of the same theme, but are, at the same time, elements that identify the story. This "storytelling" occurs on two levels: The bowl and the action of washing feet are enough for us to *know* that we are seeing a representation of a specific passage of the Gospel – that is, if we are familiar with it already. But the work also *tells* that story anew, and the difference between, on the one hand, reading from previous images and from the Gospel – that is reading iconographically and pre-textually – and on the other, reading directly, narratively, can be important.

For the drawing tells the story in a way that is different from, and not necessarily congruent with, the Gospel story. As a visual narrative the drawing juxtaposes a story of a footwashing with the literary one, with which it bears comparison but from which it cannot but differ. I want for a moment to describe the drawing with narratological concepts, hence as a narrative *without* recourse to iconographic recognition. Doing so will show us that the work tells the story according to the different levels of narrative signification briefly outlined in Chapter 3.

The two figures and the action taking place between them constitute the elementary narrative syntagm of the fabula – subject–action–object, or figure–washes–feet (of other figure). The contiguity among these three elements is itself the sign for the syntagm. When we look at the figures Peter and Jesus, we get a specific vision of that fabula – that is, its focalization. We notice the surprise and confusion of the former in the bowing of his head and the clasping of his hand, as well as the tension of the shoulders which narrativizes the scene by introducing time: The figure is not stably seated; he might get up, has just sat down, or hesitates between the two.

So far, the representation functions quite like a verbal description of a character. The figure of Jesus, likewise, can be described as a character. He is eagerly tending to his business, a feature that is signified by the attitude of his body, especially his knee and his laboring hand. Both knee and hand signify unnecessarily laborious action by the distance between them, between Jesus' foot and the bowl, which puts the figure at risk of imbalance and, therefore, produces a narrativizing tension in the figure's back. The two descriptions of these figures, attributive or adjectival, join "adverbially" in the action itself, which is thus respresented emphatically as an event. It is this adverbial clause specifying the event which constitutes the narrative focalization. This focalization is represented before us and emphasized self-consciously in the tense looks of the bystanding apostles – the internal, delegated focalizers –

unseen by the two figures but seeing *with* and, if we let them, *for*, us.

The manner of narration, finally, is specified in the combination of bold and fine lines, of sketchy and detailed lines, and the application of those choices to the particular focalization. In the first place, this can be seen particularly acutely in the elaboration of the heads of the two main figures as opposed to the sketchiness of the surrounding apostles' heads. This is not to suggest the rather banal observation that main characters receive more elaboration than secondary characters, equivalent to description in verbal works. Instead, it is to suggest that the most important features of the work are delineated in terms of the *visually narrative representation*. The tensions in the bodies – Peter's arms and back and Jesus's knee and back – are emphasized in a different narrative mode: in a few, underelaborated, yet extremely "telling," strokes. They are telling precisely because they work together. They make specific sense or they make no sense at all. Here they work as specific signs, that is, as signs of this particular focalized representation of this fabula.

Although it colludes with the verbal text recounting Jesus' footwashing, this narrative interpretation is not verbally based, but neither is it "purely" visual. The signs are visual, but the code that correlates these signs to specific meanings is not. The interpretation rests on principles of decoding proper to narrative structure: As I hope to have shown in Chapter 3, the structure of narrative is not medium-bound.[34] This narrative decoding supplements iconographic decoding. The two modes of reading work together to help us recognize something: the iconographic reading, to recognize a particular traditional story; the narrative reading, to recognize "story" as a mode. But as this analysis, as well as the following one, should make clear, recognition in turn needs to be supplemented by narrative interpretation if we don't want to miss the distinctive effect of each work. Many Footwashings have been depicted, and all can be recognized on this basis of combined iconography and narrative, but the differences between them, in narrative terms, are not simply recognizable; they must be processed in each particular encounter by a narratively engaged viewer.

So, for example, in the drawing of Jesus washing the feet of his disciple, the iconographic recognition of the event as the mythical Footwashing does not contradict the narrative reading. It gives more, rather than different, information, and the story we read becomes richer. The aspect of hard work, of effort, which we saw in the specific focalization and narration in the drawing, is not signified in the Gospel, but is not incompatible with the latter either. Rather, it gives a specific sense to the idea of humility, thus highlighting the dignity of labor. The mythical, and therefore ahistorical, notion of humility is thus given a historical specificity.

There is not always such harmony between iconographic and narrative reading, however. The relations between the two juxtaposed readings can vary greatly, from specification as in the *Foot-*

washing, to deviation, alternative semantic fields, opposition, contradiction. In the *Adoration*, represented in Figure 5.9, a narrative reading based on the same principles as used for the previous drawing might lead one to a more deviant interpretation compared to the iconographically determined subject.

NARRATIVE AGAINST RECOGNITION: SIGNS FOR A DIFFERENT STORY

First of all, the idea that the drawing of Figure 5.11 depicts one of the Magi is recognized only by the humble attitude of the old man, paying his respect to the child, while his mantle distinguishes him from the other possible adorers, the shepherds, who, in turn, would be identified – Bryson would say "recognized" – by their staves and sheep. The child being held by the woman can only be the Christ child being held by the Virgin. We do not need the halo, the cradle, or the other traditional attributes to catch on to this.[35] So far, the signs are iconographic-denotative.

The conjunction of figures – a kneeling old man, a woman holding a child before him, the woman herself – functions again as the skeleton of a fabula recognized as the core event of a well-known story. But we may try to take one step back and stay with the slightly more abstract formulation of the conjunction. What if we suspend for a moment the reference to the Adoration, and decline the cultural and contextual invitation to recognize this fabula?

What we have, if we disregard the story, is a fabula built up from a diagonal series of elements:[36] From right-top to left-bottom we see three heads bowing, three bodies, divided into two opposed groups. The two groups are separated and linked again: subject – action – object as one group, complicated in this case by an indirect object at the other side of a separation. The woman sits with her knees open and holds a baby that has no strength to stand on its own; its arms, for example, hang like those of a doll (Figure 5.12). The feet of the baby are continuous with a very bold line, almost a blot of ink, between the woman's thighs. In terms of bold versus light lines – say, the image's textuality – this blot is the central

5.12 *One of the Magi Adoring the Infant Jesus*, detail

focus of the drawing. The woman is holding the baby up to the man, as if to hand it over to him. This action is clearly distinguished from a static pose by, again, a tension in the arms signified by the distance, just a little longer than necessary, between the woman's body and her hands, which also affects the representation of the arm.[37] The veil covering her head is transparent, as her garment seems to be; her legs are clearly visible. The man looks old. He does not look up to the child the story wants him to adore. He is not kneeling either; he is squatting. He has his hands ready to take the baby and put it into his lap (Figure 5.13).

If we link these elements together to form a narrative syntagm sufficiently coherent to form a fabula, without skipping over any of these details, we hardly come up with the standard scene of the ostentation and adoration of the child. Action, not a still pose, is being depicted. The bold line-blot, the effort represented in the arm, and the emphatically powerless infant can be processed as a delivery scene. The woman is "right now" pulling the baby out of her body and handing it over to the elderly man. In other words, this fabula is not congruent with the iconographically recognizable scene, which in fact tends to obliterate rather than emphasize the elements I have been describing. Yet it is a fabula, and if it needs to bracket the official story temporarily, it certainly does not contradict that story, but only conflates the Nativity with the Adoration; by representing both in one scene, they shed an unexpected light on both. Let us see how the other narrative strategies help substantiate this claim.

Again, focalization helps us see, not what is represented, but how it is represented – what view of the scene is proposed to us. Some of the previously mentioned features are, in fact, already constructing focalization. In terms of the description of the figures, the bodily details of the woman support the view that a bodily event is being represented. The infant's feet are not visible; they seem to be still in the birth canal. The woman's face is elaborated while her eyes are not; she must come across as actively laboring at birthgiving.[38]

I am tempted to push this reading even further – and may or may not get my readers to go along. If I did, I would contend that the heads of the infant and the elderly man are strikingly similar. This similarity, signified in the identical attitude of the head, is further enhanced by the bald, round, and slightly flattened top and by the diagonal line running from ear to chin, identical in each. It would be both tempting and, if we were inclined to avoid conflict

5.13 *One of the Magi Adoring the Infant Jesus*, detail

with the iconographically recognized idea of Christ and one of the Magi, shocking to see in this detail a sign of the idea that the man is the child's father. Although completely human, Christ could not have an earthly father, and for those who like to remain consistent with historical readings, it seems that invoking a Freudian denial of that theological dogma at this point would be unnecessarily forced. Leo Steinberg (1983) taught us how to avoid such anachronisms a propos the sexuality of Christ, which he explained in relation to contemporary theology. Similarly, it is not impossible to argue that the implicit family resemblance, just like the details of the bodily process of birthgiving, only emphasize the Christ child's human nature, thus confirming rather than contradicting the dogma of incarnation, although in a highly idiomatic manner. Handing over the baby to the old man, the woman, whose fine, youthful features and transparent veil set her off from the "ordinary" human being the man stands for, delivers the child to (a representative of) those for whom it was incarnated in the first place: the human race, exemplified by this impressed and submissive elderly man.

That this representation of the theological dogma speaks to us modern viewers, at all may, in turn, very well be due to our familiarity with Freudian theory of the unconscious and the central place of the problematic of family relations therein. I would personally like to leave room to speculate that this particular manner of insisting on Christ's humanity, by making him resemble an elderly man, can still be projected as an unconscious reading of the Gospel's "family romance," especially in connection with other instances of the representation of the problematic relations between fathers and sons in "Rembrandt." Hence, in my reading of it, "Rembrandt" – the oeuvre as a "text," a cultural whole – accommodates much of today's (by definition, anachronistic) Freudian reading.

Focalization is also at stake in the presentation of the two groups in relation to profile, and again it is our willingness to see the image as other than unified that will help us to see striking and significant details here. The man is seen from the side, and therefore the narrative makes a statement on his pose only. The woman, in contrast, is represented in three-quarter view, between profile and facing the viewer, so as to include her opened womb in the representation. If we read the image realistically, this would be a technical mistake, for as a consequence of this difference much of the iconographic as well as the narrative story is suspended. The man's hands do address nothing in particular, nor does he face the child; if technique is taken to coincide with realism, the drawing would be a failure.

Narratologically speaking, however, it is a successful deviation, for it makes us confront signs and construct a narrative. The slight mismatch between the two sides of the scene emphasizes the radical separation between the man who can only receive the child, and the woman who is actually producing it: between human and divine groups, between natural and supernatural events. The mismatch is the most radical – because self-conscious – narrative sign on the level of focalization. This mismatch bears comparison with the women-in-excess in figures of the Tobias drawing and again in the sketch of *The Last Supper*. Whereas iconography would normalize both excess and mismatch by ignoring them, narrative reading highlights precisely these "failures." Thus this mode of reading foregrounds how "failure" is produced over female bodies, thereby obstructing attempts to get rid of them as a "nuisance" or as "noise."

As in the *Footwashing*, the narrative manner or "text" specifically enhances this vision of the Nativity-cum-Adoration scene. The strongest lines are those that determine the woman's pose as the attitude of birthgiving, including the strange bench she is sitting on and which would be very uncomfortable if she were merely resting. The blot obscuring the child's feet and indicating her vagina is continued in a strong line toward her left foot; this foot in turn has detailed toes firmly planted on the ground. The man's hands ready to receive the child, his knees strongly displaying the pose of squatting, not of kneeling, and his bowed head are all drawn in bolder lines than the rest of him. Finally, the careful delimitation of the two groups' spaces literally draws a line between them and separates radically the self-absorbed face of the woman and the firmly drawn face of the man. Over this line the infant is to be handed.

That separation, and the mismatch mentioned earlier, are quite emphatically signified by the bold line circumscribing the old man's space. But once we have noticed and processed the signs of separation and especially the delimitation of the man's space, the line between the two separated realms, a little higher up at the level of the man's knees, is so incongruous that it draws attention to its own futility, thus again accenting its sign status as well as the sign status of the other lines. This line, I would suggest, can work as a hyphen (and almost literally looks like one). A hyphen is relevant in this context: By convention it is a minimally semanticized grapheme that separates *and* connects at the same time. Iconically it is a sign that "looks like" its meaning, thus representing separation and connection simultaneously. Is it visual or verbal? As the fine line between verbal and visual signification, this hyphen demonstrates that that fine line ultimately cannot be drawn.

Thus read, the image becomes much more interesting than a simple iconographic reading would suggest initially. The dogmatic views of theological traditions, or of iconographic traditions that limit us to the story not told, can blind us to other possible readings, including, paradoxically, readings that are equally acceptable even if we wish to remain within the context of theology. Reading for the narrative can be done in conjunction with reading for the theme, whenever the theme is a story. But narrative reading is fundamentally different from pre-textual and iconographic reading. It is a reading, rather than a recognition, of a narrative structure. And it is a visual reading, based on the visual signs of a nonvisual, but equally nonverbal, manner of representation.

CONCLUSION

Iconography is based on recognition, but to call recognition-based signification denotative is to reinstate the priority of denotation which literary scholarship has been hard-pressed to justify. The reassuring hierarchy between the "real" and the ideological which the denotation–connotation pair implies is ideological in itself. Yet if recognition is not denotative, what can it be?

On the one hand, recognition-based reading is unavoidable, since it is the cultural memory on which not only language but also other semiotic systems are based. Recognition operates on the basis of an ever changing, yet relatively intersubjective vocabulary which the memory of a given culture builds up, modifies, and, if necessary, breaks down or turns against itself. This aspect of recognition had doubtlessly led to its identification with denotation. Moreover, iconographic, recognition-based interpretation is not only a "natural," that is, a readerly mode of reading functioning as a language; it is also an indispensable tool for critique. It is because artists and readers/viewers know, and recognize, older stories, figures, themes, and doxas, that each art user can turn the tables on those pre-texts and change their meaning. Meaning is fundamentally unstable.

On the other hand, there are risks that iconography seems to avoid only with difficulty. These difficulties, responsible for the recent questionable reputation of iconography, are threefold. First, this mode of reading is so much based on pregiven idioms that it tends to be conservative and to privilege tradition over innovation, rather than focusing on the tension between the two. Second, the tendency to trace motifs back to traditions and sources tends to preclude active interpretation. Often, recognizing a motif is enough; interpreting it, in relation to the pre-text, the cotext, and the context, is a step not always taken. This reluctance to interpret precludes further the critical potential of iconographic reference from being developed. The third negative aspect of iconography is its eclecticism, which is a consequence of the reluctance to interpret. Referring an image back to a predecessor opens the door to an "anything goes" attitude that is close to a certain apolitical version of postmodernism: Citing loose elements and avoiding commitment to specific meanings entails a highly problematic plurality of elements outside of space and time, hence, mythical.

A fourth characteristic feature of iconography cannot be held against the method, and here my agreement with the adversaries of iconography stops short. It is a verbal mode of reading. As I noted at the beginning of this discussion, iconography reads the image as what it is not. My response to this characteristic is not negative. Reading is precisely that: replacing the signs with the absent item they stand for. It is only to the extent that the second and third negative aspects count that this becomes a problem. In fact, iconographers who stop before interpretation have not understood iconography as a mode of *reading*. Shunning a verbal response to a visual work partakes of an ideology that opposes the two arts in order to maintain the superiority of one or the other. The superiority of the visual in terms of directness, density, and realism, the claim to objective truth inherited from positivism, may not be often heard anymore in overt declarations; it is certainly inherent in the refusal to grant visual art the status of a semiotic system, if not a language.

CHAPTER 6

TEXTUALITY
AND REALISM

INTRODUCTION

WHEN using the realistic mode of reading, one searches for a content that is modeled by reality, but does so at the expense of awareness of the signifying system of which the work is made. The problem with using a realistic mode of reading and looking exclusively is that it helps to pass off content as "natural" and thus fosters ideological manipulation. Yet realism has itself succeeded in becoming so "natural" a mode of reading that denying or ignoring its pervasiveness will not help. In the preceding chapter, I argued that the tension between iconographic and narrative reading is productive. In this chapter, I shall defend a similar contention. I shall argue that the blinding effects of the realistic mode of reading can be countered by opposing realistic to textual reading and by maintaining, rather than resolving, the tension between the two. But only by first foregrounding the difference between these two modes of reading will we be able fruitfully to juxtapose them and make them interact.

The realistic mode of reading is particularly powerful because of its complicity with other oppositions that pervade modern culture. First, realism finds support in textual details for its construction of a holistic content. When we rephrase the opposition between this chapter's two modes of reading as "reading for the textual whole" versus "reading for the realistic detail" we can begin to see this tension. In addition, realism's predominance has been maintained on the basis of two other oppositional pairs: unity versus fracturedness of the work and visual versus verbal modes of expression. In addition, they do not overlap as neatly as this presentation of their complicity might suggest.

Those who read with the presumption that the work constitutes a whole, that it is coherent and well-structured, have been hard-pressed recently to justify this approach. Primarily under the influence of deconstruction, the assumption that works constitute a unity has been shown to stimulate strongly ideological interpretations, to erase disturbing details that do not fit, and to impose a Romantic conception of organic growth that is not relevant to works unrelated to the Romantic tradition.[1] The "convention of unity" is a powerful ideological weapon because of the pressure it brings to bear on one's choice interpretation. This is fostered by the presupposition of single-handed authorship and the related authority that accompanies such single-handedness.[2] The kinds of problems such a presumption can pose have recently been brought to the fore regarding the apparent practice of "Rembrandt" as a studio artist. In addition, the convention encourages the projection of "masterplots" that colonize the marginal.[3] As I suggested earlier, however, using the challenge to unity as a cover – or pre-text! – for a resistance to interpretation may well be based on the same unifying fallacy it tries to avoid. The suggestion, for example, that a detail in *Madame Bovary* is merely a sign of verisimilitude may be motivated by a sense that the detail does not fit otherwise. And such a judgment would rely in turn on a sense that the rest of the signs do fit, that the narrative is a whole that has no use for this particular detail, but does smoothly accommodate most of the others. Paradoxically, such a judgment awards the signs a status inalterably textual rather than readerly: It exerts the "effect of the real" on readers precisely because it is out there in the work.

As Naomi Schor (1987) has demonstrated and the works studied have corroborated, the aesthetic of the detail is not gender neutral. "Details" that do not fit become even more challenging if they happen to be the arena in which battle over the marginality of women is fought. Take, for example, the women-in-excess in the Tobias drawing and the sketch of the *Last Supper* (Figures 6.1 and 6.2, respectively); the mismatch between woman and man in the *Adoration* drawing; the discordant levels of reality in the Washington *Joseph*, which isolate, but also foreground, the female figure; and the empty fist in the Berlin *Susanna*, which foregrounds the status of misogyny as a cultural center in which the complicity of art and science must be acknowledged.

If we reverse the usual perspective and begin at the reader's end, it is still possible to see in the early Barthes (e.g., 1968) a contrast between "functional" details – details that we can integrate into the reading of a fabula or theme – and details promoting an "effect of

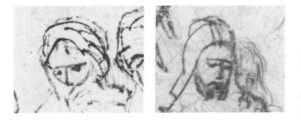

6.1 (*left*)   *The Farewell of Tobias,* detail

6.2 (*right*)   *Last Supper, After Leonardo da Vinci,* detail

the real." When Barthes coined that phrase he initially meant that
the connotation "reality" takes over the denotation and invades the
entire semantic realm of the detail. But in Barthes's use the "effect
of the real" was a reading strategy; and it was here not inevitable,
stable, or intersubjective. The difference is not just a matter of
words; acknowledging the contrast between a functional and a realistic detail affects the power of the reader and thereby enriches
the interaction between work and reader so as to increase the work's
effectiveness.

In this chapter, I shall explore the implications of a mode of
reading that I call "reading for the text." The concept of text, here,
is close to, but not identical with that of "work" (on which more
in the next chapter). A work is the artifact before us, framed and
all, exhibited in a museum or reproduced in a book, perceived by
the reader as the thing to appropriate in the act of reading yet still
outside of her or his grasp. A text is what we make of a work when
reading it; roughly, it is a meaningful, well-structured whole with
a beginning and an end. Of course, such a concept of text, however
commonplace, has been challenged by deconstruction (e.g., Derrida, 1987). But that challenge concerns the object status and the
resulting autonomy of the work. As a mode of reading, this concept
of text remains undeniably active, shaping sign events continually,
perhaps precisely because it is illusory.

One difference between "reading for the text" and reading realistically is that reading for a sense of textuality, and of the wholeness
this textuality entails, does not necessarily preclude awareness of a
fundamental lack of unity, whereas reading for the effect of the real
as it is traditionally practiced tends to do so. But although incompatible, making them interact by activating both modes concurrently is in itself a critical endeavor: Using them in combination
helps us avoid the unifying fallacy. Just as the difference between
iconographic and narrative modes of reading helps us assess what
is at odds in a work, so, too, does the difference between textual
and realist readings make a problematic and thereby fruitful combination. In this chapter, I shall explore the ideological underpin-
nings of the idea of wholeness, and the way in which textuality
and realism construct wholeness differently. The issue of wholeness
is important because it necessarily entails blindness. The desire for
wholeness, with its roots in the unconscious (see Chapter 8), informs the compulsion to project unity on the image or text, and
thus to ignore details that don't fit, that threaten to fracture desired
unity. It is perhaps the desire for wholeness that underlies much of
Western culture's preference for visual representations of the female
nude. Modes of reading that look for details that do not fit are
potentially useful tools for antirealist, critical readings. But reflection on the status of details and their relation to the whole is necessary if we are to prevent the appropriation of details as signs for
the real. The success of Barthes's concept of the effect of the real
is suspect, precisely because of this danger of appropriation.

SIGNS FOR TEXTUALITY

W. J. T. Mitchell (1985) has convincingly argued that the often alleged opposition between verbal and visual art as between discrete and dense sign-systems (proposed by Nelson Goodman, 1976), although appealing as the most sensible and the least hierarchical of the current formulations, is not entirely without problems.[4] One problem lies with the conflation of the theoretical status of signs and the way they actually function. As I argued in the Introduction, verbal art – although composed of discrete words that can normally be described individually as signs – does not *function* by a reader discerning words individually. In order to "tell" a narrative syntagm of the form subject–action–object, a text needs more words than just the three that fill the slots in the syntagm.[5] In fact, a work needs many words that do not function as discrete literary signs at all, but do contribute to the emergence of sign events by working in concert with other elements. As a sequence of mere words, then, language may be discrete; as a form of representation it is not.[6]

The same can be said of visual works. While many elements are not significant, they cannot be spared. Many of those are part of what Bryson would call "connotative elements" – that is, they fill up the surface in such a way that the representation passes for realistic. Goodman would probably see there aspects of the density of visual images. Shapiro (1969; see also Shapiro, 1973), in his attempt to assign meaning to elements like the frame, background, color, by turning them into discrete signs, thus reducing the realm of the meaningless, provides evidence that it is the reader who decides which elements are discrete signs and which are not; and this holds true for verbal as well as for visual art.

In the painting *The Toilet of Bathshebah* (Figure 6.3), in the Musée du Louvre in Paris, we can see many elements we might call "connotative," "meaningless," "effects of the real," or "parts of the image's density": the curtain, the cloth in the background, the cloth the woman is sitting on, but also the woman's bracelet and necklace, which might be seen as part of her adornment, but can also be there, simply, as visual filler. In literary texts, all of these would be called descriptive elements. Unless I have specific reasons to do so, I would not call such elements signs, nor would I undertake a forced attempt to interpret them, even if these elements in isolation would immediately be interpreted as representations of the objects they denote.[7] That critics tend to respond to such assertions of meaninglessness by immediate interpretation, as if the claim were too good a challenge to let pass, suggests that the locus of meaning is in the interaction between text and reader, not in the text alone.[8]

On the other hand, there are many elements, in both verbal and visual texts, that are neither iconographic-denotative – because they do not contribute to the recognition of the theme – nor narrative, because they do not "tell"; they seem to have no particular meaning at all, although they are clearly and insistently significant. In this section I want to discuss a few of those elements. I shall discuss those elements as signs, or, more precisely, as sign events, that contribute to our awareness that the work is processed as something we may call a *text*, even if no specific meaning can be assigned to them. The concept of text will be used in a rather casual but vitally operative sense here to mean a combination of elements leading to semiotic events – acts of reading – a combination that is structured enough to be perceived as a whole and materially presented as complete. Thus defined, novels, poems, drawings, and paintings are texts. In verbal art, the clear delimitation of the work by be-ginning and ending, problematic as such a delimitation is, serves the purpose of producing the idea – illusionary but functional – of

6.3 *The Toilet of Bathsheba*
1654, Bredius 521, canvas, 142 ×
142 cm (Paris, Musée du Louvre)

text. In visual art, the frame, or the arbitrary delimitation of a piece of paper, does the same.[9]

This flexible and functional definition of text is not a pointless passe-partout; it works to shape readings, and as such it can be shown at work with the limit case of Figure 6.4. This drawing has not been recognized iconographically as a representation of any known story or theme.[10] Nor does it convincingly tell a story of its own, although it would not be impossible to read a story into it. At first sight it appears to be a sheet of sketches, not necessarily related, nor coherent; a study sheet made at a time when paper was expensive; a fragment. For most readers, such a study sheet is not,

6.4 *Different Listeners* ca. 1537, Benesch 140, drawing, 190 × 125 mm (Berlin, Kupferstichkabinett)

a priori, a text; they would not bother trying to read it. Reading is unifying in itself: As soon as one adopts a readerly attitude, however, some sense of formal coherence, produced by the way in which the figures are proposed as a group, contradicts the sense that the sheet contains just a random set of sketches.

There is, for example, a triangular form of the seven figures so intertwined that it is hard, in spite of our overt assumption that they are random, not to see them as a group of people who are not too happy to be stuck together. The figure at the top enhances this effect. The eyes of the figure have the same narrative temporality as those of the preparatory drawing for the *Susanna* (Figure 6.5), although they look more to the side and eventually introduce potential narrativity by looking suspiciously at a viewer whom we cannot see. This viewer is not ourselves, the viewers of the drawing, but appears to be more to the left of the sheet, not in front of the representation. Diegetic focalization thus emerges, entailing a sense of narrative and responding to a single visual occasion rather than to a stable object of sight.[11] Maybe this imagined viewer is the viewer of a theatrical spectacle his looking brings into being; this idea brings the curtain into play and so makes it meaningful, although it had been only meaningless filler previously.

But then, something happens in the interaction between the reader and the image. The possibility of spectacle draws attention to the fact that the group of seven below are also looking. Are they spectators in their own right? They are sitting, five of them looking in the same direction. Their common directionality produces another hypothetical character, an implied focalizer whose invisible look they return. But the two who look in the opposite direction would then produce a problem of unity.

These figures must be accommodated, and thus they can be interpreted as talking to the figures they are very close to, maybe commenting on the spectacle. Whatever it is they are watching, they do not seem thrilled by it. This is about all we can tell. Among the choices of a boring play, a distressing event, an unpleasant obligation to wait, a sermon provoking bad conscience, or a negative response to the awareness of being viewed – by the implied focalizer, representative of the species of viewers of which we, too, are members – I shall not predict what any particular reader will decide, nor do I wish to decide for myself. This discussion is relevant precisely in that it uncovers the impossibility and, indeed, the impropriety of interpreting any further.

6.5 *Woman Standing Up
(Susanna?)*, detail

What is at stake here is the curious notion that there are signs at
work in this viewing of a drawing whose meaning is nothing in
particular. The signs – the composition, the group of seven and
the isolated figure atop the triangle, the direction of their looks,
the curtain – are there, whether we consider them connotative
filling, Goodman's density, or Barthes's random presence for the
effect of the real. Yet they are signs, for I was compelled to interpret
them, even if my attempt to do so was ultimately frustrated. And
the very fact that my interpretive effort was curtailed in the middle
made me aware that I was putting forth that effort at all.

Signs like these make readers process, not a particular text, but
a general sense of "text": A sense of coherence, of structure, of
narrativity, of meaningfulness emerges, but no specific meaning,
or rather, a plurality of possible meanings emerge – whose undecidability is precisely the token of meaningfulness.[12] The signs that
produce this sense are what I would like to call signs for text. They
undermine randomness by generating a set of possible stories, possible meanings, that are left undecided, but that mercilessly emerge
in the act of looking as soon as we grant more looking time than
a quick glance.

Signs like these contribute to the commonplace response to things
around us, the response that saves us from the destructive awareness
of chaos. But the awareness of randomness, the notion that the
sheet was made as random exercise, can provide a different sense
of unity. In the case of this sheet of sketches, there is no contradiction between the signs for text and the notion that the sheet is
composed of random sketches, exercises in drawing sitting figures,
facial expressions, and maybe, more specifically, figures too close
to one another to be completely represented. If there is conflict, it
occurs between the two reading attitudes, not between the readings
and the text.

What is the status of these signs? Again, the signs are clearly
produced by the viewer – in this case, by myself. Thus, it would
be absurd to assert that "Rembrandt" set a semiotic trap for us,
that he meant the composition to produce the sense of coherence
I just described while leaving the specific meaning uncertain, in
order to make us reflect on semiotic problems. Yet it would be
equally absurd to defend passionately the arbitrariness of the composition in view of the elements just foregrounded; the very fact
that I was able (and compelled) to go halfway toward an interpretation of the sheet as a whole is enough evidence of that absurdity.
Even Benesch's iconographic interpretation of the drawing as a
study for the Saint John derives from the same desire for textual
coherence.[13] So while the issue of authorial intention is clearly irrelevant, so, too, is the debate over the existence of the signs themselves: The signs exist when readers grant them existence. Nor will
many be willing to go so far as to see the drawing as a full story,
a cleverly composed thematic work, a semantic unity of whatever
kind, because signs for text are not inscribed in the drawing; they

are brought into existence by the reader. And once they have been brought into existence, processing the drawing without them will require a great deal of effort. That is the status of these signs: The reader can fail to grant them existence, but once that existence has been granted, their claims for textuality persist.

TEXTUALITY AND/AS SUPPLEMENT

The sketch sheet was a good example to demonstrate the notion of textuality as a mode of reading, if only because its textuality was dubious to begin with. But most representational works in the Western tradition pose the opposite difficulty: that of self-evident textuality. No one will deny the textual status of the *Bathshebah* painting, for example, at least according to my broad definition of text. The work has a frame that delimits it, a subject that gives it semantic coherence, and a composition that gives it formal structure. It is meaningful, even if interpretations vary, and it is full of signs.

In this case, the sense of unity passes unnoticed because it is not clearly contradicted by other signs. This sense of wholeness is also strengthened by recognition: The subject fits the tradition of representations of the Biblical Bathshebah, a favorite subject of painting in the Renaissance, and again a subject based on a story of problematic viewing. The story in II Samuel 11 narrates how David, after sending his army off to battle, remains idle in Jerusalem. Strolling on the roof of his palace, he sees a beautiful woman bathing. He sends a messenger to fetch her and has sex with her. When she becomes pregnant, he calls her husband, Uriah, back from the front, supposedly to cover up the rape/adultery. Uriah, however, three times refuses to enjoy the comfort of his home while his comrades at the front are fighting. This refusal seals his fate. David sends him back to the front with a letter for General Joab, in which he orders that Uriah be placed in military danger so that he will die. This happens, but at the cost of major losses. Joab sends a message with the bad news of the losses, but mitigates it with the good news of Uriah's death. God condemns David, and the prophet Nathan admonishes him through a fable. The child born of this event dies. True, we may not immediately recognize the iconographic subject of Bathshebah. But even if we don't, we still get a sense that something is happening; we get a sense of narrative.

Bathshebah's Bath is a complex work in terms of the various modes of reading it gives rise to. In the first place, viewers who know about "Rembrandt"'s work and life, who are interested in the connections between them – in other words, readers of the text "Rembrandt" – may see in it a portrait of his common-law wife Hendrickje Stoffels. This kind of noniconographic recognition requires knowledge, not of pictorial tradition but of biographical data and is not acquired separately from acquaintance with "Rem-

brandt": We know Hendrickje's face only through the representations of it in "Rembrandt."[4] Reading the painting as a portrait
of Hendrickje is a realistic reading, even if the quality of the information it is based on makes it quite dubious as a "truth." That
such a realistic reading may be no less legitimate than any other
reading should not concern us here.

A second mode of reading this work is as a traditional nude; thus
it can be discussed, in the terms of Chapter 4, as a potentially
voyeuristic work. There is surely a connection between the verbal
story, the pre-text in which voyeuristic vision determines the
events, and the popularity of the subject in painting. In the history
of Western art the theme of Bathshebah's bath is as often depicted
as Susanna's bath, and, I am afraid, for the same reason: Although,
and in some sense because, viewing is represented in these stories
as disturbing, they both lend themselves to voyeuristic purposes –
as well as to a critique of voyeurism.

It is easy to see right away that in terms of my analysis of voyeurism in Chapter 4, *Bathshebah's Bath* could qualify as moderately
voyeuristic. First, it exhibits the woman's body without representing either for identification or for ridicule the voyeuristic gaze
itself. Second, it does not thematize any contact between the naked
woman and the viewer, proposing neither an appeal for help nor
acquiescence. Third, just as in the Susanna case, the pre-textual
story itself mentions the woman's nakedness, the enticing effect it
has on the voyeur, and the subsequent (attempt at) rape. The story
is utterly doxic, so much so that even serious and sophisticated
scholarship fails to do justice to the details of the text. For the
knowledge the viewer may have of the Biblical text is not innocent
of later readings superimposed on it; as I have more than once been
able to check, most people have a vague "memory" that Bathshebah
was responsible for her own rape. This is a frequent response which
demonstrates the risks of the notion that recognition is denotative.
For it is an interpretation that II Samuel 11 does not at all call for,
but that has in effect been imposed on the story through an unacknowledged word–image interaction.

The iconographic reading, which travels from the text via the
preceding images that interpret and reinterpret it to the image at
hand, will identify the subject relatively easily if the reader possesses
enough familiarity with the tradition. The naked woman, the vague
suggestion of a roof in the background, the servant occupied with
the woman's toilet (not mentioned in the story of II Samuel 11,
but present in the iconographic tradition), and the letter in the
woman's hand – all are firmly established in the pictorial tradition.

That letter suggests a third way of reading the work; it promotes
the sense of textuality, but *not* because it is textual itself. The letter's
function depends on the reader's knowledge of the story and the
mode of reading adopted: It is what links an iconographic reading
with a biographical one on the one hand, and with the narrative
one on the other. As Gary Schwartz (1985:292) points out, the

work was painted in the year Hendrickje was summoned before the council of the Dutch Reformed Church for "living in sin with Rembrandt the painter." In a biographical interpretation, the letter in the woman's hand might be taken to refer to the letter Hendrickje received, and this biographical reference might account for the figure's melancholic look (Figure 6.6). For those who adopt this interpretation, the iconographic interpretation of the subject as Bathshebah is not plausible because a different story superseded the Biblical one. But Schwartz points out that the biographical event may have happened the other way around. The church councillors might have seen the work and interpreted the painting as a provocation, their indignation making them take action. This suggestion makes the letter meaningless for the biographical interpretation, while it establishes a biographical relation between the voyeuristic flavor of the work and the subsequent events. But since we cannot know the exact dates of the painting's composition and exhibition in connection with the letter's receipt, the question has to remain unresolved.

Nevertheless, if we bracket the iconographic tradition, it is at first sight not easy to interpret the work as a visual narrative in the way I suggested in the previous chapter. The scene is rather static, and no action takes place other than the routine manipulation of the woman's foot by her servant. Yet, even if one is unacquainted with the Bathshebah tradition, there is a strong sense of narrativity, which, I contend, can therefore be accounted for neither by mere iconographic nor by thematic recognition, nor by narrativity alone. As for the pre-text, reference to the Biblical story is scarce. We do not see any sign of the spying king. One might argue that whereas the Biblical story has the king send a servant, a messenger, to bring the woman whose view had kindled his desire, instead we have the letter, delivered by the messenger. However, this seems a rather arbitrary way of connecting the painting to a story where no letter delivered by the king's messenger to Bathshebah is mentioned. The letter is superfluous, a supplement, a detail, that nevertheless seems so "natural" that it calls the reader-for-the-text's attention to the unnaturalness of the sense of wholeness it disturbs.

But, in fact, recognition of the subject rests more probably on a somewhat uncomfortable logic, which reverses the relationship be-

6.6 *The Toilet of Bathshebah*, detail

tween the visual text and its pre-text. The fact that the woman is naked, and that her toilet is being attended to, seems to be enough to suggest that she is being prepared, "made beautiful," for a man, and that connection suggests that the image be interpreted in terms of the doxa. Out of reach of a critical response, the power of this implied viewer hovers over the woman's visual existence.

No alternative, text-internal narrative structure counters this effect – which is one of the reasons this work would qualify as quite voyeuristic. For it is not easy to construct a fabula, Bryson's (1983:56–66) minimal schema around the painting's syntagms: Elderly woman cleans nails of naked woman's foot? Woman holds a letter she just received? There is a sense of focalization in the woman's pose; her body, not her gaze, is slightly turned toward the viewer. While this serves the voyeuristic purpose, it does not connect to an alternative fabula that would thus be focalized. Only when the viewer identifies with King David, the voyeur – when, in other words, the body is offered to both the king and the customer – can a fabula be constructed, but that would bring the viewer into an uncomfortable position.

On the other hand, the woman's look is remarkable. She is undeniably melancholic and reflective. The reflectiveness is enhanced by the fact that her head turns away from the viewer while her body does not. These features remain nonnarrative, however, because they are related neither to one another nor to a fabula. But they do counter the voyeuristic effect in that the woman's unwillingness to communicate with the viewer problematizes the latter's position.

None of the attempts to construct a fabula outside of the Biblical doxa result in a naturalization of the image.[15] Although the image clearly makes sense as a whole, what sense it makes cannot easily be decided. We are left with a sense of narrativity that is not fulfilled; with a sense of wholeness that does not satisfy; with a frustrated need to position ourselves in relation to the viewing situation the narrative should bring forth but doesn't. These dead ends leave us with a strong awareness of textuality as not quite appropriate, as alien: Somehow, the image's textuality remains out of place.

THE LETTER'S SPECULATION

Still, the letter remains. Women writing, reading, or receiving letters are often represented in seventeenth-century Dutch genre painting, notably in interiors by de Hoogh, ter Borch, and especially Vermeer. Their occurrence is then embedded in the genderedness of this genre, where the household is the affair of women, and the men – often visitors, teachers of music, soldiers, or seducers – are intruders.[16] The occurrence of a letter as the central sign in a painting whose iconographic and narrative status is ambiguous is almost enough to make the work shift genres, from history painting to genre painting, perhaps in the same way as the dog did in the Last Supper sketch. The letter would then function in a different, but equally radically textual way: as an indicator of genre, even as a theoretical pun (Figure 6.7).

That does not make it any easier to decode, however. Iconographically, the letter is a type sign referring to clandestine love.[17] So it is possible to relate the letter to the melancholic look on the woman's face. Once that connection is made, within the practice of word–image interaction that informs our cultural attitudes, the impulse is to go to the Biblical story to establish such a link, as the iconographic tradition is likely to have found it there. And, if one looks for a letter that is linked to "infidelity" in II Samuel 11, one will indeed find one; but Bathshebah never sees it. It is the letter that David writes to the leader of his army, and in which he orders the latter to expose the bearer, Uriah, to mortal danger.[18]

That letter is, literally, the harbinger of death. After Bathshebah's appropriation by the king, it ushers us into the second, grimmer part of the story. Assigning that sinister function to it, then, is a way of dealing with the Biblical images that we have seen at work before – for example, in the proleptic woman-in-excess in the Tobias drawing. What happens in such an interpretation is that elements of the story get rearranged, motifs striking in their dramatic function are combined with motifs that have a stark effect on visual imagination. This way of reading the Biblical story visually, of taking up its motifs in juxtaposition and rearranging them in the space of the paint surface, leads us to ignore the place of each motif in the narrative sequence. In other words, reading the letter in Bathshebah's hand as an allusion to the letter condemning Uriah to death endorses the view that the iconographic tradition is based on such a doxic, rather than a literal, reading, in which a number of assumptions regarding gender relations in the story are also endorsed. From this perspective, Bathshebah is implicated in Uriah's death.

Relating that pre-textual reference to the letter in the painting can help the reader account for Bathshebah's melancholic look, but at the cost of semantic blurring and narrative complexity in the interaction between verbal and visual texts. Given this reading,

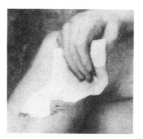

6.7 *The Toilet of Bathshebah*, detail

228

Bathshebah's look becomes narratively proleptic. This interpretation of the letter and the look, however, changes their status radically. Since according to the verbal story the female figure cannot have knowledge of the function of the letter, indeed, of its very existence, the letter becomes *the* sign for pictorial textuality, affecting the other signs related to it. It is a false sign of narrativity, and through its influence the melancholic look itself becomes a sign for textuality. It counters the painting's verisimilitude and displays the figure's function as semiotic object, as machine for generating meaning.

Starting with the other letter, one notices that it is a conspicuous, indeed, central sign in the work. It is placed in the center of the surface; its color sets it off from the softer colors that surround it; and by the many possible, yet equally deceptive associations it evokes, it seems saturated with meaning, without having any specific meaning. This is what makes the letter a sign for textuality. By an endless specularity, there is a tiny detail, the little red spot, hardly visible, on the left corner of the letter, that mirrors precisely these characteristics.

It is a strange spot; what does it signify – sealing wax or blood? If one takes it as a seal, it becomes a detail that enhances the reality of the letter: It becomes a sign for the real. The letter as a represented object is made to "look like" a real letter, and, in agreement with Barthes's concept of the effect of the real, this connotation of reality accounts for the red blot's occurrence as detail. But this interpretation does not quite work once we come to consider it more closely. For if the red blot is a seal it is strangely placed, not in the middle but in the corner of the letter. And the very contrast of red against white, as the white of the letter contrasts with the surrounding colors, calls attention to its strangeness. If the red blot cannot logically be a seal, perhaps it can be blood. And this possibly sets the speculating turmoil in motion again: Like the letter itself, the spot can be interpreted as a proleptic sign of impending violence, conferring this sense of violence onto the letter that contains and generates it. It refers, then, to the violent appropriation of the woman by David, the subsequent murder of her husband, and later, the death of the child born of the rape.

And again, that proleptic meaning refers to the textuality of these sign events: The woman holding the letter and the letter containing the spot have in realistic terms no bearing on the events the other signs predict, the signs for a doxic interpretation. The semiotic status of the spot is thereby self-reflexive: Dependent for its functioning on the signs that hold it and which it textualizes in turn, the spot is nothing in itself, has no positive meaning, and thereby foregrounds its semiotic nature. The spot mirrors the letter but it can do so only because the letter has already announced violence. The red spot also activates the letter as a sign for text in that it mirrors exactly the letter's position in the painting: central yet decentered, focal point on which all other details converge, yet a detail

229

that can remain buried under a realistic reading. The spot is to the rest of the letter what the letter is to the rest of the painting, to Bathshebah's melancholic look, among other things: It is a symptom of "text."

By their insistent suggestion of meaning, the signs discussed here demand a coherence that is not, after all, substantiated by the work as a whole. In fact, the strangest thing about them is that by their very function of indicating textuality, these signs denounce the lack of coherence, the lack of a particular meaning within the painting. Thus they indicate the irreducible gap between signifier and signified that Saussure insisted upon and that triggered Lacan's reworking of Saussure's semiotics. Signs like these, signifying at once their suggestion of meaning and meaning's deceptiveness, cannot be understood in terms of any of the usual categories of signs. They resemble most closely, while at the same time being most radically opposed to, Bryson's connotative signs, the signs for the real, to which we shall now turn briefly.

SIGNS FOR THE REAL

Originally, Roland Barthes's "effect of the real" was produced by elements that resisted meaning. Thus, it is tempting to consider as such all textual or visual "stuff" that is not indispensable for the production of the thematic or narrative meaning, but that does not attract attention to the work of representation or the textual status of the painting, as "effect of the real." In literary theory, the examples alleged are invariably descriptive details, considered superfluous to the narrative. But this tacit conflation between "signs for the real" and description seems to me unwarranted and confusing. Such a conflation is symptomatic of a problem in narrative theory that stems from a taxonomic tendency, in which events are privileged over other fabula elements, and fabula elements are privileged over representation.[19] This implicit hierarchy between events and other narrative elements is extremely tenacious, and is partly related to a cultural habit, partly to the influence of early structuralism.[20] But from another point of view, the conflation itself may be evidence of the effect of the real: Assuming, as alert readers of fiction, that the narrated events are fictitious, our need for a sense of a reality in which to place the events makes us welcome description as explicitly reality-based, even if it is, as support for the imagination, precisely not. In this case, we would have reason to privilege description under the rubric of *signs* for the real after all, without, however, making that privilege exclusive.[21]

Bryson relates the effect of the real to his revised concepts of denotation and connotation. My reluctance to adopt his proposal – to distinguish denotation and connotation as iconographic elements versus everything *not* required to make immediate sense of the image – stems from a long-standing quarrel with the logocentric

hierarchy between narrative and description, mentioned above.
Theoretical terms, whatever their intrinsic theoretical status, have
a positive heuristic effect, but they can also be quite stultifying in
that they maintain notions that hamper new insights and new
interpretations. Problematic concepts that reconfirm hierarchies between important and unimportant, between indispensable and dispensable elements, can have a temporary usefulness when
reformulated, but must always be challenged in their basic tenets,
or they will be utilized in support of reversionist positions.

If I delayed discussion of the better known effect of the real until
after the introduction of the effect of text, I did so to prevent the
effect of the real from falling back into the status of the "rest" or
of the lower half of a hierarchical dichotomy. Signs for the real
should not be defined negatively, as what they are not, but positively, as what they are, or rather, what they do. I would like to
approach them, not as a category like "description," which is too
much contaminated by its opposition to narration to stand outside
the hierarchy, but as an element within narration.

In his seminal essay "Vraisemblance et motivation" (1969b), Gérard Genette discussed narrative motivation, not description, when
he argued that the act of Madame de Clèves, heroine of Madame
de Lafayette's *La Princesse de Clèves* (1961), who told her husband
about her love for another man, was in urgent need of motivation
to make her action believable. This "plausibilization" was needed
because culturally, in terms of the current ideology of love and
marriage, the act was incongruous. But this insistence on verisimilitude is tricky; too much verisimilitude undermines its own
effect and makes the work ostensively textual.[22]

For the purpose of my analysis, the most prominent feature of
realism is its being mustered in the service of politics – in our case,
gender politics. Indeed, there is no better case to demonstrate this
alliance between realism and politics than the famous *querelle du
Cid*, started by the publication of the *Sentimens* in 1638 by the
Académie Française.[23] The relationship between state politics and
gender politics becomes particularly clear in the outright condemnation of Chimène's decision to marry the hero who has killed her
father, as *invraisemblable*. The Académie found it unthinkable that
in "real life" a woman would act in this way. *Bienséance* – how one
should behave, under specific political circumstances – thus completely overruled *vraisemblance*.[24] This seventeenth-century case is
comparable to both Pels's classicist response (in Schenkeveld, 1978)
to the excess/lack of realism in the nude in "Rembrandt," and to
Sir Kenneth Clark's connoisseurship (in Clark, 1978), appealing to
Rembrandt's love for truth to accommodate his, Clark's, personal
taste in matters sexual.

Thomas Mann (1948) played with this need for motivation in
the narrator's commentary on the gruesome evocation of the blood-
bath produced by Joseph's beauty in *Joseph in Egypt*. But the explicitness of his play reverses the effect, and makes the sign work

to arouse a self-reflexive awareness of fictionality. The very insistence of the narrator's claim to truth and verisimilitude accompanying the episode undermines any sign for the real the reader might have processed in the passage:

This oft-described scene has by some been thought to be apocryphal, and not belonging to the story as it happened. But they are wrong; for it is the truth, and all the probabilities speak for it. We must remember, on the one hand, that this was the most beautiful youth of his time and sphere; on the other, that those were the sharpest little knives the world had ever seen – and we shall understand that the thing could not happen otherwise – I mean with less shedding of blood – than as it actually did. (Mann, 1948:802)

Mann's protestations of reality and truth abound in protestations of literariness: The scene is *described*, thought to be *apocryphal*, and although he claims it *happened*, he still calls it a *story*.[25] Before alleging any argument for his claim, Mann merely repeats the authoritative truth-claim, displacing his obligation to justify it in an endless chain of truth claims: They are wrong (why?), for it is the truth (why?), and all probabilities speak for it (he has just acknowledged that the story is hard to believe). The latter phrase especially demonstrates Mann's play with *vraisemblance* as a literary device. When he finally comes up with an argument, he offers not a realist detail, but two universalistic judgments that undermine each other: If it was already hard to believe that someone could win the world contest for beauty, it is doubly hard to believe the stronger claim that these little knives were the sharpest ever (are there sharper big knives?).

The narrator, of course, couldn't care less; he is not really interested in making us believe his facts, but in combining them into something textually coherent. The combination of the two, beauty and knives, beauty and bloodshed – the resulting violence of beauty – is the "truth" the text generates. And if that truth can be conveyed only by the insistent textuality of his truth claim, so much the better. For this truth whose nature is psychoanalytic is a well-structured combination, a coherent event that "makes sense." The truth is framed by the fearful anticipation, the inevitable uniqueness, and the incurable loss, of initiation. In other words, "the truth" is a text itself.

But this is, historically speaking, modernist fiction; and in its self-reflexive self-undermining parody, it is even postmodernistic.[26] Moreover, in my interpretation at least, this fiction responds polemically to its own historical embeddedness, to the emerging Nazism by means of a critique of the realism that dominated art ever since the time of *La Princesse de Clèves* and "Rembrandt"'s *Bathshebah*.[27] Yet the parodic aspect of Mann's insistence on reality demonstrates what effective signs for the real must do. They must convince *without* insisting, they must be self-effacing, and divert us from, rather than drawing attention to, the textuality of the text. Signs for the real must not be explicit *as* signs for the real, even though they may be explicit as signs for something else. A convincing descriptive detail must not be explicit *as* description; an argument for the verisimilitude may be explicit as an argument for the righteousness of a decision, but not for its own verisimilitude. In Genette's examples, the signs for the real were not descriptive as opposed to narrative, but discursive and narrative at the same time, and that combination, although it diverted attention from the one in favor of the other, made them work.

A relevant example of this paradox is the reception of Flaubert's work. His work is generally considered the model of realistic writing, and the author's explicit poetics encourage such a reading. But his work is also considered the beginning of modernism, and its influence on Proust shows that this reception is also plausible. Yet modernist subjectivism is polemically opposed to realism's objectivism, to the claim of the narrator's self-effacement. Modernist subjectivism in turn entails the textual self-consciousness which, once radicalized, leads to postmodernism. It is in the allegedly realistic descriptions of visual space that the conflict between realism and textual self-consciousness betrays its inevitability.

The famous description of the city of Rouen in *Madame Bovary*, which so many literary theorists use as their privileged example, presents the view of the city from a diegetic focalization. The description is also emphatically perspectival, which makes it a good case for the discussion at hand. On the one hand, the description is doubly visualized; on the other it is doubly textualized. Provided with an emphatic viewer's position, inscribing an act of viewing that is in itself narrativized, the description is introduced by a metaphor of painting. Provided with an emphatic focalizer and a narrative structure, the description is constructed on linguistic tensions. The view of Rouen is thus narrativized by its embeddedness in a textual tension, visible in details like conflicting verb tenses, between narration and description. Narration is textually signaled by the *passé simple*, and description is visible in the "inappropriately" used, and thereby highly effective, *imparfait*, which betrays the boredom that overwhelms the phony surprise. The tension is resolved, or enhanced, by a "naturalizing" phrase which is, however, immediately followed by a renewed effort at narrativization by activating verbs:

Ainsi vu d'en haut, le paysage entier avait l'air *immobile comme une peinture*; les navires à l'ancre se tassaient dans un coin; le fleuve arrondissait sa courbe au pied des collines vertes, et les îles, de forme oblongue, semblaient des poissons noirs arrêtés.

Seen from above like this, the whole landscape looked still as a painting. In one corner ships crowded at anchor. The river curved round the green hills, the oblong islands looked like great dark fishes resting on its surface. (Flaubert, 1982:564; transl. 273, adapted)

The insistence on the stillness of the landscape, the invocation of the metaphor of a painting, is as unreliable as Mann's appeal to truth. The metaphor of the painting intervenes to harmonize the conflict instated by the opening sentence when insistent suddenness is brought to bear on stillness: "Puis, d'un seul coup d'oeil, la ville apparaiss*ait*" (literally, though ungrammatically: "Then, all at once the city was appearing"). The sentence transgresses all rules of grammar and style: The words *puis*, indicating the suddenness of the event of seeing, and *d'un seul coup d'oeil* ("in a single glance"), indicating the subjectivity of the act of seeing, are embedded in the narrative situation[28]; but the tense of *apparaissait* challenges not only these other signs of suddenness but even the semantic value of its own verb, *apparaître*, which implies suddenness.

The description of Rouen is, indeed, both radically realistic and radically textual. It is realistic in the two ways that this concept traditionally indicates: It depicts a "real" setting, and it is motivated by its embeddedness in the subjective narrative situation. These two forms of realism have in fact no inherent relation to each other, the one being based on text-external considerations, yet supporting imagination, the other on text-internal consideration, yet supporting the realistic effect. It is textual in that it insists on a sense of conflict. The metaphorical comparison "still as a painting" thereby fulfills a supplementary function: Its difference from the personified, activated elaboration that follows emphatically demonstrates that the constructed landscape is *not* still under Emma's gaze; and neither is, of course, the equally constructed painting it is supposed to resemble. As a sign for the real, this metaphor is like the red spot on Bathshebah's letter. As a symptom that something strange is at stake with the element these signs synecdochically signify – the description of Rouen, the letter – they burden the reality effect with a self-defeating rhetoric that points to the paradox of realism: That realism as a device undermines the sense of reality.

TEXTUALITY AND REALISM

The kind of signs at stake in the effect of the real signify the ideas of reality, plausibility, naturalness, truthfulness, and truth. One element in the truth status of a work is the sense of wholeness. When this sense of wholeness is brought about by signs for the real, it is overlooked, taken for granted; when brought about by signs for text, it is seen as constructed; everything that triggers awareness of the arbitrariness of the frame breaks the illusion of reality. Read as signs for the real, textual details convey the idea of the real only by effacing their own status as signs; signs for text can only emphasize that status. But it is the reader who decides which effect the signs will produce. While the realistic reading is often the more tempting, because smoother and more facile, more reassuring reading, the textual reading is more empowering because the sense of wholeness that remains implicit within the realistic reading is the more vulnerable to any sense of fracture within the text. The sense of textuality can accommodate such a sense even in realistic terms, provided the reader is open to the fractured state of reality.

This paradoxical state of affairs becomes understandable once we realize that Lacan's lesson is relevant in a broader context than a limited psychoanalytic one. Lacan (1966a) contended that the basis and source of experience, thought, and feeling is the symbolic, not the real. What is real, for Lacan, is not accessible and can be described only as being minus representation, description, or interpretation; minus symbolization, that is. Realism, in Elisabeth Bronfen's terms, describes the moments in a representational text that do not cover up the translation of the real into representation, but that show the real as fractured and emphasize that fractured state.[29] In this sense, realism becomes identical with textuality.

But this redefinition does not leave room for the *illusionary* realistic effect as it has been traditionally defined, so it precludes a serious critique of realism as an ideological, obscuring device that readers can but need not endorse. In a realistic reading, as traditionally considered, the position of the author as the critical agent tends to be conflated with that of the reader as the passive follower. Instead, I would like to suggest that the conventional sense of realism as effect be incorporated into Bronfen's new sense of realism as the unmasking of that effect. When the two are combined, a new, critical realistic mode of reading emerges. The combination occurs when the reader decides not to take for granted the wholeness enhanced by the detail, but instead to open the detail to the subversion that makes it, rather than the whole, the dominant element.[30] The realistic detail is then not conflated with the textual detail. So the two effects can collaborate with or work against each other, according to the activity of the viewer.

As Bryson and others have convincingly shown, the interpretation of art in the modern West has been so thoroughly contingent upon the ideal of a perfect reproduction of reality that it is not always easy to see how the sense of reality itself is constructed. Arriving at this recognition is even more difficult since these signs are conventionally assumed to work against awareness of their occurrence. And because the signs for the real are the most difficult to isolate, they often become relegated to a category of "leftovers."

The most obvious and powerful sign for the real in modern Western art is perspective. Even in Flaubert's description of Rouen, perspective played a major, albeit deceptive, part. The passion with which perspective is not only taken for granted, but also taken to be an absolute, scientific basis for all paintings and a reliable starting point for a scholarly argument about what the work "really" represents, is in itself evidence for the semiotic power of perspective as a sign.[31] A good example of the signifying power of perspective is the recent discussion of *Las Meninas*, where the question of perspective gave rise, on the one hand, to a passionate defense of Velázquez's scientific reliability while on the other was criticized at least by one viewer for "scientific mistakes." Although I shall hold this debate in reserve to be the verbal core of the next chapter, I shall just mention here that the debate demonstrates that perspective is perceived not as a sign but as a truth.

The impulse to read realistically is strongly promoted by the *Bathshebah*. For example, we noticed the conflict that makes the letter stand out. Let us start, now, not at the letter but at the look, a humanistically more appealing place to begin. The woman's melancholic look, directed nowhere, requires psychological motivation. The need for motivation is produced by the lack of connection between her look and the old servant polishing her nails. When two figures are facing each other, we expect them to look at each other, to be somehow involved with each other. The composition of the painting emphasizes this expectation by a straight diagonal line from the heroine's head to the servant's, underscored by a lower diagonal formed by Bathshebah's arm and leg, with the letter in the middle. But instead of communicating with each other, the two women here are preoccupied with something else. The intensity of their preoccupation is equally emphasized. The veiled old woman, humbly sitting at the heroine's feet, looks intensely upon the object of her care. Her hand displays the tension that we have come to know as a sign of "work" and that we can now see as a double sign for realism and textuality. The pressure of the hand refers at first sight to the "real" work of taking care, but the effect is slightly overdone, thereby referring back to itself *as* sign for the real.

Realistically speaking, the intense pressure could not but hurt

6.8 *The Toilet of Bathshebah*, detail

Bathshebah's toes and distract her from her self-absorption (Figure 6.8). Bathshebah, similarly, undermines the expectations of the narrative mode of reading by denying the sequence of events. She is staring so intently that she is clearly not about to act. Visually, her position as much as forces her to direct her gaze toward the elderly woman, but she is instead equally intensely engaged in staring vacantly. But her line of sight is broken, and the letter is the locus of its breach. If the letter were not there, the painting's line of sight would make almost no sense at all. The staring is the sign that produces the sense of need for the letter.

But this is a reversal of the function of the letter as discussed previously. If it is the deviant inward look of the woman that gives the letter its purpose, we are far removed from the letter's power to turn the look into "text." As a sign for the real, then, the look does its job. The look as sign, as rival of the letter, overwhelms the letter's role as psychological motivation for an act – staring – which is culturally considered odd – or meaningful. This is the ideal sign for the real: Powerful and overwhelming, the look asserts itself, against all odds, without necessarily being noticed as such. All the problems are swept aside: That the reference to (and the subsequent recognition of) II Samuel 11 contradicts the letter as motivation, that in fact the letter stands out as a sign more clearly than does the look precisely because the letter is less easy to explain, and that the sign status of the letter is emphasized by the red spot which mirrors it – all this is swept aside, suppressed, by the interpretation of the inward look as melancholic.

VISUAL SIGNS AND VERBAL IMAGES: THE INSTANCE OF THE LETTER

The problems raised by the tensions between the two modes of reading at stake in this chapter are intimately related to the ideological consequences of the cultural attitudes toward verbal and visual media; to the fact that these are seen as media rather than as modes of reading. With this in mind, we are now ready to consider these tensions between signs for textuality and signs for the real in direct relation to the subject of this study: the interaction between the verbal and visual arts. We cannot overlook the fact that the troublesome sign in the *Bathshebah* is a letter, not just any sort of sign but a text, a self-reflexive sign for textual coherence; but it is also a verbal text, visually representing "verbality." The most fascinating aspect of this tension between the letter, as sign for text appropriating the look for its cause, and the look, as sign for the real appropriating the letter for its effacement, comes to the fore when, and only when, the viewer knows II Samuel 11 *as a text*, not as a doxa; in other words, and punning on a Lacanian punning title, the instance of the letter is the reason for the contradictory effect.[32] The icon is thoroughly verbal, but in its verbality, thoroughly visual. We may or may not appeal to an iconographic tradition that makes the letter a more effective iconographic sign in the standard sense. That is, the opposing signs bring us back to the kind of iconography that I have called pre-textual reading. But an attempt to incorporate the actual pre-text while eliminating the imposition of its diffuse readings – its connotations in Barthes's sense, its doxic version – is more rewarding for a *visual* assessment of the work than is merely relying on the pictorial tradition. The "instance of the letter" is the shifter, the little detail that hooks us and imposes the text alluded to, that lets the text spread out and take over.

If we look at the pre-text to which the letter refers us, we shall find that it is as troublesome as the painting; it, too, has a detail that doesn't fit. The tension there is elaborated between a verbal but quite visual image ("Who smote Abimelech the son of Jerubbesheth? Did not a woman cast a piece of a millstone upon him from the wall, that he died in Thebez?") and a text (the letter from David which contains Uriah's death sentence and which the victim carries himself to the executioner). This image (occurring in verse 21) is a metaphor that does not make sense in any "logical" way, in terms of the fabula as a sequence of events, that is. It thereby symptomatically insists on the text as *other* than a story. The image deserves special attention, also because it is so starkly and, indeed, disquietingly visual. Finally, it is ideologically troublesome. Displacing the issues raised in the text in which a rapist needs to cover up, first his rape, then the subsequent murder he brings about, this metaphor attempts to pass off as self-evidently true a negative judgment on the woman in the story that no detail in the text supports. For this metaphor suggests that Bathshebah has provoked her own rape, that she is the real culprit, that the murder was caused by her sheer visual existence. The image may be taken as a symptom of the narrator's hidden agenda; the subsequent doxic versions of the story provide evidence of the success of that agenda. The relation between the painting and its "out-of-place" letter and between the text and its "out-of-place" image is emphasized by the coincidence of *the place of the letter* in the two works. Indeed, that place is as conspicuous and thereby as invisible as that of the letter purloined in Poe's famous story.[33]

As a metaphor, or allegory, of literality as discussed in Chapter 3, the letter must be given full weight. Visually speaking – in terms of distribution of space – the letter is both the visual center of the painting and the textual center of the story. Since the letter holding Uriah's death sentence in the story literally occupies the middle verse of the chapter, we might consider it in terms of Mitchell's four levels of spatial form in literature (Mitchell, 1984:283–5).

These four levels are the material form of the text, the represented space, the form in the structural sense, and the meaning that we "see" – before our mind's eye – when we understand a text. We have already seen that the verse in which the letter figures is literally central. The letter also occupies a middle position in the represented space, since the text is divided between events taking place in the palace in Jerusalem and events taking place at the front. The letter being transferred between these two spaces stands between them and, rather than connecting, separates them. And it is also structurally central and mediating because in terms of the aspects of narrative, it represents an intermediate position.

This intermediate position of Uriah's letter can be described as follows: The letter as spoken but not directly quoted discourse stands ambiguously between narrative voice and direct quotation, spoken discourse. In terms of speakers, David, the "speaker" of the letter, needs the messenger, the victim of his scheme, in order to reach his addressee who is to carry out the scheme. The event, of which the letter is the center, its transmission from one place to another, is the only moment in the story where focalization is excluded: Uriah holds the letter, but does not read it; failing to connect visuality with textuality by reading, he will die. The letter comes to stand as an emblem of the painted letter: It can be seen but not read; it functions visually but not verbally. The letter, then, is an *image*: a visual sign autonomous enough to work as a sign, yet embedded in a framework which it supports, and also by which it is supported. In terms of action, the letter stands between private violence (rape) and its concealment, and public violence (murder) and its concealment, as a brief moment of suspension. As a central event, the letter is also an emblem of a specific view of storytelling: a story that tells itself, that happens as it unfolds.

Given this central position of the letter in the text, the central position of the letter in the painting can be seen as a visual reference to the spatial position of the letter in the text. But by taking it that way, we can come to see even more. For in II Samuel 11 the letter killed. This murderous quality is both obvious and invisible, as the text surrounding it employs all possible means to conceal it. The major devices of this concealment are twofold: It uses breaches of narrative logic and also metaphor as symptom that becomes allegory. The content of the letter does not correspond to the events that fulfill its orders; instead of killing Uriah alone, the letter kills many soldiers. Thus the story line is problematized. But the metaphor, on the other hand, poeticizes the story. By its form it underscores a textual mode other than narrative. Thus metaphor becomes the alien element, the *allos* of de Man's (1979) concept of allegory, which operates the reversal of the story's meaning. Its effect is comparable to that of Bathshebah's melancholic look in the painting: Both can be taken either to explain away and reassure, or to enhance the strangeness of the letter and thereby trouble the reader.

The comparison in verse 21 seems to juxtapose, in an exasperatingly complex structure of embedding which in turn foregrounds its own fictionality, the victim Uriah who has been killed by Dav-

239

id's letter and the tyrant Abimelech who is deservedly killed by a heroic woman. The comparison is a starkly visual and exceedingly metaphorical image:

20 And if [it] so be that the king's wrath arise, and he say unto thee, Wherefore approached ye so nigh unto the city when ye did fight? knew ye not that they would shoot from the wall?
21 Who smote Abimelech the son of Jerubbesheth? Did not a woman cast a piece of a millstone upon him from the wall, that he died in Thebez? then say thou, Thy servant Uriah is dead also.[34]

The comparison is displaced, since Bathshebah, the woman in the story, is the victim, not the victor: Raped, she loses her husband in the aftermath of the struggle between the two men for her possession, and she will lose the child born of the rape. Uriah is a victim, too, since he loses his wife and his life. Abimelech, in contrast, is a usurping king: a tyrant. That the metaphor is both strongly motivated and at the same time absurdly unmotivated produces a sense of displacement. It is overdetermined thematically, since between the two murders there are at least six common elements: death, woman, wall, battle, shame, folly. All six motifs connect the metaphor to the letter as well: With the letter containing a sentence of death due to a woman, a death that is to take place at the wall and in battle, the letter's carrier brings shame on himself by being foolish enough to be honest.

On the other hand, the metaphor is unmotivated narratively, since these motives do not relate the metaphorical woman, the vehicle (the woman with the millstone, of Judges 9:53–4, who killed), to the woman referred to, its tenor (Bathshebah, the victim who is first raped and then widowed). Instead it should relate the

6.9 *David Receiving the News of Uriah's Death* ca. 1652, Benesch 890, drawing, 195 × 290 mm (Amsterdam, Rijksprentenkabinet)

shameful and foolish victim of Judges 9:53–4 to David the mighty
king of Israel. But the displacement is so emphatic that it is both
difficult and urgent that we make sense of it, and we can, if we
allow ourselves to read the patriarchal text as possessing, hidden
in its symptomatically confused detail, a critical, perhaps self-
critical, potential.

The visuality of the image invoked in II Samuel 11:21 can help
sort out these confusing aspects. The comparison is highly visual
even in it own pre-textual reference: the impressive pre-textual
image of Judges 9:53, evoked "iconographically," of a woman
standing high on top of the threatened tower of defense, dropping
her weapon – a millstone, instrument of her peaceful work, displaced in the military situation – on the head of the usurper. The
image is also highly gendered. In Judges, the fallen tyrant is so
ashamed of being killed by a woman that he orders his armbearer
to kill him quickly so that nobody will be able to say that he was
killed by a woman. In retrospect, then, it is tempting to read into
the visuality of the image the geography of the female body and
the intimidating impression it makes on the scared male: the tow-
ering woman, threateningly impressive in the eyes of the bluffing
tyrant who is approaching the entrance to the city, figuring the
woman's entrance, too closely. We can argue that this visualization
of the female body informs the comparison of II Samuel 11, which
in turn informs the "Rembrandt" painting. In fact, bluff is exactly
what Joab, the frightened man who comes up with this image,
anticipates David will reproach him with.

This reading of the verbal text receives some unexpected support
from a drawing that is assumed to represent the moment when
David receives the news of Uriah's death – the moment anticipated
by our comparison, that is (Figure 6.9). David seems surprised by
the messenger who has come to bring him the "good" news: the
murder by letter. Why would he be surprised? The soldier-
messenger bends his body as in fearful anticipation of David's expected anger. But no anger, no display of power is represented on
David's face; surprise, and maybe fear, are shown instead. The king
is standing on the balcony, the roof from which he spied on the
innocently bathing Bathshebah, and perhaps, given the narrative
device of condensation, the elevated place cannot but evoke the
tower of Abimelech's death in the comparison in II Samuel 11:21.
In the entrance, we see "already" the prophet Nathan, coming to
admonish the king for his crime of usurpation and to announce his
punishment. His position at the entrance is a literal embodiment
of the figure's entrance into the story. This conflation of three
moments of the story, and of the figurative representation of the
meaning that we "see" (Mitchell, 1984) when we acknowledge the
confusion of the comparison rather than explaining it away, makes
this drawing a particularly effective one.

The function of the metaphor, with all its distortions and irrelevancies, is to displace the guilt for the violent event from the king onto his victim. The metaphor, rather than Uriah, carries the letter over, transforming the story from a literal into a figurative, allegorical reading. And true enough, the issue that motivated the entire story is, indeed, the power of the female, a power that brought about the moral fall of Israel's king of kings, a power that only the most absolute, tyrannical power of the male can supersede. And what is that power? Nothing but the visual power of her body. Seeing her naked, David the voyeur *must* have her, regardless of the price he has to pay: his moral integrity, his best soldiers, and later, the life of his son. The metaphor drives home the "truth": that readers have the reassuring option of salvaging the reputation of the king by blaming vision and the woman, an option readers in the modern West eagerly adopt. The *image* of Bathshebah brought the king down.

This text is not just a defense of voyeurism and the ensuing rape, although on one level of reading it comes close to that, exactly as does the painting.[35] When read at face value, as most critics do who fall into the trap of its metaphoric motivation, the image stands for the woman's responsibility in the event.[36] The difficulty of disentangling the figure's structure makes ignoring its status as sign attractive. Thus conceived, the comparison functions as a sign for the real, but the "real" in question carries with it a specific gender ideology. In order to step outside of this ideology, we must reverse the perspective and look at the image *as sign*: take it *à la lettre*.

The image signifies displacement, and in that respect resembles the spot on the letter in the painting. Displaced out of the center while representing a central concern, and displacing the guilt of the violence from perpetrator to victim, the displaced image not only displaces, but also draws attention to displacement. The complexity of its own structure, which counters any attempt to disentangle it by narrative logic, refers back to the letter, which made possible both the event and this response to the event. The comparison in II Samuel 11:21 was produced by the letter's having been carried over, in the middle of the text, from one side of the represented space to the other. In other words, the letter also stood for displacement, for transition, for reversal. As the figural crux of the text, the letter engendered all subsequent textual figurations. The comparison of verse 21 is predicated upon the letter. And the letter, itself such a central figuration of the narrative text, is a sign for "text," rather than for the "real" which that text might also evoke. This is not so because the letter happens to be itself a representation of a text but because, as an image, it structures the set of signs around it into "text." The sophistication of the letter's central position draws attention to the sophistication of the comparison it produces, and whose apparent confusion may be very significant. Less than real, its meaning is ideological, and its means of conveying meaning, textual.

READING DISTORTION

If we now return to the letter with the red spot in its corner which Bathshebah holds in the painting, we discover that it, too, exposes another detail; the painting has its own "verse 21" – a detail that doesn't fit, a distortion of structure, a voyeuristic tendency, and a geography of the female body. For those who are willing to read with the text, not with the doxa, and with the detail, not with the "official story," the painting holds a surprise.

Bathshebah's body is where I suggest we finally look. After all, the painting is, on one level, just a female nude, as gorgeous as the *Danae* and as intriguingly strange. If we look at the body, without taking for granted that it is just a female body presented for our delectation, we notice that the body is twisted. It thereby reminds us of the overexhibited female body in the Joseph etching. But this time it is only slightly twisted, hardly perceptibly: Textuality is almost, but not quite, overruled by realism. The twist has the same function as the metaphor in II Samuel 11: It allows us to endorse the ideology of voyeurism and, siding with David, to blame the exposed woman. Her legs are crossed, and their crossing, made conspicuous by the letter that partly covers it, is the locus of the distortion. It is there that narrative and ideology, and textuality and realism, collide and collude (Figure 6.10).

Realistically/narratively speaking, the legs are crossed so that the servant/procuress can fulfill her duty and prepare the woman for royal rape. At the same time, rhetorically speaking, the body is turned toward the viewer who stands in for the king as the voyeur whose act of vision prepares *him* for the rape. The distortion comes to preclude this smooth appropriation. For if coherent and unproblematic voyeurism were the point, crossing the figure's legs the other way would have been much more convenient. Although the figure's right leg is crossed over her left leg, the right foot remains at the right side of the knees. Had the figure crossed her legs the other way, no awkward twisting would have been necessary. But then the body would not have been turned as much toward the viewer. So the twisting seems to be the point, and we

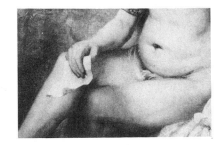

6.10   *The Toilet of Bathshebah,*
detail

can read that twist as the shift from realism to textual self-consciousness.

Indeed, this reading becomes quite plausible in the face of the letter. First, in the middle of the diagonal line leading from Bathsheba's melancholic look to her foot in the servant's hand, there is a text: a letter. Second, the line from Bathsheba to the servant only highlights the fact that she does not *look* where her eyes are directed. Her inward look goes nowhere, rigidified as it is in melancholy. Is she already mourning her murdered husband? Or her appropriated body? Or her not yet conceived son? That in itself is a highly self-conscious textual construction, for she is only being prepared for the insemination whose success will *then* lead to the murder of Uriah and the death of the offspring. Both her melancholy and the letter are radically out of place as well as absolutely central.

Until this very day, readers eagerly adopt the notion that *since* the Biblical text lets the murderer blame the victim by metaphorization, she *must* have provoked the event; thus, for example, readers retrospectively accuse her of exhibitionism, rather than David of voyeurism. But the painting's textuality disturbs such an illusion. This is why the body had to be twisted and the legs crossed in a less than handy way: This pose was necessary to expose the "geography" of the female body as well as that exposure itself. At the center of the painting is the letter; at the center of the body is the navel. The navel, the center of the body, had to be displayed so that the viewer could collude with David's voyeurism, but the display itself – its artificiality – had to be emphasized. The navel, then, functions like the empty space at which the Elder in the Berlin *Susanna* stares. The twist foregrounds textuality, constructedness, contradiction. The woman's navel is not quite the navel of the text. The letter – a text evoking a text in order to distort one – and in the corner of the letter, the little red blot, both constitute the trace of a genesis void of meaning that diffuses meanings throughout the text. Could the red spot be explained as the letter's seal? Surely, if you like. But then, it is displaced in its turn, from the middle where seals tend to be applied, to the corner, marginalized. And then, it is void in its turn, for the secret which seals are meant to warrant is unveiled: The letter is open, its metaphoric hymen broken.

If we assume that the spot denotes blood, announcing the bloody events the sealed letter is meant to bring forth, then the fact that the wrong figure is holding it calls into question the effectiveness of the seal, of the letter, of the text. In other words, the little spot points to a confusion that in its similitude to the one in the text denounces the confusion in the text and those persistent readings it has triggered. The confusion pervades the image, infecting the delectable body and the navel thereof, for the sake of whose exhibition the entire body had to be twisted, so that we could realize the difference between a realistic navel as a center for erotic viewing and a textual navel as a diffusing and confusing void center – a trace or *gramme* of the image's genesis in pre-textuality.

CONCLUSION

In conjunction with this very literary reading of the literary pre-text, what can we conclude about the painting's signs and the modes of reading they allow us to endorse? The two readings of the letter as sign for text and the look as sign for the real are mutually exclusive, incompatible yet competing because they each appropriate the other sign within their reach. The simultaneous occurrence of both sign events is impossible. Yet both interpretations are possible. In other words, another commonplace about the distinction between visual and verbal art has to be sacrificed: We must discard the notion that verbal works are processed sequentially, in time, whereas visual art can be viewed in a single moment.[37] The viewer who wishes to reflect on both possibilities of interpretation needs to shift alternately from one mode to the other. So does the reader who wishes to account for both the realistic-ideological appeal of the metaphor in II Samuel 11 and for the textual effect of the letter, which undermines that appeal. Both readings are non-sequential and nonsimultaneous.

The incompatibility and the irreducible gap between them makes the entire painting hinge on a gestalt shift, makes the painting akin to the rabbit-or-duck drawing: Is this a text or a scene, a narrative or a display, a painting or a woman? It cannot be both at the same time, for the power of signs for the real resides in this exclusiveness. Thus we must conclude that signs, indeed, are events, and that we viewers are the subjects who bring about these events. We choose between the rabbit and the duck, the text and the woman. And we have the possibility of choosing both, although not within the same reading event.

But these readings are not *imposed* by the work; realism as a mode of reading can help us *not* read in this way. For the Washington *Lucretia* can surely go a long way without the attention to rhetoric that helped reading into it a statement about rape, representation, and the subjectivity of the victim. The shadow of the dagger can be motivated by a concern for the representation of speed: as a sign for the real, which makes the act plausible. The fact that the sleeve is blurred makes the speed interpretation even more compelling. And yes, the woman in the etching of Joseph and Potiphar's wife *is* holding a fold in the garment. The gesture of her hand is a powerful sign of the real that attempts to efface the traces of the representation, which are, in that case, the absence of traces of the "real" meaning. The second head behind Christ in the sketch of the Last Supper could be just a discarded first draft, and the empty fist of the Elder in the Berlin *Susanna* could remain empty.

There is no reason to argue that signs for the real are more descriptive, more visual, less narrative, than other kinds of signs. They participate in the narrative, descriptively or otherwise, and they are visual or verbal according to the work and the element in which they function. If they tend to overwhelm other signs, it is because of the cultural habits with which we approach the works, not because realism is inherently powerful. It depends on us viewers to interpret the doubling of the end of Bathshebah's left braid either as a shadow of the braid or as a painterly trace, as a thing that effaces the work of the representation or as a symptom that foregrounds it.

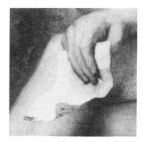

CHAPTER 7

SELF-REFLECTION AS A
MODE OF READING

Perhaps there exists, in this painting by Velázquez, the representation as it were, of Classical representation, and the definition of the space it opens up to us. And, indeed, representation undertakes to represent itself here in all its elements, with its images, the eyes to which it is offered, the faces it makes visible, the gestures it calls into being. But there, in the midst of this dispersion which it is simultaneously grouping together and spreading out before us, indicated compellingly from every side, is an essential void: the necessary disappearance of that which is its foundation – of the person it resembles and the person in whose eyes it is only a resemblance. This very subject – which is the same – has been elided. And representation, freed finally from the relation that was impeding it, can offer itself as representation in its purest form. (Michel Foucault, *The Order of Things*, 1973:16)

INTRODUCTION

FOUCAULT's final words of his introductory chapter of *The Order of Things* are a beautiful expression of a mode of reading that has become quite common, even predominant, with the rise of poststructuralism and postmodernism. Self-reflection in art is today highly valued because it reacts against realism, drawing attention to the making of art, to its constructedness. The tensions between modes of reading I have discussed in the previous chapters – between iconographic recognition and narrative construction, between realistic recognition and textual construction – are productive tensions precisely because they make us aware of the choices involved in processing art. Self-reflection, then, is at first sight just another possible mode of reading.

But within the framework of a reading-oriented theory of art, self-reflection as a mode of reading entails a complication, rendered in its simplest form by the question, Whose self is being reflected, anyway? The identity between the work and its subject – between work as labor and work as product – is not unified; it is fragmented by the intrusion of the reader/viewer whose position is inherently paradoxical: Is she or he part of the self being reflected or reflected on? If so, then the self-reflective mode of reading, which subsumes the viewer into the work, does not encourage the viewer to reflect on self; hence, the self remains whole, while only the reflection becomes fractured; if the viewer is not part of the self that is being reflected (upon), then the self is disrupted from the start, and again, the viewer will not be encouraged to reflect on his or her self. This paradox is the subject of this chapter.

Svetlana Alpers begins her article on *Las Meninas* (Figure 7.1) with the following appraisal:

Along with Vermeer's *Art of Painting* and Courbet's *Studio*, Velázquez's *Las Meninas* . . . is surely one of the greatest representations of pictorial representation in all of Western painting. (Alpers, 1983:31)

It seems that we are to turn to the Spanish masterpiece, rather than to "Rembrandt" where, in spite of an abundance of self-portraits, there is hardly a representation of painting, and only a few of the artist's self as painter. Yet, the cover of Georgel and Lecoq's book on self-reflexive painting, *La Peinture dans la peinture*, has "Rembrandt"'s little panel *The Artist in His Studio* (Figure 7.2), not the more obvious Velázquez, on its cover. This very early painting, and one certainly not in the category of masterpieces Alpers refers to, stands alone in the artist's oeuvre. The modest size and thematic simplicity of the "Rembrandt" compared to the proudly huge and insistently complex Velázquez makes the evocation of the former in relation to the latter seem almost inappropriate – if it were not for the mode of reading we are inclined to bring to both works and whose mission it is to question such appraisals. Indeed, it is to this little work, along with *Las Meninas*, that Leo Steinberg refers in his analysis of Picasso's lifelong obsession with simultaneity, his effort to overcome the limitations of perspective:

Or else the foreground motif is a canvas in progress – as in Rembrandt's *Painter Before His Easel* (Boston), and in Velázquez' *Las Meninas*. In both pictures, our attention turns on the glance of the painter; behind the reverse of the canvas, we see its obverse observed. (Steinberg, 1972:182)

Steinberg's formulation – "Our attention turns on the glance of the painter" – is as enigmatic as it is to the point. For the eyes of the represented painter are exactly the point: Those eyes are not depicted but turned into signs. Self-reflection counters realism.[1]

As we have seen, the effect of the real, in its pursuit of unproblematic representation, is resisted by the mode of reading that privileges textuality, which insists on the constructedness of wholeness. Only to a limited extent can a reader who wants to believe in the illusory transparency of realistic art and fiction ignore disturbing countersigns; beyond that, a viewer/reader holding such a belief will be annoyed by the unlikeliness of the representation and sometimes even condemn the artist as lacking skill.

The *Bathshebah* is not likely to elicit such a reaction, for the painting can accommodate both realistic and textual readings; but the *Joseph* etching (Figure 3.6) might. Viewers who respond to the work's narrative strategy are forced to see the collusion and collision of the story of desired initiation and the story of fatherly jealousy making the woman's body deviate from a "real" body, by depriving it of its wholeness. But the viewer who is not ready to attribute the strangely distorted body of the woman to a narrative strategy

7.1   Diego Velázquez, *Las Meninas* 1656, canvas, 321 × 281 cm (Madrid, Museo del Prado)

249

will find it oddly drawn. In addition, those viewers who are aware of the work's narrative strategy will also necessarily become aware of representation as manipulation. Once the woman is seen as the product of the two men's imagination, then the fabula of the narrative itself is instantly modified. But again, the viewer who overlooks the work's narrative strategy will miss this complication as well. I shall argue in this chapter that viewers who engage in a narrative reading, when we push it a little further, will be led to reflect on the work itself and its work upon us: Those viewers will be led to self-reflection. But this self-reflection is by definition double-edged.

This mode of reading is made double-edged by its relationship to narcissism. The effectively antirealistic reading strategy favored in postmodern criticism, the mode of reading I want to explore in this chapter, is self-referential: It is a reading for the work itself, the mode that makes us read, to use Linda Hutcheon's term, for the narcissism in the work.[2] The term admittedly has its drawbacks;

7.2 *The Artist in His Studio* ca. 1629, Bredius 419, panel, 25.1 × 31.9 cm (Boston, Museum of Fine Arts)

although Hutcheon warns us not to take it negatively, the sense of self-closure and death conveyed by its psychoanalytic framework is hard to avoid. However, compounding the mythical, visual, and psychoanalytic connotations of narcissism, the term also illuminates the particular pictorial quality and the erotic near-gratification of self-reference. The concept of narcissism will be used here as a bridge between the self-reflective mode of reading and the problems inherent in a psychoanalytic approach to painting, which will be the subject of the following chapter. But in order to allow for such a leap from pictorial self-reflection to psychoanalytic narcissism, the very idea of self-reflective reading needs elucidation.

THE STILL LIFE OF MIRRORING:
SELF-PORTRAITS

In Velázquez's *Las Meninas* the detail that elicited the responses analyzed in this chapter is the mirror, the typical device for self-reflection. I shall show that this mirror is the screen on which the critics project their desires. In the "Rembrandt" panel, the mirror is not represented, but neither is it absent: The panel contains, among other things, a self-portrait, and self-portraiture implies mirroring. In this sense alone, can self-portraiture as a genre be taken to be self-reflexive by definition.

Many of the "Rembrandt" self-portraits-without-mirror foreground the self-representational aspects of the works. Either the work emphatically explores the face, as in the set of early etchings, or it foregrounds the constructive aspect of the posture, as in the two late self-portraits representing the self as painter, or as in the impressive self-portrait of 1658 in the Frick Collection where the self assumes royal status not only by posture but also by dress. In the following chapter, I shall say more about the way in which narcissism in the stricter sense is at issue in these works. Here I invoke them because, rather than an implied viewer, they suggest an implied mirror, in which viewer and painter are identified (Figure 7.3).

The early etchings and the late self-portrait are opposed, yet complementary. The etchings might be seen to emphasize the exploration of the face, the discovery of its "ugliness" as part of the act of representing it; as Chapman (1989:160) put it, they represent extreme facial expressions. The etchings narrativize the self-exploration and representation. The first one especially relates the shock of self-reflection, representing the face so close to the work's surface that the figure seems to draw back after literally hitting the mirror. Here, the viewer's place is absorbed, the piercing eyes of the figure discouraging a comfortable viewing position. Pain is also the central motif in the second etching, which emphasizes all the figure's "ugly" features: the wild hair, asymmetrical eyes, broken nose, and wrinkles between the tense eyebrows. The Frick painting,

7.3 Collage of series of self-portraits. Top row, left to right: *Self-Portrait* 1660, Bredius 53, canvas, 111 × 85 cm (Paris, Musée du Louvre); *Self-Portrait* 1658, Bredius 50, canvas, 133.7 × 103.8 cm (New York, The Frick Collection); *Self-Portrait* ca. 1661–2, Bredius 52, canvas, 114.3 × 95.2 cm (London, Kenwood House, The Iveagh Bequest). Middle row, left: *Self-Portrait with Hagard Eyes* 1630, etching (Paris, Bibliotheque Nationale). Middle row, right: *Self-Portrait with Wild Hair* 1631, etching (Amsterdam, Rijksprentenkabinet). Bottom row, left: *Study: Self-Portrait, Beggars, Heads of Old People, Profile of Beggar in Half-Length* ca. 1632, etching (Haarlem, Teylers Museum). Bottom row, right: *Beggar Seated on a Hill* 1630, etching (Haarlem, Teylers Museum)

on the other hand, although not embellishing the face, does not explore it; the face radiates a calm self-assurance. The fourth etching, representing the figure we know to be the artist as a beggar whose open mouth is almost screaming the figure's poverty at us, shows again a self-conscious discomfort at the discovery of the face to be represented.

The painting in the Frick Collection shows the royal figure sitting back, powerfully enthroned, so that the viewer is not addressed as aggressively as in the first etching, yet cannot but feel diminished by the figure who is in control. This painting displays the tokens of power and wealth: costume, belt, and staff, in collusion with the tokens of painterly mastery. These indices of class superiority signify the superiority of painting: The staff is being held like a brush, the play of light and dark make the dress shine like gold, the golden brushstrokes are covering the figure's breast like honorific medals. This royal self is the dressed-up version of that other famous self-portrait in the Kenwood House in London, dated 1660, where the painter's prestigious position is derived not from dress and pose but from maulstick and palette (Figure 7.3).[3]

The royal quality of the Frick painting and the insistently mirroring quality of the first etching supplement each other. The two aspects of the mirror in *Las Meninas*, to be discussed shortly – its being filled by royalty at the viewer's expense, and its distorting effect which both allows the viewer to identify with the image and wounds the viewer's narcissism – are represented in these two contrasting works. Together, they illuminate the Boston panel (Figure 7.2). The insistently implied mirror of the etchings, signified by the strong facial expressions, is not so obvious in the paintings. What makes these paintings self-reflective in a more complicated way is the left hand of the figure, strangely distorted in each painting.

The detail that strikes in the three paintings is, indeed, that hand: Clutched around the instrument of the artist in the first; loosely holding a staff but leaving a gap between index and middle finger in the second; the left hand invisible, having been replaced by the palette in the third. In addition to the Boston panel, the first and the third of these paintings are the only works where the artist represents himself as a painter. I contend that he does so in the Frick work as well, but metaphorically. The figure in the work from the Louvre, which shares the light border of the dark canvas with the Boston panel, holds the brush as loosely as the royal self in the second work holds the staff, thus conveying its equally symbolical meaning. The figure in the Kenwood House painting does not even hold anything; the hand has *become* the instrument of painting, and as if to emphasize this sign, the other hand is invisible as well.

If the middle painting is the symbolic version of the two others, discursively arguing for the nobility of painting as an art, the self-reflection on the work of painting must be signified there as well. A striking detail confirms that intuition: the gap between the two fingers. I was immediately drawn to this gap because of the cover of Naomi Schor's (1987) book on the detail, where a hand with a gap between the same fingers is reproduced.[4] Schor discusses this detail in her chapter on Roland Barthes's aesthetics, "Desublimation," and suggests that the gap represents erotic desire by its reference to castration (96–7). Her close reading of Barthes's fragment on this detail reveals that the gap evokes the lover's cigarette that might fill it, which becomes for Barthes the erotic value of the striking detail or *punctum*. The Barthean punctum is then a void comparable to the empty area in the Berlin *Susanna*, the navel that I filled with a magnifying glass and that Barthes in this case filled with a cigarette.

The gap between the two fingers in the Frick painting, then, became for me the painting's punctum through intertextual contact with Barthes via Schor. Schor discusses the punctum in terms similar to my definition of myth in Chapter 3:

[F]or Barthes the detail becomes the privileged point of contact between reader and text: the discursive punctum is the hook onto which the reader may hitch her own fantasies, fasten his own individual myths. Located at the intersection of the private (Barthes's lover) and the public (the painting of Tobias), Barthes figures emblematically his aesthetic project. (Schor, 1987:96)

But instead of a lover's cigarette, the painter's brush, metaphorically evoked by the staff between thumb and index, is metonymically implied by the gap. Why would this double signification be needed? Why this redundancy? In fact, there is no redundancy here; the two signs work in two opposed directions. If the staff metaphorizes the painter's brush as royally successful, the gap signifies it as failing the act. If art is a royal occupation – an argument that *Las Meninas* clearly makes as well – it also poses a threat to the artist's self, dangerously at stake in the act of painting. The hand was distorted in all three of these paintings because precisely this dignified art of painting can never be taken for granted.

The self-portrait takes on a novel meaning in this respect. First, self-portrait is a genre that accommodates many different endeavors. Using the cheapest available model, the artist can use it for the purposes of study; as such, it is one way among many in which the self-portrait enhances the representational *work*. The self-portrait can become self-reflexive, not because it shows us the face we know to belong to the painter, but because it stands for study – for the practice of painting and its difficulties. Second, it is a genre based on the mirror image: Only by watching his own face in the mirror is the artist able to represent it. Therefore, such a representation is always dubious as a "natural" image, as a "perfect copy"; most probably it is reversed and thereby potentially subversive of realism itself.[5] The mirror image is by definition distorting, as Lacan was well aware when he elaborated the concept of the mirror stage as formative of the self in alienation on the basis of that distortion.[6]

But the self-portrait gains in self-reflexivity when the reflection on painting is not signified in the study, in the exaltation of the self but in the detail that demonstrates the danger to the self. Both the early etchings and the late paintings do this. In the etchings, the closeness to the surface which makes the viewer withdraw, or the awkwardness of a detail of the face, problematizes the conflation of represented self and successful representation. In the paintings, the pose and the face are not threatened, but instead, the bodily integrity of the subject, represented as engaged in representation, is put at risk. The body at risk is the representation of the threat to subjective wholeness that self-reflection poses. I will contend further on in this chapter that this threat is so real and emotionally problematic that most participants in the debate on *Las Meninas* shy away from endorsing it, but leave their discourses inscribed with the traces of the fear.

SELF-REFLECTION AND
ITS DISCONTENTS

Self-reference has invaded the arena of interpretation so pervasively today that it needs further specification. As an antirealistic and critical, if not self-critical, mode of reading, it focuses on details in a work that are interpreted as referring to an aspect of the work itself; these details then become signs that counter smooth, realistic interpretation of the subject matter. Self-referential signs may, therefore, either escape notice or bother viewers solely interested in a realistic reading of the represented subject. But for those in-terested in the challenge self-conscious works of art address to the readers' views of the world – including their position in it – these self-referential signs may stimulate reflection on representation and its tension with the represented object, and, by extension, stimulate reflection on the viewer/reader's own realistic impulses. Thus con-ceived, self-reference is the royal road to critique.

The paradoxical entanglements within the concept of self-reflection entail that we take the subject of this chapter – self-reflexivity as a mode of reading – at its own word, and use as the verbal "other," not a pre-text as in the analysis of the *Bathsheba*, not a posttext as in that of Mann's *Joseph* (1948), not a cotext as in that of *Uncle Tom's Cabin*, but an intertext in the narrow sense: a reader's/viewer's response to, and reflection of/on, a self-reflexive work. No such text is more revealing than that of the heated debate that focused on Velázquez's *Las Meninas*, around 1980, between philosophers and art historians.

The revival of interest in *Las Meninas* is occasioned primarily by the fact that Foucault, a philosopher and hence a professional discursive self-reflector, opened his study of the classical age with a thirteen-page reflection on it.[7] He saw inscribed into the work the invisibility of the viewer, whose place is taken by the royalties. Searle, another philosopher, significantly a philosopher of language and hence of discourse, took the work as typically paradoxical, precisely because the viewer *cannot* be in the same place as the royal couple, yet must be precisely there (see Searle, 1980). The term "paradox"[8] upset two other critics and amused others, thus setting off the responses to both this interpretation of the painting by Snyder and Cohen (1980) on the one hand, and by Steinberg (1981) on the other, and a few years later, Alpers presented her own response obliquely in connection with these predecessors.

The issue of the first three papers is the position of the viewer in relation to the mirrored image of the king and queen in the center of the work. The second round seems much more distanced. Steinberg declares that he had written his piece years before the debate broke out, and Alpers only casually refers to the three papers of the first round. The debate makes a good intertext for self-reflection because, at least in the articles by Searle and by Snyder and Cohen, there is a striking discrepancy between the positions the critics argue for in their discursive reflections and those they reflect – mirror – in their discourses. In other words, the critical texts lend themselves to the kind of specular and speculative reflexive reading that makes self-reflective reading genuinely relevant.

As it happens, then, the discourse of my colleagues is the object of analysis in this chapter. This can, of course, become quite an unpleasant situation. In order to put myself as well as my colleagues on the spot, and in order to satisfy the requirements of self-reflection, which oblige me to reflect on myself as well, I shall follow up, in the next chapter, with a little piece of self-reflection on my own discourse.

However, such a reading strategy might also lead to a self-sufficient sense of triumph, a self-congratulatory pleasure in discovery. This sense of triumph would then not only cancel out the critique itself by offering the contradictory persuasion that one has dicovered the "truth in painting" without seeing the dissemination of meaning that the very idea of truth entails.[9] It might also distract the viewer/reader from historical and social issues art addresses as well. In other words, once self-reflection as a possibility has become commonplace – as it has with the rise of postmodernism – reading for "narcissism" is in danger of becoming narcissistic itself.

Two other drawbacks could be induced against self-referentiality as a mode of reading. First, self-referential reading could be accused of being ahistorical. This accusation can be countered easily in two ways. The first has to emphasize the parodic quality of intertextuality, which transforms it into a device for self-reflexivity. Linda Hutcheon suggests, in the Preface to her book *Narcissistic Narrative* (1980), that the parodic effect and the intertextuality it entails seem to save us the trouble of situating a work in history; this is both a reason for its attraction and, as she rightly points out, a reason for suspicion. For if self-reflective reading relieves the reader of the trouble of placing the work in its historical context, it is precisely because the intertextual reference specifies the work's historical position. Intertextual reference is not just a self-contained self-reference. It may also clarify the problematic relations between the work and its predecessors – the kind of reading that iconography at its best produces.[10] And if it does this, then intertextual references like parody relate the work – *as work*, hence, as nonrealistic – to something else. And that something else, the "other" work, is historically positioned. The relationship between the two works thus produces the diachronic perspective that positions the parodic work historically, as well. In other words, this kind of intertextuality proposes its own historicality at the same time that it calls into question the very notion of historicism implicated in a deceptively simplistic mimeticism. As Foucault pointed out, history has the paradoxical usefulness of protecting us from historicism – the historicism that calls on the past to respond to questions of the present.[11]

Second, self-referential readings could be accused of presuming that they are an end in themselves. But self-reference should be not a conclusion but a starting point for further specification. This is one of the differences, for example, between Alpers's and Searle's interpretations of *Las Meninas*. Alpers's piece is more relevant than Searle's for two reasons: First, the author is willing to see more than one meaning in the painting; and second, in relation to that openness to ambiguity, she attempts to make the self-referential meanings historically meaningful. She points out two different, and in a way incompatible, modes of reading – narrative and descriptive – and does not try to harmonize them. In other words, she avoids two limitations to the interpretation that the hypothesis of self-reference sometimes seems to encourage, the limitations brought forth by the illusion that saying "this work is about itself" is saying a good deal. This is one reason why the seemingly odd comparison between the Velázquez and the "Rembrandt" does make sense: Simply concluding that both are "about painting" makes us confront the poverty of this mode of reading if the historical context is left unspecified, and the possibility of ambiguity ignored.

Another criticism of self-referential readings is related to that articulated above: Self-reflective readings are criticized for diverting attention from issues concerning "the world." Obviously, one could respond that such a tendency rests on a distinction, even an opposition, between work and world which it is the mission of self-reflexivity to challenge. If thought through carefully, self-reflection proposes a radical view of the world as itself constructed – which entails a critical perspective on the world and its changeability. This kind of criticism is precisely the reason why the concept of self-reflexiveness is in need of specification. In this chapter, I shall argue that among the modes of self-reflexiveness by which works of art are read, the more specific, and thus more productive, ones incorporate reflection on the relations between work and world, whereas the more global, nonspecific ones tend to be used to obliterate those relations.

As I suggested at the beginning of this chapter, self-reflectiveness as a mode of reading seems paradoxical; it seems that way because the self-reflective mode leads the viewer/interpreter to submit to a position perceived to be determined by the work. As in a Hegelian master–slave dialectic, the viewer is so overwhelmed by, so triumphant over, the "discovery" of self-reflexivity, that she or he tends to set her or his own position aside and submit totally to the self-reflective position seemingly proposed by the work, at the cost of self-reflection of the viewing or reading subject. The result is a paradox as classic as the Cretan liar's. Much of self-reflexiveness addresses the position of the viewer, and thus seems to define and circumscribe that position. But if reflection of/on the work entails reflection of/on the viewer's position, then any submissive response is paradoxically nonsubmissive; it refuses to obey the command of reflection. In other words, an order of nonsubmission can be neither obeyed nor disobeyed.[12]

The paradoxes and possible confusions the concept of self-reflection proffers are produced by the ambiguity of *both* parts of the term: self and reflection. The element "self-" requires the reader/viewer to consider which self is at stake in the reflection: that of the work and/or that of the reader? I shall assume that self-reflection needs to risk the viewer's entanglement within the work and thus must endorse the reflection of/on *both* selves. This is suggested by the ambiguity of the word "reflection," meaning both mirroring and thinking.[13] Taking self-reflection as mirroring leads one to considerations of the Lacanian mirror stage as a first, visually based construction of the self *in* self-alienation, whereas discursive self-reflection leads to self-critique. Again, I advocate a position that holds these two aspects of the term in tension, as long as they first are distinguished clearly.

The two ambiguities of the word "reflection," coupled with the two possible selves to be reflected, lead to four possible positions. The mirroring and the analytical, discursive form of reflection differentiate between nonreflective, possibly unconscious doubling of the work, and a conscious position toward the work that problematizes representation. In the first case, there are two possibilities again, according to the meaning of "self" involved. If the critic responds to the self of the work only, taking it as radically other and leaving him- or herself safely out of reach, the result will be pure description. Snyder and Cohen's response to Searle and to *Las Meninas* reflects this attitude. If, in contrast, the two selves are conflated in the mirroring, while the reflection remains nonreflective (i.e., nonanalytical, nondiscursive), the result will show symp-

toms of primary narcissism as described by Lacan in his paper on
the mirror stage. Some elements of Searle's paper on *Las Meninas*
can be interpreted in this way.

The discursive mode of self-reflection, which entails that one
take an explicit position on the reflexive qualities of the work and
the self, can again take two distinct forms. If the reflection is limited
to the self of the work, the work is taken as a theoretical statement
about representation. The text or painting becomes a theory. This
is how Foucault reads *Las Meninas*. This mode of reading is quite
frequent in the wake of poststructuralism, in spite of the fact that
it is quite reductive, using the work of art only as an instrument.
The second mode in this category, and the fourth mode of self-
reflective reading, is the one in which discursive, reflective reading
involves both the self of the work – the way in which it problematizes itself as representation – and the self of the critic, whose
position as, say, an art historian or a philosopher is also the subject
of reflection. The articles by Steinberg and Alpers come closest to
this.

The distinction between visually and discursively based forms of
reflection clearly must not be taken to hierarchize the visual and
the discursive. On the contrary, since this hierarchy was undermined in the previous chapters, I can now further elaborate the
thesis that both visual and verbal texts – both paintings and pieces
of literature, criticism, and philosophy – have both visual and discursive aspects, and appeal to both visual and discursive modes of
reading. These modes should therefore not be conflated with the
respective media. In order to avoid misunderstanding, I shall show,
first, the visual-mirroring sense of reflection in the discursive texts
under scrutiny.

Reading the critical texts self-reflexively as the same kind of
verbal–visual texts as any other text invoked so far, I shall draw,
first, from a reading of Searle's article, the reflective issues of the
debate and formulate them in terms of the problem of "narcissistic
representation." The second paper, Snyder and Cohen's, will confirm and strenghten, in effect *repeat*, the central preoccupation of
Searle's text, which they had set out to attack, while at the same
time trying to avoid the mirroring by staking out their position as
cut off from the work. I shall close with a reexamination, in light
of these analyses, of the concept of narcissism as a label for this
mode of reading. Then, adopting *faute de mieux*, the paradox of
obedience to self-reflexiveness, in the next chapter I shall return to
the repressed in the history of my own interpretation of the etching
Joseph and Potiphar's Wife.

And this will bring us back, via what may seem a long detour
on *Las Meninas*, to "Rembrandt." But the detour will prove highly
relevant because it will demonstrate another kind of self-reflection,
a kind that remains confined to the visual works while modulating
between self of work and self of other, as well as between visual
and discursive self-reflection. The two paintings that are the main

characters in this chapter, the Velázquez and the "Rembrandt," will be seen as responding to, and reflecting (upon), each other through their own selves. The detour is also relevant precisely because the quality of the *Las Meninas* debate allows us to notice "narcissism at work" in ways that no debate on any "Rembrandt" demonstrates with equal subtlety. Although "Rembrandt" criticism generally neither goes so far nor transgresses disciplinary borders so vigorously, self-reflection, and subsequently narcissism, in "Rembrandt" are less conspicuous but all the more effective. Indeed, the status of this artist in the history of Western culture, the label "high art," which popular culture attaches to this body of work, has been directly related to the self-reflection the work displays, and this thesis has elicited as much passion as the *Las Meninas* debate.[14] The psychoanalytic concept of narcissism is a productive reading hypothesis with which to approach "Rembrandt." In the following chapter, in turn, I shall argue that the reception of this body of work, including its status as "high art," can indeed be related to the viewer's inevitable entanglement in narcissism.

THE LOOKING GLASS REVISITED

Juxtaposing *Las Meninas* and *The Artist in His Studio* is like juxtaposing brilliant sunlight and morbid shadow, or a crowded stage to a near empty dressing room. *Las Meninas* is self-reflexive in the most obvious sense: It is a painting about painting. The question of self-reflection in *Las Meninas* is, in its simplest formulation, What is the position and the identity of the viewer in relation to the mirror representing the king and queen of Spain and in relation to the canvas the represented painter is working on? And the problem in the responses stems from the assumption that this question is answerable. There are two visual modes of self-reflection involved in this question: the mirror and the canvas. In the "Rembrandt," these are replaced by the canvas and the palette. The two modes in *Las Meninas* stand in relation to each other as does "natural" to "cultural"; as do given, mimetic, realistic to constructed, artificial, textual; or, in a different vein, as does narcissistic-imaginary to symbolic. It is precisely this duality of the self-reflection that distinguishes this work, not only from the modest and relatively simple "Rembrandt" panel, but also from its more glorious rivals. But the two aspects of the self-reflection are incompatible, and the mismatch between the two, reflected in the troubling question of what is to be seen on the canvas we cannot see, is precisely the locus of the problem.

Hence, there are two concerns that tend to be conflated in the responses to *Las Meninas*. The first key concerns the painter's canvas, strangely huge, foregrounded yet displaced into a corner, which makes it easy to overlook. We must realize that the real painting on which this huge but overlookable painting is represented is equally huge. The oversize of the represented canvas is also obvious in the little "Rembrandt" panel, although in that work the canvas does not match the size – nor the material, the work being painted on wood – of the framing work itself. The disproportionately large canvas in the "Rembrandt" painting conflates, so to speak, the functions of the mirror and the canvas in the Velázquez: Like the mirror, it stands in the place of the viewer, displaces the viewer's place; like the canvas, it makes us reflect on what is reflected on its invisible side only to leave the palette unemployed.

Next to the canvas in *Las Meninas*, the second instance of self-reflection, and key to the painting's problem, is the mirror in the middle of the painting in which the royal couple is represented. The question the mirror evokes is, Where are the royal intruders standing, and where is the viewer standing? In other words, what is reflected in the mirror, and what is the position of the viewer in relation to this reflection? Thus the mirror poses the very question of self-reflection, including the absorption of the viewer within the question. As represented in this mirror, the royal couple, the masters of all represented characters, are strangely small, unclear, and secondary to the scene depicted in the representation. Nobody is looking at them. While invisible but "real," the royal couple, in their presumed position just to this side of the picture plane, is the focus of sustained attention from six out of nine characters and interrupts the narrative of peaceful work in the studio, imposing the rival narrative of the couple's decisive displacement. There is no such diverting mirror-presence in the "Rembrandt" panel. The artist, there, is alone.

Between the royal masters representing themselves by posing in front of a mirror, and the powerful servant representing them with his own hands on the canvas in the Spanish painting, there seems to be a competition. The painter's talents define him as a Hegelian slave toward the masters whose self-definition requires the slave's unslavish willingness to represent them; he does their bidding, but not without including in his work the master–slave dialectic through which he, his work, and they are defined.[15] The competition between the royal couple and the painter is enhanced by the tension between the two narratives, one of which – the work in the studio – is durative, hence poor as a narrative. As is evidenced by the surprised scrutiny on the part of six characters, the other – the couple's presence whose image is in the mirror – is punctual, hence supplying suspense. In the "Rembrandt" the stillness of the painter's pose contradicts the sense of narrative inherent in the idea of work. To anticipate a little, we, the viewers, will have to work hard to make this work productive as a narrative of work – and of power. In contrast, in the Spanish work the distribution of power is powerfully suspended – thus insisting on its presence. And this suspense has to do with self-reflection, the mirror, and the critical response.

Foucault's goal is to understand classical representation, and the conclusion of his analysis, quoted at the opening of this chapter,

demonstrates that he finds self-reflection the key.[16] His thesis, as it
has been taken up by his respondents, is relatively simple. Taking
the work to reflect the typically classical attitude toward pictorial
representation, Foucault argues that the painting represents the absence of the viewer. Searle argues, on the basis of an analysis of
point of view, that the viewer is both where and not-where the
royal couple is, whereas Snyder and Cohen find fault with the
technicalities of point of view by which Searle reaches his paradoxical conclusion.[17]

First, then, Foucault: For Foucault the viewer's absence is signified by the fact that the obvious place for the viewer, the mirror
in the middle of the painting, is occupied by somebody else. Foucault's reading is based on the hypothesis of self-reflexivity in its
double meaning of visual mirroring and discursive thinking. He
takes the first as a metaphor for the second, staying, himself, on
the side of discursive reflection on the work's self(-mirroring). I
contend that it may be the most powerful aspect of the idea itself,
that these two meanings tend to be conflated in self-reflection.

In contrast, the little ''Rembrandt'' at first sight seems clearly to
signify the presence of the viewer. The tiny painter is not only
looking out of the framed scene right into the viewer's eyes, but
also ostentatiously posing for him/her (Figure 7.4). No mirrored
image of another subject takes the viewer's place here. Yet the
distance between the little man and the huge canvas, and the angle
of vision represented, muddles the line of vision between viewer
and represented painter. It is hard for viewers not to feel that the
canvas stands between them and the painter, with this twofold
effect: We become less certain that the painter is looking at us, and
we realize that it is the work, not us, that makes the subject – the
painter – visible. So actually both works make a place for the
viewer, only to undermine it immediately. And they do so by using
the formulaic genre of the *portrait*: the token of irreducible individ-
uality (Figure 7.3). It is this basic insecurity of the viewer's position
that proposes self-reflection to the viewer, and it is perhaps because
of an inability or unwillingness to expose oneself to this insecurity
that it is overwritten in some of the critical texts – hence the displaced tone of anger.

7.4 Velázquez, *Las Meninas*,
details; *The Artist in His Studio*,
detail

262

Foucault's reading is also based on another paradox: By *representing* the absence of the viewer, the work does represent the viewer, albeit negatively. "Verbality" helps to show how. Some claim that visual representation has difficulty representing syntactic connections, shifters, and negations; and the latter seems the most resistant of these three negative indicators of visuality; see, for example, Gombrich (1949) and Burke (1968). However, if Foucault is correct, then the Velázquez work does represent this negation visually. If the work functions in this way – which it does only within an extremely limited conception of visuality – we might say in the line of Foucault's argument that by working for the negation of the viewer, self-relfection makes the work discursive, and what we "see" is a *discourse* on representation. This would then be an instance of visual discursivity (i.e., a discursive mode in a visual medium). This metarepresentational discourse triggers a philosophical response to the work: It allows Foucault to use the painting to drive home his theoretical point about classicism, and the painting becomes a philosophical text.

But what also characterizes Foucault's response is a triumphant sense of understanding that is related to the unifying impulse of criticism, especially acute in self-reflexive reading. This unifying tendency is also readable in the quote that opens this chapter. Indeed, by taking up the aspect of the work that accommodates a classical dogma, the philosopher has unified the work against all odds. Reflecting on it discursively, he keeps his own self out of reach. By responding to this aspect of the Foucaultian response, Alpers and Steinberg are able to overcome its limitations.

SELF-REFLECTION AND REALISM

In contrast, Searle's attempt to grasp the nature of the self-reflexivity in the painting, besides its obvious discursivity, is also mirroring. So while he also uses the painting as a theoretical text, he does not keep the critic's self at bay. Searle begins with a paradox and ends with an unexpected realism that characteristically points to the limits of self-reflection in its current, frequent mode of application. He starts where Foucault ended; he problematizes the unity Foucault achieved by introducing the typically ambivalent idea of paradox. Paradox, like irony, is a tricky concept. It helps to overcome a naive sense of unity, while still accommodating the problematic unity in an *Aufhebung* that resolves the conflict. It does so by relapsing into realism. In these two respects, it is a modernist rather than a postmodernist concept.[18]

Here is how, at the end of his introductory section, Searle reformulates the question of the meaning of *Las Meninas*:

At one level the picture is indeed about Margarita and her entourage; at another level the picture is about two things, one of which lies outside the picture and the other of which is invisible. (Searle, 1980:480)

263

It is important to note that Searle does not deny or ignore the first level – although we have to wait for Alpers to integrate that into the whirlpool of self-reflexive meanings. Searle sets it aside, brackets it, and fails to take it up later. Why does he mention it here? If we take the sentence as an iconic representation of the outlined project, we shall see that there is an interesting syntactic structure. While opening up the unity of the work, the division into two levels ensures that the subsequent distinction between two "things" will not disturb the unity within that second, self-reflexive level. Thus, the sentence has already accomplished "visually" what the rest of the argument sets out to do discursively: It has replaced a naive and monolithic unity with a sophisticated, dialectical one.

And, to continue the dialectical parallel with the "Rembrandt": While this work contains no characters other than the painter, Searle's point applies nevertheless. On one level, the painting is a portrait, a painting about "Rembrandt"; on another level, it takes up two issues, one of which – the emphatically excluded viewer – lies outside the work, and the other – the meaning of the represented work – is invisible, too much inside the work, so to speak. If we wish to overcome Searle's limitations, we have to counter his two divisions: We must interpret the first level in relation to the second and so break up the implied unity of the second. In other words, we have to address the question of what the portrait of the royal couple is doing in the narrative of painting and what the irreducible difference is between the references to the viewer and to the invisible work. They may reflect each other, but they cannot be conflated.

Searle's position depends on the theory of meaning he is advancing, and in this sense his position resembles Foucault's. His style symptomatizes the other mode of self-reflection. He develops his theory of meaning thus: Meaning is intentional, and pictorial meaning is inherently – intentionally – based on resemblance, which in turn is contingent upon point of view. While stating this theory discursively, the modifier slips in, again, in a syntactically interesting way:

And since the intentionality of pictures, *at least within the conventions of classical pictorial representation*, relies on resemblance between the picture and the object depicted, the form of intentionality that exists in pictorial representation is crucially dependent on point of view. (Searle, 1980:481; my emphasis)

The syntax presents casually what Searle takes as self-evident, as given ("at least"), that which is precisely the alleged object of self-reflection in the work under scrutiny. If the work is proposing a reflection on pictorial representation in the classical age, then the conventions casually evoked are part of what is being reflected upon. And their center is repressed into the margin, so as to become unarguable. Searle's interest in doing this seems twofold.[19] He needs to safeguard the paradox of the painting as well as the universal validity of the rest of his statement: his theory of meaning.[20] In this sense, his discursive use of *Las Meninas* is rigorously metadiscursive.

The points of Searle's argument that were to be explicitly or implicitly challenged by his opponents were already inscribed in this syntactic structure, beginning with paradox itself. As I mentioned earlier, Snyder and Cohen criticized Searle's account of point of view, whereas Alpers challenged the eventual unification of the self-reflexivity that the sentence proleptically signifies.[21]

Searle (1980:252) repeats his realistic assumption: "It is the first painting as far as I know to be painted from the point of view of the model and not from that of the artist." Two elements in this statement point precisely to the problematic aspects of the theory on which Searle bases his argument. First, his statement implies a distinction between model and painter, ruling out self-portrait, in some sense a self-reflexive genre that conflates the points of view of the model and artist.[22] More crucially, rather than claiming that the "model" – assumed to be the king and queen – has to be other than the viewer, Searle does not rule out the possibility that the two are metaphorically identified, though neither does he explore this possibility. It may be interesting to dwell on Foucault's view a little longer in order to see the consequences of the fragility of the royal couple's existence (Foucault, 1973:14) for an identification of the viewer with them. Instead of gratifying the viewer's narcissistic impulse, such an identification might seriously wound it. The viewer, then, cannot win: On the one hand, the king and queen are the only legitimate and possible viewers of the painting; on the other, they cannot see the work as is, while their representation in it is dubious, fragile, and minimal, both in size and in clarity. Where is the viewer to turn in the face of this paradox?

Searle's conflation of model and represented figure reduces to a denial of the representational status of the work – a denial, informed by realistic reading, that leaves little room for self-reflection. That is, regardless of the previously mentioned possibility of identification between the viewer who should be, and the royal couple that *is*, reflected in the mirror, the fact that it is a *mirror* that is represented does not mean that we have to fall into the trap of the mirror, imprisoning ourselves within the self-reflexion of primary narcissism. The mirror could be, for example, a metaphorical mirror, suggesting self-reflection in the discursive sense, a sign of the same status as the letter in the *Bathshebah*: a textual navel.[23]

Here we begin to see how the "Rembrandt" panel can serve as another intertext to the Velázquez. We can now assign a meaning to the apparently clumsy pose of "Rembrandt"'s represented self and, in the same move, overcome Searle's realism. The artist's pose emphatically suggests a self-portrait, a nonnarrative work whose generic conventions contradict those of the studio narrative, which is equally emphatically presented in *Las Meninas*; in comparison, the "Rembrandt" is almost a still life. Of course, so are parts of *Las Meninas*, especially the field filled by the painter's palette and the hair and ribbons of the attendant contiguous with it. But in the "Rembrandt" this stillness is central: The palette on the wall, the distance between painter and canvas, the pencil or brush still pointing elsewhere – all denote that the painter is *not* at work – not yet, that is (Figure 7.5).

These details in the "Rembrandt" comment on the distance, in *Las Meninas*, between painter and canvas emphasized by the interposition of the servant offering the princess a drink, to which I shall return. Reading with the "Rembrandt," we cannot ignore that Velázquez's painter's pose is also just a little too much arrested to be that of a plausible artist-at-work.[24] There is in the "Rembrandt" a sense of play with proportion and light which suggests that the "clumsiness" of the represented artist can itself be taken as a self-reflexive device; it foregrounds the fact that the figure is a *representation*, a construction, thus initiating the self-reflexivity of the work that needs us to be aware of this construction in order to make its complex argument. No conflation between model (the real artist posing as a constructed artist) and representation (of the idea of the artist, laden with multiple meaning as we shall see) is encouraged here.

The turn of Searle's argument toward paradox is unfortunate and fortunate at the same time. It is unfortunate that Searle is trapped in his own paradox and thereby seems to make a convincing case for realism as the most powerful mode of reading – powerful enough to undermine the explicit self-reflexive effort. But his argument also *demonstrates* – both self-reflexively in the specular sense, and "visually" through the iconic syntactic structure – the power of a self-reflexive painting to absorb the position of the viewer to the point of paralyzing the latter's ability to reflect on the self. By his syntax, Searle shows his involvement in specular self-reflection.

The realistic turn the argument takes is fortunate, then, because it is rooted in the very mirroring that makes the painting self-reflexive, and thus helps us "see" what self-reflection can do. The mirror image of the royal couple, the key to the work's problematic status and the key by which all our critics are locked into the work, mirrors itself: It is not only the mirror of the "real" viewer of the scene, of the viewer's intrusion upon the scene, of the invisible work on the canvas, and of the visuality of that work; but, because it mirrors all of these, it mirrors its own status as mirror. Hence, it is the *mise en abyme* of self-reflection. And thus it includes in its

7.5 Velázquez, *Las Meninas*, details; *The Artist in His Studio*, detail

266

specularity the social aspects of painting in the historical age it positions itself in: It mirrors the interdependence of opposed classes, to which I shall return. If it is clearly a mirror, it must yield an image of "self," thereby identifying to one another the royal masters narratively intruding and the painting servant engaged in self-reflection.

This is why Foucault's position need not be rejected too easily, although its neat theoretical status must be undermined. The historical specificity of the problem of *Las Meninas* cannot ignore the *situation of painting*. As a court painter, Velázquez is both a servant and a master, mastering the immortality of his master. That painfully problematic place of royalty is represented in the representational rivalry: The painter's self-portrait, foregrounded, well executed, and expressing pride, outbids the blurred, small, and backward mirror image of his masters (Figure 7.6). But the royal couple and the viewers are conflated. Hence, it is not viewing royalty alone that is subordinated to making (them). The *function* of the viewer is filled in by the *identity* of the particular viewer, the only one meant to look at the work. This raises the question of who is in control, a question that entails a dialectic near-gratification, and then wounding, of the viewer's narcissism. Class difference, then, is potentially subverted. Who made the Infanta, the king, or the painter?

THE CONSTRUCTION OF THE MIRROR

We are now in a position to ask how we can work self-reflection into the "Rembrandt" panel, despite the absence of the mirror – or, for that matter, of any character other than "Rembrandt" himself. Does this panel manage to embody the class difference that Velázquez integrated so convincingly into the question of representation?

The Velázquez displays the distorting aspect of the mirror image doubly. It does so by the blurred quality that presents the mirror image as inferior to the other, pictorial representations; and it gives the mirror image a rival in the invisible canvas – the painterly construction – and by the other framed image in the background,

7.6 Velázquez, *Las Meninas*, details

267

the man who, as an actor, enters or exits the scene. As an index of theatricality, this man highlights the scene intruded upon by the supposedly entering royal couple. Representing the mirror *with* the self-portrait is one way of foregrounding the two-sidedness of self-reflection that is implied, through the implied mirror, in self-portrait as a genre.

As with the other self-portraits, in the Boston panel the mirror is inscribed in the painting in two complementary, albeit negative, ways. The palette, represented precisely in the place of the mirror, is as tiny, proportionally, as Velázquez's mirror. It is also as central and as remote. The palette is empty and thus proleptic, introducing time and suspense. Its emptiness is made visible, illuminated by the amazing source of light this painting works with: the light coming from the invisible canvas. The canvas thus substitutes the idea of the lamp for that of the mirror (Abrams, 1953), but this is not clearly a substitution, as the ambiguity of the key word "reflection" shows. If the canvas reflects light, then we are led to assume that it is empty itself, and if, as Steinberg argues for Velázquez's mirror, "Rembrandt"'s palette mirror reflects the painting that we cannot see, then the canvas is arguably empty, as well as mirroring.

This mirroring quality illuminates one other detail in relation to this emptiness, a detail that refers back to self-portraiture and hence to mirroring: the look of the represented painter, relatively tiny. The man is looking at the viewer, but his eyes are not focused. Like hollow black blots of paint, holes perhaps, they may also be looking obliquely at the canvas. Significantly, the reason we cannot be quite sure of the latter possibility lies in the line of light: Although its light fully illuminates the empty palette, the canvas does not quite illuminate the artist's face (Figure 7.7). A triangle emerges from this difficulty, among the canvas, the artist, and the viewer, introducing a complexity that foregrounds the comparison with *Las Meninas*. The tension in the work stems from this problem: Who dominates, and thus defines, whom? The painter is represented as looking at the viewer, who thus becomes the model of a self-portrait – a situation at least as paradoxical as the mirror wherein the royal couple stands in for the viewer.

7.7   *The Artist in His Studio,* details

Searle's identification, presumably based on a technical error but, as Steinberg argues, nonetheless plausible, of the viewer with the king and queen of Spain introduces a slightly embarrassing narcissism into the act of viewing. But something even more embarrassing threatens to happen with the "Rembrandt." The viewer is led to identify with the painter who has not painted anything yet, but who is posing as a great painter, defined as he is by the size of his work, which thereby promises to be literally great. This identification is more embarrassing, not so much because it is a transgression of class boundaries; it is embarrassing because it is primarily and directly a transgression of subjective boundaries, of the irreducible but unstable opposition between the "I" and the "you."

This transgression shows the threat of collapse inherent in what Benveniste (1966) helped us see as the personal language situation with its inevitable role reversals – a threat that makes representation of otherness, the distancing mode of the "third person," such an urgent impulse. The transgression suggested in the identification of viewer with painter thus instills in the act of viewing a sense of regression to the imaginary stage, delimited by the experience of the mirror and its alienating effect. Rather than trying to escape this troubling effect by deflecting it toward criticism of the painter's "clumsiness," the artificial pose can be allowed to enhance this alienating effect.

What does this reflection on/of the "Rembrandt" allow us to say about Searle's blissful realism? By stepping into the realist fallacy – moving *inside*, not *through*, the looking glass – which the work so deceptively offers for reflection, Searle necessarily blinds himself to the critical function of the mirror, which proposes reflection on historically specific boundaries of class but also, intertwined with that reflection, reflection on boundaries of self and self-definition.[25]

ON MIRROR TALK

In order to measure this blindness to the critical function of the mirror and its consequences for the relations between discourse and image, we must listen to Searle again:

> We know that the paradoxes *must* have a *simple* solution because we know that the scene depicted is a visually possible scene. (Searle, 1980:486; my emphasis)

His submission to the work is indicated by his taking the painting, as it were, at its word: Visual evidence is privileged positivistically. Taking the picture tautologically as proof of itself, the self-reflection is turned into self-nonreflection. Rather than taking the work as questioning itself, it is taken to affirm itself.

This realism in turn simplifies, unifies, the solution to the paradoxes. Again, the desirability and the possibility of the solution are implicit in the syntax of Searle's sentence, rather than explicitly

stated. Although the self-evidential effect of the painting is attributed to its visuality, the solution to the paradox proposed by Searle
is, not surprisingly, linguistic.

Drawing upon speech-act theory, Searle (1980:487) proposes the
following simple solution:

> Just as every picture contains an implicit 'I see', so according to Kant every
> mental representation contains an implicit 'I think', and according to
> speech-act theory every speech act can be accompanied by an explicit
> performative, for example, 'I say'. But just as in thought the 'I' of the 'I
> think' need not be that of the self (in fantasy, for example) and in speech
> acts the 'I' of the 'I say' need not be that of the speaker or writer (in
> ghostwriting, for example) so in the *Meninas* the 'I' of the 'I see' is not
> that of the painter but of the royal couple.

Rather than cite the obvious and relevant – but problematic – cases
of "third person" versus "first person" narrative, Searle uses the
unlikely, irrelevant, and hardly illuminating case of ghostwriting
to argue that the "I" can be different from the declared speaker.[26]
In ghostwriting, the *speech act* performs the identification of one
speaker, the subject of the utterance, with someone she or he is not
but chooses to be for the time of the utterance. The word "ghost"
in that expression suggests the uncanniness of the doubling of the
subject and proposes to see the subject of writing as an image, albeit
an image of the invisible – which is what ghosts are. The reason
that different narrative structures are more problematic as well as
more relevant is precisely because in those structures sheer subject-
identity is not assumed but challenged. That is why the comparison
between "Rembrandt"'s panel and Velázquez's canvas can help us
understand these issues.

In "first person" narrative, the speaker shifts within an unchang-
ing identity among the subject positions that identity can variously
occupy.[27] This is another sense in which the stiff pose of "Rembrandt"'s painter is meaningful. It is a self-portrait that foregrounds
its own constructedness in order to challenge identity itself. To
solve this theoretical problem, speech-act theory has had to posit
a set of characters doing things that fall under the heading of speech,
but that are quite different from it: looking, for example, or
thinking.

The concept of "third person" narrative, on the other hand, is
paradoxical in itself because it leads to the absurd identification of
a "third-person narrator." Such a narrator would cancel him-/her-
self out, the narrator's voice supposedly disappearing behind the
narrative that "tells itself."[28] The term "third-person narrator" is
at best an abstraction as impossible and as ideological as the perfect
copy of the world that realistic painting supposedly strives for.
Searle, a major voice of the school of speech-act theory, fails to
examine the implicit parallels between *Las Meninas* and these forms
of narration. Such parallels are quite relevant, however. If we think
in terms of the "Rembrandt" panel for a moment, the notion of a

"third-person narrator" appears detachable from the issue of realism and related to self-portrait as a genre, in spite of the apparent necessity for a "first-person" narrator in such a genre. The way Rembrandt, as Alpers argues, makes value out of his face, thus promoting the construction of something like a genre of nonautographic "self-portraits," bears comparison with "third-person narrative." Such a notion is already relevant for this early work. The self-portrait hovers between self and other, challenging the distinction between the categories of first and third person as it challenges subjectivity and its illusion of wholeness.

Searle effectively absorbs the fallacious concept of a "third-person narrator" into speech-act theory with the analogy to the Kantian thinking subject, with its assumption of an implicit "I say." The problem that remains, however, is the one that also remained in "first-person" narrative to which the third-person narrator is now theoretically identical: It is the problem of representing, *within* the speaking voice of the now safeguarded unified narrator, the views, thoughts, and (mis)conceptions of other subjects. These subjects, for which narratology has devised the term "focalizers," can be embedded characters whose point of view the narratorial voice adopts and, in free indirect discourse, even absorbs to the point of confusion. But these focalizers can also be the diffused ideologies or doxa that the speaking subject would like to disavow, as well as the speaker's unconscious views, fantasies, and preoccupations. This is, again, foregrounded in "Rembrandt"'s little man who, by means of his stiffness – which he shares with the painter in *Las Meninas* – is both self and other, in relation to (our image of) the artist as well as in relation to ourselves. He literally *mediates*, that is, sees for us what we cannot see; since we are reflected in and by him, our emptiness can be filled by his narcissistic fantasies about grandeur – which, likely enough, we all share. The central device for this confusion, the painter's eyes, backfires nicely on the viewer. Although the artist can see the work to come – he can see the canvas, but he can also (fore)see what will be represented on it – his hollow eyes need our eyes to "see" and be seen, to acknowledge the status of this artist with whom we identify.

The solution based on speech-act theory rests on the assumed analogy between seeing and speaking. This analogy is particularly vital in the semiotic analysis of visual art in the line of Benveniste, represented principally by Louis Marin. In its simple form, this analogy is untenable for two reasons: It conflates different modes of perception without examining the implications of that conflation – thinking and seeing; speaking is hardly an act of perception – and it conflates different subject-positions in relation to acts: Visually representing, not seeing, would be the act parallel to speaking.[29]

To be sure, the insight that vision is subject as much to the social construction of the visual fields and the modes of semiosis we are trained to adopt, as speech is to the social construction of discourse, has been an important impulse for a critical approach to visual art.

But assuming an unargued analogy among "I see," "I think," and "I say" is not the same thing as criticizing and undermining an unwarranted opposition between two media; rather, it obscures the issues involved in such a critique. As a consequence, the conflation enables Searle to account for a visual paradox in a fundamentally verbal way, while, as we have seen, bracketing crucial problems with reference to the reliability of seeing on which he must rely. The conflation is mediated, rendered invisible, by the interposition of thinking, a mode of semiosis without a clearly defined medium. That mediation also allows another conflation, that between acts of production and acts of reception, to pass unnoticed.

The latter conflation reduces the unstable I–you interaction of the personal language situation to one stable and unified. There is a world of difference between interaction, which leaves the subjects distinct but distributes their respective power, and conflation, which blurs and entangles the identities of the individuals concerned. This difference justifies my insistence on the two meanings of "self" in self-reflection. Taking the one for the other reveals a particular kind of response to self-reflection. Strictly speaking, the act analogous to speaking would be painting, not seeing the result, and the act analogous to representing something visually "out there" would be "third-person narration." Thus, Searle also represses the verbal aspects of his response by repressing his own position as a viewer.

The conflation of representing visually with viewing demonstrates again paradoxically the absorption of the critic into the work: Denying his own position, he increases his own importance. He conflates what *Las Meninas* distinguishes so exemplarily: the master and the servant, whose interdependence can be assessed only as long as a minimum of autonomy is preserved for each. The "Rembrandt" demonstrates why this conflation is such an attractive (non)position: In spite of the narcissistic frustration entailed by the lack of self, identification with the artist gratifies narcissistic dreams of grandeur. Snyder and Cohen's (1980) text suggests susceptibility to this impulse; these critics push the confusion further by identifying in their turn with Searle, their opponent, while distancing themselves from the painting.

VISION ON THE RIGHT SIDE OF SIGHT

There is a paradoxical sense in which self-reflexivity encourages reflection of, rather than on, reflection; Searle's critics locate these limitations of discursive self-reflection, but, in my interpretation, only to be more deeply engulfed by them.[30] Their thesis is that Searle is wrong, that there is no paradox in *Las Meninas*, and that Searle's thesis is based on a technically incorrect analysis of the painting. Their discursive argument aims at self-reflection of the third type: discursive reflection on the painting's self only. Had they succeeded in their goal, a shallow descriptive piece might have been the result; but the literary, or unconscious, dimensions of their text make it fascinating as they reveal the symmetrical counterpart of their discursive reflection on the work of art: mirroring reflection of the selves of both critics and work – type two. The tensions between these two will be demonstrated in this section where I shall argue that discursive involvement, entailing blindness toward the inevitable entanglement of the self, precludes self-reflection of the fourth type.

The very title of Snyder and Cohen's (1980) response to Searle's response to Velázquez's painting, "Reflections on *Las Meninas*: Paradox Lost" is revealing. Its first word, "Reflections," points to the explicit issue, while stripping it of its ambiguity. The mirroring reflection yields to rationalist discursive reflection. Or so it seems. The second part of the title, "Paradox Lost," might be read to suggest an implicit stake: the threat of merging inherent in the paradisiacal imaginary stage and the subsequent compulsion to disentangle the self from it, through primary narcissism.

The primary allusion in the second part of the title is, of course, to Paradise Lost – the myth – as well as the poem. And this allusion gains meaning from being related to the idea of narcissism through the imaginary blissful wholeness culminating, and at the same time undermined and irretrievably lost, in the mirror stage.[31] This imaginary bliss has aspects of both an image and a fiction. The mirror stage establishes wholeness precisely through these two aspects.[32]

These two critics respond to Searle's bliss lost at the outset. In terms of this text's pre-text, the loss of paradise satisfies those who, with Lucifer, were exiled from it. In the opening paragraph they write:

Velázquez's *Las Meninas* is paradoxical, *according* to John Searle. There has accumulated a staggering literature discussing the mysteries of this painting, and so, *presumably*, the contribution of Searle's essay is its *quasi-technical* exposition of the paradoxical character of the painting. (Snyder and Cohen, 1980:429; my emphases)

Distance is introduced ironically in the first sentence with the qualification "according to," and in the second sentence with the suggestion of misplaced arrogance. Clearly, Snyder and Cohen propose a duel that Searle cannot win. I shall contend that the motivation for their anger can be found by confronting the subtitle of the essay ("Paradox Lost") with the title of the final section, "*Las Meninas* Regained." It is not surprising that the key to this retrieval of the paradisiacal state is the mirror.

In eighteen pages the authors claim to prove what Steinberg (1981:46) says in one sentence: "The first, written by a paradox-loving philosopher, erred (like Foucault's) in its initial assumption about the viewer's implied position." To be sure, Snyder and Cohen, as well as Steinberg, are right – discursively, that is – in their basic claim that Searle's position is not based on the standard visual-technical notion of point of view; instead, it reflects a mode of seeing perhaps promoted, but misleadingly so, by the painting itself.[33] But if this mistake was as obvious as they claim, it could be put more lightly. Clearly there must be another issue. The underlying issue seems to be, How could Searle "err"? The issue of perspective in *Las Meninas* bears comparison with the problem posed by the metaphoric image in II Samuel 11:21. Being trapped by it, one buys into the doxa; seeing through it, one triumphs over it discursively, but fails to explain the effect of a structure complex enough to make sophisticated respondents err.

Instead of addressing the issue of the painting's seduction, the truth-in-painting argument is invoked. But the relevance of truth, and the question of what kind of truth one is talking about are quite uncertain. Because paradise is already said to be lost, there must be a subject and a crime – a fall – but a limited fall that excludes the critics and makes possible their offering a redemptive final paragraph. The mirror will be the locus of redemption: It is through the mirror that the critical position will be constituted, first rescued from the traps of childlike, imaginary bliss, and then allowed to accede to rational, symbolic truth, based on a radical separation of the critics' selves from that of the work.

Let me try out a reading of this text that reverses the hierarchical relationship between "literal" and "figurative" language – while remaining aware of the impossibility of disentangling these terms and their distinction from the verbal–visual cluster we are dealing with. Early on, the two critics develop the hypothesis, meant to be absurd but in effect deeply visual, that Velázquez painted two pictures,

each of a mirror, both with points of view appropriate to someone looking directly into the mirror: one with the mirror showing Velázquez (in the act of painting, if you like) and the other with the mirror showing, say, Searle (also painting, if you like). On Searle's account, the first painting is not paradoxical but the second is. (Snyder and Cohen, 1980:431)

I don't believe that this argument "mirrors" Searle's. On the contrary, Searle's solution is based on the obliteration of the distinction alleged here, which amounts to that between "first-person" and "third-person" narrative. But the statement does symptomatize a mirroring relationship between the critics and the philosopher, via the painter whose crucial function for the establishment of the viewer's identity I have already shown by comparing it with "Rembrandt"'s panel. Their argument is, indeed, quite narcissistic, introducing an absurd set of mirrors only to dwell on, and drive home, a reflexion of their own – a narcissism only slightly obscured by their implied accusation of narcissism in Searle.

The second phrase, "painting, if you like," implies either of the following implicit propositions:

1. /Searle has "painted," reflected, just like Velázquez – that is, equally convincingly – in his essay;/ or

2. /Searle has pretended to be as good a reflector as Velázquez./ In other words, the critics are trapped by the Platonic impossibility of disentangling the reflection from its "real" object – thus granting more to Searle's argument than they seem to intend. The symptom of this aggrandizing of their opponent is its denial.[34] They must deny the disturbing homage they imply: "Searle is not the artist." Or is he?[35]

In a vocabulary that mirrors and outdoes the unifying tendency in the philosopher's formulation, pairing it with positivistic truth claims, Snyder and Cohen (1980:433) propose their alternative:

There is a *simple* procedure that allows us to *establish*, for paintings like *Las Meninas* that are projected in one-point perspective, the *single* point on the canvas that is, *by definition*, exactly opposite the eye that *establishes* the projection. (my emphases)

The plural in "paintings like" shows that the critics aim at a discursive/one-self reflection (type three) à la Foucault: painting as theoretical example. They are wrong: Steinberg shows how the painting plays on the possibility of more than one-point perspective.[36]

On the narcissistic level, they conflate the critics' position with that of the painter who dictates what they ought to see. We have seen how this same conflation occurred toward the end of Searle's paper, and it is interesting that his two critics push the same fallacy further, narrowing the point of view to a *single* point opposite a single eye. This delimitation of point of view to a single eye – a single retina – is, of course, also a symptom of the repression of the body involved in viewing.[37] The tendency to delimit vision to a disembodied gaze is similar to the tendency to remain within a strictly discursive position – to save the self from mirroring. As such, it provides evidence of the attraction of mirroring. We must conclude, then, that the two critics not only fail to disentangle themselves from the work of the painter, but by trying to do so – by trying to keep their own selves at bay – they fail to disentangle themselves from the work of their opponent.

The absorption this text displays has already been presented to us: "Rembrandt"'s little panel clarifies this point even more successfully than does *Las Meninas* where the issue is diffused into an issue of class, although the intertwinement of classes, there, also challenges individualistic subjectivity. Compared to the mirror stage, the absorption in the Snyder and Cohen text is regressive: It signifies the possibility of the subject falling back into imaginary identification – and "imaginary," within a Lacanian framework, has at least four possible meanings: fictionality (to imagine), visuality (image), subjectivity (the subject's imagination), and wholeness (perceiving the body as whole, as unified). The word brings all these aspects to "reflection," adding at least one more ambiguity to an already ambiguous word. The regressive tendency to absorption – so contradictory to, yet so provoked by, the self-reflexive image – arouses a specific kind of anxiety that only partially overlaps with Bloom's "anxiety of influence," and that can best be named the anxiety of mirroring.

The difference between these two anxieties points toward a gender problematic. As is well known, Bloom's concept is defined in solely Oedipal terms and makes art a history of fathers and sons. The anxiety of mirroring, in constrast, will be shown in the next chapter to stem from narcissism and the problems of the subject's constitution of self in primary narcissism, before the construction of gender. Significantly, this pre-Oedipal anxiety is related to the mother from whom the subject needs to disentangle itself in order to achieve subjective integrity, not to the father with whom the Oedipal son competes.[38]

I wrote earlier that Snyder and Cohen try to make the transition from imaginary paradisiacal bliss to "adult," symbolic happiness, from a self-contained paradise ("Paradox Lost") to fulfillment in the relation to the Other ("*Las Meninas* Regained"). But this transition is not as smooth as they set out to prove. They are detained by the attractions of the mirror, by the mirror stage where the transition is dramatically staged in a self-referential moment. It is the mirror stage that challenges their superiority and endangers their voyage to scholarly adulthood; and an interruption of this voyage is what the critics seem to fear most of all.

The reason the mirroring aspect of self-reflection seems so dangerous lies in its primary visuality. "Rembrandt"'s face, in the first etching of illustration 7.3 (2a), may be read to represent this shock at mirroring, at *seeing* the self. Visuality mediates between the two basic meanings of reflection, but also threatens to pull the reflector back from discursive-symbolic reflection into visual-imaginary reflection, and the more so if the reflector is both interested in visual art and committed to denying the discursivity of that art. For this very anxiety rests on a symmetrical repression of the visual in discourse and of the discursive in the visual. In other words, it rests on a defensive attempt to deepen the gap which the present study is trying to bridge by positing the irreducible difference between the *media* as a coverup of the negotiable differences, and mobilities of the *modes*, which are more difficult to handle. Everything that comes close to visuality is seen as threatening because not discursively satisfying.

As a consequence, Snyder and Cohen adopt a defensive attitude toward Searle's competence as a philosopher and toward his philosophical vocabulary – "[A] persistent oddity in discussions of *Las Meninas* is the use of technical-sounding terminology ('paradox,' 'ambiguity,' 'self-referential,' 'axioms')" – which is routine in monodisciplinary responses to interdisciplinary perspectives; their anxiety is reflected in the charge of arrogance (What does he take himself to be? Velázquez perhaps?), which hides a much more dramatic insecurity than the professional one: the anxiety of mirroring, which threatens the reliability of the arbitrary sign. It is this profound semiotic anxiety that has to be remedied by being theoretically on the right side, a position formulated as rigid righteousness that excludes reflection on the position of the self.

THE CHALLENGE OF SELF-REFLECTION

One reason both Steinberg and Alpers are more successful, at least from my perspective, in their attempts to explain *Las Meninas* through self-reflexivity is that they are not in the least disturbed by the apparent lack of unity in the painting. Another reason is that they recognize the failures of previous critics and discuss those failures in terms of the works themselves: the painting as well as the critical discourse. Thus they are able to integrate into their interpretations not only the work itself but also the discourses about it, integrating, at the same time, discursivity into the very center of visuality. In a vein similar to that proposed in my discussion of the *Bathshebah* pre-text, both critics assign responsibility for the critical miasm to the work, and rather than locating what the work is supposed to mean in a stable conception of the sign, they explain the work as what I call a sign event, occurring between the canvas and its critics.

Here the similarities between the two critics end, however. Steinberg (1981:48) merely uses previous criticism to frame his own interpretation which, for all its brilliance and persuasiveness, its pluralism and its comprehensiveness, is still presented as an account of what *Las Meninas* actually shows, and once this protective frame is set up, the critical discourse of others barely comes up again. Thus Steinberg's self-reflection remains more along the lines of Foucault than it need do; it remains a type three, discursive reflection of the painting's self only.

But this is the case only on the explicit level. What the picture actually shows (him) turns out to be the possibility that both points of view, so antagonistically opposed by the two previous papers, coexist; and indeed, just like the empty eyes of "Rembrandt"'s painter, Steinberg (1981:51) shows that "the picture's focal center keeps shifting." This acknowledgment of the work's visual mobility implies a willingness to renounce a statement of the work as theory, and thus Steinberg comes closer to full self-reflection (type four) than he sets out to do.

Steinberg's attention to dispersion – one is tempted to say, dissemination – makes his interpretation fascinating. Among the many aspects he makes us see with him is the trio of triangles formed by the characters, each building up a different center for the work: the eyes of the Infanta, the mirror image, and the man standing in the doorway at the back of the space.

One way in which this dissemination is signified quite explicitly is in the representation of inattention. As Steinberg points out, the

Infanta is not interested in the drink offered to her; the dog does not bother to respond to the foot teasingly put onto his back; the man to whom the woman in the middle distance talks is not listening. Three senses are represented here as failing to work: sight, hearing, and touch; three ways of communicating are ineffective: communicating visually, verbally, and physically. The representation of inattention can hardly be ignored in a work that represents attention so sharply that the viewer, strongly implicated, needs to divert attention from him-/herself by indicating the royal couple as the real addressees of the looks. It alone introduces dissemination; it alone gives the lie to Snyder and Cohen's plea for unambiguous truth.[39]

Steinberg does not fail to notice the sense in which the painting includes, in its self-reflexivity, reflection on class positions. But he does not seem to see the implications of these divisions for the tension between narrative and vision on the one hand, and the relations between gender and power on the other, and the relevance of both for the painting's view of painting. There are, to begin with, three "attentive young persons in triangular disposition" who look out of the picture, straightforwardly interested in the royal intruders, thus privileging the extradiegetic level to the diegetic one in which they are positioned themselves. These three youngsters are then framed by three characters inattentive to the king and queen precisely because they are paying attention to some diegetic agent. While the former group is able, but also obliged, to see beyond their own world, they are thereby made unable to participate in the narrative that is played out there. Together, the two groups demonstrate the tension between narrativity and visual stillness: Alpers will call this "description." The latter group, in contrast, disqualified by age and status from participating in the royal act of seeing beyond immediacy, acts out the story of everyday life and its material conditions: As Steinberg (1981:53) puts it, they are "caught up in play, in service, and in conversation."

I am not terribly convinced of the futility of these occupations, however, since they not only represent three ways of communicating, but also constitute the narrative of the dignification of the sovereigns, which would not be noticed at all without its interruption: Royalty derives its meaning from what it is not. This is, I think, an important point about the significance of social status which the tension between narrative and stillness is making.

Among the many triangles Steinberg sees in the painting, he mentions three adult men as a triangle which by its very dispersal directs the attention emphatically outside the painting. They are privileged not only as focusing devices, but also as focalizers. Of the three groups "ranked according to what they see" (Steinberg, 1981:53),[40] the three adult men alone see

a complex of interrelations, or two worlds at a glance – their own and another; a stage to serve in and a painted equivalent purely visionary.

Without elaborating on the choice of characters for each of these functions in vision, Steinberg (1981:53) sums up the result of *Las Meninas*'s self-reflexive meaning when he states:

The painter gives us the real, the reflected, and the depicted as three interdependent states, three modalities of the visible that cause and succeed one another in a perpetual round. Reality, illusion, and replication by art conspire in ceaseless recirculation.

First, it needs to be emphasized that the "real" that Steinberg includes in his interpretation is strongly staged, thus becoming an art form itself, another mode of representation. The social hierarchy is thereby presented as a theatrical performance. Second, the implication of this division of labor is obvious: The proud status of the painter who "masters" all of this is narrowed to the one gender exclusively chosen to represent complex vision, the others being disqualified by age, class, and gender.

Only Alpers hints at this link between different modes of hierarchization. Yet it is here that we can shift from the issue of class in the narrower sense to that of social hierarchy in general. For there is a sense in which it is not the painter who is the principal character of this work but the Infanta – in the double sense of being central both spatially and functionally. And her position, in turn, recalls the question, Who made the Infanta? – a question that expresses the competition between king and painter.

The way the princess looks cannot be equated simply to the other characters' inattention to the diegetic events in favor of the visual one. To the indifference of the dog and the man in the middle ground, she opposes an active refusal to her maid's gesture – as active as that of the woman in the second drawing discussed in Chapter 4, who opposed her objectification by the gaze (Figure 7.8). By the very contradiction in the Infanta's position between high and low, powerful and powerless, as it reflects (on) the contradiction between reflecting/seeing and reflected (upon), she represents by herself alone the dialectic of mutual self-definition: both the speculative possibilities of art and its ruthless limitations. This specialty signifies her uniquely mediating position, signified in the absolute centrality of her eye. As Alpers (1983:39) puts it:

7.8 Velázquez, *Las Meninas*, detail; *Female Nude Seated*, detail

Velázquez questions her role: she is a princess, but at the same time a little girl; she is most marvellously self-possessed in bearing, but is herself possessed by the court and by the royal lineage marked by her placement just below her parents's mirrored image.

Two points remain to be discussed here: the out-of-focus eyes of the painter, which match the eyes of "Rembrandt"'s painter in their ambiguity, and, in contrast, the centrality, which can only be a false lure or pretext, of the Infanta's eyes (Figure 7.9). In other words, in spite of Steinberg's brilliant account of the ways in which the dissemination of the foci work for self-reflection, there remains a dissemination which, while hardly visible, is persistently troubling because it affects the status of the two rivaling main characters.

Both the represented artist and the Infanta seem slightly cross-eyed; their looks are just a tiny bit out of focus. The artist's look hovers between his canvas and the intruding pair, thus challenging the realistic view of art, which would require absolute coincidence between them. The distance between the two – the real and the represented, as Steinberg would call them – is emphasized by the interposed body of the attendant. As Alpers points out, this woman's ribboned hair, matching the palette in color and brush stroke, is finely contiguous with it. The idea of *work* as craft, as process – as opposed to *the* (completed) work – is thus introduced; the maid's failure to communicate, her unsuccessful service, is, precisely, work: honest, well-placed, subordinate but necessary. Steinberg puts this servant in the category of distracted characters, whose sight is limited to the narrow sphere of the diegesis of every day life. But perhaps we are confronting here the "breach toward a latency" that allows us to break through Steinberg's beautifully triangular construction.[41] Steinberg's view depends, I think, on how "work" is represented.

SIGNS FOR WORK

Alpers convincingly argues that Velázquez does not reject the humble work of craft, and therefore there is a sense in which Steinberg adopts too easily the hierarchy of seeing and fields of visibility as

7.9 Velázquez, *Las Meninas*, details; *The Artist in His Studio*, detail

a statement made by the painting rather than a question raised by the critic in interaction with the work. Within my typology of self-reflection, he overstretches the work's self in order to keep his own self out. Comparison with "Rembrandt" may be illuminating here. Alpers (1988) has emphasized sufficiently the notion that Rembrandt spent much energy on promoting the craft of painting. In the present study, we have seen the example of the *Footwashing* (Figure 5.10). In the royal self-portrait in the Frick Collection (Figure 7.3), the gold that assigns royalty to the self is explicitly crafted, not assigned by the social hierarchy; it is made by the self, out of brushstrokes. However, such attempts are necessarily ambivalent. They rest on a sense of humble, honest work whose humility they aim, at the same time, to subvert. It is a mistake to believe that craft and art are in opposition. Art subsumes craft as its necessary but insufficient condition.

The ennobling representation of work is present throughout the "Rembrandt" corpus. We shall see other examples in the next chapter, but we have already seen in the *Footwashing* Jesus' competent and concentrated labor countering the Biblical message of humility in order to subsume humility – craft – into the higher, proud work. This drawing also identifies the worker with the main figure. "Rembrandt" promotes the figure of Jesus to the heights of art, built upon the foundations of humble work: craft. The drawing thus turns the moral issue into a semiotic and social one. Jesus is *made* by "Rembrandt," just as the king is made by Velázquez.

In the Boston panel (Figure 7.2), this same dialectic between humble craft and proud work is apparent. Although the painter is tiny, his canvas is huge, and although he has not done the work yet, he is already, as the subject he proposes himself to be, qualified to do it. Thus, both visually and narratively, he is predestined to be a great man. While there are few explicitly self-reflexive works, and none that pull together so many aspects of self-reflection as *Las Meninas*, I would like to contend that self-reflection is, if I may say so, disseminated throughout much of the "Rembrandt" corpus, not only in the self-portraits.

It is in this respect that, I submit, both class and gender are inscribed differently by "Rembrandt" than by Velázquez. For Velázquez an ambivalence toward work as craft and service is not surprising, for *Las Meninas*'s focus on social roles makes it less than likely that the painter will manage to repress entirely his own position as a servant. The very effort to define royalty through those who make it, is a symptom of this awareness. The bodily contiguity between painter and attendant symptomatically signifies the return of the repressed.

The maid as a figure is as contiguous to the painter as her ribboned head is to his palette (Figure 7.10). Her gesture makes sense, not only as a sensible thing for an adult to offer – food and drink are basic necessities of life – but also because it makes possible the Infanta's refusal of the drink. Thus it displays her childlikeness as a token of her high position. Social role thus becomes a semiotic tool for representation, rather than just its product; the Infanta's sharp looking-away also suggests the spoiled child.

But her look, in turn, painfully reminds us that we are what the child looks at. And the silence about this may demonstrate that herein lies the real blow to the viewer's narcissism. This triangle, formed by looking as an act, here equivalent to a speech act, deprives us of our focus. The new triangle formed here is that among painter, child, and viewer. Two out of these three are looking at two things at the same time; aren't we, then, too? The center of the constitutive mutuality between looking and being looked at is a spoiled child, mistaken about priorities of life – although also, as we have seen, well-trained in social hierarchization. Her slightly cross-eyed look distracts us from any possible realistic reading of this figure; rather, it alerts us to the contradictions the figure represents. This is also the mission of the work of the painter: Rather than deceive us with a transparent representation, he alerts us to the deceptiveness of appearances. And that includes, of course, the image in the mirror.

Why would the idea of *work* be particularly sensitive to all figures involved, including the viewer? The social relevance of work as defining status in the hierarchy is not sufficient to explain why hierarchy is called for in the first place. The self-reflection that I have called "mirroring" has also been shown to subsume, to engulf, to draw in the viewer. The anxiety, then, concerns the contiguity that mirroring entails. If discursive reflection turns out to encourage a safeguarding movement that excludes the critic's self, it is because the three critics of the first round shied away from that threat. Work leaves traces, affects the worker, and so does looking as work. The blow to our narcissism also has a background that can be defined in rhetorical terms.

Work as a process makes dirty hands, and those dirty hands, contiguous with the image or text, put the self on the spot. In contrast, the kind of representation that shuts out the representer's self – artist and critic alike – presents work as a neat product, effacing the traces of the process. As a metaphor of its represented object, a discursive self-reflection without reflection of the speaker's self is clean of work – a white-collar production, so to speak. In contrast, a self-reflection of and on both selves produces a complex metonymic work, contiguous with the process that made it. Looking

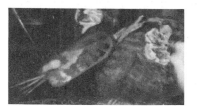

7.10 Velázquez, *Las Meninas*, detail

282

as work, then, can safeguard those traces, but one needs to endorse the dirty hands of the painter – the bifocused eyes of the viewer he has set before us.

This self-reflection challenges us to endorse the regressiveness involved in the mirror stage. The one triangle of painter, maid, and princess is figuratively a closed group, screened off, on both sides, by an instrument of ostentation: on one side, the enormous canvas; on the other, a female figure whose hands display the enormous surface of her body. Above them hovers the ambiguous image of the parents. Between all these forms of representation, I cannot blame the little girl for looking away. Nor, for that matter, can I blame the powerful painter for identifying with her.

CONCLUSION

This dialogue between two paintings, through that between one painting and its critics, has suggested that self-reflection as a mode of reading is appealing and at the same time threatening. The danger comes from the sense that when the viewer allows him- or herself self-reflection, the viewer is subsumed in the work. Self-reflection in the mirroring sense defies self-reflection in the discursive sense. The locus of this danger is the place where the position of the viewer gets blurred – the mirror in *Las Meninas*, the self-portrait in the "Rembrandt"; but the danger also resides in the self-portrait in *Las Meninas*, equally stiff, equally antinarratival, yet representing the narrative of representation as a socially relevant practice.

The selves in these self-reflections are defined and delimited by work. The work in question is hard to perform: It is the work of representation as a contradictory effort, as an effort to make what is not there yet, to define the new world in which these representations exist. Critics do this: They represent the work they work on. Artists do it, too: representing their own work, involving their own craft as well as their service for patrons. Velázquez had a patron when he painted this work and had to handle his own position in terms of this servicing work. "Rembrandt," one would think upon looking at this painting, had no patron, and yet the Boston panel demonstrates the need for patrons in the loneliness of the tiny figure confronted with the immense task posed by the empty canvas. Even this little lonely man is there as a social being, a worker. Representing painting as royal and as work, and work as ennobling and as socially defining, these two works by artists classified as "great" by the selections of "high culture" undermine the distinction between "high" and "low" art through the insistence on work as central.

In a similar vein, the drawings discussed in Chapter 4 showed an insistence on work that undermined that other ideological opposition current in thinking about art: that between ugly and beautiful. There, the question of the beauty of the female body was made irrelevant by the inherent beauty of the work of representation, in a gesture linking gender, work, and nobility similar to the gesture in *Las Meninas*, which posits the painter's work as contiguous with the woman servant's ornaments. And finally, if these two old masters represent the anxiety of the self enmeshed in working conditions, our contemporary critics, who also derive their social status from the work of writing their responses, are no more immune to this challenge to their dignified selves.

The question remains, Who is in control? In my reading, this question perhaps informed the tone of Snyder and Cohen's response. They, as rationalists who can solve problems by technical rigor, who can make them *simple*, seemed to feel dethroned by Searle's "loose" terminology. The prestige of academic rationalism they implicitly relied on is their version of social hierarchy. In their response, as in the painting, social hierarchy with its clarity and its delimitations – here the competence of the art historian posed against the incompetence of the philosopher – is the remedy against the threat posed by the mirror, against the anxiety of mirroring.

This anxiety is also the source of the appeal of self-reflection. Offering a "simple" solution to problems, paradoxical or otherwise, posed by fascinating works of art, self-reflection as a concept enables the critic to understand, to objectify, to grasp and hold, that which by its complexity threatens to absorb the critic and make him or her powerless. What is at stake, then, is narcissism, at the various different levels discussed here. Hutcheon's (1980) term "narcissistic work" was more appropriate than she probably anticipated. The reasons narcissism turns out to be so crucial a concept in an approach to art beyond the word–image opposition will be discussed in the next chapter.

I shall put narcissism, then, in the center of a reflection that cannot be but self-reflexive in its turn: a reflection on the appropriateness of psychoanalytical reading of art. Such a reflection has been proposed by many before me, especially for verbal art.[42] What others have done less frequently is emphasize the concept of self-reflection as the core – let's call it the navel – of psychoanalysis's relevance for art. Shoshana Felman has beautifully summarized the radicality of Freud's originality in his foregrounding of reflexivity and Lacan's reflexive return to that Freudian novelty:

What Lacan thus brings to light is the fact that what Freud's "inaugural step" – his constitutive procedure – inaugurates and later institutes is a new and unprecedented *mode of reflexivity* – of the process through which something turns back upon itself: a new mode of reflexivity that necessarily incorporates a passage through the Other, not as a reflection of the self but as a radical difference from the self, a radical difference to which, paradoxically, the very movement of reflexivity is addressed; a reflexivity whose self-reference, whose process of turning back upon itself, is not based on symmetry but on asymmetry: asymmetry between the self departed from and the self returned to; asymmetry between the turn and the return; a reflexivity, therefore, which, passing through the Other, returns to itself without quite being able to rejoin itself; a reflexivity which is thus untotalizable, that is irreducibly dialogic, and in which what is returned to the self from the Other is, paradoxically, the ignorance or the forgetfulness of its own message; a reflexivity, therefore, which is a new mode of cognition or information gathering whereby ignorance itself becomes structurally informative, in an asymmetrically reflexive dialogue in which the interlocutors – through language – inform each other of what they do not know. (Felman, 1987:60)

The narcissistically informed lack of interest in the informative ignorance to which Felman is alluding here is the locus of the failure of critics using self-reflexivity as an interpretive device. Narcissism, then, is the central place where psychoanalysis can help.

CHAPTER 8

BLINDNESS
OR INSIGHT?
PSYCHOANALYSIS
AND VISUAL ART

The fantasy... is there in front of me, in the mode
of *Vor-stellung:* I (re)present it to myself. Better still,
I (re)present myself in it through some "other," some
identificatory figure who enjoys in my place. But the
point from which I contemplate the scene – the fantasy's "umbilical cord," we might say, through
which it is linked with what is invisible for the subject
– is not offstage. I am *in* the fantasy, there where I
am the other "before" seeing him, there where I am
the mimetic model even "before" he arises in front
of me, there where I am acting out before any distancing, any drawing back: a nonspecular identification (blind mimesis) in which consists (if he/it
consists) the entire "subject" of the fantasy. (Mikkel
Borch-Jacobsen, *The Freudian Subject*, 1988:44–5)

INTRODUCTION

THE enigma of art, of artistic sensitivity and creativity, has
long intrigued psychoanalysts. But their attempts to "psychoanalyze" visual art have been mostly as unsuccessful as
were Freud's own comments on Leonardo da Vinci and Michelangelo.[1] For when the psychoanalyst understands art solely in terms
of its motifs and models, the result is generally reductive, biographical, and sexist, with its most important result being a sense
of futility, of irrelevance, and even of an imperialistic colonizing
of the visual by a hostile discourse. The primary – and deadly –
problem with these attempts to psychoanalyze art is that of the
status, or location, of the two partners in the encounter. What does
it mean to "psychoanalyze" a "patient" who cannot talk back, and
who is the patient anyway? In other words, what exactly is being
psychoanalyzed: the work, the artist, the critic's response?[2]

However, not all psychoanalytic criticism of art is doomed from
the start. The recent work of the more daring art critics is beginning
to make a convincing case for a classical Freudian psychocriticism
which, far from being reductive, is immensely intriguing, enrich-

ing, and original.[3] Moreover, there is a strong interest in visuality itself among contemporary psychoanalytic critics and theorists, mostly of Lacanian inspiration.[4] And the field where psychoanalysis has most successfully been brought to bear on works of art is that of film studies, where, significantly, the question of visuality and the question of fictionality are strongly intertwined. This intertwinement, I shall contend in this chapter, accounts for the appeal of visual art as a mediator for the unconscious of the viewer.

The questions that I perceive to emerge from this oversimplified survey of the state of things address the relationship between psychoanalysis as a discursive practice and visual art as a visual practice. This formulation suggests already that we should examine the relationship between the two as those between two practices, two arts if you like, rather than as between an object and an "approach" or mastercode whose mission it is to master its object through understanding. This equity is an indispensable precondition for overcoming the many ideological impulses to domination inscribed in the psychoanalytic endeavor – impulses that, in spite of the fundamentally dialogic structure of psychoanalysis, threaten to strike any attempt at insight with blindness at the start. This threat is, of course, not unrelated to verbality and its imperialistic repression of the irreducible visuality – and nonverbal aurality, for that matter[5] – inherent in the discursive understanding of working through.

The negative influence of overweening verbality can easily be seen to underlie the failures of a psychoanalytic approach to visual art. Reductive criticism, for example, comes with the presumption that understanding is one-sided mastering; its mastercode sets out to subdue the visual work, first, by translating it into a meaning, and then reducing that meaning to its origin. For example, Gentileschi's *Judith and Holophernes* denotes "hatred of men" because its author experienced rape.[6] The psychoanalyzed work can from then on do very well without itself and its visuality: It has become a document of the artist who in turn becomes a case of something that the psychoanalyst is interested in, say, the question of misandry. All the steps to get rid of the visual work of art, as visual, as work, and as art, partake of a systematic repression of the visual. This is logocentrism; in the Gentileschi case, and in others, it is logocentrism in the service of male obsessions. Given the passion with which this is pursued, the stakes must be high.

According to Freud, the stakes are high indeed. As it happens, visuality is the key experience that leads to castration anxiety. Verbal accounts about how castrating Gentileschi's painting is supposed to be only display what they set out to master: Castration comes into the little boy's mind after seeing the mother's "lack," and seeing becomes tainted with a trace of the fear he feels when he imagines he might share his mother's fate.[7] Visuality thus becomes the site and origin of danger. As a consequence, vision will be either rejected or controlled by those who have a stake here. Thus art critics betray their residual fear when they invoke discourse to overcome the fright of this primary visuality. No wonder there is a more than reasonable acknowledgment of the irreducible difference between the arts.[8]

Clearly, then, the importance of visuality as the experience that generates castration anxiety is gender related. For men would have a defensive interest in controlling vision. So it ceases to be surprising that the discursive practices that deny the importance of visuality, notably the possibility of visual art as a signifying practice, lack respect for difference, utterly; in fact, antagonism or opposition between the arts is still today ferociously defended by many. Visual images are taken to illustrate discursive mental constructs. So the visual is thereby necessarily in an inferior position.

In this negative ideology of the visual, discursive articulation is idealized: The visual is merely an inarticulate illustration of a more sophisticated verbal structure. Even Goodman's (1976) allegedly value-neutral distinction between dense and discrete semiotic systems partakes of this ideology, or at least sustains it. The counterpart to this negative ideology is the positivist's privileging of sight as the most reliable sense organ; this position denies the interpretive moment in vision as well as visual discursivity, and is, therefore, equally negative.

If recent film theorists have so happily rallied around psychoanalysis, it is precisely because in film, their object of study, the visual and verbal are profoundly intertwined. In addition, the fantasy character of film suggests to the theorists that they question the above ideology of the visual, taking it as a problem that informs film and its theory alike.

If we understand theory in its etymological background (which is, after all, visual), we can understand why such an approach is useful. Theory, understood as "insight," is radically different from what it was in the above-described classical and vulgar Freudianism. It ceases to be a dominating discourse and becomes rather a willingness to step into the visual, and to make discourse a partner, rather than dominant opponent, of visuality.

Given this understanding of theory as insight, as what Mitchell (1984) suggested to be a form of visuality, it is no coincidence that film studies today are at the forefront of feminist theory.[9] It is also not surprising that Lacan, with the complexity of his discourse, his tendency to design crazy diagrams, and his resistance to genetic reductionism, is the background theorist of choice.[10] Because of his idiosyncratic style, Lacan is impossible to "apply." One can enter into a dialogue with his discourse, one can evoke it, resist it, or follow it for a while; but its very form – its iconic relationship to the complexity of the object – continuously resists being turned into a mastercode.[11] And that is so much the better.

Another area in which psychoanalysis and visual art have been productively brought together is represented by works like Fried's *Realism, Writing, Disfiguration* (1987) and comes out of what I called

"Comparative Arts" in Chapter 1.[12] Although he does not extensively thematize the issue of discursivity in painting, his long and thorough analysis of largely a single painting by Thomas Eakins is informed by a concern with writing as a preoccupation of visual art, while his essay on Stephen Crane's short stories centers upon the theme of drawing and enhances the visuality – the visual figurativity of the self-reflexive field of writing. The very terms of Fried's own discourse – writing, realist representation, castration, disfiguration, the relationship between self and the making of images – suggest a thoroughly integrated encounter among visuality, verbality, and the critical endeavor.

Writing is the very term denoting a process whereby the opposition between visual and verbal melts into a nonanalytical, nonbinary acknowledgment of difference. Writing is a privileged Derridean *trace*; it is as visual as the *trace of castration* which the "lack" of the female body is said to display for the ignorant little boy whom so many critics still seem to want to be. So writing is the ideal "navel," the decentered center, the trace of genesis cutoff, the shallow cave, and the ungendered bodily sign of the text–image complex as it is understood here. Writing is the primary combination of discourse and visuality that indicates the basic intertwinement of the two media in one of the most prestigious and truth-oriented media of Western culture. Because of all these features, it is the medium, the activity, and the precondition of the very possibility of psychoanalytic criticism as a culturally embedded activity.

In this chapter, I shall position psychoanalysis as a discursive "tool" which the art critic can, under certain conditions, bring to bear on works of visual art in productive rather than reductive ways. The most important condition is that the critic overcome the utilitarianism implied in this very idea of "tool" and its correlates, "use," "application," and "object." In keeping with the discussion in Chapter 7, the two points I shall address most emphatically are the critical and self-critical potential of psychoanalysis, and its status as a semiotic theory, both evoked by Shoshana Felman's epigraph to Chapter 7. Both features are problematic, easily repressed, and must be situated beyond the word–image opposition.

If theory renounces the domination of visuality that classical psychoanalysis tends to embrace, it will have to relate to the visual in another way. The difference will be, if I may say so, spectacular and will subsume the issues raised in the preceding chapter. The spectacle of that spectacular difference will be that of the difference between the blindness of mastery and the insight of its renunciation. It is in this direction, I shall contend, that blindness as a central theme in visual art and in psychoanalysis seems to point.

But mastery is, as I have argued, a narcissistic protection against the threat of contamination, whereas its renunciation entails the acceptance of the two-sided constructedness of an image's unity. Narcissism, at the center of the debate on how to bring psychoanalysis to visual art, will have to be called upon to protect us against the temptation to latch onto psychoanalytic themes that are too obvious to be fruitful.

Precisely because castration is so much a favorite of classical, not to say vulgar, psychoanalytic criticism, it is the most vulnerable of Freudian ideas, open to the simplification of typological thematics. I have hinted at some of the relationships between blindness and castration anxiety that are carried by the act of blinding. As it happens, much of the "Rembrandt" corpus is about blindness, an obviously crucial and self-reflexive theme in visual art. To avoid the danger of a simplistic application of psychoanalysis to "Rembrandt," then, I need to prepare a complicating framework. The issue of blindness as both a Rembrandtian preoccupation and a general source of self-reflection in the visual domain, as both a symbolic-psychoanalytic and a metavisual problem, as both a written trace and an image, needs to be set off against the background of the need for self-reflection discussed earlier. For these reasons, the present chapter will focus on narcissism, reserving the theme of blindness for the next chapter.

COLLISION AND COLLUSION OF PSYCHOANALYSIS AND VISUAL ART

If we wish to do anything to narrow the generally alleged gap between psychoanalysis as a verbal discourse and visual art as irreducibly different because visual, we have to look toward semiotics, since the concept of sign is transmedial. Psychoanalysis *is* a semiotic theory. For it works on signs (symptoms, dreams), on codes (condensation, displacement), on the phatic dimension (the "talking cure," dialogism and its problematics: transference and countertransference), and, first and foremost, on meaning. It tends to share with semiotics the imperialism inherent in any discourse that can be used as a hermeneutic mastercode. Objects of art, or the process of production and reception of art for that matter, consist of, or work with, signs. Any theory of art has therefore a potentially semiotic status; to some extent, it is only a matter of vocabulary whether we speak of composition, brushstrokes, style, or iconographic traditions as codes, or not.

On the basis of this double semiotic status, psychoanalytic discourse on art cannot avoid at least touching upon semiotic issues. But psychoanalytic theories of art and creativity are of interest, not only because of this semiotic potential, but also because they share with semiotics the attempt to overcome both deterministic, mechanistic views of culture, and idealistic speculations about it.

More practically, semioticians have borrowed psychoanalytic concepts and sometimes psychoanalytic style, while psychoanalysts are sharply aware of the overall importance of symbols and signs for their discipline. Methodologically speaking, this is about as close as semiotics, art criticism and interpretation, and psychoanalysis have gotten. That critics hover between explanation and interpretation is symptomatic of the problem inherent in bringing these fields together; that critics struggle with the problems of the other disciplines, with how to persuade psychoanalysts to be less speculative, semioticians to be less positivistic, or art critics to be less idealistic, is another indication of the rocky relationship among these disciplines.

These intricate relationships among the three domains suggest the need for a more systematic, theoretical account of their relative positions; attempts to construct a general theory are fraught with problems of method. Let me briefly enumerate these problems:

In the first place, the premises underlying this general theory are currently vague. The relationships among the disciplines are more or less based on an implicit analogy, which suggests more specific relationships than are argued for. This is one of the problems of the distinction between the gaze and the glance as proposed by Bryson, which implies an analogy between the painterly trace and the bodily implication of the viewer that is less than satisfactorily argued for.

Furthermore, the concepts of art and creativity cannot be defined without recourse to a theory of the same type as the one that it is meant to support; hence, circularity is inevitable. For example, the hypothesis of narcissism as a force urging artistic self-reflection, the hypothesis that informed Chapter 7, rested on narcissism as a force urging self-reflection in the first place. In spite of the insight such a hypothesis may incidentally yield, as a foundation for a theoretical argument it reflects a circularity which remains an embarrassing glitch that might hamper theoretical development.

Next, there is no a priori reason why one should assume that a general theory can account for a phenomenon as ill-defined as creativity or art. Like "literature," "art" is an ideological term that implies its exclusionist mechanisms as well as its deceptive unificationism. It seems clear that the narcissism which I argued informed *The Artist in His Studio*, if only because the work is embedded in the context of rising bourgeois individualism, could hardly account for, say, the function of totemic sculpture in Africa, religious sculpture in ancient Egypt, or post-Freudian play with narcissism as in the contemporary genre of nonautographic "Rembrandt self-portraits" in postmodern art.[13]

A further problem is that the resulting lack of specificity makes such theories virtually irrelevant. On what basis can one expect to illuminate the question of art in general, given the varied forms, media, and historical and ideological contexts of an individual work? Universalism narrows empirical content down to unacceptably little.

In addition, methodologically speaking, there is no hope of ever reaching falsifiability. We can never know whether there are sub-jects who have the features defining the creative psyche, yet do not create art. Theories therefore remain necessarily speculative: I shall never be able to "prove," for example, that my account of the tension between looking and touching in the *Susanna* tradition has anything to say about "what the works really mean," precisely to the extent that nobody will be able to prove that I am wrong.

A related problem is that the discourse of such theories is strongly metaphorical, borrowing from ideological domains like the familial and the military. Each of these metaphors used brings in a number of uncontrolled features with it. Moreover, metaphorical equations tend to replace others, like the causal, functional, or synecdochical, which would make the theory less vague and more readily falsifiable.

One example from Susan Deri's (1984) book clearly demonstrates this problem. The study draws heavily upon metaphors such as behavior of mother = behavior of child, toys = the world, and the like, where a more functional relationship either would have had more explanatory power or would have been more easily re-jected. And the metaphorical equations are stated, of course, and can hardly be argued for: Psychoanalysis as a whole is based on a number of such metaphorical premises that have become so com-monplace that we no longer question them.

A final problem of the domain from which psychoanalysis bor-rows its metaphors overlaps with the object of the theory (i.e., that the formation of the subject is strongly anchored in family relations) as well as with an ideological view of that domain (i.e., that moral values are linked to the way in which the family forms the subject). In general, theories that deal with "good" things like art and beauty easily become moralistic. Freud tried hard to overcome this ten-dency, and he managed better than many of his followers who fall back into pre-Freudian connotations attached to key Freudian terms.[14] The premise of much work done in the object–relations school of psychoanalysis, for example, presumes that creativity is a good thing. The origin of that good thing is, then, explained by good origins, which introduces another of those metaphorical re-lationships. The good mother is, not surprisingly, the first and foremost requirement for the development of a creative person. The Lucretia theme convincingly shows just how closely moralism and metaphor collaborate. There, the metaphorical interpretation that takes the suicide to stand for the rape obliterates the murderer, the rapist, and encourages blaming the victim for her own death, if not for the rape. Here, the metaphor of the good mother as image of what the child shall be confines women to motherhood as their primary task, and inversely, turns artistic work into something predetermined.

These are problems enough to make one wish to abandon the attempt to develop a psychoanalytic theory of art, with the result that art critics either use psychoanalysis without worrying about the methodological framework and its requirements, or reject psychoanalysis as useless, irrelevant, and methodologically unsound. And, thus, we are left with a false dilemma: We can either accept psychoanalysis *with* its flaws or reject it altogether.

From a feminist perspective, this either/or position is clearly unacceptable. For it implies that either we have to accept the Freudian biases, including those against visuality which are informed by a fundamentally male and childish position, or we must remain closed-mouthed before a discourse that has so much to say about the relationship between gender and visuality and, as we shall see, about visuality outside of, or before, sexual difference. From a semiotic perspective, the above flaws may not matter so much. Rather than seeking to explain art, in the strong, genetic sense, which is what psychoanalysis sets out to do, a semiotic view of "psychoanalysis and art" will undermine precisely the geneticism while strengthening the hermeneutic potential of the theory. Shoshana Felman (1977) has suggested that we begin by making explicit what we mean by the ambiguous conjunction "and," which creeps into any interdisciplinary self-justification.

The conjunction "and" means "behind" in the sense of "before" for many psychoanalysts; it means "about" or "in" for many pre-poststructuralist critics; it means "in dialogue with" for optimistic deconstructionists; whereas it may mean "functioning as a go-between in the process of" working with art, for semioticians. For the semiotician, then, the relationship between psychoanalysis and art is neither a one-sided master–slave relationship as the arrogance of positivist epistemology would have it, nor an egalitarian dialogue as Felman prefers it; in a different perspective, it is neither a Hegelian master–slave dialectic, as a transference-centered psychoanalysis would make possible, nor a free-standing encounter. It would be, rather, a mutually necessary, existence-threatening suspension of mastery. It would be a discursive practice fully self-conscious about the implications such a practice holds for the assumed specificity of each. And it would be an attempt to "use" psychoanalytic concepts as more or less random beginnings rather than as codes, let alone mastercodes. In short, it would be an attempt to "semiotize" art, to assess its discursive status along with, or in terms of, its visuality, at the same time that it attempted to visualize psychoanalytic discourse. Psychoanalysis could initiate, through some of its concepts, an account of the dynamic process of art by mediating the relationship among sender, work, and addressee in the otherwise noncommunicative process dominated by fixation and delay. It could turn art against itself by letting art challenge *its* own fixities. "Psychoanalysis and art" together would launch our voyage into the territory that lies beyond the word–image opposition.

Unfortunately, however, those who apply psychoanalytic concepts to art all too often fall back into the traps outlined above.

They do so by presuming that a message, or a set of signs, links genesis and reception by conveying meaning. We interpret the work of art as the message containing the record of the psychic state of the artist during the making of the work.

A first revision in this conception already makes all the difference. Instead of such a direct cognitive connection, we might suppose that the artist's psychic force leads to the making of the work and finds expression in that work. The artist's creative process then "translates" that force into meaning, which retains the forcefulness of the process within it. Force, in such a revision, is the power pressure occurring at the intersection of energy, drive, imagination, and symbolization. Force is not meaning but a surplus attached to meaning, an illocutive aspect. As such, this revisionist psychoanalytic approach partakes of a theory of performativity.[15] In this theory of the affective nature of art, the addressee is assumed to be sensitive to that force-in-meaning, reacting by identifying, protesting, denying, or accepting the affect. Response to art, then, would be an emotive, mostly unconscious response to the traces of the force that informed its making or, rather, that will turn it, for the respondent, into art. Popular art could be as affective as "high art."

The expression, the work of art, is the only accessible part of this process: It is result and trace of the force-in-meaning. Through these traces or signs – or symptoms, if you like – psychoanalytic theory would then be able to propose a way of looking at art. The trace, then, would invert the genetic perspective: As the first and only access to the supposed force, from which art begins, it would lead us most probably to the dis-semination of meaning. The force, which leaves only the work as its active writerly trace, sets the process in motion; it refers, prospectively, to what will happen, rather than retrospectively, to what had been created. And this line of thought leads us away from psychoanalysis as mastercode.

In contrast to a genetic, explanatory theory, psychoanalytic concepts must be situated somewhere between signs and codes, thus undermining the privileging of both. As signs, they can signify the background on which the above assumption of the force–meaning interaction rests. As codes, they can mediate on one level between interpretation and explanation, on another level between sender and addressee, and on yet another between force and meaning. In order to keep open the transition between these levels, I shall refer to the concepts discussed in this light as *views* – with the visuality of the term intended. Since these views will be identified with familiar concepts from psychoanalysis generally considered as hermeneutic "tools," interpretations elaborated in terms of these concepts will have to be open-ended and interdisciplinary. Whatever its other features, a view is a view, inexhaustible by discourse. But as it provides (in)sight into the event of art, such a concept can also be seen as a room with a view.

The voyage through *Las Meninas*, its cotexts and its posttexts, has provided some insight into the complexity of self-reflection as a quadruple mode of reading that inescapably confuses visual and discursive modes of reflection and entangles the selves concerned even in the very attempt at disentangling them. But the road is still, so to speak, a little too well-constructed, a little too smooth to be the royal road to self-critical reflection, which cannot but be tortuous and perhaps circular, but certainly with many points of access. With "Rembrandt" as our principal guide and object – master and servant, if you like – we may now wish to venture upon a less royal, less masterable, less happy path, that will lead us not to a conclusion but, appropriately, to a new set of questions. Its starting point is the loose end that has remained dangling at several points in the preceding discussion: It is the question of narcissism and, through that, the question of how we are to use psychoanalytic discourse in formulating our response to art. In this section I shall bring the concept of narcissism more explicitly to bear upon the self-reflexive modes and open up the subject of psychoanalytic discourse.

Let us begin with Figure 8.1. The scene represented here is Biblical: the murder of Sisera, a Canaanite leader, by Yael. Like Judith, Yael is in the ambivalent position of being both a national heroine and a gender enemy. The well-known conflation of Judith and Salome (Panofsky, 1955:36–9) attests to the conflict of interests and betrays the priorities of Western culture. Judith beheaded Holophernes to save her people; she used her feminine charm to gain entrance to his tent, but she explicitly remained chaste: Here the issue is primarily political. Salome, on the other hand, danced for her stepfather Herod and was enticed by her mother Herodias to ask for the head of John the Baptist as a reward. The issue is not so much political as sexual, although no sexual intercourse is involved. Yael received the enemy leader into her tent – a reversal of the Judith situation – put him to sleep, and drove a tentpeg through his temple. In this case, the issue is political, but whether Yael used sexuality to gain that political end remains unanswered.[16] Despite this ambiguity, Yael is identified with Judith both by the Biblical language and by subsequent criticism. In the Bible she is described positively with the phrase "Blessed among the women be Yael" (Judges 5:24, 26), a phrase that is applied to the three major Biblical heroines – Yael, Judith, and Mary. But the evolution of what is considered good for a woman, from murder to self-negation, obscures the fact that all three figures earned their title of honor by eliminating a man.[17] Judith mediates between the two others. For Yael, the elimination is acted out by plain murder – the active and positive elimination of the man. For Mary, this is done by plain virginity – the passive, negative elimination of the man.

For Judith, both murder and virginity are at stake: As a murderer of a male enemy, she is emphatically virginal. The change in the norms is honored by the fact that in later criticism Mary is praised, Judith is conflated with the purely sexual murderess Salome and thereby obliquely criticized, and Yael is violently and directly attacked.[18]

8.1   *Yael Killing Sisera* ca. 1659–60, Benesch 1042, drawing, 100 × 172 mm (Amsterdam, Rijksprentenkabinet)

8.2   *Tobias Curing His Father's Blindness* ca. 1649–50, Benesch 646, drawing, 175 × 133 mm (Berlin-Dahlem, Kupferstichkabinett)

Although it is not entirely without antecedent, the motif of Yael's heroic act is not frequently represented in the tradition of Western painting. And nowhere is it represented as *the* image of work, even though the Biblical text suggests the meaning of /work/ by referring to Yael's access to the weapon as the tool for her work. This drawing uses that reference to work. As an anti-Pygmalion, we see here a visual artist, a sculptor, at work on something that can at any moment become alive.[19] The suspenseful narrative of murder (e.g., will he wake up before he is killed?) is replaced by the equally suspenseful narrative of representation (e.g., is the work destructive or creative?). Just as the seduction of Adam by Eve was reversed into that of Eve by Adam (see Figure 4.11), so here a murder scene is reversed. The modification of life into death becomes a scene of creation, of the perfect creation the Pygmalion myth stands for: the modification of death into life through art. But this transformation through art becomes a kind of work that leaves dirty hands.

Work is also relevant in another way here. While the Song of Deborah, assumed to come from a tradition of Judges 5, evokes the pleasure of violence quite gruesomely, and while the (male) epic tradition (Judges 4) conveys disturbing imagery of reversed rape, this drawing of the scene, although equally forceful, is stunningly *quiet*. Utter concentration and hard work, harmoniously combined, subsume, justify, or replace violence.

The metaphor that operates in this work's relation to the pre-text and that makes the reversal possible, is obviously the notion that Yael's act was in some sense productive, even creative: It contributed to the creation of Israel, as a unified and monotheistic people, the difficult formation of which is the focus of the Book of Judges.[20] The reversal this drawing presents rests on a reading of the pre-text of Judges 5, rather than 4, wherein Yael's act is specifically praised as an act of women's *work*. This is the most plausible historical meaning of the phrase "Blessed be Yael among the women *in the tent*." The final qualification has often been assumed to indicate the limitations of the space, the radius of action women were assigned to. This is certainly an aspect of its meaning; but through that limitation, the phrase also indicates specific kinds of work – raising the tents, for example – that provide Yael the instrument of her act, while establishing a metaphoric and a metonymic link between her daily life and the act which at the same time it made possible and unlikely.

What we want for the moment to retain from this representation of work is both the respect for craft and the double reversal: from male to female artist, from female to male object, and from life–death to death–life, from destruction to creation. This double reversal has a subversive aspect, which we can also see in Velázquez's painter's contiguity with women, work, and childlikeness.

In terms of narcissism, the drawing's positive mood self-reflexively represents the artist's identity as an ideal maker. The connection with femininity, to which I shall return, is not irrelevant to this positive view of the self-identity of the artist. The drawing of *Yael* is supposed to be about murder, but murder is not seen as violent and destructive here; murder is, according to the drawing's metaphorical argument, as necessary for the creation of Israel as the work of craft is necessary for the creation of a work of art. As the *Footwashing* (Figure 5.10) has already shown us, "in the Beginning was the Work"; in this light Mary's labor of birthgiving in the *Adoration* (Figure 5.11) can now be seen self-reflexively as well. Now compare the Yael drawing, for a moment, to the following drawing, one of the many works responding to the apocryphal Biblical story of Tobias (Figure 8.2).

In the Tobias scene, we are told, the young Tobias operates upon his father, who had been blinded by a veil that a bird had dropped upon his eyes, a veil that needs to be removed. What we see, however, is a displacement of the sort "Rembrandt" displays so often. True enough, if we read iconographically, we recognize the characters: We see Anna, Tobias's mother and the blind man's wife, leaning on her stick as if to emphasize how *her* old age produces impotence; we see Tobit, leaning backwards, immobilized by the right hand of his son; we see Raphael, the angel who has accompanied Tobias throughout his initiation quest, spreading his wings for protection for the last time; and finally, we see Tobias, ready to begin the operation.

It has not passed unnoticed that, in a primary "deviation" from the Biblical story, Tobias uses an instrument for the operation, an instrument that is usually seen as an allusion to the cataract oper-

8.3   *Tobias Curing His Father's Blindness* 1636, Bredius 502, panel, 47.2 × 38.8 cm (Stuttgart, Staatsgalerie)

298

ation.[21] This instrument, a sharp, pointed little thing, is represented in all of the many "Rembrandt" versions of this scene, as an obsessional figure (see, e.g., the early painting of 1636 in Figure 8.3). The frequency with which it appears suggests that it has greater significance than the allusion to the cataract operation provides. As a consequence of this "deviation," the operation is altered from the removal of the veil to the penetration of it. The instrument fits oddly with the story, since removing a veil is the opposite of piercing one, unless we venture to take literally the structural suggestion in the pre-text that the removal of Tobit's blinding veil is somehow connected with the piercing of Sarah's so far unconquered veil of virginity; this connection, loaded with gender, is proposed by the emphatic simultaneity between the two endeavors Tobias sets out to accomplish.

I have already suggested this much in Chapter 5, but we are now better equipped to see this connection in relation to the motif of self-reflection. Rather than cure his blindness, Tobias, with his frighteningly sharp instrument, seems to be about to blind his father. Moreover, whereas in Figure 8.1 the subject of violence was gendered feminine, here the mode of violence is gendered masculine, but in relation to the feminine *as well as to the father.*

This gender aspect is the more remarkable as blinding is often related to castration in the history of Western culture. This scene would then metaphorically represent castration, Julius Held argued long ago in *Rembrandt's Aristotle* (1969). Held's argument was convincing, but he did little more than repeat the typical gesture of early pychoanalytic criticism: He collected examples of a motif (blindness) and assigned it in passing a fixed and fixing meaning: castration.[22] This mode of criticism is itself castrating, in that, denying the mobility of the text, it too is blinding.

Should we then overlook the traditional connection between blinding and castration? Not in the least. Let us assume for a moment that the little instrument has to do with castration. If this metaphor is acceptable, then the imagery of castration is quite frequently evoked in the "Rembrandt" corpus, often through blindness or blinding. I shall cite examples in the next chapter. But it also shows up in a more literal sense, and this may lead us to wonder about the effect of its metaphorization.

An example of a more straightforward castration motif can be seen in the drawing of the near sacrifice of Isaac (Figure 8.4), where the knife threatens to fall directly "in place." The knife, a more commonplace instrument than Tobias's pointed instrument, looks like the one in the *Blinding of Samson* – on which more shortly. It is not pointed; it does pierce, but slices; it cuts off. The motif is classical because the castrator is the father – as it should be if the work is to represent castration anxiety – and the son's body is represented as smooth, feminized. One detail does connect this classical castration with the deviant Tobias: The father's eyes, compared with those of the angel, are blurred. The castrated son's face is entirely empty, but the father is not a well-equipped see-er either.[23]

The difference between this classical castration and the possibly metaphorical one in the Tobias connects with two other motifs frequent in "Rembrandt": the aggression of the son toward the father, which is acted out through competition and role reversal, and which the *Isaac* seems to justify and provoke; and the feminization of the male body, which the *Isaac* displays through the smooth emptiness of Isaac's body, and which points to a role reversal between the sexes.[24]

In "Rembrandt"'s Tobias story, the son pierces the father's veil, rather than removing it. Not only does this act turn curing blindness into blinding, but if blinding is to stand for castration, the work also reverses generational roles. In addition, Tobias's act becomes a metaphor of the piercing of the bride's veil. Just as the pre-text, by its emphasis on simultaneity, generates the metaphorical connection between Tobit's disease – blindness through the veil, through becoming a virgin so to speak – and Sarah's disease – killing husbands, by being an incurable virgin – just so "Rembrandt" connects the "curing" of both diseases. The similarity between these two interpretations, castration and defloration, the way in which the one might stand as a metaphor for the other, needs, of course, further elaboration, for the connection is far from obvious. For the moment, however, I am content to map out a context for another

8.4 *Abraham Withheld from the Sacrifice of Isaac* ca. 1630, Benesch 90, 194 × 146 mm (London, British Museum)

detail that has passed largely unnoticed or, if noticed, has remained unexplained.

This detail is quite striking: In Figure 8.2, Tobias is pointing his instrument, not toward the father's eyes, but toward his beard (Figure 8.5). This oddity is easily explained away. Thus Held (1969:115) states: "Tobias is not caught performing the "operation" but examining closely his father's eyes, preliminary to the actual cure." But this explanation only displaces the problem, for now we are saddled with the unexplained, the careful almost tense gesture of Tobias's hand manipulating the instrument. Rather than naturalizing the detail within a realistic interpretation, the combination of the beard, the father–son interaction, and the gesture makes the oddity available for reading as a textual navel. It becomes the locus of the shifting of meaning, the entrance into another possible story. As Freud (1900:525) put it, in *The Interpretation of Dreams*, the navel is "the spot where it [the dream] reaches down into the unknown."

Within the theme of competition between generations, the beard is a sign of age, of the elder position in the generation conflict. Thus is it a marker of fatherhood, turning the young, beardless Tobias into the son. This is not superfluous, as it underscores the reversal in the power relation between the two, preparing the ground for attention to violence, if not castration. But when taken "literally" first – that is, visually – as merely a surface, the beard looks less like a beard than like a sheet of paper. Its emptiness makes it a place for speculation of the caliber of the emptiness around which the Elder in the Berlin *Susanna* clutched his fist (Figure 4.6). And indeed, Tobias's instrument itself looks pretty much like a pen, brush, or pencil. Are Tobias's eyes, like the gesture of his hand with the instrument, directed toward the locus of the instrument's point on the beard, rather than toward his father's eyes, or toward both? We cannot quite tell.

As the navel of the text, the beard generates self-reflection. Drawing becomes work par excellence. The surrounding figures who are holding their breath in tension about the story's climax – the curing of the father's blindness – may as well, in this other story, be holding their breath because an artist is coming into being. That this self-reflection is acted out over the token of the father's old age, his beard, emphasizes a particular view of (self-)generation: The father needs to be eliminated in his vital capacity for the son to come into his own. If the son is to become a great visual artist, then the father must not be able to see. Castration, then, is not just metaphorically represented through blinding. Castration as the de-

8.5 *Tobias Curing His Father's Blindness*, detail

struction of the power to create, gendered male, is made to *be* blinding.

Thus three relations among the elements of meaning in this drawing emerge, with all three being more than metaphorical. The relationship between father and son, represented at the moment of the son's liberation by the father's undoing, metaphorically stands for the relationship between groom and bride, brought in by the pre-text with its insistence on simultaneity and with the similarity it evokes between the two diseases and Tobias's two tasks. Sexuality has given the son the strength, finally and symbolically, to do away with his own castration anxiety. And these conflated relations take shape in, and coincide with, the relationship between the novice artist and his old predecessor.

This drawing allows us to imagine, then, the Tobias story as a shifter between preoccupations – as the story that bridges the gap between the "work of life" and the work of art. The work of life is presented as the difficult task of initiation and the subsequent displacement of the father. The work of art is presented both in its aspects of social and personal ambition and in its craft, its work. I do not want to say simply that the life story is a metaphor for the work story, although that is one possible way of looking at this complex. Rather, it is the possible metaphorical conflation of these stories that makes the drawing so dynamic. We must give up trying to discriminate which, in this triple-layered metaphor, is the vehicle, and which the tenor.

Just like the Yael drawing (Figure 8.1), this one represents for us visually the problematic inherent in "life" and "art," both seen as work. To put this in provisionally simplistic terms, the ambition of the painter is represented as working through the castration of the father which, in turn, is conflated with the defloration of the woman that made it possible. That the latter is a formidable task toward which the young man is ambivalent is obvious from the pre-text, where seven prospective husbands lost their lives in the endeavor. It is this element of the story – including the structural identification with the father's and the bride's ordeal – that is most widely known.

Our culture seems to have endorsed, then reversed, this identification in the expression "Tobias night." This expression does not, as we might expect, refer to the anxiety of the deflowering husband, nor does it refer to the exploit of the groom who succeeds after all. Instead, it refers to the *ius primae noctis*, the right of the father to deflower the son's bride. This is how a patriarchal culture appropriates, in the name of the father, the moment of role reversal Tobias acts out in the myth.

But the trace of the pre-textual meaning remains in this drawing. That Tobias precisely does *not* delegate to the father the formidable task is shown by his *coup d'état*, his usurpation of the fatherly power as well as the power to represent his own version of the story. We may say that he deserves it, for that the task is formidable is suggested by the Yael drawing. And this is where the father–son problem encounters the man–woman problem.

Yael is a good example of the formidable woman. She is not just the source of creative strength here, in an idiosyncratic view of the Muses,[25] but also the male artist's rival, or companion, in creation. Yael's quiet and forceful effort echoes Tobias's quiet and forceful concentration. Both Yael and Tobias concentrate in forceful suspense. They concentrate with eyes that are the central organs of their bodies. And their eyes concentrate on what they direct their hands to do. The one artist is a son figure assisted by his mother; the other is a woman. Both use a pointed instrument and perform their art on the surface of the impotent, blind body of a man.

In the arrogation of artistic and social mastery, Velázquez gave the woman attendant the humble, yet indispensable, assignment of representing work. He did so in order to confine to manageable proportions the forceful presence of woman in the ascension to artistic and masculine power. "Rembrandt" proceeds otherwise. Even less inclined to discount the place of women, he makes their images as formidable as those of the father in more typical representations, as we shall see shortly. The effect of this valuation of women and of this subjugation of the father works, of course, to increase the young man's own pride. This is what makes the Tobias figure so strong in this drawing: self-confident, concentrated, spatially and narratively central. But the conquest is difficult because it is plural. It is plural because what is at stake, narcissism, is itself plural.

NARCISSISM AND ITS DISCONTENTS

Narcissism, in psychoanalytic discourse, is not the clearest of concepts. It points to a love relationship whose object is the image of oneself. The image one has of oneself is, however, founded on the model of other persons. As Mikkel Borch-Jacobsen (1988) brilliantly points out, narcissism is already predicated upon the imitation of the other which narcissism is supposed to short-circuit.[26] Here lies the psychoanalytic paradox and its parallel with the paradox of representation. The hypothesis that art is a function of narcissism rests upon the amorous captivation of the subject by this self-image, the internalization of a relationship, which is externalized in the work of art. And the work of art is not only an externalization of an internalized relationship, but is also made *for* others – patrons, viewers – so that this relationship with the external world is inscribed within power relations that affect the narcissism of the painting self. The work of art comes to stand for the loved self-image that is represented to others; it becomes a sign of the self-image loved for its otherness. If the self is initially fully internalized, short-circuiting others, it is subsequently fully externalized, made other. This tension illuminates in turn the concept of narcissism itself: Rather than defining an attitude toward a specific object, the self, it refers to a relationship in which "self" is defined, or produced. As Borch-Jacobsen (1988:71) puts it, "[T]he elaboration of the concept of narcissism does not escape the effects of narcissism."

Yet the concept of narcissism has come to stand for a variety of phenomena, for different stages in the development of the subject. In what is called "primary narcissism," the subject is imagined as not yet having gained awareness of difference, so there cannot yet be a relationship to objects since objects are still indistinct, unified. This objectless state is seen as both complete unity and complete fragmentation: The nondelimited world cannot be whole, for wholeness does not apply. A subject that is indistinguishable from an object cannot be a subject, for separation is what defines subjectivity. In Freudian terms, the *ego* cannot yet exist because it is not yet distinguished from the *id*; only after the *id* emerges can object relations commence.[27]

As you recall, primary narcissism constituted the threat in *The Artist in His Studio* (Figure 7.2), where the insecure yet proud painter threatened to contaminate the viewer; there the threat could be defused by reference to the artist's clumsiness. But since narcissism is relational, it cannot apply to the structure of primary narcissism. As Jean Laplanche among others has remarked, the conflation between object and subject, presupposed in primary narcissism, a conflation in which everything inheres in the subject, presupposes in turn a minimal delimitation of the self.[28] Hence, this primary narcissism cannot be entirely primary. Nor can the subject of it be merged with the environment, basically the caring mother. Instead, the state of primary narcissism is rather a retrospective projection, a hallucination of what the beginning of the self must have been. The sense of threat emanating from *The Artist in His Studio*, then, arises from the fear of this imagined merging.

The tension that arises when the subject fantasizes a need to liberate itself from this imaginary state of confusion is considered by Kristeva (1982) the most archaic form of narcissism capable of being the force of art.[29] The narcissism that arises when the effort to separate is strong enough to initiate the completely negative relationship to the mother (the first relation to the self as non-mother, as m/other), features the duality of the representation of self as nothingness. The self is that which separates from the mother by becoming unified. This beginning subject is modeled on the only possible object. As Green (1983:113) writes: "La mère couvre l'auto-érotisme de l'enfant" (the mother covers the child's autoeroticism).

This moment of separation is not without a profound effect upon the generation of signs, of meaning: it is based upon both similitude as its metaphor, and of contiguity as its condition. But *it is not itself a meaning*. This becomes particularly clear in Green's analysis, when he defines the position of the mother:

The mother is caught in the empty framework of negative hallucination, and becomes the framing structure for the subject itself. The subject builds itself there where the investiture of the object was consecrated in the place of its investment. (Green, 1983:126, my translation, emphasis removed)[30]

The position of the mother becomes thus the condition for semiosis, a code if not a mastercode, and Green concludes:

[T]he negative hallucination of the mother, without being in any way representative of anything, *has rendered possible the conditions of representation.* (Green, 1983:127, my translation; emphasis in text)[31]

But the moment of separation is also a moment of effort, struggle, and pain. *Work,* as the incredible effort of creating, is contaminated by the imagined memory of this moment.

It is no wonder that labor, the work of birthgiving, comes to mind as the metaphorical, but also metonymical sign representing this moment. Between state and process, between subject and object, between destruction of the bond with the mother and creation of the self, this moment figures as the founding sign for art as an endeavor for which words like "difficult" and "ambitious" now sound hilariously repressive.

The single most disturbing painting in "Rembrandt," *The Blinding of Samson* (Figure 8.6), can now be read as a stunningly successful representation of this imaginary moment. The exceptionally forceful presence of violence in this work contrasts sharply with the representations of work that we have seen so far. But this violence illuminates the way in which the repression of violence in the depiction of Yael's murder of Sisera returns as a symptom in the very choice of pre-text. In the *Samson,* the archaic experience burdens the subject, both painter and onlooker, with the trace of absolute effort: Everyone but Delila is engaged in the effort, which accumulates in Samson's right foot.

The importance of this work for the present argument rests in the way it can illuminate the different strands discussed apropos of the Tobias drawing (Figure 8.2). The *Samson* can be seen as a mediation between, and a conflation of, pre-Oedipal and Oedipal dramas. This work shows us one possible connection between blinding as the feared moment of castration and blinding as the fantasized moment before the separation from the mother, the terminal moment of primary narcissism. The moment that is at stake here, the transition from inside to outside, is blinding: There can remain an image of nothing but the transition itself, and the purely negative subject cannot have eyes to see. The moment represents nonexistence and, on another level, obliviousness of that terrible nonexistence.[32] As a topic for a work of art, it offers enough occasion for artistic pride to appeal to an ambitious artist who wishes to show the art of work through the work of art; for representing this nonrepresentable state – nonrepresentable because invisible to the blinded subject – is the paradox of primary narcissism as self-reflection. It is the metaphor of the creation of the self through a distinction that obliterates the self.[33]

Primary narcissism is given a slightly different cast in Lacan's (1966b) theory of the mirror stage. The *mirror stage* is the moment in which primary narcissism ends and the subject emerges. In this experience, the subject relates for the first time to another, and losing its initial blindness, internalizes the first image it sees: the image of the self. As is well known[34] and dramatically exposed by Lacan in his seminal essay "The Mirror Stage as Formative of the Function of the I," this self-construction is based on an imaginary image: a fundamental alienation, a fiction that generates the representational impulse. The itinerary can be described as a voyage from the subject-to-be to the other, identification with that other, and return to the subject with the self subsuming the other. If relationship there is, it is with imagination rather than object. Image forming is the basic experience that follows separation, and this image forming leads to self-reflection in every possible sense. In visual art, this stage leads to the sense that there is not so much a represented object but an image, a nonreflexive yet self-conscious *image* of the self.[35] The self-portrait as a genre, and many "Rem-

8.6   *The Blinding of Samson* 1636, Bredius 501, canvas, 205 × 272 cm (Frankfurt am Main, Städelsches Kunstinstitut)

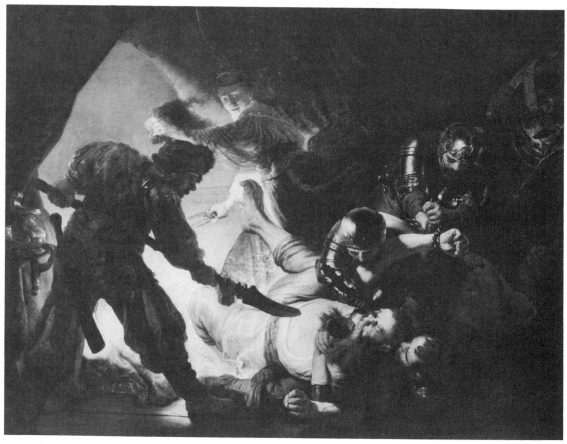

306

brandt" self-portraits in particular, can be at least partly related to this experience.

We may elucidate this process, this itinerary from the subject to the self, through the series of etched self-portraits "Rembrandt" did supposedly at the beginning of his career, a selection of which is reproduced here, in addition to that in Figure 7.3 (Figure 8.7). Usually, the variety of facial expressions – from laughing, through merry, sad, and clownish, to angry, with an exaggeratedly ugly or idealized nose – is explained by considering these portraits as studies. But this down-to-earth explanation, plausible as it is, fails to account for the slight sense of discomfort the etchings give the viewer. Chapman (1989) provides a stronger explanation, interpreting these etchings as depicting facial expressions "against the background of his early activity as a history painter and seventeenth-century ideas about representing the emotions or, in the terminology of the period, the passions of the soul" (160). Precisely because they also stand in the tradition Chapman mentions, the etchings stand apart by the sense of uneasiness they provoke, at least for me. This uneasiness might be caused by the excessive differences among them, which can be accounted for in terms of the primary narcissism of the mirror stage. The discovery of the self as a first possible object/other to relate to is preceded by the realization of the otherness of the image, which a beginning and self-conscious artist is likely to experience at the moment of his artistic mirror stage. "Rembrandt"'s habit of practicing his craft in front of a mirror, then, is not only an attempt to develop his skill, as in the interpretation of the etchings as studies, but also a way to recover that primal experience of emerging selfhood by re-presenting the self as other, by making art.

Another concept of narcissism, referred to as *secondary narcissism*, is the later, regressive relationship from subject to self as exemplified by the myth of Narcissus. This regressive relationship constitutes a reversed narrative of the formation of the subject, in which the self is identified with the other, or the self-image is invested with

8.7 Left to right: *Self-Portrait* 1630, etching (Haarlem, Teylers Museum); *Self-Portrait* 1630, etching (Amsterdam, Rijksprentenkabinet); *Self-Portrait* 1630, etching (London, British Museum)

8.8 *Self-Portrait* 1629, Bredius 8,
panel, 89.5 × 73.5 cm (Boston,
Isabella Stewart Gardner
Museum)

the features of the love object. Looking for the love object, Narcissus returns to the mirror, invests the self with the love directed to the object, then, discovering the self-image in its contradiction, returns to nonseparation, to the womb where he, and it all, came from.

Secondary narcissism, unlike primary narcissism and the mirror stage, implies a story. As such, it subsumes in its reversal the two other moments with which it forms a series of moments, of events whose agents gradually merge into nothingness. This process is painfully contradictory because the subject of secondary narcissism "knows" the object status of the self as well as of others. In the myth, the story leads to death; in art, it leads to the sense of alienation inherent in the representation it informs, a representation that leaves the viewer unsure of what s/he sees: object or self, self as object. It should be clear by now that "clumsiness" is instrumental in this process of (self-)representation.

Let us now look at a self-portrait that is not simply a study, and yet is profoundly a study in self-reflexive art (Figure 8.8).[36] This very early self-portrait of 1629, dated the same year as *The Artist in His Studio*, evokes uncertainty. The face features the symptoms of vanity that make one want to categorize the painting as idealized. If moustache and mouth, arrogant eyebrows and straight nose alone are not telling enough, hairstyle and hat, gown and light, hardly leave room for doubt that the painting is idealized. It is so, not in relation to some "real" model, like the artist's legendary ugliness, but as representation.[37] Its object is a handsome and proud young man, the self. On the other hand, this very feature signals insecurity, as does the hesitant eye directed almost, but not quite, at the viewer who, insofar as s/he coincides with the subject of the work, functions as a mirror.

Of what, however, does the self consist in the case of a beginning artist? The idealization of self and the insecurity about it refer not only to the self as image, but also to what this subject wants to be: a subject making objects, a subject whose identity is *in* the work. The painting has the features, not only of the presentation of a proud and insecure young man, but also of the masterpiece as required by the guilds or, more likely in the case of this artist, by the court or urban patrons. The painting has the carefully accomplished strokes that display his craft: the varied surface-substances of the hair, the feather, the scarf, and the chain, the velvet, the jewel, the tender wrinkles, and the slightly shiny reflection on the nose (the Freudian shine/glance on the nose is not far away). And it also offers the features through which this painter will create his own painterly image: It offers the empty background, the decentered light, the almost monochrome palette. The proud and insecure young painter aspires, through this work, to the status and the identity of a master.

The representation of the self here conflates that of the self as being and as doing. The self is represented as both conforming to the standards of quality – both handsome and skilled – and being different – insecure and original. It places the artist as a disclosing subject: as talented, yet inexperienced, still with a soft moustache, and eager to gain a place in relation to the world, to others, as the overly skillful details betray. His is an attempt to acquire intersubjective status, to establish his existence. As such, the portrait contains the contradictions of narcissism itself. It constitutes the relationship with the self in otherness; the resulting object, the work, displays by its sheer existence as object that the narcissistic subject loves an *image* of the self that is intersubjectively acknowledged as other.

The semiotic aspects of narcissism are based on the relation of representation that the image of self as other entails. The narcissistic subject relates to an outside object, but this object is represented as the self. This profoundly metaphorical relationship invites the viewer to see him- or herself in the mirror of the self-reflexive work, and simultaneously makes the viewer shrink away from that identification.[38]

The different types of narcissism, however, entail different motivations for this metaphorical relationship of representation. Only secondary narcissism leads to full representation of the self, since the self has already been formed via the mirror stage before secondary narcissism can occur. The self-portraits relating to (but by no means identifiable with) that stage represent the self as other rather than as self.

But even within the broad category of secondary narcissism, the image can be based on what the subject is, what it used to be (thus introducing time), or what it would like to be. Only in the first case would the relationship remain fully metaphorical. In the second case, the temporal relation, virtually narrativizing the image, motivates the metaphor metonymically. In the third case, a temporal relationship pointing toward the future insinuates itself, though it remains slight, overwhelmed by the descriptive urge to give form to fantasy. Roy Schafer (1967) recalls that Freud distinguished a fourth possibility: the image as modeled on what was once part of it.[39] The resulting motivation of the metaphor would be, then, synecdochical. If at all, it would be doubly so: The stage at which the limits of the subject were different is that of primary narcissism, and then there was not yet self-image, for there was not yet image at all. The self was part of the wholeness whence it needed to disentangle itself in order to accede to selfhood. This relation can be established only through the reversed narrative of secondary narcissism, as the self regresses toward the preseparation moment and its struggle. The narcissistic metaphor, then, would represent the self not only as what was once part of the subject; it does so also through a previous part of its story.

At this point we need to ask how this view of narcissistic painting relates to more socially oriented interpretations. The question implicit in this one is, How universalistic is psychoanalysis? The self-portrait is a socially and historically specific form of artistic self-expression, and that it flourished in the seventeenth century is not a coincidence. In this age emerged the self-consciousness of a class without hereditary nobility as a self-evident basis for self-confidence; the age also marked the rise of individualism. Unlike Velázquez, "Rembrandt" was emphatically not a court painter.

The genre of the self-portrait flourished in the context of social attitudes that made the urge for contradictory self-reflection through the object/other in intersubjectivity into a phenomenon typical of the cultural environment. At most, then, the self-portrait exemplifies a typical genre of the time, but other modes of representation can be chosen for self-reflection, and can reach a similarly significant dual self-reflection. The considerations of class that frame the self-reflection of *Las Meninas* are not absent from "Rembrandt"'s self-reflexive works, but they are concentrated in the one major problem of "Rembrandt"'s identity: how art *is* class, and how generation-cum-gender is another form of class. The artist who hovered between social classes all his life embraces this particular mode with more than conventional enthusiasm. Social factors may account for "Rembrandt"'s choice of the genre of self-portraiture, but not necessarily for the ambiguity and the insistent feeling of alienation that these self-portraits convey; nor for the onlooker's sense of recognition of that urge and the fantasy of the archaic experience it rests on.[40]

NARCISSISM AND SELF-REFLECTION

What does the psychoanalytic discourse on narcissism have to do with the problems and fallacies of self-reflection? We have seen how Foucault, and then Searle, were arrested in their self-reflexive interpretations because they did not include their own position as critics into their analyses. Hence, they rejoiced in, rather than reflected on, the unity they "discovered" in *Las Meninas*. Upset by the paradisiacal self-gratification transparent in Searle's conclusions, but unaware of the source of their discomfort, Snyder and Cohen were trapped by the very mirroring self-reflection that inspired their fears. The immediacy of their response is not irrelevant to this collapse. It took the efforts of other critics to split asunder the newly won unity of *Las Meninas*, that was achieved by the initiators of the debate, in order to reach a fuller, because fourfold self-reflection.

The psychoanalytic concept of narcissism helps to show how self-reflection can be self-gratifying, even erotically so, and at the same time why the impulse to self-reflection can be harrowing. Insight into this fear, if worked through, can help us overcome it and so allow us to endorse the gratification. To illustrate this, let

311

us briefly return to the little etching of *Joseph and Potiphar's Wife* (Figure 8.9).

In my first interpretation of this etching, I dwelled mainly upon the fracturing of the image into two mutually connected, but radically different narratives: those of the jealous father and the fearful son. In light of the Tobias problematic, the relationship between the two narratives gains depth. The anxiety this work provokes becomes understandable when we realize that the etching is precisely the medium of the penetration of the sharp styles that represents both defloration and, in Tobias's reversed version, castration. Even the smallness of the work contributes to the harrowing effect of this etching.

I have also pointed out the place and mode of the two phalli in the etching. The one, the powerful fatherly phallus, stands between the viewer and the scene, as a Freudian symbol. The second, the son's imaginary penis, is an exemplary Lacanian icon: hidden yet conspicuous for whoever has eyes to see. Those who can see this are likely to feel affected by an urge to blind the father, as part of the endeavor to reach maturity.

A third story can be projected into this etching, but before I set out to present it, I want to reflect for a moment on my own position in all of this, as I promised to do in Chapter 7. My own history with this etching is fraught with repressions. When I set out to work on the etching, I almost at once processed the bedpost as a phallic symbol, illustrating the reductive deceptiveness of Freudian-symbolic reading in the old mode. But it was only when my whole paper had been written[41] and I was, so to speak, ready to go, that somebody else – my brother – pointed out the second phallus to me. I did, however, manage to develop an argument that saved my narcissism, threatened as it was by the commitment to a public performance: The various ways in which the female genitals are inscribed in the etching, and also their sizes, had attracted my attention, as had the possibility that the curtain, as in the *Danae*, represented a gigantic vagina, hence making the scene *also* a birth narrative.

The third episode of my story with the *Joseph* was the moment

8.9 *Joseph and Potiphar's Wife*, 1634, etching (Haarlem, Teylers Museum); *Danae* 1636, Bredius 474, canvas (Leningrad, Hermitage); *The Blinding of Samson* 1636, Bredius 501, canvas (Frankfurt am Main, Städelsches Kunstinstitut)

312

when a most attentive interlocutor suggested a third narrative.[42] She suggested that my dual story and its major symbols were disturbing in two respects. First, she noted that although the sheer maleness of the two phalli and the emphasis on masculinity gave me the sense that the woman was just being used as text (although neatly displayed), I had not really criticized this. Second, she pointed out that the two focalizers come to a full stop at the navel of the woman. Thus, the navel becomes central; but this, of course, leads to a new unification of the text. Or does it?

The navel here stands for displacement itself. It is a center on the surface of the body and has no function other than being the useless trace of a history: the history of, precisely, the subject's separation from the mother. Between genesis and structure, between story and text, its false centrality, its futility points to, criticizes, the false centrality of the phallus whose doubling had already neutralized it as the center of the image. The navel of the female body is the meetingplace of the two masculine perspectives, but actually, they do not even really meet there. The navel prevents them from seeing beyond it into the realm of the other.

Now, and here comes the repressed third story, if we take the navel's ostentatious pointlessness literally, we can also erase it. Erasing the navel turns the woman around: She now turns her back to us, associating us viewers with the male voyeur (Figure 8.10). But what, for goodness sake, is she doing at the other side? At the far side on the bed, in the shaded part of the work, hidden from those who are not interested in this story, we see a body, lying on its belly, and whose bottom is clearly distinguishable – again, for whoever has eyes to see (it). The "official" story, the Biblical pretext, would accommodate this body, suggesting we see in this other body the fantasized young man – the unreal but desired Joseph – whom the woman dreams of making love with. This dream of pleasure takes place *inside*, within the gigantic female body formed by the curtain. Why was it so hard to see that?[43]

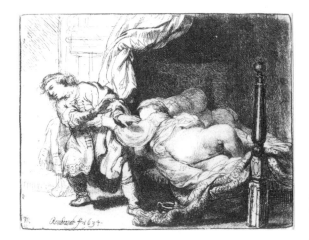

8.10 *Joseph and Potiphar's Wife*, modified

313

The way in which narcissism is involved in this repression has to do with self-reflection as identification, the crux of the narcissistic paradox as analyzed by Borch-Jacobsen. Not only are the two phalli now utterly ridiculous, pointless so to speak, since the woman turns her back on them; but also, if the woman turns her back on the men, she turns her back on us as well, implying that we, as viewers/voyeurs, do not matter. And it is not impossible to analyze this irrelevance of the viewer, brought about by the woman, as a radical version of primary narcissism: as the separation from the mother.

In this disquieting mode of reading, then, the mother becomes the primary agent of the work. In keeping with the other role reversals based on specific fantasies, it is the mother who is doing the separating. As we have seen, primary narcissism comes into focus as the end of the reversed story of secondary narcissism. From the perspective of secondary narcissism, it is up to the viewer, not the mother, to make the separation. By stripping us of the initiative, the reversed figure wounds our narcissism. She who, in the double interpretation elaborated in Chapter 3, was rendered superfluous and torn, distorted, for the sake of two male fantasies is now taking over completely. In agreement with Green's pointed formulation of the mother as empty frame, yet constitutive of the self, the woman now figures the relation of primary narcissism. This relation is both totally gendered, in that the mother takes primacy, and totally ungendered, in that every subject, male or female, needs to construct him- or herself in this way. The woman thus revised overshadows the two male positions with which the viewer could identify, leaving no alternative position easily available for the viewer – unless the viewer is willing to identify with this woman.

This secondary narcissism informs scholarly and other socially validated forms of work as much as artistic work. Inasmuch as criticism shuns self-reflection, it unwittingly displays its vulnerability to this threat against the narcissistic sense of self. Although, as psychoanalysis teaches us, insight alone is insufficient because the repressed experiences have to be wholly worked through, insight into psychoanalysis can certainly help a little bit. So let us explore a little further the ways in which the discourse of psychoanalysis "helps."

ECCE EGO: SUPEREGO, SUPERMAN

The narcissistic impulse that informs both these works and the responses they trigger is related to yet another psychoanalytic concept that is similarly suited to take on the visual aspects of the work of art as it simultaneously introduces both narrativity and conflicting modes of representation within the work. It is now easy to see how narcissism, the trap of self-reflection, can lead to stagnation and to a tension that reaches beyond the self. This can happen because the self to which the subject relates is represented for him or her as an image. The image of the self is the starting point for an inquiry whether art and its inherently ambitious quality can be seen in relation to ideals and idealization.

The self that becomes the object of relational investment in narcissism can be described as the "aggregate or organization (so far as it exists) of all the self-representations" (Schafer, 1967:145). It is important that we keep in mind the plural form of the noun "self-representations." Self-representations are numerous and changing, and occupy different roles in the psychic system. They are constantly tested against the standards the subject holds and against the subject's representations of reality. The hypothesis that the process of art derives its dynamism from the tensions brought about by the confrontation between representations of self – and of objects, for that matter – and standards the subject holds, partially subsumes the hypothesis of narcissism. The two meet when the idealization to which the confrontation often leads concerns the self. But idealization, in turn, must be confronted with the relationship between the subject and his or her ideals.

Ideals are standards of, for example, perfection, beauty, excellence, gratification. The concept of ideals is goal-oriented and thereby apt to narrativization, related to an event – that of the achievement sought – rather than to a static situation. In itself, an ideal is morally and socially "neutral." One may maintain standards that are socially unacceptable, like standards of racial purity, domination, absolute gratification, or standards that are socially valued, like self-sacrifice, productivity, personal commitment. Although an ethical evaluation of these standards is of course possible and necessary, their ethical difference does not influence their status as standards or ideals. In the following remarks, this should not be forgotten.

Standards are defined by the tension that occurs between them and actual reality; they are almost always impossible to meet, and if they are met, they become more demanding. In trying to do something about that tension, one can either change the standard, or change reality. Pushing toward the limits of reality in order to make one's ideals meet it more closely is different from changing (one's representation of) reality in order to make it coincide with one's ideals. In the first case, one is pursuing an ideal and trying to get the best out of it; in the second case, one is idealizing. This difference is not socially neutral: The ambition inherent in the pursuit of ideals influences the social realm according to the social values attributed to the particular ideas, whereas idealization changes the relationship between the idealizing subject and his or her environment. The relationship between ideals and idealization is not inclusive and not symmetrical.

Ideals may or may not stimulate idealization. A subject in a secondary narcissistic stage will tend to idealize him- or herself by constructing self-representations that meet the subject's standards for an investable love object. Since matching this ideal is easier if the object is left vague, the narcissistic self-love goes through more than usual difficulty in establishing a satisfying match; hence the tendency to idealization.

A less narcissistic subject will idealize another object, and construct representations of the other that are better than reality in order to make the object meet the standards set for it. But this is not meant to suggest that loving someone else is necessarily a non-narcissistic love, nor that stretching the limits of reality, hence, idealization, is necessarily a narcissistic gesture. Let us return briefly to the idealized self-portrait (Figure 8.8). The self is made better, more impressive or more beautiful, as it was in the royal self-portrait in the Frick Collection (Figure 7.3 top row, right-hand piece) or in the self-portrait in Figure 8.8. The quality of the portrait as representation, the insistence upon making it as good as one possibly can, is not idealization: One can idealize one's image, but one's performance tells the truth of the limitations of one's work.

In order to assess what such a view can bring to our experience of visual art, let us take as acceptable the suggestion that "Rembrandt"'s numerous self-portraits sometimes seem to propose that some features of his looks did not meet his own standards. The feature to fall short most noticeably is the nose. In the light of the idea of mirror-stage narcissism, the ugliness of the nose seems to have made the artist feel "other" more than any other feature. The idea of idealization suggests an antithetical relationship between these etchings and the painted self-portrait of the same period. The experience of alienation at the moment of the mirror stage leads to the standard of physical beauty that, in this case, would then be likely to include a straight nose.

The etchings, then, signal the failure to meet that standard, and the exploration or the cynical mocking of that failure. The insistent look in the mirror constitutes the trace of the effort to make real and ideal meet which results in distortion one way or the other. The painting, in contrast, represents a solution to the tension through idealization: The limits of reality are stretched. As we have seen, the ambition to be a good painter which this work so ostentatiously displays fulfills the function of making good for the lack of realism in the representation, which in turn is "faithful" to the experience of alienation. Pursuing the ideal of excellence in painting successfully, the artist "deserves" the idealization of his face.

Whether or not the pride in the young man's face is realistically justified or not is not our concern; there is no way really to judge. But the fusing of the beauty of the face and that of the painting as representational work indicates an attempt to compromise between ideal and idealization. The good artist manages to meet the standards of excellence closely enough to allow himself to idealize his face without going too deeply into illusion and delusion. The excellent painter cannot but produce beauty, and the nose is part of that beauty; that is what the perfect match of both ideals and idealization in the work signifies.

The persistence of this idealization despite the sharp awareness of its illusionary quality can be seen more clearly in another early painting, representing a rarely painted episode of the Samson saga (Figure 8.11). It is in itself interesting that "Rembrandt" represents himself as the young Samson, the ideal of masculinity. At first sight, the orientalism (Said, 1978) in the painting is quite strong and, for contemporary standards, is not without racist overtones: Note the two black witnesses, so much smaller in size than the hero and with excessively Negroid features, and the stereotyped old Jew as the father-in-law.

The Biblical story has it that Samson fell in love with a daughter of the Philistines, so "logically" speaking, this father figure should look more "pagan" than Jewish. But these remarks are anachronistic and realistic. In terms of the problematic of idealization, the "nose problem" has been solved here quite radically. Keeping his striking eyes, the artist gives himself not only beautiful hair for which the narrative provides the pre-text, but also, in keeping with the same stereotype about Jews, here in a positive version, a slightly Jewish, aquiline nose.

In the painting as well as in the represented scene, the father figure is confined to a marginal place. Visually speaking, he has only a little corner of the painted surface, his face and hands being the only parts of the figure to be represented, while the son's body, foregrounded, is hugely present. In the visual narrative, the one

8.11 *Samson Threatening His Father-in-Law* 1635, Bredius 499, canvas, 158.5 × 130.5 cm (Berlin-Dahlem, Gemäldegalerie)

317

fist of the son contrasts with the two hands of the father, which both represent powerlessness. The one hand is confined in the ring on the window shade, the other in a gesture of begging or holding off. The father is confined to the house, whereas the son stands in the world. As the pre-text has it, this distribution will be fatal: Whereas Samson survives, the father will die in the house – and through Samson's doing at that.

More than an anecdote from Samson's prehistory, the painting represents a competition between father and son. This father has to be as Jewish as the son, for it is important that he resemble him visually, so that he can authenticate the son as son, thereby enabling the latter to win the generational competition. The father's fatherhood is more important than is his personage as alien Philistine father-in-law suggested by the narrative.

Between the two tendencies of psychoanalytic reductionism, the appeal to fixed schemas – for example, Oedipal tales – and to biographical details, this painting is deceptively attractive, so much so that it seems worthwhile to address those tendencies explicitly. In the first place, the excessive threat in the painting is aimed at the father, and, according to the pre-text, its stake is the conquest of the bride. Nothing is more directly and simply Oedipal. In the second place, it is tempting to attach this painting to the scarce biographical facts known about "Rembrandt." The artist was interested in the growing Jewish population of Amsterdam in the midst of whom he chose to live, and he was intensely preoccupied with the Hebrew Bible of which Samson and Joseph were among his favorite characters. Perhaps these interests were related to this entirely different dimension of narcissistic lack and tendency toward idealization. Moreover, the works we are dealing with are all early works, and this particular one is probably from 1635, a year after his marriage to a woman of a higher social class. Perhaps this is why the story of the Jews appealed to him for self-representation. But these speculations, however attractively they may seem to "fit," are suspect and beside the point precisely because they fit too well. Fitting with (our image of) the artist, they leave the viewer safely out of sight.

Whether the encounter between the concept of idealization and the painting reveal "Rembrandt"'s sense of some inacceptable ugliness is irrelevant. What is relevant is how these two illuminate the viewer's sense of idealization. In other words, our analysis of the work should account not only for the ambition of the figure as an image of the artist, but also for the metonymic bond the figure is engaged in establishing with the viewer. The psychoanalytic concept of idealization must help us deal with three aspects of the work: First, Samson slightly turns away from the diegetic addressee of the threat toward the viewer, who is thus implicated in the work and appealed to for confirmation of the son's outclassing of the father's power. Second, "beauty" is the locus of the competition, which binds the work of life to the work of art. And third, the role of the navel hovers between the oversized, fleshy fist and the over-elaborated handsome nose, thus threatening with a solid punch in the nose any viewers willing to stick out their necks – knocking them out of the representational illusion.

MEDUSA'S SPELL

Before we can let the work address these three issues, however, we must take another detour to reach such an illumination, a detour that first leads through a false track of biographical psychoanalysis, but that soon leads us to a clash, not between a painting and a supposed reality, but between two paintings. Compare the *Samson* and its less than attractive father figure, with Figure 8.12. In a painting dated 1633, now in the Metropolitan Museum of Art in New York, we see a traditional Bellona or war goddess.[44] Gary Schwartz (1985:125) commented on this painting: "Very much in the pose of Rembrandt himself in a self-portrait of 1631 . . . Bellona casts her less-than-fiery gaze upon us."

Schwartz pinpoints the two fascinating and clashing aspects of the work: the pose of "Rembrandt himself," and the unfiery gaze that fits poorly with the idea of Bellona. The word "clumsiness" is on the tip of our tongues. But before we take that easy way out, let us take seriously these two features of the painting. First, the woman in this picture may be less than fiery; she is in any case also less than elegant. Second, the supposedly frightening shield of Me-

8.12 *Bellona* 1633, Bredius 467, canvas, 127 × 97.5 cm (New York, Metropolitan Museum of Art)

319

dusa, on which more shortly, is turned slightly to the side, while her own face confronts the viewer directly. Her bulging eyes are strikingly peaceful indeed; almost pacifying, domesticating the viewer.[45]

Again, the two risks of psychoanalytic criticism are close; it is appealing to see in this figure a portrait of "Rembrandt"'s fiancée Saskia, whom he married in 1634 and whose face as we know it through the many portraits of her is not without similarities to Bellona's. Succumbing to this temptation, one would foreground the intriguing question of whether she posed for the painting or whether, on the contrary, the artist sought out a woman for marriage who looked like his painted Bellona/Medusa. As in the case of Hendrickje's relationship to the *Bathshebah*, there is no way of knowing. Whichever way the influence went, the idea would be that the young painter was afraid of women: Biographic and thematic reduction go hand in hand.

Nothing seems more plausible, indeed, and at least one critic, Fernandez (1982), has suggested this much apropos of the ghostly girl in the *Nightwatch*.[46] Nothing seems less relevant either, I am afraid. This hypothesis would "explain" the preference of the psychoanalyzed subject "Rembrandt" for the story of Tobias, who domesticated the lethal Sarah, of Joseph who was treated so wickedly by Potiphar's wife, and of Samson who was victimized by the woman he loved.[47] And sure enough, that thematic centrality is undeniable, and it would be foolish to ignore the theme it suggests. Yet the perspective on the Joseph story in "Rembrandt"'s representation which I have developed hardly warrants such a reductive hypothesis; "Rembrandt"'s Tobiases, too, are much richer than such a reading would suggest, and there will be more to say about the Samson works as well.

If we read the *Bellona* visually *and* discursively, there are several features that we can make interact with the *Samson*.[48] The woman, although not fiery looking, appears quite impressive *as* woman. The sheer largeness of her body yields, so to speak, room for two, and her right hand emphasizes the size of the body. Moreover, her dwarfed proportions add to this effect. Since it is not by her gaze that she represents war, this emphasis on her large body is not irrelevant. It may be the locus of the other story; it may be the navel of the text. But if Bellona is not fiery herself, she is holding a Medusa shield. In effect, this other representation of a traditional frightening female is juxtaposed against the empty, shiny space that covers the place of her navel.

We cannot, however, take Medusa's fieriness for granted any more than we can take Bellona's herself. Here, too, the visual conflicts with the verbal, the representation not quite matching the pre-text. Medusa's face on the shield, rhetorical as it may otherwise be, does not look more fiery than its twin sister.[49] Nor does it look specifically female. On one level, the open mouth fulfills its traditional function as a symbol of the vagina dentata which, as an exteriorized projection of castration anxiety, petrifies the enemy[50]; on another, in combination with its eyes, this mouth is screaming for help.

In a way, the eyes on the shield look angry perhaps, but they also look helpless, as helpless as the eye of the father in the *Samson* looked. A helpless, older figure, gendered ambiguously if not male – that is what we can see in this Medusa. Maybe this figure, doubly fixed by its status as representation within a representation, is screaming for help, appealing to the viewer, not frightening but frightened. The helplessness of this figure seems to be caused by surprise: Neither the father nor the Medusa head seems to understand what the danger is about, why the threat is necessary. To turn this confrontation between the two paintings into one story – a story of ideals and idealization that supersedes the other stories, just as the allegorical tradition and the idea of ornamental rhetoric were superseded – we must now take into account the *pose* of the woman. Her pose, as Schwartz points out, in additon to repeating a work by Rubens, repeats that of an earlier self-portrait.

If we explore the possibility of the meaningfulness of such a repetition here, we can see in the woman's repeating the pose of the artist in the earlier self-portrait a figure who combines the features of a mother and those of the self who, if I may say so, has disappeared within her. There is, after all, room for two within her body. Her pose signifies the self's position – including his struggle with the ideal – and the alliance with the woman that he needs in order to cope with that struggle. The form of identification signified here takes care of the position of the father even further.

The shield Bellona holds, and holds off – aside – represents *en abyme* the terrified, because beaten, father figure. According to the pre-text, the father is defeated, murdered, by Samson's doing. The peaceful eyes of the woman reassuringly pacify the fiery eyes of the young hero in the *Samson*. And if we now look back to this young man, we can see that although he may be handsome, he is not finished with his struggle to attain his ideal self-image. First, his fist clearly invests more force in the threat than is required to overrule the less than impressive father. Second, he displays the by now characteristic cross-eyed gaze. The left eye looks at the father; the right eye is directed toward the viewer. The addressee of the threat is thus an integration of the father and the viewer. This integration makes sense for an ambitious artist: The viewer *is* a father figure, the social father who must become a patron if the artist is to exist. We only need to imagine the fist holding a brush to see the tension of the early self-portrait reemerge (Figure 8.8). What the slightly arrogant expression in combination with the masterly paint did there is made explicit here: The fist is shaken toward the men in power. These men – father, the father-in-law holding the desired bride as well as the viewer holding the desired commissions that enable the acquisition of the desired bride – are advised to acknowledge the idealized self and thus turn it into ideal reality.

If the woman in the *Bellona* is given the pose of an earlier self-portrait as Schwartz suggests, and if she also takes on the double ambition of the other earlier self-portrait (Figure 8.8) as I suggest, she is given the features – eyes, shape, hair, and perhaps nose – of a later self-portrait, the disguised one of the *Samson*. But, given the complexity and the unconscious force of this identification, it is no wonder that it had to be disguised.

Bellona's remarkably peaceful, resigned eyes do, after all, resemble the fiery ones of the young hero. This woman figure not only assimilates in her image that of the young "Rembrandt," idealized as a monument of beauty and as a tower of strength (Samson's identity); she also holds in her hands – in her power – the domesticated image of the defeated father. This Medusa is not petrifying but petrified: Thus the structure *en abyme*, wherein the visual representation on the shield is represented *as* a visual representation, is brought back to a renewed literalness.

The woman figure capable of all this combines the image of a frightening mother with that of a reassuring mother. Stronger than the father, she collaborates with, rather than threatens, the son who is, as Samson, strong enough to cope. But the balance remains delicate, and the price for the magic that turns an idealized self-image into an ideal "reality" remains negotiable: The possibility of both inflation and deflation protect "Rembrandt" against the petrification of the psychoanalytic perspective.

CONCLUSION

Ideals originate in varied sources. For a semiotic perspective of what they bring about, it is not enough to realize that ideals are at stake in representation. The reason a work is effective, the reason why the traces which the work sets forth affect the viewer, can be suggested by the hypothesis of idealization. This reason, located in the force with which ideals and "reality" clash, makes that idealization and the pursuit of limits so urgent that they become part of the representation. The force of the clash between ideals and idealization is in its turn heightened or diminished by the variable force with which ideals are maintained, a variability caused by their compromised character.

A subject can experience an unusually intense need to idealize because that subject must repair extremely ambivalent feelings and the destructiveness they entail. Between the *Samson* and the *Bellona*, the risk of damage from such ambivalence seems to be at stake. The craving for "something extremely good" (Klein, 1975), a source of fierce ambition, may be seen as the desire for "reparation" of damage feared. Since few of us escape ambivalent feelings toward the powerful fathers and mothers who circumscribe our lives, the paintings discussed – which evoked the idealized self-portrait, the pointless threat to the powerless father figure, the reassuring warrior-mother – touch us in our own cravings, fears, and resentments and thereby trigger a forceful response. In contrast, a mere display of vanity, a hatred of elderly men, or a fear of impressive women would only irritate.

The Kleinian concept of reparation integrates the two aspects of standards mentioned above into a convincingly dynamic although not harmonious whole: It integrates the idealization of the (self-) representation and the pursuit of the standard of excellence in the execution of it, which draws idealization nearer to reality and reality nearer to the ideal. Westlund (1987) explains the effect of Shakespeare's comedies in terms of this aspect of idealization, thus offering an explanation for the genre of romantic comedy as a whole. Whether or not such a genre will, in the case of specific works, be effective – in other words, whether such works will be experienced as a successful specimen of the genre – depends on the intensity with which the above clash has been turned into (idealized) representation. Not just any idealized representation will appeal to the need, in the viewer, to go about repairing him- or herself; yet sharing this appeal between artist and addressee is indispensable if the works are to have this effect. Hence the work cannot function if the addressee does not bring to it the needs it helps to fulfill.

Nor is comedy or its idyllic visual counterpart the only generic form in which reparation through idealization can take place. When involved in more painful endeavors, comedy and the idyllic can become features of works, rather than remain free-standing genres. We can clearly see, for example, that both the *Bellona* and the *Samson*, although not comic or idyllic works, are not without features partaking of those genres. The caricatural aspects of the *Samson*, primarily aiming at the father but not entirely sparing the son, insert comic overtones into a work whose pre-text is sharply tragic, while the woman's peaceful gaze in the *Bellona* turns the warrior into a Good Shepherd.[51] The force of the clash, pushing toward, and transgressing the limits that the work can plausibly display, pervades all aspects of the work and becomes its decentered central meaning. It is only by this duality that the psychoanalytic hypothesis, subsuming both ideal setting and idealization as well as the relations between them, can inscribe the discourse of contradiction in what is otherwise "just" a painting.

The account of the connections between the last two paintings I have discussed is neither purely visual – if only because I needed so many words to demonstrate it – nor simply discursive. It was a reading in which the discursive dimensions like pre-text and iconography were discounted in favor of the works' more directly visual features. The discourse of psychoanalysis that makes room for the related concepts of ideals and idealization enabled us to *see* aspects of the works and so account for the works as visual, as works of art, and as "Rembrandt." In addition, these aspects together formed a discourse, filling in the one work with a propositional content derived from what it is not: the other work.

From self-reflection to narcissism to ideals to idealization – the subject's investment in her or his own quality is the relevant factor. The passion with which the gratification of self-love is pursued by the work, the passion that affects the viewer, is based on two different moments of touching. The first is identification, an identification evoked by the metaphoric impulse. I shall have more to say about identification in the next two chapters, but here it suffices to say that when a viewer is confronted by a work of art as insistent as these paintings, identification with the self on display – whom we can easily pinpoint as the painter, the Master Himself – is obviously an attractive position. But there is more to this affect than metaphor. The second moment of touching is strongly apostrophic; there is a metonymic connection in which the viewer does not identify with the subject of the painting, but allows this subject to *touch* him or her: to disconcert, confuse, undermine the viewer's sense of self.

This second support for the affect these works can produce is neither gratifying nor pleasurable. It resides in the sense of *difference*, of nonidentity, which in turn affects our sense of a stable identity. Like the etched self-portraits which insist on the alienation, the noncoincidence, between subject and represented self by including the astonishment at what the mirror image presents to the viewer, the *difference within* both the *Bellona* and the *Samson* strikes us as an inevitable blow to our wholeness, our narcissistic security. Green among others has pointed out the intimate bond between primary narcissism and the construction of the subjective unity. This construction, however, carries with it a sense of its constructedness, thus founding our sense of wholeness, of unity upon its loss. As Green (1983:116) puts it:

The time of separation from the mother and the time of repression can join in retrospect, but they are not joint from the beginning, since this temporal conjunction is retrospectively inferred from the search for the lost object, which unites the real loss of the object at the moment of separation and the loss undergone by repression. (my translation)[52]

The figure of Samson is and is not the subject "Rembrandt" as we imagine him; Bellona is and is not frightening, is and is not like Saskia, is and is not like "Rembrandt." This difference within, then, strikes the viewer, too: Affected by the labor of these works, we are and are not what we take for granted that we are.

The problem of narcissism, therefore, not only entails the increasingly positive view of the self as this chapter has shown it. There is another side to narcissism, a negative, frightening, and unsettling side. "Rembrandt" not only represents himself as a strong, handsome, or competent subject. He also represents himself as the weak, ugly, or incompetent subject in a large number of works. These negative features join in a motif that is pervasive in the "Rembrandt" corpus and that cannot but have a special meaning in the case of visual art: They enter into the motif of the incompetent subject who cannot see. Narcissism that remains ungratified, an

ideal that cannot be matched, idealization turned against the self —
these are the aspects of a negative narcissistic thematics that is at
stake in those works where the subject is shown unable to see, to
focus, to reach a visual goal.

But here, again, this view is not unambiguous. While the works
discussed in this chapter remain ambiguous and, because of the
fragility of the idealization accomplished by the represented subject,
never entirely gratify the narcissistic impulse of the viewer, the
works that represent the failure of looking have, in turn, another
side to them: The blindness they represent, as we shall see shortly,
also entails insight. The next chapter, then, will propose yet another
aspect of self-reflection, as a reflection on vision and visuality as a
product of and precondition for the formation of selfhood.[53] But
in order to be in a position to assess that complicating form of self-
reflection, the positive aspects inherent in narcissism should be kept
in mind along with the negative aspects being developed. And as
we saw in Chapter 7, the self being reflected (upon) is also the
viewer's self. With the view of narcissism developed so far, this
progression becomes inevitable.

In all the works discussed in this chapter, there is a surplus, a bit
left over. That surplus spills out of the paintings into the viewer's
response. The idealization that I have been assigning to "Rembrandt" is also our own idealization *of* "Rembrandt." Both separately and collectively, these works are texts in their strongest
pragmatic efficacy, in that they disseminate and dis-seminate meaning — on the condition that we are willing to use psychoanalysis to
see them. To put it differently, Bellona has no navel, she has only
the shiny surface that covers the place of the navel and that inscribes
the navel's elusive centrality.

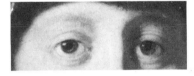

CHAPTER 9

BLINDNESS AS
INSIGHT: THE POWERS
OF HORROR

To be penetrated is to abdicate power. (Leo Bersani,
"Is the Rectum a Grave?" 1989:212)

INTRODUCTION

THE psychoanalytic concepts discussed in the previous chapter in effect shed some new light on several works that have
traditionally escaped critical understanding, either because
they were experienced as "mysterious" (i.e., beyond discourse), or
because they were judged "clumsy," immature (i.e., not really
worth critical discourse), or, in still other cases, because they were
too "horrible" (i.e., disempowering critical discourse). In each of
these cases, criticism may have failed because the critics were unable
or unwilling to deal with the works in terms of their visual self-
identity, while the discourse composed of the conjunction of discursive theory and visual signification was able to overcome these
limitations.

Our central psychoanalytic preoccupation so far has been narcissism. The central position of this concept in part reflects Freud's
opinion that narcissism is the most general element in the formation
of the subject.[1] Two additional arguments also underlie my focus
on narcissism. The first is the wish to explain the sense of creativity
and the impulse to make "something extremely good" (Klein, 1975)
in terms of the problematic emergence of the subject, rather than
in terms of a romantic view of the artist as a neurotic loner. Neither
ignoring "Rembrandt"'s forcefulness – as those interested in de-
bunking the romantic view tend to do – nor taking that forcefulness
as a sign of individual genius – which would not explain anything
since the authorship of these works is neither certain nor monolithic
– is acceptable.

Second, I wanted provisionally to privilege narcissism so that I
could explain the works' affective force for viewers of either gender.
Unlike Oedipal problematics, which emphasizes sexual difference
in terms of the boy's relation to the father, primary narcissism
derives from a phase traversed by every subject, male or female.

Narcissism may not be gender neutral; but the gender problematic is directed toward the subject from which the narcissistic subject is taking distance, not necessarily toward the latter's own sexual identity. In addition, the position of femininity is not secondary: The force of primary narcissism is aimed not against the father but against the mother, the figure from whom subjects of both genders must separate themselves.

I would like to bracket the emergence of sexual difference in these analyses in order to speculate about the *affective force* of these works of visual art for viewers of both genders. Yet, rather than ignoring gender, I wish simultaneously to position the works themselves – their subject agent and their subject theme – in the realm where gender is a major aspect of subjectivity. In other words, while the affect of the works touches both men and women, the thematics of the works differs along gender lines. It is hoped that the dialectic between affect and thematics, which can never be separated but only temporarily distinguished, will help us to overcome simplistic psychoanalytic criticism and to reach an understanding of what happens in the paintings through what happens in the viewer.

To that end, in this chapter I wish to focus more closely on a particular theme in the "Rembrandt" corpus, understanding that theme in psychoanalytic terms. This theme has a strikingly self-reflexive quality in visual art, and its relevance for the Tobias works has already been demonstrated. The theme is that of seeing and its negative counterpart, blindness.

The frequent occurrence of blindness in "Rembrandt" is well known. Many of these works directly refer to stories of blindness and blinding. For example, in *David Playing the Harp for Saul*, in The Hague (Figure 9.1), the covering of Saul's one eye emphasizes the other eye and the uncertainty of seeing. Other works suggest the obsession with blindness by exaggerating the pre-textual reference, as in the *Oath of Claudius Civilis* (Figure 9.2), where Claudius's one blind eye is disturbingly displayed. Other works that do not appeal to a pre-text thematizing blindness also suggest a problem of vision. Finally, even when no thematic reason for attention to problematic sight is called for in an insistently pre-text-based work, the figure seems represented as blind, as in the *Return of the Prodigal Son* in Leningrad (Figure 9.3). Thus many of the drawings

Left to right:

9.1 *David Playing the Harp for Saul*, ca. 1655, Bredius 526, canvas, 130 × 164.3 cm (The Hague, Mauritshuis), detail

9.2 *The Oath of Claudius Civilis* 1661–2, Bredius 482, canvas, 196 × 309 cm (Stockholm, Statens Konstmuseer), detail

9.3 *The Return of the Prodigal Son* ca. 1662, canvas, 262 × 206 cm (Leningrad, Hermitage), detail

of older men, especially in the early period, suggest bad eyesight, inattention, or inability to focus.[2] Among the famous paintings, some refer, again, to pre-texts about blindness, and the predilection for such a thematics may be worth speculating about.

Traditionally blindness has been related by psychoanalysis to castration. Freud himself speculated that the Samson story was an example of this connection. And "Rembrandt" created quite a few works in response to those stories that originated in the deeply antivisual culture of the ancient Hebrew texts. Among the many works in "Rembrandt" where seeing or blindness is explicitly or indirectly foregrounded, several are related to a Hebrew pre-text: the story of Susanna and the Elders, evidently about looking and its illegitimacy; the Samson saga, wherein the repeated transgressions of the hero end in blinding; and the Book of Tobit, where the son cures his father's blindness.

The position in the Oedipal triangle of the "blind" figure is, however, not consistent in all of these works. In the first of these groups, the figures who look and represent "bad looking" are Elders – father figures – and their victim is a young woman. We saw in Chapter 4 that the problematic of visuality is turned into a central *mise en abyme* in one of the works devoted to that theme by the misplaced gaze of the one Elder who touches Susanna. The theme of castration is not absent here, since the old men are taken down a peg by young Daniel who saves the mother figure. In the Samson saga, the hero's blinding is the doing of a woman he is said to love. Is Samson a father or a son figure? He cannot be identified with the position of the Elders, and the Philistines who blind him are clearly not so much older than he to turn him into a son figure. In the Tobit works, the father is blind and the son helps him overcome his blindness, deflowering a young woman in the same endeavor. Again, there is a tension between father and son, but this tension is not easily placed in a straight Oedipal schema.

The deceptive simplicity of an interpretation of blindness as castration does justice neither to the works as works of visual art, nor to psychoanalysis as a dialectic discourse. But this flaw inheres not in psychoanalytic interpretation but rather in thematics. As I have tried to show elsewhere, thematic approaches may perpetuate and justify ideological readings.[3] So while I may point out a theme in "Rembrandt," I shall certainly struggle to avoid treating it as a fixed, petrified semantic unit defined as what I want it to be. My goal in these pages is, on the contrary, to revitalize the theme by dynamizing it, by turning it into a story itself, the story of visuality and of painting.

In visual art, the theme of seeing and not seeing ultimately belongs to the thematics of self-reflexivity, a favorite theme of deconstructive criticism.[4] I shall let "Rembrandt" suggest that the Biblical culture's resistance to seeing stems from an awareness of its attractions and the dangers of its unqualified admission. Seeing is a consequential act that needs to be performed with care and responsibility so that it can yield gratification without entailing danger for either see-er or seen; without turning into a weapon of domination, that is.[5] That this is not easy to achieve, never unambiguously possible, and always accompanied by risk, is precisely the point.

Therefore, seeing is, must be, and needs to be culturally framed, a framing that is censoring, controlling, and safeguarding, preventing both chaos and abuse. The negative view of seeing, as discussed in Chapter 4, relates irresponsible and unjust seeing to power, power to gender, gender to age and generational position. It is in this triangular connection that we shall now be able to construe the complex and unusual position toward women readable in "Rembrandt."

In order to escape the rigidity of thematics, we must allow the various conflicting modes of interpretation discussed in Chapters 5 and 6 to exercise their interplay. On the one hand, we cannot ignore recognition, since the very titles of these works, appended in later ages, reflect the work of recognition performed by previous viewers. Rather than questioning these superimposed titles, I shall show that they make more than superficial sense as soon as we let the works illuminate the problematic of visuality in the stories. On the other hand, we shall have to give priority to visual narrative if this illumination is to take place at all. Similarly, just as the realistic and the textual readings were shown to be in tension in Chapter 6, we shall see that this tension is crucial here as this tension is necessitated by the textual shifts needed to accommodate realism.

Narcissism, the shifter between self-reflection as a mode of reading (Chapter 7) and psychoanalysis as a discourse helpful in such a reading (Chapter 8), will be an inevitable subtext in this chapter where the self-reflexive theme of seeing is at stake. But whereas in Chapter 8 narcissism was mainly presented as an impulse of the ambitions – as a positive force, that is – we shall see here why Freud also established a strong and disquieting connection between narcissism and a more negative element: melancholia, or failed mourning. This negativity, which leads from narcissism to mourning to death, will demonstrate the place of gender in narcissism. In the analysis of the painting central to this chapter, *The Blinding of Samson*, the relationship between narcissism and the related psychoanalytic concepts will be further complicated by the relationship between psychoanalysis and semiotics through the complex concept of sublimation. These subjects will evolve into a knot that I shall refrain from untangling, because my aim in this study is not to make "Rembrandt" simpler but more complex.

SAMSON AND SUBLIMATION

Sublimation is the concept that occurs most frequently in attempts to define art psychoanalytically. It is a central, yet admittedly vague concept.[6] Like the other concepts discussed, sublimation is not specific to art; it is meant to explain social life and civilization in general, of which art is a "sublime" extension. The concept points to human activities that have no apparent connections with sexuality but are assumed to be motivated by the force of sexual or aggressive drives. The instinctual force of the drive remains, but is diverted toward a different, nonsexual aim.[7]

The objects of the sublimated instinctual force are socially valued ones like artistic and intellectual creativity. Hence the somewhat idealistic term "sublimation" which should be confused neither with its everyday correlate "sublime," used as a general evaluative term, nor with the historically specific, romantic aesthetic term "sublime." In fact, the adjective "sublime" has no relation either to the active verb "to sublimate" or to the latter's generic noun "sublimation," both of which imply an activity, an aim, and displacement.

The idea that art in some cases may come from the repression of sexual or aggressive drives, which is what the simplified sublimation hypothesis amounts to, is obviously bound to scandalize art lovers. Attempts to counter it with more "positive" views have been numerous, some of them more or less successful, others total failures. These attempts betray an erroneous conviction shared with many a psychoanalytic art critic that a hypothesis can be valuable only if it is totally generalizable, although such a generalization is actually unnecessary and grossly ahistorical. I would like to assess the merits of the sublimation hypothesis through its capacity for interdisciplinary illumination of specific works of art and the visual specificity it conserves in its very discursivity.

An analysis of the concept shows that it rests on two tensions, one between *force* (the force of the drives) and *meaning* (its sublimated aim), and the other between *symbol* (the disguise of the repressed) and *meaning* (the repressed). These tensions must not be resolved. Susan Deri's (1984:43) polemic stance distorts and simplifies Freud's perspective when she argues that he tried to resolve these tensions by claiming that an irreducible opposition exists between the poles of the latter tension. Her alternative, however, is already inherent in Freud's semiotic theory itself: "Only by considering symbols as *revealing* and *communicating*, as well as *concealing*, can their full meaning be understood" (Deri, 1984:44; italics in text). Freud's interpretive practice, in spite of its reductionist drawbacks, shows that he could not agree more happily with this; in fact, Deri shows in her polemic that she is as specularly engaged with Freud as Snyder and Cohen were with Searle.

In fact, what distinguishes Freud's semiotics from, say Saussure's is the motivatedness of the relationship between signs and meaning; it is motivated, precisely, by the force wherein it originates. Concealment is revealing in itself, and what is concealed can be revealed; whereas the arbitrary relationship Saussure postulated leaves the connection between sign and meaning unreadable.

What makes the sublimation hypothesis both difficult to grasp
and relevant for semiotics is that the tension between force and
meaning is dialectic as well as irreducible. When an unavowable
desire is repressed, it leaves traces of its instinctual background –
traces that project that background into the work. Through the
indices these traces constitute, the force becomes meaning: This is
Freud's representation *avant la lettre* of Derridean writing.[8] The
meaning conveyed in the process of sublimation cannot but carry
the force that is their signifier; the meaning *is* force. It is perhaps
for this reason that the ambiguity inherent in any semiosis seems
to be so vital in works of art. Ambiguity implies that what is
conveyed by the ambiguous sign has been condensed. Lacan (1966a)
and many others equate condensation with metaphor: the cluster
of one sign and many meanings.

One reason why semiotic theories of metaphor are always slightly
inconsistent – as argued by Ricoeur (1979), by Silverman (1983),
and by others – may be due to the illusion that the above equation
(condensation = metaphor) is valid. If condensation in semiotic
analysis has this metaphoric aspect, its psychoanalytic background
implies that it must also possess, in the form of traces of the instinctual force, a metonymic aspect as well. In addition, condensation is not a single sign but a cluster of signs passed off as single.
Finally, since the meaning, revealed and concealed, is metonymically related to the signs of the work of art, the sublimation
hypothesis implies that some meaning related to sexual or aggressive drives must be traceable in the work. It is precisely here that
the reductive tendencies of the hypothesis will surface and must
(and can) be countered. According to the semiotic perspective,
these meanings are figuratively signified; metaphor subsumes
metonymy.[9]

The *Blinding of Samson* (Figure 9.4) provides the most dramatic
illustration of this concept of sublimation, not in itself but in the
response it triggers. Sir Kenneth Clark finds the *Samson* "an extremely disturbing picture," and he adds, "Only a man of genius
could have done something so consistently horrifying" (Clark,
1978:50). Clark describes the painting in terms such as "ugly,"
"horrifying," "appalling," and "grotesque." Clark's strong terms
and their negative connotations have more force than usual in
Clark's discourse; his self-confident claim to good taste regarding
feminine beauty is far away. I venture that something has happened
between Clark and the painting that belongs to the register of shock.
Like Searle's bliss and Snyder and Cohen's anger, I take Clark's
horror as a symptom that the successful criticism of the painting
requires a psychoanalytic perspective; in this case the sublimation
hypothesis needs to be understood in its full complexity and power.

First, in understanding this work we should realize that there is
no direct need to interpret the work with reference to the Biblical
pre-text; indeed, such a reference can obscure aspects of the work,

because the intertextual relationship with the Samson story can only make the choice of subject, as well as the composition, accents, and execution, more disturbing. The sexual meanings which the Biblical story hardly conceals are overruled in the painting by the aggressive violence of the represented event.[10] And it is this displacement that I want to focus on. As I hinted before, it has been suggested that the conspicuous preoccupation with blindness in "Rembrandt" refers to the artist's repressed Oedipal castration complex; see Held (1969). But such a suggestion is problematic in terms of the painting as it stands before us because the Oedipal positions are far from clear.

As distinct from the *Prodigal Son*, the various Tobits, and the portraits of blind or seemingly blind old men, the situation is reversed here: It is the men in power who blind the lover Samson who is less than fatherly in position, costume, and behavior.

Again, biographical data — or myths about them — threaten to disturb the visual experience by invoking a story instrumental to reductionism, and the terms of the debate illuminate the issue at stake here. The painting was not commissioned, according to Rosenberg (1948) and others, but was conceived as a present for Rembrandt's patron Huygens, as compensation for the artist's lack of punctuality in the execution of a commission of a series of Passion scenes for the Prince of Orange, Huygens's employer.[11] The work, too, was not graciously accepted, but imposed on Huygens against his will. We have here a good example of the problem of the notion of "context." Let us assume, for the sake of the argument, that this story is historically accurate. But it is not "raw data" and requires interpretation in its turn. Even then, the basic question, the one that relates the painting itself to the story, remains unanswered. Why did "Rembrandt," apparently unable to execute the commission – the best he ever got – and aware of Huygens's reluctance to accept the gift, have to substitute the one scene of suffering for the other, while the one was welcome and the other hardly acceptable?

If this story is to make sense, the substitution of the one figure by the other must be meaningful in terms of the issue of blindness. This is indeed the case. The opposition between the two suffering heroes is revealing. The passion scene has the victim on the erect cross, his body fully exposed. The innocent victim willingly accepts his suffering. Instead, Samson, guilty of his own undoing, is nevertheless in revolt; he is lying down, in a sort of cave guarded by the woman, formed by hardly recognizable curtains. According to Clark (1978:53), instead of the classical style of the commissioned series, he paints here in a wild Baroque or Jacobean style. Indeed, "Rembrandt" is doing the opposite of what he is expected to do, and this as punctually as he possibly could: One is tempted to say that he is acting as does a child who opens the door when asked to close it.

The artist is seen not as a neurotic genius but as the normal naughty child; this is going further in demystifying the great artist than anybody else seems ready to go. Gary Schwartz (1985), whose study aims largely at doing away with the Romantic view of the unhappy, sensitive, loving, and misunderstood genius, and displays a vested interest in giving a rather unpleasant picture of the artist, stops short of endorsing the picture as I have just outlined it here, thus making an interesting case for the work's affect. The violence of the work has not passed unnoticed, and the aggression implied in such a gift is obvious. Schwartz in his unexpected kindness finds it an embarrassment even to conceive of such a gesture; as the gift and its refusal are documented but the precise identity of the work is not given, so Schwartz happily substitutes another painting for this gift. Schwartz's (1985:130) argument runs that Rembrandt would not give such a painting to "a man (Huygens) who wrote: 'No one can depict something ugly so that it gives pleasure'."

This argument is based on the assumption that the artist would not contradict and annoy such a powerful patron. Thus it is a case of interpretation of the context, in terms of a view of unproblematic social power according to Oedipal lines. Schwartz thus discounts the artist's notorious ambition that might very well have led him to contradict Huygens visually, in favor of accepted standards of social hierarchy. Moreover, the argument requires that Rembrandt acknowledge a statement that denies the very fact of this painting; for this work does precisely what Huygens thought impossible. Again, it is not the historical facts but the resistance discernible in the critic's investment in the question that seems the locus of the work's work.

As it happens, Schwartz proposes that Rembrandt gave to Huygens "Rembrandt's most succulent painting of a female nude" (129), the *Danae* (Figure 9.4). Sure enough, this is "a more attractive gift

9.4   *The Blinding of Samson* 1636, Bredius 501, canvas, 205 × 272 cm (Frankfurt am Main, Städelsches Kunstinstitut); *Danae* 1636, Bredius 47, canvas, 185 × 203 cm (Leningrad, Hermitage)

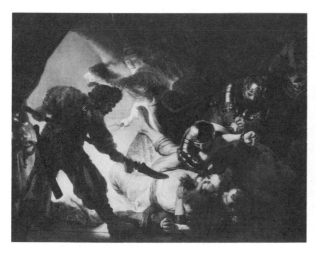 

suggestion" (Schwartz, 1985:131), but choosing the "right" gift is not necessarily the most likely thing for Schwartz's nasty Rembrandt to do. Moreover, as Schwartz (1985:131) does not fail to mention, "in the absence of all further mention of Rembrandt's gift in Constantijn Huygens's well-documented life, we are forced to conclude that he returned it." This point, of course, undercuts the argument of the substitution: If the artist was out to please Huygens and gave him the attractive *Danae*, there is no reason why Huygens should have returned it. If, on the other hand, "Rembrandt" was out to rebut Huygens's views on visual art, then the latter, as displeased with the gift as Schwartz would have been, is more likely to have rejected this insulting gift.

The illogical twist in Schwartz's argument is the symptom of the work's affective force. What interests me here is, first, Schwartz's obvious reluctance to let the Rembrandt persona, which he first built up as extremely unpleasant, do something really unpleasant by giving what Schwartz sees as a truly horrifying gift; hence we can see the extent to which Schwartz partakes of Clark's emotional response. Second, I am interested in Schwartz's assumption of the radical *difference* between the two works that are competing for the status of gift. I contend that the visual similarities between the two works are far more striking precisely because of the thematic opposition. In other words, I shall argue that, affected by the work, Schwartz is unable to *see* the work; thus he is metaphorically conflated with the figure who is being blinded.

The *Danae* can be said to be, as we saw briefly in Chapter 4, about seeing, about the transgression of the taboo on access to the woman's body, and about the interdiction against seeing. Seeing in this work a most succulent female nude ignores the work's narrative, which bars the viewer's sight by the powerful arm of the woman, used as an index referring the viewer elsewhere. This power is as insulting as contemporary critics have found Manet's *Olympia*'s gaze to be, and Schwartz defends himself against this assault on his narcissism – how dare the painting forbid him, a prestigious art critic, to see? – by ignoring it, and thus declining to see, in paradoxical obedience to the work as he refuses to see it. But the work, like the *Samson*, is not only about the interdiction against seeing; the similarities go further. The structure and composition of the *Danae* are identical to that of the *Samson*. Where Samson lifts his right foot, Danae lifts her right hand, forming a similar line, displaying *force*. Although the *Danae* is an attractive and, as is often claimed, sensuous work wherein the reclining body of the woman in the cave formed by the curtains yields self-confidence and power, it cannot be denied that the *Samson*, almost contemporaneous with the *Danae*, is structured by and large in the same way: a body, from which force emanates, reclines in a cave formed by curtains. And again, as in the interaction between the *Bellona* (Figure 8.12) and the other *Samson* (Figure 8.11),[12] the ostentatious thematic changes hardly obscure these identifications.

In order to deepen these similarities, we must substantiate the claim that the *Danae* is not so much about the woman's vulnerability as about the man's difficult visual access to her. To that end we must emphasize the maturity of the woman in the *Danae*, who hardly suggests the young virgin-daughter of the mythical pretext, of the "official" story of female initiation; we must also note the presence of the blind child in the putto who is represented *en abyme*, thus doubly fixed to immobility, as well as the strangely male features of the "officially" female servant: Dressed as a woman, s/he has the face of an elderly man. Thus the nuclear family is ready: for reductive interpretation, that is. Let me stop here, and add only that the painting focuses on the woman as the central, narrative, and visual subject – the mother figure – and thereby alone escapes simplified Oedipalism. The servant-man, on the other hand, dons the beret we know from numerous "Rembrandt" self-portraits, and is holding keys. Pre-textually, these keys refer, of course, to the iconography of confinement and stand for the virgin's being barred from sexual intercourse; it is quite possible to leave it at that.[13] But within the thematics of looking and in connection with the features that suggest self-portraiture, one may want to go further; these keys might be taken as an index of a correct understanding of the indispensable framing of seeing. As the keys to the correct forms of framed visuality, they are a sign of the artist who knows how to look properly. And looking properly, in this painting, is looking away from the female nude body.

The *Samson*, on the other hand, shows the male figure, the proud, invincible hero, in the reclining position, identified with the mother only in the force emanating from his foot, but for the rest utterly different: victimized, blinded, deprived, like the viewer in the *Danae*, of seeing the mother. This deprivation, however, is represented not only through blinding itself, but also through metaphorical identification: Samson reclines in the same position as the mother figure in the other work and is *thereby* also unable to see the mother. This conflation is blinding, and it alludes to primary narcissism.

SAMSON AS WOMAN

What can the sublimation hypothesis do for the understanding of this disturbing painting and the stories surrounding its reception – the work and its disturbing work – and how can we meaningfully establish connections between castration and narcissism? In the first place, throwing such a work into the face of his benefactor – a father figure – is so obviously an act of aggression that the very "success" of biographism in this direction precludes its effectiveness. For sublimation to be at stake, the aggressive impulse must be repressed. But it is hard to speak of repressing the aggressive impulse. Huygens was so effectively offended that he returned the painting, and Schwartz, identifying with this blow, doesn't even want to hear of this painting being the gift. But if the aggressive impulse is not repressed, then there is no need for the displacement inherent in sublimation, and the unstable relation between the work and the unconscious is definitively broken.[14]

Yet psychoanalytic response criticism analyzes not what Rembrandt did to Huygens, but what the work of "Rembrandt" did to Clark, Schwartz, and myself – to all those who are emotionally affected by the work and, while disturbed, can hardly do more than call it "disturbing." In other words, psychoanalytic response criticism can help us understand why the painting strikes the viewer with a muteness that is the discursive equivalent of his or her blindness. But to account for that blindness, we may need to look at something other than aggression per se.

Under analysis the overt aggression of the painting moves to the semiotic side of our analysis of the concept, where it becomes a meaning /aggression/ which must contain some trace of its initial force, a force that may be other than aggressive. In other words, this meaning becomes the sign of another possible drive, signified through the mechanism of connotation.[15] This other drive may be sexual. So let us turn to the sexual aspects of the painting, which are of a different order than the aggressive ones.

Of course, this approach requires that a reader, reading in this way, endorse psychoanalysis as a language, an idiom one can learn and use. Let us see what happens to such a reader. If we read forms within the psychoanalytic idiom, we can begin to notice that if the soldiers, for example, are narratively aggressive – on the level of diegesis, they are actually attacking the figure – the weapon of the soldier at the left *means*, by its form (through iconicity) and direction (through indexicality), the penis. This is one way to interpret the *round* point of this most visible of weapons. This soldier does not wear the harness and helmet of the others, but looks, in fact, quite like a "normal" young man. As a young man he can be identified with Tobias, acting carefully, ready to penetrate his father's eyes. The form of his weapon, on the other hand, is reminiscent of the more directly castrating knife held and dropped by Abraham, ready to fall right into place to castrate his son Isaac in Figure 8.4.

All this seems to point to castration. But hardly does that motif come into sight before it is displaced by other features. If we see the weapon as penis, then Samson's body is threatened not so much with castration as with rape. This, then, shifts the gender position of his body, and we begin to notice that his body is gendered feminine in a number of ways.[16] The color of the soldier's dress is red: the color of blood as much as of passion. The position of the weapon in relation to Samson's opened legs is not without sexual overtones; nor is, when viewed in a totally different way, the position of the body in relation to the cave itself. Sexual penetration is thus represented on various levels and with various means – as violence, as rape. What impels such a reading? The discursive input is double: Reading with the other painting, the *Danae*, is one way of reading the picture as what it is not; reading it with psychoanalysis is another one. The two collaborate, mediated as they are by the painting's own insistence on vision and visual trauma. The similarity with the overtly erotic *Danae* foregrounds the sexual aspects of the *Samson*, while the obvious opposition in mood between the two becomes meaningful in its turn. The sexual aspects brought into focus in the *Samson* signify another level of meaning where they both conceal and reveal the relationship between aggression and sexuality: the representation of sexuality as frightening, and as effortful. The soldiers who do the blinding not only handle their phallic weapons relentlessly; they labor. This is hard work. Not surprisingly we shall see, labor, albeit another kind, is ultimately what is at stake here.

The sexual aspect we just saw in the soldier's weapon is visible only if we look in a particular way, namely at the surface, not the depth of the painting. *Work*, the self-reflective theme par excellence that we already have seen so frequently in "Rembrandt," is foregrounded by the contrast between the various readings this painting allows. If we look in the mode of classical perspective, the painting is reassuringly narrative. The weapon, then, points at Samson's breast. If we look at the surface, suddenly the scene becomes much more frightening. "Rembrandt" is in general not very keen on perspective, and we can read in this painting a statement of his reasons. More than in any other work, perspective is here set up as the deceptive, realistic art that "Rembrandt"'s predilection for enhancing the painted surface endeavors to question. Depth is here opposed to surface, as deceptive reality is to unconscious reality, as theory is to practice, as ground is to figure. Thus we can read a collusion between the sexual instability of the Samson figure and the representational instability of visual art. The art of the surface, according to this self-reflective statement, is advocated as the more adequate visual mode of representation that can represent what the art of perspective seeks to obscure.

With this in mind, we cannot be surprised by a second ambiguity. Thus far we have seen aggressive and sexual impulses represented in this work, and intertwined with each other at that; there is also a third level of meaning where the two meet to explain each other. The shifter between the two distinct but related isotopies is the structural element that makes the painting deeply ambiguous, in both the psychoanalytic and the semiotic sense. Samson's foot, lifted to kick Delilah (Figure 9.5), is this element we noted earlier as similar to the arm of the powerful woman of the *Danae*. It resembles two things at once, but in order to see both, one needs to hold this gestalt shift in tension, and so see two totally different compositions.

Let us look once more at the composition of the painting. On one level, the cave suggested by the curtains can now be read as a gigantic womb. Although this is not systematically the case in "Rembrandt," it is not the first time that we have encountered this possibility.[17] If we let this figuration determine the other figures, an ambiguity begins to evolve. If the cave is a womb, then Samson is a baby who is at this very moment and before our very eyes being born.

In either case, there is a metonymical relationship between the curtains as womb and the figure's effort as birth. Given the reversibility of this relation in the process of reading, the relation cannot be causal. It is, rather, metonymical in a visual sense: The curtain/womb is spatially contiguous to, and thereby contaminates, the figure/baby. Being born is a painful experience: This pain is represented in the figure's struggling his way out. His foot pushes the mother aside in order to push himself out of her body, to pave his way toward being. Thus seen, the foot is that of a baby laboring to distinguish himself from the mother's body; it is a depiction of primary narcissism in turn symbolized by a birth scene. The effort, the pain, the labor of birthgiving make that primal scene precisely suitable to represent the projected, retrospective fantasy of the delimitation of the self from the mother. The scar of this painful moment is, of course, the navel.[18]

But now, let us take the same foot as an element in a different scene, wherein the cave is once again a room. Seen this way, Samson also represents a woman giving birth. In this spectacular way his body is gendered feminine. He is reclining, held, bound, by a "midwife": the man lying underneath him, who represents a less than realistic image of a fighter, and whose spread legs are about to let the baby through, to push it out. From this perspective, his cramped foot represents the effort of the suffering woman giving birth – an undeniably painful experience. It is as painful as the rape suggested on the other level of meaning, an experience in which the subject's wholeness is also threatened.[19]

9.5 *The Blinding of Samson,*
detail

338

Samson, then, is either a subject trying to emerge from the mother's body, or he is identified with the mother. The painting suggests that there are only two positions: the metonymic conflation with the mother, or the metaphoric identification with the mother. In both cases, the position of primary narcissism is presented as the central moment of the formation of subjectivity, a formation that is strongly determined by the subject's relationship to the mother. In both cases, Samson's masculinity is neither ignored nor discounted, as is traditionally the case with the figure of Christ, but actively problemized.

This problemization unfolds in time. The subject is not formed *yet*; its formation is about to take place, and with it will come the genderization of the figure. What is captured in this work is the moment when that gendering is not yet accomplished; what is depicted is the suspended state of the subject lacking itself. A sign of this lack will remain on the body, male or female, as a scar of this trauma: That sign is the navel.[20] Here the figuration of this scar is displaced onto the eye, the eye being blinded. What the subject in this state of suspense cannot, will not, see is the lack of wholeness which the primary narcissistic experience can put to an end only after acknowledging it. The scar, the memory, will feed into the subject's later, secondary narcissism, which is called upon to compensate for this initial experience of lack.

THE STORY OF SIGHT

The suggestion of a relationship between the *Samson* and the *Danae* finds support in a number of compositional details. The putto in the *Danae*, for example, rhymes with the man at the upper right in the *Samson*. Both seem to have bound hands; and for the soldier whose function it is to bind Samson's hands (the suggestion created by the rope framing his tied wrists), this similarity entails a contamination of him by Samson, the nonsee-er. And indeed, the man does not look competently: He does not look at the body on display, any more than does the putto. Another similarity between the two paintings can be seen in the woman's hand whose bent fingers rhyme with Samson's unnaturally bent toes. The way in which this work complements the *Danae* cannot but be grounded in the respective themes of each: the interdiction against looking at the nude and blinding. The *Danae* forbids looking, and the interdiction is gender specific. It is not just looking but looking at what does not belong to the public domain of cultural display: the body of the mature woman or the mother. In the *Danae* the direction of looking thematically conveyed the propositional content, whereas in the *Susanna and the Elders* it was the *mode* of looking that was called into question: the myopic, "scientific" competence, based on a polemic narcissism that claims to possess what cannot be possessed. In the *Samson*, the interdiction is both more fundamental and more

339

general: Looking as such, the very physical capacity to see, is taken away from this man, problematizing his gender in the same move. The interdiction is again related to gender, but there is no nude to figure the transgression and the punishment. So how is this proposition figured?

The work is about looking in more than one sense. The intensive looks of Delilah and the soldiers are quite meaningful in both these interpretations. In the one view, Delilah's look represents the displaced metaphor of the woman to whom the gigantic womb belongs – a token woman, so to speak. That metaphor is metonymically suggested and supported by the blue color of her dress which mingles with the bluish background of the curtain and the sealike, dreamlike world outside. In the second interpretation, she is also a midwife, one who, filled with concern for the suffering woman whose life is in danger, fulfills her practical duties.

It requires a discursive a priori input from the pre-text to see in this woman's looks anything like aggression. Her look, instead, is remarkably pacific, no more fiery than the gaze of Bellona whom she resembles. But it is not in the viewer's interest to accuse her of cruelty on the basis of the doxa, for she is related to the viewer through the way she rhymes with the soldier at the right. This man shares with her not only his position and facial expression but also the raised arm. Both hold Samson in (visual) power: They take him under arrest – *prendre sous garde*. The hair and the sword that cut it off have the same function. And this man, whose bulging eyes and open mouth remind us of the flabbergasted father-Medusa on Bellona's shield, is clearly impressed by what he sees – as is the viewer he represents. The soldier with the phallic weapon does not look aggressively any more than the other figures, while the second soldier on the right looks at the man on the left, rather than at the fallen hero.

If the *Samson* is about seeing, the first thing that matters is the fact that Samson is deprived, like the viewer in the *Danae*, of seeing the mother. In that respect he is a continuation of the servant of the *Danae*. In both paintings this interdiction against seeing the mother's body is signified by the use of point of view, albeit in opposed manners. In the *Danae* the point of view is high, so that the viewer "comes down on" the naked woman; this attraction is first aroused, then deviated by means of the arm. In the *Samson* the point of view is low, so that the viewer looks *with* Samson toward Delilah, only to realize that Samson, precisely, cannot see her.

But in spite of the similarities between the two works, the sexual aspects of the *Samson* are of a different order. Whereas the *Danae*, problematizing facile gender identities, constructed gender only to undermine it by narrativizing vision, the *Samson* uses the same compositional structure and the same theme – vision – to construct gender by pitting it against aggression.

Take the soldiers, for example: By definition and by virtue of the pre-text, they *are* aggressive, but their aggressiveness is not unproblematic. They are aggressive to the same extent as the woman in the *Danae* is on display as a nude. Their aggression is gendered, I have suggested, to the extent that the weapon of the soldier at the left can be read as "the penis." It is this soldier whose profile stands out against the light coming in from behind, from the opening to the outside, thus emphasizing the darkness of the scene; it is this soldier, therefore, who stands for the surface of the painting, which I earlier set off against the reassuring depth of perspective; and it is this soldier who insistently *looks*. He looks and thus establishes a line of focalization which leads from his eyes via the weapon/penis to Samson's eyes. There, the look stops short, because Samson is being deprived of his sight.

We can now see how the concept of focalization as defined in Chapter 4 is more than the limited concept of line of sight. Whereas sight stops short, focalization continues; the look here is interrupted but attention continues; sight is replaced by violence, and the force of this violence directs us further, via the forcefully kicking foot, to the woman standing in the back.

If we take the soldier on the left as an internal focalizer, the focalization is gendered as male. As we have seen, the position of the weapon in relation to Samson's opened legs is not without sexual overtones; nor is, in a totally different way, the position of the body in relation to the cave itself. Sexual penetration is thus represented on various levels and with various means, as the theme figured by the line of focalization. It is clear then that Samson is not at all constructed as unproblematically male.

Focalization is also shown to be more powerful than the mere line of sight because it is focalization that holds together the double composition: The composition is held together by the lines between the figures who look and what they look at. Both the figure of the woman and the position of the foot turn out to be key elements in this construction of focalization. The scissors the woman is holding point backwards, but her bulging eyes look outward – at us. Thus the line of sight that started with the first focalizer at the left, and that was continued problematically by the force that replaced Samson's sight, ends with the viewer. In between are the blinded eyes, the forcefully pushing foot, and the woman who takes over the looking that Samson can no longer perform.

But this line of sight is not the only one. The sense of over-crowding we get here, compared to the balanced *Danae*, stems not from the sheer number of figures but from the overwhelming representation of vision. This is a multifocalized painting. In the first place, there is one figure at the right whose sole function is to stand at the margin and watch – a stand-in for the viewer. Like us this soldier with bulging eyes and open mouth, is clearly impressed. His representational function is doubly signified, too. This soldier locks the viewer within a frame of vision. He does so by the similitude between his eyes and Delilah's, with whose face his face rhymes, and by the ambiguity of the direction of his eyes, which

341

seem almost to look at the horrible act he is witnessing. His eyes hesitate, just overlooking Samson's face in the move from there to the viewer. We can now see that the soldier with the phallic weapon who does not bear an aggressive expression any more than the other figures, actually looks rather concerned. And the second soldier on the right looks at the man on the left, rather than at the fallen hero. His look, emphasized by the light, is a typical example of the stealthy, quick, self-conscious, and anxious glance. Of these four looks, none shows either aggression or pleasure, whereas the three other figures, whose eyes we do not see, are engaged in forceful labor: What are we to make of such a representation of seeing?

The decision to endorse provisionally a psychoanalytic theme as a discourse by which to read this painting has taken us a long way. We can now see the *Samson* as responding to, or offering the other side/sight of, the *Danae*. The female body offered for voyeuristic noncommunication took over and made visual communication the thematic center of the self-awareness the work promoted. In terms of the communication model, the message short-circuited the sender's attempt to dominate the viewer at the expense of the female figure.[21] The *Samson* makes the woman and the man change places, putting the ambiguous servant of the *Danae* in the foreground and the woman who was on display in the background.

The woman who dominated vision by delegating the servant to direct our look, now takes the place of this servant. She directs our look, not away from a beautiful body but away from a frightening body. The ambiguous servant who looked so much like a man, and like the artist, while representing *not being able to see*, now represents total blindness and total effort, while remaining sexually ambiguous. The posture of Samson's body, especially his foot, identifies him with the mother he is struggling against, with the female who directs the eye, and with the artist who, as a maker of visual art, as yet distrusts vision.

In psychoanalytic terms, we can interpret the aspects of doubling, of struggle, as representations of the struggle that comes with sexual ambiguity. The frightening coincidence of two fearful experiences turns sexuality into something horrifying, and the more so because it is inevitable. The two experiences on which this conflict is based are that of the violence which the too fearful human being sees in male sexuality, and the imprisonment, the suffocating enclosure, feared in female sexuality: This conflict is based on the fear to do harm and the fear to suffer harm. The latter fear stems from the association between sexual penetration and birth, the association with the mother's body. According to Kristeva's (1982) view of primary narcissism, this association between sexuality and the omnipotence of the mother causes a struggle between life and death in which the existence or the destruction of the emerging subject is at stake.

Collapsing the *Danae* and the *Samson*, we can now see how, and why, the woman and the man have changed places. The servant in the *Danae* had already been blinded, the taboo on vision already being established. Imagine that the accents are displaced onto the next episode: The woman of the *Danae* disappears from sight, and the servant, now completely blind, takes her place. For not resisting the temptation to look, Samson is condemned to become central, to be put on display in his turn, for others to look at, without being able to look back. Like the woman in the *Danae*, he tries to defend himself against that horror. But his defense seems to miss its target, for it is directed away from the viewer. It is not entirely futile, however, for if it cannot protect the figure from the viewer, it definitely spoils the viewer's pleasure of looking.[22] But whoever said that visual art was sheerly for pleasure? The reassuring realist, perspectival art perhaps; not "Rembrandt" 's art which proposes as an alternative to the "window on the world," the "self on the surface."

The woman in the back holds in her hand a pair of scissors. And scissors serve to cut off, not only hair, but also umbilical cords. The midwife's function in the psychoanalytic birth of the subject in primary narcissism is to secure the healing of the scar. There is again, in this painting, a space for the figuration of the work's navel, an empty surface that asks to be filled. It is the space between the two loci of the violence done to this subject, the locus of castration "covered" by the phallic weapon and the locus of blinding "covered" by the pointed weapon: the eye. The empty surface of Samson's breast is the only light spot in the dark half of the work, and thereby mirrors, or rhymes with, the light outside that promises subjective wholeness *after* this birth. Between this surface and the blue sea there is a line of light: a light available for sight when, after the scar has healed and the navel has been produced to remind the subject forever of this moment with the mother, seeing in the right way will become possible. As the navel of this work as text, this surface generates the story of sight.

This view suggests why the painting accommodates the double perspective I have been describing. We see in the reclining, bearded man a being trapped in two intertwined positions that can neither be disentangled nor harmoniously combined. On the one hand, he, the man in the painting, *is* the birthgiving mother. His open thighs; the effort of labor represented in his distorted foot; the opening of the cave which recapitulates the opening of his body; the scarlet of the curtains, of the soldiers' tunics, and of the blood that spouts out of Samson's eyes – all of these details support this metaphoric interpretation. On the other hand, the man fights the birthgiving mother, with the same distorted, kicking foot, with the same force. This ambiguity is shaped by the unusual mutual perspective that we may also want to see in the *Joseph* etching. We see a cave whose entrance/exit – entrance of penetration, exit of birth – is guarded by Delilah. We see the reclining body of Samson in the cave, which is a gigantic body. Within this second perspective we see inside this

343

all-encompassing body the body of a baby being born and giving birth, who replaces the mother and fights her. How can this representation remain in touch with the pre-text?

Seen in this way, the scene does seem to lose touch with the Biblical story in which Samson is subdued by the Philistines. True, the passage in which he is described as sleeping on Delilah's knees does have overtones of the child–mother scene, especially when read visually. In "Rembrandt" there are enough indications that the story has been read as a visual figuration of mothering, as was the case with other representations in the seventeenth century.[23]

In Figure 9.6, for example, a painting now in Berlin, Samson is sleeping on Delilah's lap. That representation suggests that he is lying between her knees, which is a literal visualization of the wording in Judges. There, the expression "between her knees" in turn alludes to birthgiving. And indeed, although the sleeping male figure is, on one level, of adult size, on another he is smoothly

9.6 *Samson and Delila* 1629,
Bredius 489, panel, 61.4 × 40 cm
(Berlin-Dahlem, Gemäldegalerie)

344

contiguous with the body he seems to be sliding out of. The two
bare feet are there as silent reminders of the cramped, effortful foot
in the Frankfurt painting. And the soldier coming in with the pair
of scissors, carefully and fearfully, is shown what to cut. The hair
Delilah is pointing at is a string of curled hair, which is visually
quite similar to an umbilical cord. Again, another soldier, peering
around the curtain behind which he is standing, is looking both at
what is going on within the picture and at the viewer, including
the latter within the scene.

So perhaps "Rembrandt"'s *Blinding of Samson* is not so detached
from its Biblical pre-text. But in fact there is a later scene in the
story to which the Frankfurt painting proleptically alludes. The
final scene of the Biblical story, and its most directly visual one, is
the destruction of the temple of Dagan, in which Samson both dies
and gives his greatest performance. In that scene, Samson is actually
blind but symbolically clear-sighted, visionary; God has allowed
his hair to grow back, and thus his strength to return. Standing
between two columns – gigantic thighs, we can venture – he pushes
them aside, or, in the terms of this interpretation, forcefully expands
the too narrow opening, thus destroying the birthgiving mother
and making her superfluous.[24] Secondary narcissism responds to,
and compensates for, primary narcissism. But that passage requires
a detour: that of the specification of gender in culture wherein the
mother is more than a fantasy to be rejected. As Borch-Jacobsen
(1988:115) puts it:

"Something" – "something" that narcissism is not, itself, and that Freud
calls "parents" here – has to bring it [the subject] into the world, has to
enable it to be born to itself, has to present it to itself by giving it a "form,"
a "figure," a *Gestalt*.

I hope it is clear that the horribly suffering Samson is a more
suitable signifier for this painful experience, for this complex of
intertwined fears, this forceful event, than is Christ, sublimely erect
and already past his suffering; he is related to the father rather than
to the mother, and accepting his fate so that the force of the struggle
is gone. Christ would be a metaphor for his own suffering; Samson
is that, too, but because the force is still at work *within* the metaphor,
his aggression and his suffering strike the viewer, metonymically.
The solely metaphoric interpretation, then, would consider aggression as the concealing sign of something else, say, sexual ambiguity.
But the sublimation hypothesis also requires a metonymic link.
Aggression, then, becomes subsumed by the sexual impulse. In the
picture, the aggression is directed toward the already powerless
man. He is the victim of male (the soldiers and their weapons) and
female (by being imprisoned in the cave) sexual impulses as seen
from the perspective of the young man. The aggression returns
from the victim to the woman, from the victim as woman/mother,

to the woman as victim. The violence of the conflict between these two impulses, deriving from these different identifications, is what constitutes the trace of the force that, disturbing the viewer, she or he will see as "ugly" or "horrifying." It is here wherein lies the "touch of horror" of this work, a horror that signifies the meeting of force and meaning.

The sublimation hypothesis, then, can be used within an interpretive process that is reluctant to jump to biographical conclusions, thus reducing the work's meaning to one schema. Of course, it is not impossible to integrate biographical data; the story of the gesture toward Huygens, if it is historically accurate, certainly enhances the effect of the painting as another pre-text. But there is no need to assume that artists are neurotic, or more neurotic than we all are. There is also no need to limit the reading to the overtly instinctual features of the work, which would, in a sense, opposing the sublimation hypothesis, in that they would ignore repression in the concept and the semiotic detour it entails. Nor do we need to ignore the instinctual features, for the sublimation hypothesis itself requires that those signs be there, as traces or *grammata*.

What this response to the painting has set out to demonstrate is the dynamic effect of the interaction between visual and discursive languages. If I invoked psychoanalysis and its most common concepts – castration, aggression, sexual impulses, sublimation – at the beginning of this analysis, it was not to use it as a mastercode by which to reduce the work's complexity and affective excess; on the contrary, it is the psychoanalytic beginning itself that has been educed by the painting, the details of which never quite fit the interpretation. Psychoanalysis has been complicated by the visual experience at least as much as the other way around.

MELANCHOLY, BEAUTY, AND THE NARRATIVE OF LOSS

In his short essay on disturbances of vision, Freud (1910a) suggested that psychogenetically caused blindness is a form of melancholia. Melancholia (Freud, 1917), in turn, is related to primary narcissism and the threat of the loss of self. As Jean Laplanche points out, these relations are far from clear, although their importance for psychoanalysis as a whole is overwhelming: The primacy of primary narcissism would displace and decenter castration and the Oedipal moment from their centrality. In both castration and narcissism, sight, in the form of mis-seeing, plays a fundamental role in the construction of gender, and the insistent presence of problematic visuality in the cultural constructions of constantly shifting gender ideologies might be based on either moment.[25]

What is at stake with this displacement is the status and nature of gender as the founding category of psychoanalysis and the derivative status assigned to women within that category. If castration is the founding moment of gender awareness, then the view of

woman's "lack," or the idea of castration, is what constructs masculine self-identity, while feminine self-identity is asymmetrically
constructed. If, on the other hand, primary narcissism is the founding moment, then gender is constructed in relation to the mother
for both sexes, and both femininity and masculinity are constructed
primarily on the basis of a lack: the lack of wholeness. The imaginary moment of primary narcissism, then, would be the founding
moment in which sight blinds the subject; thus it is not the other
who is perceived as lacking but the self perceived as not-whole.
The loss inherent in primary narcissism, the loss that turns this
moment into a secondary reaction rather than a truly primary experience, thus narrativizes blindness as initiating the subject. In
relation to this moment, castration and the genderization derived
from it are secondary repressions of this primary secondariness.

The reason melancholia is made central to Freud's discussion of
blindness is then twofold: On the one hand, the melancholia is
Freud's own, emerging at the realization of castration's secondariness and the subsequent realization of the belatedness that conflicts
with his obsession with origins. On the other hand, primary narcissism is a moment of loss, a loss that can be repeated only in later
phases.[26] The *Samson* is therefore the crucial work on blindness,
the work that subsumes all other works precisely because the figures
in it are *not* distributed according to Oedipal positions.

But if Freud is right, then melancholia is the narrativization of
primary narcissism, programming all subsequent losses according
to its founding model. And if that is true, then melancholia must
be a central element in the cultural process of art in our culture.
That this is indeed the case is suggested by the hypothesis, formulated by Kofman (1984), that the process of art is melancholic
mourning. Melancholia is, in Freud's definition, failed mourning.
Melancholia is related to loss; if there were no losses to suffer, there
would be no need to mourn, and if all mourning were successful,
there would be no melancholia. But primary narcissism is the model
of mourning that includes its failure; so there will always be melancholia. In case of a loss, the process of detachment from the lost
love object may be hampered by the overwhelming force of the
identification of the subject with the object. As a result, the subject
cannot free him- or herself from the object, nor can he or she invest
other objects; there is no space left. This is the shadow that primary
narcissism casts over the subject, as a primary *grammè* that cannot
be written away.

Given the powerlessness that results from melancholia, the hypothesis just formulated is paradoxical from the outset, not because
it relates beauty to sadness and loss, but because it relates the creation or investment of an object with the incapacity to relate to
objects. This paradox is central in the affective work that art practices on the viewer. The viewer is compelled both to relate to the
object and to suffer from the melancholic inability to relate by which
the work contaminates him or her.

On one level, melancholia entails a general aesthetic theory. Greuze's *Girl Weeping Over Her Dead Bird* is not, according to Kofman (1984:22), about a girl mourning her dead bird. It is about mourning beauty. Making or otherwise relating to beauty is an attempt to escape from the elusiveness of all things, which, according to this argument, is what we spend our time mourning. But while seeking consolation in beauty, we discover that beauty itself is elusive. We create art in order to create a beautiful object that gives us simultaneously the illusion of eternity, the awareness of elusiveness, and the mournfulness of that clash. Art, then, mourns itself. And Greuze's girl does not mourn anything concrete, for she *is* the mournfulness that gives us occasion for mourning. This is Kofman's central thesis in *Mélancolie de l'art*.

On another level, this melancholic aesthetic is modeled upon the initial experience of melancholia that results from primary narcissism and the lack that the subject knows, but fails to *see*. Repressing this foundation in primary narcissism, this aesthetic may be itself an aesthetic of blindness. Acknowledging the foundation of melancholia in the primary experience of blindness then becomes the royal road to insight. In this section, I shall argue for such an interpretation of the theme of blindness as the acceptance of not-being-able-to-see, which is required in order to achieve insight.

The semiotic implications of Kofman's melancholic aesthetics are complex, indirect, and difficult to grasp, and, as we shall see, that is all for the better. They touch upon representation. Kofman describes Aristotle's double conception of mimesis as both copying and supplying but, in any case, displacing reality, and relates it to the fascination with and fear of resemblance. This view adds meaning to the problematic of the mirror as outlined in Chapter 7. The dead body, the antique colossus (Vernant, 1976), and the mirror image exemplify the surplus meaning (i.e., the *atopia*) inherent in the object that represents, through resemblance, something which it both is and is not. This *atopia* necessitates that something – something magical – be done to reinstate the reassuring categories of being:

Art concerns, not a simple annihilation of the real (which would still be a way to control it), but its sacrifice in the sense that Bataille says that the sacrifice changes, destroys its victim, but does not neglect it. It concerns a slippage of the real, its suspension where all immediate meaning gets lost. (Kofman, 1985:16; my translation)

It is in this sense that Kofman can equate the sacrifice of the subject who loses him- or herself in an overinvestment in the lost object, and the loss of that object which triggers melancholia. Resemblance creates a loss of identity similar to that caused by overinvestment in the lost object by the melancholic subject who, in the process, sacrifices him- or herself.

Conceived in this way, the hypothesis concerning the relationship between the processes of art and melancholia has an interdisciplinary background that exceeds by far the simple borrowing of concepts. The psychoanalytic side requires that an object be lost; hence, we need to identify the object and the event of its loss. In Kofman's view, beauty, the ultimate resource for the sufferers of loss, constitutes loss by its elusiveness. Mourning, then, becomes melancholia because the lost object was the last resource, and losing beauty shows the subject that all objects are lost beforehand. But what is this concept of beauty? When is art beautiful enough to trigger melancholia? And, what is to be gained by this undeniably Romantic view? A link, here, or maybe a leap, brings us to the semiotic side. The feeling of loss is related to, perhaps *is*, the atopia that characterizes resemblance.

The double concept of mimesis which is described in an almost Peircean language in Aristotle's *Poetics* provides a way in the problem.[27] As Kofman rightly states, the duality of Aristotelian mimesis is not an opposition; instead, the opposition is a feature of what it describes and what constitutes its intrinsic fictionality. This antithetical interpretation has brought about a stream of fictionally based arguments, traditions, aesthetic philosophies, and that displacement onto the concept is precisely its force.

Resemblance, then, is both similarity and difference, representing both what the object stands for, but also what it is not; something else. Its status as sign is what constitutes, inaugurates, its being lost. Thus the atopic loss is represented, among other things, in the Lacanian mirror experience, which in turn represents primary narcissism's visual aspect, where wholeness is produced by loss of self.

If we accept the melancholia hypothesis as a discursive mediator, art is effective when it is self-reflexive – but self-reflexivity gains a new dimension and a new set of nuances. The effective work of art will present an object lost by definition; hence, it will offer signs that stand for something else and that simultaneously represent the resulting *atopia*. This is what makes the early "Rembrandt" self-portraits so powerful, and their effect slightly embarrassing. The duality of such works triggers in the addressee the uneasy feeling which uncannily suggests that we are not simply looking at one thing, but rather that something is happening on another level different from the one with which we are consciously preoccupied.

MASCULINITY GENDERED FEMININE: *THE POLISH RIDER*

The *Polish Rider* (Figure 9.7) is one of "Rembrandt"'s most enigmatic paintings, and the enigma includes more than the identity of the work's painter. The discourse that defines the work includes the enigma of its autographic wholeness: Doubts about its authenticity focus on particular parts of the work, like the horse, the background, the body. Moreover, the circumstances of its genesis, the identity of the sitter, and a possible commission are so enigmatic that careers are built on attempts to solve these problems.[28] The painting stands alone in the "Rembrandt" corpus, although it shares features with several of his "periods."

We can first note an encounter between the work as painting and the work of melancholia in the tone of the critical discourse about the painting, which displays the very mood with which the painting affects the viewer. Again, critical discourse that is more than usually periphrastic, repetitive, and avowedly powerless, works as an indexical sign of the critic's affective encounter with the work. Sir Kenneth Clark phrases his admiration for the painting in a way that seems to me to confirm the workings of the melancholia hypothesis.

9.7   *The Polish Rider* 1657, Bredius 279, canvas, 116.8 × 134.9 (New York, The Frick Collection)

350

He calls it "one of the most *personal* and *mysterious* of [Rembrandt's]
later paintings" and "one of the great poems of painting" (Clark,
1978:59–60). The latter statement suggests a sense of textuality
based on a romantic view of poetry. Others react equally strongly
to the "strange" quality of the painting. Held (1969:45–84) begins
his essay on the painting by describing it as having "mystery" and
"special fascination," and being "enigmatic," "puzzling," thus at-
testing to the work's affect.

One possible response to the affective attack by the painting on
the critic/viewer is denial, expressed in attempts to explain the
strangeness by tracing the sitter's identity (Broos, 1985) or by qualifying it as orientalism (Slatkes, 1983).[29] The painstaking effort of
Slatkes's book for example, in no proportion to the weight of the
conclusions, is akin to Snyder and Cohen's emotional scientificity:
Almost an entire book is devoted to the question of Rembrandt's
orientalist sources, to unverifiable suppositions about possible
models, and, ultimately, to a striking evasion of a view of the work
as a whole. This move to naturalize the strangeness of the work
(see also Campbell, 1973) is clearly an attempt to strip it of its
otherness by seeing in it what it is not.[30] It is an attempt to insert
between work and viewer a reassuring discourse in order to avoid
the work of a more troubling discourse. It reveals an urge to replace
the possibility of melancholia with positive "data" about the work's
genesis. In other words, while this painting may not be thematically
about blindness – although I shall contend that in a way it is – it
seems to strike the critics with blindness. If we wish to understand
a work not as the product of historical accidents but as the locus
of cultural interaction, we shall have to account for the painting
and its strangeness, for the work itself *and* the responses it provokes.

The mystery of the *Rider* is not unrelated to gender, and, more
specifically, again to the sexual ambiguity of a male figure. One
feature that, according to Clark (1978:60), accounts for the painting's strangeness, is the "almost feminine beauty" of the rider. This
sexual ambiguity is naturalized immediately by reference to the
sitter, who might be the same as the person who sat for Potiphar's
wife in the two paintings devoted to that subject. Indeed, s/he
might. We have already seen (Chapter 3) to what extent the two
represented women are different, according to the status of the
representations as fictitious, imaginary, or theatrical, in spite of
the coincidence of character and (who knows?) model. Referring
the rider to this woman – hence, to these two figures – is not without
interesting intertextual resonances, and I can imagine how this hypothesis could lead to an encounter between the rider as overdetermined by femininity, and the women as identified with the
young heroic figure in the *Rider*. But as an attempt to do away
with the work's strangeness, such an "explanation" seems utterly
beside the point. All it can do (and that is all for the good) is raise
questions about the relationship between the "strangeness" of the

351

work and the beauty of the represented knight, beautiful "because" almost feminine, and yet a knight – a model of masculinity in the feudal tradition, albeit of filial, not fatherly masculinity. Thus we may want to reconsider this cliché about feudality, and emphasize *its* strange affinity to fatherly power and prolonged filial dependency.

A second feature invoked for an understanding of the work's strangeness is the gaze of both rider and horse, each directed toward some unattainable goal. This formulation suggests a narrativization of this portraitlike painting, whose narrativity is both obvious and problematic. These gazes, and the discursive response to them, will provide a key to the solution of a problem that Kofman leaves unresolved. This problem has to do with the relationship between narrativity and melancholia, a relationship that may explain why Freud relates melancholia to primary narcissism as its originating experience, its narrative navel.

For our purposes, the key position of melancholia springs from the conflation between the visual problematics of primary narcissism and the narrative problematics melancholia itself presupposes. Thus the concept will help us understand the tension in visual experience which the thematics of blindness elaborates. Melancholia refers to a story: the loss of the loved object, the attempt to mourn it, the failure of the attempt, the process of investment of the object in the self, and the subsequent fixation that closes off new object relations: All this implies a temporal process. How, then, can a single work of visual art signify, or be, the loss and its mourning, as well as the failure of that process, all at the same time? In other words, how does the discourse of psychoanalysis narrativize a painting?

The gazes of horse and rider are directed, spatially, toward some unattainable goal, unattainable because irretrievable, lost in space because lost in time. The object is outside the representation itself. Moreover, the gazes diverge. The split between the subject of gazing/longing and the lost object is represented within the representation. The unity of horse and rider, one of Freud's favorite metaphors for the unity of *Ich* and *Id* that constitutes the subject, is broken by the divergence of the gazes. Spatially, the directions diverge; visually, directions and aims are separated; narratively, the aims, the objects differ. On all these levels, gaps result. The contiguity of horse and rider and the divergence of their desired objects are represented in their negative coincidence: in their loss. In narratological terms, the object of focalization is *nothingness* (not the same thing as *nothing*). This structure of focalization, the insistent concentration on nothingness and the divergent reaching outside the work, represents the limit of focalization itself. This is one way in which "blindness" is narrativized.

The gazes, in their dual relationship to time and space, introduce a tension between the narrative and the descriptive modes of representation. Alpers (1985) argues that Rembrandt explores the limits of the descriptive mode that distinguishes Dutch art in the seventeenth century from Italian art, which is much more directly narrative. This view suffers from the binary opposition presupposed between narrative and description. As I have argued elsewhere (Bal, 1981–2), description itself is rarely devoid of narrativity; more often than not, a descriptive work or passage inserts narrativity through narrative devices such as tense, voice, and focalization, and through rhetorical devices such as metaphor and metonymy. Here, the directionality of the gaze entails description, the mode of representation of what is seen.[31]

But nothing is seen, and rider and horse see "it" in a different space. The horse looks straight ahead, while the rider looks obliquely back. The teleology of the gazes, their object-orientedness, entails narration, the mode of representing what has happened and what will happen. But what has occurred is loss, the loss of beauty's duration, and what will occur is the unattainability of the object. Melancholia, by its fixating and paralyzing power, makes the story into nothingness, into description. It is this tension that allows the melancholic reading to work. Where object and time, implied by loss and mourning, produce narration, the unattainability of the object, rendering the gaze pointless, triggers melancholia. And this melancholia is contingent upon *not being able to see*: It is contingent upon blindness.

What does looking come to when the thing looked at sends the viewer back to nothingness? The blindness contaminates the viewer who cannot but reflect on what it means to look at beauty. For this reason, the knight representing beauty should be beautiful himself, but ambiguously so: The rider is made ambiguous through femininity, through otherness. In this way, *he* becomes *it*; the beautiful man whose identity at one level we might want to uncover becomes beauty itself, ungraspable and anonymous. The represented object becomes representation, and the activity set in motion is caught in a self-reflective cycle.

This "cross-eyed" gaze so characteristic of *The Polish Rider* – not of the rider as a character but of the rider and horse as a unified yet conflicting image – may shed new light on the frequent representation of blind men. The paradox of the blind gaze, the divergent set of eyes, the dead, the blurred, and the fixated eye, is particularly acute in some of the paintings where the blind men are, perhaps, not blind at all. Intensity of looking – gazing – seems to equal blindness. There is invariably something wrong with looking. We have already seen that in the *Danae*, for example, the gaze is as objectless as in *The Polish Rider*, although there the subject of looking is at first sight presented as a false object of looking; the nude is as fully represented as possible, but she is represented only as a lure. Strangely enough, the woman, the mother, the nude, exposed to the viewer's gaze as she is, need only lift her powerful arm to strip the onlooker of his identity. Subjected to her direction, the voyeur whose identity depends on gazing, looks away in a

Hegelian dialectic from the very object that constitutes himself. Looking is also criticized in this way in the *Susanna*, and, as I shall argue shortly, in the *David Playing the Harp for Saul*, in the Mauritshuis, The Hague. *Direction*, then, is the key to the narrativization of the problematic of vision, and the bidirectional gaze in the *Rider* concentrates the thematics of vision entirely in directionality.

In *Return of the Prodigal Son* (Figure 9.8), at the Hermitage, the ambiguity is even more striking. There is no mother figure in this painting as there is in the Tobias works, not even by implication or as a secondary figure, as in the *Samson*, nor by conflation as in the *Rider*. Gender identity here is not absent as an issue, but is fought over between men. At first sight, the father looks down upon his retrieved son. A second glance, however, shows us that his eyes are empty, blind. In connection with the pre-text we may ask, Should the departure of the son have had that castrating consequence? Is a father without his child a father no more? Visually, the empty eyes oversee a unity between father and son. But what is the status of this unity, and how does it relate to vision?

When we look further into the father's apparently empty eyes, his eyes suddenly seem empty no longer (Figure 9.3). He does see; his eyes are not entirely dead (although the result may be equivalent). The father looks away from the son. Where the head of the son turns slightly to the right, the father's eyes turn in the opposite direction, signifying the irretrievable loss of the relationship between them. Directionality is again the locus of the representation of the problematics of vision. This is why the insistent unity between father and son is needed: It serves as the signifier of the gap that fractures it. Like the unity of horse and rider in the *Polish Rider*, the unity of father and son is there only to be imperfect, an imperfection that is signified by the divergence of looking.

The consummation of this irretrievable loss of unity becomes melancholia. For the father the loss is signified by the departure of the son. This departure is definitive. Upon the son's eventual return, the old man turns into a different state of himself as father: A son who is able to go away is not part of the father's self. For the son,

9.8   *The Return of the Prodigal Son*, detail

354

the departure functioned to shape his sense of self, and looking away from the father, not sharing in the direction of the father's eyes, is a move away from the unity that is both safe and blinding. Conceived of as a unity, the loss revealed in this composite figure becomes the fixation that is melancholia, and blindness.

THE FRAGILITY OF MASTERY

In the *Return of the Prodigal Son*, the bidirectionality of the gazes of father and son represents the split inherent in unity, while it is the father who represents blindness in the first place. Like Tobias, the son is willing to return to the father after his travels, but unlike the latter, not to cure his blindness. If Tobias, in turn, is willing to take it upon himself to cure his father, the pre-text suggests it is for two reasons: Tobias can afford to be generous toward his father because after his successful sexual initiation he is ready to become a father in his turn; he is ready to join the guild, so to speak. Second, the operation has been commanded by another father figure, the divine father who presides over fathers and sons alike.

The last two works I shall briefly discuss in this chapter again present the father as ambivalently blind, and in both cases the fatherly power and the threat to or loss of it seem to be related to the problematic of vision. Both in the *David Playing the Harp to Saul* and in *The Oath of Claudius Civilis* the father figure is represented with a phallic headdress, a phallic token of real power – scepter or sword – but only one eye (Figures 9.1 and 9.2). Whereas the former work has only two figures and an insistent visual split between them, the latter is crowded, yet the father figure is isolated here as well.[32] According to Schwartz, the *David* could be composed of two single panels that have been joined together later. And voicing this possibility shows that the critic is sensitive to this sense of a split in the work. Regardless of the material correctness of Schwartz's suggestion, in terms of the melancholia hypothesis this split is significant. In a different way, this picture represents the same problematic unity between father and son as did the *Prodigal Son*.

The meaning of the split in the *Saul* (Figure 9.9), represented by a large, dark curtain, and materially enhanced by the sewing together of two fragments right across that curtain, is again a narrativized lack. The work suggests that the antagonism between Saul and David is not a state, but the result of a narrative development: the loss of a unity. First of all, the obvious differences between the father figure and the son figure in this painting should not obscure the similarities between them. David is holding a phallic object, too. The front of the harp seems to grow right out of his body. Moreover, his vision as well as Saul's is problematic. His eyes are directed to the side, not toward a clear and visible aim but, on the contrary, toward no ostensible aim: not toward his harp, not toward his patron, not toward the viewer. If, as the pre-text has it, Saul suffered from melancholia, this David seems to be contaminated by it.

Saul is, in fact, much more similar to David than to Civilis of Figure 9.2. Civilis is grand, superhuman, and upright; his hand is holding the sword strongly. Saul's body is not erect; he seems burdened, and his hand, although holding the staff, grasps it almost accidentally. Saul's single eye is staring. It stares at the viewer, but does not relate to the viewer; it does not seem to see. Compared to the single eye of Civilis, Saul's eye is empty, turned inward, folded back upon itself.

Saul is the only character of all these defective lookers who is already melancholic in the pre-text. There his melancholia is related to, although not caused by, his fear of David's rivalry. And rightly so, as the Biblical reader knows, for David will in effect be the next king, in spite of Saul's various attempts to kill him. In the painting, this rivalry is not represented in any obvious way, and so begins the tension between the verbal and the visual stories. If melancholia is represented by loss, the loss here is a loss of touch with the young man who shares so many features with him; it is a loss represented here by the curtain, the curtain which, according to Schwartz, challenges the work's authentic status and unity. And it is certainly meaningful that it is this very splitting curtain that Saul uses to cover his other eye.

In terms of the story, this covering is a gesture of wiping an eye that cries. The melancholia is then quite concretely represented. But covering one eye is also a way of indicating a defect of vision, especially in connection with the other eye's empty stare. The central detail, the navel of the text, is then not the one eye that we see, but the other eye that we cannot see, or rather, the piece of cloth that covers it. Like Tobit, Saul has a blinding veil over his eye. The sloppiness of his body and of the hand that holds the token of his power, results of a loss, suggests his castrated state.

9.9 *David Playing the Harp for Saul*, detail

356

We do not see the hand that is supposedly being used to cover the invisible eye. Strictly speaking, we do not even know for sure that Saul is manipulating the curtain himself. The lack of muscular tension in his entire body does not promote a sense of action. The piece of cloth alone suggests that for Saul it is the object of an action and the locus of an event, the token of a narrative. But what the event is exactly cannot be made out. What matters visually is that the curtain, by virtue of its being suspended where it is, visually closes off the two men from each other. By this event, David is visually out of Saul's reach. The loss of visual contact, then, entails the loss of vision as such. And as we can see, this loss triggers the paralyzing melancholia that castrates this father figure. What is fascinating is that in this work as in the *Prodigal Son*, the father's lack does not shift power to the son. They both seem to lose in the bargain.

The *Claudius Civilis*, finally, has been considered a symptom of "Rembrandt"'s revolt against the fathers above him (Figure 9.10). As his latest known commission, it seems to have been less than successful and was returned to the painter who subsequently cut it down. It is also his latest representation of the blind eye, and the most explicit one at that. The one eye is ostentatiously, provocatively blind; the other eye is provocatively, aggressively looking. In her essay on this work, Carroll (1986:23) briefly describes the psychoanalytic issue of the work in these words:

Rembrandt has invested the scene with an architypal quality as well. A Freudian interpretation could be adduced to account for this, attending to the patriarchal aura of Civilis: to his superhuman size and the phallic aspect of his upraised sword and single eye. From the viewpoint of comparative mythology, one can note that the one-eyed god or hero is a recurrent figure of sovereignty in Indo-european myth and legend, wherein the single eye of a leader betokens divine wisdom, magic power, and the capacity, in the words of Georges Dumézil, of the "guerrier-fauve" to render his enemies "aveugles et sourds, ou comme paralysés de frayeur."[33]

9.10 *The Oath of Claudius Civilis*, detail

357

According to this view, the figure of Civilis offers an alternative view of power, meant to challenge the power of the city magistrates; Civilis's own patriarchal power would be affirmed wholeheartedly.

Although Carroll's interpretation is on the whole compelling, however, I doubt the monolithic wholeness of the fatherly aspects of this figure, and the submission to the Oedipal father this wholeness would entail. True enough, when compared to Saul, the figure is extremely powerful. Yet his one blind eye is insisted upon: His sighted eye addresses the viewer, but so does the other, blind eye. And although the mythological background adduced by Carroll makes the patriarchal figure comparable to the Medusa mother figure in that both castrate the son, I am not convinced that this castration of the son is the exclusive stake in the painting.

Just as in the *Prodigal Son* and in the *Saul*, the woman, the mother, is absent from this work. But with these works we do have a sense of split. Even this powerful father figure is not able to maintain the unity with the son. Although the work is crowded, on the right and left side of Civilis there are empty spaces. The figures sitting next to him both look intensely, but not at Civilis. Whereas the look of the older man on the left seems to be turned inward, that of the younger man on the right seems, again, blind. The man at the extreme left is putting his sword on top of that of Civilis. This gesture is supposedly part of the ritual being played out. But then, this man is looking at Civilis. And what is more, Civilis, although looking at the viewer, may also be seen as returning this look. Is this man challenging Civilis's total power, and if so, is Civilis's power represented so insistently in order then to represent that even such power is challengeable?

In spite of the enormous proportions of this royal leader, of his powerful pose, and of his royal attributes, the one-eyed father figure does not strike me as frightening. He, too, is vulnerable to being blinded; he, too, has difficulty focusing his vision. The defect of vision outweighs the possible mythical allusions to total power.

CONCLUSION

What Civilis's problematic eyesight overrules in the first place is the predominance of the Oedipal moment that Carroll suggested is overwhelmingly represented in the positive view of Civilis's power. The Oedipal moment fades away under the pressure of what the insistence on Oedipus represses: the moment that came before and that already staged the problematic formation of gendered subjectivity. The absence of the mother in the three works under consideration here is only one aspect of this tension. The split between father and son embodies the melancholic paralyzing mournfulness of the loss of unity and the problematic of vision: It all reconstructs the moment of primary narcissism in which the mother is present not so much as a figure, but as the framework, the background, the ground upon which the self emerges. One cannot see one's own background; this is a blindness we can only acknowledge.[34]

Melancholia, then, is mourning – failed mourning, as Freud taught us – and that failure is, precisely, a blindness. Blindness is the inability to see what is being mourned. Thus the subject, in primary narcissism, emerges already in loss, in death. Death itself, the event upon which the concept of mourning is metonymically contingent, is nowhere explicitly present in these works, but is continually suggested as the background of the primal experience informing melancholia. We shall see in the final chapter that death, in "Rembrandt," has everything to do with the tension between pre-Oedipal and Oedipal blindness and with the emergence of gender identity.

Through the mediation of the concept of mimesis, the idea of melancholia suggests how absence, loss, and the failure to relate to the outside world can be represented in the gap between descriptive and narrative representation, brought about in these cases by the divergence of focus, a divergence that sets the limits to narrativity itself. No medium is more appropriate, of course, to elaborate this problematic than visual art, visual representation; no theme is more challenging – appropriate as well as problematic – to embody its visual discourse, than blindness. And no tool for understanding is more appropriate than the discourse that, for all its contributions to the repression of visuality, has also contributed more than any other to documenting the crucial place of visual experience in the formation of the subject, in its pregendered first confrontation with gender.

The psychoanalytic discourse is, then, a discourse that does not in itself simplify and reduce the work, although more often than not it is used in such negative ways. Rather, it makes the work more complex, inserting modes of discursivity within the visual experience, and even, in the above cases, thematizing that discursivity through a thematized visuality. This encounter brings about responses to the work within the work, lending a new dimension to the psychoanalytic concept itself: Melancholia becomes a mode of representation as well as its motivation. Whether the motivation originates in the painter's irretrievable psyche or in the viewer's unacknowledged response is utterly beside the point. Instead of concentrating on these moot points, we need a dynamic view of semiosis wherein the critic tries to understand the nature of the sign event, rather than a fixed, monolithic, and universal correlation between sign and meaning. Within such a view, the understanding of the possibility of the melancholic event (whose traces can be seen in standard critical discourse, and whose origin is repeated in every one of its occurrences) would emerge from an encounter between, rather than from an "application" of, psychoanalysis and the visual work.

The paradoxical relationship between the negativity of loss and the sacrifice of the subject that melancholia entails, on the one hand, and the representation through the breaking of limits of semiotic modes and means, on the other, is illuminated by the paintings, at least as much as the paintings are illuminated by the psychoanalytic reflection. And reflection, then, takes on its multiple meaning that alone protects the work of art against reductionism and utilitarianism. Reflection here means discursive thinking as well as mirroring, the mirroring of psychoanalytic discourse in the work of art. And the latter reflection works to visualize melancholia as a "fixating" as well as a narrativizing mode of representation.

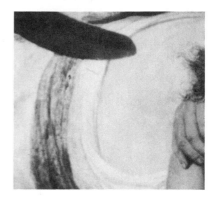

CHAPTER 10

DEAD FLESH, OR THE
SMELL OF PAINTING

But when I knelt down next to her in order to comfort her, I saw that the wound of the belly was an
enormous cavity, almost everything had been removed from the abdomen and on the bottom, like a
tool left behind in carelessness, was the razor. (Willem Brakman, *Heer op Kamer*, 1988:108)[1]

INTRODUCTION

I N a paradoxical sketch, "Rembrandt" represented the central
scene of the Biblical story of Judges 19 (Figure 10.1). The sketch
is paradoxical because it is a statement about death signified by
the movement of the dead body. This paradox can be understood
as we shift attention from the represented content to the mode of
representation. Then, by the incongruous twist that brings death
itself to life, the pictorial sign of movement becomes a crucial token
of self-reflexivity. But reversing this perspective, we can also say
that reflection on pictorial representation is in an important way
focused on death.

Pulling together the many threads of this study, this final chapter
is about both death and representation. It is also about gender.
Returning to some of the issues raised in the opening chapter, I
wish to address more explicitly the question that arose there in a
more cursory way: I want to consider the relationships, in "Rembrandt," among death, women, and representation; among silence,
speech, and gender; among violence, art, and culture. This exploration will lead to reflections on violence, on the materiality of
paint, and on the act of opening. Opening bodies is, I shall suggest,
the very project of painting. But to say this now is to skip several
stages.

"Rembrandt," as I have been arguing in the previous chapters,
sometimes allows for the reading of an extremely subtle view of
women. Yet the body of Rembrandt criticism provides evidence
that the works also allow for readings partaking of the cultural
commonplaces, the doxas of the enculturation of misogyny. This
shows that ideology is a matter of interaction between work and

viewer, not a matter of the work alone. Moreover, the resulting interpretations have been, more often than not, ambivalent. Take the *Lucretia*s for example: Although the very subject matter of these paintings, representing suicide as the metaphor of rape, colludes with the masculinist doxa regarding rape, the victim's view is also there to problematize that doxa. In addition, differences among works are considerable: indeed, so far we have seen works where women can be read as represented sympathetically as in *Samson's Wedding* and in the Berlin *Susanna*, or ambivalently as in the *Bellona* and *The Blinding of Samson*. Finally, the number of works in which gender boundaries are transgressed, like the *Blinding of Samson*, *Bellona* and her medusa, and *The Polish Rider*, add to the sense that gender in "Rembrandt" cannot be pinpointed easily. I suggest, then, that the cultural fascination with "Rembrandt" is related not to an affirmative, monolithic ideology of gender, but to the plurality of ideological possibilities the works leave open.

But it becomes necessary, then, to assess whether we can leave this decentralized vision as is and take it as evidence for the non-coherence of the subject "Rembrandt." That oeuvre would in this case be a forerunner of the postmodern challenge to coherence. In spite of its blatant ahistoricism,[2] such a position has its attractions, if only because it fits the plural view of ideology and subjectivity that contemporary theory argues for. It has in its turn ideological problems, however. Stopping short at ascertaining noncoherence may also be just a little too easy and may cause us to neglect a dimension of the work that tells more about verbal and visual interpretation than we have so far been able to hear. What I would like to do in this chapter is to assemble the diversity of "Rembrandt"'s representations of women and connect them, and their diversity, with the representational strategies discussed so far. This assemblage will not unite the diverse views of women into some artificial whole, but will position the nonconsistency itself within a framework that makes this very lack of coherence understandable. "Rembrandt"'s discourse on gender is a discourse on representation, and vice versa.

I shall pursue this question through the discussion of a few works (not *on* women in particular) that relate to the most frightening aspect of life and the most urgent motivation for, yet challenge to, representation: *death*. Death is a challenge to representation to the extent that the experience of death is a moment that nobody can describe, an event that nobody can escape, a process that nobody can narrate. Representation, especially portraiture, partakes of the attempt to quell the fear of death and to compensate for the loss of identity and material existence death entails. The representation of death as both gendered and representational, therefore, can shed new light on the diverse aspects of the ideological positions toward gender that "Rembrandt" enables the viewers to project onto the works. In a third turn, then, I shall discuss a few of the more celebrated representations of death that help us to reach such an understanding: the slaughtered oxen and their human and scientific counterparts, the anatomies.

LANGUAGE AND A MURDEROUS VISION OF DEATH

I have already mentioned the undated drawing now in the Kupferstichkabinett, Berlin-Dahlem (Figure 10.1), in which the scene in the Book of Judges, chapter 19:26–8 is depicted. As it is about rape, this story has been briefly discussed in Chapter 1. The drawing represents the moment when the traveling Levite, who has exposed his wife the previous night to gang rape in order to avoid being raped himself, finds her the next morning on the threshold of the house where he has spent the night. It is one of "Rembrandt" 's most acute representations of death, which, paradoxically, is full of movement and life, full of narrative, and full of speaking hands.

The drawing is less famous than "Rembrandt" 's painted works on death, like the Paris *Slaughtered Ox*, renowned for its bold brush strokes, often quoted in modern painting, and recently discussed in a little book whose title I borrow for this chapter: *L'odeur de la peinture*;[3] it is also less famous than the two anatomy lessons of Dr. Tulp and of Dr. Deyman. Yet this little drawing, once we let it

10.1 *The Levite Finds His Wife in the Morning* 1655–6, Benesch 997, drawing (Berlin, SMPK, Kupferstichkabinett)

363

interact with, and read it through the textual story it is supposed
to depict, provides an indispensable perspective on "Rembrandt"'s
urge to paint death in a specific way in the famous works: It illuminates "Rembrandt"'s propensity to depict death as stinking dead
flesh, representing the dangers of representation and the ambivalence of gender. I shall argue that this view of death is deeply
connected with women as "Rembrandt" inscribed them in some
of his works.

As I suggested in my brief presentation of the story of Judges 19
in Chapter 1, the young women who are the victims of sexual
violence in Judges are, for reasons that have to do with their sexual
maturity and their institutional background, disruptive of the social
structure as well as of the narrative. Their rape and/or murder work
to cure both: to bring about a return of social order and to lead the
narrative to its next phase. In the first chapter, I focused on the
former; here I shall concentrate on the latter.

The drawing (Figure 10.1) depicts the victim at the threshold of
the house, and thus positions her literally as a liminal figure, as the
embodiment of transition. In spite of the sketchiness of the representation as a whole, the steps that constitute the threshold and
signify the house as real and as stone are particularly clearly drawn.

In order to stretch the verbal–visual interaction to its limits, I
would like to present here one semiotic aspect in the verbal narrative
that is directly related both to the social issue and to representation:
It is the use of language for violence, and the way in which this
particular aspect is represented in "Rembrandt"'s nonlinguistic
work. The moment in which language and violence are intricately
related is precisely the one that our drawing represents: the moment
where the woman is no longer able to speak, where her dead flesh
is *seen*, misunderstood, addressed, and ultimately, misused in a
radical perversion of speech.

Vision also plays a crucial role in this horror story. Mis-seeing,
un-seeing the woman is what is painfully represented in the sketch,
thus showing that this central scene of failed vision has a special
meaning for visual representation.[4] Her death and the story of it
are not only violent but also narratively ambiguous. She dies, we
might say, several times, or rather, she never stops dying.[5] It is
this aspect of her dying that makes this drawing so central in the
reflections on death readable in "Rembrandt": An event that is
punctual and nonnarratable is turned into a slow process represented
as the climax of narrative that then becomes the visual work challenging the limits of visual representation. This woman's dying is
a semiotic force; in Peter Brooks's (1984) terms, it is the motor of
the narrative.

Whereas in the pre-text the event is turned from punctual into
durative, the representation of this already perverted death in an
allegedly static medium further explores and undermines the limits
of the realm of the speakable. The asumed limits of the speakable
suggest what this apparently casual sketch explores: It makes us

ask how the already paradoxically continuous process of death can be represented visually, *as process*.

In the pre-text, the agents of the woman's death are as unclear as is its moment; the act keeps being displaced from one man to the next. Not only is this woman the object of the body language of rape, a language that bespeaks her death; her body is also subsequently used *as* language by the very man who exposed her to the violence. Where the narrative seems to fail to construct history, rape becomes the sign that does, it becomes the generative event of Judges. The relationship between semiotic behavior *in* the book, and the narrative that *is* the book is what I take to be the motor that drives the dynamics of this drawing. In this respect it is important to notice that the moment chosen to narrate this murderous, continuous rape, is a moment of vision, of mis-seeing, and the agent who unsees the woman to death is the one who speaks through her body.

The moment of this endless deferral of death which a visual artist chose to represent is the one in which vision becomes a speech act. The morning after the gang rape, the woman's husband opens the door to go his way, and "*behold*, there is his wife, fallen down, and her hands are on the threshold" (Judges 19:27).[6] Two words, then, generate this drawing: "open" and "behold."[7] Opening the door for sacrificial violence, then, the man contemplates the body of the wife he had disposed of, and what he sees is here for us to see: "Behold, she is fallen." I shall take up this complex to account for some uncanny and gendered effects of the paintings of death, and their putrifying stench.

Next to Genesis, Judges is one of the major texts "Rembrandt" responds to throughout his corpus, and, perhaps significantly, it is

10.2 *Samson Posing the Riddle to the Wedding Guests* (*Samson's Wedding*) 1638, canvas, 126 × 175 cm (Dresden, Gemäldegalerie)

a book that problematizes language by proposing uncanny kinds of speech acts to challenge language as purveyor of meaning. I wish to contend that Judges is an attractive venue upon which the ambition of visual art can explore the limits of representation, precisely because it explores the limits of *its* medium. Judges is, for example, full of riddles, the speech act of the *lack* of meaning.[8]

In addition to riddles, Judges is also full of speech acts based on an *excess* of meaning, acts that emblematize the power of words in the most radical way; they are vows. Their meaning being death, they bring death, they kill.[9] Between the lack of meaning and an excess of meaning, speech is overruled by the force that motivates it. This overruling of meaning by motivating force happened in the *Blinding of Samson* as well, and we can now see what the special attraction of such a speech event is for "Rembrandt." In the gap left by this view of language as deficient, visual representation inserts itself and becomes an alternative language.

It is this alternative language that is "spoken" in "Rembrandt"'s sketch of the woman in Judges 19 who, in the Bible, is killed in and as speech. This particular linguistic murder occurs several times there. Before her death by the gang rape she is surrendered linguistically, and after her death she is dispatched as language, when her body is cut into pieces and sent to the tribes of Israel, as a *letter* – a piece of writing not containing but embodying a message – and as a slaughtered piece of meat. Butchering equals writing here; death equals vision. This is a case, if ever there was one, of the scandal of the speaking body.[10] Between the two moments of her murder by multiplication and publication – multiple rape and publication of her body – is the climactic, breathtaking moment of vision during which the husband-opener fails to see, thus adding to, and consecrating, the murder.

LANGUAGE AND THE SEMIOTICS OF MIS-SEEING

In order to account for the crucial position of this drawing in terms of the paradoxes of visual narrative, I shall briefly demonstrate through *Samson's Wedding* (Figure 10.2) that verbal narrative is no more self-evident than visual narrative; this we can come to understand when reading visual narrative for its commentary on verbal narrative; and we can also come to understand, through the same process, that speech acts tend to cross over, and cross out, the narrative line of the fabula.

During the seven-day party preceding his wedding, Samson "put forth a riddle" to his thirty Philistine companions at the feast. As a speech act, the riddle is based on power. The subject who proposes the riddle knows the answer, while the addressee does not. The riddle's answer/meaning is Samson's secret performance and transgression, the killing of the lion and the eating of honey out of the corpse's belly in controversion of the dietary laws. The answer is his anatomical lesson, so to speak.

The all-male company in which the speech act is accomplished, the generic feature of the riddle's insolvability, the use of the future tense to point toward the wedding to come which necessarily fractures the unity of the group by the introduction of the woman, the crisis that cannot but break out because of the dissymmetry of interests – all this suggests a problematic of possession in the future where a woman is at stake, and at center stage. This is the theatrical-representational motivation for the strange isolation of the bride in the painting, a motivation I integrated iconographically to the position of Christ in Chapter 5.

The painting responds to the problematic discrepancy in speech-act theory between force and meaning, which I showed could be transferred to the visual domain through psychoanalysis, in Chapter 9. This distinction not only fails to distribute the field of meaning; this failure is also itself thematized *in* the meaning. This is a crucial insight into representation, but it leaves us with a kind of perplexity when we transfer it to "Rembrandt" 's drawing of Judges 19. There, too, the meaning – the woman's death – and the force – its narrativization in movement – confront each other in the paradox of representation: In order to represent the narrative of death, the drawing requires a movement – in the woman's right hand – that denies death precisely while pointing to its agent.

According to Eco (1976), signs are those things that can be used in order to lie. This definition helps us understand the "lies" in the drawing: the movement of a dead woman, signified by the lines under her slightly blurred right hand, and the ghostlike transparency of the living man, signified by the continuous line of the stone on which he is supposed to stand.[11] Neither sign is merely a lie; both are representational paradoxes. The latter is an example of the solidity of objects Alpers mentioned as one device of self-reflexivity. In this case, the solidity of the stone negates the man's realistic solidity. Just as the speech act of the riddle in Judges undermines the narrative plot line, so too does a line here undercut the drawing's realistic quality: The force of the speech act of drawing cancels out its own realistic meaning.

Jonathan Culler (1983) reformulates Eco's definition of the sign from the reader's perspective. He tells us that a sign is everything that can be misunderstood. This reformulation is important here, for it is the act of reading that the present study is both focusing upon and demonstrating. Misreading, then, is the key to semiosis, just as mis-seeing is the key to opening the woman's body and to representing her death.

If we now take another look at the painting of the riddle, we are better prepared to appreciate the importance of the woman's gesture. She wards off the attempt to open her body, which is the definition of marriage at stake in Judges and, perhaps, in "Rembrandt." Referring this painting back to its narrative precedent, the lion in the scene generating the riddle is not Samson but his antagonist. The one whose belly yields sweetness like honey is combined, conflated, with the strong one. One answer to the riddle is, then, "the formidable woman." Identifying her with the lion does not bode well for her: The lion can yield sweetness only when dead. Given such a reading, the painting illuminates, in turn, the drawing of Judges 19, where the inevitable next step – the sweetness yielded in death – is represented. The theatrical quality of the painting emphasized by Alpers[12] clearly must not be related to the alleged hypocrisy of the woman; instead that quality must be related to the representational noncoherence of the work which sets the woman apart from the surrounding characters. This quality of isolation is sharply foregrounded in the drawing.

"Rembrandt"'s affinity for Judges, his depictions of these two of its scenes, suggests a split, a deep and unbridgeable gulf, between two projections of women. On the one hand, there are women who are feared and therefore hated, who need to be appropriated by violence. These women are potential mates – the brides who must be violated in order to be *opened*. On the other hand, there are women who are harmless because they have already been violated. These are the victims, women as social figures of marginality with whom the subject "Rembrandt" can identify. With the first class of women, the subject has a relation of contiguity, which implies a continuity he fears; with the second, he has a metaphoric relationship which implies the distance and separation that allow sympathy without entailing danger. Both these projections meet in the representation of these two scenes from Judges; they meet in death, that is: Ultimately, the one woman must be killed, and the other has been killed already.

She must be revivified, but only if she is already dead: The woman in the drawing is not easily placed on either side of this split. That difficulty is precisely why I present this drawing as crucial and generative of meaning for "Rembrandt" as a whole. Since these two classes of women have to be kept apart, the very act of severance that operates the separation becomes the subject of painting in the death works.

As we have seen in our confrontation between psychoanalysis and art, there is no story without motivation, the force that pushes the subject to tell it, and that lies both in the past and in the present of the speech act. In Judges in general and in this riddle episode in particular, there can be no riddle without a story, and there can be no story without a riddle; there can be no present tense without a past tense that predicts the future. The urgency of this narrativity also affects the drawing, making it, in turn, a burning story. It is in the future that the word of the speech act becomes flesh, burned flesh; and the flesh is female. It is this gendered flesh, I shall argue, that we smell in "Rembrandt"'s famous death paintings.

368

STAGING DEATH: THE WORD
BECOME FLESH

Samson's riddle produces the story in which is embedded the par-adox of the rape victim's continuous murder: It produces the rep-resentation of death as narrative. This dynamic aspect of death is also visible, narratable in its visuality, in the drawing of Judges 19. The gesture of the woman's hand on the threshold is important in both the text and the drawing. It has often been explained symbolically.[13]

Beyond the dichotomy of literal and figurative-symbolic,[14] the detail of the hand can be taken as a metastatement on the text's narrativity: The gesture, as the drawing presents it, is the self-reflexive "lie" that counters the grave misreading both text and drawing thematize. That misreading is represented in the compo-sition, which we can now read as a metastatement on the work's theatricality. Narrativity and theatricality are two conflicting modes of representation resolved in a dialectic narrativization of vision.

The moment selected for visual representation is well chosen because it is the painful one that produces doubt and fear in readers who, from the perspective of a pernicious and utterly ideological partiality, have a stake in the moral righteousness of the character of the Levite, the husband of the victim. It is deeply confusing to see the theatricalization of this door-opener's behavior. Reading theatrically, as the introductory exclamation "Behold" suggests we might, we see how he almost steps over the body of his wife – his first misreading of the sight presented to him – then orders her to stand up – a second misreading, now of his position of power. When no body (!) answers, we see him tie her (body) to his donkey to take her home and, in his most vicious moment of deception, cut her up for semiotic misuse.[15] Attempts to redeem this man are numerous, but they are condemned to fail from the outset.[16] Most of these passionate apologists claim that the woman must already have been dead. This outlet leads, however, to another dead end, because the Levite, a priest, would have had to break the taboo of touching the dead by butchering her – the very transgression on which Samson's riddle is based. The relationship between vision, in the epistemological dubiousness inherent in its semiotic nature, and touch, as the metonymic attempt to escape semiosis, prob-lematizes this scene even further.

Given the obvious fact that the misreadings of this scene are motivated by the desire to see the woman as dead, hence, to partake of the diegetic misreading of the Levite, it is remarkable that the drawing adds to this confusion rather than helping the viewer to master it, by adding the short lines under the woman's right hand.[17] This representation of movement seems to suggest that the drawing contradicts the standard apologies by emphasizing movement, hence, life. But these lines do not depict the woman as "really" alive; they suggest only that she is acting out her story, the story of her continuous death – her death as a process that challenges the epistemological basis of our conception of death as a knowable event. In order to represent her death, then, the drawing must let her move.

The question of the realistic status of the movement of the hand, then, is also an epistemological question: It raises the question of knowledge, on both the diegetic and the semiotic level. Who knows what? Does the husband know that the woman is dead? No, for if he had, he would not have ordered her to stand up. Does the reader know she is dead? I think not, for the forcefulness with which her death is argued betrays that the reader does not, cannot, know. This lack is a blow, not only to the scholar whose mission is purported to be knowledge, but also to the reader who feels conflated with the ignorant character, the Levite.

But there is more to knowledge than meets the eye. To know and to possess are both expressions for the sexual encounter from the male perspective, and are thus intimately related to each other and to gender.[18] This equation is possible because knowledge is itself a thing one can possess: One *has* knowledge. But one cannot possess what one does not know, for how can one know whether or not one possesses it? And one cannot give what one does not possess, hence, giving the unknown is a priori an act of semiotic abuse. To know, furthermore, is also an epistemological act whose relationship to vision is at stake, both in Judges and in "Rembrandt." Does the epistemologically defective man, in the drawing, *know* his wife, sexually and existentially, if he cannot even know if she is alive or dead? In other words, is he her husband at all at this point? It is this that his intense act of looking lets us question. From this perspective, the line that makes him transparent also makes him unreal: As the woman's husband he does not exist. This line shifts the work from realistic failure to semiotic adequacy.[19]

My reading of this drawing is based on the refusal to endorse the separations between "literal" and "figurative," between visual and verbal, along with the acknowledgment of the impossibility of "pure" meaning – of meaning without force. We can read this refusal of the distinctions that have dictated much of Western representational and interpretive practice in the lines moving the hand in "Rembrandt"'s drawing. The hand of this woman is crucial: It tells about death and about representation. It does not "see," but it speaks about mis-seeing. More "real" because more alive than the body of the husband, the hand is about to point in accusation at her murderer. It accuses him not only of multiple and durative murder, but also of misreading, mis-seeing, and misrepresentation.[20]

The woman's gesture is not acknowledged as semiotic, as an initiator of the phatic function. The hands on the threshold that both accuse and implore are misread by the husband to whom they are addressed – while they are polemically enhanced by "Rembrandt." The drawing insists that the husband's misreading is wrong. It demonstrates that her gesture is phatic, enforcing se-miosis. The woman addresses her husband from below, implying a radical repositioning of vision. The husband, who is represented in the drawing as wringing his hands eloquently as in despair – speaking with his hands – cannot *see* the movement of the woman's hand, as the hand itself blocks the sight of the lines underneath it.[21]

By interrupting the represented line of vision, hence, both em-phasizing and problematizing diegetic seeing as much as in the Berlin *Susanna*, the work does several things at once. It represents the very moment of suspension between life and death, action and inaction, thus raising the question of the husband's response and generating the following episode. It theatricalizes the visual mo-ment, by inscribing in it the dimension of time. And it emphasizes its own status as a work of representation, willfully misreading the conventions of representational art. The husband *looks* at the wom-an's hand, but the *representation* of its telling movement is not for him to see.

The sacrificial gift of this woman led to the public opening of her body; it led to rape, death, and dismemberment; instead of qualifying her subject position, it destroyed it. The husband lives by this destruction: He stands over her, fails to see her, ineffectively and abusively speaks to her, and steps over her. The woman can speak only as body. This body will be used to speak, but it is no longer the woman who speaks. As an inevitable consequence of the scene of vision outlined by the drawing, her body, utterly robbed of its significance as herself, is "divided, limb by limb, into twelve pieces, and he sent her throughout all the borders of Israel" (19:29). The dead body can speak, but by a perverse twist it is the man who totally subjected her, not herself, who speaks. Begging for the merciful interpretations of his crime against women and life which will in effect be granted to him in the history of Biblical interpretation, the man's hands overshadow the speaking power of the woman's. But by opposing the lie of her hands to that of his, the drawing lets her speak against this cultural defense of rape and murder.

This defense, like all speech, leaves a rest, a gap in which the repressed motivation can return: The drawing helps us see how and why. The man's begging hands can also be read as his fear of the threat coming from the side of the father. Instead of siding with the daughter who, after all, took his side earlier in the story, he submits to the father and sacrifices her. His weakness and his fear are exposed and, with an ambivalence that is a misreading in its turn, the drawing shows a man who, rather than a die-hard cynic, is so weak that he loses his substance, while his fear is projected onto the object of sight. Whereas Judges simply quotes the Levite's subsequent lie, and whereas Biblical criticism subscribes to that lie, "Rembrandt" also exposes us to the fright that motivated the re-jection of the woman.

Judges 19 ends with an imperative – *speak*, a masculine plural –

response to the visual speech of the woman's divided flesh. The tribes address their order to speak, not to the "speaker," but to the husband. The speaking body itself is misread: The tribes blame the Benjaminites, not the husband and what he stands for. The speaking body fails to speak because it is not listened to. We face again the scandal of the speaking body; it is denied the power to speak. To this subsequent scandal, the drawing opposes the prefiguration of a response. The man may be the opener of doors and bodies, but he is depicted as so weak in the drawing that his perverted speech will indeed be misread, yet in a way opposed to the misreading of the tribes. The drawing, already erasing him while enhancing the dead woman, will not let his lie be read at all. The navel in this work is taken by lines: the line cutting through the man's substance, undermining his reality, and the lines producing the woman's movement that he cannot see. The collusion and collision among these lines generate the drawing's diffusion of meaning.

STAGED DEATH: THE WORK BECOME STONE

We have now come a little closer to the ambivalence I speculated was readable in "Rembrandt." If the "Rembrandt" who emerges from this reading partakes of the fright of the woman as mate-to-be, hence, as body to be opened by force, he also competes sharply with the fathers, who weaken him from behind so to speak, and he seems to stick to a son position throughout his work. The Tobias drawings; the many blind fathers depicted; plus the Berlin *Susanna* with its harsh critique of the father figures and the intense sympathy with the woman, in her vulnerability and youthfulness, as daughter rather than mother – all these instances point to a strong ambivalence resolved by the splitting up of women into two radically different positions. The fascination of the scene represented in the Judges 19 drawing stems from the ambiguity of the man: He is a son who loses the competition, a husband who fails as such, but he shares behavioral features with the father, narratively by his act of gift, visually by his bent body.

The drawing's composition is ultimately self-reflexive. It enhances the dialogue between the woman's moving hand and the man's begging hands in a diagonal that interrupts the line of sight. The discrepancy between the diegetic begging hands and the hand that blocks the sight of its own representational movement is another instance of distortion that breaks with realism for the sake of representation, comparable in this respect to Bathsshebah's unreal body-twist discussed in Chapter 6 (Figure 6.3). Kept in sexual ignorance to the very end, the husband will not be able to *know* the meaning of the woman's speaking hand. His intensely looking eyes underscore the more strongly his visual failure.

It is interesting to look from this perspective at a drawing, dated

1647 and purported to represent the sacrifice of Iphigenia, but which can as well represent the Hebraic equivalent of that Greek story, the sacrifice of Jephthah's daughter (Figure 10.3). The composition is emphatically theatrical, set on a stage in which the stone altar is as strongly foregrounded, oversize for the small body next to it. The division of the scene, with the military men on the one side and the female mourners on the other, emphasizes the central position of the daughter's body, about to be opened, about to be burned, generating the ghastly stench of fried flesh. The small dagger held by the soldier is only slightly displaced in relation to the more common instrument of body opening, the penis. Its position in relation to the soldier's body as well as to the bride-victim's body is more than casually suggestive of this metaphorical quality. The woman is (s)lain on her bridal deathbed by the man who embraces her in order to kill better, under the watchful eye of a fatherly figure. The difference between this representation of death and that of Yael killing Sisera (Figure 8.1) is subtle but crucial. Both victims seem asleep, but the *work* of killing, self-reflexively sculptural in the Yael drawing, is decidedly sexual in this one.

Yael's sculpturing killing takes on additional meaning in light of the death drawings of Figures 10.1 and 10.3. Not only does Yael become the reflector of the creator, producer, artist, thus crossing traditional gender boundaries wherein making is masculinized, as we have seen. Not only is sculpture a mode of visual representation that works through touch, and that is thereby ideally suitable to

10.3 *The Sacrifice of Iphigenia* ca. 1647, Benesch 586A, drawing, 248 × 197 mm (Paris, A. Normand)

373

represent the ambition of the artist "Rembrandt" as Alpers has described it. In relation to death, this sculptural quality also becomes the token of durability, of duration beyond death. In addition, as we can now see in drawings 10.1 and 10.3, stone is also the token of theatricalization, the setting against which "real" and "symbolic," or "real" and "fantasy," as well as narrative and visual are measured. The threshold and its symbolic meaning – of both solidity beyond the "real" and boundary crossing – is overdetermined by its similitude to the altar, on which Jephthah's daughter is sacrificed and on which the other woman's body, already opened many times, will be butchered by the man who could not *face* her speech. Finally, stone is what cannot be penetrated by the violence of rape and murder, only by that of representation, of sculpture. In the drawing of Judges 19, the stone of the house is stronger, as a sign, than the Levite's body: This is why the line of the step turns the husband into a ghost.

The act of opening the body is, then, the emblematic act that "Rembrandt" will make us work with in other representations of death. Against the light of the outlined interaction between "Rembrandt" and Judges, his more famous paintings may well add to the uncanniness of the connection between self-reflexivity in death and gender.

STAGED DEATH: LIFE BECOME WORK

In this section, we shall move from dying women to dead women, and from the strange, semifictional Biblical women to a "real" but foreign woman – the executed Elsje Christiaens, a murderess who had slain her landlady with an axe, and whose dead body is the subject of two drawings – and a doubly fictional but familiar woman – the sculpted wife/muse in *The Goldsmith*. In spite of the differences between these two women, their deadness cannot be questioned.

In our attempt to understand death in "Rembrandt" we have been confronted with an increasing number of related paradoxes, all readable through the interaction between the works and the pretext. These paradoxes fall into three sets. The first set concerns representation. Death is represented through movement, language is represented in visual art, and speech is represented as silence. The second set concerns subjectivity. Although the works in question are attributable to a male *hand*,[22] the fear and hatred of women are represented from the inside, from *her* inside, thus questioning the monolithic concept of the subject this very notion of "hand" implies. This exteriorization of the inside experience through the inside of the other occurs on two levels. It occurs through the identification with the woman, not only as the subject matter but also as focalizer of the diegesis of the work – that is, with her subject position. And it occurs through the literalization of her inside-turned-outside: through the opening of her body.

The third set of paradoxes concerns theatricality. The most intimate, hence "absorptive" experience – fear – is offered for contemplation in a strongly, but perhaps deceptively, theatrical mode. This mode is depicted as strongly theatrical: It is depicted through ritual, the ritual of sacrifice – that ritual which Scarry defined as the turning outside of the inside. Ritual is theatrical in more than one respect. Historically, the theater may have emerged from ritual, and so ritual would be theater's "purest" form. Systematically, ritual is the most extreme form of role playing, of signifying in the elusive ways of symbolism,[23] of exchanging subjectivities. But this theatricality is deceptive in that, unlike most works in which theatricality is thematized, no eye contact with the viewer is represented. Therefore, the works remain utterly absorptive.

This latter paradox is informed by the paradox of death itself. This paradox is at the heart of Foucault's "theo-/necrology," as Denis Hollier has reminded us in an article with the telling title "The Word of God: 'I Am Dead' " (1988). Only by "God" – that is, only radically outside of human language – can death be spoken. For death is that which cannot be spoken in the first person, simple present. This impossibility has major consequences for the status of narrative in representation. Death cannot be represented in this narrative mode because, like fire, it hovers between a state and an event.[24] Hence, the representation of death will hover between narrative (the story of an event) and description (the description of a state), breaking down one of the most dogmatic, but also most problematic dichotomies of narrative theory. It will also hover between the two aspects of its own impossibility: the first person and the present tense.

That death should challenge narrative structure makes perfect sense if we believe Peter Brooks's (1984) suggestion that narrative as a form acts out the theory of *Beyond the Pleasure Principle*: It acts out both the desire for the end – for death – and the compulsion to delay that end by repetition. This connection becomes more meaningful if we also incorporate Elisabeth Bronfen's (1989) radical reinterpretation of Freud's text in terms of gender. The impulse underlying narration, then, is the repression of the mother as the ground of primary narcissism, the repression of the deadly memory of the wound inflicted as the subject creates itself, and the repression that leaves a scar as trace in memory: the navel.

Separating provisionally the two aspects of the impossible representation of death – the first person and the present tense – we can resolve the paradox of the deceptive theatricality in the two drawings through the paradox of subjectivity. Although the deaths of the women in drawings 10.1 and 10.3 are set on a stage, they are not staged. They are, rather, proposed for *absorptive* imagination. Staging a figuration of murder as an inevitable next step, or next stage, these works are encoded in the future tense: Death is coming, but it has not yet occurred. This staging of "death," then, is problematic as a representation. One step removed from "real" death, from the representation of the corpse that is the only convincing form of death, it allows us to read "I am dying" – the present progressive tense – rather than "she is dead." In other words, the first person is more basic to the drawings than the simple present tense. And this is so, I would like to speculate, because in some way gender is more crucial for representation than time.

In other works, however, the paradox has been solved in the opposite direction, as in *The Goldsmith* and in the two drawings of the executed woman, Elsje. There, the representation of death is focused on the present – she is dead – rather than on the subject – I am dying. But the representation is not based on an easy, clear-cut choice between these two alternatives. By way of the self-reflexivity of these works, the inscription of the repressed, or sacrificed, aspect has been attempted, and the readability of the traces of those attempts provides a key to the readability of the symmetrical other, the trace of the present tense in the subject-centered drawings.

The Elsje drawings and *The Goldsmith* have in common that they are both about "making" and about dead women. As it happens, the Dutch verb for "killing" is, literally, "to make dead." Although this emphasis on causality and agency is semantically obscured in the English word, the syntactical property of the verb as a verb of action retains it.[25] And syntactic relations will turn out to be the motors of semantics in the death works. In all three works, an instrument of violence is emphasized. In *The Goldsmith* (Figure 10.4), the sculptor, like Yael, wields a hammer to fix the statue to its base, while embracing it tenderly with his other hand. In the drawings of Elsje's corpse, Figures 10.5 and 10.6, the instrument of violence is the axe, assumed to be the instrument with which the dead woman has murdered her landlady. As it is represented, however, it looks like the instrument that has killed Elsje. But this conflation of murderer and victim through the instrument may be necessary to enable "Rembrandt" to make this statement on death.

The hammer and these axes cannot be unproblematically taken as signifying the same thing, however. One reason is the difference in placement. The hammer of the goldsmith points downward, more toward his own body than toward the statue/woman, whereas in the Elsje drawings, the axes are both strongly emphatic, but, syntactically speaking, placed differently in the two drawings. In Figure 10.5, it is directed inward, with its upper point, like an arrow, functioning as an index, pointing toward the woman's mouth, the silenced organ of speech. In the other (Figure 10.6), it points outward.

But of course, there are similarities, especially if we see the instruments not in isolation, but partaking of a syntagm. In the etching, we cannot ignore, for example, that the goldsmith's gaze is directed toward his hammer, hence to the part of his own body this instrument substitutes for. This line of sight might affect the quality of the tender embrace of his other hand, which begins to look like a gesture of bodily appropriation. In the frontal drawing of Elsje, the woman's head is framed, violently confined, by the transversal beams from which the axe hangs. This confining function is taken over, in Figure 10.5, by the central trunk of the gibbet, that, in concert with the ropes, holds her body in place. In each of these three works, the confinement of the body is emphasized by the resistance to this confinement. The sculpted woman's upper body seems to draw back from the man's firm hold, whereas the Elsje drawings demonstrate the need for holding a body that tends to escape the limits designed by the ropes. And in all three cases the woman's hand is the counterinstrument.

The woman in the etching is holding onto her children, one in each hand, and although her grasp is embedded in that of the man who dominates her, in terms of both dimension and existential status, the autonomy of her hands cannot be ignored. The hands of the murdered criminal also seem to escape the hold of the very ropes that cause her arms to move upward. This is especially striking in the profile drawing, where a sense of movement even seems inscribed in the woman's right arm. If the right arm is the one that wielded the murdering axe, the left arm is, by comparison, the dead one, contained by the axe that is hung on its side.

In all three works, emphasis falls on the woman's abdomen. In the etching, she is holding her baby at the precise site where babies come from, where they are "made." In the drawings, the very deadness of the body, its quality of "hangedness," makes the ab-

10.4 *The Goldsmith*, etching
(Haarlem, Teylers Museum)

377

domen protrude and thereby at least visually escape the confinement of death. The striking position of the hammer, wielded to confine, to fix, the woman and her children to their base/place, in turn sheds some new light on the position of the axe as the instrument of confinement in the drawings. This confinement points outward in the one and inward in the other drawing, containing and guarding the body in the one and the mouth in the other. In these respects it makes sense to read the three works as a set, to read making and killing as conflated.

Yet reading them separately is also illuminating. For the syntactic spin-offs of "making dead" are differently signified in each. Placing the etching within the Pygmalion tradition, for example, the artist simply seems to seek to convey the making of life. But in this etching, as in the Tobias drawing and the Yael drawing, the gender positions of the Pygmalion theme are filled in untraditionally. The standard positions – the master sculptor and the young girl as his object – are replaced in the etching, with the woman as mother,

10.5 (*left*) *A Woman Hanging from the Gallows* 1654–6, Benesch 1105, drawing, 176 × 93 mm (New York, Metropolitan Museum of Art)

10.6 (*right*) *A Woman Hanging from the Gallows* 1654–6, Benesch 1106, drawing, 142 × 81 mm (New York, Dr. A. Hamilton Rice)

the master position not belonging self-evidently to any of the figures. In the Tobias, the artist is the son, the father figure being turned by the son's artistic action into a castrated, blinded, impotent old man, whereas in the Yael, the artist is a mature woman killing/making a man.

As a traditional token of representational ambition, the sculpted woman in the etching is expected to say "I am alive," not "I am dead"; yet her embeddedness in the artist's enterprise emphasizes her status as dead matter. But we have seen that this is problematic in two ways: First, the statement "I am dead" can be uttered only in the future, whereas any statement in the simple present must be in the third person – "she is dead." This problem addresses the paradox of tense and of time. Only by focusing on the deadness in the present can the miracle of bringing something inert to life be made meaningful. Second, between dead and alive, the person must shift from identification to objectification, from "I" to "she."

The etching, by virtue of its traditional symbolism, clarifies this most explicitly. The Pygmalion theme represents the outrageous ambition of art, but it also represents the danger of art, of the competition with God, a danger embodied in the Frankensteinian escape from the grasp of the maker. This flipside of power has been resolved in ways that are distributed according to gender lines.[26] The frightening power over life is equaled only by the power to deal death. In the face of the threat of freedom that life entails, "making dead" is a safer, and yet equally powerful, enterprise. The two enterprises are not just juxtaposed, then, in the emphatic representation of the womb next to the instrument of death, but also, the life-bringing organ is syntactically subordinated to the death-dealing implement, as the etching makes the woman a dead thing in the hand of her/its maker.

Bringing this to bear upon the Elsje drawings, we shall recall that syntactically, the axes are juxtaposed to the women's abdomens, the vicinity of their wombs, but as the instruments of confinement they also subordinate the "clause" of Elsje's body. In the frontal drawing, the axe wards off attempts from outside to bring the body to life by gaining access to it – "she is dead" – whereas in the profile drawing, the axe prevents the body from coming to life, from speaking, from saying "I am dying." What is warded off, in both cases, is the theatricalization of this death.

Oddly, in warding off theatricalization, these two Elsje drawings allude to two aspects of theatricalization. Alpers, among many others, rightly points out that the public execution of criminals and the subsequent display of their dead bodies were meant as an exemplum, a moral lesson to the public. In that sense, they were part of a theatricalization of guilt whose ritual character was meant to exorcize evil from the public. "Rembrandt," however, interiorized this display, thus interiorizing both the guilt and the gender of the culprit. As display, the dead woman is utterly theatrical, but the theatrical setting has been voided. This affects the narrative mode and makes it paradoxical in its turn, again making narration and description compete.

These drawings, Alpers (1988:79) writes, display a kind of descriptive ambition. Description is supposed to be the mode that differentiates still states from narrative events, and outer from inner. In a way we can say it differentiates death from life. Whereas narration represents events, including inner events like thoughts and emotions, description represents exterior, perceptible states. This makes description doubly unfit for the representation of death as experience, in spite of its fitness for representing still states. Yet Alpers is right in her diagnosis of these drawings as descriptive, despite the fact that they are obviously about death as more than an outer state. For description is used here as the mode that helps bridge the gap between the evenemential yet inner "I am dying" and the descriptive yet outer "she is dead," thus getting as close as possible to the impossible "I am dead" through the interiorization of guilt. Description, then, serves here to moderate the inner experience and the outer display, turning the drawings into uniquely self-divided wholes.

Through this mediation the ritual is stripped of the exorcizing effect that would block the identification. By diverting the temporal mode of narrative, which proposes the ritual identification as a provisional rite of passage, to the descriptive stillness, stripped of this reassuring temporality, death is ambiguously between state and event. As with the affect of melancholia, the guilt-ridden death of the other is turned inward, thus killing, threatening to kill, or at least affecting, the "I."

DEATH AS STILL LIFE

Description in painting is best isolated in the genre of still life. With still life as a cotext, then, we should be able to reach a different way of looking at the "effect of death"[27] in the highly theatrical murder of Iphigenia (Figure 10.3).[28] For one thing, the stiffness of the victim's body, the sense that her death has both already been accomplished (she is dead) and is being staged (I shall die), make the drawing shift genres, from history to still life. This shift makes sense in that in an obvious way, still life is about death: about dead objects, about lifeless display, about mortality.

There are almost no still lives in "Rembrandt." But the works we are focusing on in this chapter come closest through the exteriorization of the exemplum of death on display, traditionally represented in *vanitas* still lives but also perhaps in those works where display encompasses death by definition, the luxurious tables of *Pronk-stillevens*. Those categories are limited in the representation of displayed bodies of criminals in the Elsje drawings and, of course, also in the anatomies discussed below. In still life, all traces of human life are obliterated, and it is only in the very radicalness of their excision that those traces may be read back into that most descriptive of painterly modes. This is how narrative returns into description; it returns as the repressed.[29] The Judges drawing of Figure 10.1 and the play with lines overruling realistic life gain more depth from this perspective.

When read as a literalization of the idea of still life, the drawings of Elsje come close to the slaughtered oxen. And thus, by metonymic implication, they come close to the subject of slaughter, to the butcher, as well as to the subject of display, to the law. By means of metonymy, the representation of the law as butcher, and of butchery as the display of its result, brings the experience of death closer to visual experience. The butchery, for visual display, of the woman in Judges 19 exemplifies the statement on visuality which these works suggest. The law, in turn, represents the social order that structures class difference and, hence, that need of *pronck* or ostentation.

Through the idea of still life, then, the active subject of sculpture in *The Goldsmith* returns as stilled-life's trace. The etching, although full of life, confines life within the stillness of the work of art. And it is this work of confinement, of death, that is, that provides the work with the sense of activity in the double work – making art and making life – of the represented subject. Display, the precondition of still life that turns the genre into a generic emblem becomes itself staged death. Thus art is once more connected to death, this time on the level of its making.[30]

In agreement with Alpers's analysis, "Rembrandt" comes to the fore as both representative of tradition and maker of it. The skulls that decorate many of the traditional *vanitas* still-life paintings as a sign commemorating death function as a *mise en abyme*.[31] These skulls, in agreement with the function of this figure that never quite fits and thus tends to overflow the whole which it is supposed to summarize, can be seen either as redundant, since painting itself is intricately linked with death, or as highly significant, as something that overturns the work as a whole.

And what the skull does for a traditional still life, the hammer and the axe do for the etching and the drawings under consideration here. The sculptor's hammer, so practical, yet so symbolically phallic at the same time, as both a tool of art and a tool of life, fixes the sculpted woman onto the plate on which she will be displayed. The sense of confinement of the body read in the Elsje drawings is similarly emphasized and summarized by that tool, yet the hammer's significance is also supplemented with violence and thereby tainted with life, by the axes.

This notion of supplement, so vigorously actualized by Derrida in his acute analysis of Rousseau's *Confessions* in *Of Grammatology* (1976) challenges the hierarchy between whole and part, between work and detail, between central and peripheral concerns. Given this analysis, we are compelled to question the status of the tool as detail in all three works.[32] The sexual aspect (in the strictly visual sense) of the hammer, combined with the castrating connotation of the axe, raises the question of sexual identity that has lurked throughout the present investigation.

Sexual identity is itself both a "detail" and a totality at the same time, signified as it is in a tiny part which, as the synecdoche par excellence, in important ways stands for the whole of human identity in a culture based on binary opposition: a *mise en abyme*, which provides sight of, or insight into, the abyss of the representational urge. Sexual identity as *mise en abyme* is the figure of displacement that undermines the clarity of that very concept: What, in displacement, must be placed, what eliminated, for the prefix and the root to make sense? And what is the cost of such "dis-placement"? These questions bring us to the work that is in an important sense the dis-play of displacement: *The Slaughtered Ox.*

DEATH AS STAGE:
PAINT BECOME FLESH

A century ago, Eugène Fromentin put the ambiguity of still life thus apropos of "Rembrandt"'s *Slaughtered Ox* in the Louvre:

[It is] the flayed ox from the Louvre, whose exactness is so great and whose quality so extraordinary that this incomparable piece makes all still lives look pale... (my translation)[33]

Fromentin's language is astonishing. I have to wonder how exactness could be measured in this particular painting, and I stopped short at the relevant choice of the word "flayed" rather than "slaughtered." But more importantly, I was amused by the ambiguity of the words *morceau incomparable*, "incomparable piece," of which we might ask the author to which they refer, the piece of art or the piece of flesh. Significantly, the ambiguity allows both, and the comparison turns out negative for "all still lives" precisely because of that ambiguity. In addition, the metaphor "look pale" reverses the literal perspective of the comparison in a most colorful way: That it should be the representation of the pallor of death that makes still lives look pale in comparison suggests something of the killing power of this work.

Let us once again confront two works, finding that, in the gap left by the difference between these two similar works, the crucial effects emerge. The first *Ox*, now in Glasgow (Figure 10.7), is supposed to be a relatively early work, dated in the late 1630s, whereas the one in the Louvre (Figure 10.8) is dated 1655. The works are similar in their design and iconography, rather than in their execution, and that is why they make a good case for the argument of self-reflexivity.

Both works display the opened body and represent the naked flesh of death. The "personnel" is the same in each work: Both have a gigantic, dominating mass of dead flesh and a woman in the background, apparently a maid. The colors are also similar: Both paintings work with the colors of the pallor of death and of the blood of violence. Both works are paradoxical in that the substance of the body is emphasized as strongly as is its opened quality, although this paradox is not equally obvious in each. The compositions are more or less alike spatially: The direction of the "gibbet," and consequently of the body, does not brutally face the viewer. This receding direction does not spare us the sight of the dead body, however, but allows us to see the outside and the inside at the same time, thus working in the same way as the twisted lemon peel in still life. But dead flesh is very different from a lemon.

The two major differences I wish to focus on are the substance of paint and the distribution of semiotic labor between the members

10.7 *Slaughtered Ox* 1643(?), Bredius 458, panel, 73.3 × 51.8 cm (Glasgow Art Gallery and Museum)

of the "personnel." The first work is painted neither extremely "finely" nor extremely "roughly." As a consequence, the substance of the paint does not strike the eye, nor does the work of painting draw attention to itself. The work remains representational, realistic, in the way a "third person" novel without narratorial intrusions does. The deictic traces of the subject of representation, although never really absent, are secondary. The dead body is clearly circumscribed, and although it is flayed as much as its sister in Paris, the paint confines it like a skin. We see death as a given, not as a construct, so we can overlook it. Since it goes without saying, death does not impose itself.

Similarly, the maid is represented at work, turning away from us as well as from the corpse, as if her presence in the represented space were just a coincidence. She seems to be there merely as an

10.8 *Slaughtered Ox* 1655,
Bredius 457, panel, 94 × 69 cm
(Paris, Musée du Louvre)

effect of the real, as a token of "life" within the scene of death. She becomes the paradoxical female presence of still life that, according to Bryson, is repressed – no women are represented within the works – yet whose traces return in the very subject matter of the genre – food, domestic gear – which is the fruit of her activity, of her life. She has to be in the background, so as to be part of the display. The spatial continuity between her body and the mass of flesh is slightly troubling, especially since she, too, has her head down and her bottom up, but this can easily pass unnoticed.

In terms of the stage, the dead body could be an element of the decor, the maid a figurant, leaving the stage itself void of the main figures: the butcher, and/or the subject of "I am dead." And although the contiguity between the body of the maid and the dead body could make an imaginative viewer shiver, the activity of work obscures the syntagm "she is dead" which is so predominant in the Judges and the Elsje drawings.

On the other hand, the stage of this scene is empty in a disquieting way. For the play of display, there are remarkably few actors on stage. The space looks empty, and this emptiness is part of the bareness that the dead and emptied body displays. Nothing really happens, and nothing can happen, as the stage is almost void of props, actors, and narrative. It is almost empty, but not quite. In the right-hand corner of the stage is a heap of clothes, unnecessary and meaningless, which allow for an effect of the real, an effect of the stage, or an effect of fantasy. The very shapelessness of the heap facilitates projection of the forms we need to bring the stage to life: the clothes of dressing up – for the stage – or of undressing, the skin of the ox, the cloths used to clean up the blood.

If the Louvre painting is so much more famous, it is primarily because of the daring roughness of the handling of the paint, which allows for different interpretations. In spite of the directness, the imposing quality of this paint, it is possible to shy away from this paint's radical implications. For example, it has been interpreted as expressive, evocative; Alpers rightly points out that Soutine obviously reoriented the motif in his *Flayed Ox* of 1939 in this way. By implication she claims that Soutine was blind to the imposing self-referentiality of paint handling which, as the French say, *crève les yeux*, "pierces the eye." This should not surprise us: We know from our reflections on blind fathers that what pierces the eye also blinds. And we know from Freud's metaphor of the name of regions on a map as well as from Lacan's (1988) analysis of the "Purloined Letter" that the overly visible can become invisible. The drawing of the *Entombment* (Figure 10.9) similarly foregrounds Jesus' head so much that it becomes invisible.

Soutine, then, despite his strong response to the paint handling, behaves like Poe's Prefect who is too scrupulous and too invested in discursivity not to be blind to the visual. He has treated the impasto as if it were a "third person" narrative mode: Displacing the relationship between the work and its subjectivity, hence also, his subjectivity, he took the work as expressing *something else*, as expressing the corpse, rather than itself.

But there is more to the interpretation of expressiveness than just offering a different viewpoint. Evocative painting is not just different from constructive, self-referential painting; it is its opposite. Evocativeness thus stands for elusiveness, avoidance of realism, possibly avoidance of the crude reality of death; it is a token of death, rather than its spelling out. In other words, on the level of textuality (rather than fabula), Soutine has looked at the Louvre *Ox* as if it were the Glasgow ox.

In contrast, a self-referential interpretation raises the question of the relationship between this painting-self and the representation of death. It is not enough to claim that the case of art as work dictated the "rough" mode. The substance of the paint is also the substance of death. And the substance of death is dead, stinking flesh. What we have to deal with – what the work does not spare us from – is the effect of the putrifying smell of paint. The medium of overcoming death, which painting was in the age of portraiture, becomes here the medium of overcoming the nonrepresentability of death.

The substance of paint as flesh affects every aspect of the dead body. The roughness not only conveys the making of the work; it also loosens the boundaries of the body – its outside – conveying the fusion that is inherent in rotting. The flesh represented, therefore, stinks, and its stench contaminates the representation itself. We can criticize here one relationship to gender: the relationship

10.9 *Entombment* ca. 1640, Benesch 482, drawing (Amsterdam, Rijksprentenkabinet)

386

established by the doxa. Whereas masculinity tends to stand for clarity, boundaries, and separateness, femininity tends to be related to fusion, transgression, and connectiveness. In addition, whereas the relatively "neutral" brushwork in the Glasgow piece allowed us to differentiate between inside and outside of the body, the Louvre work exposes dead flesh on both sides. This is why Fromentin's word "flayed" is so appropriate: The opened body is openness itself. It is literally the body turned inside out; there is no outside left; all we see is inside. Instead of being inside a butcher-shop, we are within a body. The position of the maid partakes of the same effect. The reassuring distinctness of the maid from the ox in the early work secures boundaries: She is alive; it is dead. The seamless contiguity between the two bodies in the Louvre painting disturbs this neat division.

From this perspective, it is meaningful that the butchered body in the earlier work is more filled, less empty than in the later work. As it is also slightly more removed from the spectatorial plane, the confrontation with dead flesh is decidedly less emphatic and less self-imposing there. That the increase of the substance of dead flesh comes with an increase of emptiness, hence a decrease of *represented* substance, only makes the case for self-referentiality more convincing. This increase-cum-decrease is a "dis-play": a display that unplays the fabula of the play.

The emptiness of the body in the Louvre painting is emphasized in yet another way. In the lower part of the body are two pins or nails. As Dessons (1987) points out, these nails are not necessary for fixing the body to the stand; that is taken care of by the ropes with which it is attached at the top. The body is in fact hanging freely – in contrast to Elsje's confined body. The nails' function, then, is to hold the body open. Although the body in the other work is equally open, there are no nails there. Apparently, the nails are not necessary for a realistic effect. And since they do not serve an effect of the real, they may be assigned an effect of openness. But they also entail an effect of violence, bringing the work one step closer to a crucifixion.

The nails emphasize the openness of the body which is not really greater in this work, but which is represented more self-consciously. It is in this framework that the decrease of represented substance functions to increase deadness. The body is here an empty body, and this emptiness is elaborated by the nails, which dis-play the inside of the body, and the nothingness it reveals. And as Dessons remarks, what body could be more appropriate for representing the nothingness inside the body than the castrated, degendered ox. But degenderedness is not exactly what the castrated body represents. Nor is castration a degendering concept.

The maid is not working in this painting. Or rather, she is not working as maids do, cleaning up the blood of the massacre. Yet she is active, more active in a sense than the other one. Whereas the other maid is doing the work that defines her in a timeless present, this maid's intrusion on the scene is a narrative event. The one maid is described, the other narrated. The first is a figurant, the second a character, perhaps even the main character.

This character is looking or trying to look. The intensity of her effort to see is emphatic, but the direction of her look is unclear, her eyes empty; she narrativizes the work by bending her head. Her eyes are not quite focused on the dead flesh. She also seems to look at the viewer, but does not do that quite clearly either. Her eyes are intense, yet empty, no less empty than the eyes of the father in the *Prodigal Son* or of so many other figures in "Rembrandt," where "looking" is a problematic activity. Between state and event, emptiness is narrated here.

Although the maid's head is fully represented, her body is not quite so clear. Owing to the typically Dutch double door, she seems to be cut off beneath her bosom, at the beginning of her belly. The white apron that makes the top of her belly protrude disappears in the dark background farther down. But where her body ends, that of the ox begins. There is contiguity here again, but this time the contiguity is more problematic to process, less easy to ignore, than in the other work. The similarity in position between the maid and the ox in the earlier work is replaced here by complementarity. Where the outer representation of her body recedes, the gigantic inner body seems to take over. Here the opened inside replaces the woman's body, the emptiness of the ox's body representing the womb: Only announced, alluded to by the woman's apron, it "pierces the eye" in the dead body. This is how this work is, in a complex sense, on dis-play. Death is, here, the very stage on which gender and representation exchange roles.

"She is dead": It has been stated already in the drawings, but here the staging of death reaches a more disturbing proximity. For the woman looks at the viewer, while also, through the emptiness of her eyes, she takes on an iconic relationship of signification with the empty body. In other words, she becomes "us" while becoming "it." If the viewer is willing to go along with this effect, the miracle is accomplished, and the painting says: "I am dead." But as this statement requires the violent representation of emptiness – through the nails – simultaneously with the radical representation of decay – through the substance-in-fusion of rotting flesh – it can be said only in the grammar of emptiness, in the feminine form.

THE STAGE OF DEATH:
DIS-REPRESENTATION AND MASTERY

The miracle accomplished in the Louvre *Ox*, however, leaves one dimension unexplored. Although staged, the representational event and its uncanny effect remain unaffected by reality, as if confined to the unconscious. The toll taken by their radical statement on representation of (or as) gendered death is an abstraction from the social construction of reality, albeit a concretely necessary one. To be sure, such an abstraction is part of the "argument": The centrality of the secrecy of the empty female body is necessary in order to challenge representation. In addition, both *Ox* panels partake of the display of still life, a display that cannot be detached from the social context of class and gender; both are put on display through being dis-played. These maids, thus, foreground these works as socially anchored. Yet, in a way, these two works, staged as they are in a liminal, intermediate space, position death outside of life. The limbo of the dark stable seems as far removed as possible from the theater of social life. The unreality of the maid in the second work, who seems cut in half just as the husband in the Judges drawing was crossed out, contributes to this impression. The husband was crossed out by a line so that he became merely lines, pure representation; so, too, is the maid here cut through by the metonymy of the gigantic, blown-up version of her body. However, the isolation of the woman and her "other half" on the stage of death obliterates the radical contrast between death and life, between dead

10.10 *The Anatomical Lesson of Dr. Nicolaes Tulp* 1632, Bredius 403, canvas, 169.5 × 216.5 cm (The Hague, Mauritshuis)

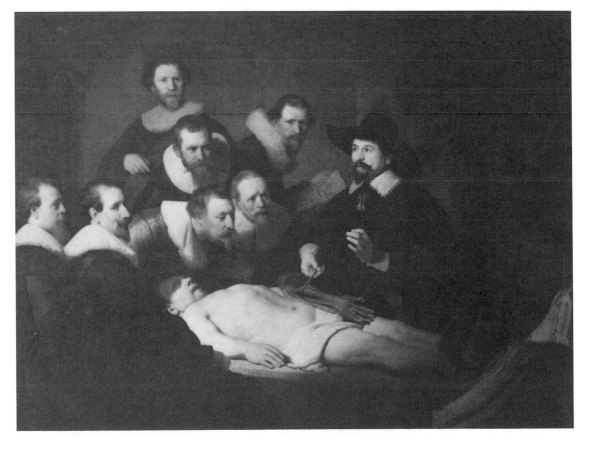

flesh and the life of the masterful manipulation of representation, leaving a vacuum of meaning.

This vacuum leaves the potential subject of the statement "I am dead" a place to which to withdraw – a paradigmatic space that lacks historical syntagm, for the present tense and the first person leave a third deictic dimension, the "here" of reality, which is signified in relation to the second person. The second person is the metonymic extension of the subject, against which the subject needs to be defined, demarcated, and confined. This dimension is highlighted in a final pair of works, where the dis–play of death and self-representation are staged in the social theater of mastery, but where the genderedness so uncannily foregrounded in the late *Ox* is repressed. As an alternative, imperfect yet powerful representation of death and of representation, the *Anatomical Lesson*s of Dr. Tulp (1632; Figure 10.10) and Dr. Deyman (1656; Figure 10.11) allow us to bring the present reflection to a conclusion.

The *Anatomies* are in an obvious way about death. Yet the very qualities that defined death in the Louvre *Ox* – the genderization and the loosening of boundaries – seem less obvious here. In neither *Anatomies* is the paint handling particularly striking, and the social

10.11   *The Anatomical Lesson of Dr. Jan Deyman* 1656, Bredius 414, canvas, 100 × 134 cm (Amsterdam, Rijksmuseum)

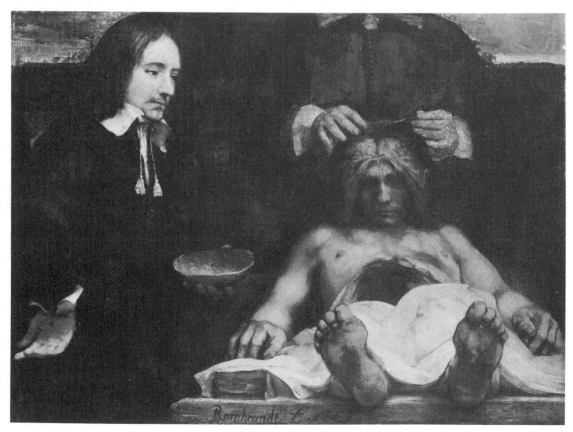

setting, although suggesting the stench of death, does not emphasize the force of the representation, the stench of painting. These works share with the *Ox* panels the two colors of death – pallor and blood – as well as the shape of death – bodily openness. But unlike the *Ox* panels, the corpses being dissected are human; in each of the *Anatomies* the place, meaning, and function of the open wound differ. But as we shall see, these differences are complementary.

The *Anatomies* are representations of a conventionalized theatrical event. And although this study's goal is not historical reconstruction, the very problematic of the *hic et nunc* at stake in this section requires that we position the works in relation to the conventions. I wish to emphasize, however, that the place of historical considerations in these reflections is strictly circumscribed, limited to the construction of a reading of the works in which "history" is represented. This limitation is necessary if we are to avoid projecting present-day concerns onto a past that can exist only as the confluence of "givens," along with the urges and desires of the interpreter. As Foucault formulated it:

History protects us from historicism – from the historicism that calls on the past to respond to questions of the present. (In David Couzens Hoy, ed., 1986:250)

This clarified, let us look at the tradition of public anatomies, the very conventional character of the scene represented in the *Anatomies* inevitably forming part of the way we read such works.

The festive anatomies of the seventeenth century were theatrical performances: performances where actors played fixed roles, where the public watched, thrilled, "willing to suspend disbelief," an attitude that characterizes the processing of fiction, and paying an entrance fee as part of the social ritual and selection that comes with "art." But these anatomies were theatrical, also, in an older sense: They carried with them the meaning of the antique theater in three respects.

First, they were ritualistically structured; the order of events was fixed, with the opening of the thorax being routinely the first step. It is significant that the *Tulp* shows a different order: Here the hand is being dissected while the thorax is still intact. This deviation from the ritual routine only works to emphasize the self-reflexive meaning of this handling of the hand. Second, as we noticed earlier apropos the Elsje drawings, the anatomy was also part of the public exorcism of guilt. Thus it had or was meant to have an effect similar to that of catharsis in Greek tragedy. In his monograph *Rembrandt's "Anatomy of Dr. Nicolaas Tulp,"* William S. Heckscher (1958:8) ascribes this conventional effect to the anatomies, relating it to the ritualistic character of the event:

[T]he corpse [was] so callously displayed before the eyes of fascinated spectators, each one of whom felt, dumbly or inarticulately, that he witnessed a cathartic ritual enacted for his own good.

The key notion here is *fascination* – a concept often related to Greek drama, originally conveying the dumbfounded petrification of horror and attraction at the same time. The term refers to the impossibility of detaching one's gaze from the spectacle which, however much good it does, initially petrifies like Medusa's head.[34] Fascination related to primal visual experience, is, then, a gendered concept, as well as a narrative concept, referring as it does to the blockage of narrative that results in description. Thus fascination turns vision into something both vital and annihilating; it is a form of death itself presented as necessary and good.

A third aspect of the public anatomies was the successive *nomination* of the organs, thereby turning the corpse into a text, into a descriptive discourse as Philippe Hamon (1981) defined it: as a syntagmatic articulation of the paradigmatic *nomenclature*. The ritual of circumscription of the body by nomination of its parts comes close to a discursive form of fascination: Not only is the eye attached to and absorbed in the corpse; the ear is, too. This connectedness of vision and language in the display strictly speaking defines the event as theater. In the *Tulp* the intense stares of all the figures, combined with the emphatic presence of books, of book knowledge, of book reading, can be read as referring to this generic theatricality which doubles the pictorial theatricality.

According to Dessons, the dissection of a female corpse was an even greater attraction. Given the urge toward catharsis that informed this attraction, we can see that the connection between display and gender we saw earlier would then be confirmed in this convention as well. Discounting the frightening aspects and the negative view of women implied here, Dessons sees in the *Anatomies* a "contexte de drague," a context of erotic pursuit. Heckscher quotes a contemporary text which shows that this link was overtly appealed to. The fragment is worth quoting here again, because it evokes a concatenation of preoccupations – vision and language; sex and power; money and art; sex and death – all of which have recurred throughout this study, and in the preceding section in particular. The text plays on the location – the *hic* – of the anatomical theater, across the street from a meat hall (Heckscher, 1958:31).[35]

The two meat halls which you see here are well equipped with beautiful "meat," beautiful inside and out, and so much of it that one hardly knows where it all goes. Come on, little ladies, please come spending your money here, buy as much as your heart desires. From this kind of "flesh" a husband won't grow horns. Who enters pure will exit pure as well. Do you desire to know what people are there upstairs? Those are the surgeons who make fresh wounds and who are trained in the noble art. At the same time this is a peaceful meeting place of Rhetoricians. The ones show the wounds in the human body, the others try to cure the soul.

By an amusing coincidence, the meat hall and the anatomical theater link our two sets of paintings to each other. In a sense, the description fits the Louvre *Ox* better than it fits the *Anatomies*. The exhilirating explicitness with which flesh and meat – dead and live flesh, that is – are juxtaposed suggests that the denial that the former will make husbands grow horns is meant to be taken "Freudially" as suggesting its opposite. The "fresh wounds" made by the un-specified "noble art" (of medicine or of love?) could then sound almost appealing rather than repulsive.

There is no dissection of a female corpse in "Rembrandt," at least not literally. But it may be worthwhile to consider gender when examining the differences between the early and the late *Anatomies*, while also keeping in mind the similarities between the anatomical theater and its private counterpart, the butcher's stable.

The *Tulp* has been subject to more extensive analyses and inter-pretations than the *Deyman*.[36] Considered the artist's first com-missioned painting, the *Tulp* appears to have been an instant success – a historical feat in the artist's social construction of self – whereas only a fragment of the *Deyman* remains. This difference makes a juxtaposed reading difficult, of course, at the same time that it also accounts for the less vigorous interest this work raises. But as we have seen with the *Claudius Civilis*, the reduction of format can also yield particularly insistent effects.

Both works are reassuring as well as unsettling paintings. The *Tulp* demonstrates both the mastery over death and death as a source of knowledge. The surgeon being the *other* within the artist, the other artist, or the *you* in relation to whom the subject of painting is positioned, this mastery is irretrievably elsewhere. The generalized looking focuses and disperses the addressed audience's attention, directing it toward a definite object yet away from the corpse. Fascination is combined with the impossibility of *facing* mastery over death. The surgeon's left hand, making the gesture of understanding, of subtle grasping – the gesture of holding and wielding the painter's brush, the knower's pencil, or the surgeon's knife – forms a triangle with the other two hands: One is his own right hand, the hand that actually makes the gesture rather than representing or imitating it; the other is the dissected hand of the corpse.

The surgeon here is unambiguously represented as holding a position of mastery: He masters the corpse, the doctors present and eager to learn, the public drawn in by the eager looking of one of the doctors – the only one of the tight group higher than Tulp, if I discount the badly integrated man in the back. But the intensity of this looking betokens as well as disperses Tulp's mastery. This looking narrativizes the scene, but concentrates that narrativization elsewhere, in the hand of the surgeon opening the body. What is unsettling, among many other things, is the narrativization of this demonstration of opening the body. Tulp is about to pull the corpse's muscles so as to make the dissected hand replicate – or figure – the surgeon's gesture; the surgeon is about to move beyond the domain of knowledge to that of action: He will make the corpse move, he will bring the corpse back to life. This must be the case if we are to be able to make sense of his left hand, a hand that bespeaks the surgeon's superhuman knowledge. This rivalry with the Divine Maker is also a competition with the artist solely capable of resolving the paradoxes of representation. No wonder the men watching this surgeon are holding their breath.

Dessons's (1987) essay was inspired primarily by this painting, a choice of focus that is fascinating, given the fact that the main theme of the book is the opening of the body. If this painting is of an anatomy, it presents the dead body as remarkably closed. The fleshy belly and thighs have a substance that is as far removed as possible from the Louvre *Ox*. The flesh is not rotting at all. The skin is intact except for the arm which is clearly set off from the rest of the body both by its color and by its disproportioned size.

The emphasis on the navel, the site of the body's closure, is an emphasis on this closedness. But then, the navel is a significant detail: This work is the only one of all the works discussed here where the represented navel coincides with the textual navel of the work. As we have seen, the navel is the site of bodily closure, but also the scar of bodily openness. It is the scar of birth that connects primary narcissism with the anxiety of openness, with the vagueness of the birth fantasy. That the navel in this work exemplifies both clarity and closure is an interesting appropriation of primary narcissism in favor of mastery. The boundaries between dead corpse and live doctors is clear-cut so to speak, in terms of both composition and color.

When writing briefly on the *Deyman*, Dessons finds that later work less daring. What is he repressing? To uncover this we must examine Dessons's fascination for the *Tulp*, which is buried under his philosophical interpretation, an interpretation that serves to repress his fascination. He writes:

In the form of a double experience, painting and classical philosophy are situated together in the domain of metaphysics, the one stating that the body is a text, the other that the text is a body. (my translation)[37]

Time and again he verges on the (in)sight of the "indecency" of the *Ox* as well as the *Deyman*. Thus he speaks of the white and red stuff that fills the "abdominal (and abominable) cavity" of the *Ox*. Yet ultimately, Dessons turns the *Tulp*, and by extension the series of works on the opened body, into a statement on art alone, stripping it of its disquieting references to the issues at stake in the death works altogether. In order to open up his closing statements into a more complex perspective on the fascination these works exercise, I shall in my turn wind up through this text.

The reason for Dessons's blindness, and for my discussion of it, becomes obvious when we juxtapose two quotes, one on the *Ox* and one on the *Tulp*. Speaking of the maid in the Louvre *Ox*, whose deadly, because intransitive, look he has just evoked, he writes:

Her indefinite status: she does not have the social authority of the surgeons of Amsterdam, and her ambiguous status: half visible, she is half hidden, inscribing the painting within the violation of a taboo. (my translation)[38]

In contrast to this guilty violation of clarity that comes with the opening of the body in slaughter, in sex, and in representation, the *Tulp*, a bit gratuitously related to *jouissance* because dealing with the body, becomes an exemplary discursive representation:

Model for the discourse on death and on *jouissance*, model . . . for the constitution of a writing of the body, the surgical practice proposes for the painter a model of manipulation, where the right usage of the hand is *figuring, not decomposing.* (my translation, my emphasis)[39]

Figuring, when opposed to decomposing, not only stands for design, for drawing, as opposed to paint handling that is so central for "Rembrandt"; it also stands for writing, insofar as drawing is so much closer to writing than paint handling. Strangely enough, what Dessons is doing here in his essay on the body is trying to get rid of what "Rembrandt" proposes as the *body* of representation in favor of an unfleshed writing. This move is disturbing, as it allows Dessons to revert to an old version of the word–image opposition that privileges the word. If we look at the impasto paintings – in which Alpers draws attention to the uncanny thickness of the blood on the wound of the second *Lucretia*, for example – the *Anatomies* can hardly compete with these in power of representation. Against Dessons, then, I would contend that decomposing *is* the right usage of the hand, and if only the social authority of the surgeons could be integrated into the physical authority of the inside of the female body, we could have surmounted the last remnant of resistance, a resistance that hampered the representation of death as it hampered an understanding of representation beyond the word–image opposition. This resistance resides in the social place as source of knowledge, as the model of art.

This surmounting of a limited, superficial concept of the social as the model of art is accomplished in the *Deyman*. It is often noted that the opened abdomen demonstrates that this anatomy progressed conventionally, but that the surgeon is dissecting not the body but the brain.[40] Obviously, this is true. It is also true, however, that this either/or schema might obscure an important connection between the two body parts – and what they stand for. The dark red cavity of the abdomen is symmetrical with the yellowish substance of the brain. Not only are they of the same size and shape; the latter would nicely *fit inside* the former. If we recall the two colors of the substances in the *Ox*, it becomes possible to read this complementarity of form as another token of self-referentiality.

This can be done when we take the theatricality of this scene at its word. The figuration on the dissection stage is a triangle, not a binary opposition. For the doctor on the left is an important participant in the cast. Attentively looking *into the cavity*, he is respectfully and subserviently holding the basin of the skull. This cup is commented upon by his left hand which figures its shape in a striking pose. The skull cup is juxtaposed to the abdomen as its metonymical metaphor, and thus it draws attention to the importance of looking as a rhetorical device of figuration.

This brings us to the eyes of the dead man. The eyes of the corpse are shadowed, invisible; and the aggressive directness of the pose – the arms, feet and head turned toward the theater's absent fourth wall – allow us to imagine that the corpse itself is looking – at the viewer. The body is thus inscribed with indices of ambiguity: Iconically signifying death, it carries an index of possible life. In a similar way, the body, although on one level clearly male, carries an index of femininity: The left breast looks quite fleshy. Death loosens gender boundaries, but in the same way as the Louvre *Ox* which the immense abdominal cavity recalls here.

The confrontational pose of the cadaver can be read in two distinct ways. In the first place, the body's pose is an iconographic rewriting of Christ after his descent from the cross. But it can be read in this way only because of the frontal pose, which also foregrounds the index of femininity. Thus this work also iconographically feminizes Christ, just as *Samson's Wedding* did. "He" becomes inscribed with "she," a "she" that, as a truly Derridean supplement, cannot be removed without undermining the "he." In the second place, the pose draws the viewer into the work and draws the work into the experiential world of the viewer. What it works with is the opposition "I"–"you," now embedded in the "he" supplemented with "she." What we have here, then, is an integration of the *Ox* as the experience of death's intensity, through its collusion with femininity – "I–she am/is dead" – with the anatomy as the knowledge of death, its authority displaced elsewhere. The surgeon has been cut off, so that for the modern viewer, the "you" has merged into the "I." This effect did not, of course, occur when the painting was whole. But perhaps it is fortunate that it has been severed: Its intensity has been increased by the decrease of its size. Thus this work which Dessons does not see, accomplishes what the author himself writes toward the end of his essay, apropos of the programmatic quality of the *Tulp* but in important ways *mal à propos*:

[It was necessary that] the subject be no more the practice of mimesis, but painting itself in its materiality and its gestures, its libidinal relations with the painting subject. It was necessary to make a painting where the subject [was] no more defined as an act of imitation, in allegiance with the order of the sign, but as a conflictual subject, taken in a double relation to the social and the unconscious. (my translation)[41]

What this work and, by extension, all the death works suggest is precisely this *conflict within* that, in the age of Descartes and the great anatomies, inaugurated modern representation; this double relation is not a matter of juxtaposition, but contemporary theory has a good deal of trouble not keeping it confined within an opposition. To escape such a dichotomy, we may take the Louvre *Ox* as a pre-text for the *Deyman*, and then use it as a commentary by which to read the earlier *Tulp* as a work struggling to shun the genderedness of death and of (its) representation. If we accept what this reading of "Rembrandt" suggests, what will become of the mastery of painting beyond the social mastery of the surgeon?

CONCLUSION

> En peinture comme en morale, il est bien dangereux
> de voir sous la peau. (Denis Diderot)

For Foucault, death is the key to reading.[42] According to the works examined in this chapter, this key opens the body of a practice of painting that is as far removed as possible from discursive writing, yet highly discursive in its own way. On the one hand, the "rough" style of painting moves away from the pencil of design toward a representation of substance, where touch and vision tend to coincide. On the other hand, the self-reflexivity this practice incorporates makes statements assertively that only discourse can try to grasp in their full complexity.

Death ends life, and thereby makes life meaningful. Thus it subverts the sequentiality of life, of discourse, and of history, while lending all three meaning. The mutual need that visual and discursive representation display, even in their polemical attempts to claim priority for one or the other, makes death an appropriate metaphor for representation. Van Gogh, that brilliant painter and writer, knew this when he wanted to paint "something voluptuous and grievously afflicting," once more indicating the closeness of death, representation, and gender.

Indeed, by virtue of death's signifying impact on life, it cannot be less gendered than the latter. Subverting the order of events and the distinction between state and events, the end – death – recasts the beginning of life – birth. And birth is the painful moment where the relevance of gender is magnified by the might of the mother like the body of the *Ox*. The most acute representation of this deadly painfulness I have discussed in this study is, of course, *The Blinding of Samson*, but other works suggest the same.

Gender is not just motherhood, although the overwhelming motherhood in birth marks each subject until death – the navel being the scar remaining to remind the subject of birth. Motherhood is a gender position that marks both men and women alike. Throughout life, gender strikes us unexpectedly, wounding us incurably. Merging social doxa, unconscious structure, and punctual experience, gender also merges the actants of fantasy, the actors of role playing, and the individuals of the varying moments of a life history. Sensitive to the complexities of gender between s/he, you, and I, "Rembrandt" confronts the viewer with a discontinuous,

397

apparently incoherent, practice of representation through gender. Perplexity in the face of this ever changing vision, and fascination in the face of the total hostility and the total identification, have informed much of the preceding reflection. The dialectic, or dialogic, interplay between visual and discursive aspects alone allowed us, at times, to creep beneath the skin of painting, according to Diderot a dangerous endeavor. And in agreement with the death works, what I found beneath that skin was a world where "Rembrandt" and I – *s/he* and *I* – could no longer be distinguished. And *I* and *you* are in turn exchangeable positions, so that *you* are contaminated by *s/he*. That is all for the good, for I have tried to take *you* along into this realm of suspended distinctions beyond the word–image opposition.

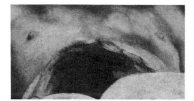

NOTES

INTRODUCTION

1. See Salomon's interpretation of this painting. See also Mary Jacobus's fascinating discussion of Raphael's *Sistine Madonna*, with reference to the Arezzo *Pregnant Madonna* of Piero della Francesca. Jacobus discusses the Raphael as it is read by Freud's patient Dora. See "*Dora* and the Pregnant Madonna," in Jacobus's *Reading Woman* (1986).

2. When speaking of literary history, Culler (1988:xv) phrases the problem in the following way:

    If history is the name of the discrepancy between intention and occurrence, then literary theory has a pertinent model to hand in its debates about the problematical relation between meaning as intentional act (of a writer or reader) and meaning as textual fact (the product of grammatical, rhetorical, textual, and contextual structures).

3. See especially White's essay "Interpretation in History" (1978). Emphasizing the impossibility of reaching "pure" historical knowledge is not the same thing as denying that historical events really occurred. The knowledge of the events, the possibility of describing them outside of the present and hence of ascertaining their significance, are what is questioned, not their having really occurred.

4. See Martin Jay (1988), Svetlana Alpers (1985), and T. J. Clark (1985).

5. The phrase is Griselda Pollock's. She used it to explain her view of the social history of art during the N. E. H. Summer Institute on "Theory and Interpretation in the Visual Arts" in 1989.

6. Among recent reader-oriented studies of visual art I mention here only two: Kemp, ed., *Betrachter* (1985), a collection of essays representing various approaches of the reader; and Freedberg, *Power* (1989), a sustained effort to analyze the effect of images from a number of different angles.

7. See Silverman (1988) and Penley (1989). Both of these authors juxtapose avant-garde and popular films. See also the work of Anneke Smelik (e.g., 1989), who analyzes popular feminist films. This is another way of undermining the opposition insofar as the opposition rests on the unwarranted and often implicit assumption that high art is subversive whereas popular art is ideologically damaging.

8. In my work on literature I have myself mainly, though not exclusively,

contributed to a rereading and critique of the male canon. But what I then set out to do is not to critique those works and dismantle their inherent sexism, but to argue that although no less sexist than the culture they stem from, these works tend to be misread in a way that obscures even the symptomatic signs of struggle with the sexism they cannot but display. I will pursue a similar goal here: Although on many occasions I will situate "Rembrandt" as just another case in a broadly male-oriented culture, I will *at the same time* argue that we make it worse than it need be. Thereby, we miss the opportunity to use these prestigious works to make statements about gender relations – statements that can be more productive than constant denunciation.

9. In fact, the same strategy should be followed for other names of authors. I have refrained from doing so to avoid burdening the text with too many signs of self-consciousness, which might hamper a pleasant reading. Since "Rembrandt" is the main focus of this study, that name cannot possibly be written unproblematically.

10. The library comes closest. But although the purchase of books for a library surely partakes of the exclusions inherent in gathering, the distinction between the museum's display and storerooms is unparalleled. The National Gallery in Washington, D.C., went so far as to remove a challenged "Rembrandt" from the exhibition rooms, thus bowing to the authority of the scholars, rather than leaving it to the public to decide whether a disattributed "Rembrandt" is still worth seeing or not.

11. For a subtly dialectic view of the relation between Freudian theory and the Sophoclean model, see Verhoeff (1984).

12. An overview of this discussion is offered by Culler (1981).

13. Culler's argument can be found in "Stories of Reading," in *On Deconstruction* (1983).

14. See Ernst van Alphen (1988b), ch. 6, for a full account of the problem of reading. A shorter version in English appears in a special (1989) issue of *VS Versus* on reading. That issue also has other important contributions on the problem at issue here.

15. Rosi Braidotti (1991) makes this point when speaking of the problematic relationship between feminism and philosophy. Her argument does not compel us, of course, to return to the authoritarian practice that the poststructuralist argument rightly discarded. Instead, the challenge we are facing is to embrace the vulnerability of interpretation, arguing for a more democratic and critical practice of it, a practice in which its status is radically changed.

16. If we want to assess to what extent we can circumscribe the signifying units called signs and understand our dealings with them, we must delimit the field of signs and meanings in two directions. At one extreme there are the subsemiotic technical aspects of the works of art. Although they all contribute to the construction of signs, stylistic variation, light and dark, composition, or more technical aspects like brushstrokes, paint thickness, and lines are not, a priori, signs in themselves; not any more than in a literary text sheer ink on the page, mere punctuation marks, and syntactic structures are. Although they are part of what make us interpret the work, we do not give them meaning in themselves, except in some truly special cases (cf. Meyer Shapiro's attempt to theorize the sign status of these subsemiotic elements).

At the other extreme, there are the suprasemiotic holistic aspects of the works. Although there has been a tendency to conflate the concepts of "text" and "sign," and, by extension, of "work" and "sign," I think such a conflation only displaces the problem of what kinds of encounters signs and meanings are. This conflation has an unexpected and unfortunate consequence.

The consequence of such a position is that the compound sign will be subdivided into discrete units, and this division will become a gesture at best either of articulation or of slicing up, delimiting, what supposedly adds up in the whole. This subdivision is held more acceptable for verbal than for visual art; indeed, the distinction between the two is often based on the very assumption that verbal works are composed of discrete units whereas visual works are "dense." The distinction is deceptively self-evident and can be deconstructed only by reversing it and arguing that to some extent verbal texts are dense – the sign of the effect of the real cannot be distinguished from the work as a whole on which it sheds a specific meaning – and that visual texts are discrete, which sometimes, and in some respects, they are. The distinction is untenable, but it nevertheless reflects different attitudes of reading that operate conventionally for each art. Attempts to assign to verbal details whose point is not obvious the function of producing an effect of the real or an effect of verisimilitude can be seen as efforts to promote a reading of verbal art that seems more appropriate for visual art.

17. In the *Tractatus Logico-Philosophicus* (1921), Wittgenstein gives a visual dimension to verbal propositions and regrets language's cloudiness, thus suggesting that density is by definition visual, which it is not. In the later *Philosophical Investigations* (1953), he rejects his nostalgia for purity in the early work and argues that language is no less dense than pictures are. Here, he endorses language's ambiguity as one of its most basic features. See Allen Thiher's *Words in Reflection* (1984), for an account of Wittgenstein's views of language for the transition and break between modernism and postmodernism in literature. The assumed visuality of language plays a key role in that change.

18. A clear example is the historical-critical school in Biblical scholarship, which holds an even more dogmatic position than iconography in art history. Historical-critical scholarship works from the premise that the texts that today form the canon of Biblical texts have been composed out of fragments of diverse "layers" of various origin. Convincing as the hypothesis is in itself, the following step – slicing up each text into "layers" that can each be assigned a place in the history of the text – does not make the least sense in terms of the hypothesis itself. "Separation of sources" may be the phrase preferred by the historical-critical school for this approach, but Edmund Leach's killing phrase "unscrambling the omelette," with its unwitting Lacanian overtones, is far more telling. See Richter (1963) for an example of the sterility of this approach which I critique extensively in my *Murder and Difference* (1988b). In more up-to-date semiotics, however, this accumulative concept of text is still vital. Among many examples, the meager results of Greimas's detailed analysis of a short story by Maupassant (Greimas, 1976) show the limits imposed by this fallacious approach.

19. *Dissemination* (1981) is not only one of Derrida's most intriguing and richest books, but it is also provided with a brilliantly clear introduction by Barbara Johnson.

1. This is true regardless of whether the challenge is real. Some of these challenges are meager attempts to safeguard art history by giving it a new coating of self-reflection, mainly by attacking prestigious "fore-fathers." See, as an example of this attitude, Rees and Borzello, *The New Art History* (1986).

2. This is even the case on the institutional level: If the College Art Association invited, as it did in 1988, an "alien" (Norman Bryson) to organize a panel on deconstruction in the visual arts, an "alien" approach to be introduced to the most important gathering of art historians in the United States, what happened was a recuperation, an embedding of deconstruction within art history, not a challenge put to it from the outside. By the same token, neither Bryson nor deconstruction can be considered outsiders.

3. Among the best known examples are Foucault (1973) and Searle on *Las Meninas* (1980); Bryson on French art; Buci-Glucksmann on Baroque art (1986); Marin on Poussin (1988).

4. See Bakhtin, *The Dialogic Imagination* (1981). Among the many recent studies of Bakhtin, the volume edited by Morson and Emerson (1989) can serve as a useful critical introduction.

5. The terms of Bloom's analysis as well as of Bryson's reorientation of it remain entirely Oedipal. As a consequence, the model does not make room for, nor does it explain the blatant absence of, women artist-emulators. Rather than rejecting the model, then, it should be refocused once more, and be used to explain how an Oedipally structured practice of the arts perpetuates the exclusions that an uncritical use of the theory would take for granted. Although he does not explicitly address this issue, Bryson's analytical practice is at times quite sensitive to it (e.g., his analysis of David's *The Oath of the Horatii* and *The Intervention of the Sabine Women* in *Tradition and Desire*).

6. This presentation is meant merely to place in context the subsequent discussion of the field and its approaches, not to assess and hierarchize the respective merits of these studies, let alone to judge the many relevant studies not mentioned here.

7. On the one hand, I emphasize that my "Rembrandt" study is basically *not* art historical because it is more reception-oriented, literary, and theoretical than historical, while it hardly inserts itself in the traditions of the discipline. Yet the works I engage with "belong" – if such a colonizing term can be appropriate – to the field of art history, and therefore, my disclaimer cannot be unqualified. On the other hand, then, I also feel the need to specify what I mean by "art history." By that I mean simply the whole range of activities of departments traditionally named so. This includes some sort of history – be it of the institution of art, including economic and social history; of particular works or styles, including the analysis of works, more or less emphatically placed historically; or of the discipline itself, in a kind of metahistory in the Hayden White fashion. The most interesting representative of the last approach seems to me Michael Holly (e.g., 1984, 1989, 1990). I agree with Holly that art history should not be distinguished from art analysis: No analysis can be entirely ahistorical, nor can historical explorations do without some sort of analysis of works. The term "art criticism," not exactly parallel to literary criticism,

usually refers, but shouldn't, to the more journalistic mode of review-ing art currently on exhibit. But this catches my own endeavor in a paradox. Although not art historical in the disciplinary sense, I cannot entirely disclaim allegiance to the term I just eliminated: art criticism, but then, on the model of academic literary criticism. And criticism cannot be outside of history. The historical dimension in this study, then, is primarily that of my position as a feminist academic in the 1980s, engaged with works that are historically double-edged: Orig-inating in an age long gone, they receive a new historical dimension as I focus on their functioning and their embeddedness in contemporary culture. If I cannot save myself from these aporetic dilemmas, it is a telling case of the Babelonian confusion that disciplinary boundaries and historical terminology entail.

8. This debate, which marked a turning point in art history's increasing involvement in interdisciplinarity, will be discussed extensively in Chapter 7.

9. Martin Jay (1988) adopts Alpers's distinction, and thus juxtaposes the descriptive mode as an alternative to, albeit in continuity with, per-spective, hitherto considered the sole dominant regime until the late nineteenth century. Alpers's historicism in this book can be charac-terized as social history, but only if one considers the visual culture, as she finds it, to have major social implications. I think it does, but these implications remain to be specified.

10. The term "doxa" refers to the unargued commonsensical assumptions about a story's meaning, in Bourdieu's (1977:168) terms. "the universe of the undiscussed."

11. This is emphatically my interpretation of Alpers's enterprise, not her own. Her goal is to define the *visual* culture in which Dutch art emerged, and, therefore, she argues against the emphasis on verbal sources (e.g, Alpers, 1988:xix). I would slightly rephrase this claim, which I find altogether problematic in light of the sources Alpers uses: She attempts to define the visual culture as it is laid down in verbal discourse about vision as well as visual images about the culture as a whole. Verbal discourse about vision is necessarily culturally framed by other discursive considerations – for example, philosophical, po-litical, and religious. Visual images make statements about their own status as record of a culture, but that status itself is heavily implicated within philosophical, political, and religious considerations. Thus phrased, neither the verbal sources nor the visual sources are "pure" of each other, and the visual culture is a *culture*, thus by definition, mixed.

12. It is with this view of Vermeer that I have implicitly taken issue in the introduction. Not that I think Alpers is wrong to see Vermeer as fitting in with a descriptive visual culture. Within the opposition she sets up, Vermeer is the best case she could have chosen. Rather, neither Vermeer nor for that matter the visual culture in question is as pure of narrative and other forms of discursivity as Alpers's very opposition suggests.

13. It seems significant to me that there is a parallel crisis in Biblical scholarship, where the historical-critical dogma hampers development. The so-called literary approaches to the Bible do not help, unfortu-nately, precisely because they do not engage with the state of the discipline, but simply reject it and position their novelty outside of it.

Alter and Kermode's *Literary Guide to the Bible* (1988) demonstrates the inherent sterility of such an attitude.

14. Alpers's view should not be overstated, at the risk of making it unnecessarily untenable. The suggestion that Rembrandt single-handedly invented capitalism is, of course, a gross overstatement. For Alpers, Rembrandt profited from a trend that he made more vital to the art world. I am not in a position to assess the exact historical merit of this view, and I am not interested in such an assessment. Rather, I find the attempt to view the works from the perspective of their making and dealing a productive innovation, a fruitful reading strategy.

15. The term "diegetic" comes from French narratology (Genette, 1980; Bal, 1985) and refers to the level of the represented objects – for narrative, a fabula consisting of actors and events – as distinct from the level of representation, where the specific ordering of the fabula elements yields the particular structure of the work. In painting, the depicted actions of the figures are diegetic, as are the figures themselves in relation to the events the actions constitute. In this study, the term rigorously refers to a level of analysis, not to a "real" thing, nor to a "deep structure" (in the linguistic sense). For example, the status of the nail and the hole in the Vermeer painting discussed in the introduction, is diegetic if we consider it part of the story of decorating the room or as one of the loci for emphasizing the sunlight; it is not diegetic when considered a trace of the painter's preparation of the studio, nor is it diegetic when related to the emphasis on balance as a visual issue. Similarly, the shower of gold in the *Danae* is diegetic when taken as a token of Zeus's invasion; it is not insofar as it is a form of illumination of the space. It is, however, diegetic, but within a different fabula, when taken as the locus of the viewer's enforced exit.

16. See, for example, Darrel Sewell's catalog for the 1982 exhibition (Sewell, 1982:38). I shall return to this issue later in this chapter.

17. Bryson's next book is now also available: *Looking at the Overlooked: Four Essays on Still-Life* (1989). I limit myself to the earlier books here.

18. See Hubert Damisch's monumental, indispensable study of perspective, *L'Origine de la perspective* (1987). Panofsky's famous essay, "Perspective as Symbolic Form" (1927), makes the same claim, but remains ambivalent.

19. The shortest text in which Peirce defines all three grounds can be found in Innis's (1984) collection. That text also demonstrates the difficulty of Peirce's idiosyncratic style of theorizing. I would like to emphasize, in keeping with my reader-oriented approach, that the three Peircean terms are best used to refer to grounds, not to signs; to the reason why a sign event occurs, not to a thing out there in the world. The interest of Holly's analysis does not lie in the truth of her claim, which could easily be used to disqualify the forerunners of cultural history in favor of a contemporary, more "scientific" history. Rather, it rests on the very possibility of interpreting these texts in such a way that fundamental questions arise regarding the possibility of keeping separate the visual and the discursive.

20. I am not sure that the concrete proposal should go under the name of materialism. I guess there is some sort of tradition-and-desire problematic at stake here. See also Bryson's article "Intertextuality and Visual Poetics" (1988).

21. Indeed, an attempt to do this was published by Louis Marin (1988).

Unfortunately, Marin fails to make the case, a failure that is due to a number of problems in his argument. Given the status of this article which has been often reprinted, I shall briefly enumerate these problems, most of which remain implicit and may easily pass unnoticed:

1. Marin subordinates the image to (the meaning of) the discourse.
2. He equalizes enunciation to looking, thus subordinating the addressee to the sender.
3. He lends superiority to *récit* over *discours*, to story over enunciation. The goal of representation then becomes transparency. "Meaning" becomes the ultimate and objective truth, while the sender is universalized. Emblematically, the word *ego* becomes for him the center of the visual text.
4. The term "iconic" is made equivalent to "visual." Thus indexicality is obscured, and the prejudice that images are iconic is reinforced.
5. The Jakobsonian theory of communication, flawed in itself, is further reduced.

Thus Marin ends up celebrating transparency and subordination to the sender.

22. In this study, I shall draw upon a limited set of examples, for various reasons that are, again, part of my argument: The works are not meant as mere (visual) illustrations of a more important (verbal) argument, but constitute an argument in tension, in a relation of nonoverlapping, with the propositional argument.

23. Obviously, this summary is less than reliable, which cannot be helped. In Chapter 3, I discuss the Genesis story in relation to Freud's *Totem and Taboo* (1914), to Thomas Mann's novel *Joseph and His Brothers* (1948), and to Rembrandt's etching of 1634. I shall argue there for the inherent impossibility of myth as stable meaning. Here I can only happily endorse the inherent failure of my attempt to summarize the story faithfully.

24. This is a case where the iconographic detail works connotatively, although denotation is required for the connotation to work. Visual or verbal, the problem of this pair remains the same (see Chapter 5).

I chose to consider the Washington painting the first work, the Berlin one the second. There is no historical reason to do this: It is likely that both works date from 1655, but no more is known (Schwartz, 1985). There is, however, a narrative reason – which brings my argument into the word-and-image endeavor. In the Washington piece, the gesture of accusation seems primary; in the other one, we already see Joseph's reaction to the accusation. If the two works were to be considered as a sequence, as a kind of comic strip, this would then be the "logical" sequence. Schwartz relates the works to Vondel's play *Joseph in Egypt*, written in 1640 and successfully performed in 1655. The repetition of the theme could be due, according to Schwartz (1985:275), to a change in cast. It could, or it could not. I don't find the facts alleged by Schwartz relevant for a discussion of the paintings in relation to a reading of them; at most, they shed some light on the context of their making. But for such a purpose the information is too loosely supported by evidence to be convincing. On Rembrandt and theater, see the following section.

25. Even though, for simplicity's sake, I shall focus on the visual signs that contribute to recognizability, it is clear that prior knowledge of

some version of the story is indispensable. Stories like this, circulating in allegorical and other modes, are part of the cultural common knowledge and background, or they will not be representable in painting. But this doxic knowledge does not entail a priority for the verbal, for this common cultural knowledge is not in itself verbal. What circulates is the interiorized imagination of the story, including its visuality. Brian Stock's concept of "textual community" is useful here if "text" is not assumed to be totally verbal. See Stock, *The Implications of Literacy* (1983).

26. On visual simultaneity, see Kibédi Varga (1988) and Steiner (1988).

27. The word "pre-text" is meant to be ambiguous, referring to the previous "text," the desire and anxiety toward the mother figure, who proposes sexuality to the initiate son; as well as to the occasion, the excuse for the central confrontation between father and son for which the woman is used.

28. So far I have treated the two works as similar. Later on I shall propose radically different readings for each, but here that differentiation is irrelevant. The relation between a shift in meaning and a radical change in affect is itself problematic. I shall return to this issue later.

29. I am not claiming that this counterreading is feminist. At most, it can be reread now, again in a countermove, for a feminist perspective. The point I am making is a general theoretical one, but it has obvious implications for a political reading.

30. The term "interpretant" is used in the Peircean sense. See De Lauretis, "Semiotics and Experience" in *Alice Doesn't* (1983). I shall have more to say about this concept in Chapter 2.

31. But that distinction itself is ideological, and subject to deconstruction, as any attempt sharply to delimit the realm of the literal will show. See van Alphen, *Bang voor schennis?* (1987), for a semiotic concept of ideology; "Literal Metaphors" (1988) and *Bij wijze van lezen* (1988b), for a deconstruction of the opposition of figurative versus literal.

32. I mean notions like spatial versus temporal, simultaneous versus sequential, et cetera. The problematic status of these distinctions, which invariably turn, first, binary, and, next, hierarchical, has been sufficiently demonstrated. See, for example, Mitchell (1985).

33. I insist on the particular status of interpretation. I can imagine art historical approaches that would (try to) refrain from interpretation in the semiotic sense, and limit themselves to the study of commissions, material state of the canvases, attribution, et cetera. To what extent interpretation can be totally bracketed is, of course, questionable; neither Schwartz, who claims to do so, nor Alpers, who seems to desire to do so, can do without interpretation. In Alpers's case, her "slips" into speculative interpretation constitute the stimulating moments that have been generative of much of my own thinking.

34. Of which Bryson is one of the leading critics; see his *Vision and Painting* (1983). I consider this theoretical and polemical book the least convincing of the three, precisely because of the tradition-and-desire problematic. If it provides evidence of anything, it is primarily of the necessarily personal motivation of scholarly work, which I take as an excuse for my own, as displayed in the present chapter. The impulse to claim radical newness precludes clarity, and thus obscures some of the most interesting ideas advanced. For example, the idea of relating the semiotic concept of deixis as a specific form of indexicality to

painting in a kind of first-person/third-person distinction is fascinating and should be embraced; the connection between deixis and bodiliness remains unnecessarily unclear, thus resulting in a failure to persuade, which is due, in my view, to a desire to break more radically with predecessors than is substantiatable.

35. Just to show the inescapability of his own point in the later book: His scarce references to Fried's *Absorption and Theatricality* (1980), a predecessor that deals partly with the same material and partakes of a similar project, subtly display a tradition-and-desire problematic.

36. Although in Corneille, too, this notion is problematic, and precisely because of the Oedipal tradition-and-desire problematic. See Verhoeff (1974, 1980), for a psychoanalytic analysis of Corneille's tragedies and the concept of *gloire* in that framework. Verhoeff's approach provides the best available literary context for Bryson's book.

37. The problem has been addressed more explicitly in anthropology, a discipline whose burden of colonialism made this reflection more urgent (see Fabian, 1983). Two collections of essays on reader-response theory are Suleiman and Crosman (1980) and Tompkins (1980). See Jauss's (1982) concept of the horizon of expectation as an attempt to reconstruct contemporary readership; Iser's (1978) concept of gap as an attempt to construct an ahistorical, ideal model of readership; Culler's (1983) analysis of the paradox theories of reading and van Alphen (1989), for an attempt to solve the paradox systematically, with a built-in account of historical readership. The latter account seems so far the most plausible, comprehensive, and noncontradictory.

38. This particular relationship between words and images is frequent, especially in the sites of cultural leadership where canonization is effectuated. Studying this relationship is a very relevant, though of course not exclusive, approach.

39. Holly (1988, 1989). I discussed Holly's thesis earlier in connection to iconicity. Here her work presents another case of the pervasive transgressions of the boundaries between discursive and visual signification.

40. See my (1981–2) account of this problematic, and a typology of description in the context of rhetoric. Hamon's (1981) book remains the only major work on description from a literary-theoretical perspective. On narration, Alpers's most relevant source is Banfield (1982).

41. For the notion that apparently semantically empty codes like dichotomies constitute ideologies, see van Alphen (1987:40). In Chapter 10, I hope to show that "Rembrandt" provides a good case for, and demonstration of, such a deconstruction.

42. Alpers gives herself a powerful argument for the impossibility of distinguishing the two modes in her (1983) article on *Las Meninas*, one of the best analyses of that overanalyzed work. The special status Alpers assigns to Velázquez's painting, which also holds for "Rembrandt," would appear less special if it was not built on a preestablished dichotomy. This paper, incidentally, also provides evidence of the collaboration between words and images: It is through the activation of the concepts of descriptive versus narrative, a distinction and its deconstruction, that Alpers is able to *see* the painting differently from those who remain unaware of the steering agency of words in their account. This is an instance of the as yet termless symmetrical coun-

terpart of visual poetics: a verbally informed, yet basically visual, seeing.

43. Moreover, as I have argued in the introduction, Alpers's emblematic case also suffers from the dichotomy. Being defined as descriptive, Vermeer's work misses being read narratively; worse, it misses being read as a visual narrative event.

44. Of course, I am not suggesting that Alpers shares misogynistic views that condone rape; only that at times she borrows its ideologies un-awares, as we all do, inevitably to some extent. At other times she is sharply aware of the misogynistic potential of some of the works (e.g., in her discussion of the etching *The Goldsmith*).

45. In a personal communication, Alpers argued that hair does not have for Rembrandt the relevance I attribute to it in the interpretation ex-posed in Chapter 4. I am not convinced by the objection, but more to the point is the difference in focus. For Alpers, images in this art are more maker-oriented than viewer-oriented, whereas I maintain that this is not the way to put it. For me, the difference lies not in the artist's intention but in the approach. Although on the one hand I can appreciate this difference in focus, on the other hand I am troubled by the potential projection in the intentionalist project. How can we know whether hair counts for Rembrandt or in "Rembrandt," rather than for this particular critic? The overhistoricization of the art obscures the underhistoricization of the critic's own position.

46. In Bal (1989), I have proposed this term to indicate stories that are apt to promote ideological investments by virtue of their binary structure, even if this structure itself is ideologically empty.

47. Fried does not claim to be a semiotician, but I would argue that his dis-tinction is at the heart of semiotic thinking. On the one hand, he is writ-ing about signs: signs of the relationship at stake, at the crossroads of semantics and syntactics. On the other, he is discussing these signs in use, in their affect, thus bringing in the pragmatic perspective. The in-terpretive impulse becomes self-reflective as we realize that the seman-tics of painting and beholder include our own pragmatic position.

48. I am using these theatrical terms in order to radicalize Fried's concept, but I am aware that I am thereby distorting his text. He does not seem to intend the concept to have this literal meaning. I feel, however, that taking it literally helps to reduce the metaphorical status of the concept, at the cost of reducing its range. The latter reduction is in my view more profitable than the former; it increases the precision and the "empirical content" of the concept.

49. The narratological term "focalizer" does not coincide with either of these two functions. Both the Brechtian narrator and the represented beholder *also* function as focalizers, mediating the represented *view* of the diegesis proposed for the reader/viewer's adoption. See Bal (1985), and Chapter 3 here.

50. This care is particularly notable in Fried (1980), 104–5, 121.

51. Fried calls attention to the fact that, strictly speaking, the sex of the patient is indeterminate because the sexual organ is invisible. I suggest that the shape of the thigh suggests that he is male, but I agree with Fried that the invisibility of the organ as the *sign* of the sexual identity as well as its replacement by the probed wound turns the male son into the ambivalent son under threat of castration and sexual undif-ferentiation. Hence, the organ is not blocked from sight to keep the

gender indistinct but to show the male gender at the moment of danger
of dissolution into indistinctness, and thus identified with femininity.
In Chapter 8, I shall relate this ambiguity to primary narcissism. The
contrast with Eakins's other clinic painting, *The Agnew Clinic* of 1889,
is striking. Here the patient is unambiguously female, as is the onlooking nurse. Thus this painting robs the scene of the profound ambiguity that makes the earlier one so fascinating.

52. Although the direction of the gaze of the doctor at the lower right is
ambiguous (he could be looking at Gross as well as at the wound, or
at the mother [?]), if we take it that this polyvalence is a sign in its
turn, this man's eyes become shifters between the three levels of diegesis: that of the primary action of the operation and its ambiguous
object, that of the female (?) outsider, and that, intermediate, of the
resting master surgeon.

53. The words in a letter to Huygens of January 12, 1639 are "die meeste
ende die naetuereelste beweechgelickheijt" (the greatest and most natural movement); Alpers (1988), 49. The seven letters by Rembrandt
have been edited by Horst Gerson (1961). Alpers reproduces the elements of the discussion of this phrase, in *Enterprise* (1988), 126, notes
37–41.

54. The other figures are engaged in interaction and constitute a unity
from which the bride is emphatically excluded. Fried's book is not
mentioned in this chapter on theatricality. Alpers uses the concept in
a way opposed to Fried's: For her, theatricality in Rembrandt "is not
engaged with addressing the viewer but with constituting a self by
performance and by commanding performance" (Alpers, personal
communication). The opposition between the two uses of the term
does not affect my view that the men, not the bride, are being theatrical, in both Fried's and Alpers's sense.

55. Who, strictly speaking, neither tricks nor lies either. See my *Lethal
Love* (1987) for a detailed analysis of Judges 14–16. This is the second
case where Alpers borrows a misogynistic element of the doxa. This
is unfortunate, as she has shown elsewhere (e.g., Alpers, 1983, 1985)
a fine sense of gender problematic and its exclusions.

56. In general, irony is a tricky concept that always comes in handy if
we don't see what we should be seeing. But in order for irony to be
meaningful, it requires a set of consistent indications. Genre is one
such indication. I shall argue later that the painting does play on genre
reversal. But even so, the reversal is not located in this figure.

57. One of the points I hope this discussion conveys is that robbing theoretical discourse of its status as mastercode, and making the works
of art interact with theory on an equal position are feminist issues.
The theoretical terms of Alpers's and Fried's discourses stand in the
way of their own validity as well as of the insight into gender positions
they can provide, once they are liberated from their mastery.

58. The reflections proposed in this study have institutional backgrounds.
The verbal–visual integration is much in the air, and various journals
devote special issues to it (*Style, Poetics Today*) or discuss such inte-
grations as a matter of fact (*Semiotica, October*), while new journals
have emerged that explicitly address these issues (*Representations, Word
and Image*). More importantly, universities are starting to endorse programs along this line, like the undergraduate majors Woord en Beeld
at the Free University of Amsterdam (see Varga, 1984, 1985, 1986,

1988, 1990) and Comparative Arts at the University of Rochester. Research groups are active in and between various European universities (see, e.g., Scott, 1988).

CHAPTER 2

1. On the ambivalent attitudes toward allegory in contemporary scholarship, see Owens (1984). For an excellent understanding of the allegorical impulse, see Fineman (1980). The basic text is, of course, Benjamin's *German Tragedy* (1977).

2. In a very broad sense, we can speak of Dutch culture in the seventeenth century as a *textual community* in Stock's (1983:90–1) terms. The best description to date of this community is Simon Schama's wonderful *The Embarrassment of Riches* (1987). The *visual* culture of that community as analyzed by Alpers (1985) can best be imagined as partly overlapping with Schama's description. Hence, the visual culture of that community forms that part of the *textual* community that is concerned with visuality. In order to confront my analyses in this book with historical evidence, a similar analysis of the culture's textual base would be needed: What did people read, and about which texts did they talk, not only the *burger* elite but also the larger community? Sermons held in churches are a powerful source for such an inquiry. Although this is, for the time being, only an idea for a project, its relevance could demonstrated by the sheer number of scholars who base their claims on unexamined assumptions about this textual community. Several examples can be found in Schwartz (1985); for example, his assumptions about the Samson myth.

3. I am well aware of the difficulty of analyzing rape in terms of semiotics only. The all too real horror of rape thus seems to be left out of the discussion. However, my claim is not that semiotics exhausts the subject, but that it should be included.

4. No further argument is needed for this untenability since the appearance of Hayden White's *Metahistory* (1973) and *Tropics* (1978). The classic on argumentative rhetoric is Chaim Perelman's *Rhetoric* (1979); on rhetoric as *l'art de bien dire*, as ornamental language, and the tropes and other figures of style, I. Dubois (1981).

5. Let me emphasize once more that claiming that rhetoric touches, has an effect on, reality is not the same as claiming that reality is only rhetorical.

6. Masson's *Assault on Truth* (1984) contains the relevant fragments; the correspondence he edited (Freud, 1985) provides the complete material. The case has become famous through, among other publications, Janet Malcolm's (1984) journalistic presentation of the Masson story. My use of the Emma story does not imply full agreement with all of Masson's statements on Freud, although I do agree in the case of Emma Eckstein.

7. For a brilliant analysis of the concept of displacement and its development in Freud's work, see Samuel Weber's *The Legend of Freud* (1982).

8. One of the most interesting analyses of the Emma case that I have come across is hidden in a 1984 article by H. U. E. Thoden van Velzen

on the famous dream of Irma's injection. Thoden van Velzen convincingly identifies Irma with Emma. He analyzes the case into four "scripts" or agendas, two of which are overt and two covert. The covert scripts are identified as "Ambivalent Feelings Towards a Friend" and "Identification with Emma." The author also identifies the group examination as rapish ("Emma feels frightened by a group examination that may turn into a rape"; Thoden van Velzen, 1984:280).

9. The term "hysterics" or "hysterical poetics" means a search for the displaced, the unsaid, but often visible, sign of the unspeakable experience. It is not unlike Naomi Schor's notion of "clitoral hermeneutics" in its systematic displacing of accents (see Schor, 1984, 1987), but it is not identical with that either, as hysterics is not limited to the reversal of detail and main line advocated by Schor. Hysterics focuses on the possibility of systematic redisplacement and exploits "considerations of representability." The latter term is, again, an exploitative appropriation of a Freudian term. See Weber (1982), for an excellent critique of it. Here, the term does not refer to the "dreamer" or writer or painter, but to the reader or viewer who will, within hysterics, exploit the representation's visual or otherwise imaginable status.

Needless to say, the use of the term "hysterics" does not in any way refer to the debate about idealizing hysteria that took place in the 1970s and was effectively rebutted then. I thank Susan Suleiman for pointing out the need to emphasize this. The term refers to the notion that the repressed will force its way out, through hysteria or otherwise; similarly, I will force the story of rape as a female experience out of the men's accounts of it that repress the women's stories. This metaphorical term alludes to an *image* of hysteria – that of the wandering womb – which it proposes to read literally – exactly as a hysterical poetics aims to do.

10. See Teresa De Lauretis's seminal analysis of the rhetoric of violence in "The Violence of Rhetoric: Considerations on Representation and Gender" in *Technologies of Gender* (1987). De Lauretis's starting point is Breines and Gordon's denunciation of the complicity of the language/rhetoric of the social sciences with gender-related violence – here, family violence. De Lauretis (1987:34) writes:

> And they [Breines and Gordon] counter the dominant representation of violence as a "breakdown in social order" by proposing instead that violence is the sign of a "power struggle for the *maintenance* of a certain kind of social order" (1983:511). But which kind of social order is in question, to be maintained or to be dismantled, is just what is at stake in the discourse on family violence.

Meijer (1988) proposes a stunningly powerful reading of the work of a Dutch poem within the framework of family violence, more specifically, father–daughter rape. Ironically, the poet in question, Neeltje Maria Min, had been blamed for writing too familiarly. Her style was said to be affected by "family sickness" because of her intimate, unpompous imagery. Meijer is now able to write: "It is not family sickness; it is the family that is sick."

The present analysis is meant to be a next element in this chain of feminist analyses of the thorough intertwinement of semiosis and asocial reality.

11. I am not suggesting that the event actually *was* a rape; I am saying that as a text it can be read in such a way that it can become an allegory

of rape. That is, it shows the most characteristic features of the semiotics of rape.

12. Gary Schwartz confesses his lack of data to reconstruct the circumstances under which the late history paintings were made. About the
*Lucretia*s he provides no clue. About the subject of Lucretia he writes
nevertheless confidently: "The story of Lucretia, appearances aside,
was pure political allegory in the circles of Rembrandt's patrons"
(Schwartz, 1985:330). The notion that allegory explains away an entire
subject is alien to my enterprise in this study. I have argued at greater
length for a literal understanding of the rape scene in Judges 19, equally
subject to being explained away as mere allegory, in *Death and Dissymmetry* (1988c). Svetlana Alpers's (1988) book on Rembrandt makes
a powerful use of a detail of the second *Lucretia* on its cover. Alpers
focuses on Rembrandt's handling of paint. Her remarks on the second
Lucretia (e.g., Alpers, 1988:80) will be discussed later.

13. In Dutch, the two earlier rape scenes would not be referred to as rapes,
but "simply" as abductions. An abduction is not, in the legends of
antiquity, systematically represented as against the will of the abducted
woman, whereas actual rape is against her will by definition. See,
however, Carroll (1989).

14. As I suggested earlier, the way I deal with the paintings allows me to
dispense with inquiring into the difficult problem of their authenticity.
Moreover, the whole discussion seems highly problematic to me and
cannot be seen outside the situation of power and the economy, and
the investments art historians have therein. Semiotically speaking, the
endeavor to tell a "real" from a "false" Rembrandt falls flat when
confronted with its own premises. If the production of art in the
seventeenth century was as much based on studio work, teaching, and
collaboration as the researchers claim, then the whole notion of authenticity loses at least part of its meaning. In the face of this frustrating
research, Svetlana Alpers provides answers to the authenticity problem
by displacing the question, turning the very deceptivity of Rembrandt's
hand into a feature of his art.

15. Reading a work in one way or another is only partially an option. A
reader inserts him- or herself within a set of cultural attitudes which,
together with the personal baggage the reader brings to the work,
direct ways of reading. My own readings of "Rembrandt," for example, are informed both by my personal and political experience with
the issue of rape and by the possibilities opened by contemporary
feminism. Even this is, of course, an artificial distinction, as the personal experience is in turn informed by the collective historical moment. Yet, within all these constraints, one can be eager or reluctant
to read in certain ways. As feminist theorists put it, one can be an
obedient or a resistant reader. The best account of reading to date I
have found is van Alphen's brief article on "The Complicity of the
Reader" (1989).

16. And to make my own position clear: Just as I read Masson's selection
of Freud's letters with the idea of rape in mind, so too did I have my
first experience of "Rembrandt"'s first *Lucretia* in a situation that felt
"rapish." In 1985 I was allowed to look at the painting in the workshop
where it had just been cleaned. The canvas was covered by a cloth,
and when the cloth was removed and the scene suddenly revealed, I
could not help feeling indiscreet.

I am very grateful to Professor Arthur Wheelock, curator of the Department of Northern Baroque at the National Gallery in Washington, D.C., for showing me the painting and sharing his views of it with me. In fact, his remarks on Lucretia's reanimation largely triggered my own reading of the work.

17. Regretfully, both details are hardly visible on the copies printed here. They do come out quite strongly on the canvas, although they are definitely details – of the "clitoral" kind, as Schor would say. A comparable detail is the blurred sleeve of the arm holding the dagger. This blurring emphasizes both movement and foregrounding. The frontal lighting is functional in bringing out the sense of display and the ambivalent address of the viewer.

18. This meaning of realism is not to be confused with considerations of the historical reality of either the event or the production of the painting. The best source for the latter aspect of "Rembrandt" is Alpers's (1988) account, which is more analytical than Schwartz's (1985) anecdotal one. Alpers proposes an interpretation of the second *Lucretia* that is entirely different from, but not in the least incompatible with, mine.

19. There are, in fact, visual representations of the act, as for example, in Titian's *Rape of Lucretia*. In instances where the act itself is represented, the ambiguity lies either in the grotesque quality of the representation as a whole, as in a painting by Christiaen van Connenbergh (Vandenbroeck, 1987), or in the theatricality of the representation of resistance. Again, there, the rape tends to be represented as the victim's own doing. But I shall argue that the metaphoric representation of rape as suicide is even more pernicious than that.

20. "Under conditions of sex inequality, with perspective bound up with situation, whether a contested interaction is rape comes down to whose meaning wins" (MacKinnon, 1983:652). There are reasons enough to prefigure whose meaning has a chance of winning, by inserting focalization as the figuration of the woman's experience within the evidence. Tania Modleski (1987:28) analyzes how unselfevident this is apropos Hitchcock's *Blackmail* and its critics:

> Patriarchal law can hardly consider her innocent, nor can it possibly offer her real justice, since its categories precisely exclude her experience – an exclusion to which the critics we have quoted amply bear witness as they strain the limits of patriarchal discourse in order to subdue the truth of this experience.

21. There is an enormous literature on metaphor. A powerful introduction is provided by Lakoff and Johnson's *Metaphors We Live By* (1980). Lakoff's later book, *Women, Fire, and Dangerous Things* (1987), is also important, as is Lakoff's most recent book, *More Than Cool Reason* (1989), coauthored by Mark Turner. Perhaps the best known theory is Ricoeur's *The Rule of Metaphor* (1979). See also Holland and Quinn (1987), and the collections edited by Ortony (1979) and Sacks (1977). Particularly relevant for this chapter is Sweetser, *From Etymology to Pragmatism* (1989). Mark Turner offers an unorthodox account in *Death Is the Mother of Beauty* (1987), whose title alone is pertinent to this chapter.

22. The question, Who acts?, is one of the three key questions of narratology as I see it. See especially my *Death and Dissymmetry* (1988c),

ch. 1, for an overview with a justification of the relevance of these questions.

23. This possibility is implied in Peirce's distinction between dynamic object and immediate object. For a discussion of Peirce's view of the object, see Umberto Eco (1979); for a discussion of Eco's paper, see De Lauretis (1987), 38–42. See also De Lauretis's seminal "Semiotics and Experience" in *Alice Doesn't* (1983), to which I shall return in the conclusion of the present chapter.

24. Although Hasenmueller's analysis of the *Rolin Madonna* is convincing and shows how important semiotics is for analyzing visual art, I find it unfortunate that she conflates here the concepts of metonymy and synecdoche that I shall separate from each other in my analysis of the *Lucretia*s.

25. The concept of *gaze* as opposed to *glance* has been revitalized by Norman Bryson in his *Vision and Painting* (1983). The abstraction from the spatiotemporal position of the onlooker that is implied in the gaze is precisely what makes it voyeuristic. This distinction will be discussed at length in Chapter 4. There I shall also question the notion that the gaze is by definition voyeuristic. Feminist film theorists have criticized the assumption that the gaze is by definition male. See Kaja Silverman's seminal "Fassbinder and Lacan" (1989) for a brilliant revision of the Lacanian concept of the gaze.

26. In the seventeenth century, the bowels were often considered the seat of feeling. For an audience holding that view, there would not have been metonymy here; for contemporary viewers, there is. Since I am mostly addressing issues of work–viewer interaction, this historical change only limits the validity of the metonymical interpretation, but it does not undermine it.

27. I wish to thank the participants of the conference "Theory Between the Disciplines," at the University of Western Ontario, April 1988, for their eager discussion of a shorter draft of this chapter. The remarks on the hand with the dagger were proposed by Robert Browne of the Université de Montréal.

28. Note that the term "iconic" is meant here in a specifically Peircean sense as referring to signs that relate to their meanings on the basis of a formal analogy. As I wrote before, I do not want to suggest that the visual is by definition the domain of the iconic. On the contrary, in this chapter I am making the case that Peirce's three modes of signification, the iconic by analogy, the indexical by contiguity, and the symbolic by convention, are unevenly and unpredictably distributed both in visual and in verbal works. For example, the interpretation of the wound as an iconic representation of the vagina does not appeal to visuality, any more than taking the wound "literally" does. Both interpretations are starting from the visual sign and giving it verbal meaning, complex and plural in the first case, singular in the second.

In spite of its sharp insights into the process of semiosis, I find Eco's (1976) rejection of Peirce's three concepts not altogether convincing; nor do I find his alternatives, useful in themselves, sufficient to replace them. I prefer to define and relativize them carefully.

29. This interpretation receives support from Alpers's (1988) remark on the thickness of the paint as representing the artist's physical engagement with the violence. The use of red paint in thick layers for the

representation of already thickening blood makes of the painter a *sculpteur manqué* (Alpers, 1988:31). In a later chapter on performance in the studio, Alpers relates the question of impasto with that of theatricality and the work in the studio. Comparing a sketch of the dead body of an executed woman with the *Lucretia*, she draws attention to the pragmatic dimension of the work. She writes: "But for the blood which stains the pleated cloth over her breast red, the three-quarter format and the figural authority are characteristic of Rembrandt's later works." And: "In his studio, death becomes an event: description (of Elsje) is replaced by enactment (on the part of Lucretia)" (80).

30. Painterly canvas or theatrical curtain, in Dutch the word (*doek*) is the same. Hence, even the appeal to history and authorial intention cannot decide here. For a historical study of the relationship between painting and the theater in Italian Renaissance art, see Damisch (1972).

31. The idea of visual narrative must be sharply distinguished from that of the visual rendering of a verbal narrative. One of the major arguments of this study is for the importance of a specifically visual, yet decisively narrative, mode of signification. This issue will be elaborated in Chapter 3, and taken up again in Chapter 5.

32. This is a good example of the critical potential of Bryson's theory of the logic of the gaze. In his terms, the gaze would here be broken and the glance would take over, thus engaging the viewer's own bodily presence and, I would add, instating visual narrative.

33. I published a much longer version of this comparison in Dutch in 1988 under the title *Verkrachting verbeeld: Seksueel geweld in cultuur gebracht*. The concept of ideological postion is problematic. It suggests a conscious choice which I do not mean to imply here. I take the concept of ideology in the sense elaborated by van Alphen (1987), that is, as a fixed code perceived as natural and limited to the interests of one group. When I speak about ideological positions, I am not referring to the author-painter's position, but to the extent to which the latter allows for a disruptive reading. In that sense, I would not claim that "Rembrandt" takes a critical position, but that these works certainly let us take one. With Livy, the critical position can be taken as well, but in a more antagonistic way. In other words, if we wish to act upon Livy's text in a relevant way, we must become more "resisting" readers. If I were asked whether I approve of these works ideologically – a question that I find disturbingly simplistic, but that I address here to avoid misunderstandings – I would answer that I prefer "Rembrandt" and Shakespeare to Livy and Ovid. But this judgment, of course, ignores historical difference. I wish to emphasize that ideologically informed aesthetic judgment of the works is not the purpose of this study; rather, it is the ideological aspects of acts of reading that are relevant.

34. On the one hand, the historical Rembrandt had a classical, if incomplete, education; on the other, no evidence exists concerning what he actually read. Even for a remotely historical view, it seems safer to assume that he partook of the general humanistic spirit of his days, knowing about the classical stories rather than reading them, and, more importantly, taking for granted that representing them was a culturally meaningful act. If the allegorical impulse was part of that self-evidence, one still could not predicate an overt purpose for the sole meaning of the work, let alone for its complex interpretive afterlife. For infor-

mation about Rembrandt's education and the alleged relations to verbal sources, see, for example, Emmens (1979).

35. Although it would be both anachronistic and inappropriate to declare "Rembrandt" a protofeminist, I am willing to state that some of the works attributed to him allow for feminist readings in a more sympathetic manner than do Livy's and Ovid's texts, for which a feminist reading would have to be more resistant.

36. "Logorrhea": a stream of logos, both in the broader sense of words and in the narrower sense of preestablished, fixed meanings, the doxa of male possession of the female body. The word "logorrhea" is here used to mean the sickness inherent in this exercise of power through words, a power both in terms of representation – the capacity to produce a powerful enough image to entice the listener – and in terms of social power – Collatine's right to speak and be listened to versus Lucretia's reduction to being an object of evocation and desire. The sickness is contagious, thus passing from Collatine to Tarquin. It is also fatal, killing not the sick, but those submitted to the sick one's power.

37. The passage is also quoted by Vickers (1986:215).

38. See Hertz for a pertinent analysis of the image of Medusa and its relation to social revolution and the military. On the "Rembrandt" *Bellona* as an image of (the domestication of) Medusa's power, see Chapter 8.

39. I have studied this story, as well as the other stories in Judges, where young women are raped and/or murdered, in *Death and Dissymmetry* (1988c).

40. The phrase "women as spectacle" reminds me of Lisa Tickner's (1988a) seminal study of imagery as used by the suffrage movement in Britain. Tickner demonstrates that women have been able to reverse the situation described in this chapter and to use spectacle instead of being one. The images she studies have so long been neglected possibly because women are doxically considered to *be*, rather than *have*, images to wield power – just as in regard to that other power tool, the phallus, psychoanalysis told them they *are*, rather than *have*, that power.

41. This incident shows clearly, if such were needed, that the conversation rapists are often so eager to sustain with their victims (see also French's *The Women's Room*, 1977) does not in the least soften the experience. On the contrary, it is a kind of second rape: The victim has to talk kindly while she is dying of fear; the man holds his power over her, and often just uses the time taken up by the conversation to get ready for a second rape. Moreover, the conversation is used to make the victim believe that she has not struggled enough and to make her feel guilty or make others believe she was guilty. The conversations are often used in court as evidence for a "friendly" relation between rapist and victim. Leta's illusion that she could prevent the second rape was so deceptive, yet understandable, that, instead of preventing the second rape, it caused a third, metaphorical self-rape – or should we say a self-murder?

42. This sentence shows an intimate relationship between the intuitive fright and horror the girl feels and the visual image of the man which triggers these feelings. As such it is neatly symmetrical with the use of the image of the woman as enticement in the Lucretia tradition.

43. On the illusionary quality of framing, see Derrida, "Parergon" in *Truth in Painting* (1987a).
44. Winifred Woodhull (1988), 168. This article provides a good brief introduction to the current state of the debate on rape. Woodhull is critical of Foucault's position, while using his theory of power to get away from essentialist accounts of rape such as Brownmiller's, and from an overemphasis on socialization which often verges on the brink of essentialism, exemplified by Griffin (1979), Russell (1982), and Medea and Thompson (1974). Foucault's statement appeared in the Change Collective publication *La Folie Encerclée* (1977); Monique Plaza's response in *m/f* (1980).
45. Mitchell (1985) demonstrates that the distinction between verbal and visual inevitably brings with it a hierarchy, in which either one or the other sense is superior, and a chain of related dichotomies, like time and space, intellect and sense, and, of course, male and female.

CHAPTER 3

1. Much has been written on the question of how images tell. See, for example, Varga (1988) and Steiner (1982). The perspective I shall adopt in this chapter is not quite the same as in these studies. I shall address the question of how to represent time in a spatial medium only to leave it aside. Not that I consider it irrelevant in itself, but I contend that it is skipping over the question of *visual* storytelling in favor of that concerning *translation* from one medium to the other. Storytelling is in these studies conceived primarily as a verbal act, which images can at best only approach.
2. Mann's explicit metatextual polemics (e.g., Mann, 1948:667, 816, 987) and, more importantly, the very choice of a Hebrew myth at the historical moment when he wrote the novel (1932) make both misplaced and futile the attempt, inherent in myth criticism, to insert the text as another *case* in either Hebrew or Greek tradition of the "universal content." Such an insertion says precisely nothing about the book, and what it tries to say is wrong, in the sense that the claim that the statement refers to the novel is false; the novel does not recount an already known story; it does not address the characters of Yohannan's universal story as he describes it, since Mann makes a point of questioning explicitly both qualifiers attached to the nouns. Joseph is not innocent and the woman is not lustful. This judgment implies that although interpretations can never be proven "right," let alone exclusive, they can be proven wrong. There can be no question of trying to deal with the novel as a departure from the historical reality of the day, as many scholars have done (see, e.g., Apter, 1978); if Mann's novel has a mythical flavor, it can be accounted for only within the metatextual discussion the novel offers.
3. The persistence of the object of study (myth) in its approach (myth criticism) is indeed quite general; it is obvious, for example, in structuralist approaches to myth, as in Lévi-Strauss's (1963) statement that a myth consists of all its versions (217). This allows him to proceed to the analysis of what these versions have in common. Edmund Leach (1983), one of Lévi-Strauss's followers in Biblical analysis, defends this view and refers to any attempt at rehistoricizing and specifying the

discursive situation of the texts as "unscrambling the omelette." As I mentioned before, I share Leach's skepticism concerning the historical-critical attempts to divide up the Bible into strands attributed to different authors and periods, and the phrase "unscrambling the omelette" does render the aporia of the enterprise fairly well. It is to the consequences he draws from it that I object. The historical-critical method suffers from flaws comparable to those that limit the reliability of the results of the Rembrandt Research Project: a division of the work into fragments based on the preconception of unity that the very division undermines. For a critique of the historical-critical school of Biblical research, see Bal (1988b). Leach's claim is derived from Malinowski's (1926) functionalist view that myths function as charters for social action. This view should logically lead to a study of the historical position of myths, but this is not what Leach deduces from it. In myth criticism, as in the structural study of myth, a myth is a myth because, under the layers of dust of historically changing signifiers or as a common denominator of all versions, it remains the same signifier-independent signified, a universal story. The relationship between this view of myth and the concept of collective unconscious is more or less taken for granted. The expression matters only as a symptom of its content, and variation matters only as evidence of similarity. No wonder today's psychocritics rarely bother to study myth for its own sake.

4. I claim that this new current can be understood only against the background it tries to reject. See my (1986b) review of Brooks's book.

5. Gallop's view is based on Felman's introduction to the special issue of *Yale French Studies* (1977), where the latter defines the relation between text and interpretation, or between literary and scholarly texts for that matter, as nonhierarchical, both in time and in authority. Felman's brilliant practice of her own view in *Le scandale du corps parlant* (1980) shows not only the relevance of her idea but also the close relation between language and myth. (The French book has appeared in English, but nothing remains of its wonderful title which, literally translated, reads in English "The Scandal of the Speaking Body." The English title, *Literary Speech-Acts*, denies the book's uniqueness, putting it into the category of textbooks. Fortunately, the book itself has not suffered excessive "damage" or "distortion" in the process of translation.)

6. It is here that psychoanalysis joins, without, however, coinciding with it, the kind of critique Habermas (1968/1972) advocates. In an earlier book, *Femmes imaginaires* (1986a), I have perhaps overemphasized the aspects shared by Habermas and psychoanalysis. For a convincing argument against Habermas's illusion that they coincide, see Rose (1986:1–163).

7. If we agree with Lévi-Strauss's statement that a myth consist of all its versions, we should be willing to take that statement to its logical consequence: There is no myth "underneath" (historical criticism) or "within" (structuralism) these versions; there is no myth other than each version, each representation, just as there is, as we shall see, no primal fantasy less personal and less narrative than any other fantasy.

8. The titles of the "Rembrandt" works are later impositions. But, as in the case of the *Lucretias*, I wish to emphasize once more that the artist's intention matters less than the possibility the works offer the viewer

for projecting in his or her turn. Nevertheless, in the case of these particular works, no doubt that I know of has ever been raised to suggest that the three works do indeed refer to Genesis 39. The motivations for the making of the works, however, remain unclear. See Schwartz (1985:274–5) for an attempt to explain the existence of the two paintings, probably of the same year, by a change in the cast of the performance of Vondel's play *Joseph in Egypt*.

9. Often it is not; many works were produced on commission. See Schwartz (1985) for a first systematic study of Rembrandt's patrons, and Alpers (1988) for a much more thorough and challenging analysis of mutual influence between the works and the artist's relations to the marketplace. It will be obvious by now that I do not share the assumption underlying Schwartz's study that the circumstances of a work's genesis determine its meaning. This assumption rests on an unwarranted identification, first, between genesis (i.e., commissions) and intention, and then, between intention and meaning. As for the former identification, even the strictest commission leaves room for personal input, if only of a personal interpretation of the relation between mythical subject matter and allegorical-circumstantial extension. Furthermore, intention should be separated into conscious and unconscious elements. Assumptions, warranted or not, regarding "Rembrandt"'s intentions are in my approach relevant only to the extent that they are part of the viewer's cultural baggage.

10. Even to cancel time out. As Lévi-Strauss suggests in *The Raw and the Cooked* (1969), myth is, with music and dreams, a "machine for the suppression of time." Hence, the case of myth is a suitable one for examining how verbal and visual narrative meet in the use of devices for rendering time.

11. The concept of *gap* is meant as a conflation of the literary notion promoted by Iser, the psychoanalytic-semiotic one (e.g., Rose, 1986:49–81) and the ideological one (Hamon, 1984). It goes without saying that the status of a gap is readerly, and not textual (*pace* Kemp, 1985a).

12. "Angels" in the Hebrew Bible are better viewed as messengers of the Lord. Their postal function is crucial. Only in Christian mythology do they become endowed with a moral function. This change, which the translation "angel" in both traditions obliterates, contributes to the moralistic projection of Christian values onto the Hebrew Bible which can then only fail to meet those anachronistic standards and, thus, gave rise to the development of Christocentric, if not plain anti-Semitic, views of the Hebrew Bible. For an analysis of the Genesis text, see Barthes, "The Struggle with the Angel," in *Image–Music–Text* (1977).

13. The gender of angels can still become a signifying element in a chain of meanings. Although ambiguity and femininity are frequent, explicit masculinity is also attributed to angels. See van Alphen (1987) for an analysis of a play popular in Rembrandt's time, Vondel's play *Lucifer*, in which angels are male, as opposed to both God and humans, who are represented as female.

14. Otto Benesch (1970:93–4) claims that in both paintings Joseph was originally represented kneeling at the foot of the bed. This is quite possible and makes the later choice more relevant. Yet Benesch's argument that this must have been so because in the Washington painting the woman's hand is gesturing toward the bedpost, is not convincing

at all. The woman is pointing to the red cloth, Joseph's coat, which is the evidence of his misbehavior – and her desire. This shortsightedness of the critic is a case of the unfortunate conflation of genesis, (presumed) intention, and meaning.

15. It is also theatrical in Alpers's sense.

16. The dialectic between origin and articulation is central to the problem of the status of psychoanalytic criticism. See Pavel's (1984) commentary on Brooks.

17. The pervasiveness of this objectifying fallacy is particularly clear in Freud's theory of femininity (e.g., see his 1931 article, "Female Sexuality"; see also Kofman, 1985a) and is given concrete status in Freud's (1905b) theory of jokes (see also Kofman, 1986). Here is one example of the kind of discourse that operates to exclude women by the interplay between second and third grammatical persons:

> Throughout history people have knocked their heads against the riddle of the nature of femininity. . . . Nor will *you* have escaped worrying over this problem – those of you who are men; to those of you who are women this will not apply – you are yourselves the problem. (Quoted in Felman, 1981:19)

18. *Mise en abyme* is the French term, ascribed to Gide, that refers to a story-within-the-story that summarizes the main story. A single sign can also serve this function. See Bal, *Femmes imaginaires* (1986a), ch.4, for an extensive account of the concept and its uses.

19. This pun was proposed by Harai Golem from the Porter Institute of Poetics and Semiotics at the University of Tel-Aviv.

20. "Bare" only in regard to Mann's work on it. The Biblical sentence serves as an introduction to the episode, as a motivation for the woman's love, and is as far as Genesis goes toward "humanizing" that figure.

21. Viewed through Mann's novel, the angel in the painting of *Jacob Wrestling with the Angel* foreshadows Joseph's sexual ambivalence and the difficulty Jacob will have with this particular son.

22. This aspect of the character turns the novel into a work that hinges on the limits between modernism and postmodernism, as these two movements are defined by Brian McHale (1987). For McHale, *modernism* is defined by epistemological skepticism, whereas *postmodernism* is characterized by ontological skepticism. Thus, uncertainties about perception, the projectional nature of interpretation, and the variable description of identical entities like characters are modernist features; the suspension of the limits of *being*, the identification between characters that are normally distinct, and the radical changes within one character are postmodern aspects of the novel. The metanarrative status bestowed on the character is also typically postmodern. McHale rightly emphasizes the profound similarities between postmodernism and Renaissance poetics. The metatextual status of postmodern texts on the one hand, and the metarepresentational aspects of much seventeenth-century painting on the other, makes for an affinity between them, although by no means an identity.

23. This scene occurs in the Quran version (Appendix 3) as well as in Rabbinical commentaries. If we take it that the passage refers to the Quran, that is in itself a meaningful political signification whose resonance is particularly striking today.

24. The concept of catharsis is better known than understood. See Dupont-

Roc and Lallot (1980) for a clear interpretation. If the act is cathartic, it also points up a cathartic possibility for the reader.

25. After his actual birth, Joseph has to be delivered from the pit in which his brothers had cast him, and from the prison in which the woman has him cast.

26. What follows bears comparison with a formalist reading. Note that this recourse to a formalist description is not meant to be based on the same ontological status of the image's form on which formalism claims form to be based. I use this description to foreground the difference between this *attempt* to read intersubjectively and the subsequent voluntary transgression of that attempt, when later on I shall emphatically endorse the position argued in the previous chapter, wherein the boundaries between social and individual semiosis shaped by experience are constantly undermined.

27. This looking back with a figure is the visual equivalent of free indirect discourse, to which I shall return in the next chapter.

28. For a brief introduction to this concept, see Bal (1985); for a more extensive argument, Bal (1986a). I shall justify the transposition of this term onto the visual domain in Chapter 4.

29. See Rimmon (1977), Perry and Sternberg (1968), and Gombrich (1960/1968).

30. Is there any historical support for my reading, the kind of evidence we are in the habit of demanding when interpreting historical images? There might be, but only because the desire for such evidence is part of the habit (in De Lauretis's sense) of interpreting historical images. Is there any evidence, for example, in the Biblical text? Actually, in the seventeenth-century Dutch, as the Staten translation particularly shows, the double status of the man within the closed space of the house gets emphasized. Although there is no evidence as to which translation Rembrandt possessed – or even that he actively read the text before setting to work – it is likely that the influence of both the Lutherian and the Staten translations imbued the cultural context defining the textual community, in much the same way as the polemics surrounding Keplerian optics, as Alpers (1985:26–70) claims, were in the cultural air. This "version" of Genesis 39 informs the textual community of which Rembrandt was a member. I have tried to enhance the meeting places of the Hebrew text and of this Dutch translation in the working translation appended to this chapter, because the historical specificity of "Rembrandt"'s Joseph might be related, among many other things, to the polemical background of these very literal translations, translations that were political acts. I would further venture to speculate that in the "Rembrandt" we can read this discursive context as part of his screen. (Compare, e.g., both translations of verse 11: The house is a *closed house*, as the Hebrew word for "prison" indicates.)

31. My further reading is predicated upon the projection of contemporary feminist views of voyeurism. This projection is unlikely to have any historical support, yet is quite central for the history of contemporary dealings with images. Therefore, I would contend that in spite of its purposeful anachronism, this reading is nevertheless historical. Not that voyeurism is a twentieth-century invention; it is the feminist critique of it that is rigorously contemporary.

32. The Quran version does say that Joseph, at the moment of seduction, saw the face of God:

    > And (with passion) did she desire him, and he would have desired her, but that he saw evidence of his Lord.

    Note that he saw his spiritual father, not Potiphar, his social father. The passage is provided with a footnote that puts particular emphasis on ways of seeing:

    > But he had a sure refuge – his faith in God. His spiritual eyes saw something that her eyes, blinded by passion, did not see. She thought no one saw when the doors were closed. (*Quran*, 558)

    In Mann's novel, the considerations Joseph goes through at length involve all three fathers: Jacob, Potiphar, and Jahweh. It is toward the last that there is a consideration of sexual jealousy. But the object of this jealousy is Joseph himself, not the woman. Jahweh does not have claims on her, since she is devoted to an Egyptian god. But he owns Joseph, just as the other god owns the woman.

33. Responses to earlier versions of this chapter are rather skeptical regarding this point. It does not seem obvious to some that the body's weight should logically rest on the foot held back, and the foot indicating the direction of the flight should be lighter, maybe already in the air. Yet my interpretation can easily be tested in "real life." The interesting point is not, of course, that I claim to be right against many objections, and certainly not that "real life" proves it, but that this particular detail struck me, while seeming farfetched to others. If I were wrong, it would be evidence of my share in the dialectic of projection. But even if I am right, the divergence between my view and that of others is equally convincing evidence of the same point. In both cases, there is divergence, which is precisely the issue in this chapter. The realistic argument I am invoking is, of course, no more decisive here than it is in cases where I refute it on the basis of its irrelevance.

34. See Emmens's (1977:73–7). The major source for this criticism is Pels, discussed in Alpers (1988:53) and in Chapter 4 of this book.

CHAPTER 4

1. Not only did art history emerge largely from nineteenth-century connoisseurship, but even today, the prestige of an endeavor like the Rembrandt Research Project, whose conclusions led immediately to changes in the museum, indicates this central position of connoisseurship. The doubts about the conclusions, which are predicated upon stylistic analysis much more substantially than was expected even by the members of the team themselves, do not seem to undermine the firmness with which they are acted upon. And that is, precisely, the indication that connoisseurship has not been dethroned from its central place.

   On the case of Gentileschi, see also Garrard's (1988) book-length study. Garrard can be characterized as a revisionist, rather than a radical, feminist art historian. She argues for insertion of Gentileschi into the canon, not for a fundamental critique of the canon. See Gouma-Peterson and Mathews (1987) for an overview of feminist art history, divided according to generations. Tickner's (1988b) overview in *Gen-*

ders works with a systematic division based on Michèle Barrett's (1987) seminal analysis of the problems of feminist uses of the category of difference. Gouma-Peterson and Mathews's contribution is an indispensable source; Tickner's article provides very useful insights.

2. Among others, by Bissell (1968) and Harris and Nochlin (1976).

3. The term "pre-text" is again intentionally ambiguous, referring to the ordinary sense of "occasion" as well as to the temporal sense of "prior text."

4. In turn, the Eve story had to be rewritten for this meaning to become the bone of mythical rigidity in Genesis traditions. See my *Lethal Love* (1987), ch. 5. If the name Eve serves here to characterize the type of the lustful and seductive female, it is only in its later Christian interpretation.

5. Such a view of pornography can be found in Kappeler (1986), among others.

6. This reference is utterly missed by Donaldson (1982:19–20) when he criticizes Artemesia Gentileschi's painting *Tarquin and Lucretia* for *not* expressing Artemesia's own experience of rape. The *Lucretia* painting was done decades after the rape, whereas the *Susanna* is almost cotemporal with the experience. The intriguing question that remains, then, is why Gentileschi chose the subject of voyeurism and near-rape to express her experience of real rape – that is, the Susanna rather than the Lucretia story. It is the purpose of the present chapter to suggest a possible answer to this question, an answer that takes storytelling itself into account.

7. The other one is earlier, dated 1634 (Mauritshuis, The Hague).

8. See Schama (1985) for an account of this problem of response. Schama confirms from his historical perspective some of the points I am making about systematic aspects of viewing.

9. The passage incidentally provides a good case for my point about projection; words like "wished" and "love of truth" prove it. Clark's response, whatever it is, is attributed to the artist: *He* wanted to make a statement on beauty, but *he* was too honest to disregard truth. A variety of implications become clear when we try to dissect the statement. The net result is that the artist will always be a clone of the critic: a woman lover, a connoisseur of female beauty, an honest person, and all for clinging to the "truth" of women's deficient beauty without reflecting on the standards by which her beauty is measured; sensitive to the visual appeal to the senses and aware of the difference between artistic beauty and sexual attraction. An astonishingly modern "Rembrandt" and a surprisingly self-centered and simple man emerges from this picture.

10. Gombrich (1986) describes how in the Italian High Renaissance "the conquest of natural appearances went hand in hand with the realization of a human ideal of Beauty," so that realism lost its antagonism to beauty and idealization. In "Rembrandt" this tension seems not to have disappeared at all. I am, of course, not referring to the historical shifts in taste, for example, contemporary preference for plump, versus modern preference for slim bodies. Between the sketches that I am about to discuss and the *Danae*, the difference is semiotic, not natural, and the insistence on beauty (in the *Danae*, although qualified) and on visuality and gender (in the sketches) is a matter of meaning, not of taste.

11. Bryson (1983:93–4) relates the term to the French *regard*, which he decomposes into *re-* (=repetitively) and *-gard* (=*prendre sous garde*, "taking hold of").

12. The terms are based on a Lacanian theory of looking. See Lacan (1979:65–119); also Rose (1986) and Silverman (1989). I shall return to the Lacanian–Silvermanian terms below.

13. In a book already mentioned, van Alphen (1988b) discusses the prevailing currents in reader-response theory as criticized by Culler (1983). The author is happy with Culler's conclusions concerning the aporia entailed by both positions' compulsion to grant more importance to the factor – text or reader – for they initially deny any stability; but he is not satisfied with the state of powerlessness in which those conclusions leave us. Van Alphen then proposes that we abandon the idea that we are always talking about one concept of meaning. Instead, he distinguishes between what he calls "two moments of meaning" (van Alphen, 1988b:235) which are not congruous with each other. A summary of these thoughts appeared in English in the Italian journal *VS Versus* in 1989.

14. This variability allowed within the socially prescriptive gaze also makes sense within classical psychoanalysis, where variations can be related to the stages of development. Explaining the interest psychoanalysis thus takes in the *aims* (unfortunately conflated with the *meaning*) of looking, Ellen Handler Spitz distinguishes these Freudian looks as follows:

> Within each stage there is variability of aim so that, for example, in a visually oriented child who might later develop into an artist, the oral-incorporative motive might be displaced onto looking (note the ordinary expression "he devoured it with his eyes"), as might the anal-sadistic motive ("a killing look"), or the phallic ("a penetrating glance"). (Handler Spitz, 1985:43)

15. In other words, the position of the viewer is represented and included in the image, in order to preclude the easy and uncommitted gaze. As John Ellis suggested in 1980, this is one possible way of countering the disturbing aspects of pornographic films.

16. In the last chapter of *Sexuality* (1986), Jacqueline Rose cites a fascinating drawing by Leonardo da Vinci which shows to what extent the desire to see is often used to override a fear of seeing.

17. For a political analysis of bodily and facial beauty, see Lakoff and Scherr (1984).

18. Of course, both critics must have been aware of this, had they been asked. The point is that their discourse conflates the issue of female beauty with that of its representation. The title of Clark's book alone confirms this (*Feminine Beauty*).

19. Even today, the trace of this relation remains in that drawings are seldom on exhibition. They can be viewed only by special permission, often under surveillance of a member of the museum staff. The viewer is then in turn being viewed. This reproduces the position proposed by Ellis for undermining the pornographic effect for the pornographic viewer.

20. "Pornographic" is meant in a specific sense here, of writing the sexual lust within the text–reader relation, resulting in the impulse to appropriating the object of that lust.

21. Quotations are from the *New English Bible with the Apocrypha,* Oxford Study Edition (New York: Oxford University Press, 1976). Since I

am not assuming a direct influence of the text on the "Rembrandt" paintings, the question of translation is irrelevant.

22. In Biblical literature from the Hebraic tradition, causal connections are hardly ever made explicit. Juxtaposition is the dominant mode. Hence, the sequentiality of the two sentences is plausibly generative of causality.

23. Terms like "aberrations," "perversions," and "pathology" sound today so anachronistic that one can easily simplify Freud's gender prejudices. In fact, he used these terms in order to insert his discourse into the medical discourse of the day rather than to deny the sexual ambiguities that he was, indeed, the first to have foregrounded.

24. I am not suggesting here that all viewers of visual art are pornography lovers; I am trying to make the case that there is a similarity in *position* that makes it easy to use visual images for pornographic purposes. There is a continuity between the two positions, not an automatic overlap; the degree to which they overlap must be examined for each particular case. See also Freedberg, "Arousal by Images," in his 1989 book.

25. In Freud's positive view of looking, shame is the counterforce that has to be overcome in order for voyeurism and its counterpart, exhibitionism, to be possible. Note that the symmetry Freud assumes between voyeurism and exhibitionism suggests a more or less "democratic" division of labor, ignoring power relations and the dissymmetry they entail. According to Freud, the active and passive tendencies of what he calls "perversions" are two sides of the same thing. He claims that every voyeur is also an exhibitionist. Unexpectedly, the Biblical story supports this assumption, as we shall see.

26. See, for example, Mulvey (1975); De Lauretis (1987).

27. According to Eco (1976:7), providing the possibility of indulging in lying is the very defining feature of the sign: "Semiotics is in principle the discipline studying everything which can be used in order to lie."

28. I have made an extensive case for this cynical view of Biblical literature elsewhere; see Bal (1988c). The most disturbing story in the Book of Judges, for example, the gang rape and murder of a young woman in Judges 19, which I have briefly evoked in Chapter 2 and shall discuss again in the final chapter, is too easily appropriated by allegorical readings. Such readings do not exhaust the story's effect, and their hasty endorsement may implicate the bad conscience of the reader.

29. I am referring here to the distinction between *general vision* – everything visual in the sense of visible (medium) – and *visuality* as a specific semiotic mode that can be employed in both visual and verbal media. The distinction is discussed in Foster, ed. (1988). The term "mode" is borrowed from linguistics, where it serves to distinguish, for example, the affirmative from the interrogative and imperative modes. The visual mode appeals to visual imagination, not to physical perception; to seeing before "the mind's eye," as well as to seeing real objects. Seeing a represented figure in a painting is imaginative as much as seeing a literary figure is, and both acts of seeing are different from perceiving a real person. However, the perception of a real person, in turn, also leads to the construction of an image before the mind's eye.

30. The concept was first proposed by Genette (1972; English translation, 1980), and it was meant to distinguish narrative *voice* (Who speaks?)

from *vision* (Who sees?). Genette did not give the concept the systematic stature it deserved because he failed to ground it in a systematic
theory of narrative. I have tried to solve that problem in my *Narratology*
(1985), an attempt that generated an incredible amount of response,
too much, indeed, to hold the theoretical aspects of my proposal accountable for it. The critical, hence feminist, potential of my amend-
ments became clear much later, and I now think it is that potential
that gave rise to such strong reactions. I elaborated that aspect of the
theory later (see Bal, 1986a) in the framework of my feminist analyses
of Biblical love stories. In that French book, I reworked the discussion
with Genette and related it to ideological issues. The English version
of that book, *Lethal Love* (1987), does not contain this theoretical
discussion.

31. The term "diegetic" is derived from "diegesis," an alternative term
for "fabula." Both fabula and diegesis refer in this terminology to the
– presupposed but nonexistent – sequence of events that, in modified
form, is represented in the story. "Diegetic" is convenient since "fabula" does not allow for an adjectival form.

32. The literature on free indirect discourse is abundant. See McHale (1978)
for a useful summary. Banfield (1982) proposes a linguistic theory that
raised many criticisms but that is, in my opinion, the best account of
the phenomenon to date. Banfield ignores the concept of focalization,
however, which sometimes leads to stretching the realm of "pure"
linguistics a bit far.

33. The murders of heroes by female characters in the Bible tend to be
represented in sexual imagery. Yael's manner of killing Sisera in Judges
4 and 5 comes close to a rape, and I have argued elsewhere (see Bal,
1988c) that it is indeed a revenge for the rape and murder of young
women in the Book of Judges.

34. These two suggestions do not overlap. As recent feminist films have
demonstrated, the gaze can be undercut by a redirection of internal
focalization as well as by blocking it. The first strategy is used by
Karen Arthur (1987), in the film *Lady Beware* where the man's focalization of the store windows alternates with the designer's focalization
of the same, thus opposing his erotic interpretation with a postmodern
play of signifiers. The second strategy is used in Marleen Gorris's film
Broken Mirrors (1984), where, as Anneke Smelik (1989) has demonstrated, internal focalization is first proposed and then cut off, so that
the traditional parade of women, maintained on the level of the fabula,
is undermined on the level of focalization. This example shows clearly
that focalization is constitutive of meaning itself, not a dispensable
comment: the event of the parade still takes place, but there is no sense
of parade.

35. The detail of the raised finger in "Rembrandt"'s etching has also been
pointed out by Christine van Boheemen in her book *The Novel as
Family Romance* (1987), in which many of the issues discussed here are
also raised, albeit in a different context.

36. For Freud, looking is derived from touching, an inferior and preparatory version of it.

37. I use the term "ideologeme," which I take from Jameson (1981), in
the sense of an ideological unit, comparable to the semantic unit called
"sememe." When I am speaking of ideologemes, the semiotic domain
is that of semantics.

38. I cannot delve into the complex question of canonically accepted body types in the seventeenth century. The issue here is not the discussion within the art world but the response by viewers as it is documented by these two texts, Pels's poem (see Schenkeveld-van der Dussen, 1978) and Clark's (1980) essay. In fact, the body image in the *Danae* can as well be seen in many respects as an ideal of beauty as Gombrich (1986) described it.

39. To be precise, this is an example of Peirce's category of the metaphoric icon. In his subdivision of icons Peirce writes:

> Those which partake of simple qualities, or First firstnesses, are *images*; those which represent the relations, mainly dyadic, or so regarded, of the parts of one thing by analogous relations in their own part, are *diagrams*; those which represent the representative character of a representamen by representing a parallelism in something else, are *metaphors*. (Innis, ed, 1984:10)

None of these three terms can be taken in their standard sense. "Image" is not necessarily visual, but just iconic in the sense defined earlier; "diagram" is a relational icon, relations within the sign corresponding to relations within the meaning/concept; and "metaphors" are metaphorical icons, which are mediated through "something else." In the case at hand, the iconic relation is mediated, because there is no analogy between hair and paint unless mediated through the idea of elaborateness.

40. Exceptions are Alpers (1988) and Silverman (1989), who mention the genderedness.

41. This iconographic reference was pointed out to me by Eugene Vance and Tom Mitchell. I thank them and the other members of the audience at the University of Chicago for their stimulating questions and suggestions.

42. "This is that Rembrandt, responding to the oft-made challenge to paint the inner man or the soul, portrayed himself as a man of melancholic temperament" (Chapman, 1989:165). I am not convinced by Chapman's argument that the early self-portraits are specifically related to melancholia, nor that the idea of melancholia should be related to the person of the artist and his view of self. This individualistic conception entails a romanticized view of melancholia as a temperament fit for artistic genius (Chapman, 1989:167). But melancholia is also a dangerous state, a psychic paralysis that makes the subject suffering from it unfit for action. In the case of the Susanna story and its suggestion of impotence, this negative concept of melancholia, closer to the Freudian analysis of melancholia as failed mourning, seems more illuminating. See also Chapman (1990).

43. I thank Eugene Vance for insisting on this detail whose interest had escaped me.

44. This idea was suggested to me by Elizabeth Helsinger from the University of Chicago. My assessment of the *Susanna*s is opposed to that of Miles (1989:124), who finds the later one more complicitous with male voyeurism than the earlier one.

CHAPTER 5

1. Bryson was in a good position to launch such an attack; he had already published, two years earlier, his *Word and Image* (1981), which provides

an example of a radically different, yet convincingly historical approach to French eighteenth-century painting. And *Tradition and Desire*, published in 1984, must have been well underway. In the two books that frame *Vision and Painting*, the author shows persuasively that a radical renewal of the theory and practice of art history can be achieved, without threatening the overall goals of the field as such, attributing an explicit place to history in general and to the history of painting in particular, and displaying in his analysis the finest interpretive skills.

Interestingly, the interpretations, brought about within a strong theoretical framework, also lead to implicit and explicit aesthetic judgments that are mostly convincing. Hence, Bryson implicitly argues not only that interpretation is helped rather than hampered by theoretical reflection, but also that "connoisseurship," the most antitheoretical stance art historians endorse, is assisted as well.

2. See Erwin Panofsky (1955) for an introduction to iconography and iconology; and Michael Ann Holly (1984) for an illuminating presentation of Panofsky's ideas in relation to his cultural background and predecessors. See also Moxey (1986) for a critical presentation. Broos (1977) would be a helpful tool for an orthodox iconography of "Rembrandt."

3. Holly's (1984) point in her attempts to connect Panofsky's ideas with innovative art history and hermeneutics of his time is well taken. Not only does she reinsert "newness" within history, thus giving innovation both the dignity it deserves and the relativity it needs, but also she implicitly justifies discursivity as crucially productive *within* the discipline, whose interdisciplinary nature she thereby proclaims.

4. For an illuminating deconstructionist reversal of the concept of influence in the context of visual art, see Baxandall (1985), 58–62.

5. For a summary of the most important arguments against this distinction and the hierarchy it entails, see van Alphen (1987).

6. One reason to look for a different term for what Bryson wants to point out is the possible confusion caused by Barthes's definition of connotation as the voice of the cultural context. Bryson does not mean to include this in his definition of denotation; for him, the denotative sign works by an absolute and pointed reference, which does not necessarily entail its opposite, a diffuse reference.

7. The drawing is most often said to represent the farewell of Tobias when he leaves home; sometimes it is related to the arrival of Tobias at the house of his distant relatives, or to the farewell from that house when he has married the daughter. I adopt the first of these possibilities here, not because I deem it the best or the most plausible reading, but because it seems to be the most frequently alleged one. Hence, it clarifies my point about iconographic reading. The third reading is proposed by Schatborn (1987), 63. Benesch's (1973, V:245) catalog has the least plausible reading: "Raguel Welcomes Tobias." For that reading, which bypasses the farewell aspects, the veiled woman also constitutes a "problem," an element that hits the limits of iconography and requires surplus decoding. A similar proleptic reading, which interprets her as already prepared for the travel of which nothing can yet be known at the moment Tobias enters the house, is thus the most likely interpretation to occur.

8. This feature is central in initiation rites according to van Gennep (1960).

428

This theory has been reformulated within a structuralist framework by Turner (1969). Turner's theory has in turn been criticized from a feminist perspective (e.g., Bynum, 1984); yet once revised it can still be useful, as Gerstein (1989) demonstrates. I have discussed the problems and the heuristic value of the concept of rite of passage extensively elsewhere (Bal, 1988c).

9. The concept of intertextuality has been introduced into Western criticism by Julia Kristeva. See Culler's (1981) article "Presupposition and Intertextuality" for a fine account of its uses and misuses. The use of a term related to textuality for visual art seems amply justified after Bryson's *Word and Image* (1981), and in the case we are discussing, it is even quite pointed and indispensable for a distinction important for the assessment of visual signs. Bryson discusses the concept further in "Intertextuality" (1988c). An example of intertextual analysis (although carried out unawares) is Baldwin's (1989) article.

10. This is only apparently a difference between visual and verbal art. In verbal art, too, we do not know which elements of the sequence we are reading will eventually turn out to be significant; *pace* Perry (1979). The alleged sequentiality of verbal art is as illusory as is the stillness of images.

11. Not any more than that of psychoanalytic reading, as Freud warned us often enough. Reading any dog as a metonymy for "Tobias" is as pointless and erroneous as reading a phallus into any oblong object.

12. Both class (Hagar was a slave) and ethnicity (she was Egyptian) are ideologically troubling factors in this story which received such a venerated place in both the Judaic and the Christian canon. Working exclusively with iconography tends to obliterate the disturbing and ambivalent aspects of the representation that can be processed only by a different mode of reading. In this case, iconography tends to collaborate with mythical reading as described in Chapter 3.

13. In Chapter 3, I have demonstrated the dangers inherent in this notion of recognition. Here my argument is different, but complementary. The idea of recognition can be useful and not push us into the trap of mythical reading, only if its quality of culturally based recognition, as distinct from both direct visual decoding and interpretation, is carefully kept in mind.

14. Another sign, less strongly iconographic but equally visual and proleptically referring to the pre-text, is Hagar's hand on her face, expressing despair. There is also Abraham's hand which seems to bless the boy who, expelled as he is, is nonetheless the patriarch's son. The habit of interpreting hands as "speaking," as carrying dramatic meaning, discussed in Chapter 3 as one of the devices for narrating the subject disposed of by visual semiosis, is also part of the iconographic mode of reading. And finally, there is the isolated figure of Sarah, the jealous wife whom the textual tradition holds responsible for Hagar's dismissal. Her arms crossed and firmly resting on the fence surrounding the house, she is clearly in possession of the house in both the material sense and, more importantly, the historical sense of "the house of Israel." Her isolated position in the visual representation can be read as a sign for the other side of her jealous and possessive behavior. Between the one wife who is expelled and the other wife who is alone, the patriarch with his two powerful hands is represented in his place

of power over both. The emphatically isolated visual position of Sarah is in some way a critical response to the text which leaves it to the reader to judge – which readers eagerly did, at Sarah's expense.

15. The term "cotext" refers to the body of texts with generically similar thematic structures. Alter's concept of type scene, proposed in *The Art of Biblical Narrative* (1981) is not without serious problems, notably for its illusory projection of the reader's own thematic unifications onto the corpus. Yet it can be useful if handled in productive tension with other modes of reading. It should be used as a relatively empty structure, not filled in with "typical" divisions of labor according to class or gender, as Alter tends to do. For example, the type scene of farewell seems acceptable to me; the type scene of the betrothal as proposed by Alter does not, and needs to be replaced by the more open formulation of "selection of sexual partner," thus extending the type scene to accommodate scenes where the partner selected is male, or where the "betrothal" is ironic and implicit. Similarly, "murder through cunning" is acceptable, whereas "woman murders man through cunning," underlying Zakovitch's (1981) interpretation of Judges 4 and 5 is not. See my *Murder and Difference* (1988b), for a more detailed discussion.

16. Genette uses the term "archtext" here, but I prefer pre-text because its double meaning keeps reminding us of the active work on preceding texts, rather than the obedient repetition of them. Moreover, the term "archtext" suggests origin, rather than a living tradition. See Baxandall (1985) for a critique of the search for origin.

17. To complicate matters even more, responding to *Tom* is in turn impossible without a postcolonial critique of *Tom*'s difference from that other strand of writing on slavery, the slave narratives themselves. For a representative, although in some ways problematic, overview of these issues of difference, see Gates, ed. (1985).

18. See, among many commentaries, Tompkins (1985) and Lang (1987) for a critical assessment of the novel as partaking of the genre of the sentimental novel. Spillers (1985) also undermines the gender politics inherent in the definition of the genre, while critiquing the obvious racism in the novel. I prefer the genre concept of the social novel, which subsumes both the "sentimental novel" à la *Tom* and the "realist" novel à la Dickens – whose sentimentality no one would deny – thus ridding the genres of their genderedness which inevitably turns hierarchical.

19. This passage has been reprinted in the introduction to the Penguin edition of the *Narrative of the Life of Frederick Douglass, an American Slave, Written by Himself*. I quote from the 1982 edition. The introduction is by Houston A. Baker, Jr.

20. The terms of this opposition remind one of Flaubert's ambition to write an unimpassioned novel – a standard, that is, for realism. Eloquence would then be the opposite, the trace of the dramatized narrator that destroys the realistic effect. The interest of this passage is thus the argument that the authentic realism of the autobiography is enhanced by its literary realism, thus by its illusion of fictionality.

21. This is why the assessment is simply wrong. There is remarkably little focus on love; neither the persecuted slaves nor the tormented masters seem to have the energy to indulge in love relationships. Eva's death is described in detail, whereas Tom's death is not described in itself.

Religion does indeed play an important role, but not in the "typically female" sentimental way Larner suggests. Action, fights, and feats of heroism – those so-called nonmelodramatic, masculine themes – are not absent, but take just slightly different shapes from what Larner's horizon of expectations allows him to recognize; those expectations are clearly derived from the genre of the Western. How else could we describe Eliza–Hagar's and George's flights, Tom's refusal to beat a fellow slave if not as heroic? It all depends on the preconceived notions used, whether they allow the critic to recognize these as heroic acts.

22. In spite of her pointed critique of the "politics of literary history" which systematically underrates and excludes women's novels, Jane Tompkins continues to use the genre name which inherently evokes negative connotations in her book *Sensational Designs* (1985).

23. Shakespeare did not limit the use of the white-sheet effect to comedy; it also works in *Hamlet*, the exemplary tragedy, which, in turn, also adopts comical elements. Most of his tragedies have comic elements – for example, the gatekeeper in *Macbeth*.

24. In much the same way, today's feminists prefer to speak about alternative strategies and women's cultures than about oppression, and they prefer the term *survivor* to *victim* for those who were raped.

25. That Tom's heroic death is prefigured by little Eva's sweet and redeeming death does not make the genre effeminate, but instead appropriates the honorable position of Christ for both women and blacks. Tompkins (1985:127–8), demonstrates that Eva's and Tom's deaths, heroic and redemptory, represent a philosophy of power that is both religious and political. The scene of the death of an angel-like child may be standard in the literature of the period – in Dickens's *Dombey and Son*, the death of little Paul is in many respects similar to Eva's death – but in *Tom* the scene is much more politically effective than in other cases.

26. For an example of a syntactical analysis in visual art, see Benesch's comment on the structure of a set of drawings representing the departure of the angel in the Tobias story, drawings of Hagar in the desert, and drawings of the departure of the angel after Manoah's sacrifice (Benesch, 1973:235–43). This analysis is hardly an iconographic reading, however, because Benesch does not assign meanings to the signs. Baxandall (1971) uses the concept of syntax in a more specific way. He argues that Giotto's compositions endorse the syntactic structure used by contemporary orators. Thus he makes a good historical case for the project of "discursive viewing" as symmetrical to "visual reading."

27. This was a standard procedure and gives evidence for the particular ways in which artistic traditions were transmitted. The historical Rembrandt never went to Italy; hence, he never saw the original fresco. This situation alone makes a case for iconography as a reasonable approach, because only through art-internal dynamics can he have known the Leonardo; it also sets the limits to iconography. If the compositions and the figurative details such as body posture were eagerly copied and then imitated, this situation does not prove that imitation for its own sake was the most important goal for the artist. Framework rather than work, the predecessor's choices provided the artist with a language the audience was likely to understand; but the work "written" in that language was not identical to the work from

431

which that language was borrowed. The difference between language and utterance, between system and actual signs, makes plain the limits of the iconographic mode. For the need to transform the copied models, see, for literature, Bloom's *Anxiety of Influence* (1973) and, for visual art, Bryson's *Tradition and Desire* (1984). On Leonardo's fresco and its copies, see Steinberg's "Leonardo" (1974) and the literature there; on the "Rembrandt" drawings after the fresco, see Gantner (1964).

28. The engraving is ascribed to Giovanni Pietro da Birago, ca. 1500. Its attested popularity makes Rembrandt's knowledge of it plausible. For the attribution to Birago, see Oberhuber (1966). My interpretation does not depend on whether the dog was already in the model.

29. Steinberg (1974:360–72) attributes seven functions to the hands of Christ in the fresco. I fully agree with his passionate and persuasive plea for polysemous interpretation. He argues that copyists tend to disambiguate their models. This is certainly true of the copies made to memorize the composition, like Birago's. It is the more revealing that the hasty "Rembrandt" sketch contains so many aspects that extend polysemy far beyond his alleged model. More than memorizing the copy, then, "Rembrandt" memorized the ideas that the copy gave him for future elaborations, in a spirit, not of imitation, but of compositional allusion.

30. The only reference to the Brueghel that imposes itself is the stillness of the bride. However, through the compositional allusion to the Leonardo, our painting foregrounds this stillness, and gives it a meaning that is absent or marginal in the Brueghel (*pace* Gantner, 1964: 111–16).

31. I have analyzed this episode at length in *Death* (1988c). This bride is one of the three young women who are sacrificed in the Book of Judges, as victims of a struggle between fathers and husbands, and between two types of marriage connected with these positions. The aftermath of this failed wedding clearly points to this different type of marriage, where the wife stays in the house of her father.

32. Because the possession of the offspring by either father or husband is the major stake of the competition acted out in Judges, this gesture takes the story beyond seventeenth-century Christianity, back to ancient Judaism, and by the general theme of male competition it thus also refers to present-day feminist issues. For an iconographic precedent of the figuration of offspring as the meaning of the wedding, one can think of van Eyck's *Arnolfini Wedding*.

33. Hagar's image haunts Eliza's precisely because it requires the detour via the Jordan and Elijah. Hence, the Biblical Hagar becomes more densely charged with symbolic meanings. The confusion of different Biblical images does not make for a holistic sign; it signifies a confusion in the religious morality of the day, whose direct connection to the problem of slavery is its meaning. It is the double standard that is taken in, in *Color*, to bear upon the problem of women.

34. According to my opposition to Susanne Langer in Chapter 3, the *content* of a narrative, if we can speak of such thing in isolation at all, is different for each narrative, hence different also when the media differ. But that is not the issue at stake here. When I say that narrative structure is not medium-bound, I mean that each medium has the potential to *tell*,

that each can be read narratively if the addressee is competent and willing to do so.

35. On the importance of traditional attributes and "Rembrandt"'s deviations from the tradition, see the engaging analysis of the *Holy Family* in Kassel, by Wolfgang Kemp (1986).

36. See Steinberg in Mitchell (1984), for a good example of the signifying possibilities of the diagonal line. The diagonal often works as a syntactic connective.

37. As I shall argue in the next chapter, "Rembrandt" often highlights bodily tension as a sign of the idea of work in thematic contexts where work is not otherwise foregrounded. The device is so frequent that it becomes a self-reflexive sign, idiomatic of the oeuvre. This is consistent with common understanding of "Rembrandt" as a subject keenly interested in the status of art.

38. In Chapter 9, I shall give another example of the relation, established in "Rembrandt," between birthgiving and blindness.

CHAPTER 6

1. Nor do Romantic works themselves fit this idea of unity too neatly. It is striking that much work in deconstruction focuses on Romantic works in particular; Paul de Man (1979, 1984) and Chase (1986) are good examples. See Culler (1981, 1983) and van Alphen (1987) for illuminating discussions of the convention of unity.

2. On the problematics of authorship in connection with textual unity, see Derrida (1984, 1987b, 1988b) and Kamuf (1988).

3. See Habermas (1968/1972) and Jameson (1981) for critiques of the masterplot. Freud's predominant masterplot of the Oedipus complex has been sufficiently criticized, and the alternative of a pre-Oedipal plot in which the mother is central has convincingly been advanced. I shall refer to the latter in Chapter 9.

4. Mitchell argues that Goodman's blind spot is rooted in his fundamentally apolitical attitude, which makes him unaware of the conventions and value systems underlying representational practices. See especially Mitchell (1985), 70–4.

5. This is a problem with Bryson's chapter "Perceptualism" in *Vision* (1983). His theorizing of connotation in painting as what is superfluous for the sheer recognition of narrative syntagm seems to suggest that minimal narrative syntagm is linguistic. In addition, this entire section of the chapter is based on a wrongheaded interpretation of photography, inspired by Barthes's claim that photography is indexical by nature. Bryson misreads Peirce when proposing a sliding scale between indexical as based on resemblance (!), and symbolic, neglecting to account for the iconic in Peirce.

6. This is why much of the scholarship on word-and-image relations, however valuable in other ways, is theoretically based on the wrong premises. See, for example, Camille (1985), who, in spite of his opposition to verbocentrism, constantly seeks to map the *equivalent* visual signs to match the words. The problem is enmeshed with the confusion between ideas and propositions on the one hand, and sentences on the other; thus, also, are Gombrich's statement that images cannot distin-

guish the universal from the particular (review of Morris) and Burke's similar statement that images cannot represent the negative (Burke, 1968). To be sure, the fundamental difference between illustrations of a text, as in Camille's material, and representations of a (doxic) story, as in many of the "Rembrandts" here discussed, cannot be overestimated. Nevertheless, the matching, even as "literally" (!) as possible, between image and word will have to pass through the common idea that each of these represents within the possibilities of its own medium. Matching is never quite translation.

7. And that is not the same thing as meaningless. See Hamon's classic *L'Analyse* (1981); Kittay, ed., *Yale French Studies* (1980); and my own (1981–2) article. All these studies argue against the prejudice that only bare narrative syntagm is the skeleton of meaning, and what cannot be attached to that syntagm is meaningless. This privileging of narrative syntagm is a form of logocentrism.

8. I have myself done this in *Narratologie* (1977) and subsequently in "On Meanings" (1981–2), responding to Genette's use of Barthes's concept of the effect of the real. I do not feel that there was much wrong with my interpretation of the passage in *Madame Bovary* – nor was there much wrong with Genette's interpretation, for that matter – but the compulsion to take up such a challenge is interesting in itself for the discussion here. Today I would emphasize that these meanings originate in the reader, not the text.

9. On framing in literature, see Brombert (1980), D. A. Miller (1981), Piwitt (1965) for more traditional approaches; Herrnstein Smith's *Poetic Closure* (1968) seems to me the best of its kind; Derrida's remarks on framing throughout *Dissemination* (1981) and *Truth* (1987a) challenge the very notion of framing.

10. Benesch (1973:I, 40) lists the drawing as number 140, calling it "Different Listeners." He assumes it to be a study for the painting of *Saint John the Baptist Preaching*, in Berlin.

11. Richard Wollheim (1987) refers to something like this when he uses the idea of an image-internal spectator who is not represented. I find some of the interpretations he constructs quite illuminating, but his theoretical concepts too general. I prefer to theorize such an internal spectator as a focalizer whose appearance introduces narrativity, and who can be connected with diegetic focalizers. I also have basic problems with the theoretical and ideological framework of Wollheim's concept, which is an attempt to define art as work-immanent, as high art, as universal, as elitist, and, inevitably, implicitly as male.

12. I wish to insist, at this juncture, that undecidability is not the same thing as indeterminacy, let alone randomness. For a clear and short exposition of the difference between these two, see the Afterword to Derrida's *Limited Inc.*:

> I want to recall that undecidability is always a *determinate* oscillation between possibilities (for example, of meaning, but also of acts). These possibilities are themselves highly *determined* in strictly *defined* situations (for example, discursive – syntactical or rhetorical – but also political, ethical, etc). They are *pragmatically* determined. (Derrida, 1988b:148; emphases in text)

13. In fact, Benesch's source was H. Kauffmann (1926).

14. How deceptive such a circular knowledge can be is demonstrated by Alpers's (1988) comparison of Rembrandt's own self-portraits and Jan

Lieven's portrait of Rembrandt. We think that we know "Rembrandt"'s face, and use that knowledge to identify self-portraits in details of his history paintings. Since we like Rembrandt's art better, we believe his self-representations more accurate than Lievens's representation of "Rembrandt," which presents us with a quite different face. I find this conflation of aesthetics and realism quite telling.

15. Naturalization is the impulse to integrate a representation within our own sense of "normality," of what is possible and "natural" in our life experience. Thus there is a close connection between naturalization and appeal to doxa, or "common sense." See Culler (1975).

16. On de Hoogh, see Sutton (1980); Gerson (1966). On Vermeer, see Gowing (1970), Wheelock (1981), Blankert (1978), van Gelder (1958), and de Jongh (1976). A very acute interpretation of one of Vermeer's women with letter was proposed by Annie Leclerc (1977). Bryson (1990) connects interiors to still life precisely in this respect. His analysis of the marks of male intrusion in still life also holds for domestic interiors.

17. Annie Leclerc (1977) wrote perhaps the most congenial contemporary response to the love letter in Vermeer's *Woman Writing a Letter*. In this essay she attempts to reorient the traditional iconographic interpretation of the motif away from the cliché of marital infidelity into the direction of a women's sphere. Jane Gallop (1988:165–78) criticizes Leclerc's feminist reading/writing for its repression of class consciousness.

18. As I shall argue shortly, the letter is a shifter in the Biblical story, too. The story is, moreover, curiously confused where it deals with relations among signs, women, and death. See my *Lethal Love* (1987) for a detailed analysis.

19. See Alexander Gelley's attempt to bring the analysis of description beyond the taxonomic dichotomy: "Premises for a Theory of Description," in *Narrative Crossings* (1987). Gelley tries to overcome the dichotomy by moving from description to space to fictional worlds without clearly delimiting the scope of these concepts. I would contend that he would have succeeded better if he had assigned a proper place to visuality.

20. For a critique of this hierarchy, see Herrnstein Smith, *Margins of Discourse* (1978); and Culler, "Story and Discourse in the Analysis of Narrative," in *The Pursuit of Signs* (1981). Culler's position is based on Chase, "The Decomposition of the Elephants: Double-Reading *Daniel Deronda*," in *Decomposing Figures* (1986); and Peter Brooks, "Fictions of the Wolfman," in *Reading for the Plot* (1984).

21. In my (1981–2) article on description, I discuss the input of metaphor, metonymy, and other figural structures into description, a fact which in itself suffices to show the fictionality of even the most realistic description. I also argue, there, for the integration of description within the narrative, an argument I don't want to repeat here.

22. A most substantial and coherent account of realism to date seems to me Pavel's study of possible world poetics. A fine historical account of the development of realism in the service of politics is DiPiero (in press).

23. See DiPiero's pertinent analysis of this document. DiPiero writes in conclusion:

The Académie Française contributed to the definition of *vraisemblance* as political didacticism, as the promulgation of an officially sanctioned ideological vision of the world. (DiPiero, in press, ms. 99)

This vision of the world clearly included a gender politics.

24. One of the spokesmen of this realism was La Mesnardière. DiPiero quotes a telling passage:

> Pour la propriété des Moeurs, le Poète doit considérer qu'il ne faut jamais introduire sans nécessité absolue, ni une Fille vaillante, ni une Femme savante, ni un Valet judicieux. (DiPiero, in press, ms. 137)

DiPiero writes that La Mesnardière goes on to enumerate his cases of assaults on realism with a faithful African, a truthful Greek, a subtle German, or an uncivilized Frenchman. He then concludes:

> The development of *vraisemblance*, then, is a historically and politically determined literary mode that served to naturalize parochial representation, to narrow the ever widening schism separating an aristocratic ideal from elementary reality. In short, *vraisemblance* helped to reassert the ostensible adequation of ideal and real, of art and nature, while systematically eliminating any trace of political motivation. (DiPiero, in press, ms. 101)

We may think that we have, today, overcome these blatant prejudices, but that kind of evolutionism is itself a prejudice. In addition, even if the content of prejudices has changed, the use of realism to pass them off as the truth has not.

25. The argument is simultaneously serious – realistic – and parodic – textual. In the first interpretation, Mann sides with the Quran over and against the Bible. In the second, he is exaggerating in order to mock the kind of argument itself.

26. McHale (1987) argues convincingly that the "dominant" (a term borrowed from Jakobson, 1960) in modernism is epistemological skepticism, which, when pursued to its extreme, becomes ontological skepticism, the dominant of postmodernism. He alleges examples from novels by Faulkner and Joyce, but *Joseph and His Brothers* could be argued to demonstrate this transition within a single novel. For a seminal overview of current conceptions of postmodernism, see van Alphen (1989b).

27. Nazi methods to tell the difference between a Jew and an Aryan are no less ridiculously entangled in the impossibility of realism, and the all too real consequences of that realist craze demonstrate the urgent necessity of acknowledging this impossibility.

28. The term "narrative situation" refers to the specific combination of narrative agents that utters a narrative sequence: narrator, focalizer, and character actor. The description of Rouen is embedded in a sequence wherein the external narrator utters the words whose content is Emma's experience, mainly visual, of her voyage(s) to Rouen in anticipation of the already boring encounter(s) with her lover Léon. The tension between suddenness and routine is also signified by the highly implausible oscillation between exciting surprise and boring routine.

29. Elisabeth Bronfen (1990) analyzes a novella by Theodor Storm in this paper. Her words are:

> Wenn das Reale – in Anlehnung an Lacans Typology – nur bezeignet werden kann als Sein minus Repräsentanz, Beschreibung oder Interpretation, wird der Begriff "Realismus" adäquat für jenen Moment in einem darstellenden Text, der nicht nur die notwendige Uebersetzung des Realen ins Repräsen-

tatorische aufdekt, sondern das Reale nur in Bruchstücken zeigt, in jenen "Details", die das Scheitern und Stolpern jeglicher sybolisierender und imaginärer Versuchte zu manifestieren suchen.

30. Again, Naomi Schor's (1987) work on the detail is exemplary in the sense.

31. In *Word and Image* (1981), Bryson convincingly argues that there is no continuity in the importance of perspective from the Renaissance to the period of modernist art, and that notably rococo art ignores it almost completely. See Damisch's extensive analysis of thinking about perspective in *L'Origine de la perspective* (1987).

32. One may want to elaborate on Lacan's title: "L'Instance de la lettre" (1966). I shall not do so here, but let me just evoke three of the many associations generated by the word "instance": *example*, in straight English; *agent*, in reversed "Franglais" (e.g., as a translation of the French "les instances du récit"); *insistence*, as a filling and enhancement of a graphic gap. For the *Bathshebah*, all these meanings are relevant.

33. When speaking about the place of a letter and the displacements it can produce, I cannot, indeed, help thinking of the debate centered on this short story; comparable in passion and intellectual quality to the debate on *Las Meninas*, it extends from Lacan, via Derrida (1988a), to Barbara Johnson (1988) and beyond. The pieces of the debate have been published as a collection by John P. Muller and William J. Richardson (1988).

34. The translation is taken from *The Holy Scriptures of the Old Testament: Hebrew and English* (1976). There is discussion of the weapon: "millstone" or "piece of millstone." The translation might also be "one millstone," with emphasis on the singular, which alludes to the one stone with which Abimelech killed all his brothers save one. See my analysis of this issue in "The Displacement of the Mother," in *Death and Dissymmetry* (1988c).

35. Needless to say that nobody in her or his right mind will attempt to excuse David fully. But blaming him individually is a more pernicious way of staying outside of the ideologeme which informs the story and to which the viewer is subjected as much as the king.

36. In *Lethal Love* (1987), I analyzed in detail two critical responses to this metaphor, one (Perry and Sternberg, in Sternberg, 1985) entirely falling into the trap and eagerly buying into a superficial sexist interpretation; the other, more subtle and technically "correct," which, after carefully mapping out the complex structure, is nevertheless unwilling to interpret its very complexity along with its overt meanings (Fokkelman, 1981). As a result, even this careful critic misses the point of the sign for the real, the image's self-effacement. Compared to the *Las Meninas* discussion, the first of these interpretations would be comparable to Foucault's (1973) and Searle's (1980) "naive" (read: nontechnical) assumption about perspective, and the second to Snyder and Cohen's (1980) more sophisticated mapping of the "real" perspective; both, however, miss the point that Steinberg (1981) highlights, which incorporates the passion for technical righteousness.

37. This commonplace view persists in spite of overwhelming evidence that viewing necessarily takes time. See Goodman (1976:12) and Pritchard, Heron, and Hebb (1960) for psychological evidence, quoted by Goodman. For a theory of sequential reading of verbal art, see Perry (1979).

437

CHAPTER 7

1. The most extensive analysis of this little panel that I have found is in Bruyn et al., *Corpus* I (1982), 208–13.

2. See Linda Hutcheon, *Narcissistic Narrative* (1980) and her more recent *A Poetics of Postmodernism* (1988).

3. The painting has been seen as a reference to Apelles. See Broos (1983).

4. The cover represents a detail of *Tobias and the Angel* by the School of Verrochio, National Gallery, London.

5. See Bryson's devastating critique of the ideology of the "perfect copy" in *Vision and Painting* (1983).

6. The key text is "Le stade du miroir comme formateur de la fonction du Je" (1966b). See also Jacqueline Rose, *Sexuality in the Field of Vision* (1986).

7. Foucault (1973), 3–16. The critics who took up the challenge of Foucault's self-confident *placement* of the work within his own argument made little of the specific intertextual relation between the painting and the philosophical argument, which was reversed in comparison with the subsequent critical arguments. Foucault's purpose was not to say anything special about *Las Meninas* but to make *Las Meninas* say what he, Foucault, had to say about the classical age. It seems to me that this apparent use of a "masterpiece" as a mere example is partly responsible for the emotional responses. But in Foucault's way of writing, there is no such thing as a mere example. *Las Meninas* provided the philosopher with the discourse that he needed: a visual discourse. This detour was quite functional: It enabled him to escape the charge of simplification (which, ironically, is precisely what he was charged with). Foucault (1973:9) relativizes this view of visuality by a strong emphasis on the irreducible difference between words and images:

> But the relation of language to painting is an infinite relation. It is not that words are imperfect, or that, when confronted by the visible, they prove insuperably inadequate. Neither can be reduced to the other's terms: it is in vain that we say what we see; what we see never resides in what we say. And it is in vain that we attempt to show, by the use of images, metaphors, or similes, what we are saying; the space where they achieve their splendour is not that deployed by our eyes but that defined by the sequential elements of syntax.

8. These authors' dismay seems to stem from the well-known discomfort brought forth by interdisciplinary discourse. Here is one out of many defensive reactions to the very language Searle uses:

> In the first quotation Janson seems in the Foucault–Searle line, although he does not note a "paradox" wrought by this way of seeing the painting. In the second quotation he settles for an "ambiguity," a less exotic logical crux. (Snyder and Cohen, 1980)

Indeed, this seems to me primarily a reaction to philosophical terms. The irony is just a little too heavy-handed for such a casual issue, emphasized as it is by the quotation marks which disqualify the terms they frame – the word "exotic" related to "logic," the unnecessarily ironic "wrought." The focus of the irony, however, is not only alien discourse but also, precisely, the threat emanating from "wrought by this way of seeing the painting."

9. See Derrida's preface to *Truth in Painting* (1987a), where the author

"disseminates" the meaning of the phrase so as to preclude any attempt to give it meaning. "Truth in painting" has no truth to reveal.

10. There are two different and even opposed, postmodern positions at stake here, which have been disentangled in the illuminating article by van Alphen (1989b): the eclectic position, which takes historical styles as a playground of available elements to be adopted; and the critical position, which uses historical styles polemically in responding to them, thus making statements of historical interest. Eclectic postmodernism, then, bears comparison with some excessive forms of iconography, which only traces provenance without interpreting the meaning of a reference. Critical postmodernism bears comparison with a critical iconographic practice; for example, Mary Garrard's reading of Gentileschi (see Chapter 4).

11. In David Couzens Hoy, ed., *A Foucault Reader* (1986), 250.

12. Van Alphen addresses this paradox in his book on reading attitudes by differentiating between the reading attitudes proposed by the text and those adopted by the reader. He distinguishes four possible attitudes in relation to it: the realistic text read realistically, the postmodern text read postmodernistically, the postmodern text realistically, and the realistic text read postmodernistically. Given the corpus my study works with, the fourth attitude is at stake. A realistic text is then a work that is not wholly realistic, but that both fits the conventions of realism and has elements that enable, or even encourage, a "postmodern," self-reflective, reading attitude. See van Alphen (1988b), 59.

13. The different spellings – *self-reflexion* referring to mirroring, *self-reflection* to introspection – are not consistently differentiated, and do not hold in French, where the same word is used to denote both meanings and thus carries even greater ambiguity.

14. This is an admittedly radical interpretation of Alper's book, *Rembrandt's Enterprise* (1988). In a discourse that is more historical and intentionalist than I deem she is able consistently to substantiate, Alpers discusses four ways in which Rembrandt determined the status of his work as "high art." The first of these, "The Master's Touch," or self-reflexive devices of paint handling, will be discussed in Chapter 10 of the present study. Another, theatricality, has been briefly presented in relation to *Samson's Wedding* in Chapter 1. The two others are the mastery over the studio and the marketing of art. The irritated, often angry, responses Alpers's book has received resemble some aspects of the *Las Meninas* debate. They point to the problem of the lack of self-reflection in Alpers's critics, who get upset without realizing how their motivations for anger are connected to the very subject of Alpers's book. The irritation invariably concerns Alpers's characterization of Rembrandt as a shrewd businessman rather than as a lonely genius; yet her critics cannot help but accuse Alpers of falling back into the romantic view of the genius that they, her critics, have set out to undermine. Given Alpers's picture of Rembrandt as a businessman, the opposite seems rather to be the case. It strikes me as relevant for the discussion here that Alpers's critics, hardly concealing their irritation, tend to criticize her "tone." Being in disagreement with some of Alpers's statements, but not in the least irritated that she makes statements at all, I see the tone they attribute to her in her critics' discourse, not in hers; a good case of nonreflective self-mirroring.

15. See, for example, Jonathan Brown (1986) and Madlyn Millner Kahr (1976); also Emmens (1961).

16. This is one common element between classicism and postmodernism, at least in Charles Jencks's (1987) view of the latter.

17. Note that the propositional content of Foucault's and Searle's interpretation is basically the same. If, for Foucalt, the essence of classical representation is the absence of the viewer, then to *signify* that absence *in* the painting is already to enter into Searle's paradox. This signification of absence is, by the way, a case of pictorial negation, deemed impossible by Kenneth Burke (1968). I shall return to this negativity shortly.

18. Modernism is sometimes conflated with postmodernism; for example, see Melville (1986). As mentioned before, McHale (1987) sees modernism as embodying epistemological doubt and postmodernism as embodying ontological doubt. Jencks warns against a conflation of what he calls "hypermodernism" – modernist principles taken to their extreme – and postmodernism; between the two there is a radical schism.

19. I use the word "interest" in the strong, Habermassian sense of motivations that orient a discourse and relate it to the historical and bodily subject of the speaker/writer/painter. See Habermas (1968/1972). Using the term in this sense by no means implies that I adopt Habermas's idealistic normative critique. I insist on this point because in *Femmes imaginaires* (1986a), where I use Habermas's view to substantiate my own claims about narrative and reading, I have not differentiated my views clearly enough from his.

    A statement on Searle's interests does not refer to intention but to the orientation-guided agency. The relationship between orientation and agency is not predicated upon the unconscious either. It can be *explained* with reference to either intention or the unconscious, but I shall refrain as long as I can from speculating about a colleague's psyche. If I wind up using a psychoanalytic vocabulary to interpret the critical texts, this must be seen in consistency with the position I take in this book: as the product of the interaction between myself and these texts.

20. His investment in both is equally strong, obviously, because the existence *and* the resolution of the former, the paradox of the painting, must prove the validity of the latter, his theory of meaning. That Searle is sensitive regarding his theory is public knowledge and to a certain degree understandable, given extensive attacks on it by Derrida. The pieces of Derrida's contribution to this debate are published in *Limited Inc.* (1988b); Searle's reply to the first piece, Derrida's "Signature Event Context," appeared in *Glyph* as "Reiterating the Differences: A Reply to Derrida" (1977).

21. Whereas Snyder and Cohen respond to the philosopher's intrusion into the field of art history, Alpers, known for her involvement in interdisciplinary discussions on representation, addresses precisely the limitations of art-historical discourse. Alpers is one of the founders and editors of the journal *Representations* which endeavors precisely to examine questions of representation in different media.

22. For Georgel and Lecoq, this is the reason why self-portraiture is a central genre within their categorization of self-reflexive art.

23. At first sight, Searle's statement might enjoy the benefit of a (possibly) productive doubt. If it is meant ambiguously, the word "model" is the shifter between the two possible readings of the statement: Is Searle speaking of the royal pair as "really" present at the invisible side of the room – as present as the viewer is – or as the models of the represented painting scene? Such a reading of the statement would have a truly self-reflexive potential, involving the viewer – Searle – in breaking down the work's unity. The description of the painting, however, precludes such a reading and, to the contrary, suggests a generalizing statement almost comparable to Mann's ironic one about Joseph's beauty and the little knives. Searle's analysis relies heavily on the conflation of model and representation, which turns the discussion into a realistic endeavor. (I need this irony to make my own argument clear; but I am well aware of the injustice done to Searle in the move. Maybe it will help to realize that my own analysis of self-reflection is meant to be self-reflexive: I am setting up an intertext as well as a set of characters – Searle being the first victim of this fictionalization – apt for demonstrating the mechanisms of self-reflection.)

24. Granted, the "Rembrandt" is on one level just an early work, and it is easy – too easy for my taste – to attribute the stiff pose to "real" clumsiness. But what if this early date is appropriated into the interpretation, and what if, by the time he did this work, the artist had already painted dynamic narrative works? The issue here is that of the problem of "high art." It is hard, sometimes, not to be a connoisseur and therefore evaluate the paintings. Yet this chapter sets out to undercut precisely that impulse.

25. It is as if the need for realism has something to do with this: It allows the critic to jubilate about self-reflection while totally escaping its threatening, because self-questioning, effect of mirroring: the reflection of the painter's self in the viewer's.

26. Rather than ask the obvious question why seeing, thinking, and speaking should be identical in structure, I want to address the symptomatic choice of examples. Searle's example of the "I think" structure in fantasy is problematic; his "I say" example is highly surprising.

27. Take, for example, Proust's Marcel as the adult writer; this persona is linguistically indistinguishable yet representationally radically different from the young boy experiencing the anxiety produced by his mother's uncertain availability; from the adolescent exploring social and sexual roles; even from the adult thinker, self-reflexively worried about the endeavor he is involved in.

28. In an illuminating discussion of this problem, Genette (1969) advocated Benveniste's distinction between *discours* and *récit*.

29. Louis Marin's *Études sémiologiques* (1971) contains wonderful analyses; yet the assumed analogy between speaking and looking often confuses the issues unnecessarily. Sharon Willis's sharp and convincing critique of Diderot's art-critical position and of Michael Fried's (1980) reiteration of that position, which also refers to Marin's "Arcadian Shepherds" (reprinted in Bryson, 1988b), at one point delineates this dubious analogy explicitly:

> Any speech event, then, constitutes an implicit mapping of positions with respect to a context. The same is basically true for the look. (Willis, 1984:92)

30. Again, I have to apologize for using the critical discourse as a sample

rather than as a text in its own right and for the inevitable distortions such a use entails. I strongly encourage the reader to read these texts for their own argument.

31. Lacan insisted on the ambiguous but central aspect of identification in the mirror stage when he wrote:

> Il y suffit de comprendre le stade du miroir *comme une identification* au sens plein que l'analyse donne à ce terme: à savoir la transformation produite chez le sujet quand il assume une image. (Lacan, 1966b:90)

But the transformation, which later on becomes a retrospective source of anxiety, is overwritten by the experience of wholeness in vision:

> L'Assomption jubilatoire de son image spéculaire par l'être encore plongé dans l'impuissance motrice et la dépendance du nourrissage qu'est le petit homme à ce stade *infans*, nous paraîtra dès lors manifester en une situation exemplaire de la matrice, symbolique où le *je* se précipite en une forme primordiale, avant qu'il ne s'objective dans la dialectique de l'identification à l'autre et que le langage ne lui restitue dans l'univers sa fonction de sujet. (Lacan, 1966b:90)

These aspects of the formation of the subject through the endorsement of the assaults on his or her narcissistic wholeness can be read in the literary features of Snyder and Cohen's article.

32. The irony of the article's title seems to have Searle's happy solution to the problem of *Las Meninas* as its target; only the philosopher's blissful "simple solution" justifies such an ironic allusion. The bliss was achieved, for Searle, when his argument reached the solution of self-reference. The concluding sentences of Searle's essay are, indeed, interesting in that they locate the source of the bliss in self-containment and the unification of the work in its simplicity, and the gratification awarded to the narcissistically absorbed critic:

> There is no way to answer the question What is the picture a picture of? that does not include reference to the picture. But that is *simply* a *consequence* of the *fact* that the picture is self-referential. On the representational reading, its conditions of *satisfaction* include it. (Searle, 1980:488; my emphases)

The syntax of the first sentence reflects the self-containment it describes: The question whose answer has to be included in the picture is embedded in the sentence that reflects (on) the picture. The second sentence restates the same thing simply as "simply," the repetition as logic ("consequence"), the self-reflexive interpretation as a "fact" about the work, thus demonstrating the critic's absorption. The bliss itself, for which the ground has thus been prepared, is represented in the very end, where the slightly misplaced word "satisfaction" replaces the more usual "felicity." The effect of this deviation from traditional terminology is enhanced by the grammatical separation of conditions and satisfaction, where the more conventional speech-act theoretical expression would have been "felicity conditions."

Obviously, Searle's philosophical position cannot be reduced to the unifying impulse; I am not reading his text as philosophical-discursive, but as literary. And the unifying impulse is represented strongly enough in his text when read as literary – which includes visuality. Reading the article as literary is not only meant to undercut the prestige of philosophical discourse itself which lends it more credibility than is "logical." This reading is also an attempt to gain further insight into the problematic interaction between verbality and the visuality in both verbal and visual texts. In addition, the reading I have ventured was meant to pave the way for an understanding of the discrepancy between metacritical distance and precritical passion.

33. The possibility that the work promotes the "wrong" use of point of view might have led to reflection on the impulse for technical propriety. The technical notion of point of view is itself predicated upon an ideology of abstract, disembodied seeing, which Bryson (1983) called "retinal."

34. Freud's (1925) essay on negation provides only a psychoanalytical framework for a well-known aspect of everyday life. The signifying power of denial is precisely why negation can, indeed, be visually represented. Denial is not absence; it is the statement of an absence, thereby its re-presentation.

35. As I have argued, Searle's claim about the painting is less than "stunning and wide-ranging"; on the contrary, it is quite narrow, a limitation represented by his word "simply." Understanding the work as simple, Searle's triumph also appropriates it, thereby claiming, indeed, that he is (as clever as) the artist.

36. Snyder and Cohen themselves have reflected Searle's happy simplicity, his sweeping certainty, and his embedding syntax that presents the crucial qualifier as unquestionable. But the sentence quoted above reflects more than that: It avows the inherently tautological, hence noncritical, position of criticism, its paradoxical absorption within the self-critical work that is being criticized. On the rational level, the insistence on certainty is already telling: The "procedure" (the theory, the critic's instrument) allows the critics to "establish" (implying certainty) a point that in turn "establishes" (for sure) the "projection" (presumably unambiguously dictated by the work).

37. See Bryson (1983), for a critique of the idea of a disembodied look; see Thiher (1984) for a characterization of modernism and postmodernism in terms of the view of, and attitude toward, vision in language theory and in fiction.

38. In a footnote about the mirror, Snyder and Cohen display an anxiety of mirroring. Criticizing Foucault's loose (read: literary rather than technically pictorial) use of terms which they claim to be able to use more "appropriately," they write:

> It will not do, even if spoken very loosely, to say that we are opposite the whole wall when we are at our point of view, for then one would be *obliged* to *admit* that if, say, the mirror and one of the rear wall's paintings were interchanged, 'we' would still be reflected in the mirror. (Snyder and Cohen, 1980:437, n. 9; my emphases)

This obligation to confess our sins is less painful than the critics seem to assume, for the relation between pictorial representation and mirroring is precisely what the work in its self-reflexivity proposes. Therefore, the mirror and the painting within the painting are, indeed, interchangeable semiotically. Qua meaning, they are readable as synonymous. In addition, the "we," including the ironic quotation marks, betrays another anxiety: the anxiety of the visual side of reflection, of mirroring, of being mirrored, of being conflated between "reality" and representation. The "we" is as symptomatic as a genuinely Freudian parapraxis, for no one claims that "we" are reflected; our position is flatteringly taken by the royal couple, and the couple is mirrored. The "Rembrandt" panel shows this more clearly, again, than the Spanish work, precisely because the "we," here, is radically alone. The lack of narrative, of characters involved in action, is also a lack of the Other, the symbolic order that saves the subject from the nauseating specularity of the mirror.

39. The inattention can be seen to support several meanings, different but convergent in each case. The Infanta, ignoring the drink offered to her, substitutes her parents as a more important center of interest, thus complying with her role as obedient child, while also playing her social role of mistress, free to say "no" to a servant. The man in the middle ground similarly confirms social roles: He refuses to listen to a fellow servant, equal in status but lower in gender, while paying homage to his divinely ordained superiors. The third indifferent character, the dog who would be well placed to enhance narrativity by responding to the supposed arrival of the royal couple, does nothing of the sort. Is this signifying a lack of respect for royalty, due to the dog's lack of humanity, hence, of understanding of social structure? I would rather assume that narrativity in the episodic sense was to be subordinated to a narrativity inscribing the social hierarchy. In this vein, the dog as sign teaches the boy a lesson about the inappropriateness of *his* inattention to the entrance or presence of the king and queen, to which all episodic action is to be subordinated.

40. The connection between social rank and vision is especially relevant in relation to the construction of gender. See Bryson's illuminating essay (in press) on the construction of masculinity in Géricault through a genderization of rank.

41. The phrase is from Jean Delay's now classic psychoanalytic study of Gide, *La jeunesse d'André Gide* (1973–4).

42. Psychoanalytic work on visual art is less current. Examples are offered by Handler Spitz (1985) and by Fuller (1985). In contrast, film studies rely heavily on psychoanalysis, especially its feminist vein, arguably the most powerful one. See for example, Rose (1980) and, of course, Silverman (1988).

CHAPTER 8

1. See Freud (1910b, 1914b). Peter Fuller's (1985) critique of Freud's art criticism is only one example in a long series of comments. Particularly relevant is Rose's brief comment at the end of *Sexuality* (1986).

2. Shoshana Felman has pleaded convincingly against the notion that the work is the patient in all her writings on psychoanalysis; see especially "To Open the Question" (1977) and *Jacques Lacan* (1987). See also Brooks (1987). See also Gallop (1984).

3. An example of both enriching and reductive work can be found in Michael Fried's publications, already discussed in the first chapter. I am referring positively to Fried's (1987) Eakins interpretation. I find most of his article "Courbet's Femininity" (1988), in contrast, both reductive and overly idiosyncratic. For a wonderful analysis of those of Freud's writings that suggest fiction and art, see Kofman (1973, 1985b).

4. For a more or less Freudian perspective, see Handler Spitz (1985). For a Lacanian perspective, see Rose (1986) and Silverman (1988, 1989).

5. See, for example, Etty Mulder, *Freud en Orfeus* (1987). Mulder draws

upon Jean-Joseph Goux's *Les iconoclastes* (1978). The very notion of nonverbal aurality immediately evokes, of course, Kristeva's concept of the maternal chora and the related distinction between the (preverbal) semiotic and the symbolic. Kristeva uses these in *Revolution in Poetic Language* (1984) and in *Desire in Language* (1980). An introduction to Kristeva can be found in Toril Moi's *Sexual/Textual Politics* (1985) and her introduction to *The Kristeva Reader* (1986) which she edited. Rose's essay "Julia Kristeva: Take Two" (1986) is also important. The best critique of the concept of the chora is "The Fantasy of the Maternal Voice" by Silverman, in *The Acoustic Mirror* (1988).

6. See Elena Ciletti, "Questa e la donna terribile!" (1988) for an account of the case of Gentileschi, and her "Patriarchal Ideology" (in prep.) for a study of Judith iconography. Ciletti points to the stunningly reductive and *thereby* sexist interpretations, in *American Imago*, by Joseph W. Slap (1985), Graeme J. Taylor (1984), and Martin S. Bergmann (1976), all three of vague, undigested psychoanalytical inspiration.

7. See the stunning case of a drawing by Leonardo da Vinci, invoked by Rose (1986) in her concluding essay. This drawing displays the fright itself, its source in vision, and its result in the mutilation of the female body. Visual disgust is the overwhelming expression on the face of the male subject in this drawing.

8. This is, I would like to speculate, why film studies are so central for the psychoanalytic criticism of visuality, and also why this strand of film studies started out from the concept of castration anxiety. See, for example, Mulvey (1975). It all holds together.

9. See, for example, *Camera Obscura*, a journal for feminism and film theory.

10. Lacan's diagrams and illustrations by themselves make the point about the interaction between verbal and visual. His famous set of ladies' and gentlemen's room doors as an "illustration" of his version of the Saussurian sign displays the irreducible overflow of meaning brought into discourse by the visual sign.

11. An example of a dialogue with equal partners is Silverman, "Fassbinder" (1984). Examples of more orthodox accounts are Sullivan, *Lacan* (1986); and Rose, *Sexuality* (1986).

12. As I wrote there, "Comparative Arts" is meant as a term that endorses the positive aspects of Comparative Literature: its theoretical perspective, its systematic confrontation of works coming from different cultural backgrounds, and its questioning of elitist and logocentric assumptions; not its negative aspects, like its imperialist tendencies and its narrow humanism.

13. One example among many is Harvey Breverman's *Printer* of 1970. The catalog of an exhibition of Breverman's work in the Jean Paul Slusser Gallery at Ann Arbor shows the artist's photograph. A self-portrait on the cover of the same catalog presents the face recognizable from the photograph, yet also resembling the face in *The Printer*. On the other hand, the face in that work is clearly "Rembrandt." Thus this work is a self-portrait – of Breverman – and a portrait of "Rembrandt," but not a "Rembrandt" self-portrait. *The Printer* is owned by Raymond Federman at Buffalo.

14. An obvious example is the term "perversions." Although the term itself does suggest deviation, Freud clearly and repeatedly presents the

perversions as the norm, the key to normal sexuality, the mastercode that helps him to formulate his major discoveries. Yet the term has never been emancipated from its negative connotations.

15. Theory of performativity itself has suffered from problems similar to those of psychoanalysis. The theory, which includes Austin's initial proposal, criticized by Derrida (1988b), defended by Felman (1980), clearly summarized by Culler, and taken up by deconstructionists of the second generation (e.g., Kamuf, 1988), is most productive when viewed as a temporarily suspended set of uncertainties. See my *Death and Dissymmetry* (1988c), ch. 5, for a less than blissful version of it.

16. The most insistently sexual interpretation of this story is by Zakovitch (1981).

17. See Fokkelien van Dijk-Hemmes, "Gezegende" (1986) for this evolution, and "Interpretaties" (1989) for a detailed analysis of Judges 4 and 5. Van Dijk has contributed substantially to the feminist insight which understands the very praise of these female figures, in their intertextual connections, as displaying a negative development of gender relations in the chronology of the Biblical literature.

18. See my *Murder and Difference* (1988b), where I discuss Yael's case at length, and bibliography there for evidence of the negative view of the character.

19. The Pygmalion tradition is present in "Rembrandt" in the little etching "The Goldsmith," where the male artist is also represented as a sculptor and as a lover.

20. See my *Death and Dissymmetry* (1988c) for a critical analysis of this construction, which is systematically carried out literally over the dead bodies of young women. See specifically Judges 11:30–1 and 34–40 the sacrifice of Jephthah's daughter; Judges 15:1–6, the murder of Samson's first wife; and, most disturbingly, Judges 19, the gang rape and murder discussed in Chapter 2 and again in Chapter 10 of the present study.

21. See Louise S. Richardson, "A Rembrandt Drawing" (1970). I thank Dr. Richardson for her assistance in the study of this drawing. Seymour Slive dates this drawing 1640–5.

22. To be fair to Held, I must add that his is not a psychoanalytic endeavor. He mentions the theme of castration only in passing. Of course, this casual encounter with psychoanalysis brings with it its own problems. Held tends to idealize Rembrandt's motivation in regard to his preference for the Tobias story. While Held (1969:117) notes that "it is certain that in most cases Rembrandt dealt with the story of his own volition," the critic nevertheless claims that love between father and son is the attraction of the story for Rembrandt (Held, 1969:120–4). Thus he affirms: "Indeed, stories demonstrating the ties of affection between father and son always appealed to Rembrandt" (Held, 1969:121). One wonders how Held envisages the precise relation between this love and the castration motif, and the relationship between volition and the unconscious.

23. The emptiness of the surface of Isaac's smooth body and eyeless face is even more striking in the painting of the same theme.

24. And, speaking of knives, we must not forget the other side of Tobias's endeavor which so pointedly reminds us of Mann's little knives: defloration. And this suggests yet another crossing of gender boundaries.

25. For an analysis of the ambivalence of the fantasy of the muse, see Bronfen (1988).

26. Borch-Jacobsen's entire book is devoted to the disentanglement of the consequences of this paradox. Although I do not believe that his analysis undermines psychoanalysis as a whole, the paradoxes of narcissism are at the heart of the problem of the subject. Borch-Jacobsen rightly argues that the subject, dislodged from the ego, is neatly moved to the unconscious, thus leaving the individual's autonomy basically intact.

27. See André Green, "Le narcissisme primaire: structure ou état," in his (1988) study on narcissism, for a brilliant analysis of the problem of primary narcissism. Green concludes that primary narcissism cannot be a state or phase but must be a structure. It is only imagined as a phase.

28. See Laplanche (1976), ch. 4. For a comprehensive study of the problem of narcissism one can best begin with the entry in Laplanche and Pontalis (1973); next read Freud's essay "On Narcissism: An Introduction" (1914c); and then read Laplanche's chapter, Borch-Jacobsen's chapter "Ecce Ego" (1988), and Green's chapter "Le Narcissisme primaire" (1983). On primary narcissism there is also Kristeva, *The Powers of Horror* (1982).

29. See, for a good presentation of Kristeva's view, Cynthia Chase's (1983) review of the book. See also Jacobus, "Dora and the Pregnant Madonna," in *Reading Woman* (1986) for a discussion of it. Jacobus brings Kristeva's view to bear upon the material Steinberg brings in, in his *Sexuality of Christ* (1983), and she succeeds in adding a fascinating dimension to Steinberg's interpretation.

30. "La mère est prise dans le cadre vide de l'hallucination négative, et devient structure encadrante pour le sujet lui-même. Le sujet s'édifie là où l'investiture de l'objet a été consacrée au lieu de son investissement." (emphasis removed)

31. "L'Hallucination négative de la mère, sans être aucunement représentative de quelque chose, *a rendu les conditions de la représentation possibles.*" (emphasis in text)

32. André Green emphasizes this dual status of the structure of primary narcissism as *existence in nonexistence*. Borch-Jacobsen explains this duality by, precisely, the inherent mimeticism of *any* narcissism.

33. On the cultural status of distinction and contemporary views of how to achieve distinction, see Bourdieu's *On Distinction* (1984). Although Bourdieu does not address this issue, the very notion of distinction as aesthetic superiority suggests a relationship between the fantasy of primary narcissism and the social valuation of taste.

34. One of the best brief presentations of the multiple meanings of the term "imaginary" that are bound to the concept of the mirror stage is Jacqueline Rose's *Sexuality* (1986), 53.

35. See Banfield (1982) for a linguistic analysis of discursive nonreflexivity.

36. Bruyn et al. discuss this work in *Corpus* I, (1982), 218–24. They find the work "has less of the painted study about it, and has a rather more representational meaning" than other self-portraits of the same period. I fully agree with this assessment, and my purpose here is to clarify that sense of semantic plenitude. For an illuminating account of the "face-value" in "Rembrandt," see Koerner (1986).

447

37. This ugliness is in turn, of course, the product of the artist's struggle with self. The portrait of Rembrandt by Lievens, in the Rijksmuseum in Amsterdam, presents him perhaps not as more sympathetic but certainly as less ugly, than many of the self-portraits. Yet the discourse on "Rembrandt," entirely based on the work as it is, has constructed an ugly artist, believing "Rembrandt" rather than Lievens. See Alpers (1988), ch. 1.

38. The metaphoric object choice of narcissism is contrasted with the metonymically based anaclitic object choice, based on identification – hence, also metaphoric – between the object of love and the parent anaclitically invested. See Laplanche and Pontalis (1973), 33.

39. Freud lists these four forms of narcissistic investment in his essay "On Narcissism: An Introduction" (1914c). See also Borch-Jacobsen's (1988) commentary, 102–7.

40. For a social perspective on visual art which addresses questions like this one, see Janet Wolff (1981).

41. The initial paper was published in the volume of papers from the conference for which I wrote it; see Rimmon-Kenan, ed. (1987). The conference took place in Jerusalem, and as I was writing on the Hebrew Bible then, I felt uncomfortable speaking on the Bible at that particular location. It was by this experience of strange involvement that "Rembrandt" became my way out: The etching enabled me to speak on the Bible through the etching, thus bringing together two cultures instead of appropriating the other.

42. Special thanks to Milena Dolezelova-Velingerova to whose voice as female other I owe *seeing* what my blindness would not let me see before, maybe because it was frighteningly attractive.

43. Some of my readers still find this hard to see. In Figure 8.10, I have tampered with the etching so as to demonstrate what my respondent in Toronto saw, and what I was willing to see after a long hesitation. Even after it was pointed out to me, it took me weeks to see it, because, I can now say, I had to conquer another repression, which had to do with narcissism. On one level, of course, I would have liked to discover this possibility myself; hence my narcissism was wounded. But this kind of self-accusation is a way out that is just too easy.

44. Bruyn et al., who discuss this work in *Corpus* II (1982), 321–32, doubt that Saskia was the model for this Bellona. This question can never really be answered of course, since we know Saskia only from "Rembrandt"'s representations of her. With that caveat I am inclined to see at least some similarity with "Saskia"'s face, whether Saskia sat for the painting or not.

45. The pacifying eyes are needed to neutralize the frightening, threatening effect of frontality which Jean-Pierre Vernant sees as a systematic mythologeme in his *La mort dans les yeux* (1985). It is striking that "Rembrandt" has other ways of making frontality meaningful. In the two *Lucretia*s (Figures 2.1 and 2.2), the frontality does have the stark effect Vernant posits, but instead of frightening the viewer, it signifies the figure's fright of the viewer.

46. Fernandez in fact concludes that the painter's assumed "horror feminitatis" led to homosexuality, a conclusion that amounts to an unwarranted homophobic generalization. Fernandez's judgment is based not only on anachronistic ideals of female beauty – along with the critics whose comments were discussed in Chapter 4, he finds many

of Rembrandt's women ugly – but also on offensive views of homosexuality as gynophobia. In addition, it rests on a superficial reading of the *Nightwatch*, in which he fails to see the relationship, constructed by light, color, and diegetic focalization, between the girl in yellow and the "hero" of the painting.

47. Held explains the predilection for the Tobias story in a similarly biographical though more positive vein, by suggesting that Rembrandt was deeply attached to his father. Such a view is resolutely incompatible with the psychoanalytic framework of the Oedipus complex which Held invokes in support of it.

48. In order to avoid any misunderstanding, I initiate this play between the paintings as a visual reading device, not on the basis of "real" connection – which can be based only on biographical data, if at all. I see possibilities of establishing a connection that is largely discursively informed (based on psychoanalytic thought about ideals and idealization) but visual in effective labor; the connections are visual. As for biographical background, the issue is not whether the woman "is" Saskia: Maybe the artist chose his wife according to his image of powerful women, and/or chose to make some of the Saskia portraits, especially the *Saskia as Flora* of 1635 (London, National Gallery) resemble the *Bellona*. The London painting is very close to the *Bellona*, and the woman's gaze is almost identical, while the color of the hair makes the reference to Saskia a little more convincing. Between the two paintings, "Rembrandt" married. The apparent contradiction between these two paintings – the one representing war, the other idyllic spring and fertility – is dissolved once we make more of Bellona's peaceful gaze and her large body, as I am doing here on the one hand, and, on the other hand, notice the weapon that the x-rays have revealed to have been held in Flora's right hand, but which was painted over. Flora was Judith in her former life!

49. Schwartz (1985), 125. As I hope to have made clear in Chapter 2, I believe that rhetoric is a discursive "language," a way of conveying meanings, and not, as is often assumed, an ornamental and futile addition to the "real" signs, hence, meaningless. Schwartz's use of the word "rhetorical" points to this negative connotation of the term, hence the reference to "clumsiness" I ventured earlier.

50. For a fascinating – *c'est le cas de le dire* – analysis of Medusa imagery in the literature of the French Revolution, see Hertz, *The End of the Line* (1985).

51. According to an early Freudian account, comedy as a genre is characterized by the defeat of the father, whereas tragedy endangers the son. Both genres, in this view, are elaborations of the Oedipus complex, but the radical difference in *mood*, which entails the difference in *mode*, stems ultimately from the position of the son. See Verhoeff (1974, 1980) for an account of this problematic. The male-centeredness of this view, again, conflicts with the intense attention to women and their positions in "Rembrandt." An account of the Oedipal complex from the perspective of the mother is called for in the case of a male artist who does not merely love the mother, but also does not fear identification with her.

52. "Le temps de la séparation d'avec la mère et le temps du refoulement pourront se rejoindre après coup, mais ils ne sont pas confondus à l'origine, puisque cette conjonction des temps est rétrospectivement

inférée par la recherche de l'objet perdu, qui réunit la perte réelle de l'objet lors de la séparation et la perte subie par le refoulement."

53. The distinction between vision as sense perception, and visuality as a culturally framed mode of behavior is the theme of a (1988) collection edited by Hal Foster. The terms are not meant to suggest that there is such a thing as "pure" or "neutral" vision; the former term just emphasizes the physical aspect of seeing, whereas the latter focuses on the cultural determinations of the same.

CHAPTER 9

1. See Freud (1914c). For a critique of this alleged centrality, see Laplanche (1976), ch. 4.

2. This is particularly striking in the first volume of Benesch's (1973) edition of the drawings. As a sampling of the theme's occurrence, I submit that the following numbered drawings can be related to problems of vision, either because of the pre-text or because of the representation of the eyes: 2, 7, 17, 23, 23A, 35, 38, 40, 42, 56 recto, 82, 93, 127 recto, 128, 129, 131, 150, 154, 167, 174, 189, 190.

3. See my *Murder and Difference* (1988b). The special issue of *Poétique* devoted to thematics clearly demonstrates the regressive, positivist tendencies of thematics. Although some of the articles in that issue are historical and/or interdisciplinary enough to escape these tendencies (e.g., Leroux, 1985), the overall endeavor strikes me as regressive and defensive.

4. See Culler, *On Deconstruction* (1983). Two examples of self-reflexive thematics that are similar to my endeavor here are Schor (1984) and Fried (1987). In the opening chapter of *Breaking the Chain* (1987), Schor proposes a self-reflexive thematic reading of *Madame Bovary* that focuses on writing, speech, and difference. And as mentioned previously, Michael Fried's *Realism, Writing, Disfiguration* emphasizes writing in the painting, and drawing in the text he analyzes.

5. Seeing is thus part and parcel of sexual politics as analyzed, for example, by Leo Bersani in his seminal article "Is the Rectum a Grave?" Bersani (1989:218) writes:

> [T]he self which the sexual shatters provides the basis on which sexuality is associated with power. It is possible to think of the sexual as, precisely, moving between a hyperbolic sense of self and a loss of all consciousness of self. But sex as self-hyperbole is perhaps a repression of sex as self-abolition. It inaccurately replicates self-shattering as self-swelling, as psychic tumescence.

Bersani's analysis of sexual politics in view of the AIDS crisis is timely and convincing. Precisely because of its compelling importance I must point out occasional dangers in the paper, notably when the author seems to fall into the trap of cheap liberalism by equating child *abuse* with childhood *sexuality*, and identifies the struggle against the former with a psychotic resistance against the latter (Bersani, 1989:215). This is a rhetorical trap, justifying the very equation of violence and pastoral Bersani sets out to denounce.

6. See Laplanche and Pontalis, *The Language* (1973), 431-3. The most thorough discussion of sublimation by Freud is in *Three Essays on the Theory of Sexuality* (1905a) and, in relation to art, in *Civilization and*

Its Discontents (1930). The concept has rarely been taken up in more recent psychoanalytic criticism, probably because it is so easily misunderstood as an elitist idealization of art.

7. The standard translation for the German word *Trieb* – "instinct" – is unsatisfactory, as has often been noted. I adopt the more suitable translation "drive," which has fewer animalistic connotations and implies the force which I want to discuss here. Since "drive" has no accompanying adjective, I resign myself to using "instinctual" in adjectival constructions when referring to the nature of the force; "instinctive" when referring to the source of a form of behavior.

8. In "Freud and the Scene of Writing," in *Of Grammatology* (1976), Derrida shows how Freud stages, in the course of his writing career, the scene of writing as the founding metaphor for the work of the unconscious in the psychic apparatus as a whole. The outcome of this development is, according to Derrida, the short essay "Note Upon a 'Mystic Writing-Pad' " (1924), wherein, to my own mind, both the psychic apparatus and writing become hopelessly confused.

9. The interdisciplinarity of the concept of sublimation can best be demonstrated by the failed attempt to force its different aspects into two sets of monodisciplinary concerns, which would result in the following division:

PSYCHOANALYSIS	SEMIOTICS
Force	Meaning
Trace	Ambiguity
Metonymic aspect	Metaphoric aspect
Sex or aggression	Work of art

This ordering shows that neither set is self-sufficient. The need to clarify each concern through one or more of the other set is characteristic of interdisciplinarity as necessitated by the concerns of this study.

10. See my interpretation of the story in *Lethal Love* (1987). I shall argue shortly that the "Rembrandt" corpus hardly worked with the Delilah episode; or to the extent that the episode is represented, it is profoundly "distorted."

11. The correspondence does not identify the painting's subject, only its size. Rembrandt's letter remarks that it should be hung in strong light. Schwartz (1985) contends the gift was the *Danae*, not the *Samson*, for implausible reasons I shall discuss below.

12. The two Samson works are exceptional, not only within "Rembrandt" but within all of the Western iconographic tradition. Although the capture of Samson, his nap on Delilah's lap, and the cutting of his hair are very often depicted, the two scenes of these early Rembrandt paintings are virtually without precedent.

13. Intertextually, the keys provide the Washington *Joseph* (Figures 1.2 and 1.4) with a meaning that seems quite adequate. The keys Joseph carries there, which an image–text iconography would relate to Joseph's power in the household, now come to represent his confinement in the bedroom at the threshold of sexual maturity.

14. This is the key problem of Freud's interpretation of Sophocles's *Oedipus the King*, the key pre-text of psychoanalysis. For a brilliant interpretation of this case, see Verhoeff, "Does Oedipus Have His Complex?" (1984).

15. Barthes, in *Mythologies* (1972), defined "connotation" as a second meaning built up out of the first sign and *its* meaning. Such a second meaning is not secondary in importance; on the contrary, it may overwhelm the initial meaning entirely. Neither is it more vague, less specific, or belated. In spite of serious problems with Barthes's use of the pair denotation–connotation, I find the terms useful under specific conditions. See also Chapter 5.

16. The following interpretation focuses on the aspects of Samson as gendered feminine. As Bersani (1989) rightly points out, the abdication of power that being penetrated entails is not a privilege of either sex or rather, of any gender. What Bersani underilluminates, however, is the position of either sex toward choice in this matter, hence the question of being penetrated as abdication or as deprivation of power. In other words, the gender positions of "woman" and of "homosexual man in a passive position" are not identical. In acknowledgment of Bersani's timely focus on this gender position outside of the predominant either/or constructions, I see in the *Samson* various reasons, in addition to the body's rapeability, to read the body as gendered feminine.

17. The curtain/cave/womb motif is obvious in the *Danae*, but also plausible in the *Joseph* etching. Again, this may be just a compositional device void of meaning. While any reader may feel compelled to interpret it as a token of theatricality, for instance, the advantage of my reading is its integration within the work as a whole.

18. Green's (1983:131) analysis of "primary narcissism between structure and state" is again relevant here:

> There is no contradiction in considering it [primary narcissism] at the same time as a state of absolute quiescence of which all tension is abolished, as the condition of independence of satisfaction, as closing of the circuit by which negative hallucination of the mother gets fixed, thus opening the way to identification as well as the way to appropriation of the ultimate perfection whose invulnerability is the final goal. The phase which necessarily follows that invulnerability is surely the *self-engendering which suppresses the difference between the sexes*. (my translation, emphasis in text)

19. See Chapter 2, for this interpretation of rape. The idea that rape is suggested here is understandable only if we realize that culturally, rape has become a powerful metaphor for the threat to the subject in general. The very allegorical reading of the classical myths of rape – Lucretia as well as Judges 19 – proves this point, as well as justifies my reluctance to use allegory as escape.

20. The reader is reminded here of Elisabeth Bronfen's seminal interpretation of *Beyond the Pleasure Principle* (1989), in which the author explains Freud's repression of the role of his daughter as a mother – of the grandson whose game triggered the theory – and as a daughter – whose death intervened and coincided with the formation of the theory – by reference to the central trauma of birth as a deadly trauma inflicted by the mother. Freud called that trauma, referring to his daughter/mother's death, "eine schwere, narzisstische Kränkung," a deep narcissistic wound.

21. The allusion is to the communication model of Roman Jakobson in "Linguistics and Poetics" (1960), an improvised sketch at the closing of a conference which, as I have suggested earlier, has come to dominate literary studies for over twenty years.

22. This deprivation of the pleasure of looking is precisely what Schwartz

refuses to accept as an act of aggression against Huygens. I would think that if a powerful man proclaims that it is he, the political holder of power, who sets the limit to what artists can do, an ambitious artist would jump at the chance to challenge that usurpation of power. The magic performed is that the pleasure is spoiled on one level but returns more strongly on another: The fascination remains.

23. The mothering aspect is quite noticeable in Rubens's representations of this scene. See, for example, a preparatory drawing, represented in my book *Femmes imaginaires* (1986a) which contains a detailed analysis of the fragment of the Biblical text narrating the scene of the haircutting.

24. I have suggested elsewhere (Bal, 1986a, 1987) that this final scene, a representation of autogenetic performance, is a polemical statement against the power of the mother. The entire story is about the problematic power of the mother. Earlier in the Samson saga, at the moment of the conception of the future hero, his mother overrules and outwits his father. Thus the first moment of the genesis of the hero is fatherless. These aspects make the story of Samson an excellent pretext for the struggle with vision in terms of primary narcissism and the problematic emergence of the subject. The importance of this moment in the genesis of the hero cannot be more adequately described than in Green (1983), quoted earlier in this chapter.

25. See the concluding chapter of Rose (1986) and the stunning Leonardo drawing brought into the discussion there.

26. Elisabeth Bronfen's (1989) analysis of Freud's *Beyond the Pleasure Principle* (1922) argues this, too. Bronfen's analysis confirms and substantiates my intuitive sense that the struggle, in Freud, to keep castration in its founding place rather than surrendering to the evidence of the primacy of the scar of primary narcissism, is the very force that affects the readers of these texts. The navel not only displaces the phallus; as the mark of the primary cut, programming all other cuts, it also subsumes it.

27 See Bal (1982), for a Peircean interpretation. Many studies have tried to overcome the binary opposition between imitation and creation which riddles the traditional interpretation as a trace of a mode of thinking alien to the *Poetics*. See, as one example among many, Prendergast (1986).

28. Broos devoted much of his (1985) dissertation to the latter problems. The question of the relevance of these questions is not addressed. For the literature on the *Rider*, Broos's study provides the most important elements; Slatkes (1983) provides another, perhaps more comprehensive list.

29. The meaning of orientalism as a sign of reassuring distance that helps to neutralize the affective contamination of the viewer by the (often female) model has been pointed out by David Scott among others: See his "Ecrire le nu" (1989). The seminal text remains Said's *Orientalism* (1978).

30. For a discussion of the compulsion to naturalize, and the various modes of naturalization in the reading of literature, see Culler (1975), 131–60. An acute critique of the attempt to naturalize otherness by defining and generalizing "it" is offered by Trinh Minh-ha. She (1989:75) writes:

> Trying to find the other by defining otherness or by explaining the other

through laws and generalities is, as Zen says, like beating the moon with a pole or scratching an itching foot from the outside of a shoe.

31. Since Alpers does not explicitly provide a working definition of description, I cannot be quite sure to what extent the following account colludes with her view of descriptivity. It seems that it is primarily in the mode of focalization that description is specified, seeing being the favorite mode for description, whereas any other mode – for example, remembering, thinking, imagining – can be at stake in narrative.

32. Margaret Deutsch Carroll interprets this work in terms of political ideology, as a revolt against the power of the city magistrates. Carroll (1986:25) clearly sees the links between this political issue and the issue of familial patriarchy, when she writes:

> We know that from the onset of his career he [Rembrandt] depicted fathers whose power was attenuated or under stress – as in his many representations of the blind Tobit. Rembrandt's sense of the insufficiency of the conventional image of the all-powerful father – as a false, impoverished representation of family experience – must have become even more acute in the 1650s, when he was divested of his legal status as parent and property-owner.

If one wishes to relate thematic obsessions with historical, personal experience, I can imagine that this experience was not new to Rembrandt, but uncannily repeated the experience of the young man, coming of age yet fully dependent on patrons. Blinding Claudius Civilis is a repetition of blinding Samson.

33. Carroll refers to classical psychoanalytic sources that give a straight Oedipal interpretation of this motif: Rank (1913), Eder (1913), and Reitler (1913). For Dumézil, she quotes his publications of 1948, 1959, and 1974. Another source is Scott Littleton (1982). I mention Carroll's sources here because they do join the inquiry in this chapter, although in a more classical and less textually oriented manner.

34. Again, Green (1983:126) explains why the very absence of the mother constitutes her total power:

> *The mother is caught in the empty frame of negative hallucination, and becomes framing structure for the subject itself. The subject constructs itself there where the investiture of the object has been consecrated instead of its investment.* (my translation, emphasis in text)

and he concludes:

> Can we not infer that the negative hallucination of the mother, without being representative of anything, *has rendered the conditions of representation possible.* (Green, 1983:127; my translation, emphasis in text)

This notion of the frame can be productively juxtaposed with Derrida's problematization of the frame as a token of the work's autonomy, in the chapter "Parergon" (1987).

CHAPTER 10

1. Dutch text: "Maar toen ik naast haar neerknielde om haar te troosten zag ik dat de wond van de buik een geweldige holte was, bijna alles was uit de buik verwijderd en op de bodem, als een slordig achtergelaten stuk gereedschap lag het scheermes." This contemporary novel can be read as a postmodern elaboration of the relationships among death, gender, and representation which I shall suggest in this chapter to be relevant for "Rembrandt."

2. It can, however, be argued that the basic tenets of postmodernism are present throughout the cultural history of the West.

3. See Gérard Dessons, *L'odeur de la peinture: Essai sur une question posée par Rembrandt à la peinture représentative* (1987). The essay is rhetorical and speculative, and the sometimes interesting ideas are not elaborated sufficiently to be convincing. However, I shall pick up some of its ideas in this chapter. Owing to the unelaborated character of Dessons's discourse, it is difficult to assess and acknowledge precisely the extent of my indebtedness to the text; this note will have to serve as a general acknowledgment where specific reference is not made.

4. This Biblical story is not frequently depicted, for the obvious reason that its horror is quite unspeakable and hard to convey strongly enough.

5. It is impossible to tell, on the basis of the Judges text, when she dies. She is raped and tortured all night – "night" being, of course, a symbolic stretch of time – and falls on the threshold of the house. Dead or alive? As she does not respond to her husband's summons to stand up, he takes her home. Dead or alive? Once home, the husband cuts her up. Dead or alive? This is a story of violent death as a continuing process, not a punctual event.

6. The noun translated here as "wife," usually rendered as "concubine," refers to a wife within the tradition where women live in their own father's house after marriage. Strictly speaking, the translation should be "patrilocal wife." See my *Death and Dissymmetry* (1988c).

7. The verb form used for the act of opening is *jiphtah*, the word that rings in the name of Jephthah, the murderer of the virgin daughter sacrificed in violence for the sake of (military) violence in Judges 11. The importance of opening as the act that allows vision while dealing death is thus emphasized by the pun on *jiphthah*/Jephthah; so is the murderous quality of opening, vision, and the body.

8. Riddles ask for meaning because without an answer, they don't have meaning. Samson's riddle at his wedding – the pre-text of a major "Rembrandt" work discussed here – barely conceals its sexual meaning, but it rests on a confusion – a who is who? – that calls this answer into question. And in this lack of clarity lies the riddle's force: the motivation of its utterance the trace of which the riddle *is*.

9. Jephthah is the hero of this killing kind of speech. He is also, according to his name, the opener of bodies (see note 7).

10. *Le scandale du corps parlant* (1980) was the original striking title of Felman's brilliant book on speech-act theory. As mentioned previously, the English translation bears the innocent title *The Literary Speech-Act* (1983). Devoid of its force, the translation has undermined the speech act of the book.

11. Obviously, these details that I read as signs can easily be explained away: The lines under the woman's hand can be taken as a shadow, the lines through the man's body as a token of the drawing's sketchiness. I fail to see *why* one would want to do that, thus precluding the possibility of interacting meaningfully with the work, of taking it seriously *as it is*.

12. As I argued in Chapter 1, Alpers here misreads the Judges text and, subsequently, the painting. This misreading also of the painting is caused by the priority given to the word, not the written word in its materiality but the logos turned doxa, the general cultural interpre-

tation of the text which is, in *its* turn, a misreading. Alpers's view that the work is theatrical is nevertheless convincing. But instead of relating the theatrical quality to the moral issue of hypocrisy, which she must do once she has compared the painting to the *Judas*, it can be more interestingly related to the representational issue of realism, in other words, to the unresolvable dialectic between force and meaning.

13. It is a detail curiously emphasized in criticism on Judges, which otherwise tends to domesticate the story's horror and to overlook the durative narrativity of death. In Biblical criticism, the gesture is generally interpreted as symbolic, because realistic readings have trouble integrating it literally. If it simply indicates that the woman is still alive, the husband actually murders her. Symbolically interpreted, it can more pleasantly be taken to mean a silent appeal to justice, which can then, in a scandalous reversal, be used to justify the subsequent civil war.

14. See van Alphen (1988a) for a pointed critique of this dichotomy. The ideological nature of dichotomy as a structure of thought, and of this particular one as a tool to delimit the domain of "reality" according to one's needs, is especially noticeable in the use of the concept of allegory as I have discussed it in Chapter 1.

15. Not knowing whether a person is dead is a well-known theme in horror literature. In Poe's story "Berenice," the character tears out the woman's teeth, not seeing that she is alive in her grave. Live burial is a favored representation of unsure death. In Judges 19, the woman is not buried alive, for even that fate, in all its horror, is a one-time event, albeit durative. This woman is condemned to death and then executed in various ways which all presuppose that she is already disposable: The host takes her to be expendable, the husband takes her to be expendable, the rapists take her to be public property, and then dead, the readers of the message her flesh constitutes take her to be her husband's property. Because of all these misreadings of her, her death cannot be punctual, nor acknowledged, or even ended.

16. A most flagrant, because quite sophisticated, apologetic misreading of the story is in an article by Susan Dinitch (1982). This article is a distressing example of the misuse of anthropology and of the authority of cultural-historical relativism. Dinitch misreads the story in such a disturbing way, perhaps because she completely ignores its visuality. This is how precedence for the "word" over the image becomes utterly logocentric.

17. The literature is abundant. Although some critics notice that the Levite, in the following episode, bluntly lies when he states that his life was threatened, while denying his own role in his wife's horrible fate (Judges 20:5), they persist in defending him. The idea of the lie as the token of semiosis, then, is devoid of its radical sting. A similar evacuation of the work results from the explanation of the lines as shadow, however "logical" or "realistic" such an explanation may be.

18. In *Death and Dissymmetry* (1988c), I have developed this view at length through a parallel analysis of Judges 11 and Freud's "Taboo of Virginity" (1918). This double reading yielded a perspective on the intricacy of vision, knowledge, and memory. Arguably, these three together make narrative.

19. The relationship among knowledge, gender, and death is exploited in yet another Judges drawing which represents the problematic quality

456

of speech. I am alluding to Figure 8.1, the drawing of the murder of
Sisera by Yael, already mentioned in Chapter 8. Let me quote the text
once more, because it can serve as a reading of the Levite's
transparency:

> And he said to her: "Stand in the door of the tent, and it shall be, when any
> man comes and asks you, saying: 'is there any man here?' that you say:
> 'none'." (4:20–3)

The exhausted chief Sisera, on his flight after the defeat of his
army, is invited by Yael to seek refuge in her tent. He prepares to
go to sleep, and then, Sisera, like the Levite to his wife, gives Yael
an order. But as an order, it misfires as flagrantly as the Levite's
"up!" Sisera's circumstances do not give him the authority required
for ordering. His unsuccessful order embeds a question of identity
that assimilates it to the riddle. The question is not, this time, *who*
the subject will be, but *what* he is: a man or not a man, "none."
Typically, the negation allows for indeterminacy, and in the space
created by that property, both characters respond to the speech act
differently.

For Sisera, the answer is obviously meant to deny his presence; it
is an order to lie; but ordering someone to lie is a lie in itself when
the commander is not in a position to command. Yael willfully misreads the order. For her, the speech act is a riddle, and riddles have
perfect truth value. The answer to the riddle must consist, then, of
finding out how a man can be no man. When she arrives at her answer
– as a dead man – she acts upon it. In "Rembrandt" this act is a self-
reflexive representational act. This drawing can serve as a symmetrical
counterpart to the Judges 19 drawing. Yael's act is represented as hard,
serious, specialized work, and Sisera's death as peaceful sleep. Paradoxically, while the woman's hand moves to represent her ongoing
death, Sisera's stillness represents life.

20. Here is the scene of the pre-text that the drawing responds to, and its
narrative follow-up which, I submit, is also inscribed in the drawing:

> And her lord rose up in the morning and opened [*jiphtah*] the doors of the
> house and went out to go his way; and behold, his patrilocal wife was fallen
> down at the door of the house, with her hands on the threshold. And he
> said to her: "up!, and let us be going" and none answered. And he took her
> upon the ass; and the man rose up and went to his place. And when he had
> come into his house he took the knife and laid hold on his patrilocal wife
> and divided her limb by limb into twelve pieces and sent her throughout all
> the borders of Israel. (*Holy Scriptures*, 1982, 19:27–8)

21. This reading is based on a refusal of realism, and on a privileging of
visuality. Thus the man is a figure, but the line underneath the woman's
hand, realistically speaking just a device for representing movement,
is taken to be a figure on the same level. My point in this reading is
that these lines are as semiotic as the man and the line signifying his
transparency.

22. The notion that works of autographic sign systems are bound to a
subject is expressed in the word "hand." If the hand in "Rembrandt"
has been interpreted as the painting hand (by Alpers) and the speaking
hand (by myself), these interpretations are consistent, I shall argue,
because in such sign systems one speaks with hands. On the other
hand, as Judges has demonstrated and as the legal system through its
judges continues to confirm, one can kill with words.

23. Turner (1967:19) defines ritual in a structuralist framework. This definition is illuminating for my purposes in this chapter:

> By "ritual" I mean prescribed formal behavior for occasions not given over to technological routine, having reference to beliefs in mystical beings or powers. The symbol is the smallest unit of ritual which still retains the specific properties of ritual behavior; it is the ultimate unit of specific structure in a ritual context.

24. Fire is Austin's favorite example of this narrative impossibility; see his *How To Do Things with Words* (1975). See Felman's illuminating discussion of Austin's theory: *Le scandale* (1980). Koerner's essay, "The Mortification of the Image" (1985), presents a survey of the problems of representing death and the solutions proposed to those problems. His view that death is the basic *hermeneutic* of Christianity comes close to the view I propose here, but it stops short of including the relationship with gender as the other side of that hermeneutic. Moreover, Koerner takes for granted that death *is* a state and is represented only as an event. I would refrain from such a leap, which tends to throw us back into the simplistic idea of symbolicity as a one-to-one relationship of signification.

25. See Kress and Hodge (1979), for an analysis of the ideological aspects of syntactical form. In this study the authors show how syntactical forms like the passive or reflexive forms obscure the agent as well as the active aspect of the act, thus ultimately displacing responsibility from the agent onto the victim.

    French has the verb *tuer*, the equivalent of "to kill," while it also allows for the phrase *faire mourir*, with a different meaning. The difference is a displacement of the agent, which is present and active – in the present tense – in *tuer*, whereas the act occurs *par procuration* – indirectly – in *faire mourir*. A murderer *tue* his victim, whereas a king who exposes soldiers to death – as David does in II Samuel 11 – *fait mourir* his men.

    For a relevant analysis of the Pygmalian tradition, see Gross (1989).

26. Nancy Jay (1985) makes a convincing case for the life-giving versus death-dealing privileges of the two genders as inscribed in the practice of blood sacrifice. See also Barbara Johnson's wonderful analysis of Frankenstein in relation to life, death, and gender in her chapter "My Monster, Myself," in *A World of Difference* (1987).

27. The term is an allusion to Roland Barthes's "effect of the real" (1968), whose possibilities Philippe Hamon further explored in his study of "the character effect" (*effet-personage*) in his book *Le personnel du roman* (1983). In Hamon's terms, the death drawings are managed by two "characters," the I-future and the she-present, which it is the project of the works to merge.

28. On still life in seventeenth-century Dutch culture, see William B. Jordan's catalog of the recent exhibition, entitled *A Prosperous Past* (1988). In his (1990) book on still life Norman Bryson makes a strong case for a gendered quality in the genre. I think this gendered quality is so strong, although in more than one way, that I would consider still life a mode rather than a genre, the extreme instance of description but including the associations of the very word "still life," nicely complemented by the French all-but-equivalent *nature morte*.

29. See Bryson's *Looking at the Overlooked* (1990), for an interpretation of still life that concurs with the present one in more than one respect.

30. See, in this connection, Elisabeth Bronfen's analysis of Snow White, in her forthcoming book on representations of death.

31. *Mise en abyme* is a concept that seems suitable for this analysis on more than one level. It comes from heraldry, a visual domain, and it has become a standard term in literary studies, where it has come to mean any sign that signifies the work as a whole. See my *Femmes imaginaires* (1986a), 159–79, for a detailed analysis of the concept. There I reinstate the term within its visual origin, thickened by its detour through literary use, by referring to contemporary visual artist Danielle Keunen's work entitled *Mise en abyme* (1981; owned by the Nederlandse Kunststichting).

32. The major study of the status of the detail is Naomi Schor's *Reading in Detail* (1987). The concept of *mise en abyme* in itself undermines the idea of the detail, as it refers to those signs that are by definition details, yet, equally by definition, refer to the whole.

33. "Le boeuf échorché du Louvre, dont l'exactitude est si grande et la qualité si extraordinaire que ce morceau incomparable fait pâlir toutes les natures mortes . . . " in *Maîtres d'autrefois*, cited by Dessons (1988), 73.

34. See Neil Hertz's fascinating analysis of male hysteria and its relationship to sexual politics in *The End of the Line* (1985). Hertz's view confirms the connection I have established between death and genderedness, and also relates this complex to vision.

35. Heckscher's translation is slightly directive – for example, "desire" where "wish" would also be possible – but since it clarifies the relevance of the fragment for my purpose, I leave most of it. The ambiguity of the Dutch word *vlees* compelled Hecksher to decide between "flesh" and "meat," which could not be helped although it unfortunately suppresses an acute confusion of dead and alive bodily substance, not only in this text but also in the death works which focus so closely on flesh.

36. Heckscher's study details the iconography of the work, and relates it to traditional scenes of lamentation, of martyrdom, and of justice. He emphasizes the sacrificial character of the work. William Schupbach (1982) examines the paradoxical representational practice in the painted muscles of the hand, which he refers to the goals of anatomical knowledge as knowledge of the human body and knowledge of its divine architect. Alpers makes most of the dissection of the arm in the *Tulp* as reference to the hand which is, after all, the instrument wielded by both artist and surgeon. Within the context of the emphasis on books and the status of the anatomist as a scholar, we might take this double reference as a paradoxical identification between the "I" who "writes" and the "he" written about in a third-person narrative. Bruyn et al. discuss the work in *Corpus* II, 172–89. See also Riegl (1971).

37. "Sous la forme d'une double expérience, la peinture et la philosophie classique se situent ensemble dans le champ de la métaphysique, en disant l'une que le corps est un texte, l'autre que le texte est un corps" (44).

38. "Son statut indéfini: elle n'a pas l'autorité sociale des chirurgiens d'Amsterdam, et trouble: visible à demi, elle est à demi cachée, inscrit le tableau dans la violation d'un interdit" (76).

39. "Modèle pour le discours sur la mort et sur la jouissance, modèle . . . pour la constitution d'une écriture du corps, la pratique chirurgicale

propose au peintre un modèle de la manipulation, où le bon usage de la main, c'est figurer, non triturer" (49). I translate *triturer* as "decomposing" because that verb allows me to retain *triturer*'s double meaning which the French verb shares with decomposing: the passive one related to death – a decomposing body – and the active one related to productivity, which is exemplified by Cynthia Chase's study *Decomposing Figures* (1986). The title of Chase's book can be read as polemically confronting both terms of Dessons's opposition.

40. Horst Gerson (1984:398) relates the *Deyman* to the first modern *Anatomical Lesson*, J. J. van Calcar's title page for Andreas Vesalius's *De Humani Corporis Fabrica* of 1543. Vesalius is represented dissecting the uterus of a woman – considered the site of evil – while Deyman dissects the brain, the site of the soul. Needless to say, this comparison becomes much more relevant in the present context.

41. "[Q]ue le sujet ne soit plus l'exercice de la mimesis, mais bien la peinture elle-même dans sa matérialité et sa gestuelle, dans ses rapports pulsionnels avec le sujet peignant. Il fallait un tableau où le sujet se définisse non plus comme acte de copie, allégiance à l'ordre du signe, mais comme instance conflictuelle, prise dans un double rapport au social et à l'inconscient" (71).

42. Both *Death and the Labyrinth* (1986) and *The Birth of the Clinic* (1975) – a work of reading and a work of history – appeared in the same year as if to underscore Foucault's double-edged vision, based on this premise.

REFERENCES

Abrams, M. H. 1953. *The Mirror and the Lamp: Romantic Theory and the Critical Tradition.* London/Oxford/New York: Oxford University Press.

Académie Française. 1912 (1638). *Les Sentimens de L'Académie Française sur la tragi-comédie du Cid.* Paris: Picard & Fils.

Allende, Isabel. 1985. *The House of the Spirits.* New York: Alfred A. Knopf.

Alpers, Svetlana. 1983. "Interpretation Without Representation." *Representations* 1, 1: 31–42.

    1985. *The Art of Describing. Dutch Art in the Seventeenth Century.* Chicago: The University of Chicago Press.

    1988. *Rembrandt's Enterprise: The Studio and Market.* Chicago: The University of Chicago Press.

Alphen, Ernst van. 1987. *Bang voor schennis? Inleiding in de ideologiekritiek.* Utrecht: Hes Publishers.

    1988a. "Literal Metaphors: On Reading Postmodernism." *Style* 21, 2: 208–18.

    1988b. *Bij wijze van lezen: Verleiding en verzet van Willem Brakmans lezer.* Muiderberg: Coutinho.

    1989a. "The Complicity of the Reader." *VS Versus* 52–3, 121–32.

    1989b. "The Heterotopian Space of the Discussions on Postmodernism." *Poetics Today* 10, 4: 819–38.

Alter, Robert. 1981. *The Art of Biblical Narrative.* New York: Basic Books.

Alter, Robert and Frank Kermode (eds.). 1988. *The Literary Guide to the Bible.* Cambridge, Mass.: Belknap Press of Harvard University Press.

Apter, T. E. 1978. *Thomas Mann.* London and Basingstoke: McMillan.

Austin, J. L. 1975. *How To Do Things with Words.* Cambridge, Mass.: Harvard University Press.

Bakhtin, Michail. 1981. *The Dialogic Imagination,* edited by Michael Holquist, translated by Caryl Emerson and Michael Holquist. Austin: University of Texas Press.

Bal, Mieke. 1977. *Narratologie: Essais sur la signification narrative dans quatre romans modernes.* Paris: Klincksieck.

    1981–2. "On Meanings and Descriptions." *Studies in 20th Century Literature* 6, 1–2: 100–48.

461

1982. "Mimesis and Genre Theory in Aristotle's Poetics." *Poetics Today* 3, 1: 171–80.

1985. *Narratology: Introduction to the Theory of Narrative*, translated by Christine van Boheemen. Toronto: University of Toronto Press.

1986a. *Femmes imaginaires: L'Ancien Testament au risque d'une narratologie critique*. Utrecht: Hes Publishers; Montreal: HMH Hurturbise; Paris: Nizet.

1986b. "Tell-Tale Theories." *Poetics Today* 7, 3: 555–64.

1987. *Lethal Love: Literary Feminist Readings of Biblical Love Stories*. Bloomington: Indiana University Press.

1988a. *Verkrachting verbeeld: Seksueel geweld in cultuur gebracht*. Utrecht: Hes Publishers.

1988b. *Murder and Difference: Gender, Genre and Scholarship on Sisera's Death*, translated by Matthew Gumpert. Bloomington: Indiana University Press.

1988c. *Death and Dissymmetry: The Politics of Coherence in the Book of Judges*. Chicago: The University of Chicago Press.

1989. "Introduction." In *Anti-Covenant: Counter-Reading Women's Lives in the Hebrew Bible*, edited by Mieke Bal, 11–24. Sheffield: Sheffield Academic Press/The Almond Press.

Baldwin, Robert. 1989. "Rembrandt's New Testament Prints: Artistic Genius, Social Anxiety, and the Marketed Calvinist Image." In *Impressions of Faith: Rembrandt's Biblical Etchings*, edited by Shelley Karen Perlove, 24–71. Michigan: University of Michigan–Dearborn, Mardigian Library.

Balet, Leo. 1962. *Rembrandt and Spinoza*. New York: Philosophical Library.

Balzac, Honoré de. 1971. (1833). *Le Père Goriot*. Paris: Editions Garnier.

Banfield, Ann. 1982. *Unspeakable Sentences: Narration and Representation in the Language of Fiction*. Boston, Mass.: Routledge & Kegan Paul.

Barrett, Michèle. 1987. "The Concept of Difference." *Feminist Review* 26: 29–41.

Barthes, Roland. 1968. "L'Effet de réel." *Communications* 4: 84–89. [English: "The Reality Effect." In Roland Barthes, *The Rustle of Language*, translated by Richard Howard, 141–54. New York: Hill and Wang.]

1972. *Mythologies*, translated by Annette Lavers. London: Jonathan Cape; New York: Hill and Wang, 1973.

1977. *Image–Music–Text*. Essays selected and translated by Stephen Heath. New York: Hill and Wang.

Baxandall, Michael. 1971. *Giotto and the Orators*. Oxford: Oxford University Press.

1985. *Patterns of Intention: On the Historical Explanation of Pictures*. New Haven: Yale University Press.

Belting, Hans. 1987. *The End of the History of Art?* translated by Christopher S. Wood. Chicago: The University of Chicago Press

Benesch, Otto. 1970. *Collected Writings*, Vol. I: *Rembrandt*. London: Phaidon.

1973. *The Drawings of Rembrandt*. Complete edition in six vols. by Otto Benesch. Enlarged and edited by Eva Benesch. London: Phaidon Press. (Orig. publ. I and II, 1954; III and IV, 1955; V and VI, 1957.)

Benjamin, Walter. 1977. *The Origin of German Drama*, translated by John Osborne. London: New Left Books.

Benveniste, Emile. 1966. *Problèmes de linguistique générale*, Vol. I. Paris: Gallimard.

1970. "L'Appareil formelle de l'énonciation." *Langage* 17: 12–18.

Berger, John. 1980. *About Looking*. New York: Pantheon Books.

Bergmann, Martin S. 1976. "Love That Follows upon Murder in Works of Art." *American Imago* 38, 1: 98–101.

Bernheimer, Charles. 1985. "Introduction." In *In Dora's Case: Freud – Hysteria – Feminism*, edited by Charles Bernheimer and Claire Kahane, 1–18. New York: Columbia University Press.

Bersani, Leo. 1987. "Is the Rectum a Grave?" In *AIDS: Cultural Analysis, Cultural Activism,* edited by Douglas Crimp, 179–222. Cambridge, Mass.: M.I.T. Press.

Bible. 1976. *New English Bible, with the Apocrypha*. Oxford Study Edition. Oxford: Oxford University Press.

1982. *The Holy Scriptures of the Old Testament: Hebrew and English*. London: The British and Foreign Bible Society.

Bissell, R. Ward. 1968. "Artemesia Gentileschi – A New Documented Chronology." *The Art Bulletin* 50: 153.

Blankert, Albert. 1978. *Vermeer of Delft*. Oxford: Phaidon Press. (orig. publ. 1975).

Bloom, Harold. 1973. *The Anxiety of Influence: A Theory of Poetry*. Oxford: Oxford University Press.

Boheemen, Christine van. 1987. *The Novel as Family Romance: Language, Gender, and Authority from Fielding to Joyce*. Ithaca and London: Cornell University Press.

Borch-Jacobsen, Mikkel. 1988. *The Freudian Subject*, translated by Catherine Porter. Stanford, Cal.: Stanford University Press.

Bourdieu, Pierre. 1977. *Outline of a Theory of Practice*, translated by Richard Rice. Cambridge: Cambridge University Press.

1984. *Distinction: A Social Critique of the Judgement of Taste*, translated by Richard Nice. Cambridge, Mass.: Harvard University Press.

Braidotti, Rosi. 1991. *Patterns of Dissonance: Feminism and Philosophy*. Cambridge, U.K.: Polity Press.

Brakman, Willem. 1988. *Heer op kamer*. Amsterdam: Querido.

Bredius, Abraham. 1936. *Rembrandt Harmenszoon van Rijn 1606–1669: The Paintings of Rembrandt*. Vienna: Phaidon Verlag.

Brombert, Victor. 1980. "Opening Signals in Narrative." *New Literary History* XI, 3: 489–502.

Bronfen, Elisabeth. 1988. "Dialogue with the Dead: The Deceased Beloved as Muse." *New Comparison* 6: 101–18.

1989. "The Lady Vanishes: Sophie Freud and 'Beyond the Pleasure Principle'." *South Atlantic Quarterly* 88, 4: 961–91.

1990. "Leichenhafte Bilder, Bildenhafte Leichen." *Die Trauben des Zeuxis*, edited by Hans Korner. Koln: Olms Verlag.

in prep. *Over Her Dead Body*.

Brooks, Peter. 1984. *Reading for the Plot: Design and Intention in Narrative*. New York: Alfred A. Knopf.

1987. "The Idea of a Psychoanalytic Literary Criticism." In *Discourse in Psychoanalysis and Literature*, edited by Shlomith Rimmon-Kenan, 1–18. London: Methuen.

Broos, B. P. J. 1977. *Index to the Formal Sources of Rembrandt's Art*. Maarsen: Gary Schwartz.

1983. "Fame Shared Is Fame Doubled." *Rembrandt: Impact of a Genius.* Amsterdam, Rijksmuseum.

1985. *Rembrandt en zijn voorbeelden / Rembrandt and His Sources.* Amsterdam: Rembrandthuis.

Broude, Norma and Mary D. Garrard (eds.). 1982. *Feminism and Art History: Questioning the Litany.* New York: Harper & Row.

Brown, Jonathan. 1986. *Velázquez: Painter and Courtier.* New Haven: Yale University Press.

Bruyn, J., B. Haak, S. H. Levie, et al. 1982– . *A Corpus of Rembrandt Paintings.* Stichting Rembrandt Research Project. The Hague, Boston, London: Martinus Nijhoff Publishers (Vol. I, 1982; Vol. II, 1986; Vol. III, 1989).

Bryson, Norman. 1981. *Word and Image: French Painting of the Ancien Régime.* Cambridge: Cambridge University Press.

1983. *Vision and Painting: The Logic of the Gaze.* London: Macmillan.

1984. *Tradition and Desire: From David to Delacroix.* Cambridge: Cambridge University Press.

1988a. "The Gaze in the Expanded Field." In *Vision and Visuality*, edited by Hal Foster, 87–114. Seattle: Bay Press.

1988b. *Calligram: Essays in the New Art History from France.* Cambridge: Cambridge University Press.

1988c. "Intertextuality and Visual Poetics." *Style* 22, 2: 183–93.

1990. *Looking at the Overlooked: Four Essays on Still-Life.* Cambridge, U.K.: Reaktion Press.

in press. "The Construction of Masculinity in Géricault." In *The Politics of Looking*, edited by Norman Bryson, Michael Ann Holly, and Keith Moxey.

Buci-Glucksmann, Christine. 1986. *La Folie du voir: De l'esthétique baroque.* Paris: Galilée.

Burke, Kenneth. 1968. *Language as Symbol.* Berkeley: University of California Press.

Bynum, Carolyn Walker. 1984. "Women's Stories, Women's Symbols: A Critique of Victor Turner's Theory of Liminality." In *Anthropology and the Study of Religion*, edited by Robert L. Moore and Frank E. Reynolds. Chicago: Center for the Scientific Study of Religion.

Camille, Michael. 1985. "The Book of Signs: Writing and Visual Difference in Gothic Manuscript Illumination." *Word and Image* 1, 2: 133–48.

Campbell, Colin. 1973. "The Identity of Rembrandt's 'Polish Rider'." In *Neue Beiträge zur Rembrandt-Forschung*, edited by Otto Simson and Jan Kelch, 126–36. Berlin: Mann Verlag.

Carroll, Margaret Deutsch. 1981. "Rembrandt as Meditational Printmaker." *The Art Bulletin* LXIII, 4: 585–610.

1986. "Civic Ideology and Its Subversion: Rembrandt's *Oath of Claudius Civilis.*" *Art History* 9, 1: 10–35.

1989. "The Erotics of Absolutism: Rubens and the Mystification of Sexual Violence." *Representations* 25: 3–30.

Change (Collective). 1977. *La Folie Encerclée.* Paris: October.

Chapman, H. Perry. 1989. "Expression, Temperament and Imagination in Rembrandt's Earliest Self-Portraits." *Art History* 12, 2: 158–76.

Chase, Cynthia. 1983. Review of Kristeva, *Powers of Horror, Desire in Language*, and "L'abjet d'amour." *Criticism* 26, 2: 193–201.

464

1986. *Decomposing Figures: Rhetorical Readings in the Romantic Tradition.* Baltimore: The Johns Hopkins University Press.

Choron, Jacques. 1963. *Death and Western Thought.* New York: Collier Books.

Ciletti, Elena. 1988. "Questa e la donna terribile!: Artemesia Gentileschi and Judith." [Lecture: Geneva, Hobart and William Smith Colleges]

in prep: "Patriarchal Ideology in the Renaissance Iconography of Judith." In *Prefiguring Woman: Gender Studies and the Italian Renaissance.*

Clark, Kenneth. 1978. *An Introduction to Rembrandt.* New Albot: Readers Union.

1980. *Feminine Beauty.* New York: Rizzoli.

Clark, T. J. 1985. *The Painting of Modern Life: Paris in the Art of Manet and His Followers.* London: Thames and Hudson.

Culler, Jonathan. 1975. *Structuralist Poetics: Structuralism, Linguistics, and the Study of Literature.* Ithaca: Cornell University Press.

1981. *The Pursuit of Signs. Semiotics, Literature, Deconstruction.* Ithaca: Cornell University Press.

1983. *On Deconstruction: Theory and Criticism After Structuralism.* Ithaca: Cornell University Press.

1988. *Framing the Sign: Criticism and Its Institutions.* Norman, Okla. and London: University of Oklahoma Press.

Damish, Hubert. 1972. *Théorie du nuage: Pour une nouvelle histoire de l'art.* Paris: Editions du Seuil.

1987. *L'Origine de la perspective.* Paris: Flammarion.

De Lauretis, Teresa. 1983. *Alice Doesn't: Feminism, Semiotics, Cinema.* London: Macmillan.

1987. *Technologies of Gender: Essays on Theory, Film, and Fiction.* Bloomington: Indiana University Press.

Delay, Jean. 1973–4. *La Jeunesse d'André Gide*, 2 vols. Paris: Corti.

Deleuze, Gilles. 1986. *Foucault.* Paris: Editions Minuit.

Deri, Susan K. 1984. *Symbolization and Creativity.* New York: International Universities Press.

Derrida, Jacques. 1976. *Of Grammatology*, translated, and with an Introduction by Gayatri Chakravorty Spivak. Baltimore: The Johns Hopkins University Press.

1981. *Dissemination*, translated, and with an Introduction and Additional Notes by Barbara Johnson. Chicago: The University of Chicago Press.

1984. *Margins of Philosophy*, translated by Alan Bass. Chicago: The University of Chicago Press.

1987a. *Truth in Painting*, translated by Geoff Bennington and Ian Mc Leod. Chicago: The University of Chicago Press.

1987b. *The Postcard: From Socrates to Freud and Beyond*, translated by Alan Bass. Chicago: The University of Chicago Press.

1988a. "The Purveyor of Truth," translated by Alan Bass. In *The Purloined Poe: Lacan, Derrida, and Psychoanalytic Reading*, edited by John P. Muller & William J. Richardson, 173–212. Baltimore: The Johns Hopkins University Press.

1988b. *Limited Inc.*, translated by Samuel Weber. Evanston, Ill.: Northwestern University Press.

Dessons, Gérard. 1987. *L'Odeur de la peinture: Essai sur une question posée par Rembrandt à la peinture représentative.* Paris: L'Aphélie.

Diamond, Irene, and Lee Quinby (eds.). 1988. *Feminism and Foucault: Reflections on Resistance*. Boston: Northeastern University Press.

Dijk-Hemmes, Fokkelien van. 1986. "Gezegende onder de vrouwen: Een moeder in Israel en een maagd in de kerk." In *'T is kwaad gerucht als zij niet binnen blijft: Vrouwen in oude culturen*, edited by Fokkelien van Dijk Hemmes, 123–47. Utrecht: Hes Publishers.

    1989. "Interpretaties van de relatie tussen Richteren 4 en 5." In *Proeven van Vrouwenstudies Theologie*, Vol. I, edited by Jonneke Bekkenkamp e.a., 149–217. Leiden/Utrecht: IMO Research Pamphlets.

Dinitch, Susan. 1982. "The 'Sodomite' Theme in Judges 19–20: Family, Community, and Social Disintegration." *Catholic Bible Quarterly* 44: 365–78.

DiPiero, Thomas. submitted. *Formidable Masters: Imitation, Seduction, and Appropriation in Early French Fiction*.

Donaldson, Ian. 1982. *The Rapes of Lucretia: A Myth and Its Transformations*. Oxford: Clarendon Press.

Douglass, Frederick. 1982. (1845). *Narrative of the Life of Frederick Douglass, an American Slave, Written by Himself*, edited by Houston Baker, Jr. New York: Viking Penguin

Dubois, J. et al. 1981. *A General Rhetoric*, translated by Paul B. Burrel and Edgar M. Slotkin. Baltimore: The Johns Hopkins University Press.

Dumézil, Georges. 1948. *Mitra-Varuna: Essai sur deux représentations indo-européennes de la souveraineté*. Paris: Gallimard.

    1959. *Les Dieux des Germains*. Paris: Presses Universitaires de France.

    1974. " 'Le Borgne' and 'Le Manchot': The State of the Problem." In *Myth in Indo-European Antiquity*, edited by Gerald James Larson et al., 17–28. Berkeley: University of California Press.

Dupont-Roc, Rosalind, and Jean Lallot. 1980. *Aristotle: La Poétique*. Paris: Editions du Seuil.

Eco, Umberto. 1976. *A Theory of Semiotics*. Bloomington: Indiana University Press.

    1979. "Peirce and the Semiotic Foundations of Openness: Signs as Texts and Texts as Signs." *The Role of the Reader: Explorations in the Semiotics of Texts*. Bloomington: Indiana University Press.

Eder, M. D. 1913. "Augenträume." *Internationale Zeitschrift für ärztliche Psychoanalyse* I: 157–8.

Ellis, John. 1980. "Photography/Pornography, Art/Pornography." *Screen* 20, 1 (Spring): 81–108.

Emecheta, Buchi. 1985. (1983). *The Rape of Shavi*. London: Fontana.

Emmens, J. A. 1961. "*Les Ménines* de Velázquez: Miroir des princes pour Philippe IV," *Nederlands Kunsthistorisch Jaarboek* 12: 51–79.

    1963. [Review of] H. Gerson, *Seven Letters by Rembrandt*. *Oud Holland* 78: 79–82.

    1979. *Rembrandt en de regels van de kunst*. Amsterdam: Van Oorschot.

Estrich, Susan. 1987. *Real Rape: How the Legal System Victimizes Women Who Say No*. Cambridge: Harvard University Press.

Fabian, Johannes. 1983. *Time and the Other: How Anthropology Makes Its Object*. New York: Columbia University Press.

Felman, Shoshana. 1977. "To Open the Question." *Yale French Studies: Literature and Psychoanalysis. The Question of Reading: Otherwise* 55/56: 5–10.

    1980. *Le Scandale du corps parlant: Don Juan avec Austin ou la séduction en deux langages*. Paris: Editions du Seuil. [English: *The Literary Speech*

Act: Don Juan with Austin or Seduction in Two Languages, translated by Catherine Porter. Ithaca: Cornell University Press, 1983.]

1981. "Rereading Femininity." *Yale French Studies* 62: 19–44.

1987. *Jacques Lacan and the Adventure of Insight: Psychoanalysis in Contemporary Culture*. Cambridge, Mass.: Harvard University Press.

Fernandez, Dominique. 1982. *Amsterdam*. Paris: Editions du Seuil.

Fetterley, Judith. 1978. *The Resisting Reader: A Feminist Approach to American Fiction*. Bloomington: Indiana University Press.

Fineman, Joel. 1980. "The Structure of Allegorical Desire." *October* 12: 47–66.

Flaubert, Gustave. 1962. (1857). *Madame Bovary*. Edited and introduced by Claudine Gothot-Mersch. Paris: Garnier. [English transl. by Alan Russell. Baltimore: Penguin, 1950.]

Fletcher, Angus. 1964. *Allegory: The Theory of a Symbolic Mode*. Ithaca: Cornell University Press.

Fokkelman, J. P. 1981. *King David: Narrative Art and Poetry in the Books of Samuel*. Assen: Van Gorcum.

Foster, B. O. 1959. *Livy*, with an English translation by B. O. Foster. London: W. Heinemann Ltd.

Foster, Hal (ed.). 1988. *Vision and Visuality*. Dia Art Foundation, Discussions in Contemporary Culture No. 2. Seattle: Bay Press.

Foucault, Michel. 1972. *The Archeology of Knowledge and the Discourse on Language*, translated by A. M. Sheridan Smith. New York: Pantheon Books.

1973. *The Order of Things*, translated by Alan Sheridon. New York: Vintage Books.

1975. *The Birth of the Clinic*, translated by A. M. Sheridan Smith. New York: Vintage Books.

1979. "What Is an Author?" In *Textual Strategies: Perspectives in Post-Structuralist Criticism*, edited by Josué V. Harari, and translated by Donald Bouchard and Sherry Simon, 141–60. Ithaca: Cornell University Press.

1986. *Death and the Labyrinth*, translated by Charles Ruas. New York: Doubleday.

Frazer, Sir James George. 1931. *Ovid's Fasti*, with an English translation by Sir James George Frazer. London: Heinemann Ltd.

Freedberg, David. 1989. *The Power of Images: Studies in the History and Theory of Response*. Chicago: The University of Chicago Press.

French, Marilyn. 1977. *The Women's Room*. London: Sphere Books Ltd.

Freud, Sigmund. *Standard Edition of the Complete Works of Sigmund Freud*, edited by James Strachey. London: The Hogarth Press. [Hereafter *SE*; unless otherwise indicated, references listed below are to *SE*.]

1900. The Interpretation of Dreams. *SE* IV and V. New York: Avon Books.

1905a. *Three Essays on the Theory of Sexuality*. *SE* VII: 125–243.

1905b. "Jokes and Their Relation to the Unconscious." *SE* VIII.

1910a. "The Psychoanalytic View of Psychogenetic Disturbances of Vision." *SE* XI: 211–18.

1910b. "Leonardo da Vinci and a Memory of His Childhood." *SE* XIII: 59–137.

1914a. *Totem and Taboo*. New York: Vintage Books; *SE* XIII: 1–162.

1914b. "The Moses of Michelangelo." *SE* XIII: 211–36.

1914c. "On Narcissism: An Introduction." *SE* XIV: 6–102.

1917. "Mourning and Melancholia" *SE* XIV: 239–58.

1918. "The Taboo of Virginity." *SE* XI: 191–208.

1919. "A Child Is Being Beaten." *SE* XVII: 175–204.

1921. "Group Psychology and the Analysis of the Ego." *SE* XVIII: 69–143.

1922. *Beyond the Pleasure Principle.* New York: W. W. Norton. *SE* XVIII: 7–65.

1923. "The Ego and the Id." *SE* XIX: 12–66.

1924a. "The Economic Problem of Masochism." *SE* XIX: 157–70.

1924b. "A Note Upon a Mystic Writing-Pad." *SE* XIX: 227–32.

1925. "Negation." *SE* XIX: 233–9.

1927. "Postscript (to "The Moses of Michelangelo").

1930. *Civilization and Its Dicontents*, translated by Joan Riviere. London: Hogarth.

1931. "Female Sexuality." *SE* XXI: 221–43.

1985. *The Complete Letters of Sigmund Freud to Wilhelm Fliess, 1887–1904*, translated and edited by Jeffrey Moussaieff Masson. Cambridge, Mass.: Belknap Press of Harvard University Press.

Fried, Michael. 1980. *Absorption and Theatricality: Painting and Beholder in the Age of Diderot.* Berkeley: University of California Press.

1987. *Realism, Writing, Disfiguration: On Thomas Eakins and Stephen Crane.* Chicago: The University of Chicago Press.

1988. "Courbet's Femininity." In *Courbet Reconsidered*, edited by Sarah Faunce and Linda Nochlin, 43–53. Brooklyn: The Brooklyn Museum.

Frye, Northrop. 1957. *Anatomy of Criticism.* Princeton: Princeton University Press.

Fuller, Peter. 1980. *Art and Psychoanalysis.* London: Writers & Readers Cooperative.

Gallop, Jane. 1984. "Lacan and Literature: A Case for Transference." *Poetics: Psychopoetics-Theory* 13: 301–8.

1988. *Thinking Through the Body.* New York: Columbia University Press.

Gantner, Joseph. 1964. *Rembrandt und die Verwandlung klassischer Formen.* Bern und Munchen: Francke Verlag.

Garrard, Mary D. 1982. "Artemesia and Susanna." In *Feminism and Art History: Questioning the Litany*, edited by Norma Broude and Mary D. Garrard, 147–71. New York: Harper & Row.

1988. *Artemesia Gentileschi: The Image of the Female Hero in Italian Baroque Art.* Princeton: Princeton University Press.

Gates, Henry Louis, Jr. (ed.). 1985. *"Race," Writing, and Difference.* Chicago: The University of Chicago Press.

Gelder, J. C. van. 1958. *De schilderkunst van Jan Vermeer.* With a commentary by J. A. Emmens. Utrecht: Kunsthistorisch Instituut.

Gelderblom, Arie-Jan. 1988. "Allegories in the Garden." *Style* 22, 2: 230–7.

Gelley, Alexander. 1987. *Narrative Crossings: Theory and Pragmatics of Prose Fiction*, Baltimore: The Johns Hopkins University Press.

Genette, Gérard. 1969a. "Frontières du récit." *Figures II*, 49–70. Paris: Editions du Seuil.

1969b. "Vraisemblance et motivation." *Figures II*, 71–100. Paris: Editions du Seuil.

1972. "Métonymie chez Proust." *Figures III*, 41–66. Paris: Editions du Seuil. [English: *Figures*, Vols. 1–3, English selections translated by Alan Sheridan. New York: Columbia University Press, 1982.]

1980. *Narrative Discourse: An Essay in Method*, translated by Jane E. Lewin. Ithaca: Cornell University Press.

Gennep, Arnold van. 1960. *The Rites of Passage*. Chicago: The University of Chicago Press.

Georgel, Pierre, and Anne-Marie Lecoq. 1987. *La Peinture dans la peinture*. Paris: Editions Adam Biro.

Gerson, Horst. 1961. *Seven Letters by Rembrandt*, edited by Horst Gerson, transcribed by I. H. van Eeghen, and translated by Yda Ovinck. The Hague: L. J. C. Boucher.

1966. "Pieter de Hoogh." *Kindlers Malerei-Lexikon*, III, 308–12. Zürich.

1984. *De schilderijen van Rembrandt*, translated by Nelleke Fuchs-Van Maaren. Alphen aan de Rijn: Icob.

Gerstein, Beth. 1989. "A Ritual Processed." In *Anti-Covenant: Counter-Reading Women's Lives in the Hebrew Bible*, edited by Mieke Bal, 175–94. Sheffield: Sheffield Academic Press and The Almond Press.

Girard, René. 1961. *Mensonge romantique et vérité romanesque*. Paris: Grasset. [English: *Deceit, Desire, and the Novel: The Self and Other in Literary Structure*, translated by Ivonne Freccero. Baltimore: The Johns Hopkins University Press, 1965.]

Gombrich, E. M. 1949. Review of Charles Morris, *Signs, Language and Behavior*. Art Bulletin 31: 68–73.

1968. (1960). *Art and Illusion: A Study in the Psychology of Pictorial Representation*. London: Phaidon Press.

1986. "Ideal and Type in Italian Renaissance Painting." In *New Light on Old Masters*, 89–124. Oxford: Phaidon.

Goodman, Nelson. 1972. *Problems and Projects*. New York: Bobbs-Merrill.

1976. *Languages of Art: An Approach to a Theory of Symbols*. Indianapolis: Hackett.

Gouma-Peterson, Thalia and Patricia Mathews. 1987. "The Feminist Critique of Art History." *Art Bulletin* LXIX, 3: 326–57.

Goux, Jean-Joseph. 1978. *Les Iconoclastes*. Paris: Editions du Seuil.

Gowing, Lawrence. 1970. *Vermeer*. London: Faber & Faber (orig. publ. 1952).

Green, André. 1983. *Narcissisme de vie narcissisme de mort*. Paris: Les Editions de Minuit.

Greimas, Algirdas Julien. 1976. *Maupassant: Exercices pratiques*. Paris: Editions du Seuil. [English: *Maupassant: The Semiotics of Text, Practical Lessons*, translated by Paul Perron. Amsterdam and Philadelphia: J. Benjamins, 1988.]

Griffin, Susan. 1979. *Rape: The Power of Consciousness*. New York: Harper & Row.

Grimm, Brüder. 1974. *Kinder- und Hausmärchen*, gesammelt durch die Brüder Grimm, mit Vorwort von Ingeborg Weber-Ketterman. 3 Teile. Frankfurt and Main: Insel Verlag. [English: Grimm, *Selected Tales*, translated by David Luke. Harmondsworth: Penguin Books Ltd., 1974.]

Gross, Kenneth. 1989. "Moving Statues, Talking Statues." *Raritan* 9, 2: 1–25.

Guest, Harriet, and John Barrell. 1988. " 'Who Ever Perished, Being

Innocent?': Some Plates from the Songs of Innocence." *Style* 22, 2: 238–62.

Habermas, Jürgen. 1972. (1968). *Knowledge and Human Interests*, translated by Jeremy J. Shapiro. London: Heinemann.

Hamon, Philippe. 1981. *Introduction à l'analyse du descriptif.* Paris: Hachette.

1983. *Le Personnel du roman: Le Système des personnages dans les "Rougon-Maquart" de Zola.* Geneva: Droz.

1984. *Texte et idéologie.* Paris: Presses Universitaires de France.

Handler Spitz, Ellen. 1985. *Art and Psyche: A Study in Psychoanalysis and Aesthetics.* New Haven and London: Yale University Press.

Harris, Ann Sutherland and Linda Nochlin. 1976. *Women Artists: 1550–1950.* Los Angeles: County Museum of Art.

Hasenmueller, Christine. 1980. "A Machine for the Suppression of Space: Illusionism as Ritual in a Fifteenth Century Painting." *Semiotica* 29, 1/2: 53–94.

Hecht, Peter. 1989. *De Hollandse Fijnschilders: Van Gerard Dou tot Adriaen van der Werff.* Amsterdam: Rijksmuseum/Gary Schwartz/SDU.

Heckscher, William S. 1958. *Rembrandt's "Anatomy of Dr. Nicolaas Tulp": An Iconological Study.* New York: New York University Press.

Held, Julius S. 1969. *Rembrandt's Aristotle and Other Rembrandt Studies.* Princeton: Princeton University Press.

Herrera, Hayden. 1983. *Frida: A Biography of Frida Kahlo.* New York: Harper & Row.

Herrnstein Smith, Barbara. 1968. *Poetic Closure: A Study of How Poems End.* Chicago: The University of Chicago Press.

1978. *On the Margins of Discourse: The Relation of Literature to Language.* Chicago: The University of Chicago Press.

Hertz, Neil. 1985. *The End of the Line: Essays on Psychoanalysis and the Sublime.* New York: Columbia University Press.

Hirschkop, Ken and David Shepherd (eds.). 1989. *Bakhtin and Cultural Theory.* Manchester and New York: Manchester University Press.

Hofrichter, Frima Fox. 1982. "Judith Leyster's *Proposition*: Between Virtue and Vice." In *Feminism and Art History: Questioning the Litany*, edited by Norma Broude and Mary D. Garrard, 173–82. New York: Harper & Row.

Holland, Dorothy and Naomi Quinn (eds.). 1987. *Cultural Models in Language and Thought.* Cambridge: Cambridge University Press.

Hollier, Denis. 1988. "The Word of God: 'I am Dead.'" *October* 44 (Spring): 75–88.

Holly, Michael Ann. 1984. *Panofsky and the Foundations of Art History.* Ithaca and London: Cornell University Press.

1988. "Cultural History as a Work of Art: Jacob Burckhardt and Henry Adams." *Style* 22, 2: 209–18.

1989. "Past Looking." *Critical Inquiry* 16, 2: 371–96.

1990. "Vision and Revision in the History of Art." In *Theory Between the Disciplines*, edited by Martin Kreiswirth and Marc Cheetham, 151–68. Ann Arbor: University of Michigan Press.

Hoy, David Couzens. 1986. *A Foucault Reader.* London: Basil Blackwell.

Hutcheon, Linda. 1980. *Narcissistic Narrative: The Metafictional Paradox.* New York: Methuen.

1988. *A Poetics of Postmodernism: History, Theory, Fiction.* London: Routledge.

Innis, Robert E. (ed.). 1984. *Semiotics: An Introductory Anthology*. Edited with introductions by Robert E. Innis. Bloomington: Indiana University Press.

Iser, Wolfgang. 1978. *The Act of Reading: A Theory of Aesthetic Response*. Baltimore: The Johns Hopkins University Press.

Jacobus, Mary. 1986. *Reading Woman: Essays in Feminist Criticism*. New York: Columbia University Press.

Jakobson, Roman. 1960. "Closing Statement: Linguistics and Poetics." In *Style in Language*, edited by Thomas A. Sebeck, 350–77. Cambridge, Mass: M.I.T. Press.

James, Henry. 1898. *What Maisie Knew*. London: W. Heinemann.

Jameson, Fredric. 1981. *The Political Unconscious: Narrative as a Socially Symbolic Act*. Ithaca: Cornell University Press.

Jauss, Hans Robert. 1982. *Toward an Aesthetics of Reception*, translated by Timothy Bahti. Introduction by Paul de Man. Minneapolis: University of Minnesota Press.

Jay, Martin. 1986. "In the Empire of the Gaze: Foucault and the Denigration of Vision in Twentieth-Century French Thought." In *Foucault: A Critical Reader*, edited by David Couzens Hoy, 175–204. Oxford: Basil Blackwell.

    1988. "Scopic Regimes of Modernity." In *Vision and Visuality*, edited by Hal Foster, 3–28. Seattle: Bay Press.

Jay, Nancy. 1985. "Sacrifice as Remedy for Being Born of Women." In *Immaculate and Powerful: The Female in Sacred Imagery and Social Reality*, edited by Clarissa W. Atkinson, Constance H. Buchanan, and Margaret R. Miles, 283–309. Boston: Beacon Press.

Jencks, Charles. 1987. *Postmodernism: The New Classicism in Art and Architecture*. New York: Rizzoli.

Johnson, Barbara. 1987. *A World of Difference*. Baltimore: The Johns Hopkins University Press.

    1988. "The Frame of Reference: Poe, Lacan, Derrida." In *The Purloined Poe: Lacan, Derrida, and Psychoanalytic Reading*, edited by John P. Muller and William J. Richardson, 213–51. Baltimore: The Johns Hopkins University Press.

Johnson, Mark. 1981. *Philosophical Perspectives on Metaphor*. Minneapolis: University of Minneapolis Press.

    1987. *The Body in the Mind: The Bodily Basis of Meaning, Reason, and Imagination*. Chicago: The University of Chicago Press.

Jongh, E. de. 1976. *Tot Lering en Vermaak*, exhibition catalog. Amsterdam: Rijksmuseum.

Jordan, William B. 1988. *A Prosperous Past: The Sumptuous Still Life in the Netherlands, 1600–1700*, edited by William B. Jordan. The Hague: SDU Publishers.

Kahr, Madlyn Millner. 1976. *Velázquez: The Art of Painting*. New York: Harper & Row.

Kampen, Nathalie. 1981. *Image and Status: Roman Working Women in Ostia*. Berlin: Mann.

Kamuf, Peggy. 1988. *Signature Pieces: On the Institution of Authorship*. Ithaca: Cornell University Press.

Kappeler, Susanne. 1986. *The Pornography of Representation*. Minnesota: University of Minnesota Press.

Kauffmann, H. 1926. *Zur Kritik der Rembrandtzeichnungen*. Berlin: Repertorium für Kunstwissenschaft 47.

Keller, Evelyn Fox. 1985. *Reflections on Gender and Science*. New Haven: Yale University Press.

Kemp, Wolfgang. 1985a. "Death At Work: A Case Study on Constitutive Blanks in Nineteenth-Century Painting." *Representations* 10: 102–23.

1985b. *Der Betrachter ist im Bild: Kunstwissenschaft und Rezeptionsathetik*, edited by Wolfgang Kemp. Koln: Dumont Buchverlag.

1986. *Rembrandt: Die Heilige Familie oder die Kunst, einen Vorhang zulüften*. Frankfurt am Main: Fischer Tschenbuch Verlag GmbH.

Kirk, Geoffrey S. 1972. "Aetiology, Ritual, Charter: Three Equivocal Terms in the Study of Myth." *Yale Classical Studies* 22: 83–102.

Kittay, Jeffrey. 1980. "Descriptive Limits." *Yale French Studies* 61: 225–43.

Klein, Melanie. 1975. *Love, Guilt, and Reparation, and Other Works*. New York: The Free Press.

Koerner, Joseph Leo. 1985. "The Mortification of the Image: Death as a Hermeneutic in Hans Baldung Grien." *Representations* 10: 52–101.

1986. "Rembrandt and the Epiphany of the Face," *Res XII*: 5–32.

Kofman, Sarah. 1973. *Quatre romans analytiques*. Paris: Editions Galilée.

1985. *Mélancholie de l'art*. Paris: Editions Galilée.

1985a. *The Enigma of Woman: Woman in Freud's Writings*, translated by Catherine Porter. Ithaca: Cornell University Press.

1985b. *L'Enfance de l'art*. Paris: Editions Galilée.

1986. *Pourquoi rit-on?* Paris: Editions Galilée.

Krauss, Rosalind. 1985. *The Originality of the Avant Garde and Other Modernist Myths*. Cambridge, Mass.: M.I.T. Press.

1988. "The Im/pulse To See." In *Vision and Visuality*, edited by Hal Foster, 51–78. Seattle: Bay Press.

Kress, Gunther, and Robert Hodge. 1979. *Language as Ideology*. London: Routledge & Kegan Paul.

1988. *Social Semiotics*. Ithaca and London: Cornell University Press.

Kristeva, Julia. 1980. *Desire in Language: A Semiotic Approach to Literature and Art*, translated by Thomas Gora, Alice Jardine, and Leon S. Roudiez. New York: Columbia University Press.

1982. *Powers of Horror: An Essay on Abjection*, translated by Leon S. Roudiez. New York: Columbia University Press.

1984. *Revolution in Poetic Language*, translated by Margaret Waller. New York: Columbia University Press.

Lacan, Jacques. 1966a. "L'Instance de la lettre dans l'inconscient ou la raison depuis Freud." *Ecrits I*, 493–528. Paris: Editions du Seuil.

1966b. "Le Stade du miroir comme formateur de la fonction du Je." *Ecrits I*, 89–100. Paris: Editions du Seuil.

1968. *Speech and Language in Psychoanalysis*, edited by Anthony Wilden. Baltimore: The Johns Hopkins University Press.

1979. *The Four Fundamental Concepts of Psycho-Analysis*, edited by J.-A. Miller and translated by A. Sheridan, Harmondsworth: Penguin.

1988. "Seminar on 'The Purloined Letter'," translated by Jeffrey Mehlman (with "map of the Text"and "Notes to the Text"). In *The Purloined Poe: Lacan, Derrida, and Psychoanalytic Reading*, edited by John P. Muller and William J. Richardson, 28–98. Baltimore: The Johns Hopkins University Press.

Lafayette, Madame de. 1961. (1678). *La Princesse de Clèves*. Texte établi et présenté par Albert Cazes. Paris: Société Les Belles Lettres. [English:

In *Great French Romances*, edited by Richard Aldington. New York: Palat Press, 1946.]

Lakoff, George. 1987. *Women, Fire and Other Dangerous Things: What Categories Reveal About the Mind*. Chicago: The University of Chicago Press.

Lakoff, George, and Mark Johnson. 1980. *Metaphors We Live By*. Chicago: The University of Chicago Press.

Lakoff, George, and Mark Turner. 1989. *More than Cool Reason: A Field Guide to Poetic Metaphor*. Chicago: The University of Chicago Press.

Lakoff, Robin Tolmach, and Raquel L. Scherr. 1984. *Face Value: The Politics of Beauty*. London: Routledge & Kegan Paul.

Lang, Amy Schrager. 1987. *Prophetic Women: Anne Hutchinson and the Problem of Dissent in the Literature of New England*. Berkeley: University of California Press.

Langer, Susanne K. 1953. *Feeling and Form*. New York: Scribner's.

Laplanche, Jean. 1976. *Life and Death in Psychoanalysis*, translated, and with an introduction, by Jeffrey Mehlman. Baltimore: The Johns Hopkins University Press.

Laplanche, J. and Pontalis, J. B. 1973. *The Language of Psychoanalysis*, translated by Donald Nicholson-Smith. New York: Norton.

Leach, Edmund. 1983. "Anthropological Approaches to the Study of the Bible During the Twentieth Century." In *Structuralist Interpretations of Biblical Myth*, by Edmund Leach and D. Alan Aykock. Cambridge: Cambridge University Press.

Leclerc, Annie. 1977. "La Lettre d'amour." In *La Venue à l'écriture*, edited by Hélène Cixous, Madeleine Gagnon, and Annie Leclerc. Paris: Union Générale des Editions.

Leroux, Georges. 1985. "Du topos au thème: sept variations." *Poétique* 64: 445–54.

Lessing, Gotthold Ephraim. 1974. (1766). *Laokoon: Oder über die Grenzen der Malerei und Poesie*. In *Werke*, edited by Herbert G. Gopfer et al. München: Carl Hanser. [English: *Laocoon: An Essay upon the Limits of Poetry and Painting*, translated, with an Introduction and notes by Edward Allen McCormick. Baltimore: The Johns Hopkins University Press, 1984.]

Lévi-Stauss, Claude. 1963. "The Structural Study of Myth." In *Structural Anthropology*, translated by Claire Jacobson and Brooke Grundfest. New York: Basic Books.

    1969. *The Raw and the Cooked: Introduction to a Science of Mythology I*, translated by John and Doreen Weightman. New York: Harper & Row.

Lotman, Iurij. 1977. *The Structure of the Artistic Text*, translated by Gail Lenhoff and Ronald Vroon. Ann Arbor: University of Michigan Press.

MacKinnon, Catherine. 1983. "Feminism, Marxism, Method and the State: Toward Feminist Jurisprudence." *Signs* 8, 4:635–58.

Malcolm, Janet. 1984. *In the Freud Archives*. New York: Alfred A. Knopf.

Malinowski, Bronislaw. 1926. *Myth in Primitive Society*. London: Kegan Paul.

Man, Paul de. 1979. *Allegories of Reading: Figural Language in Rousseau, Nietzsche, Rilke, and Proust*. New Haven: Yale University Press.

    1984. *The Rhetoric of Romanticism*. New York: Columbia University Press.

Mann, Thomas. 1948. *Joseph and His Brothers*, translated by Helen Tracy

Lowe-Porter. New York: Alfred A. Knopf; Harmondsworth: Penguin.

Marin, Louis. 1971. *Etudes sémiologiques*. Paris: Klincksieck.

1983. "The Iconic Text and the Theory of Enunciation: Luca Signorelli at Loreto (circa 1479–1484)." *New Literary History* XIV, 3: 253–96.

1988. "Towards a Theory of Reading in the Visual Arts: Poussin's *The Arcadian Shepherds*." In *Calligram: Essays in the New Art History from France*, edited by Norman Bryson, 63–90. Cambridge: Cambridge University Press.

Masson, Jeffrey Moussaieff. 1984. *The Assault on Truth: Freud's Suppression of the Seduction Theory*. New York: Farrar, Strauss and Giroux.

McHale, Brian. 1978. "Free Indirect Discourse: A Survey of Recent Accounts." *PTL* 3, 2: 249–87.

1987. *Postmodernist Fiction*. London and New York: Methuen.

Medea, Andra, and Kathleen Thompson. 1974. *Against Rape*. New York: Farrar, Strauss & Giroux.

Meijer, Maaike. 1988. *De lust tot lezen: Nederlandse dichteressen en het literaire systeem*. Amsterdam: Van Gennep.

Meltzer, Françoise. 1987. *Salome and the Dance of Writing*. Chicago: The University of Chicago Press.

Melville, Stephen. 1986. *Philosophy Beside Itself: On Deconstruction and Modernism*. Minneapolis: University of Minnesota Press.

1990. "The Temptation of New Perspectives." *October* 52: 3–15.

Mesnardière, Jules de la. 1639. *La Poétique*, Vol. 1. Paris: Antoine de Sommaville.

Miles, Margaret R. 1985. *Image as Insight: Visual Understanding in Western Christianity and Secular Culture*. Boston: Beacon Press.

1989. *Carnal Knowledge: Female Nakedness and Religious Meaning in the Christian West*. Boston: Beacon Press.

Miller, D. A. 1981. *Narrative and Its Discontents: Problems of Closure in the Traditional Novel*. Princeton: Princeton University Press.

Miller, J. Hillis. 1981. "The Two Allegories." In *Allegory, Myth, and Symbol*, edited by Morton Bloomfield, 355–70. Cambridge, Mass.: Harvard University Press, Harvard English Studies.

Mitchell, W. J. T. 1984. *The Language of Images*. Chicago: The University of Chicago Press.

1985. *Iconology: Image, Text, Ideology*. Chicago: The University of Chicago Press.

Modleski, Tania. 1987. *The Women Who Knew Too Much*. New York: Methuen.

Moi, Toril. 1985. *Sexual/Textual Politics: Feminist Literary Theory*. London: Methuen.

Moi, Toril (ed.). 1986. *The Kristeva Reader*. New York: Columbia University Press.

Moir, A. 1967. *The Italian Followers of Caravaggio*. Cambridge, Mass.: M.I.T. Press, Vol. 1.

Morson, Gary Saul and Caryl Emerson (eds). 1989. *Rethinking Bakhtin: Extensions and Challenges*. Evanston, Ill.: Northwestern University Press.

Moxey, Keith. 1986. "Panofsky's Concept of 'Iconology' and the Problem of Interpretation in the History of Art." In *New Literary History*, 265–74.

1989. *Peasants, Warriors, and Wives: Popular Imagery in the Reformation.* Chicago: The University of Chicago Press.

Mulder, Etty. 1987. *Freud en Orpheus: Hoe het woord de muziek verdrong.* Utrecht: Hes Publishers.

Muller, John P., and William J. Richardson. 1988. *The Purloined Poe: Lacan, Derrida, and Psychoanalytic Reading.* Baltimore: The Johns Hopkins University Press.

Mulvey, Laura. 1975. "Visual Pleasure and Narrative Cinema." *Screen* 16, 3: 6–18.

Nochlin, Linda. 1988. "Courbet's Real Allegory: Rereading 'The Painter's Studio'." In *Courbet Reconsidered,* edited by Sarah Faunce and Linda Nochlin, 17–43. Brooklyn: The Brooklyn Museum.

Oberhuber, Konrad. 1966. *Kunst der Graphik III, Renaissance in Italien.* Vienna: Albertina (No. 28).

Ortony, Andrew (ed.). 1979. *Metaphor and Thought.* Cambridge: Cambridge University Press.

Ostermann, G. n.d. *Les érotiques de Rembrandt.* Paris: René Baudouin.

Owens, Craig. 1984. "The Allegorical Impulse: Toward a Theory of Postmodernism." In *Art After Modernism: Rethinking Representation,* edited by Brian Wallis, 203–35. New York and Boston: The New Museum of Contemporary Art and David R. Godine, Publisher.

Panofsky, Erwin. 1927. "Die Perspektive als 'symbolische Form'." *Vortraege der Bibliothek Warburg* 1924–1925. Leipzig/Berlin.

1955. *Meaning in the Visual Arts.* Harmondsworth: Penguin.

Parker, Rozsika, and Griselda Pollock. 1981. *Old Mistresses: Women, Art, and Ideology.* New York: Pantheon Books.

Pavel, Thomas. 1984. "Origin and Articulation: Comments on the Papers by Peter Brooks and Lucienne Frappier-Mazur." *Style: Psychopoetics at Work* 18, 3: 355–68.

1985. *The Poetics of Plot: The Case of English Renaissance Drama.* Minneapolis: University of Minnesota Press.

1986. *Fictional Worlds.* Cambridge, Mass.: Harvard University Press.

Peirce, Charles Sanders. 1931–58. *Collected Papers,* Vols. 1–8. Cambridge, Mass.: Harvard University Press.

Penley, Constance. 1984. "'A Certain Refusal of Difference': Feminism and Film Theory." In *Art After Modernism: Rethinking Representation,* edited by Brian Wallis, 375–90. New York and Boston: The New Museum of Contemporary Art and David R. Godine, Publisher.

1989. *The Future of an Illusion: Film, Feminism, and Psychoanalysis.* Minneapolis: University of Minnesota Press.

Penley, Constance (ed.). 1988. *Feminism and Film Theory.* New York and London: Routledge.

Perelman, Chaim. 1979. *The New Rhetoric and the Humanities: Essay on Rhetoric and Its Applications,* translated by William Kluback. Boston: D. Reidd Publishing.

Perry, Menakhem. 1979. "Literary Dynamics: How the Order of a Text Creates Its Meanings. With an Analysis of Faulkner's 'A Rose for Emily'." *Poetics Today* 1, 1–2: 35–64 and 311–61.

Perry, Menakhem, and Meir Sternberg. 1968. "The King Through Ironic Eyes: The Narrator's Devices in the Biblical Story of David and Bathsheba and Two Excurses on the Theory of the Narrative Text." (Orig. publ. in *Ha-sifrut,* 263–92.) [In Hebrew; also in Sternberg 1985.]

Piwitt, H. P. 1965. "Poetische Fiktion, Wirklichkeitsauffassung und Er-zählerrolle im neueren Romananfang." In *Romananfänge. Versuch zu einer Poetik des Romans*, edited by N. Miller, 173–84. Berlin: Literar-isches Colloquium.

Plaza, Monique. 1980. "Our Costs and Their Benefits." *m/f* 4: 28–39.

Poétique. 1985. Numéro spécial *Du thème en littérature*, 64.

Pollock, Griselda. 1988. *Vision and Difference: Femininity, Feminism, and the Histories of Art*. London and New York: Routledge.

Prendergast, Christopher. 1986. *The Order of Mimesis: Balzac, Stendhal, Nerval, Flaubert*. Cambridge: Cambridge University Press.

Preziosi, Donald. 1989. *Rethinking Art History: Meditations on a Coy Science*. New Haven: Yale University Press.

Prince, Gerald. 1982. *Narratology: The Form and Function of Narrative*. Ber-lin, New York: Mouton.

Pritchard, R. M., W. Heron, and D. O. Hebb. 1960. "Visual Perception Approached by the Method of Stabilized Images." *Canadian Journal of Psychology* 14: 67–77.

Quran. 1965. *Translation of the Meanings of the Holy Quran* by Abdulla Yusuf Ali, Vol. 1, 3rd edition. Presented by the Muslim World League.

Rahv, Philip. 1953. "The Myth and the Powerhouse." *Partisan Review* 20: 635–48.

Rajchman, John. 1988. "Foucault's Art of Seeing." *October* (Spring), 89–117.

Rank, Otto. 1913. "Eine noch nicht beschriebene Form des Oedipus-Träumes," *Internationale Zeitschrift für ärztliche Psychoanalyse* I: 151–6.

Readings, William and Stephen Melville (eds.). in prep. *Vision and Textuality*.

Rees, A. L., and Frances Borzello (eds.). 1986. *The New Art History*. London: Camden Press.

Reitler, Rudolf. 1913. "Zur Augensymbolik." *Internationale Zeitschrift für ärztliche Psychoanalyse* I: 159–61.

Richardson, Louise S. 1970. "A Rembrandt Drawing." *Bulletin of the Cleve-land Museum of Art* LVII: 68–75.

Richter, Wolfgang. 1963. *Traditionsgeschichtliche Untersuchungen zum Ri-chterbuch*. Bonn: Peter Hanstein Verlag GmbH, Bonner Biblische Bei-träge 18.

Ricoeur, Paul. 1979. *The Rule of Metaphor: Multi-disciplinary Studies of the Creation of Meaning in Language*, translated by Robert Czerny with Kathleen McLaughlin and John Costello. Toronto: University of To-ronto Press.

Riegl, Alois. 1971. "Dutch Group Portraiture." In *Modern Perspectives in Western Art History: An Anthology of 20th-Century Writings on the Visual Arts*, edited by W. Eugene Kleinbauer. New York: Rinehart & Winston.

Rimmon, Shlomith. 1977. *The Concept of Ambiguity: The Example of James*. Chicago: The University of Chicago Press.

Rimmon-Kenan, Shlomith. 1983. *Narrative Fiction: Contemporary Poetics*. London: Methuen.

Rimmon-Kenan, Shlomith. (ed.). 1987. *Discourse in Psychoanalysis and Lit-erature*. London: Methuen.

Rose, Jacqueline. 1980. *The Cinema in the Eighties: Proceedings of the Meeting.* Venice: Edizioni "La Biennale di Venezia."

1986. *Sexuality in the Field of Vision.* London: Verso.

Rosenberg, Jakob. 1948. *Rembrandt.* Cambridge, Mass.: Harvard University Press.

Russell, Diana. 1982. *The Politics of Rape.* New York: Stein and Day.

Sacks, Sheldon. (ed.). 1977. *On Metaphor.* Chicago: The University of Chicago Press.

Said, Edward. 1978. *Orientalism.* New York: Pantheon Books.

Salomon, Nanette. 1983. "Vermeer and the Balance of Destiny." In *Essays in Northern European Art Presented to Egbert Haverkamp-Begemann,* 216–24. Doornspijk: Dawaco.

Scarry, Elaine. 1985. *The Body in Pain: The Making and Unmaking of the World.* Oxford: Oxford University Press.

Schafer, Roy. 1967. "Ideals, the Ego Ideal, and the Ideal Self." In *Motives and Thought,* edited by Robert R. Holt, 129–74. New York: International University Press.

Schama, Simon. 1985. "Rembrandt and Women." *Bulletin of the American Academy of Arts and Sciences* 38: 1–21.

1987. *The Embarrassment of Riches: An Interpretation of Dutch Culture in the Golden Age.* New York: Alfred A. Knopf.

Schatborn, Peter. 1987. "Toelichting bij de afbeeldingen." In *Het boek Tobias. Met etsen en tekeningen van Rembrandt en zijn leerlingen,* 55–70. "Voorwoord" by Christian Tümpel. Toelichting Peter Schatborn. Zeist: Vrij geestesleven.

Schenkeveld-van der Dussen, Maria A. 1978. *A. Pels: Gebruik en Misbruik des tooneels.* Culenborg: Tjeenk Willink/Noorduijn.

Schor, Naomi. 1984. *Breaking the Chain: Feminism, Theory, and French Realist Fiction.* New York: Columbia University Press.

1987. *Reading in Detail: Esthetics and the Feminine.* New York and London: Methuen.

Schupbach, William. 1982. *The Paradox of Rembrandt's "Anatomy of Dr. Tulp."* London: Welcome Institute for the History of Medicine.

Schwartz, Gary. 1985. *Rembrandt: His Life, His Paintings.* Harmondsworth: Penguin.

Scott, David. 1988. *Pictorial Poetics.* Cambridge: Cambridge University Press.

1989. "Ecrire le nu: la transposition de l'image érotique dans la poésie française au XIXe siècle." *Romantisme* 63, I: 87–101.

Scott Littleton, C. 1982. "New Evidence Relative to One-Eyed and One-Handed Figures." In *The New Comparative Mythology,* 99 Berkeley and Los Angeles: University of California Press.

Searle, John. 1977. "Reiterating the Differences: A Reply to Derrida." *Glyph* 1: 198–208.

1980. "*Las Meninas* and the Paradoxes of Pictorial Representation." *Critical Inquiry* 6: 477–88.

Sedgwick, Eve Kossofsky. 1985. *Between Men: Homosocial Desire and the English Novel.* New York: Columbia University Press.

Sewell, Darrel. 1982. *Thomas Eakins: Artist in Philadelphia.* Philadelphia: Philadelphia Museum of Art.

Shakespeare, William. 1912. *The Rape of Lucrece,* edited, with Notes, In-

477

troduction, Glossary, List of Variorum Readings, and Selected Criticism by Charlotte Porter. New York: Thomas Y. Crowell.

Shapiro, Meyer. 1969. "On Some Problems in the Semiotics of Visual
Art: Field and Vehicle in Image-Signs." *Semiotica* 1, 3: 223–42.

——— 1973. *Words and Pictures: On the Literal and the Symbolic in the Illustration
of a Text.* The Hague: Mouton.

Silverman, Kaja. 1983. *The Subject of Semiotics.* Oxford: Oxford University
Press.

——— 1988. *The Acoustic Mirror: The Female Voice in Psychoanalysis and Cinema.*
Bloomington: Indiana University Press.

——— 1989. "Fassbinder and Lacan: A Reconsideration of Gaze, Look, and
Image." *Camera Obscura* 19: 54–84.

Slap, Joseph W. 1985. "Artemesia Gentileschi: Further Notes." *American
Imago* 42, 3: 335–42.

Slatkes, Leonard J. 1983. *Rembrandt and Persia.* New York: Abaris Books.

Slive, Seymour. 1953. *Rembrandt and His Critics: 1630–1730.* The Hague:
Martinus Nijhoff.

Smelik, Anneke. 1986. *En de spiegel brak.* Master's thesis, Rijksuniversiteit
Utrecht: Instituut voor Theaterwetenschappen.

——— 1989. "Het stille geweld." *Tijdschrift voor vrouwenstudies* 38: 235–52.

Snyder, Joel and Ted Cohen. 1980. "Reflections on *Las Meninas:* Paradox
Lost." *Critical Inquiry* 7: 429–47.

Spillers, Hortense J. (ed.). 1985. *Conjuring: Black Women, Fiction, and Literary Tradition.* Bloomington: Indiana University Press.

Steinberg, Leo. 1972. *Other Criteria: Confrontations with Twentieth-Century
Art.* London, Oxford, New York: Oxford University Press.

——— 1974. "Leonardo's *Last Supper.*" *Art Bulletin,* 297–411.

——— 1980. "The Line of Fate in Michelangelo's Painting." In *The Language
of Images,* edited by W. J. T. Mitchell, 85–128. Chicago: The University of Chicago Press.

——— 1981. "Velasquez' *Las Meninas.*" *October* 19: 45–54.

——— 1983. *The Sexuality of Christ in Renaissance Art and Modern Oblivion.* New
York: Pantheon Books.

Steiner, Wendy. 1982. *The Colors of Rhetoric: Problems in the Relation Between
Modern Literature and Art.* Chicago: The University of Chicago Press.

——— 1988. *Pictures of Romance: Form Against Context in Painting and Literature.*
Chicago: The University of Chicago Press.

Sternberg, Meir. 1985. *The Poetics of Biblical Narrative: Ideological Literature
and the Drama of Reading.* Bloomington: Indiana University Press.

Stimpson, Catherine R. 1980. "Shakespeare and the Soil of Rape." In *The
Woman's Part: Feminist Criticism of Shakespeare,* edited by Carolyn Ruth
Swift Lenz, Gayle Green, and Carol Thomas Neely, Urbana, Chicago,
London: University of Illinois Press.

Stock, Brian. 1983. *The Implications of Literacy: Written Language and Models
of Interpretation in the Eleventh and Twelfth Centuries.* Princeton: Princeton University Press.

Stowe, Harriet Beecher. 1981. (1852). *Uncle Tom's Cabin, or Life Among
the Lowly.* Edited and introduced by Ann Douglas. New York:
Penguin.

Suleiman, Susan R., and Inge Crosman (eds.). 1980. *The Reader in the Text:
Essays on Audience and Interpretation.* Princeton, N.J.: Princeton University Press.

Sullivan, Ellie Ragland. 1986. *Jacques Lacan*. Ithaca: Cornell University Press.

Sutton, Peter C. 1980. *Pieter de Hoogh*. Complete edition. Oxford: Phaidon.

Sweetser, Eve. 1989. *From Etymology to Pragmatics: The Mind-As-Body Metaphor in Semantic Structure and Semantic Change*. Cambridge: Cambridge University Press.

Taylor, Graeme J. 1984. "Judith and the Infant Hercules: Its Iconography." *American Imago* 41, 2: 101–15.

Thiher, Allen. 1984. *Words in Reflection: Modern Language Theory and Postmodern Fiction*. Chicago: The University of Chicago Press.

Thoden van Velzen, H. U. E. 1984. "Irma at the Window: The Fourth Script of Freud's Specimen Dream." *American Imago* 41, 3: 245–93.

Tickner, Lisa. 1988a. *The Spectacle of Women: Imagery of the Suffrage Campaign, 1907–1914*. Chicago: The University of Chicago Press.

____. 1988b. "Feminism, Art History, and Sexual Difference." *Genders* 3: 92–128.

Todorov, Tzvetan. 1984. *Bakhtin: The Dialogic Principle*, translated by Wlad Godzich. Minneapolis: University of Minnesota Press.

Tolnay, Charles de. 1949. "Velázquez' *Las Hilanderas* and *Las Meninas*." *Gazette des Beaux Arts* 35: 21–38.

Tompkins, Jane. 1980. *Reader-Response Criticism: From Formalism to Post-Structuralism*. Baltimore: The Johns Hopkins University Press.

____. 1985. *Sensational Designs: The Cultural Work of American Fiction, 1790–1860*. New York and Oxford: Oxford University Press.

Trinh T. Minh-ha. 1989. *Woman, Native, Other: Writing Postcoloniality and Feminism*. Bloomington: Indiana University Press.

Turner, Mark. 1987. *Death Is the Mother of Beauty: Mind, Metaphor, Criticism*. Chicago: The University of Chicago Press.

Turner, Victor. 1967. *The Forest of Symbols: Aspects of Ndembu Ritual*. Ithaca: Cornell University Press.

____. 1969. *The Ritual Process: Structure and Anti-Structure*. Ithaca: Cornell University Press.

Valentiner, W. R. 1957. *Rembrandt and Spinoza: A Study of the Spiritual Conflicts in Seventeenth Century Holland*. London: Phaidon Press.

Vandenbroeck, Paul. 1987. *Beeld van de Andere: Vertoog over het Zelf*. Antwerp: Museum voor Schone Kunsten.

Varga, A(ron) Kibédi. 1984. "La Rhétorique et la peinture à l'époque classique." *Revista di Litterature moderne e comparate* XXXVII, 2: 105–21.

____. 1985. "Un métadiscours indirect: Le discours poétique sur la peinture." In *La Littérature et ses doubles*, edited by Leo H. Hoek. *C.R.I.N.* 13: 19–43. Groningen: Faculteit Letteren.

____. 1986. "Le Visuel et le verbal: le cas du surréalisme." In *Espace et poésie*, edited by Michel Collot and Jean-Claude Mathieu, 159–70. Paris: Presses de l'Ecole Normale Supérieure.

____. 1988. "Stories Told by Pictures." *Style* 22, 2: 194–208.

____. 1989. "Criteria for Describing Word & Image Relations." *Poetics Today* 10, 1: 31–54.

Verhoeff, Han. 1974. *Les Comédies de Corneille: Une psycholecture*. Paris: Klincksieck.

____. 1980. *Les Tragédies de Corneille: Une psycholecture*. Paris: Minard.

____. 1984. "Does Oedipus Have His Complex?" *Style* 18, 3: 261–83.

Vernant, Jean-Pierre. 1976. "Figurations de l'invisible et catégorie psychologique du double: le colossos." In *Mythe et pensée chez les grecs*. Paris: Maspéro.

1985. *La Mort dans les yeux*. Paris: Hachette.

Vickers, Nancy J. 1986. " 'This Heraldry in Lucrece's Face'." In *The Female Body in Western Culture: Contemporary Perspectives*, edited by Susan R. Suleiman, 209–22. Cambridge, Mass.: Harvard University Press.

Vickery, John B. (ed.). 1966. *Myth and Literature: Contemporary Theory and Practice*. Lincoln: University of Nebraska Press.

Walker, Alice. 1982. *The Color Purple*. New York: Harcourt, Brace, Jovanovich.

Weber, Samuel. 1982. *The Legend of Freud*. Minneapolis: University of Minnesota Press.

Westlund, Joseph. 1987. "What Can Comedy Do for Us?: Reparation and Idealization." In *Psychoanalytic Approaches to Literature and Film*, edited by Maurice Charney and Joe Reppen Rutherford, 83–95. Cranbury, N.J.: Fairleigh Dickinson University Press.

Wheelock, Arthur K., Jr. 1981. *Jan Vermeer*. New York: Abrams.

White, Christopher. 1969. *Rembrandt as an Etcher: A Study of the Artist at Work*, 2 vols. London: A. Zwemmer.

1984. *Rembrandt*. London: Thames and Hudson.

White, Hayden. 1973. *Metahistory: The Historical Imagination in Nineteenth-Century Europe*. Baltimore: The Johns Hopkins University Press.

1978a. "Interpretation in History." In *Tropics of Discourse*, 51–80. Baltimore: The Johns Hopkins University Press.

1978b. "The Forms of Wildness: Archeology of an Idea." In *Tropics of Discourse*, 150–182. Baltimore: The Johns Hopkins University Press.

White, John. 1972. *Mythology in the Modern Novel: A Study of Prefigurative Technique*. Princeton: Princeton University Press.

Willis, Sharon. 1984. "Lettre sur les taches aveugles: à l'usage de celles qui voient." *L'Esprit créateur* XXIV, 1: 85–98. [In English].

1987. *Marguerite Duras: Writing on the Body*. Urbana and Chicago: University of Illinois Press.

Winnicott, D. W. 1971. "Transitional Objects and Transitional Phenomena." In *Playing and Reality*, 1–25. New York: Basic Books.

Wittgenstein, Ludwig. 1958. (1953). *Philosophical Investigations*, translated by G. E. M. Anscombe. New York: Macmillan Press.

1961. (1921). *Tractatus Logico-Philosophicus*, translated by B. F. McGuinness. New York: The Humanities Press.

Wolff, Janet. 1981. *The Social Production of Art*. New York: St. Martin's Press.

Wollheim, Richard. 1987. *Painting as an Art. The A. W. Mellon Lectures in the Fine Arts, 1984*. Princeton: Princeton University Press.

Woodhull, Winifred. 1988. "Sexuality, Power, and the Question of Rape." In *Feminism and Foucault: Reflections on Resistance*, edited by Irene Diamond and Lee Quinby, 167–76. Boston: Northeastern University Press.

Yohannan, John D. 1968. *Joseph and Potiphar's Wife in World Literature*. New York: New Directions.

1982. "Hebraism and Hellenism in Thomas Mann's Story of Joseph and Potiphar's Wife." *Comparative Literature Studies* 19, 4: 430–41.

Zakovitch, Yair. 1981. "Siseras Tod." *Zeitschrift für die Alttestamentliche Wissenschaft* 93, 3: 364–74.

INDEX OF NAMES
AND TITLES

INDEX OF TERMS

absorption, 29, 40, 45–53, 108, 153, 199–201, 261, 275–6, 375, 443n

acting (role playing), 53, 54, 55, 58

action, 211

address, 39, 51, 56, 58, 71–2, 91, 144, 167, 253, 318, 413n

aesthetic judgment (taste), 7, 96, 190–3, 197, 231, 348, 415n, 423n, 427–8n, 434–5n, 441n, 447n

affect, 6–7, 18, 31, 37, 38, 42, 54, 116, 282, 322–5, 326, 327, 333, 334, 336–60, 408n

aggression, aggressivity, 61, 143, 172, 329, 332–60

alienation, *see* strangeness

allegory, 2, 60, 74, 77, 82, 83–4, 86, 88, 91, 97, 174, 177, 238, 239, 242, 321, 410n, 411–12n, 412n, 415n, 425n, 452n, 456n

ambiguity, of gender, *see* sexual ambivalence; logical ("rabbit or duck"), 122, 123–4, 160, 245, 257; of signs, 73, 93, 107, 121, 122, 123–4, 163, 257, 258, 283, 325, 331, 337–8, 343, 364, 382, 396

ambivalence, 23, 42, 46, 48, 56, 97, 104, 117, 122–8, 162, 364, 372

anatomy (as subject), 389–98

angel, 103, 179–85, 419n

anthropology, 25, 85, 112, 183, 407n

anxiety, castration, *see* castration anxiety; of influence, 26–8, 33, 42, 276, 406n, 423n; of mirroring, 276, 282, 284, 443n

apostrophe, 71–2, 148, 324

appropriation, 82, 83–4, 85, 86, 89, 90, 143, 169, 174, 175, 194, 195, 196, 202, 218, 229, 244, 245, 302, 368, 376, 394

archtext, 430n

artifact, 218

art history, xv, 7, 25, 26, 27, 39, 40, 138, 177–8, 403n, 422n, 428n, 440n; feminist, *see* feminist art history; state of, 25–8, 29, 39, 177

articulation, 111

artist, as genius, 7, 326, 332–3, 427n; as identity, 8, 298; intention of, 5, 6, 223, 408n, 415n, 419n, 419–20n; as subject, 247–84, 394; *see also* author(ship)

attribution, 138–9; *see also* authenticity

authentication, 190

authenticity (autography), 7, 9, 29, 349–50, 356, 412n

authority, 90, 99, 111, 112, 217

author(ship), 5, 7, 8, 11, 139, 217, 326; death of, 11, 14; *see also* artist

autobiography, *see* discourse, autobiographical

autography (authenticity), 7, 9, 29, 349–50, 356, 412n

background, 219

balance (visual), 1–3, 404n

beholder, *see* viewer

Biblical scholarship, 401n, 403n, 418n

binarism, 27, 39, 41, 42, 58, 152, 181, 231, 353, 397

birth (as subject), 211–14, 338, 342, 343, 344, 345, 394, 397, 433n

blindness (inability to look; difficulty seeing), xv, 7, 11, 17, 21, 31, 48, 50, 51, 53, 104, 128, 172, 179–85, 216, 218, 269, 273, 287, 289, 290, 298–325, 327–60, 385, 388, 394, 433n, 448n, 450n

body, female, 213

body language, 61, 90, 365

calligraphy, 142

canon(ization), 400n, 407n, 422n

castration, 11, 51, 109, 184–5, 254, 289, 290, 299–303, 328, 332, 336, 343, 346, 354, 356–7, 382, 387, 408n, 446n; anxiety, 152, 287, 290, 299, 302, 445n, 321; primary, 23, 347, 453n

catharsis, 117, 391, 392, 420–1n

causality, 72, 86, 78, 89, 93, 149–50, 292, 376

censorship, 13–14, 62–4, 68

Classicism, *see* representation, classical

class, classism, 7, 87, 190, 253, 267, 269, 275, 278, 279, 281, 311, 318, 381, 389, 429n, 435n, 444n

code, 15, 16, 17, 32, 33, 36, 37, 58, 178, 209, 290, 293, 294, 305

coherence, 17, 34, 222–3, 224, 232; lack of, 53, 230, 362, 368

collective unconscious, 109, 418n

color, 2, 35, 46, 66, 75, 81, 106, 108, 121, 124, 159, 196, 219, 229, 309, 336, 340, 343, 382, 383, 391, 394, 395, 448–9n

comedy, 193, 195, 197, 322–3, 431n, 449n

"comic strip device," *see* sequential narrative

commentary, 29, 86, 397

commonplace, 103, 181, 256

comparative arts, 31, 33, 54, 55, 289, 445n

490

492

Benveniste, Emile. 1966. *Problèmes de linguistique générale*, Vol. I. Paris: Gallimard.

1970. "L'Appareil formelle de l'énonciation." *Langage* 17: 12–18.

Berger, John. 1980. *About Looking*. New York: Pantheon Books.

Bergmann, Martin S. 1976. "Love That Follows upon Murder in Works of Art." *American Imago* 38, 1: 98–101.

Bernheimer, Charles. 1985. "Introduction." In *In Dora's Case: Freud – Hysteria – Feminism*, edited by Charles Bernheimer and Claire Kahane, 1–18. New York: Columbia University Press.

Bersani, Leo. 1987. "Is the Rectum a Grave?" In *AIDS: Cultural Analysis, Cultural Activism,* edited by Douglas Crimp, 179–222. Cambridge, Mass.: M.I.T. Press.

Bible. 1976. *New English Bible, with the Apocrypha*. Oxford Study Edition. Oxford: Oxford University Press.

1982. *The Holy Scriptures of the Old Testament: Hebrew and English*. London: The British and Foreign Bible Society.

Bissell, R. Ward. 1968. "Artemesia Gentileschi – A New Documented Chronology." *The Art Bulletin* 50: 153.

Blankert, Albert. 1978. *Vermeer of Delft*. Oxford: Phaidon Press. (orig. publ. 1975).

Bloom, Harold. 1973. *The Anxiety of Influence: A Theory of Poetry*. Oxford: Oxford University Press.

Boheemen, Christine van. 1987. *The Novel as Family Romance: Language, Gender, and Authority from Fielding to Joyce*. Ithaca and London: Cornell University Press.

Borch-Jacobsen, Mikkel. 1988. *The Freudian Subject*, translated by Catherine Porter. Stanford, Cal.: Stanford University Press.

Bourdieu, Pierre. 1977. *Outline of a Theory of Practice*, translated by Richard Rice. Cambridge: Cambridge University Press.

1984. *Distinction: A Social Critique of the Judgement of Taste*, translated by Richard Nicc. Cambridge, Mass.: Harvard University Press.

Braidotti, Rosi. 1991. *Patterns of Dissonance: Feminism and Philosophy*. Cambridge, U.K.: Polity Press.

Brakman, Willem. 1988. *Heer op kamer*. Amsterdam: Querido.

Bredius, Abraham. 1936. *Rembrandt Harmenszoon van Rijn 1606–1669: The Paintings of Rembrandt*. Vienna: Phaidon Verlag.

Brombert, Victor. 1980. "Opening Signals in Narrative." *New Literary History* XI, 3: 489–502.

Bronfen, Elisabeth. 1988. "Dialogue with the Dead: The Deceased Beloved as Muse." *New Comparison* 6: 101–18.

1989. "The Lady Vanishes: Sophie Freud and 'Beyond the Pleasure Principle'." *South Atlantic Quarterly* 88, 4: 961–91.

1990. "Leichenhafte Bilder, Bildenhafte Leichen." *Die Trauben des Zeuxis*, edited by Hans Korner. Koln: Olms Verlag.

in prep. *Over Her Dead Body*.

Brooks, Peter. 1984. *Reading for the Plot: Design and Intention in Narrative*. New York: Alfred A. Knopf.

1987. "The Idea of a Psychoanalytic Literary Criticism." In *Discourse in Psychoanalysis and Literature*, edited by Shlomith Rimmon-Kenan, 1–18. London: Methuen.

Broos, B. P. J. 1977. *Index to the Formal Sources of Rembrandt's Art*. Maarsen: Gary Schwartz.

1983. "Fame Shared Is Fame Doubled." *Rembrandt: Impact of a Genius.* Amsterdam, Rijksmuseum.

1985. *Rembrandt en zijn voorbeelden / Rembrandt and His Sources.* Amsterdam: Rembrandthuis.

Broude, Norma and Mary D. Garrard (eds.). 1982. *Feminism and Art History: Questioning the Litany.* New York: Harper & Row.

Brown, Jonathan. 1986. *Velázquez: Painter and Courtier.* New Haven: Yale University Press.

Bruyn, J., B. Haak, S. H. Levie, et al. 1982– . *A Corpus of Rembrandt Paintings.* Stichting Rembrandt Research Project. The Hague, Boston, London: Martinus Nijhoff Publishers (Vol. I, 1982; Vol. II, 1986; Vol. III, 1989).

Bryson, Norman. 1981. *Word and Image: French Painting of the Ancien Régime.* Cambridge: Cambridge University Press.

1983. *Vision and Painting: The Logic of the Gaze.* London: Macmillan.

1984. *Tradition and Desire: From David to Delacroix.* Cambridge: Cambridge University Press.

1988a. "The Gaze in the Expanded Field." In *Vision and Visuality*, edited by Hal Foster, 87–114. Seattle: Bay Press.

1988b. *Calligram: Essays in the New Art History from France.* Cambridge: Cambridge University Press.

1988c. "Intertextuality and Visual Poetics." *Style* 22, 2: 183–93.

1990. *Looking at the Overlooked: Four Essays on Still-Life.* Cambridge, U.K.: Reaktion Press.

in press. "The Construction of Masculinity in Géricault." In *The Politics of Looking*, edited by Norman Bryson, Michael Ann Holly, and Keith Moxey.

Buci-Glucksmann, Christine. 1986. *La Folie du voir: De l'esthétique baroque.* Paris: Galilée.

Burke, Kenneth. 1968. *Language as Symbol.* Berkeley: University of California Press.

Bynum, Carolyn Walker. 1984. "Women's Stories, Women's Symbols: A Critique of Victor Turner's Theory of Liminality." In *Anthropology and the Study of Religion*, edited by Robert L. Moore and Frank E. Reynolds. Chicago: Center for the Scientific Study of Religion.

Camille, Michael. 1985. "The Book of Signs: Writing and Visual Difference in Gothic Manuscript Illumination." *Word and Image* 1, 2: 133–48.

Campbell, Colin. 1973. "The Identity of Rembrandt's 'Polish Rider'." In *Neue Beiträge zur Rembrandt-Forschung*, edited by Otto Simson and Jan Kelch, 126–36. Berlin: Mann Verlag.

Carroll, Margaret Deutsch. 1981. "Rembrandt as Meditational Printmaker." *The Art Bulletin* LXIII, 4: 585–610.

1986. "Civic Ideology and Its Subversion: Rembrandt's *Oath of Claudius Civilis*." *Art History* 9, 1: 10–35.

1989. "The Erotics of Absolutism: Rubens and the Mystification of Sexual Violence." *Representations* 25: 3–30.

Change (Collective). 1977. *La Folie Encerclée.* Paris: October.

Chapman, H. Perry. 1989. "Expression, Temperament and Imagination in Rembrandt's Earliest Self-Portraits." *Art History* 12, 2: 158–76.

Chase, Cynthia. 1983. Review of Kristeva, *Powers of Horror, Desire in Language*, and "L'abjet d'amour." *Criticism* 26, 2: 193–201.

464

1986. *Decomposing Figures: Rhetorical Readings in the Romantic Tradition.* Baltimore: The Johns Hopkins University Press.

Choron, Jacques. 1963. *Death and Western Thought.* New York: Collier Books.

Ciletti, Elena. 1988. "Questa e la donna terribile!: Artemesia Gentileschi and Judith." [Lecture: Geneva, Hobart and William Smith Colleges]

in prep: "Patriarchal Ideology in the Renaissance Iconography of Judith." In *Prefiguring Woman: Gender Studies and the Italian Renaissance.*

Clark, Kenneth. 1978. *An Introduction to Rembrandt.* New Albot: Readers Union.

1980. *Feminine Beauty.* New York: Rizzoli.

Clark, T. J. 1985. *The Painting of Modern Life: Paris in the Art of Manet and His Followers.* London: Thames and Hudson.

Culler, Jonathan. 1975. *Structuralist Poetics: Structuralism, Linguistics, and the Study of Literature.* Ithaca: Cornell University Press.

1981. *The Pursuit of Signs. Semiotics, Literature, Deconstruction.* Ithaca: Cornell University Press.

1983. *On Deconstruction: Theory and Criticism After Structuralism.* Ithaca: Cornell University Press.

1988. *Framing the Sign: Criticism and Its Institutions.* Norman, Okla. and London: University of Oklahoma Press.

Damish, Hubert. 1972. *Théorie du nuage: Pour une nouvelle histoire de l'art.* Paris: Editions du Seuil.

1987. *L'Origine de la perspective.* Paris: Flammarion.

De Lauretis, Teresa. 1983. *Alice Doesn't: Feminism, Semiotics, Cinema.* London: Macmillan.

1987. *Technologies of Gender: Essays on Theory, Film, and Fiction.* Bloomington: Indiana University Press.

Delay, Jean. 1973–4. *La Jeunesse d'André Gide,* 2 vols. Paris: Corti.

Deleuze, Gilles. 1986. *Foucault.* Paris: Editions Minuit.

Deri, Susan K. 1984. *Symbolization and Creativity.* New York: International Universities Press.

Derrida, Jacques. 1976. *Of Grammatology,* translated, and with an Introduction by Gayatri Chakravorty Spivak. Baltimore: The Johns Hopkins University Press.

1981. *Dissemination,* translated, and with an Introduction and Additional Notes by Barbara Johnson. Chicago: The University of Chicago Press.

1984. *Margins of Philosophy,* translated by Alan Bass. Chicago: The University of Chicago Press.

1987a. *Truth in Painting,* translated by Geoff Bennington and Ian Mc Leod. Chicago: The University of Chicago Press.

1987b. *The Postcard: From Socrates to Freud and Beyond,* translated by Alan Bass. Chicago: The University of Chicago Press.

1988a. "The Purveyor of Truth," translated by Alan Bass. In *The Purloined Poe: Lacan, Derrida, and Psychoanalytic Reading,* edited by John P. Muller & William J. Richardson, 173–212. Baltimore: The Johns Hopkins University Press.

1988b. *Limited Inc.,* translated by Samuel Weber. Evanston, Ill.: Northwestern University Press.

Dessons, Gérard. 1987. *L'Odeur de la peinture: Essai sur une question posée par Rembrandt à la peinture représentative.* Paris: L'Aphélie.

Diamond, Irene, and Lee Quinby (eds.). 1988. *Feminism and Foucault: Reflections on Resistance.* Boston: Northeastern University Press.

Dijk-Hemmes, Fokkelien van. 1986. "Gezegende onder de vrouwen: Een moeder in Israel en een maagd in de kerk." In *'T is kwaad gerucht als zij niet binnen blijft: Vrouwen in oude culturen,* edited by Fokkelien van Dijk Hemmes, 123–47. Utrecht: Hes Publishers.

1989. "Interpretaties van de relatie tussen Richteren 4 en 5." In *Proeven van Vrouwenstudies Theologie,* Vol. I, edited by Jonneke Bekkenkamp e.a., 149–217. Leiden/Utrecht: IMO Research Pamphlets.

Dinitch, Susan. 1982. "The 'Sodomite' Theme in Judges 19–20: Family, Community, and Social Disintegration." *Catholic Bible Quarterly* 44: 365–78.

DiPiero, Thomas. submitted. *Formidable Masters: Imitation, Seduction, and Appropriation in Early French Fiction.*

Donaldson, Ian. 1982. *The Rapes of Lucretia: A Myth and Its Transformations.* Oxford: Clarendon Press.

Douglass, Frederick. 1982. (1845). *Narrative of the Life of Frederick Douglass, an American Slave, Written by Himself,* edited by Houston Baker, Jr. New York: Viking Penguin

Dubois, J. et al. 1981. *A General Rhetoric,* translated by Paul B. Burrel and Edgar M. Slotkin. Baltimore: The Johns Hopkins University Press.

Dumézil, Georges. 1948. *Mitra-Varuna: Essai sur deux représentations indo-européennes de la souveraineté.* Paris: Gallimard.

1959. *Les Dieux des Germains.* Paris: Presses Universitaires de France.

1974. " 'Le Borgne' and 'Le Manchot': The State of the Problem." In *Myth in Indo-European Antiquity,* edited by Gerald James Larson et al., 17–28. Berkeley: University of California Press.

Dupont-Roc, Rosalind, and Jean Lallot. 1980. *Aristotle: La Poétique.* Paris: Editions du Seuil.

Eco, Umberto. 1976. *A Theory of Semiotics.* Bloomington: Indiana University Press.

1979. "Peirce and the Semiotic Foundations of Openness: Signs as Texts and Texts as Signs." *The Role of the Reader: Explorations in the Semiotics of Texts.* Bloomington: Indiana University Press.

Eder, M. D. 1913. "Augenträume." *Internationale Zeitschrift für ärztliche Psychoanalyse* I: 157–8.

Ellis, John. 1980. "Photography/Pornography, Art/Pornography." *Screen* 20, 1 (Spring): 81–108.

Emecheta, Buchi. 1985. (1983). *The Rape of Shavi.* London: Fontana.

Emmens, J. A. 1961. "*Les Ménines* de Velázquez: Miroir des princes pour Philippe IV," *Nederlands Kunsthistorisch Jaarboek* 12: 51–79.

1963. [Review of] H. Gerson, *Seven Letters by Rembrandt. Oud Holland* 78: 79–82.

1979. *Rembrandt en de regels van de kunst.* Amsterdam: Van Oorschot.

Estrich, Susan. 1987. *Real Rape: How the Legal System Victimizes Women Who Say No.* Cambridge: Harvard University Press.

Fabian, Johannes. 1983. *Time and the Other: How Anthropology Makes Its Object.* New York: Columbia University Press.

Felman, Shoshana. 1977. "To Open the Question." *Yale French Studies: Literature and Psychoanalysis. The Question of Reading: Otherwise* 55/56: 5–10.

1980. *Le Scandale du corps parlant: Don Juan avec Austin ou la séduction en deux langages.* Paris: Editions du Seuil. [English: *The Literary Speech*

Acknowledgments

ART RESOURCE, NEW YORK
p. 201. Fig. 5.6. Leonardo da Vinci, *The Last Supper*. 1497.

p. 249. Fig. 7.1. Diego Velázquez, *Las Meninas*. 1656.

THE BRITISH MUSEUM
p. 100. Fig. 3.1. Rembrandt van Rijn, Beheading. ca. 1640. Reproduced by courtesy of the Trustees of the British Museum.

p. 144. Fig. 4.3. Rembrandt van Rijn, *Female Nude Seated*. ca. 1630–1. Reproduced by courtesy of the Trustees of the British Museum.

p. 186. Fig. 5.3. Rembrandt van Rijn, *Hagar's Dismissal*. Reproduced by courtesy of the Trustees of the British Museum.

p. 188. Fig. 5.4. Rembrandt van Rijn, *Hagar and Ishmael*. ca. 1649–50. Reproduced by courtesy of the Trustees of the British Museum.

p. 300. Fig. 8.4. Rembrandt van Rijn, *Abraham Withheld from the Sacrifice of Isaac*. ca. 1630. Reproduced by courtesy of the Trustees of the British Museum.

ENGLISH HERITAGE, KENWOOD HOUSE, LONDON
p. 252. Fig. 7.3, top row, right. Rembrandt van Rijn, *Self-Portrait*. ca. 1661–2. The Iveagh Bequest, Kenwood.

THE FRICK COLLECTION, NEW YORK
p. 252. Fig. 7.3, top row, center. Rembrandt van Rijn, *Self-Portrait*. 1658. Copyright, The Frick Collection, New York.

p. 350. Fig. 9.7. Rembrandt van Rijn, *The Polish Rider*. 1657. Copyright, The Frick Collection, New York.

JEFFERSON MEDICAL COLLEGE OF THOMAS JEFFERSON UNIVERSITY, PHILADELPHIA, PENNSYLVANIA
pp. 30, 49. Figs. 1.1, 1.10. Thomas Eakins, *The Gross Clinic*. 1875.

METROPOLITAN MUSEUM OF ART, NEW YORK
p. 168. Fig. 4.13. Rembrandt van Rijn, *The Toilet of Bathshebah*. 1643. Bequest of Benjamin Altman, 1913. (14.40.651) All rights reserved, The Metropolitan Museum of Art.

p. 201. Fig. 5.5. Rembrandt van Rijn, *Last Supper, After Leonardo da Vinci*. ca. 1635. Robert Lehman Collection. All rights reserved, The Metropolitan Museum of Art.

p. 319. Fig. 8.12. Rembrandt van Rijn, *Bellona*. 1633. Bequest of Michael Friedsam, 1931. The Friedsam Collection. (32.100.23) All rights reserved, The Metropolitan Museum of Art.

p. 378. Fig. 10.6, left. Rembrandt van Rijn, *A Woman Hanging from the Gallows*. 1654–6. All rights reserved, The Metropolitan Museum of Art.

MUSEE DU LOUVRE, PARIS
p. 252. Fig. 7.3, top row, left. Rembrandt van Rijn, *Self-Portrait*. 1660. © Musées Nationaux.

p. 384. Fig. 10.8. Rembrandt van Rijn, *Slaughtered Ox*. 1655. © Musées Nationaux.

MUSEUM OF FINE ARTS, BOSTON
p. 150. Fig. 7.2. Rembrandt van Rijn. *The Artist in His Studio*. ca. 1629. Zoe Oliver Sherman Collection. Given in memory of Lillie Oliver Poor. Courtesy, Museum of Fine Arts, Boston.

NATIONAL GALLERY OF ART, WASHINGTON, D.C.
p. 2. Fig. 0.1. Jan Vermeer, *Woman Holding a Balance*. ca. 1622–4. Widener Collection.

pp. 34, 46, 105. Figs. 1.2, 1.7, 3.4. Rembrandt van Rijn, *Joseph Accused by Potiphar's Wife*. 1655.

p. 65. Fig. 2.1. Rembrandt van Rijn, *Lucretia*. 1664. Andrew W. Mellon Collection.

UNIVERSITY OF PENNSYLVANIA SCHOOL OF MEDICINE
p. 52. Fig. 1.12. Thomas Eakins, *The Agnew Clinic*. 1889.